New Perspectives on Languages in Contact

Félix Rodríguez González (ed.)

New Perspectives on Languages in Contact

PETER LANG

Berlin - Bruxelles - Chennai - Lausanne - New York - Oxford

Library of Congress Cataloging-in-Publication
A record in the CIP catalog has been requested for this book.
of the Library of Congress.

Bibliographic information published by the Deutsche Nationalbibliothek
The Deutsche Nationalbibliothek lists this publication in the Deutsche Nationalbibliografie; detailed bibliographic data is available on the Internet at http://dnb.d-nb.de.

Cover illustration: © Maryna Chepchur/dreamstime.com

ISBN 978-3-631-91524-0 (Print)
E-ISBN 978-3-631-91525-7 (E-PDF)
E-ISBN 978-3-631-91526-4 (E-PUB)
DOI.10.3726/b21525

Published by Peter Lang GmbH, Berlin, Germany

info@peterlang.com - www.peterlang.com

Table of Contents

Félix Rodríguez González

Introduction

1. The phenomenon of languages in contact. A brief outline and bibliographical guide

Languages are not static bodies, they are not fossils. Quite to the contrary, they are subject to multiple and continuous changes when interacting with other more dynamic ones that exert influence. In today's world, there are countless languages that share a common space and relationships of dominance or dependence, or obligatory coexistence, are established between them, with which Sociolinguistics deals. No one is completely monolingual per se, no one escapes bilingualism or multilingualism in some form or another. Contacts can be very varied in nature and thus give rise to very different linguistic phenomena. The most common and best known is "borrowing", which takes place in the epidermis of the language either from the need to fill a semantic gap in the lexicon or for reasons of prestige and influence of the dominant language.

In all cases, in some way, the predominance of English, as a lingua franca in international relations, is invariably present. Since the end of World War II, its influence has expanded, spreading to all languages through borrowing, giving rise to an extensive literature, in particular on Spanish. My interest in lexicography led me to prepare in 1997, with the collaboration of A. Lillo, the first Dictionary of Anglicisms in Peninsular or European Spanish (Gredos, 1997). Years later I conceived the idea of creating a kind of encyclopedia of Anglicism in three volumes which sparked the interest of a publishing house, Peter Lang. The first volume, *Anglicismos en el español contemporáneo: una vision panorámica* (2022), as its name indicates, investigates the presence of English in different thematic areas, from politics to fields linked to informal style such as sex and drugs and covering overseas areas, like the Canary Islands and the United States, and with an extensive study on Anglicisms in Spanish America. Due to its multifaceted nature, the volume was collective and brought together specialists in the most varied fields, as John Humbley, a leading figure in the field of neology, reported in the preface that preceded it.

The following year, I expanded and updated all my articles prepared over more than three decades, on different grammatical perspectives, gathered under the rubric *Estudios sobre el anglicismos en el español actual: perspectivas lingüísticas* (2023). Its importance was also highlighted in the prologue by the

North American philologist and specialist in the history of the Spanish Steven Dworkin.

Before the third volume appears, I have dedicated the present one to putting into perspective the role of Anglicism within the phenomenon of language contact. Due to its thematic broader scope, it has been published independently, apart from the series started previously and exclusively on Anglicisms.

Although language contacts are lost in the mists of time, they were not studied until the 19th century within the framework of linguistic history and a comparative perspective. As a discipline it is relatively young, having existed for less than a century. Pioneering studies in the study of the processes and effects of language contact include the work of Haugen (1950) and above all the seminal and more systematic work of Weinreich (1953), both classed within a structuralist paradigm. In the following years, other works followed in the wake of these two linguists on those same bases, contributing to consolidate a discipline that formally acquired status in 1979, at the First World Congress on Language Contact and Conflict held in Brussels.

The popularity of contact linguistics as a research topic of language studies that followed since then has had a reflection in the enormous bibliography existing today, especially in English and having English as a basis of comparison. Worthy of note are significant textbooks published in notable publishing houses (Appel & Muysken, 1987; Goebl et al., 1996, 1997; Thomason, 2001; Winford, 2003; Matras, 2009) and in international handbooks like Coulmas (2017), Darkennes et al. (2019), Grant (2017), Hickey (2013). Besides, journals were established dedicated to language contact research such as the *Journal of language contact,* a successful platform established in 2007 by Robert Nicolaï, which from the beginning envisioned this area of study as multi-disciplinary, encompassing a wide range of language contact phenomena and issues, linguistic but also sociolinguistic and sociological, a vision that was inspired by Weinreich (1968: 4), in the first chapter of his renowned work. Mention has also to be made of the introductory chapters and a myriad of articles that have appeared in journals of Sociolinguistics and Bilingualism.

As for the Hispanic world the first textbook worthy of mention was *Lenguas en contacto,* by the Romanian romanist Marius Salas (1988), followed later by Javier Medina (1992), *Lenguas en contacto*, of a rather pedagogic persuasion, aimed rather at students and young researchers.

Related topics and central to the study of language contact is the theme of "bilingualism" and "multilingualism". No nation is strictly monolingual in the sense that everyone living there speaks the same language natively, and the idea of considering monolingualism as the norm is a myth. In North America, speakers of Spanglish speak both Spanish and English, at times mixing the two codes and switching from one to the other (a phenomenon called "code-switching" which has developed an extensive bibliography, as Silvia Betty reports in this volume). And there are countries in western Europe, like the Netherlands where it is difficult to find a Dutch speaker living in a large city and being educated and young who is not fluent in English. A similar situation can be observed in Quebec (even Anglophone Ontarians rarely speak French).

Broadly speaking, code-switching manifests in two main ways, alternating a string of words or phrases within a conversation, where open-class content morphemes are incorporated from the source language, usually at semantically meaningful junctures and where the speaker retains the mophosyntactic frame of the dominant language; or, simply, by adopting one or more words as lexical borrowings in the recipient language. The first case can be illustrated by the classic research popularised by S. Poplak in her well-know study "I start a sentence in English y termino en español" The second is not always distinguished from lexical borrowings proper and some scholars consider both types as a continuum understanding borrowing in term of processes rather than results. When a single word is borrowed often, may be classed as a "nonce borrowing", which is a point of departure of code switching associated with the practice of bilingualism.

People view multilingualism in often conflicting ways. Some find it a psychological handicap and a political liability but in the modern world in which we live today, it is a mark of high education and prestige and a necessity of daily living in certain situations.

Although aware of the influential bibliography of language contact related to English, and inspired by it, I have consciously limited the scope of this volume basically to a specific "linguistic area", a geographic region containing a group of three languages (Spanish, French and Italian) that share some structural features a as a result of their contact with English. Consequently I have omitted reviewing peripheral aspects of language contact such as Pidgins and Creoles, for their remote application to this study, as well as many other issues, including some general like "convergence" and "interference", "globalization" and "prestige language", and more practical ones such as "language planning". However, all these topics and many more should not be overlooked when exploring the possibilities of developing an overall theory of language contact that we still feel as lacking, especially if new empirical data are collected from different language and language contact areas.

For that reason, to make up for that vacuum left, I have provided below a selective bibliography of the subject concentrating on studies with a general and even an encyclopaedic content, hoping they will be of interest to students of language contact but also to a wider audience, particularly those interested in the interaction between language and contemporary society.

References (sources and further reading)

Appel, René & Peter Muysken (1987): *Language contact and bilingualism.* London: Edward Arnold.

Coulmas, Florian (ed.) (2017): *The handbook of sociolinguistics.* Oxford: Blackwell

Darkennes, Jeroen, Joseph Salmon, & Wim Vanderbussche (eds.). (2019): *Language contact: An international handbook.* Vol. 1. Berlin/Boston.

Goebl, Hans, Peter H. Nelde, Zdenerk Sary, & Wolfgang Wölk (eds.). (1996): *Kontaklinguistik / Contact linguistics / Linguistique de contact.* Vols. 1 and 2. Berlin/New York: Walter de Gruyter.

Grant, Anthony (ed.) (2020): *The Oxford handbook of language contact.* Oxford: Oxford University Press.

Hǻkon Jahr, Ernst (ed.) (1992): *Language contact: Theoretical and empirical studies.* Mouton de Gruyter.

Haugen (1950): "The analysis of linguistic borrowing". *Language*, 26: 210–331.

Hickey, Raymon (2013): *The handbook of language contact.* Oxford: Wiley-Blackwell.

———. (2020): 2nd ed. John Wiley & Sons, Incorporated.

Ivir, Vladim & Damir Kalogjera (eds.). (1991): *Languages in contras and contrasts. Essays in contact linguistics*. Berlin/New York: Mouton de Gruyter.

Lim, Lisa & Umberto Ansaldo (2016): *Languages in contact.* Cambridge: Cambridge University Press.

Matras, Yaron (2009): *Language contact.* Cambridge: Cambridge University Press.

Medina López, Javier (1992): *Lenguas en contacto.* Madrid: Arco/Libros.

Meyers-Scotton, Carol (2002): *Contact linguistics bilingual encounters and grammatica outcomes.* Oxford: Oxford University Press.

Mufwene, Saliko S. & Anna María Escobar (2022): *The Cambridge handbook of language contact.* Cambridge: Cambridge University Press.

Salas, Marius (1998 [1986]): *Lenguas en contacto.* 2nd ed. Madrid: Gredos.

Thomason, Sarah G. (2001): *Language contact: An introduction.* Edinburgh: Edinburgh University Press.

Weinreich, Uriel (1968 [1953]): *Languages in contact. Findings and problems.* The Hague: Mouton.

Winford, Donald (2003): *An introduction to contact linguistics.* Oxford: Blackwell

2. Structure and content of this volume

Most of the studies represented in this volume refer to lexical anglicisms used in the Hispanic community, especially in the peninsular or European Spanish. They are cultural products, which are mainly developed due to reasons of prestige and snobbery, to which globalization and the growing prestige of English undoubtedly contribute.

Although the greatest contribution of English to the Spanish lexicon took place in the second half of the 20th century, its imprint in the second half of the 19th century was significant and worthy of attention, with the cultural fashions that appeared at that time, as Javier Medina highlights in his article "Aspectos socioculturales del anglicismo en España durante el siglo XIX: de *high life* y sus adláteres semánticos". This chapter complements the historical vision already advanced by F. Rodríguez in chapter I "Aspectos históricos. La introducción y el registro de los anglicismos en español", from his recent book *Estudios sobre el anglicismo en el español actual: una visión panorámica.* (Peter Lang, 2022, pp. 21–24).

Reviewing the bibliography of Anglicism, it is immediately obvious that the general trend has been for a descriptivist methodology, which is why the normative recommendations included in style books are appreciated. In this volume, two of the signatories emphasise this perspective, although with different treatment. Alberto Gómez Font, "Anglicismos resistentes y vencedores: los que ganaron la batalla a los libros de estilo", and Jesús Castañón Rodríguez, "Los anglicismos deportivos en los libros de estilo de medios de comunicación de España".

Continuing in a descriptive perspective, one aspect that should be highlighted in the field of writing is the emergence in recent years of research (articles and theses) on Anglicism in the women's magazines. That is why the contrast represented by the article by Mª Jesús Rodríguez Medina entitled precisely "Estudio de la presencia del inglés en las revistas para hombres en España: análisis comparativo" is striking due to its originality.

Also based on the press, the article by David Giménez-Folques "Presencia del inglés en las revistas gráficas satíricas", emphasises on the role of the counterculture of the 1970s, the era of the Spanish "movida", which contributed to promoting subversive and innovative language.

The Anglicisms in Spanish examined throughout this publication, as in the two above-mentioned that preceed, are of the "raw" or direct borrowing, although semantic loans and calques are less visible, and even less perceptible are the syntactic ones. Of this last class, it is worth mentioning one in the making, on which Montserrat Martínez's chapter revolves, "The woman behind the artist. Un nuevo caso de anglicismo sintáctico en español". Her corpus-based study analyzes a recent Spanish construction which is a formal and semantic replication of an English pattern (*the woman behind the artist*).

All of the contributions mentioned so far concern the lexicon of peninsular or European Spanish and have been registered in dictionaries since the 1990s, as indicated. However, the first dictionary of Spanish anglicisms, the precursor of all those that appeared later, was published half a century earlier, in 1950, in Panama, by Ricardo Alfaro, with a largely pan-Hispanic corpus, and despite these methodological limitations, it had a great influence on the Spanish speaking world. The Panamanian philologist Martín Jamieson reports on this in a recent review ("Re-visión del Diccionario de anglicismos de Ricardo J. Alfaro en el siglo XXI").

Another aspect worthy of highlighing in the current bibliography, just as in this volume, is that a majority of the loans analysed are of the "unimembre" type (Emilio Lorenzo's terminology), that is, they consist of a single lexical unit. David L. Gold's "The Polysemous Spanish Noun safacón ~ zafacón: A Borrowing from English or a Native Spanish Coinage?," the first treatment of any length or depth of the word in question, grapples with the difficulty of etymologising a word which, on one hand, could be entirely of English origin and, on the other, could consist of three Spanish morphemes none of which comes from English.

On the other hand, we must not forget phraseologisms, to which are dedicated the chapters written by Delfín Carbonell, "Bilingual phraseological lexicography: the meeting of two cultures", and Ruth Breeze and Manuel Casado Velarde "Apuntes para un análisis comparativo de la fraseología relativa a la persuasión en inglés y en español".

Most publications on Anglicisms, both in Spanish and other languages, are based on written corpora, sourced from data from newspapers and magazines, hence the uniqueness of Juan Gómez Capuz's chapter dedicated to "Anglicismos en el español oral y colloquial", with a sociolinguistic methodology.

In relation to the comparison of anglicisms with the native lexicon obtained through translation, Goretti García Morales, in her chapter "Tratamiento del anglicismo en traducciones automáticas español-inglés", points to the problems that arise with computer programs when dealing with the connotative meaning.

The studies on loans in overseas areas deserve special mention in this volume. Here, María Isabel González Cruz, drawing on a very long career in research on Canarian Anglicisms, with an ancient tradition due to the commercial contacts maintained by the islanders with the British migrants in past centuries, returns to the subject to verify the knowledge and use that is still made made of them today by the young generations of Canarian university students.

Likewise, Silvia Betti, one of the great specialists in the area of Spanglish and Spanish from and in the United States, within the context of bilingualism in that country, offers an overview of the linguistic mixture resulting from "intimate" contact of Spanish and English, especially in certain areas of the United States. Betti's chapter presents some theoretical foundations, research and part of the results of studies carried out over the years on these topics.

Also focusing on this area is Isabel Álvarez's study "El léxico del fútbol en la prensa estadounidense en español" in which she demonstrates, with empirical data that, contrary to what one might think, the reports on soccer in the US press you are not riddled with Anglicisms but rather show a preference for the Spanish term with a higher frequency than that found in Spanish-speaking countries.

2.2. A second subset of topics focus on the lexical contact produced by other languages, starting with those spoken in geographically and culturally neighbouring countries such as France and Italy. John Humbley, in his article "Peer-produced encyclopaedias disseminating loan neology: *crowdsourcing* and *crowdfunding* in French and Spanish" examines the varying treatment by these two languages when borrowing and adapting the terminology derived from such concepts.

Alicia Roffé, a slang scholar, in her article "Créativité lexicale et anglicisme dans l'argot de la drogue français", looks into the creativity French shows in the language of drugs users.

And Pedro J. Mogorrón, with his chapter " Analyse lexicale des expressions figées avec des zoonymes en espagnol et en français" looks into the lexicon of zoonyms as an area fertile in phraseology in Spanish and French owing to the close ties.

As for Italian, Virginia Pulcini, in "The ordinal superlative in Italian and English: A morphosyntactic calque" examines one particular syntactic pattern imported into the Italian language and the different semantic relations that are established among the elements of the phrases in the two languages.

In "The use of English in job advertisements in Turkey", Andreu van Hooft and his colleagues show the great extent of the penetration of English in the field of advertising, even in a very different linguistic context, just as it happens in other European languages like Dutch and Spanish. This fits in with the increase in the spread, influence, and presence of English in Turkish from 1950 to the present, which can be explained by the modernization and westernisation of Turkish society and the growing relevance of international communication in Turkey.

Finally, Amanda Roig-Marín, in her chapter "Nueva aproximación al uso de palabras inglesas en textos administrativos en latín medieval", explores the links between words borrowed from Middle English, as used in administrative texts, highlighting among other features the use of the definite article which was inexistent in the Latin of that time.

Group 1: English / Spanish contacts

Delfín Carbonell Basset

Franklin and Marshall College

Bilingual phraseological lexicography: The meeting of two cultures

Abstract: Based on the conceit that all brains are created equal, this article sets forth to explore the similarities in the phraseological discourse in languages, particularly in Spanish-English lexicography, and aims to prove that, as a result, equivalent parallel expressions in the two languages can be found. It poses further that there´s always a bilingual lexicographical solution to every phrase and idiom. To paraphrase Dr. Samuel Johnson: There´s no language problem the mind of man has set, that the mind of man cannot solve.

Keywords: ??? **

The horizon of our language is not the horizon of language, Mr. Landau

Lets start from scratch. The brains of normal newborns in England and Spain are the same. They will develop in different directions as the children grow and as they acquire a working knowledge of both English and Spanish, but, I repeat, both brains are physiologically the same. They will have the same needs, ideas, environmental responses, and fears. They will shy away from heights, snakes, darkness, and spiders. They will not fear speed or fire and will suck on anything, especially their mothers´ breasts. Language will make an imprint in the wax of the brain, shaping it, but not altering it.

Brains are created equal. The brain will differ as far as it is molded by language which, in turn, will be altered by what is called *culture,* geography, history, sociology, religion, superstition, gastronomy, literature, and climate, creating an imprint in the way it communicates with other brains, although its core remains intact.

Bilingual lexicography is the poor relation (relative), of lexicography, and it is not taken seriously by monolexicographers. Dictionary publishers –often true dictionary factories- set up teams of young interns, not dry behind the ears yet, and plunge them into compiling, for example, Spanish-English wordbooks for travelers, beginners, schools, and learners, with the idea of making a killing with the sale of such ill-made products. There are always discrepancies between the Spanish and English parts, because of the disparity of language skills among the teams of the so-called wordsmiths. To make matters worse, there is no accountability: no editor-in-chief is responsible for the fiasco. And phraseology in lexicography becomes the less, the almost forgotten relative with sparse room in every entry.

Bilingual lexicography requires a command of two languages, not some knowledge of one and a smattering of another. The result is the sorry state of two-language dictionaries which do list idiomatic expressions, in a helter-skelter way, with unhappy and sorry translations, without examples or citations that will aid the user to better understand and employ idioms that often defy proper rendering in another language. They are useless for the most part, at best. At worst, they are harmful.

In his *Dictionaries: The Art and Craft of Lexicography*, (2001), Sidney Landau deals with bilingual lexicons in 4 pages, out of 477, giving a succinct, and misleading, idea of what they are about, reinforcing my belief that such dictionaries are taken lightly -not seriously-, as the poor relation of mainstream lexicography.

Landau explains that the purpose of a bilingual dictionary is "to provide help to someone who understands one language but not the other. More, the presumption is that one of the languages is the user´s native language." He assumes that (1) the native speaker has a profound and educated knowledge of his language, and (2) the user ignores the other. I pose that the bilingual dictionary, English–Spanish, must be addressed to both native speakers, those seeking language equivalencies, English or Spanish.

Landau writes that "there is often no equivalent in the target language for entry words in the source language, not only in the obvious instances of indigenous flora and fauna but for many common words as well." This shows that Mr. Landau has expertise in lexicography, but none in linguistics or philology, and certainly none in bilingualism. I believe that there are always equivalents in any language, especially in related ones like Spanish and English which share a very common cultural background.

Bilingual lexicography must take its rightful place in lexicography at large - not just 4 pages of dismissal. Of course, being a bilingual wordsmith requires the command of two languages, not just one, which is within the reach of 98 percent of world population. Everybody speaks one language. How many speak two?

But the proof of the taste is in the pudding, and as *el movimiento se demuestra andando*, let me propose a few examples of bilingual phraseology.

Let me tell you **a shaggy-dog story**, a drawn-out story or narrative that leads nowhere and tries the patience of the listener. In *Through the Grapevine*, 2001, we read: "In a shaggy-dog story, the teller draws out the story, adding a lot of detail. When the story finally ends, some trick is involved." And another citation: "The Huntchback's Tale is, after all, a shaggy dog story that goes nowhere." (Ulrich Marzolph, et al., *The Arabian Night´s Encyclopedia*, 2004.) **WordReference** paraphrases it as "una historia larga y aburrida". **Reverso** tells us it is "un chiste malo", or chestnut, which, although true, is not the equivalent we are seeking. **Collins** insists on "chiste largo y pesado." We cannot seriously accept "historias de perro peludo" as a Google possibility. However, we must accept "**cuento de la buena pipa**" as the parallel equivalent of the English phrase we are dealing with. **El cuento de la buena pipa**, is a never-ending story that, like its English counterpart, leads nowhere. Marta Portal explains in her novel *Pago de traición* (1983): "… como el cuento de la buena pipa que consiste en quererlo contar y no en saberlo, en incitar a escucharlo y en que nunca lleguen a oírlo." And Javier Marías, in his bestseller *Corazón tan blanco* (1992), comments: "¿Quieres que te cuente el cuento de la buena pipa, decía mi abuela con malicia." A never-ending story, a long-drawn-out yarn is **a shaggy-dog story** in English and **el cuento de la buena pipa** in Spanish.

The old and truly worn-out Spanish saying **quien va a Sevilla pierde su silla**, which has the variation **quien va a la villa pierde su silla**, mostly used in America, and **quien fue a Sevilla, perdió su silla**, hints that he who is not present, those who leave stuff unattended, lose. We must keep on our toes, lest we are taken advantage of. Federico Giménez Losantos uses the saying in his *Lo que queda de España* (1995), thus: "Alberto tenía derecho a apelar al dicho de el que se fue a Sevilla perdió su silla." **Collins** has not heard of this idiomatic expression and **WordPerfect** gives "finders keepers, losers weepers" which is close, but no cigar. **Spani¡Dict** is funnier: "who goes to Seville loses his chair." There is a close English equivalent in: **Move your feet, lose your seat** which has several variations: **on/shuffle/your meat, lose your seat**, for which I offer two citations: "Move your meat, lose your seat." (Sherry A. McGee, *Skinny Women are Evil*, 2004.) And "The bull rider´s mantra is, lose your feet, lose your seat." (Jane Kubke, *Bull Riding*, 2006.)

Languages at large often have shocking expressions that become more preposterous as humanity makes forward strides in social and gender equality. **Bailar con la más fea** which I translate as **getting the short end of the stick**, is a point in question. "No sé por qué, pero a mí siempre me toca **bailar con la más fea**", I don´t know why but I always **get the short end of the stick**. We all want to dance with the pretty girl, but this guy´s tough luck forces him to dance with the "fea", the ugly one. Women didn´t have this problem because they were asked out to dance and could refuse the man who was inviting them. The expression was: "May I have the pleasure of this dance?" ¿Me permite el placer de este baile? "La fea" was a sure bet because she never refused the request. I am not sure, but I guess that Spanish-speaking women never use this idiomatic turn of phrase. I wonder why! Jesús Cacho Cortés, in his *Asalto al poder* (1988), explains a character's woes thus: "Pero de nuevo, por órdenes superiores, Rubio se ve obligado a hacer de fontanero y bailar con la más fea." Rubio gets the short end of the stick by orders from above. We must discard Google´s suggestion as a bona fide translation: "Dance with the ugliest" as not befitting a respectable solution. The cultural aspects of phraseology here point out that the Spanish idiom is no longer politically correct, but on the other hand its English counterpart may be used anytime, anywhere, as in the Winnipeg Sun of 8 Nov 2003: "You know, it´s always the victims who get the short end of the stick." We might substitute, so as not to offend, "tocar la peor parte" which may be more socially palatable nowadays.

The idea or conceit, meaning even, enclosed in a phraseological unit is not always clear-cut and easy to grasp, giving rise to confusion in its use, even among native speakers. If words may be polysemous, the same can affect phrases. This might be the case of the Spanish **tarde, mal y nunca**, defined by Manuel Seco (*Diccionario fraseológico documentado del español actual*, 2004) as "con retraso e irregularidad" which might be misused or misinterpreted due to the addition of "nunca", but this is the nature of phraseology, that it is set, even though at times it might alter its shape and appearance: "Las pensiones que se nos asignan suelen ser escasas y en la mayoría de las ocasiones pagadas tarde, mal o nunca." (ABC, 08/06/1989.) Y Augusto Roa Bastos writes: "Mejor es gozar de lo bueno de vez en cuando que tarde, mal y nunca" which adheres to a more literate meaning of the idiom. But how are we going to render this unit in English? Collins does not list it, but does insert in English "too little, too late" rendering it as "muy poco y muy tarde" which makes no sense at all. Doing a bit of research will lead us to **too little, too late** as the parallel rendering of "tarde, mal y nunca." We will find still more, a more colloquial rendering in **a day late and a dollar short**, as in "Thanks always come a day late and a dollar short but my respect has and will always be there…" (Gillian G. Gaar, *Green Day: Rebels with a Cause*, 2009.) And Gerald Baron says about Firestone (*Now is Too Late: Survival in an Era of Instant News*, 2003.): "It didn´t matter because whatever Firestone said came off as too little, too late."

Just as bullfighting has given many expressions to the Spanish language, baseball has done the same in English. **Step up to the plate** is when the batter steps up to the plate to bat, and prepares and assumes the responsibility of hitting the ball. The Oxford Dictionary explains the idiomatic expression: "Take action in response to an opportunity or crisis." The Cambridge English dictionary gives us a similar definition: "To take action when something needs to be done, even though this is difficult." "The board will have to step up to the plate and solve the monetary problems the company has" which means that the board will have to **tomar cartas en el asunto** and solve the economic situation. Manuel Seco´s *Diccionario fraseológico documentado del español* actual defines this idiom as "Intervenir (alguien que tiene autoridad)." María Moliner gives a similar definition: "Intervenir en el asunto de que se trata alguien que tiene autoridad." The *Diccionario fraseológico del español moderno* (Fernando Varela, 1996) insists on *autoridad*: "Intervenir con autoridad" which comes to show how lexicographers pilfer. The word "autoridad" flies in the face of the examples of usage: "… nosotros sí tomaríamos cartas en el asunto para obligar al estado a que proteja el inmueble." (Proceso de México, 15/12/1996.) And further: "Aunque pienses que no hay nada malo en este tipo de diversión infantil, los padres de los amigos de tu hijo pueden no opinar igual que tú y tomar cartas en el asunto." (Dunia, 07/1995.) We must be wary of definitions given by most dictionaries, and translations offered by Collins which says of "tomar cartas en el asunto": "to step in."

"I was asked to **step up the plate** and solve the problem." Me pidieron que **tomase cartas en el asunto** y resolviese el problema.

"I have been waiting for a long time for you to **step up to the plate** and fix this mess." Hace tiempo que espero que usted **tomase cartas en el asunto** y resolviese este lío.

"The government should **step up to the plate** and do something about poverty." El gobierno debería **tomar cartas en el asunto** y hacer algo sobre la pobreza.

The cultural aspects of phraseology mentioned earlier, sticks out like a sore thumb when we get into Spain and its centuries-old romance with bullfighting or *tauromaquia*, *fiesta*. Bullfighting has added many idioms to Spanish, like **estar para el arrastre**, weak, tired, and near death, which refers to the dead bull when it is dragged ("arrastrado") out of the ring. English has **be on one's last legs** which refers to the last leg of a trip – "último tramo"-, possibly the end of life, when one is exhausted and ready to exit. So, we may say: "Jack doesn´t look so good and he may be on his last legs." In Spanish, we might exclaim that "Jack no tiene buen aspecto y está para el arrastre." We can also say that someone **está en las últimas** (see a few lines down). In his play *Cementerio de automóviles* (1979) Fernando Arrabal writes: "Y si no duermo ahora, mañana estaré para el arrastre." Google insists the translation is: "be one for the drag" which we may dismiss without regrets.

"Ramsey replied he was **on his last legs**, too, and could not climb at all." (Dobald L. Price, *The First Marine Captured in Vietnam*, 2007.) Let us not forget that phraseology also has synonyms, just like ordinary words, and in this case, we could mention: be totaled, ready to drop, dead on one´s feet, ready for the scrapyard, pooped, all done in, and more.

Believe it or not, there was a time when society was crueler than now and language reflected that cruelty with expressions that today we would find hurting. Those expressions are no longer in use simply because we have made forward strides in gender equality, but there was a time when the expression **old maid (on the shelf, in the garret)** ("**vieja solterona**") was applied to women, girls really, who had not gotten married by the age of, approximately, 20. It was understood that they had remained single not by choice but because they were ugly, or their fathers did not have a pot to piss in, or such circumstances. The Spanish language came up with the expression: **quedarse para vestir santos** because unmarried girls would spend their time in church, either praying or helping around with the "santos." In English and Spanish, the old maid was always supposed to be "bitter", "amargada", and had a terrible temper, and Hugh Rawson (*Wicked Words*, 1989) says: "Old maid, from 1530, almost always appears in a negative context…" Similar to the Spanish "solterona." Luckily, such language is no longer heard but can be read in literature before 1980.

Language, phraseology, mirrors society, not otherwise, and Anna Lapine deals with the spinster, old maid, subject in depth in her doctoral dissertation *The Old Maid in the Garret. Representation of the Spinster in Victorian Culture*, where she says: "… the negative terms in which the spinster was figured, either as a grotesque body or as a homeless wanderer to be feared, ridiculed and banished from sight."

But is this attitude gone and buried?

We read in the *Daily Courier* (November 28, 20015): "Luke Kelly, who headed a traditional Irish group called The Dubliners, singing a chorus that went, "Oh, dear me, How would it be, If I died an old maid in a garret?"

Mario Vargas Llosa, Nobel Prize Winner, in his 1977 novel, *La tía Julia y el escribidor* writes: "Era una gordita cariñosa, risueña y parlanchina y yo tomaba su defensa cuando en la familia, a sus espaldas, comentaban que se estaba quedando para vestir santos."

The English and Spanish-speaking worlds have the same attitude toward visitors who stay longer than patience would tolerate, and thus we have sayings like “visitas, pocas y cortitas”, and “fish and guests stink after three days.” (Delfín Carbonell, *Dictionary of Proverbs,* Barron’s, 1998). In the Bible (Proverbs, 25:18) we read: “Withdraw thy foot from thy neighbor’s house, lest he be weary of thee, and so hate thee.” This attitude has been the butt of jokes for centuries and language has invented expressions to say for the hosts to rid themselves of unwanted, pestering visitors. One such in Spanish is: **Vámonos a la cama que estos señores se querrán marchar** which is by no means subtle, or even polite, but it has been used plenty of times. And, of course, there´s a parallelism **in here´s your hat, what´s your hurry?** Which *The Free Dictionary* defines as “A humorous phrased used to encourage someone to leave.” It has been attributed to Winston Churchill. It is the title of Elizabeth McCracken Novel (1997) *Here´s your Hat, What´s your Hurry?* Neither phraseological unit will be found in bilingual dictionaries.

When a Spanish speaker or an English speaker is provoked, they can either accept the challenge or ignore it. For example, the bullfighting expression **entrar al trapo** means that the bull goes after the lure of the red rag, “capote,” and does precisely what the bullfighter wants him to do. Manuel Seco (*Diccionario fraseológico documentado del español actual*, 2004) defines the phraseological unit thus: “Responder, como se pretende, a la provocación que le hacen.”

One of the automatic translators gives “enter the rag” as the equivalent, and WordReference (WR) goes off the deep end and whistles Dixie, saying “caer en la provocación, morder el anzuelo.” Collins simply says: “picar.” However, if we say **rise to the bait**, we find the idea faithfully reflected: “react to a provocation just as intended.” Molly, for example, was rude to David on purpose, but he did not rise to the bait and said nothing. Likening how a fish rises to take the bait dangling in the water to human behavior has been in the English language since the 1500s.

“Rather than rise to the bait, Eilish gave this succinct response just a few hours later.” En vez de entrar al trapo, Eilish dio esta breve respuesta justo unas horas después. (The Wrap, Katie Campione, Feb. 10, 2022.)

“It’s to your credit that at that stage you didn’t rise to the bait and remained calm.” “Tienes mérito que en ese momento no hayas entrado al trapo y hayas mantenido la calma”. (TechCrunch, 22/02/2021.)

If the bilingual lexicographer gives it a try, they will nearly always find parallel phraseological units in English and Spanish.

What is the bilingual lexicographer to do with the phrase: **ante el vicio de pedir, la virtud de no dar**, with its variation **contra el vicio de pedir, está la**

virtud de no dar? Collins very wisely abstains. Tureng Dictionary online poses an answer which, although not bad, gets no cigar again: "a shameless beggar must have a short denial", taken from the Centro Virtual Cervantes, which is never to be trusted. WordPerfect passes, and even Seco´s *Diccionario fraseológico* keeps mum on this one. And so on. There must be a similar way to express the rebuff we must give those "gimme pigs" in English, now that we know how to do so in Spanish. How about **I want doesn´t get**, or **I want never gets**? In *Brewtiful* (Sept. 13, 2011) a mother says: "How many times have you all heard this phrase? I was always one of these people that said I would never be like mum, I would never say the things she said and now I found myself saying them all the time… Without fail though my favorite phrase comes out, "I want doesn't get", I even annoy myself when I say it." If this mum (mom) had been a Spanish speaker she would have said to her child: **contra el vicio de pedir, está la virtud de no dar**. We still have another possibility in English: **gimme, gimme, never gets, don´t you know your manners yet?** Unfortunately, this question has a retort: **Yes, I do, but not today, so gimme, gimme anyways**.

We all have had the experience of listening to someone who talks and talks and says nothing, giving us the shaggy-dog story, and whom we are finally forced to cut short, telling him, in Spanish, **al grano**, so that he sticks to the subject and quits bothering us with long-winded details. Leopoldo Alas (Clarín), the one who wrote *La Regenta*, exclaims in his work *Apolo en Pafos*: "No, no señor, no consiento preliminares ni prolegómenos… ¡Al grano!" The origin is from thresh, (thrash) where the grain is separated from the chaff and straw, which is what the charlatan is asked, to give us grain and not chaff. **Ir al grano** is, then, to stop beating around the bush and extravagance. The English language has a phrase with the same meaning: **cut to the chase**, which has a very curious origin. In the early days of cinema, in silent movies, there was a lot of movement and constant comings and goings (moving pictures). And there were always chases, cops and robbers, good guys and bad guys. When a static scene was prolonged, they would exclaim **cut to the chase**, which is what the audience wanted to see, action and chase.

"But let's cut to the chase: who wouldn't want to work with her?" (USA Today, 2011.) "Vayamos al grano, ¿quién no querría trabajar con ella?" And, of course, we can also say: **get to the point**, which means the same thing.

"Finally, he **cut to the chase**, asking me what kind of physical shape I was in." (Katherine Skiba, *Sister in the Band of Brothers*, 2005.)

Faced with painful situations, we sometimes take the way of humor as an evasive resource to escape the pain they cause us. And as there is a phrase for every idea, the Spanish language has its own for this emotional state. When we relate to or hear of, a painful situation, we laugh, trying to mitigate the pain, while exclaiming **río por no llorar**. And the English language has created its parallel phrase in **laugh to keep from crying**. "Your story is so very sad, and, yes, I am laughing, but I am laughing to keep from crying." Freud would explain to us the relationship between the tragic and the humorous. We can laugh in stressful situations and at events that force us to cry, but we laugh to keep from crying.

"There's an old African American adage: you have to laugh to keep from crying." (The Art Newspaper, Jan. 10, 2022.) African-Americans know a thing or two about crying, and laughing to keep from crying.

Reír por no llorar, laugh to keep from crying

When we hear expressions like the Spanish **dársela a uno con queso**, we never think about giving anyone cheese, but we soak up the idea of swindle, deception, trickery, fraud, cheat. All these words (and there are more), encapsulate the meaning of **dársela a uno con queso**, but it´s not as colloquial, as picturesque, or as jocose as, for example, **take someone to the cleaner´s**, which has the same meaning as the Spanish idiom. In English we have another expression also: **take someone for a ride**, and even another, that I have written about elsewhere: **pull the wool over someone´s eyes**, defined by Webster´s New World Dictionary (1968) as "deceive or fool someone." María Moliner says that darla (dársela) con queso, means "engañar o estafar a alguien." Manuel Seco follows suit.

"Cuidado que nos la **quieren dar con queso**." Careful, they want to **take us to the cleaner´s**.

"A David se la **dieron con queso** en el banco y firmó todo lo que le pusieron delante." David was **taken for a ride** at the bank and he signed everything they placed before him.

"Esta vez **no me la dan con queso** porque ya conozco a esos estafadores." This time they are not going **to pull the wool over my eyes** because I know those swindlers.

A few centuries ago, wine merchants tried to sell low-grade wine by offering strong cheese along with it, for buyers to eat and dull their taste buds. The cheese masqueraded the poor quality of the wine and thus patrons were tricked.

To **take someone to the cleaner´s (downtown)** means to clean, wipe them out, deceive and even swindle. The cleaner´s is the Spanish "tinte" or "tintorería."

"I hate the idea I'm being **taken for a ride**. That's not making room for the fool in me; it´s merely being stupid." Me molesta la idea de que **me la den con queso**. Eso no es hacer sitio para el tonto que hay en mí; es simplemente ser estúpido. (Roger Housden, *Seven Sins for a Life Worth Living*, 2005.)

Those who compose bilingual dictionaries are bone lazy, and always take the easy way out. Perhaps this may not be out of laziness or malice, but out of ignorance or lack of time. The fact is, for example, that when a sentence is complicated, they go for the easiest or most hackneyed way. In **cortar por lo sano**, María Moliner defines as "Terminar de una vez un asunto que proporciona preocupaciones, molestias o disgustos" I give the English **lance the boil** which is, for the Free Dictionary: "to take a decisive and dramatic action that resolves or puts to an end a problematic, troublesome, or unpleasant situation." The two definitions are almost identical, but this is not known to bilingual lexicons, perhaps for the reasons I give above. They tell us that for **cortar por lo sano** we "make a clean break, cut your losses, take extreme measures, go to the root of the problem" but none cuts to the chase and gives us **lance the boil**.

"You must **lance the boil** and find yourself another job." Debes cortar por lo sano y buscarte un empleo. Ian Watson uses the phrase in his novel *Inquisitor*: "… or because he hopes you might **lance the boil** of a conspiracy without him needing to show his hand?" And "Yet when leadership has so obviously failed, there has been a marked reluctance to **lance the boil** by removing the officer." (Th. A van Baarda, *The Moral Dimension of Asymmetrical Warfare*, 2009.) And Julio Cortázar employs the Spanish idiom in his *Queremos tanto a Glenda* thus, "…el grupo se va a ir irremisiblemente al diablo si Mario no se decide a **cortar por lo sano**…" And "… decidió cortar por lo sano en el conflicto intra-partidario post-electoral." Listín Diario 4/11/1997. Rep. Dom.

Lance the boil refers to slashing, lancing, a pimple, or boil, to cure it and alleviate discomfort.

The meaning of **back and fill (backing and filling)** is to be indecisive, doubtful, hesitant, vacillate. "Such a rest is called a consolidation or a period of backing and filling… people wait to rethink." (Jeannette Young, *The Option´s Doctor,* 2007.) As it is a phraseological unit, we should not use "vacilar, dudar, titubear" but must find a Spanish phraseological unit that will fit that original.

The following citation enlightens us as to the meaning. From Jeannette Young (*The Option Doctor: Option Strategies for Every Kind of Market*, 2007): "Such a rest is called a consolidation or a period of **backing and filling**. Why **backing and filling**? Because that is precisely what the market is doing; it is going back and forth within a narrow range, gaining enough energy to continue…" And another citation: "I see that the dressmaker was able to prevail despite your **backing and filling**." (Diana Burg, *Dalliance: A Novel*, 2008.)

Although Span¡shDict translates this as "relleno hacia atrás" we must endeavor to find a more suitable equivalent, such as: **Que sí, que no**; **que si sí, que si no**;

nadar (estar) entre dos aguas. The idea of backing and filling is well expressed in Spanish in "El veterano festival británico ha estado a punto de no celebrarse por problemas de seguridad, que sí, que no, y finalmente sí." (El País, 05/07/2004.) An also in, "La cosa está que si sí, que si no…" (El Mundo, 18/05/1994.) Further: "…viven situación opaca y ambigua entre dos aguas…" (Luis Cardoza, *Guatemala. Las líneas de su mano*, 1985.)

And what are we to say about *under the wire, get off the dime, be sitting pretty, lather, rinse and repeat, bring up to speed, Chinese fire drill, cheek by jowl, get one´s just deserts, batten down the hatches, run rings around someone, tomar a uno por el pito del sereno, estar curado de espanto, por la boca muere el pez, ser culo de mal asiento, pared con pared, llevarse uno su justo merecido, apretarse los machos, dar cien vueltas a* that are to be found in daily conversation but not in bilingual wordbooks? I must again paraphrase José Ortega y Gasset: "The horizon of our language is not the horizon of language."

The brain is not a computer and although we are ignorant of its language-storing capacity, often, no matter how learned we are, it slips and makes us falter. We then seek enlightenment from tools that will aid us to remember and learn. And I contend that, as ideas, feelings, and attitudes are the same, we will always find equivalents, especially in phraseological units, in both languages. Will computer scientists find algorithms that will match idioms in two languages given a specific meaning? In the meantime, we must make do with bilingual lexicographers and hope for the best and run to improve things (last one is a rotten egg, *marica el último*) while mouthing Samuel Johnson´s words in an attempt to apologize for mistakes: "Ignorance, madam, pure ignorance."

And snip, snap snout, this tale's told out, or if you prefer: you've had your fun, the tale is done. *Y colorín, colorado, este cuento se ha acabado.*

References

ABC (1989): 8 junio.

Alas, Leopoldo (1880): *Apolo en Pafos, Obras Completas*. Madrid: Ebooklasicos Kindle.

Arrabal, Fernando (1979): *Cementerio de automóviles*. Madrid: Cátedra.

Baarda, Th. A van (2009): *The moral dimension of asymetrical warfare*. New York: Martinus Niehoff Pubs.

Baron, Gerald (2003): *Now is too late: Survival in an era of instant news*. London: Viking.

Boswell, James (1791): *The life of Samuel Johnson*. London: Wordsworth Editions.

Brewtiful (2011): September 13.

Burg, Diana (2008): *Dalliance: A novel.* London: Chesterton.

Cacho Cortés, Jesús (1988): *Asalto al poder.* Madrid: Temas de Hoy.

Cambridge (2022): English Dictionary online.

Carbonell, Delfín (1998): *A dictionary of proverbs.* New York: Barron's.

Cardoza, Luis (1985): *Guatemala. Las líneas de su mano.* Managua: Nueva Guatemala.

Collins (2022): online Dictionary.

Cortázar, Julio (1980): *Queremos tanto a Glenda.* Madrid: Alfaguara.

Daily Courier (2015): November 28.

Dunia (1995): Madrid, Julio.

El Mundo, (1994): Madrid, 18 mayo.

El País (2004): Madrid, 5 julio.

Gaar, Gillian G. (2009): *Green Day: Rebels with a cause.* New York: Picador.

Giménez Losantos, Federico (1995): *Lo que queda de España.* Madrid: Temas de Hoy.

Housden, Roger (2005): *Seven sins for a life worth living.* Amazon, Kindle Edition.

Kubke, Jane (2006): *Bull riding.* New York: Rosen Pub. Group.

Landau, Sidney I. (2001): *Dictionaries: The art and craft of lexicography.* Cambridge: Cambridge University Press.

Lapine, Anna (2011): *The old maid in the Garret. Representation of the Spinster in Victorian Culture*, Doctoral Dissertation, Ottawa, University of Ottawa.

Marías, Javier (1992): *Corazón tan blanco.* Barcelona: Anagrama.

Marzolph, Ulrich et al. (2004): *The Arabian Night's encyclopedia.* New York: Marzolp.

McCracken, Elizabeth (1997): *Here's your hat, what's your hurry?* New York: Random House.

McGee, Sherry A. (2004): *Skinny women are evil.* New York: Atria Books.

Moliner, María (2008): *Diccionario de uso del español*, CD, versión electrónica 3.0, Madrid: Gredos.

Oxford (2022): English Dictionary online.

Portal, Marta (1983): *Pago de traición.* Barcelona:, Planeta.

Price, Dobald L. (2004): *The first marine captured in Vietnam.* New York: Crown.

Proceso de México (1996): México, 15 diciembre.

Rawson, Hugh (1989): *Wicked words.* New York: Crown Publishers.

Reverso online Dictionary.

Seco, Manuel et al. (2004): *Diccionario fraseológico documentado del español actual*. Madrid: Gredos.

Skiba, Katherine (2005): *Sister in the band of brothers*. New York: Scribner´s.

Span¡shDict (2022): Dictionary online.

TechCrunch (2021): New York: February 22.

The Art Newspaper (2022): January 11.

The Free Dictionary (2003–2022): online.

The Wrap, Katie Campione: (2022), Feb. 10.

Tureng Dictionary (2022): online.

USA Today (2011): New York, Feb. 10.

Varela, Fernando (1996): *Diccionario fraseológico del español moderno*. Madrid: Gredos.

Vargas Llosa (1977): *La tía Julia y el escribidor*. Barcelona: Seix Barral.

Watson, Ian (2007): *Inquisitor*. London: Picador.

Webster's New World Dictionary (1968): New York: The World Publishing Company.

Winnipeg Sun (2003): 8 November.

WordReference (2022): online Dictionary.

Young, Jeannette (2007): *The option doctor: Option strategies for every kind of market*. New York: Offset.

Ruth Breeze / Manuel Casado-Velarde

CS, Universidad de Navarra

Apuntes para un análisis comparativo de la fraseología relativa a la persuasión en inglés y en español

Abstract: Throughout the last few decades, work on phraseology has evolved considerably. To a lesser extent, comparative phraseology has also advanced. This contribution addresses the comparative study of the phraseology of Spanish and English in the area of persuasion. The underlying schemes are analysed, and the evaluative attitudes transmitted by the respective phraseological units are compared.

Keywords: Comparative phraseology, English-Spanish, persuasion, metaphorical schemes.

Resumen: A lo largo de los últimos decenios, los trabajos sobre fraseología han adquirido un gran desarrollo. En menor medida lo ha hecho la fraseología comparada. La presente contribución constituye una aproximación al estudio comparado de la fraseología del español y del inglés sobre la persuasión. Se explicitan los esquemas subyacentes, así como las actitudes valorativas transmitidas por las respectivas unidades fraseológicas.

Palabras clave: Fraseología comparada, inglés-español, persuasión, esquemas metafóricos.

A pesar del gran desarrollo experimentado por los estudios fraseológicos durante las últimas décadas, una de las deficiencias más comunes que se observan en los diccionarios bilingües es el abandono en el que se encuentran las unidades pluriverbales (Corpas Pastor, 1996: 167), consideradas, por lo demás, la "parte más idiosincrásica y propia de cada lengua" (Corpas Pastor, 1998: 170). Son necesarios, sin duda, muchos estudios monográficos de carácter contrastivo para poder ir llenando esa insuficiencia lexicográfica.

En vivo contraste con la abundante fraseología relativa a las emociones (véase Breeze & Casado-Velarde, 2018), se encuentra la atingente a la persuasión, como se podrá comprobar en lo que sigue. Y lo mismo cabe afirmar de los estudios comparativos sobre la citada categoría conceptual[1]. Para la voz *persuasión* el *Diccionario* académico del español (*DLE*) proporciona las dos siguientes acepciones: 1. f. "Acción y efecto de persuadir". / 2. f. "Aprehensión o juicio que se forma en virtud de un fundamento". Aquí nos interesa solo la primera acepción, es decir, la acción y efecto de "inducir, mover, obligar a alguien con razones a creer o hacer algo" (*DLE, s. v. persuadir*), que en español posee también un empleo verbal pronominal: *Convéncete de que el avión es más seguro que el automóvil.*

La fraseología española relativa a la persuasión[2] se encuentra vinculada básicamente con la parte del cuerpo que llamamos *cabeza* (con sus varias denominaciones coloquiales metafóricas: *cerebro, coco, sesera, tarro, seso…*) como órgano o RECIPIENTE donde se encuentran las ideas y convicciones, consideradas COSAS. Las cuales pueden ser objeto de sustracción y, eventualmente, de sustitución por otras diferentes. El cambio de ideas en que consiste la persuasión se produce mediante la acción de un agente, fundamentalmente externo, que

- las *saca* (*sacar* [algo a alguien] *de la cabeza*); o
- las *quita* (*quitar* [algo a alguien] *de la cabeza*);
- las *sorbe* (*sorber el seso / la sesera* [a alguien]);
- se las *come* (*comer* [a alguien] *la cabeza / el coco / el tarro*)[3].

Agente que también puede *meter* las nuevas ideas o convicciones:

- *meter* [algo a alguien] *en la cabeza.*

Tras este paradigma fraseológico se oculta una concepción de la actividad persuasiva como algo que acontece de modo esencialmente pasivo en la persona objeto de la persuasión, tal y como puede inferirse de las definiciones consignadas a continuación[4]:

---

1 No aparece mencionada, por ejemplo, en Corpas Pastor (1996, 1998, 2003), ni en Leal Riol (2008). Corpas Pastor (2008) se ocupa de establecer una taxonomía general de las unidades fraseológicas "que sea válida para dos lenguas distantes genéticamente, a saber, el español y el inglés" (2008: 186).

2 Aquí se tiene en cuenta, por lo que se refiere al español, la fraseología actual tal como aparece reflejada y definida en el DFDEA.

3 En cambio, *comerse* [alguien] *el coco* [con algo] carece de significado persuasivo; equivale a 'pensar intensamente [en ello] u obsesionarse [con ello]'.

4 Menos directamente vinculados a la persuasión se encuentran otros somatismos, también centrados en la cabeza, como: *calentar la cabeza* a alguien (DFDEA) 'hacerle concebir esperanzas vanas o aspiraciones desmedidas'; *llenar la cabeza de pájaros* a

Comer el coco [a alguien] v. 'convencerle o imbuirle determinadas ideas, esp. aprovechando su buena fe o su ingenuidad' (DFDEA).
Comer el tarro [a alguien] v. 'convencerle o imbuirle determinadas ideas, esp. aprovechando su buena fe o su ingenuidad' (DFDEA).
Comer la cabeza [a alguien] v. 'comerle el coco' (DFDEA).
Sorber el seso [a alguien], *sorber la sesera* v. 'convencerle o imbuirle determinadas ideas, esp. aprovechando su buena fe o su ingenuidad' (DFDEA).
Quitar/sacar [algo a alguien] *de la cabeza* v. 'convencerle para que deje de pensar en ello' (DFDEA).
Meter [algo a alguien] *en la cabeza* v. 'convencerle de ello' (DFDEA)[5].
Lavar el cerebro [a, o de, alguien] v. 'hacer[le] un lavado de cerebro (acción de forzar, por procedimientos psicológicos y a veces también físicos, un cambio radical en las ideas y creencias de una persona' (DFDEA).

El inglés ofrece menos variedad de expresiones en este sentido, pero cuenta con unidades fraseológicas como *to put something into someone's head* ('meter algo en la cabeza de alguien') (cf. también *to brainwash* [someone], verbo que significa "lavar el cerebro" a alguien).

Un segundo paradigma fraseológico vinculado a la persuasión identifica las ideas o convicciones con la totalidad de la PERSONA física que resulta persuadida, a la que, quien persuade (persuasor), desplaza (*apea / baja / hace caer*) de la (cómoda) situación en la que se encontraba (a lomos de un *burro* o de una *burra*)[6]:

Bajar / apear / hacer caer [a alguien] *del burro / de la burra* 'convencer[le] o hacer[le] desistir de su idea' (DFDEA).

O bien el persuasor se apodera de ella (de la persona que ha sido persuadida) como si fuera un objeto; es decir, *se la mete en el bolsillo* o *en el bote*:

Meterse en el bote [a alguien] 'conquistarle o ganar su voluntad' (DFDEA);
Meterse [a alguien] *en el bolsillo* 'ganarse [su] voluntad' (DFDEA).
En esta línea la fraseología del inglés ofrece la expresión:
To be in someone's pocket (literalmente 'estar en el bolsillo de alguien'),

---

alguien, *meter pájaros en la cabeza* a alguien (DFDEA) 'hacerle concebir esperanzas vanas o ideas sin fundamento'.

5 El DLE registra la unidad fraseológica *encasquetar* algo a alguien *en la cabeza* 'convencerle de ello'.

6 Este esquema fraseológico presenta también una variedad pronominal, en la que el persuadido 'cede o desiste de su idea': *bajarse* (o *apearse*, o *caer*(se) [alguien] *del burro* (o, raro, *burra*) (DFDEA).

que significa "estar bajo el control de otra persona"; por ejemplo: "the judge was in the senator's pocket" manifiesta que el juez hacía todo lo que quería el senador. Aquí también la persona que ha sido persuadida se considera como un objeto del que el persuasor se ha apoderado.

Cuando el persuadido se deja convencer, de buen o mal grado, se expresa mediante la locución:

> *Dar* [alguien] *su* (o *el*) *brazo a torcer* v. 'ceder en una opinión, actitud o propósito en que se ha mantenido firme' (Generalmente en construcción negativa: *no dar el brazo a torcer*) (DFDEA).

Próximas a esta locución, pero con significado activo, se encuentran las frases del inglés:

> *To twist someone's arm* 'torcerle el brazo a alguien, presionar para que alguien haga algo, coaccionar'.
> *To twist someone around one's little finger* 'torcer a alguien alrededor del dedo meñique (es decir, hacer con alguien lo que a uno le da la gana, tener una influencia muy fuerte sobre alguien)'.
> *To lead someone by the nose* 'llevar a alguien por la nariz (es decir, controlarlo, muy similar al anterior)'.

En estos elementos subyace la idea de la fuerza física para representar el ejercicio de la persuasión psicológica, que refleja la metáfora conceptual "ARGUMENT IS PHYSICAL CONFLICT" (Ritchie, 2003). Ésta está a su vez relacionada con el esquema conocido "ARGUMENT IS WAR" analizado por Lakoff y Johnson (1980: 79), quienes lo consideran como especialmente característico de la forma de entender el desacuerdo entre hablantes nativos del inglés, y en un sentido más amplio, como evidencia de la prioridad del combate físico sobre el discurso en la evolución del ser humano. La referencia a la guerra como modelo básico de conflicto ha sido el objeto de crítica de parte de otros expertos (veáse, por ejemplo, Vervaeke y Kennedy, 2004), y parece claro que el esquema corporal reflejado en la noción que "el conflicto psicológico es un conflicto físico" sería más básico en la experiencia humana que la guerra como tal. En este sentido, la fraseología del español en este sentido refleja el mismo esquema subyacente de conflicto físico interpersonal. De todos modos, como explica Howe (2007), deberíamos ejercer la máxima precaución a la hora de elaborar teorías antropológicas a raíz de unas pocas expresiones lingüísticas, ya que las lenguas, como vemos aquí, ofrecen una variedad de expresiones metafóricas con diferentes implicaciones para nuestra comprensión de la sociedad humana.

Otro aspecto interesante relacionado con el entendimiento de la persuasión reside en que, tanto la lengua española como la inglesa, distinguen entre *persuadir* ("tr. Inducir, mover, obligar a alguien con razones a creer o hacer algo. U. t. c. prnl.", DLE) (inglés *persuade, convince*) y *seducir* ("tr. Persuadir a alguien con argucias o halagos para algo, frecuentemente malo", DLE) (inglés *seduce, entice*). En todos los esquemas citados, más que de *persuadir / persuade*, se focaliza la idea de *seducir / seduce*, en la medida en que no parecen mediar razones que lleven a una persona a cambiar de ideas. En todo caso, se transmite implícitamente una visión peyorativa de la acción de persuadir, en el sentido de que no se respeta al otro, sino que se ignora su dignidad de persona y se le imponen las propias ideas y convicciones.

Otras unidades fraseológicas explicitan de forma diferente el carácter de fraude seductor que se atribuye a la persuasión. Una de ellas está construida sobre una metáfora vinculada a la PESCA CON ANZUELO, en la que este está representando la idea objeto de persuasión / seducción. Y aquí es la persona persuadida / seducida la que, como si fuera un pez, *pica* o *muerde* y *se traga el anzuelo*. Es decir, es objeto de una trampa o engaño:

> *Morder/ picar (en) el anzuelo* 'dejarse engañar' (DFDEA).
> *Tragar(se) el anzuelo* 'dejarse engañar' (DFDEA)[7].

Otros fraseologismos reposan sobre la metáfora de LAS IDEAS SON ALGO QUE SE PUEDE VENDER:

> *Vender la burra / la moto* [a alguien] 'engañar[le] o hacer[le] creer falsedades' (DFDEA).

Los dos siguientes fraseologismos del inglés equivalen asimismo a "engañar":

> *To take* [someone] *for a ride* 'llevar [a alguien] a pasear'.
> *To take* [someone] *to the cleaners* 'llevar [a alguien] a la tintorería'.

En cambio,

> *To sell someone down the river* (literalmente 'vender a alguien por el río')
> responde al contenido semántico del español *traicionar*.

El carácter embaucador que tienen otros frasemas estriba en que se trata de engañar a otra persona, por ejemplo, a un comprador mediante la venta de algo defectuoso o averiado:

> *Dar gato por liebre*, ingl. *to sell a pig in a poke* (literalmente 'vender un cerdo en una bolsa'), *to pull the wool over someone's eyes* (literalmente 'tirar la lana sobre los ojos

7 La locución del inglés *to feed someone a line* no se encuentra vinculada con la pesca, sino que, probablemente, se refiere al mundo del teatro, donde los actores presentan sus "lines" (frases memorizadas) para convencer al público.

de alguien'), *to throw dust into someone's eyes* (literalmente 'arrojar polvo a los ojos de alguien').

Carece de sentido peyorativo, en cambio, el fraseologismo *poner algo* [a alguien] *delante de los ojos* "hacerle reparar en ello verbalmente o convencerle de que rectifique en su parecer erróneo" (*DFDEA*)[8].

Las siguientes unidades fraseológicas, basadas en los órganos articulatorios del lenguaje (*boca, labios*), poseen en común una acepción ("hacer callar [a alguien] a través de un argumento concluyente") y ponen el acento no tanto en el hecho de que esté convencido el interlocutor, cuanto en el hecho de la ausencia de réplica por parte de este, contenidos para los que el inglés dispone de la locución *To shut someone up* (callar a alguien) o *To keep someone quiet* (entre otros significados, hacer callar [a alguien] a través de un argumento concluyente):

Cerrar la boca a alguien v. 'hacerle callar sobornándole o amenazándole', 'hacerle callar a través de un argumento concluyente' (*DFDEA*);
Tapar la boca a alguien v. 'hacerle callar sobornándole o amenazándole', 'hacerle callar a través de un argumento concluyente' (*DFDEA*);
Cerrar los labios a alguien v. 'hacer que no hable o deje de hablar'; 'hacerle callar a través de un argumento concluyente' (*DFDEA*).

Estas expresiones también aluden al esquema del cuerpo humano y al conflicto físico (comentado arriba), aunque en un sentido más directamente relacionado con la actividad discursiva.

Observaciones finales

La fraseología de la persuasión en castellano e inglés resulta bastante similar. Muchos frasemas, como se habrá podido comprobar, remiten a los mismos esquemas subyacentes.

Los aspectos psicológicos, no perceptibles por los sentidos, se plasman mediante las acciones físicas y/o corporales.

En la fraseología de la persuasión de ambas lenguas predomina una actitud negativa de suspicacia y/o de rechazo a la actividad persuasiva, y, particularmente, a la que se considera seductora.

---

8 Cf. asimismo *abrir* [a alguien] *los ojos* [a algo] v. 'descubrírse[lo] o darse[lo] a conocer'; *arrancar/quitar* [a alguien] *la venda de los ojos* 'hacer que se dé cuenta de las cosas o que las perciba con claridad' (*DFDEA*).

Referencias bibliográficas

Academia Española, Real y ASALE (2014): *Diccionario de la lengua española*, 23.ª ed. Versión en línea: http://dle.rae.es/?w=diccionario.

Breeze, R., y Casado-Velarde, M. (2018): "Expressing emotions without emotional lexis: A crosslinguistic approach to the phraseology of the emotions in Spanish and English". En Lachlan-Mackenzie, J. y Alba-Juez, L. (eds.), *Emotion in discourse*, Amsterdam: John Benjamins, 113–138.

Corpas Pastor, G. (1996): "La fraseología en los diccionarios bilingües". En M. Alvar Ezquerra (Coord.), *Estudios de historia de la lexicografía del español*, Málaga, Universidad de Málaga, 167–182.

Corpas Pastor, G. (1998): "Criterios generales de clasificación del universo fraseológico de las lenguas, con ejemplos en español y en inglés", en M. Alvar Ezquerra y G. Corpas Pastor (Coords.): *Diccionarios, frases, palabras*, Málaga, Universidad de Málaga, 157–187.

Corpas Pastor, G. (2003): *Diez años de investigación en fraseología: Análisis sintáctico-semánticos, contrastivos y traductológicos*, Frankfurt am Main, Vervuert. Madrid, Iberoamericana.

DEA: Seco, M., Andrés, O., y G. Ramos (1999).

DFDEA: Seco, M., Andrés, O., y G. Ramos (2004).

DLE 2014: Academia Española, Real y Asale (2014).

Howe, J. (2007): "Argument is argument: An essay on conceptual metaphor and verbal dispute", *Metaphor & Symbol*, 23 (1), 1–23.

Lakoff, G., y Johnson, M. (1980): *Metaphors we live by*, Chicago, University of Chicago Press.

Leal Riol, M.ª J. (2008): "Contraste fraseológico: similitudes diferencias entre las unidades fraseológicas del español y del inglés", *Revista de Filología Inglesa*, 29, 103–116.

Ritchie, D. (2003), "'ARGUMENT IS WAR' – Or is it a game of chess? Multiple meanings in the analysis of implicit metaphors", *Metaphor & Symbol*, 18 (2), 125–146.

Seco, M., Andrés, O., y G. Ramos (1999): *Diccionario del español actual*, Madrid, Aguilar.

Seco, M., Andrés, O., y G. Ramos (2004): *Diccionario fraseológico documentado del español actual. Locuciones y modismos españoles*, Madrid: Aguilar.

Vervaeke, J. & Kennedy, J. M. (2004): "Conceptual metaphor and abstract thought", *Metaphor & Symbol*, 19 (3), 213–231.

Montserrat Martínez Vázquez

Universidad Pablo de Olavide, Sevilla

La mujer detrás del artista. Un nuevo caso de anglicismo sintáctico en español

Resumen: Este trabajo investiga un caso de anglicismo sintáctico en una situación de contacto lingüístico débil. El estudio analiza el uso de adjuntos preposicionales del nombre como en *la mujer detrás del artista* que son cada vez más frecuentes en español. La *Real Academia Española de la Lengua* (RAE) considera que son usos raros e incorrectos que se producen por influencia del inglés (*Nueva Gramática de la Lengua Española*, 2009, 858–859). Este trabajo plantea las siguientes preguntas de investigación: 1. ¿Se documenta esta construcción en el español europeo? 2. En caso afirmativo, ¿cuándo surgió y cómo se usa? 3. ¿Se trata de un anglicismo, incorrecto, como sugiere la RAE? El análisis, basado en datos de corpus históricos y contemporáneos (CE, CORDE, CREA, CORPES, EsTenTen y NOW) muestra que la construcción es de uso reciente y se ha extendido en los últimos años, especialmente en las noticias en línea. Las propiedades formales y funcionales compartidas con la construcción homóloga inglesa evidencian un caso de préstamo construccional, aunque la formación española se utiliza predominantemente en su sentido metafórico. Una encuesta realizada a 101 hablantes nativos de español pone de manifiesto la aceptabilidad de algunas de estas construcciones recientes.

Palabras clave: adjuntos nominales preposicionales, *behind*, *detrás de*, anglicismo sintáctico.

1. Introducción

El estudio de los anglicismos de la lengua española se ha centrado fundamentalmente en el léxico (Gómez Capuz, 1997; Pulcini et al., 2012). Los préstamos sintácticos son más escasos y han recibido menor atención (Pountain, 1994: 109; Sunde, 2018: 101; Matras, 2020: 234). Sin embargo, el creciente contacto de lenguas en un mundo global ha acelerado el intercambio de estructuras lingüísticas, que se extiende más allá del ámbito léxico. Como señala MacKenzie (2012: 31), "as the number of multicompetent L2 users of English in Europe grows, their L1s –and not just the lexis– are probably being slightly Anglicized." La mayoría de los hispanohablantes está expuesta al inglés a diario, ya sea de una manera activa o pasiva, y esta (de)codificación continua de expresiones inglesas lleva a interiorizarlas, lo que facilita el intercambio interlingüístico incluso en situaciones de contacto "débil", como es el caso del español europeo en su contacto con la lengua franca. El inglés es una lengua extranjera en España, sin embargo, su uso reiterado en Internet hace que incluso aquellos que no la dominen sean capaces de utilizar algunas expresiones inglesas en ciertos contextos (Balteiro, 2018: 123). Estas circunstancias facilitan la entrada de préstamos construccionales (Martínez Vázquez, 2020, 2021).

En el español actual se observa un creciente uso de sintagmas nominales complejos que incorporan adyacentes con preposiciones locativas distintas a *de*, como se observa en los ejemplos que siguen:

(1) El nuevo colegio en el centro de Sevilla no estará disponible antes de 2025. (*Diario de Sevilla*, 13/04/2023)
(2) La historia de la urbanización frente a Doñana autorizada por la Junta. (*El País*, 19/05/2023)
(3) Protestas en Georgia: ¿quién es la mujer detrás de la bandera de la Unión Europea? (*El Pais*, 10/03/2023).

La RAE en su *Nueva Gramática de la Lengua Española* (NGLE) sostiene que estos usos preposicionales son raros: "[l]os grupos preposicionales locativos en función de adjunto nominal son relativamente raros cuando están encabezados por preposiciones distintas de *de*." (NGLE, 1999: 859). Los adjuntos nominales que se construyen con otras preposiciones son considerados anglicismos incorrectos que deben sustituirse por otras preposiciones: "[p]or influencia del inglés se construyen en algunos países secuencias como *la tienda bajo mi casa* o *el cartel en ese muro*, que se consideran incorrectas y se recomienda sustituir por otras como *la tienda de debajo de mi casa* o *el cartel de ese muro*". Solo se admiten algunos casos excepcionales con las preposiciones *bajo* y *sobre* (*el puente sobre el lago*) y preposiciones con sustantivos eventivos nominalizados (*bofetada en su prestigio, guerra en Nicaragua*) (NGLE, 2009: 859).

El objetivo de este trabajo es investigar estos posibles casos de préstamos sintácticos del inglés. En concreto, se analizará uno de los usos más recurrentes: los sintagmas nominales con adjuntos preposicionales encabezados por *detrás de* (*N detrás de*, en adelante), cuyo uso es frecuente en la prensa, especialmente en un sentido metafórico:

(4) La historia detrás del jilguero de la Iglesia de San Pedro de Sevilla. (*Diario de Sevilla*, 20/03/2023)
(5) Vientres de alquiler, el negocio detrás del deseo de ser padres. (*El País*, 2/04/2023)

Este trabajo plantea las siguientes preguntas de investigación ¿Se documenta la construcción *N detrás de* en el español europeo, variedad que está en contacto indirecto con el inglés? Si es así, ¿cuándo y cómo surge? ¿Se trata de un anglicismo, incorrecto y relativamente raro, como sugiere la NGLE?

Para responder estas cuestiones se llevará a cabo un análisis mediante una metodología basada en corpus que permita documentar el uso de estos adyacentes nominales en español, cuantificarlos y señalar su fecha de aparición. Se obtendrán también datos de las construcciones análogas consideradas "normativas" por la RAE para comparar sus usos. Finalmente, se extraerán construcciones nominales inglesas modificadas por *behind* de corpus de inglés para realizar un análisis contrastivo que señale las posibles semejanzas formales y funcionales que probarían la hipótesis del préstamo. Tras el análisis se llevará a cabo una encuesta a hablantes de español europeo para que valoren la aceptabilidad de estas construcciones.

La sección 2 presenta el marco teórico: se describen las construcciones con adjuntos nominales en inglés y sus equivalentes en español. La sección 3 explica la metodología utilizada en el análisis de corpus. En la sección 4 se muestran y analizan los datos de corpus de la construcción *N detrás de*, se comparan con ejemplos de las construcciones inglesas y se contrastan con los casos obtenidos de las estructuras consideradas normativas por la RAE. El siguiente apartado ofrece e interpreta los datos de una encuesta de aceptabilidad de estas construcciones. El trabajo termina con las conclusiones del análisis y las respuestas a las preguntas de investigación planteadas.

2. Marco teórico

2.1. Adjuntos nominales en inglés

El sintagma preposicional es el adjunto nominal más frecuente en inglés (Quirk et al., 1985: 1286; Biber et al., 1999: 634; Huddleston & Pullum, 2002: 446; Conrad & Biber, 2010: 116). Datos de corpus de Biber et al. (1999) evidencian que entre el 65 % y el 80 % de los adyacentes nominales en inglés son preposicionales, especialmente frecuentes en registros académicos y en noticias. De entre los demás adyacentes nominales, los más recurrentes son las oraciones de relativo (Biber et al., 1999: 601). De hecho, Quirk et al. (1985: 1274) sugieren que los sintagmas preposicionales que modifican al nombre proceden de la reducción de oraciones de relativo (*the car standing outside the station →the car outside the station*).

Biber et al. (1999: 634) no mencionan directamente la idea de derivación, pero sí señalan la equivalencia semántica entre ambas construcciones: "prepositional phrases can be re-phrased as full relative clauses with nearly equivalent meaning". Por su parte, Conrad & Biber (2010: 116) observan que las preposiciones que modifican al nombre suelen usarse con un sentido no literal: "[u]sually these prepositions do not have their litral "physical" meaning."

La preposición *behind,* tiene un uso locativo que relaciona dos entidades. El *Oxford English Dictionary* (OED) la describe en relación a un elemento que tiene un anverso y un reverso: "[i]n the space lying to the rear of, on the back side of (a person, or object that has a front and back)." Quirk et al. (1985: 678) representan *behind* en un eje horizontal, como puede observarse en la Fig. 1. Sin embargo, esta representación falsea el sentido de *behind*, que debe ser concebido como un eje que se aleja del punto de vista, de tal manera que el punto de referencia oculte la entidad que describimos, como se representa en la Fig. 2. De hecho, el OED incluye una acepción de *behind* que toma en consideración el punto de vista de un espectador: "[o]n the farther side of (an object) from the spectator or point of reference; beyond." Es precisamente esta perspectiva la que da origen al significado figurado que señala el OED [sub 6b]: "[a]t the back of, hidden by; on the side remote from one's observation."

in front of X behind X

< -------------------------------------- X -------------------------------------->

Fig. 1. Representación de *behind* (adaptada de Quirk et al., 1985, 678).

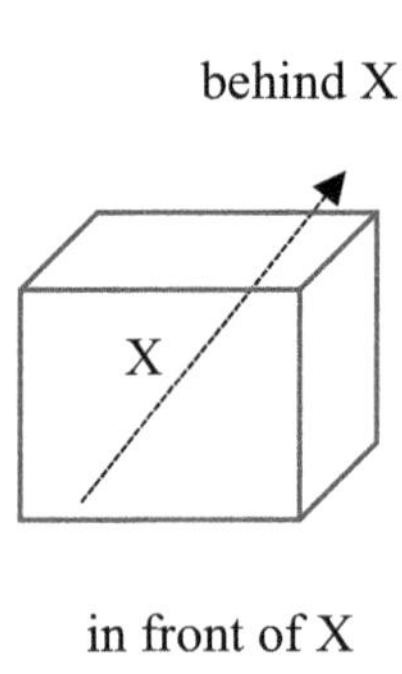

Fig. 2. Representación de *behind.*

Este sentido de ocultamiento aparece bien definido en los estudios de Lingüística Cognitiva. Así, Tyler & Evans (2003: 171) describen *behind* como ausencia de percepción y falta de seguridad sobre la ubicación de un elemento ("lack of perceptual access and lack of surety about the location of the TR [trajector]"). Por su parte, Lindstromberg (2010: 103) observa que *behind* se usa normalmente para identificar a un elemento que se sitúa por encima del punto de referencia. En su uso metafórico describe algo que queda oscurecido por el objeto de referencia: "[b]ecause *BEHIND* is particularly apt when Landmark obscures the Subject, it is used metaphorically to refer to agents that are unknown or that might wish to remain unknown" como en "*a grand conspiracy behind the assassination* of President Lincoln" (Lindstromberg, 2010: 105). Dixon (2021: 216), añade al sentido de ocultación la idea de algo inesperado: "to describe something 'at the rear of' a misleading exterior."

Otro significado figurado de este sentido locativo sugiere una escena en la que se empuja desde detrás para representar una fuerza motivadora, lo que Lindstromberg (2010: 105) identifica como "agents' motives" (*the reasons behind the assassination of Archduke Ferdinand*) o "motivating force" (*the power behind the throne*). Dixon (2021: 216) describe estos usos como " 'at the rear of' in the sense of being responsible for" (*General Joos was the man behind the coup*) o "to indicate support" (*The whole province is behind the Motion for Independence*).

2.2. Adjuntos nominales en español

En su descripción de los adjuntos nominales locativos, la NGLE (2009: 859) no menciona usos metafóricos. Tampoco cuantifica los tipos de complementos del nombre más frecuentes del español, ni los relaciona directamente con otras estructuras sintácticas. Sin embargo, en su rechazo a los complementos del nombre con preposiciones locativas distintas a *de* se señala que la construcción correcta o "normativa" debe estar encabezada por *de* (*N de detrás de*). Por otra parte, en la descripción de los adjuntos locativos, se menciona indirectamente la sinonimia con las oraciones de relativo: "*la gente de aquí* significa 'la gente que está aquí o que vive aquí'" (NGLE, 2009: 858). Por ello, cabe considerar las oraciones de relativo como alternativas a los adyacentes preposicionales del nombre, como se ha señalado para el inglés.

En cuanto a la locución *detrás de*, el *Diccionario de la Lengua Española* (DLE) no reconoce su uso preposicional, solo menciona el uso adverbial de *detrás*. Sorprendentemente, sí se incluye como locución preposicional su antónima, *delante de*. Tampoco se incluye un uso figurativo de *detrás*, aunque la segunda acepción, añadida en la última edición ("en ausencia") podría describir un uso metafórico. La falta de ejemplos impide discernir bien su uso, pero podría estar relacionado con el valor que le dan a la preposición antónima *delante* ("a la vista, en presencia de"). De hecho, el *Diccionario del español actual* incluye esta misma descripción en su acepción tercera de *detrás*: "[e]n ausencia [de una pers.]", ilustrada con un ejemplo de Delibes (*A mi tío, allá en el pueblo, le respetaban, oiga, aunque luego anduvieran por detrás diciendo perrerías*). Este sentido del uso adverbial está claramente relacionado con el sentido metafórico de ocultamiento que hemos visto en *behind*. Cabría, por tanto, asumir que existe el uso preposicional de *detrás de* –por analogía con la descripción que ofrece el DLE para *delante de*– y un uso metafórico, relacionado con algo ausente u oculto –como ocurre con la preposición inglesa *behind*. Esta locución preposicional podría compartir los mismos sentidos figurativos que señalan los lingüistas cognitivistas para la preposición inglesa.

3. Marco metodológico

Los datos para el análisis han sido extraídos de seis corpus de español. El análisis se ha circunscrito a los datos del español europeo para evitar variaciones intralingüísticas. Por otro lado, al ser la variedad que menos contacto tiene con el inglés, la constatación del préstamo favorecería la interpretación de préstamos indirectos (Peterson, 2017; Balteiro, 2018).

En primer lugar, se consultaron dos corpus diacrónicos, el *Corpus del Español* (CE) y el *Corpus Diacrónico del Español* (CORDE), para comprobar si se documentaban ejemplos de la construcción antes del siglo XX. Posteriormente, el *Corpus de Referencia del Español Actual* (CREA) aportaría los datos del siglo pasado. Finalmente, el *Corpus del Español del Siglo XXI* (CORPES) proporcionaría los datos del español europeo del siglo XXI. Aunque CORPES es un excelente corpus de referencia que incluye datos orales y escritos de diversos géneros, su tamaño es demasiado reducido (105 millones de español europeo) para obtener construcciones emergentes, cuya frecuencia inicialmente es escasa. Por ello, se optó por completar el estudio con dos corpus de español más extensos, el corpus EsTenTen18 disponible a través de la plataforma *Sketch Engine*, que contiene 8.776 millones de palabras de español europeo, y el corpus *News on the Web* (NOW) de Mark Davies, que incluye 1.442 millones de dicha variedad. Su mayor extensión y la diversidad de textos informales de Internet que estos corpus incluyen (noticias en línea, comentarios en foros, artículos de opinión, etc.) ofrecían un buen escenario para la aparición de estructuras no normativas. Por otro lado, los datos de Biber et al. (1999) muestran que las construcciones inglesas son más frecuentes en el género *news*, muy abundante entre los corpus de textos de Internet.

Para contrastar los datos del español con las construcciones análogas inglesas y valorar la hipótesis del préstamo, se consultaron dos corpus de inglés análogos: *English Web 2020* (EnTenTen20) incluido en *Sketch Engine* y *English News on the Web* (NOW) de Mark Davies.

Los ejemplos se obtuvieron con búsquedas de *detrás de* tras sustantivos ("N detrás de") y seguidamente con adjetivos pre o posnominales ("N ADJ *detrás de*"/ "ADJ N *detrás de*"). Los resultados fueron cuidadosamente analizados para descartar usos adverbiales (por ejemplo, *situar las causas detrás de las consecuencias*). Como las construcciones inglesas, que supuestamente copia el español, guardan una estrecha relación con las oraciones de relativo –bien como origen de estas (Quirk et al., 1985) o con una relación de casi sinonimia (Biber et al., 1999)– y, por otra parte, la NGLE (2009: 858) también menciona su semejanza semántica, se realizó una segunda búsqueda de adyacentes con oraciones de relativo con *detrás de* ("*N que V detrás de*"). Después, se examinaron las construcciones de adyacentes del nombre normativas, es decir, aquellas que la RAE considera correctas (*N de detrás de*), para contrastarlas con las nuevas construcciones y ver si proceden de estas o guardan alguna relación de sinonimia.

Finalmente, para comprobar la hipótesis del préstamo, se buscaron construcciones nominales inglesas con *behind* en los corpus ingleses (EnTenTen20 y NOW) y se seleccionaron los sustantivos modificados por esta preposición para comprobar su valor –físico o metafórico– y contrastar su distribución con las estructuras halladas en los corpus españoles.

Todos los ejemplos españoles que se citan, salvo que se exprese lo contrario, son de español europeo. Se incluye en la fuente las referencias que cada corpus ofrece. Algunos ejemplos han sido abreviados para ofrecer mayor claridad, pero no se han corregido errores del original.

4. Datos y análisis

4.1. La construcción *N detrás de*

Las búsquedas de *N detrás de* en los corpus diacrónicos (CE y CORDE) no dieron resultados anteriores al siglo XX. En CREA se localizaron solo tres ejemplos anteriores a 2000, pero hay que señalar que los dos últimos proceden de un mismo artículo publicado en el periódico *El Mundo*:

(6) No soy la única persona detrás de la operación. (CREA: prensa, 1995)
(7) [...] al explicarnos las razones detrás de la remodelación de la discoteca Keeper. (CREA: prensa, 1996)
(8) La iniciativa detrás de este cambio se debe a sus propietarios. (CREA: prensa, 1996).

En los textos del siglo XXI se identificó una mayor variedad de casos, lo que confirma que se trata de una construcción reciente. En CORPES se obtuvieron 125 ejemplos. La mayoría de las construcciones presentan un valor metafórico, como se observa en los siguientes ejemplos:

(9) Explicó el razonamiento detrás de su sugerencia. (CORPES: prensa, 2010)
(10) Pero la historia detrás de estas pruebas es mucho más atractiva. (CORPES: prensa, 2002)
(11) La compañía detrás de este servicio [...] (CORPES: prensa, 2005)

Los únicos ejemplos que aparecen con un valor locativo literal identifican una persona (12) y una casa (13) parcialmente ocultos por otro elemento, tal y como se representaba en la Fig. 2, que, como señalaba Lindstromberg (2010: 103) para el inglés, muestran un elemento que se sitúa por encima del punto de referencia.

(12) [...] el pequeño saltamontes detrás de la barra me dijo [...] (CORPES: libro, 2005)
(13) Le encantó la casa enorme detrás de la pequeña fachada cerca de San Felipe Neri. (CORPES: prensa, 2012)

Las búsquedas en EsTenTen18 resultaron mucho más fructíferas; los casos de sustantivos directamente modificados por *detrás de* con una frecuencia superior a 25 superan los 4000 casos, como se muestra en la Tabla 1.[1] La mayoría de los sustantivos son abstractos, por tanto, el sentido de *detrás de* ha de entenderse metafóricamente. Los sustantivos concretos suelen hacer referencia a personas –directa (*hombre, mujer, personas...*) o metonímicamente (*nombres, equipo...*)– y se representan en su mayoría mediante un valor figurativo, como en los ejemplos que siguen.

(14) [...] la gente detrás de la decisión parece pensar lo contrario. (EsTenTen18, elinternet.es)

1 Para facilitar la obtención de datos en un corpus tan extenso se limitaron las búsquedas a casos de sustantivos seguidos de *detrás de,* sin considerar un hueco para adjetivos posnominales.

(15) Areces, el nombre detrás de los grandes almacenes. (EsTenTen18, modaes.es)

Algunos sustantivos aparecen con un valor locativo, como en (16), (17) y (18). En otros, se aprecia la evolución gradual de este valor físico a uno figurativo, como en los ejemplos (19) y (20), donde un descriptor inicialmente locativo adquiere un valor caracterizador.

(16) El hombre detrás de la barra lo miró. (EsTenTen18, fanfic.es)
(17) El hombre detrás de la cámara responde [...] (EsTenTen18, motor.es)
(18) El personal detrás de la recepción no era muy amigable. (EsTenTen18, zoover.es)
(19) El hombre detrás de un pitillo que fue Santiago Carrillo constató [...] (EsTenTen18, lavozdegalicia)
(20) Él es el director, es el hombre detrás de la cámara y también el editor. (EsTenTen18, telecinco.es)

Tabla 1: Sustantivos con mayor frecuencia absoluta con *detrás de* en EsTenTen18.

N	frec.	N	frec.	N	frec.
historia	420	*historias*	68	*intención*	38
idea	314	*voz*	60	*negocio*	37
hombre	218	*concepto*	59	*factores*	35
trabajo	155	*secreto*	58	*hombres*	35
equipo	154	*filosofía*	57	*objetivo*	35
razón	153	*mente*	57	*pensamiento*	34
personas	151	*motivos*	54	*razonamiento*	33
verdad	150	*motivo*	50	*secretos*	33
persona	145	*meta*	49	*nombre*	30
razones	120	*mujer*	48	*causas*	29
gente	112	*estudio*	47	*grupo*	28
tecnología	97	*fuerza*	44	*fondo*	27
ciencia	85	*intereses*	43	*causa*	27
compañía	82	*poder*	42	*estrategia*	26
empresa	78	*genio*	40	*esfuerzo*	26
lógica	77	*inspiración*	38	*mecanismo*	26
cerebro	75	*motivación*	38	*mujeres*	26
realidad	70	*teoría*	38	*artista*	25

Son mayoritarios los ejemplos de sustantivos inanimados abstractos que expresan una causa o motivación, como *el principal factor detrás del alza de los precios* o *el motivo detrás de la decisión*. Se documentan también construcciones que desvelan propiedades intrínsecas o explicativas de un ser o una entidad, por ejemplo, *la psicología detrás del acto* o *la realidad detrás del mito de Jackie Kennedy*.

Las construcciones análogas inglesas extraídas de EnTenTen20 muestran una gran similitud con las españolas; así, los 10 sustantivos más frecuentes en la construcción inglesa (*force, idea, reason, story, reasons, man, people, science, reasoning* y *team*) aparecen también entre los más frecuentes en español (Tabla 1). Los datos contrastados de las 20 colocaciones más abundantes en español e inglés en los corpus NOW confirman esta semejanza, como se observa en la Tabla 2. La frecuencia absoluta es muy superior en los datos del inglés pues se contabilizaron los ejemplos de todo el corpus, frente a los datos del español, que se limitaron al español europeo. No obstante, obsérvese que la frecuencia normalizada por millón de palabras es ligeramente superior en español.

Tabla 2: Colocaciones más frecuentes en NOW (español e inglés).

colocación	frec. abs	pm	colocación	frec. abs.	pm
la historia detrás de	206	0.14	*the history behind*	125853	0.01
el hombre detrás de	167	0.12	*the reason behind*	31356	0.00
la idea detrás de	166	0.12	*the man behind*	21117	0.00
la compañía detrás de	101	0.07	*the idea behind*	20764	0.00
el equipo detrás de	84	0.06	*the reasons behind*	18615	0.00
la persona detrás de	73	0.05	*the team behind*	17348	0.00
la empresa detrás de	64	0.04	*the story behind*	14741	0.00
la verdad detrás de	63	0.04	*the people behind*	14002	0.00
la tecnología detrás de	56	0.04	*the company behind*	13863	0.00
el cerebro detrás de	52	0.04	*the rationale behind*	11140	0.00
el estudio detrás de	49	0.03	*the science behind*	9783	0.00
el motivo detrás de	48	0.03	*the truth behind*	9368	0.00
la mente detrás de	47	0.03	*the inspiration behind*	8738	0.00
el mundo detrás de	46	0.03	*the motive behind*	7801	0.00
la razón detrás de	45	0.03	*the reasoning behind*	7454	0.00
las razones detrás de	43	0.03	*the mastermind behind*	6814	0.00
los motivos detrás de	38	0.03	*the brains behind*	6342	0.00
las manos detrás de	36	0.02	*the stories behind*	6023	0.00
la ciencia detrás de	33	0.02	*the person behind*	5974	0.00
la mujer detrás de	32	0.02	*the logic behind*	5383	0.00

El valor de ocultamiento que expresan la mayoría de los ejemplos puede apreciarse también en los verbos que suelen preceder a esta construcción, a menudo relacionados con el sentido de descubrir. Así, en EsTenTen18 anteceden con frecuencia a estas construcciones verbos como *desentrañar, descubrir, revelar, destapar* o *descubrir* (LogDice[2] por encima de 2.5) del mismo modo que son recurrentes en EnTenTen20 verbos como *understand, explain, uncover, discover* o *reveal* (LogDice por encima de 5).

Con una frecuencia inferior (208 ejemplos) se documentaron en EsTenTen18 construcciones de *N detrás de* con sustantivos inanimados con un valor puramente locativo, como los siguientes:

(21) Las zonas de mayor peligro se concentran en el área detrás de la rodilla. (EsTenTen18, bonomedico.es)
(22) Realizará una pequeña incisión perfectamente invisible en la zona detrás de las orejas. (EsTenTen18, topdoctors.es)
(23) El cuarto solar para VPO será cedido por el Ministerio del Interior en los terrenos detrás de la comisaría. (EsTenTen18, *Diario de Ibiza*)

El uso es similar al hallado en inglés, como se aprecia en los ejemplos (24) y (25), aunque su frecuencia en español es bastante reducida. En la Tabla 3 se muestran las frecuencias absolutas de las colocaciones que aparecen al menos 5 veces en EsTenTen18, y la frecuencia de las mismas colocaciones en NOW. Los ejemplos son escasos y suelen hacer referencia a espacios abiertos de una superficie amplia que pueden verse tras el objeto que se usa como punto de referencia. Estos son los ejemplos que la NGLE considera anglicismos y que habría que sustituir por la locución preposicional precedida de *de* (*la pared de detrás de la cama*) que analizaremos en la siguiente sección.

(24) Una buena opción es pintar la pared detrás de la cama con otro color. (EsTenTen18, fotocasa.es)
(25) Have some book shelves mounted on the wall behind the table (EnTenTen20, boddunan.com)

2 Fórmula estadística que utiliza *Sketch Engine* para identificar el grado de tipicalidad de una colocación: "based on the frequency of the node and the collocate and the frequency of the whole collocation (co-occurrence of the node and collocate). LogDice is not affected by the size of the corpus and, therefore, can be used to compare scores between different corpora."

Tabla 3: Construcciones *N detrás de* con valor locativo en EsTenTen18.

	EsTenTen18	NOW
la pared detrás de	21	2
el/las área(s) detrás de	14	2
la zona detrás de	12	5
la parte detrás de	9	6
el/los asiento(s) detrás de	8	4
la/s colina(s) detrás de	8	1
la calle detrás de	7	4
el terreno(s) detrás de	7	3
el/los jardín(es) detrás de	6	1
la plaza detrás de	6	5
la explanada detrás de	5	2

4.2. Construcciones normativas

Tras analizar los ejemplos de *N detrás de,* se hace necesario investigar las construcciones alternativas consideradas normativas: las oraciones de relativo con las que se relacionan en inglés (Quirk et al., 1985: 1274; Biber et al., 1999: 634) y en español (NGLE, 2009: 858), y las construcciones precedidas de *de* (*N de detrás de*) que prescribe la NGLE (2009: 859) para los adjuntos locativos del nombre.

Las búsquedas de oraciones de relativo (*N que V detrás de*) en CORPES mostraron 333 casos con siete verbos distintos (*estar, haber, existir, latir, subyacer, yacer* y *fluir*) La mayoría de las oraciones aparecen con un valor metafórico, como en (26)y (27), aunque un 23 % (46 ejemplos con *haber* y 28 con *estar*) muestran un significado físico, como en la oración (28).

(26) el impulso que hay detrás de una canción. (CORPES: prensa, 2010)
(27) el conflicto que subyace detrás de ellas. (CORPES: libro, 2012)
(28) Claudia esperaba sola en la verja que había detrás de su instituto. (CORPES: libro, 2014)

Los datos revelan una gran semejanza entre las oraciones de relativo y la construcción *N detrás de*; ambas se usan en su mayoría con un valor metafórico y son casi sinónimas. De hecho, se puede eliminar el pronombre relativo y el verbo sin que haya cambio de significado, por lo que podrían interpretarse como modelo de las construcciones *N detrás de*, o, como señalan Quirk et al. (1985) para el inglés, versiones reducidas de las oraciones de relativo.

La construcción precedida de *de* que la NGLE considera correcta para los adjuntos locativos del nombre (*N de detrás de*), resultó ser menos frecuente y más limitada: solo se encontraron 42 ejemplos en CORPES, todos con valor físico (por ejemplo, *el colgador de detrás de la puerta*, *el piso de detrás del bulevar*, *los jardines de detrás del edificio*, *la zona de detrás del mostrador* o *los muchachos de detrás de la barra*). Solo un ejemplo puede interpretarse como metafórico: *la Europa de detrás del Telón de Acero*. La constatación de que esta construcción prácticamente solo se emplea con sentido locativo, no metafórico, demuestra que solo puede sustituir los usos literales de *N detrás de*. Esta limitación, unida al escaso número de ejemplos hallados, restringe la posibilidad de considerarla como origen de *N detrás de*.

El análisis de corpus ha revelado también un dato curioso respecto a la distribución y frecuencia de las tres construcciones: algunos sustantivos son más frecuentes con *detrás de* que con las construcciones consideradas normativas. Por ejemplo, la colocación *la historia detrás de* tiene una frecuencia absoluta de 420 en EsTenTen18, frente a los 251 casos de la construcción con relativo (*la historia que V detrás de*) y los 2 ejemplos de *la historia de detrás de*. Otra de las colocaciones más recurrentes, *la idea detrás de*, muestra 314 ocurrencias, frente a la construcción de relativo *la idea que V detrás de* que aparece en 100 ocasiones y que solo se documenta una vez con *de* (*la idea de detrás de*).

4.3. Encuesta de aceptabilidad

Para valorar la aceptabilidad de las construcciones *N detrás de* halladas en los corpus, pero consideradas no normativas, se llevó a cabo una encuesta entre hablantes nativos de español europeo. Se pedía que evaluaran la aceptabilidad de las 10 oraciones siguientes mediante una escala-likert (1. No se dice en español. 2. Apenas se dice. 3. Se dice, pero normalmente no lo diría. 4. A veces lo digo así. 5. Así es como se dice.)

1. En la calle detrás del hotel hay muchos bares.
2. Ellos son los culpables detrás del atraco.
3. Cabe destacar el incomparable "Juicio Final" en la pared detrás del altar.
4. Quiten la coma detrás de "norma".
5. Identifican al verdadero cerebro detrás del golpe.
6. La guerra es el principal factor detrás del alza de los precios.
7. El propósito detrás de este viaje es divertirse.
8. Descubre todo lo que todavía no sabes de la mujer detrás de la artista.
9. ¿Cómo saber si la persona detrás del puesto de control tiene realmente autorización para acceder a las aplicaciones?

10. Los inversores detrás del ambicioso proyecto fueron acusados de fraude y blanqueo de dinero.

Las oraciones seleccionadas para la encuesta incluían 3 ejemplos de uso locativo de *N detrás de* (1, 3 y 4) con el objetivo de valorar hasta qué punto admiten los hablantes estos usos que aparecen con una frecuencia menor en los corpus y que son considerados incorrectos en la NGLE (2009: 859). El resto de los ejemplos seleccionados presentan un valor metafórico (2, 5, 6, 7, 8, 9 y 10).

La encuesta se distribuyó mediante un formulario de *Google* entre estudiantes universitarios con edades comprendidas entre los 18 y 25 años. Se obtuvieron 101 respuestas. Los participantes contestaron todas las preguntas y dieron al menos tres respuestas distintas entre las 10 valoraciones. La Fig. 3 recoge las respuestas individuales a cada pregunta. La valoración media de cada ejemplo de mayor a menor es la siguiente:

Quiten la coma detrás de "norma".	3,98
Los inversores detrás del ambicioso proyecto [...]	3,85
Identifican al verdadero cerebro detrás del golpe.	3,71
En la calle detrás del hotel hay muchos bares.	3,67
¿Cómo saber si la persona detrás del puesto de control [...]	3,63
Cabe destacar el incomparable "Juicio Final" en la pared detrás del altar.	3,46
La guerra es el principal factor detrás del alza de los precios.	3,42
Descubre todo lo que todavía no sabes de la mujer detrás de la artista.	3,21
El propósito detrás de este viaje es divertirse.	2,68
Ellos son los culpables detrás del atraco.	1,89

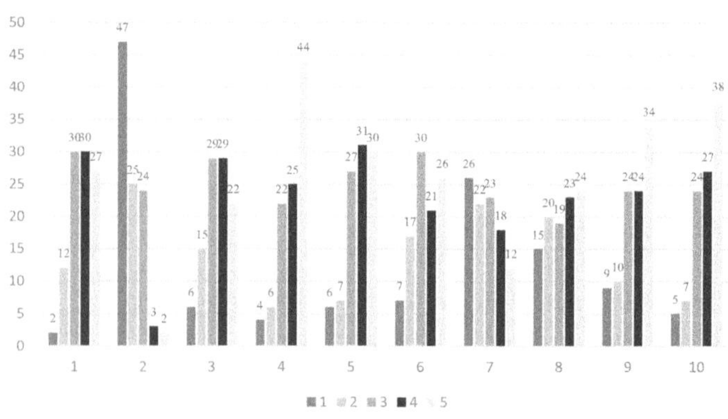

Fig. 3. Respuestas individuales de la encuesta de aceptabilidad.

Sorprendentemente, los datos de la encuesta muestran que la oración mejor valorada es la 4 (*Quiten la coma detrás de "norma"*) en la que se hace un uso puramente locativo de la construcción. Los datos de corpus mostraban una frecuencia baja de estas construcciones con valor locativo, consideradas además incorrectas por la RAE, lo que hacía pensar que iban a tener una menor aceptación. Sin embargo, 44 hablantes la valoran con un 5 y 25 confiesan utilizarla en ocasiones. Las otras dos oraciones con valor literal (1 y 3) fueron valoradas con una media de entre 3 y 4; es decir, los hablantes reconocen que se usan, aunque personalmente no las usan. Sin embargo, entre las valoraciones individuales se advierte que algunos encuestados las consideran totalmente aceptables (27 en el caso de 1, y 22 para 3). Los tres ejemplos pueden construirse con la locución *de detrás de* (*la calle de detrás del hotel, la pared de detrás del altar, la coma de detrás de "norma"*), tal y como propone la RAE (NGLE, 2009: 859), sin ningún cambio de significado.

El resto de los ejemplos de la encuesta presentan un valor metafórico que no puede expresarse mediante la locución *de detrás de*; la única alternativa sería el uso de una oración de relativo. De ellas, 5 obtuvieron una valoración bastante aceptable para los encuestados (por encima de 3). Estas construcciones muestran los distintos sentidos que se han atribuido a la preposición inglesa *behind*. Así, la segunda oración mejor valorada (*Los inversores detrás del ambicioso proyecto fueron acusados de fraude y blanqueo de dinero*) refleja un significado que se relaciona con una de las acepciones que describe Dixon (2021: 216) para *behind*, la de un grupo que se sitúa detrás ("at the rear of") para manifestar apoyo ("to indicate support"). Lindstromberg (2010: 105) identifica este uso como una escena en la que se empuja desde detrás hacia adelante. Este es el sentido de este ejemplo, que hace referencia a un apoyo financiero, un uso que no ha de entenderse necesariamente como un ocultamiento negativo o consciente, sino que simplemente alude a personas anónimas. Tampoco tiene un sentido negativo la oración que se sitúa en octava posición con una valoración media de 3,2 (*Descubre todo lo que todavía no sabes de la mujer detrás de la artista*). Este uso refleja lo que Dixon (2021: 216) describe como una caracterización que no es la esperada ("to describe something 'at the rear of' a misleading exterior"). En este caso los dos sustantivos de la construcción son correferentes. Si eliminamos *detrás* en estos ejemplos de la encuesta, el sentido de las oraciones cambia, pues señalaría a dos referentes distintos.

La oración 6 (*La guerra es el principal factor detrás del alza de los precios*) incluye un sustantivo inanimado que se concibe también como parte de la escena que Lindstromberg (2010: 105) caracteriza como un empuje desde detrás, pero en este caso para representar una fuerza motivadora ("motivating force"). Si se elimina *detrás* (*La guerra es el principal factor del alza de los precios*), como ocurriría con la oración 10 (*los inversores del ambicioso proyecto*), se interpreta como una relación causal directa.

El tercer ejemplo mejor valorado (*Identifican al verdadero cerebro detrás del golpe*) muestra claramente un ocultamiento intencionado. Por una parte, el uso del verbo "identifican" señala un elemento antes desconocido; por otra parte, el adjetivo "verdadero" sugiere la posibilidad de otro individuo que no lo era; finalmente, el punto de referencia es negativo, "golpe", por tanto, algo que razonablemente se oculta. Aunque la oración podría prescindir de *detrás* (*el verdadero cerebro del golpe*) el uso de la locución preposicional enfatiza el sentido de algo oscuro, intencionadamente oculto y que no es necesariamente causa directa.

El siguiente ejemplo mejor valorado (*¿Cómo saber si la persona detrás del puesto de control tiene realmente autorización para acceder a las aplicaciones?*) presenta un caso curioso que hemos analizado en el estudio de corpus (ejemplos 19 y 20) en el que se observa la evolución de un sentido locativo factual a un sentido caracterizador (*la persona (sentada) detrás del puesto de control →la persona que controla*). Esta interpretación no sería posible sin *detrás* (*la persona del puesto de control*) que solo ofrece un sentido locativo.

Al final de la escala, entre los que se clasifican con una menor aceptabilidad, se sitúa el ejemplo 2 (*Ellos son los culpables detrás del atraco*), con una valoración por debajo de 2 y con 47 participantes (el mayor número de consenso) que afirman que no se dice en espãnol. Obsérvese que tanto esta oración como la siguiente menos valorada (*El propósito detrás de este viaje es divertirse*), pueden construirse perfectamente sin *detrás* sin cambio de significado (*los culpables del atraco* y *el propósito de este viaje*) pues no caracterizan algo como desconocido u oculto con una relación causal indirecta, sino que señalan a personas bien identificadas y directamente responsables, en el caso de 2, o una motivación directa y natural, en el ejemplo 7, pues divertirse no se interpreta como un fin oscuro de un viaje.

5. Conclusiones

Los resultados de los análisis de datos recogidos de corpus y la encuesta de aceptabilidad nos permiten responder las preguntas de investigación planteadas al inicio. En primer lugar, el análisis de corpus evidencia que la construcción *N detrás de* se documenta en el español europeo, especialmente en la variedad de textos informales de Internet y noticias en línea de los corpus EsTenTen18 y

NOW. Los datos demuestran que la construcción surge en el siglo XXI y que es especialmente frecuente en su uso metafórico.

El significado de ocultamiento de este uso figurativo es el mismo que se describe para *behind* en el OED. Se han documentado también los distintos usos que se desarrollan a partir de este uso figurado y que describen Lindstromberg (2010) y Dixon (2021) para la preposición inglesa. Sorprendentemente ninguno de estos usos aparece recogido en el DLE, que tampoco reconoce la existencia de la locución preposicional. La lista de sustantivos más frecuentes que aparecen con este adyacente es similar en español e inglés. Del mismo modo, se observa en ambas lenguas la presencia de verbos con el sentido de descubrir que preceden a esta construcción, lo que confirma el sentido de ocultamiento.

Las semejanzas encontradas entre ambas construcciones podrían confirmar la hipótesis del préstamo, tal y como señala la NGLE para los adyacentes del nombre locativos. El origen del anglicismo podría hallarse en los múltiples procesos de traducción que requiere la sociedad actual, en la que la información fluye rápidamente de una lengua a otra. Así, McLaughlin (2011) explica ciertos préstamos construccionales del francés por la influencia de la traducción de noticias del inglés. Por su parte, Patzelt (2011) argumenta que la mayoría de las construcciones españolas prestadas del inglés son el resultado de la traducción de noticias del inglés al español. También Kranich, Becher & Höder (2012) resaltan la importancia de la traducción como origen del cambio lingüístico inducido por contacto (*contact-induced language change*).

Cabe señalar también que los ejemplos de corpus proceden de textos informales de Internet y que una característica de estos registros es la brevedad y la falta de presión normativa, factores que favorecen el uso de anglicismos (Muñoz Bassols & Salazar, 2019). La construcción *N detrás de* es más breve que las construcciones equivalentes consideradas normativas (adyacentes con oración de relativo o *N de detrás de*) por lo que cabría suponer que se prefiere por ser una simplificación de estas. Sin embargo, el análisis de la construcción *N de detrás de* muestra un uso más restringido y circunscrito a valores puramente locativos, por lo que no es parangonable con la mayoría de los usos documentados de *N detrás de,* que aparece más frecuentemente con sustantivos abstractos o con sustantivos que expresan personas o grupos humanos figuradamente ocultos o desconocidos. Aunque se ha podido constatar una evolución en el caso de algunas construcciones con sustantivos humanos, que pasan de expresar una ubicación concreta a desempeñar una función caracterizadora, esto no ocurre en el caso de los sustantivos abstractos, por lo que no parece que *N detrás de* haya surgido de la construcción locativa precedida por *de*. La coincidencia semántica de *N detrás de* con la oración de relativo podría hacer pensar que se origina por acortamiento de esta, como proponen Quirk et al. (1985) para el inglés.

Es difícil determinar con exactitud si la construcción española empieza como copia directa del inglés o si lo que copia es el mecanismo de reducción sintáctica de una oración de relativo. En cualquier caso, parece más que probable que el origen de esta construcción está en la lengua inglesa y que la estructura se ha podido extender a otras preposiciones, como en los ejemplos (1) y (2), aunque ese tema sería objeto de otro estudio. También sería interesante comprobar el comportamiento de estos préstamos en el español americano, en contacto más directo con el inglés.

6. Referencias

6.1. Corpus y diccionarios

Davies, M. *Corpus del Español: Genre / Historical.* www.corpusdelespanol.org/hist-gen.

Real Academia de la Lengua Española: Banco de datos [en línea]. *Corpus diacrónico del españo*l. www.rae.es.

Real Academia de la Lengua Española: Banco de datos [en línea]. *Corpus del español del siglo XXI.* www.rae.es.

Real Academia de la Lengua Española: Banco de datos [en línea]. *Corpus de referencia del español actual.* www.rae.es.

Seco, M., Angres, O., & Ramos, G. (1999). *Diccionario del español actual.* Madrid: Santillana.

Real Academia Española/Asociación de Academias de la Lengua Española, *Diccionario de la Real Academia Española.* dle.rae.es/.

English Corpus from the Web 2020 (EnTenTen20) www.sketchengine.eu/.

The Spanish Web Corpus 2018 (EsTenTen18) www.sketchengine.eu/.

Davies, M. *Corpus del Español NOW corpus* (News on the Web) https://www.corpusdelespanol.org/now/.

Davies, M. *English News on the Web.* www.english-corpora.org/now/

Oxford English Dictionary. www.oed.com/.

6.2. Referencias bibliográficas

Balteiro, I. (2018). Oh wait: English pragmatic markers in Spanish football Chatspeak. *Journal of Pragmatics*, 133, 123–133.

Biber, D., Johansson, S., Leech, G., Conrad, S., & Finegan, E. (1999). *Longman grammar of spoken and written English.* Harlow: Pearson.

Conrad, S. & Biber D. (2010). *Real grammar. A corpus-based approach to English*. London: Pearson.

Dixon, R. M. W. (2021). *English prepositions. Their meanings and uses.* Oxford: Oxford University Press.

Gómez Capuz, J. (1997). Towards a typological classification of linguistic borrowing (Illustrated with anglicisms in romance languages). *Revista Alicantina de Estudios Ingleses*, 10, 81–94.

Huddleston, R. & Pullum, G. K. (2002). *The Cambridge grammar of the English language*. Cambridge: Cambridge University Press.

Kranich, S., Becher, V., & Höder, S. (2012). A tentative typology of translation-induced language change. En S. Kranich, V. Becher, S. Höder & J. House (Eds.), *Multilingual discourse production. Diachronic and synchronic perspectives*. Amsterdam: Benjamins, pp. 9–44.

Lindstromberg, S. (2010). *English prepositions explained*. Amsterdam: Benjamins.

MacKenzie, I. (2012). Fair play to them: Proficiency in English and types of borrowing. En C. Furiassi, V. Pulcini & F. Rodríguez-González (Eds.), *The anglicization of European Lexis*. Amsterdam: Benjamins, pp. 27–42.

Martínez Vázquez, M. (2020). *Trump tuiteó su malestar*: English argument structure borrowing in Spanish. *Revista Electrónica de Lingüística Aplicada*, 19(2), 126–144.

Martínez Vázquez, M. (2021). Constructional borrowing through computer mediated communication verbs. En R. Enghels, D. Castilleja & A. Vande Casteele (Eds.), *Cruzando fronteras: español e inglés en contacto. Prácticas lingüísticas, ideologías e identidades*. Roma: Aracne, pp. 57–88.

Matras, Y. (2020). *Language contact*. 2ª edición. Cambridge: Cambridge University Press.

McLaughlin, M. (2011). *Syntactic borrowing in contemporary French. A linguistic analysis of news translation*. Londres: Legenda.

Muñoz Basols, J. & Salazar, D. (2019). *¿Nos hacemos un/una selfie con la/el tablet*? Cross-linguistic lexical influence, gender assignment and linguistic policy in Spanish. *Revista Signos*, 52(99), 77–108.

Patzelt, C. (2011). The impact of English on Spanish-language media in the USA. A qualitative analysis of newspaper articles. En S. Kranich, V. Becher, S. Höder & J. House (Eds.), *Multilingual discourse production. Diachronic and synchronic perspectives*. Amsterdam: Benjamins, pp. 257–279.

Peterson, E. (2017). The nativization of pragmatic borrowings in remote language contact situations. *Journal of Pragmatics*, 113, 116–126.

Pountain, C. J. (1994). Syntactic anglicisms in Spanish: innovation or exploitation? En M. M. Parry, W. V. Davies, & R. A. M. Temple (Eds.), *The changing voices of Europe*. Cardiff: University of Wales Press, pp. 109–124.

Pulcini, V., Furiassi, C. & Rodríguez González, F. (2012). The lexical influence of English on European languages. From words to phraseology En C. Furiassi, V. Pulcini, & F. Rodríguez-González (Eds.), *The anglicization of European Lexis*. Amsterdam: Benjamins, pp. 1–24.

Quirk, R., Greenbaum, S., Svartvik, J., & Leech, G. (1985). *A comprehensive grammar of the English language*. Londres: Longman.

Real Academia Española/Asociación de Academias de la Lengua Española (2009). *Nueva gramática de la lengua española*. Madrid: Espasa Libros.

Sunde, A. M. (2018). A typology of English borrowings in Norwegian. *Nordic Journal of English Studies*, 17(2), 71–115.

Tyler, A. & Evans, V. (2003). *The semantics of English prepositions. Spatial scenes, embodied meaning and cognition*. Cambridge: Cambridge University Press.

Alberto Gómez Font
Ex coordinador general de la Fundéu
De la Academia Norteamericana de la Lengua Española

Anglicismos resistentes y vencedores: los que ganaron la batalla a los libros de estilo

> «Las palabras de idiomas extranjeros, o palabras españolas extranjerizadas, que mucha gente utiliza porque se creen así más elegantes, ya que piensan que les da un barniz cosmopolita, resultan cursis, como todo lo que no es natural y sobre todo, ¿a qué aceptar la terminología extranjera si la nuestra es tan rica? Bien es verdad que hay palabras intraducibles como lo "lo cursi", "lo chic", "lo snob", pero no las tengamos siempre en los labios.»
>
> *Carmen Werner Bolín (Formación familiar y social)*

Ser autor y coautor de varios libros de estilo hace ver las cosas de la lengua desde una perspectiva de perdedor, pero no es triste, sino más bien divertido, ser testigo de cómo se pierden las batallas una tras otra, y lo más curioso es que, a pesar de todo, no se pierden las ganas de hacer algo para ayudar a los usuarios a lograr un uso de más correcto y lo más excelente posible del idioma.

En esa lucha por el buen uso del español hay muchos perfiles de personas, las más de las veces sin una relación directa con los estudios lingüísticos, pero movidas por la buena fe, y también hay, cómo no, muchos especialistas que dedican su tiempo, o parte de él, a asesorar sobre la materia.

Las batallas que se libran en los manuales de estilo son muchas y muy variadas: faltas de concordancia, equívocos léxicos, puntuación descolocada, bailes morfológicos, ortografía y tipografía erróneas, mal uso de los tiempos verbales, mayúsculas invasoras, verbos comodines, perífrasis innecesarias, orden de las oraciones, gerundios invasores, pasivas inelegantes, redundancias, desfile de preposiciones, siglas, símbolos, abreviaturas… Y, cómo no, los extranjerismos, y entre ellos el rey anglicismo, con sus lacayos los galicismos.

Los responsables de los libros de estilo de los medios de comunicación coleccionan errores lingüísticos cometidos por los periodistas, y llegan a documentar muchísimos buscando y rebuscando revistas y diarios en papel y en línea, y noticieros de radio y televisión. En esas colecciones se acumula toda una miscelánea de los errores que, bien sea por descuido o por ignorancia, cometen los profesionales de los medios, aunque también pueden deberse a que son errores incrustados en la lengua general y los periodistas se limitan a reflejarlos. Ocurre que ese tipo de colecciones adolecen de un mal incurable: hay piezas que poco a poco van perdiendo el lugar que ocuparon hasta que llegan a ser expulsadas para siempre; nunca más podrán formar parte de la lista de errores pacientemente recopilados por el coleccionista.

Otra colección propia de los autores de ese tipo de obras es, cómo no, la de manuales y libros de estilo. En el caso de quien escribe estas líneas el primero que llegó a sus manos fue el de la Agencia Efe (Madrid, Castalia, 1980, 2.ª edición), allá por octubre de 1980, y desde entonces, hasta el 2008, fue uno de los coautores de ese libro, que llegó a la 18.ª edición con el título de *Manual de Español Urgente*, y que en el 2015 se volvió a editar en una nueva versión y una nueva época. Esos manuales sufren también el mal antes mencionado: muchos de los usos incorrectos del español que en ellos se señalan llegan a ser correctos al cabo de los años, y así, el contenido de esos libros va quedándose viejo, lo que conlleva la necesidad de una continuada revisión y reedición.

Los anglicismos y expresiones anglicadas comentados a continuación provienen en su mayor parte de los libros con los que trabajaba el equipo de lingüistas del Departamento de Español Urgente de la Agencia Efe y después en la Fundación del Español Urgente (Fundéu), así como de aquellos de los que quien les habla fue autor o en los que participó como coautor.

Nada mejor para comenzar la lista de anglicismos vencedores que buscar uno para nominarlo al premio «Resistencia frente a los manuales de estilo», y el que más méritos tiene es el verbo *nominar* (de ahí que esté nominado). Durante algunos años del siglo XX, la aparición del verbo *nominar* se producía anual y puntualmente – y solo una vez al año – en todos los medios de comunicación, y era en vísperas de la concesión de los premios cinematográficos Óscar. Y cuando se creó el Departamento del Español Urgente en la Agencia Efe, en 1980, ese fue uno de los anglicismos atacados desde el principio; lo primero fue convencer a la corresponsal de Efe en Los Ángeles para que dejara de usarlo, y, tras lograrlo, su desaparición de las noticias de la agencia hizo el efecto esperado: sirvió de ejemplo para cientos de periodistas hispanohablantes de América y de España.

Después, con la creación en España de los premios Goya para la industria del cine español, se pudo ver cómo renacían *nominar*, *nominados* y *nominaciones*, pero. De momento, ahí se quedaba la cosa: era un anglicismo propio de la jerga de los premios cinematográficos. Pero de pronto irrumpió en otro terreno, el de la política, y empezaron a verse en todos los periódicos frases como esta: «comienzan los problemas en la *nominación* de candidatos de los diferentes partidos ante las próximas elecciones municipales». ¿Habría alguna razón subliminal para meter en el mismo saco a actores y políticos…?

Años después comenzaron a emitirse en la televisión unos programas-concursos en los que se encierra (siguen en antena hoy) a unas personas – en una casa, una isla, una granja… – y se las somete a determinadas pruebas, para ir expulsándolas poco a poco, hasta que una gane el concurso. Pues bien: a los designados para ser expulsados se los *nomina*. Ni unos ni otros hacían bien – hasta hace muy poquito tiempo – al usar ese verbo ya que el único significado de *nominar* era "dar nombre a una persona o cosa", definición que coincide con la segunda acepción del verbo *bautizar*. ¿Qué ocurría? Pues lo mismo que tantas otras veces: se trataba de un calco originado por una mala traducción del verbo homónimo inglés *nominate*, que en esa lengua significa "proponer la candidatura de…", "proponer a uno como candidato", "nombrar a uno para…". Y de su derivado *nomination*, que debíamos traducir como *nombramiento* o *propuesta*.

Parecía estar claro que si hablamos de políticos y de elecciones, en lugar de la *nominación* de candidatos deberemos referirnos a la *proclamación* de candidatos o la *elección* de candidatos. Y en lugar de *nominar* candidatos lo que debía hacerse era *proponer, presentar* o *proclamar* candidatos. Pero a los hispanohablantes les fascinaba tanto ese nuevo uso de *nominar* que, finalmente llegó al *Diccionario* la nueva acepción, y fue en el 2001:

1. tr. Dar nombre.
2. tr. Preseleccionar a alguien para un cargo o cometido.
3. tr. Presentar o proponer a alguien para un premio.

De nada sirvió que se luchara contra *nominar* en la mayor parte de los manuales de estilo de España y de América: el uso con su significado en inglés pudo más que todas las advertencias y todos los consejos bienintencionados.

Si los italianismos nos llegaron desde Italia y los galicismos desde Francia, la mayor parte de los anglicismos no nos llegan desde Inglaterra – o la Gran Bretaña – sino de los Estados Unidos de América, el único país a cuyos fundadores se les olvidó ponerle un nombre propiamente dicho, como Canadá, Argentina, Rumanía, Japón… Y de esa ausencia de un nombre propio, de un topónimo como Dios manda, se deriva la inexistencia de un gentilicio.

Si los *europeos* son de Europa, los *asiáticos* son de Asia y los *africanos* son de África. lo más normal sería que los *americanos* fueran de América, mas el término en inglés – *american* – se hizo sitio también mal traducido al español, pues durante muchos años muchos hispanohablantes de muchos países pronunciaron muchas veces la palabra *americano* para referirse a los habitantes de los Estados Unidos de América o a lo relacionado con aquel país.

Durante todo ese tiempo estaban cayendo en un calco del inglés *american* que en esa lengua se usa indistintamente como gentilicio del continente – América – y de los Estados Unidos. Pero eso uso era incorrecto en español, pues según los diccionarios el adjetivo *americano* solo se refería a América, y en los libros y manuales de estilo (y en los diccionarios de dudas) se explicaba que para hablar de lo referente a los Estados Unidos lo apropiado era utilizar los adjetivos *estadounidense* o *norteamericano*. Cierto es que este último – norteamericano – presenta el problema de que también lo son los canadienses y los mexicanos, pero lo cierto es que ningún hablante de español piensa en ellos cuando lee, oye o utiliza esa palabra.

Y llegó el día en el que ocurrió lo inevitable – nuestra lengua cambia y los anglicismos ganan batallas – y apareció una nueva acepción (la número 4) de *americano* en la edición del 2001 del *Diccionario*:

1. adj. Natural de América. U. t. c. s.
2. adj. Perteneciente o relativo a América o a los americanos.
3. adj. indiano (|| que vuelve rico de América). U. t. c. s.
4. adj. estadounidense. Apl. a pers., u. t. c. s.
5. m. café americano.
6. f. Chaqueta de tela, con solapas y botones, que llega por debajo de la cadera.

Más reciente es otro calco del inglés también relacionado con *american*. En el *Vademécum de español urgente* (vol. II), editado por la Agencia Efe en 1996, se decía lo siguiente sobre el anglicismo *afroamericano*, traducción tomada del inglés *afroamerican*:

«En las noticias procedentes de los Estados Unidos de América sobre la formación del nuevo Gabinete del presidente Clinton aparece repetido un nuevo término para hacer referencia a los negros de ese país: *afroamericanos*. La palabra en cuestión no está mal formada, puesto que sirve para explicar la procedencia de esas personas y tiene la misma forma que *hispanoamericanos*. Pero el hecho de que no esté mal formada no tiene nada que ver con la conveniencia ni la necesidad de su introducción como sustituta de *negros*, voz que por sí sola ya denota la procedencia de esa comunidad, ya que todos los negros de América proceden de África, al igual que los que se han asentado en otras partes del mundo.

"Quizá cabe preguntarse si los periodistas estadounidenses que escriben *afroamerican* pretenden referirse solo a los negros de los Estados Unidos, para diferenciarlos de los de Cuba, Puerto Rico, la República Dominicana y otros países de la zona. De ser así, el intento está fallido, puesto que América no es el país que hay entre Canadá y México, sino todos los que se extienden desde la Patagonia hasta Alaska, y en muchos de ellos parte de la población es de raza negra, cómo no, procedente de África, y son, pues, también *afroamericanos*.

«El elemento compositivo *afro-* se usa en Cuba para referirse a un tipo de música – *afrocubana* – en la que perviven los ritmos africanos, como en la de otros países antillanos y Brasil. También aparece en *afronegro*, voz usada para referirse a los rasgos, hábitos y costumbres africanos que perviven en las colectividades hispánicas de Américas, y en *afronegrismo*, que es como se llama en lingüística a las palabras tomadas de las lenguas de los negros africanos, y a la actitud de defensa y recuperación de elementos *afronegros* en los países hispánicos de América.

«No es necesario buscar eufemismos para referirse a los negros, y en las noticias puede decirse, sin molestar a nadie, que en el Gabinete de Clinton hay «cuatro negros y dos hispanos». Es mejor evitar esa forma poco clara (en todo caso habría que hablar de *afroestadounidenses*) y nada necesaria, y seguir hablando de *blancos*, *negros*, *amarillos* e *indios*, sin falsos pudores y si miedo de utilizar un término que solo es peyorativo si se toma como tal».

Ocurrió una vez más que tan detalladas explicaciones no sirvieron de nada, y en la edición del 2001 del *Diccionario* apareció ese anglicismo con esta definición: 'Se dice de los descendientes de los esclavos africanos llevados a América , y de su arte, cultura y costumbres'. Mas… ¿a qué *América* se refiere ese diccionario: a los Estados Unidos o al continente? ¿Y por qué no mencionan que esa voz es un calco del inglés *afroamerican*…?

También del inglés estadounidense importamos la palabra *homophobia* y la españolizamos como *homofobia*, sin pararnos a pensar que ambas estaban mal construidas si lo que se intentaba decir era 'aversión a los homosexuales' En el *Diccionario de Español Urgente* se intentó ponerle freno con estas explicaciones:

«[…] El elemento compositivo *homo-* se usa, antepuesto a otro, para dar idea de semejanza o igualdad: *homógrafo* ('que se escribe igual'), *homófono* ('que suena igual'), *homónimo* ('que tiene el mismo nombre'). *Fobia* (en inglés *phobia*) significa 'apasionada o enconada aversión hacia algo', y funciona como segundo elemento en compuestos del tipo *hidrofobia* ('horror al agua'), *fotofobia* ('repugnancia y horror a la luz'), *claustrofobia* ('sensación de angustia en los lugares cerrados'), etc.

Es decir, el neologismo *homofobia* significa 'aversión a lo semejante', por tanto, está mal formado si lo que se quiso expresar fue 'aversión a los homosexuales'. Sería muy conveniente atajarlo antes de que se asiente definitivamente en nuestra lengua, aunque la tarea será difícil si los anglohablantes lo asumen como correcto.

« […] Los anglohablantes, dada su proclividad a recortar y abreviar las palabras, han comenzado a utilizar *homo* en lugar de *homosexual*, de tal forma que para muchos de ellos la palabra griega homo ha perdido su significado de 'igual o semejante'. Pero el hecho de que esto ocurra en inglés no quiere decir que en español tenga que pasar lo mismo».

De poco sirvieron tan masticadas y detalladas explicaciones sobre el neologismo en cuestión; el español moderno se rindió una vez más ante el empuje de los redactores de noticias y de los hablantes, y la fobia a la palabra *homofobia* se quedó solamente en fobia a la *homofobia*. Y es que no puede pretenderse que todo el mundo sepa qué significa *homo* en la lengua culta.

Las palabras y los significados tomados del inglés que aparecen en este artículo forman parte de una clasificación, pues están *clasificadas* como anglicismos, pero precisamente por culpa de un calco de esa lengua, hoy las *palabras clasificadas* también podrían ser las *palabras secretas*. Hasta 1984 ninguna de las acepciones del verbo *clasificar* que podían verse en el *Diccionario de la lengua española* tenía relación con lo secreto, y el participio *clasificado* no aparecía como palabra independiente. Fue en el Diccionario de 1992 cuando esa palabra apareció por primera vez, y en su definición se dice que «dicho de un documento o una información» equivale a "secreto" o "reservado".

Lo curioso del caso – aunque deberíamos estar acostumbrados, por lo habitual que es – es que los encargados de redactar esa entrada del *Diccionario* no hicieran ninguna referencia a su procedencia… No habría estado de más informar de que se trata de un calco del inglés *classified*, es decir, una vez más uno de esos traicioneros *falsos amigos* tan temidos por los traductores.

Por eso, por tratarse de una mala traducción del inglés, los encargados de redactar el *Manual de español urgente* decidieron, en 1998, – haciendo caso omiso al *Diccionario* «oficial» – incluir una recomendación que decía: «CLASIFICADO.- Es anglicismo en frases como materia *clasificada*. En español decimos materia *reservada* o *secreta*». Y es que en ocasiones los autores de los libros y manuales de estilo alargan las batallas contra los anglicismos pensando que aún queda algún margen para cerrarles el paso, ejercicio, este, inútil casi siempre, y con *clasificado* ocurrió así.

El anglicismo *implementar* llegó al Diccionario en 1992 de la mano de la informática o computación, con el significado de – siempre hablando de cosas informáticas – "poner en funcionamiento, aplicar métodos, medidas, etc., para llevar algo a cabo". En la edición siguiente (la del 2001) decidieron quitarle la marca de jerga especializada, y pasó a ser un verbo más, sin ninguna información de por dónde había llegado a nuestra lengua… La reflexión es la de siempre que nos llega un neologismo que sirve para decir algo que ya llevábamos diciendo toda nuestra vida: ¿Nos hacía falta el verbo *implementar*? En el manual de estilo de la Agencia Efe comenzó a desaconsejarse su empleo en 1981, y se sugería que en su lugar se prefiriesen *aplicar*, *reglamentar* o *administrar*; en 1985 se añadieron otros posibles sustitutos: *cumplir*, *hacer cumplir* o *ejecutar* (un plan), y así seo mantuvo varios años más; pero de pronto, en 1994 desapareció de las recomendaciones de ese libro, en el que en 1995, con el visto bueno de la Academia, apareció esta entrada:

> IMPLEMENTACIÓN.- La voz inglesa *implementation* significa en español 'realización', 'ejecución'. *Implementación* no existe, aunque está bien formada a partir de *implementar*, que sí está en el DRAE.

Sí, los autores de ese manual de estilo decían que no existía una palabra que acaban de escribir y sobre la que estaban hablando… ¿Cabe mayor sinsentido? Sírvanos ese desliz para dejar claro que el hecho de que una palabra no esté en el *Diccionario* no implica que esta no exista.

Hoy, tanto *implementar* como *implementación* (y también *implemento*) son voces que conviven en español con otras de significados idénticos o similares; las que siguen utilizando los militantes del uso culto de la lengua: *ejecutar*, *aplicar*… Y las que siguen sugiriendo algunos manuales de estilo, aunque *implementar* sea uno más de los anglicismos resistentes y vencedores.

En el libro de estilo en línea más completo – la Wikilengua – también se aconseja evitar los anglicismos innecesarios, como en el caso del verbo *estimar* con el significado de "calcular":

> «Aunque la Academia haya aceptado ya *estimar* en el sentido de 'apreciar, poner precio, evaluar algo', es preferible no abusar de esta voz y utilizar el verbo *calcular*. Debemos evitar este anglicismo en frases tales como, '…en una media *estimada* entre dos o cuatro kilos…'. En este caso *cálculo* no es sinónimo de *estimación,*»

Se daba, ya hace bastantes años una llamativa repetición de ese verbo y de ese sustantivo en las noticias de los medios de comunicación españoles y americanos, si bien aún no era un uso propio de la lengua general, del español de los que no eran periodistas, y en el *Diccionario* no había ninguna acepción que significase eso. Esto es lo que decía:

> «ESTIMAR.- Apreciar, poner precio, evaluar las cosas. 2. Juzgar, creer. 3. Hacer aprecio y estimación de una persona o cosa.»
> «ESTIMACIÓN.- Aprecio y valor que se da y en que se tasa y considera una cosa. 2. Aprecio, consideración, afecto. 3. Instinto de los animales.»

Ciertamente es un poco raro eso de que la *estimación* sea, entre otras cosas, un "instinto de los animales"; pero lo que aquí nos interesa es comprobar que en esas definiciones no aparece ni por asomo la idea de *calcular* que sí estaba implícita en frases como estas: «Se estima que este verano atravesarán el estrecho de Gibraltar más de 250 000 personas», «Según las estimaciones del Ministerio de Agricultura la cosecha de trigo superará a la de 1984».

Y no se puede negar que avisar sobre ese uso indebido era acertado, hasta que, en el 2014, los lexicógrafos del *Diccionario de la lengua española* decidieron que esa batalla ya estaba perdida, y pusieron como primera acepción de *estimar*, la de "calcular o determinar el valor de algo", y añadieron el ejemplo de «Estimaron los daños en mucho dinero». Así las cosas, *estimar* y *estimación* en lugar de *calcular* y *cálculo* son otros dos anglicismos resistentes y vencedores más para sumar a esta lista.

¿¡Nos hacía falta la *privacidad*!? Una vez más toca poner sobre el tapete aquello de los neologismos necesarios o innecesarios, y parece estar claro que esta vez se trataba de uno de los segundos, pues durante muchas generaciones los hispanohablantes vivieron sin usar esa palabra, y aún hoy son legión los que siguen sin echar mano de ella. Pero llegó, y se empeñó en instalarse, si bien quienes se dedicaban a aconsejar sobre el buen uso del español le plantaron y batallaron contra ella durante algunos años.

Se trataba en este caso de un calco del inglés *privacity*, que nos llegó de los Estados Unidos. Su primera documentación en los bancos de datos de la Real Academia Española es de 1947, de un texto del cineasta español Néstor Almendros, en el que el autor, al describir dónde viven las grandes estrellas de cine, dice: «[…] Allí, como es zona montañosa, solo se puede llegar en automóvil, y, por lo tanto, la privacidad está asegurada».

En el *Vademécum de español urgente (II)* y, después, algo cambiado, en el *Diccionario de español urgente* se decía, entre otras cosas: «[…] Quienes "inventaron" la palabra *privacidad* lo que hicieron fue tomar el inglés *privacy* y españolizarlo añadiéndole la terminación *–dad*, sin tener en cuenta que ya existía otra palabra en nuestra lengua para expresar exactamente lo mismo que la voz inglesa: *intimidad*. Además, también en lugar de *privacidad*, podemos usar las locuciones *en privado* o *vida privada*».

El lingüista y ortotipógrafo José Martínez de Sousa, en un artículo publicado en la sección «Rinconete» del Centro Virtual Cervantes, sus explicaciones concluía con estas palabras: «[…] aunque la registren los diccionarios, y algunos no hagan ni la más mínima referencia a su origen, debemos rechazar la voz *privacidad* (así como su prima hermana *privacía*) y usar, como indica nuestra Constitución, la voz *intimidad*, que es la buena».

Pero lo cierto es que la palabra en cuestión está recogida en los diccionarios de uso – al de la Real Academia Española llegó en el 2001 – y ya cómodamente instalada en el español *moderno*…

Para saber qué es *deshonesto* basta con recordar las expresiones «proposiciones deshonestas», «actos deshonestos», «pecados contra la honestidad»… Sí, estamos hablando de lo relacionado con el sexo, así de claro, y así lo explicaba Salvador de Madariaga en un artículo publicado en el diario ABC el 20 de junio de 1971:

> «[…] ahí está, por todas partes, *honesto*, en vez de *honrado* […] De lo honesto y lo honrado ya hice valer que la frontera es la cintura. El que se conduce bien de la cintura para arriba es honrado, y si es para abajo es honesto. El que dice *honesto* por *honrado* habla o escribe *anglañol* o *hispanglés*».

Así las cosas, si es que se conduce bien de cintura para abajo es *honesto*, quien no lo haga así será *deshonesto*. Hasta aquí lo lógico y lo propio de la lengua culta, mas ya llevamos un rato viendo que en el terreno de los significados muchas veces termina venciendo la incultura y la tozudez de los hablantes.

Según la Real Academia Española, *deshonesto* era – desde 1780 hasta 1992 – "Impúdico, lascivo, falto de honestidad", "No conforme a razón ni a las ideas concebidas por buenas", "Grosero, descortés, indecoroso". Ya en la edición del 2001 del *Diccionario* quitaron el adjetivo *impúdico*, y así seguía en la del 2014. Seguramente porque ya para entonces la voz *honesto* había dejado de ser algo exclusivamente relacionado con los actos de cintura para abajo, y compartía alguno de sus significados con su hermanastro *honrado*. ¿Sucederá lo contrario y llegaremos a leer y escuchar cosas como «proposiciones deshonradas»…?

Ya en la 1.ª edición (1978) del *Manual de estilo* de la Agencia Efe había una advertencia que decía: «*honesto*.- No sacrifiquemos siempre a este adjetivo al españolísimo *honrado*». Y en el *Manual de español urgente* (también de la Agencia Efe), se avisaba desde 1985 que *deshonesto* era "impúdico, falto de honestidad", y que no debía usarse en la acepción de "falto de honradez, falso o fraudulento", por tratarse de un anglicismo. Después ya en el 2004, desapareció ese aviso del libro.

Luchar hoy, en pleno siglo XXI, contra el uso de la palabra *evento* con el significado de "suceso importante y programado, de índole social, académica, artística o deportiva" (esa es su tercera acepción en el *Diccionario*) está totalmente fuera de lugar. Nos llegó, como muchas otras, desde Hispanoamérica – allí la copiaron del inglés *event* – , y se fue haciendo un hueco entre los hablantes de España hasta instalarse cómodamente en el vocabulario de muchos de ellos, si bien, de momento, es más propia de los que están por debajo de los 40 años, y, sobre todo, de los que asisten casi todos los días a algún *evento* y se lamentan de no gozar del don de la ubicuidad para poder acudir a más de uno en la misma tarde o noche.

En principio, para los hablantes cultos *evento* funcionaba como sinónimo de *eventualidad*, es decir, de algo que podía suceder o no suceder, algo *eventual*, pero lo cierto es que es harto difícil ver u oír esa palabra bien utilizada. La lucha fue bien larga, pues ya en la 1.ª edición del *Manual de estilo* de la Agencia Efe (1978) se dejaba muy claro que no era correcto su uso con el significado que después adquiriría:

> «EVENTO.- No es sinónimo de *hecho*, *suceso* o *acontecimiento*, sino de *contingencia* o *eventualidad*. No escribamos, pues, a la inglesa: "Al conocerse el *evento*, las campanas del pueblo comenzaron a repicar". Y sí: "Puede haber una huelga de controladores aéreos. Ante tal *evento*, el Gobierno ha adoptado medidas…"».

Años después, en 1994, la advertencia sobre esa palabra cambió:

> «EVENTO.- La vigésima primera edición del DRAE incluye entre los significados de *evento* el de «acaecimiento». De todas formas, conviene no abusar de este término en lugar de *acontecimiento*».

Varias ediciones después, en la decimoséptima (2006), se cambió de nuevo lo que se decía sobre el uso de esa palabra:

> «EVENTO.- La vigesimoprimera edición del DRAE incluyó entre los significados de *evento* el de 'acaecimiento'. Se usa principalmente para referirnos a acontecimientos de cierta importancia. De todas formas, conviene no abusar de este término en lugar de *acontecimiento.*»

En el 2015 desapareció esa recomendación y ya no se mencionaba la palabra *evento*; una vez más el anglicismo contra el que se combatía fue resistente y vencedor y ganó la batalla contra los manuales de estilo.

¿Y qué mejor sitio para resguardarse de los ataques de los libros y manuales de estilo que un *santuario*?

El lingüista español Pedro García Domínguez contaba en sus lecciones magistrales sobre el buen uso del español que Jesús Hermida, periodista de Televisión Española, corresponsal en Nueva York en la década de los años 60 del siglo pasado, al informar sobre la guerra de Vietnam decía que los aviones estadounidenses bombardeaban los *santuarios* del Vietcong (o Viet Cong), y ese informador era muy importante y muy prestigioso en ese momento, de tal manera que nadie se planteó avisarlo de que quizá estaba usando mal la palabra *santuario*…

Era un problema de falsos amigos, es decir, de una mala traducción del inglés *sanctuary*, lengua en la que, además de equivaler más o menos a lo mismo que significaba en español en esos años ("Templo en el que se venera la imagen o reliquia de un santo de especial devoción"), se utilizaba, y se sigue utilizando, también con el valor de "refugio" o "asilo". No se trataba, pues, de que los estadounidenses fueran tan malvados que, no contentos con bombardear los pueblos y los cultivos de Vietnam del Norte, se dedicasen también a lanzar sus bombas sobre los templos donde los creyentes acudían a rezar.

Ese significado anglicado de *santuario* no llegó aún – de momento – al *Diccionario* académico, pero su uso está tan establecido en el español actual que ya nadie osa decir que está mal hablar de los «santuarios de ballenas» (donde van a aparearse, y no a rezar), o de los «santuarios de las mariposas monarcas», y así está recogido en otros diccionarios, y en la edición del 2015 del *Manual de Español Urgente*, donde podemos leer lo siguiente: «También es "lugar de refugio o asilo". (Diccionario de Español Actual): *santuario de criminales*.

Por mucho que intentemos *ignorarlos*, los anglicismos resistentes y vencedores vinieron para quedarse, por lo menos durante el tiempo en el que los hablantes los crean necesarios, y algunos ya llevan muchos años entre nosotros, como el verbo *ignorar* usado con su significado en inglés.

> «Cuídese de no emplear este verbo, a la inglesa, con las acepciones de 'no hacer caso de', 'desoír', 'prescindir de', 'desestimar'... Ejemplos de mal uso: "La empresa ha ignorado las demandas de los obreros"; "Allí estaba López, pero Gómez lo ignoró: pasó sin saludarlo"».

Ese era el texto que aparecía en la primera edición del *Manual de Estilo* de la Agencia Efe, en 1979, escrito por Fernando Lázaro Carreter. Y así continuó año tras año, hasta que en 1995 se cambió la redacción:

> «En español *ignorar* quiere decir 'desconocer', 'no saber una cosa'. En inglés (*ignore*), generalmente quiere decir 'hacer caso omiso de una persona o casa' ya conocidas».

Volvió a cambiarse en el 2006, pero siempre con el mismo discurso de oposición al uso procedente del inglés:

> «No utilizar este verbo con el significado de 'hacer caso omiso de una persona o cosa' ya conocidas. En español ignorar quiere decir 'desconocer', 'no saber una cosa', 'no tener en cuenta'».

Ahí ya se coló, por la retaguardia, un significado de los que en 1979 se decía que no eran apropiados: el de "no tener en cuenta". Y es que ya en el *Diccionario de la Lengua Española* del 2001 se incluyó una segunda acepción en *ignorar*, que decía: "No hacer caso de algo o alguien". Y, para rematar la faena, en el 2014 se le añadió esta coletilla: "[...], o tratarlos como si no merecieran atención".

Todos los casos anteriores forman parte de un importante *stock* de anglicismos instalados en el español. Esta última palabra – *stock* – , tras pasar por el *Diccionario Manual* en 1985 y en 1989, llegó por fin al *Diccionario de la lengua* española en el 2001, pero los lexicógrafos decidieron marcarlo con el estigma de la letra cursiva, es decir, no lo adoptaron ni lo adaptaron como una nueva voz en español, sino como un extranjerismo que se usa en nuestra lengua.

En el *Diccionario de español urgente* (2000) se decía esto sobre su aterrizaje: «[...] ocurre en muchas ocasiones, y es totalmente censurable, que se introducen términos extranjeros innecesarios, que tienen equivalentes exactos en español, y lo único que hay que hacer es el mínimo esfuerzo de traducirlos correctamente, pero ese esfuerzo parece ser excesivo para algunos. Es el caso de la voz inglesa *stock*, tan corriente en nuestros días en el vocabulario de muchos hispanohablantes que parecen desconocer palabras como *existencias*, *reservas*, *provisión*, *surtido*, *mercancías almacenadas*, *sobrantes*, *excedentes*, *almacenamiento*, *almacenaje* o *inventario*, que, según el contexto en el que aparezca, son posibles traducciones españolas. Las construcciones inglesas *to be in stock* y *to be out of stock* corresponden a las españolas *estar en existencia* o *estar agotado*».

El asunto es que el *stock* se instaló en el *Diccionario*, o sea que podemos decir que en el *stock* de palabras del español está la palabra *stock*.

¿Cuántos títulos de libros y manuales de estilo hay en el mercado y cuántas *copias* se imprimen de cada uno? ¿Siguen siendo libros útiles y de ahí que se pongan tantas *copias* en venta? ¿Hablamos de *copias* o de *ejemplares*…? Y es que hubo un tiempo en el que los libros se contaban por *ejemplares*, y luego pasaron a contarse también de la misma forma los discos – los elepés o los *singles* – . Así, se podían oír o leer cosas como «Se vendieron más de 10 000 ejemplares de la última novela de Corín Tellado» o «Ya se han vendido más de 500 000 ejemplares del último disco de Julio Iglesias».

Con esa palabra – *ejemplar* – teníamos bastante para referirnos a cada una de las reproducciones en un libro o de un disco, mas para algunos debía de ser demasiado vulgar o excesivamente larga – algún enemigo obseso del sesquipedalismo – y descubrieron que en la lengua más prestigiosa, el inglés, eso de conocía como *copy*. El calco fue inmediato, basado en una mala traducción causada por un falso amigo, y los *ejemplares* fueron convirtiéndose en *copias*.

Nadie tuvo en cuenta que una *copia* en español era, entre otras muchas cosas, la "obra de escultura, de pintura o de otro género, que se ejecuta procurando reproducir la obra original con entera igualdad", y la "imitación servil del estilo o de las obras de escritores o artistas". Otro de los significados relativamente recientes (llegó al *Diccionario* en de 1992) de la palabra *copia* era "cada una de las que se hacen de una película para su exhibición en las salas de cine, y también cada una de las reproducciones de una fotografía, de una cinta magnética, etc.". El paso de esa palabra de la cinta magnética al disco fue lógico, y se comenzó a llamar copias a cada una de las reproducciones de los discos de vinilo, también conocidos, según su tamaño, como elepés o *singles*.

El paso siguiente fue comenzar a llamar *copias* a los *ejemplares* de los libros; se trata de un uso bastante nuevo en nuestra lengua, y, como tantas otras veces, si bien comenzó considerándose como incorrecto, hoy ya no se puede afirmar eso, pues está totalmente incrustado en la lengua culta moderna, y al buscar *copia* en el *Diccionario* vemos que la nueva acepción es: "Cada uno de los ejemplares que resultan de reproducir una publicación, una fotografía, una película, una cinta magnética, un programa informático, etc."

Mas, a pesar de todo lo aquí explicado y documentado, lo cierto es que de momento no estamos en un estado de *emergencia*. Veamos algo sobre esa palabra.

No es de extrañar que pueda causar cierto impacto la etiqueta de una botella de agua mineral en la que, entre otras informaciones, figure esta: «Temperatura de emergencia, 41 grados». Y si buscamos en internet veremos más de 300 000 documentos en los que aparecen juntos «temperatura de emergencia» y «agua». Pero no se trata, como podrían entender la gran mayoría de los hispanohablantes del siglo XXI, de un aviso sobre cuál es la temperatura en la que esa agua comienza a ser peligrosa o en la que la botella puede estallar, sino, simplemente, de la que tiene el agua cuando emerge – sale, brota… – de la fuente, pues la *emergencia* no es ni más ni menos que el hecho de *emerger*.

Por eso en el *Manual de español urgente* de 1985 se introdujo una entrada sobre esa palabra, en la que se aconsejaba lo siguiente:

> «EMERGENCIA.- Conviene combatir el empleo anglicado de esa voz, que suele hacerse sinónimo de *imprevisto*, *peligro*, *urgencia*, *apuro*, *aprieto*, etc.»

Ese «conviene combatir» fue secundado por algunos profesionales del periodismo que combatieron aquel uso tomado del inglés, y aún hoy algunos soñadores siguen haciéndolo, pero ya con el claro convencimiento de la suya es una postura quijotesca. Aquella advertencia desapareció del Manual de Estilo de la Agencia Efe, porque, aunque algunos hacían como si no la viesen, desde 1947 había una acepción en la definición de *emergencia* en el *Diccionario* que iba algo más allá de la mera "acción y efecto de emerger", y decía: "Ocurrencia, accidente que sobreviene". Después, ya en el 2001, se añadió esta otra: "Situación de peligro o desastre que requiere una acción inmediata". Y, además, al hablar de los hospitales, en algunos países de América *emergencias* (en los hospitales) es lo que en otros se llama *urgencias*. ¿Y qué decir de la redundante «salida de emergencia» (salida de salida), en lugar desino «salida de socorro»? ¿Y no es mejor «aterrizaje forzoso» que «aterrizaje de emergencia»…?

Quizás el más apropiado colofón de un recorrido vital por la historia de los anglicismos resistentes y vencedores sea hacer un testamento en el que les dejemos a nuestros herederos el encargo de firmar un acuerdo de paz – un cese de hostilidades – con esas palabras contra las que nosotros batallamos durante años. ¡Pero cuidado con emplear el verbo *testar* con el significado de "hacer testamento"! Hoy eso quedaría algo anticuado y podría generar ambigüedad en el discurso, pues los hablantes del español moderno lo usan de otra forma. Hoy podemos toparnos con el nuevo uso de *testar* en la leyenda adherida en un tarro de espuma de afeitar o en los botes de cristal y tubos metálicos o de plástico de productos de belleza cuyo contenido ha sido *testado*, en algunos de ellos «dermatológicamente» y en otros, los más serios, «clínicamente».

Presentado así el asunto podría entrañar un nuevo misterio para casi todos los hispanohablantes, es decir, para los que conocían el significado tradicional de *testar*, pero ya había algunos que comenzaban a usar ese verbo sin ton ni son en los envases de los productos de belleza. La cosa consistía, pues, en descubrir qué demonios podía ser eso de *testar dermatológicamente* o *testar clínicamente*, teniendo en cuenta que en español *testar* era "hacer testamento", y que antes también significaba declarar o afirmar como testigo.

Testar clínicamente podría ser una forma de explicar que alguien hizo su testamento en la clínica, cuando agonizaba, pero eso no tiene nada que ver con lo que hay en los estantes de los armaritos de los cuartos de baño. Lo de *testar dermatológicamente* es algo más complejo, hay que establecer una relación entre el testamento y la piel de quien está testando… en fin, algo muy raro e inquietante. Pero lo cierto es que, de nuevo, nos topamos con una mala traducción del inglés, en este caso del verbo *to test* (y su participio *tested*), que en esa lengua equivalen a lo que nosotros expresamos con *controlar*, *probar*, *examinar*, *experimentar*… Y ese nuevo uso de nuestro *testar* causó furor y, a fuerza de codazos, se abrió camino hasta llegar – en el 2001 – al *Diccionario*.

Testar también resistió los ataques de los manuales de estilo, y salió vencedor, como el resto de los anglicismos aquí coleccionados.

Jesús Castañón Rodríguez

I.ES Parquesol, Valladolid

Los anglicismos deportivos en los libros de estilo de medios de comunicación de España

Resumen: Este estudio aborda el tratamiento recibido por estas voces en el lenguaje periodístico en los siglos XX y XXI. Refleja el paso del casticismo a los diccionarios de dudas, la corrección lingüística, los libros de estilo y una constante reflexión en encuentros especializados. Tras revisar su presencia en diferentes decenios, comenta el papel del anglicismo en las nuevas redacciones tecnológicas con sistemas anglosajones de redacción y presentación de noticias y su actual importancia como fuente documental para el registro institucional de usos idiomáticos. Analiza la creciente presencia del lenguaje deportivo en los libros de estilo con sus orientaciones sobre términos, expresiones, siglas y transcripción de nombres de personas, lugares y entidades. Además, aporta 107 referencias bibliográficas para ampliar conocimientos.

Palabras clave: Lexicología, anglicismos, medios de comunicación, libros de estilo.

El tratamiento de los anglicismos en el lenguaje periodístico ha sido un tema de análisis habitual en la lengua española, ya que esta forma de expresión ha sido caracterizada como una como vía de entrada de formas y usos de otros idiomas y un ámbito especialmente permeable a todo tipo de influencias foráneas.

En el caso del deporte, desde su irrupción en el periodismo especializado en el siglo XIX, esta situación ha sido abordada con enfoques puristas e innovadores y ha generado reacciones que han evolucionado desde el casticismo cerrado a los diccionarios de dudas, la corrección lingüística, los libros de estilo y la importancia de la traducción directa de noticias y de textos procedentes de agencias al adaptar a la lengua receptora elementos lingüísticos. Ha registrado desde la descripción y reflexión de sus usos a los últimos estudios relacionales para obtener datos lexicográficos y primeras documentaciones de voces para el *Diccionario Histórico de Términos del Fútbol* y el *Diccionario Histórico del español moderno de la ciencia y de la técnica* (Alonso Pascual, 1996; Álvarez Mellado, 2021; Alzugaray, 1982; Hernández, 2008; Loza y Castañón, 2010; Nomdedeu Rull, 2019 y Rodríguez González y Castañón, 2021).

Siglo XX

Puristas frente a novadores

La difusión comunicativa del deporte en el último tercio del siglo XIX y los dos primeros decenios del siglo XX se llevó a cabo gracias a dos figuras. De una parte, el *trovador deportivo*, compuesto por médicos, higienistas, publicistas y propagandistas que divulgaban la belleza del deporte y la conveniencia de su práctica. Y de otra parte, el *gacetillero sportivo* especializado en divulgar los deportes modernos y sus sociedades.

Se registró una numerosa presencia de noticias deportivas cuya creciente influencia social despertó el interés lingüístico de puristas y novadores para comentar las voces exóticas de los periodistas.

El purismo, que luchaba contra el "pestífero castellano" que abandonaba las ciencias tradicionales para entregarse a la expresión de otros idiomas, mantuvo una actitud basada en la vigilancia, el rigor prescriptivo, el proteccionismo, el estado estático del idioma, la censura, la prohibición y la corrección (Ahumada, 2012).

En el deporte presentó dos grados distintos. Por un lado, se registraba el casticismo cerrado que publicó obras para guiar a autores por un camino medio, atinado y seguro, en palabras de Juan Eugenio Hartzenbusch. Mostraba un fuerte interés periodístico por los problemas normativos del español, se atenía a la autoridad del diccionario académico y de los autores clásicos y seguía el modelo de la elegancia clásica del siglo de Oro como época dorada del romance español y del realismo español sin repetir aspectos foráneos que eran considerados como desacatos contra el romance, ni admitir la evolución del estado ideal de lengua del siglo XVII (Baralt, 1890; Mir y Noguera, 1907 y 1908). Y por otro lado, existía el purismo fiel al idioma que censuraba galicismos y barbarismos que el pueblo no usaba, se oponía a los excesos de rigidez de los otros tipos de puristas y establecía como criterio de actuación la necesidad de traducción de anglicismos con voces castizas o conformes a la índole de la lengua castellana para formar palabras derivadas. Prestaron atención a voces deportivas generales y a términos específicos de 13 deportes: automovilismo, aviación, boxeo, carrera continua, caza, fútbol, hípica, lucha, patinaje, pesca, pelota vasca, tenis y vela. Fue la etapa del encendido debate sobre el nombre en castellano que se debía dar al foot-ball con propuestas como *balompié, bola de pie, bolopié, fuboll, volapié,* o *piebalón* (Benavente, 1908; Cavia, 1908 y 1923; Cejador, 1908; Franquelo y Romero, 1910; Huidobro, 1915; Moreno, 1922).

Los novadores comentaban galicismos y barbarismos de la vida moderna, buscaban amoldarse a un vocabulario de voces exóticas y técnicas que era considerado como un caos confuso de palabras no registradas en el diccionario ni en glosarios. Entendían que el excesivo apego a los idiomas foráneos constituía una forma de indolencia, descuido e ignorancia hacia las aportaciones del pasado.

Para el mundo del deporte destacaron en esta tarea la prensa especializada de Barcelona y la labor lexicográfica desarrollada por las enciclopedias y las colecciones de libros de divulgación deportiva. Fue el caso de Antonio Viada con el serial «Sobre el vocabulario deportivo» en 1902 que logró reunir en la sala de redacción de la publicación quincenal *Los Deportes* a redactores de publicaciones especializadas, diarios de información general de Barcelona, representantes de centros deportivos y otras opiniones para crear un *patron oro castellano* capaz de sustituir la terminología inglesa y francesa por voces en español. Este abogado y periodista había proporcionado a la Real Academia Española, a petición de Víctor Balaguer, una lista de voces deportivas españolas, españolizadas por el uso o que pudiesen ser adaptadas, para su inclusión en la edición del *Diccionario de la lengua castellana* de 1899 (Nomdedeu Rull y Torrebadella, 2018; Viada, 1902).

En colecciones de divulgación como la Biblioteca Los Sports, la Biblioteca Deportiva de la Editorial Juan de Gassó o la Biblioteca de Sports y juegos de Ediciones Bauzá y en las enciclopedias editadas por Salvat, Seguí y Espasa, profesionales del deporte y de la comunicación periodística promocionaron el buen uso del idioma, ordenaron informaciones y datos y aplicaron un novedoso trabajo multilingüe para traducir voces, delimitar etimologías y encontrar equivalencias en español. Desempeñaron esta función de forma destacada Antonio Viada, Josep Elías i Juncosa y Antonio Fabregat (Castañón Rodríguez, 2011, 2019 y 2021).

Años 20

En esta década surgieron en España las Escuelas de periodismo para buscar el perfeccionamiento profesional y cultural del periodismo. En 1926 se puso en marcha la pionera Escuela de periodismo de El Debate, en la que Nicolás González Ruiz impartía las clases de redacción.

El deporte se veía como un elemento para aprender a redactar periodísticamente con un tratamiento especializado. Formaba parte del tema 34 de ejercicios y contaba con directrices específicas para las modalidades de redacción especial, más allá de la consideración de que sus formas de expresión fueran juzgadas como «galimatías antiestético y jerigonza exótica» formados por un «aluvión de palabras exóticas, vulgarísimas, ininteligibles, además de ser completamente innecesarias» (García Escudero, 1983; Gómez Aparicio, 1971–1981 y Graña, 1930).

Años 30

En 1934, la crítica al periodismo deportivo, la vida al aire libre y la exageración social del deporte se centraba en la imitación de la frivolidad extranjera y una excesiva presencia de jerga inglesa de difícil traducción sin asumir ni los valores educativos del deporte ni su influencia en la formación de un carácter tenaz y perseverante a prueba de contrariedades. Centró su mirada en baloncesto, fútbol, hockey, patinaje, rugby y tenis (Ramón y Cajal, 1934).

Años 40

En la inmediata posguerra, las instituciones lingüísticas desarrollaron un enfoque normativo y descriptivo tras la solicitud de adhesión social al buen uso en los medios, ante el anhelo de instantaneidad y ubicuidad que suponía la radio, con el fin de evitar cambios y variantes que alterasen el idioma sin mejorarlo (Menéndez Pidal, 1944).

Varios periodistas, procedentes de la Escuela de Periodismo de El Debate, favorecieron la corrección de la redacción de noticias tanto en los medios como en la formación en la Escuela Oficial de Periodismo. En el primer caso, destacó la figura de Pedro Gómez Aparicio que, como director de la Agencia Efe, acompañaba la corrección de las noticias con comentarios sobre influencias de otros idiomas desde 1944 (Olmos, 1997). También alcanzó notoriedad la labor de Nicolás González Ruiz que pensaba que la prensa podía evitar la divulgación y aceptación de términos foráneos y ser cuidadosa en la admisión a toda prisa de voces extranjeras. Entendía que la actitud rígidamente purista no tenía ningún valor práctico ni periodístico, dado que las instituciones aguardaban un tiempo a que la voz se haya incorporado de manera efectiva al léxico, y se debía apostar por una flexibilidad singular que no olvidara las normas gramaticales. Además, reflexionó sobre la carencia de cultura idiomática del periodista a la hora de discernir en el uso de un neologismo, ya que daba lugar a períodos de confusión con vacilaciones en las adaptaciones de términos y optó por favorecer la orientación del uso por parte de la clase media culta (González Ruiz, 1940).

Años 50 y 60

Estos dos decenios aportaron un nuevo paradigma en la relación entre instituciones lingüísticas y medios de comunicación.

La creación de la Asociación de Academias de la Lengua Española supuso una apuesta por ampliar horizontes y ensanchar el idioma con dinamismo, moderación y tolerancia. Favoreció la hispanización del léxico y el uso de criterios de corrección idiomática en varias resoluciones específicas en las ediciones del I, II, III y IV Congreso de la Asociación de Academias de la Lengua Española. El trabajo lingüístico se orientó a conservar la unidad fundamental del idioma, su empleo como instrumento y manifestación cultural exaltando su propiedad y expresividad y su fuerza de cohesión espiritual para atender el reto de combinar la renovación con la conservación de la pureza (Comisión Permanente del Congreso de Academias de la Lengua Española, 1952 y 1956; Rosenblat, 1969)

Era el momento de superar el viejo academicismo, el casticismo y el purismo ciego, entendidos ahora como poco eficaces, como un concepto estático del idioma y como una actitud contraria a cualquier innovación, proteccionista, reductora y empobrecedora que actuaba en la escuela, el periodismo y el libro. Era el fin de una época caracterizada por cuentasílabas, oreja-fina, contadores de acusativos, cazadores de gazapos, husmeadores de deslices y creadores de repertorios de barbarismos y solecismos. Y se daba paso a la orientación institucional y de personas capacitadas lingüísticamente para sugerir sin autoritarismos mediante una reacción anti-correccionista que contaba con la aceptabilidad social y cultural de los usos y no consideraba al anglicismo como una forma de colonialismo.

El panorama surgido tras la II Guerra Mundial trajo novedades y necesidades sociales que trajeron palabras nuevas, numerosas voces científicas, técnicas y deportivas de origen inglés para adaptarlas al idioma español. Fueron instantes para reemplazar con neologismos apropiados y para una intensificación de la intercomunicación entre continentes que requirió amoldar las voces extranjeras a los preceptos del castellano con sus correspondientes equivalencias españolas.

En esta tarea, que se consideraba más difícil que la lucha contra el galicismo porque venía acompañado de signos de progreso, tecnología, consumismo y aspectos de vida moderna, se solicitó la cooperación de la prensa periódica y la radio en el uso correcto y castizo de la lengua porque se les consideraba como un elemento positivo para evitar la fragmentación de la lengua y para frenar el localismo expresivo, aunque también facilitaban la difusión de neologismos y voces extranjeras.

En el caso del deporte esta intervención afectó a extranjerismos sustituibles por voces españolas, denominaciones de deportes y sus derivados y neologismos. En el Segundo Congreso de Academias de la Lengua Española se aportó un listado de extranjerismos innecesarios (galicismos, italianismos y anglicismos) con sus correspondientes equivalencias españolas, de los que 162 eran palabras inglesas. Entre ellas, 46 eran expresiones del mundo del deporte con carácter general y relacionadas con 20 deportes específicos: atletismo, automovilismo, baloncesto, béisbol, boxeo, camping, ciclismo, críquet, croquet, fútbol, fútbol americano, golf, hípica, hockey, patinaje, rugby, tenis, tenis de mesa, vela y waterpolo. Y además, se incluyó un vocabulario deportivo de 103 términos en el que 81 eran anglicismos.

De esta época también es el listado de 245 términos extranjeros facilitados en la Asamblea de Filología del I Congreso de Instituciones Hispánicas, de los que 67 son anglicismos deportivos relacionados con voces generales y específicas de baloncesto, béisbol, boxeo, ciclismo, esgrima, fútbol, golf, hípica, tenis, vela y voleibol (Echeverri Mejía, 1964).

En este ambiente el deporte aparecía como un rasgo de vitalidad del idioma con una terminología que se utilizaba en el habla corriente gracias a los juegos de palabras y el humorismo y sus anglicismos eran vistos como útiles, necesarios y expresivos (Rosenblat, 1960 y 1969).

Entre 1951 y 1961 se publicaron en España tres obras de interés para encauzar decisiones lingüísticas de hablantes en la comunicación pública: *Diccionario de dificultades de la lengua española*, *Diccionario de incorrecciones del lenguaje* y *Diccionario de dudas y dificultades de la lengua española* (Díaz-Retg, 1951; Santamaría, 1956 y Seco, 1966).

Estas obras buscaron el aval de miembros de número de la Real Academia Española como José María Pemán y Salvador Fernández Ramírez, quienes destacaron su sentido práctico y realista, su interés para superar el academicismo y para vivir la exigencia y la técnica de la vida moderna. Prestaban orientación en un momento de cambio de visión del idioma hacia la convivencia y la tolerancia en favor de la unidad del idioma. La norma pasaba a ser negociable y flexible y dejaba atrás el rigor preceptista del purismo con el objetivo de exaltar la prudencia y el ideal de la unidad de los países de habla hispana mediante el respeto del valor de cada una en su zona de influencia. (García Mouton, 2012).

Censuraban las formas descuidadas y su actitud ante el neologismo pasaba por voces que fueran necesarias y se acomodasen a las estructuras formales del castellano por lo que han sido consideradas como precursoras de los libros de estilo (Gómez Capuz, 1992).

Para el deporte destacó la labor del *Diccionario de incorrecciones del lenguaje*, inspirada en el capítulo «La corrupción del lenguaje» de Santiago Ramón y Cajal en *El mundo visto a los 80 años* sobre la muchedumbre de barbarismos y solecismos que afeaban y empobrecían la lengua. Pensada como expurgo del idioma, comprendió 35 anglicismos generales y específicos de 16 deportes: atletismo, automovilismo, baloncesto, boxeo, ciclismo, croquet, esquí, fútbol, golf, hípica, lucha, patinaje, rugby, tenis de mesa, vela y waterpolo.

Años 70 y 80

En los años setenta y ochenta se generalizó el descontento sobre el mal uso del idioma en los medios de comunicación con continuas críticas de errores y ligerezas en una época de aceleración de novedades de la vida moderna y la atribución a los medios de una labor educativa que fue descrita como la de un "profesorado difuso" (Zamora Vicente, 1985).

Para el ámbito deportivo en 1973 el diario madrileño *Ya* publicó el editorial «Medio para la defensa del idioma» con el fin de plantear la necesidad de una unificación de vocabulario deportivo en una tarea propia de lo que serían los libros de estilo que surgirán en la segunda mitad de la década. Y la celebración de la fase final de la Copa Mundial de Fútbol de la FIFA de 1982 llamó la atención de varios académicos para solicitar la reducción de expresiones de origen inglés (Lázaro Carreter, 1997; Luca de Tena, 1981 y Medio para la defensa del idioma, 1973).

En esta etapa, hasta 1985, se pusieron en marcha diversos libros de estilo. En 1978, Fernando Lázaro Carreter hizo el primer *Manual de estilo* de la Agencia Efe, que proponía normas y buscaba una homogeneización del lenguaje periodístico para paliar el deterioro progresivo de la lengua. Esta normalización periodística y cultural de la lengua española, tras el congreso Salamanca 80, dio lugar al Departamento de Español Urgente para atender al problema de la adopción de términos extranjeros. En las nuevas redacciones tecnológicas con sistemas anglosajones de redacción y presentación de noticias, estos principios de acción incidieron especialmente en las noticias de nacional, internacional y deportes.

En 1985, la Asociación de Academias de la Lengua Española celebró la *Primera reunión de Academias de la Lengua Española sobre el lenguaje y los medios de comunicación*. Fomentó secciones de orientación gramatical y análisis descriptivos del estado de la lengua en la prensa escrita. Activó la participación de las instituciones lingüísticas en la lengua de los medios de comunicación social con artículos de orientación para, entre otros fines, evitar la difusión de neologismos innecesarios (Asociación de Academias de la Lengua Española, 1987).

Esta reflexión llevó a la convocatoria del Seminario Internacional *El idioma español en las agencias de prensa* en 1989 que describió características y dificultades de la escritura deportiva entre las que se hallaba la proliferación de extranjerismos (Agencia Efe y Fundación Germán Sánchez Rupérez, 1990).

Fue una época de respuesta a las necesidades de la comunicación moderna, al trabajo en campos en los que no está fijada una norma lingüística y en la que surgen los libros de estilo como herramienta contra la colonización generada por la tecnología y las relaciones internacionales (Fernández Beaumont, 1987; Gallardo, García y Pons, 1992; Gómez Capuz, 1992).

Al igual que pasó con el surgimiento de los diccionarios de dudas, muchas de estas publicaciones contaron a lo largo de la historia con el aval de académicos de número: Manuel Alvar en Canal Sur, José Manuel Blecua en La Vanguardia, Fernando Lázaro Carreter en la Agencia Efe, Luis Mateo Díez en Servimedia y Alonso Zamora Vicente en Televisión Española.

En esta primera fase, entre 1977 y 1985, las orientaciones lingüísticas sobre anglicismos deportivos corrieron a cargo de los medios de información general con 3 siglas de organismos internacionales del deporte y 63 términos con voces de carácter general, olimpismo y ligadas a 18 deportes: atletismo, automovilismo, baloncesto, béisbol, boxeo, camping, caza, ciclismo, críquet, esquí, fútbol, golf, hípica, motociclismo, natación, tenis, tenis de mesa y voleibol (Agencia Efe, 1978 y 1980: Diario 16, 1976; El País, 1980; Pérez Calderón, 1985; RTVE-Radio Nacional de España, 1980).

En *Manual de estilo*, la Agencia Efe reflexionaba en 1978 sobre el deterioro progresivo del idioma en los medios de comunicación y la expansión internacional de la agencia como causas para favorecer la homogeneidad de criterios y la neutralización del estilo para defender la unidad del idioma como bien para la convivencia. Destacaba la mayor influencia social de los medios de comunicación. Planteó un nuevo enfoque para superar los excesos tanto del purismo como del academicismo que se oponían a la normativa de las academias: la asesoría frente a la censura, la recomendación frente a la prohibición, la advertencia frente a la amonestación y desaprobación… Impulsaba el propósito de buscar la contención expresiva y evitar la difusión de neologismos innecesarios. Indicaba que la Real Academia Española no sancionaba algunos usos de términos porque no reemplazaban ventajosamente a voces castellanas dando sensación de colonización. Y en el capítulo "Observaciones sobre léxico", de las 291 recomendaciones apenas un 2,06 % eran deportivas con 6 expresiones de carácter general y relacionadas con el atletismo y la hípica. En la edición de 1980 del *Manual de estilo*, Luis María Anson indicaba en el prólogo que el libro de estilo era el instrumento para evitar el colonialismo creado por las agencias estadounidenses de información, que se iba a poner en marcha el Departamento del Español Urgente para dar respuesta a dudas sobre expresiones y evitar a tiempo la generalización de anglicismos. Argumentaba que el uso de la informática en los medios de comunicación derivaría en la uniformación y simplificación del lenguaje y que era necesario crear bases de datos para superar el colonialismo cultural anglosajón y defender la unidad del idioma con el objetivo de conservar la identidad cultural. En esta edición se tuvo en cuenta para las recomendaciones léxicas el *Diccionario breve de dudas de la lengua española*, de Manuel Seco, que publicó el Ministerio de Cultura en 1979.

Libro de estilo de los Servicios Informativos, de Televisión Española, contó con una certera introducción de Alonso Zamora Vicente que enmarcó los problemas del lenguaje periodístico audiovisual en la rápida transformación que sufre la lengua con la vida moderna, la labor de la televisión como educadora de masas y como profesorado difuso en tiempos de trivialización cultural y ligerezas expresivas generadas por el cine, la industria, el comercio, los viajes y la política internacional. En el capítulo dedicado a extranjerismos y neologismos criticó la adopción de términos foráneos cuando ya existen voces castellanas que designan esa realidad. Hizo referencia al problema de su adaptación y su traducción. Argumentó como causas de estas dificultades la dependencia de las agencias informativas anglosajonas y la falta de traductores que cuidasen la pureza y la elegancia del idioma. En el apartado "Pequeño diccionario de dudas" registró 352 recomendaciones, un 8,52 %, son 30 voces deportivas relacionadas con términos generales y atletismo, boxeo, caza, ciclismo, esquí, fútbol, golf, hípica, tenis de mesa y voleibol.

Manual de estilo para informadores de radio, de Radio Nacional de España, presentó la orientación undécima del capítulo "Palabras" para evitar las palabras extranjeras aunque añadía que, si son suficientemente conocidas y correctamente aplicadas, se permite su uso. Y en el bloque "Diccionario de dudas y palabras mal empleadas frecuentemente", de las 325 recomendaciones, un 1,70 % fueron deportivas con 4 voces de carácter general y relativas a la hípica.

El diario *El País* sacó la primera edición de su libro de estilo en 1977 para uso interno, aunque desde 1980 se imprimió en forma de libro. En esta segunda, de las 3.354 recomendaciones que proporcionaba, 50 eran deportivas. Conformaban un 1,49 % del caudal léxico con voces de carácter general, olimpismo y ligadas a atletismo, automovilismo, baloncesto, béisbol, boxeo, cámping, críquet, esquí, fútbol, hípica, motociclismo, natación, tenis, tenis de mesa y voleibol. Además, incluyó referencias al uso de anglicismos en el capítulo "Normas de estilo" para abordar la transcripción de nombres sin recurrir a las transliteraciones francesa e inglesa, así como la traducción al castellano de nombre de entidades y organizaciones.

Contaba con normas internas de redacción, entre 1976 y 1980, el rotativo madrileño *Diario 16* (Rojas, 2011a).

Años 90

En el último tramo del siglo la llegada de préstamos del inglés era apreciada como una pandemia lingüística en la que el periodismo podía ejercer una labor de primer orden para acotar esa importación gracias a su influencia en la evolución del idioma y por el tratamiento de los neologismos. Se destacó la permeabilidad de las lenguas técnicas para crear un lenguaje unificado con circulación internacional y se requirió la colaboración de los medios para aportar materiales de diversa índole con los que fijar una norma léxica y gramatical, extrayéndola de los usos idiomáticos compartidos en los países de habla hispana (Lázaro Carreter, 1993).

Siguieron los tiempos de reflexión con varios congresos organizados por la Agencia Efe y el Gobierno de La Rioja. Fue el caso en 1991 de *El neologismo necesario*, en el que Pedro Riaño hizo la propuesta de crear un único libro de redacción, y en 1992 del congreso internacional *El idioma español en el deporte* en el que se elaboró un léxico de los deportes olímpicos de 435 términos, de los que 58 eran extranjerismos de uso frecuente, y se repartió en la Ciudad de los Periodistas durante los Juegos Olímpicos de verano.

Un nuevo planteamiento apareció en el congreso *El español y los medios de comunicación*, celebrado en Valladolid del 27 al 31 de mayo de 1996, al considerar que los sectores cultos no mostraban interés por el uso hablado y escrito del idioma, que existía una gran divergencia en la comunicación entre el buen uso del idioma y la práctica diaria y que la eficacia de los libros de estilo dependía de la evolución del sistema educativo y la combinación de normas y consejos de redacción con normas de las prácticas discursivas de los periodistas. Se consideraba que el libro de estilo ayudaba a combatir la ignorancia, insensibilidad lingüística, pobreza expresiva, vulgaridad, pero que también era necesario crear instrumentos de trabajo que recojan las preferencias lingüísticas en una comunidad entre las diferentes posibilidades que ofrece el sistema lingüístico (Carriazo, 2012 y Martínez Albertos, 2012).

El siglo XX finalizó con la presentación del *Proyecto Zacatecas* en México en 1997 con el fin de crear un libro común de redacción con acuerdos sobre cuestiones grafemáticas y de uso de neologismos y extranjerismos ante la incipiente globalización. De las 162 obras de referencia que formaban la bibliografía, un 3 % de su caudal guardaba relación con el deporte gracias a cuatro estudios lingüísticos y un libro de estilo.

En esta segunda etapa de libros de estilo, entre 1986 y 1998, se registraron 243 aportaciones de la información general gracias a los libros de estilo de las agencias de noticias (Agencia Efe, 1998), la prensa escrita (Abc, 1993; El

Correo,1987; El Mundo, 1996; El País, 1996; La Vanguardia, 1986; La Verdad, 1996 y La Voz de Galicia, 1992), la radio (Cadena Ser, 1989 y Onda Cero Radio, 1996) y la televisión (Canal Sur, 1991; Telemadrid, 1993 y Televisión Española, 1993). Se produjo la incorporación de la comunicación especializada en deportes entre 1992 y 1998, con 511 recomendaciones a cargo de la Agencia Efe, el diario El Mundo Deportivo y el volumen *El deporte correctamente hablado* de Televisión Española (Agencia Efe y Gobierno de La Rioja, 1992a; Bernárdez, 1998 y El Mundo Deportivo, 1995). También tuvo lugar la irrupción de recomendaciones en formato papel y digital con el *Vademécum de español urgente,* que recogió 25 dudas léxicas sobre anglicismos deportivos y su transformación en un diccionario tradicional para alcanzar la máxima divulgación con el *Diccionario de español urgente* (Agencia Efe 1992, 1996, 1997 y 2000).

Tuvieron normas internas de redacción los diarios El Correo Gallego, El Ideal Gallego, El Periódico, El Sol, Ideal, La Opinión de Tenerife y La Verdad; los rotativos encuadrados en el Grupo Promecal; el semanario Tiempo (1987); la agencia de noticias Europa Press y en proyecto el canal Antena 3 Televisión. Esta práctica de hojas de estilo de uso interno también se registró en los diarios Sport y Superdeporte, así como en el semanario Don Balón (Rojas, 2011a).

En el cruce de todos los datos, se generaron 605 anglicismos diferentes de los que 8 son siglas relacionadas con organismos deportivos y federaciones y 597 términos son de carácter general, olimpismo y que guardan relación con 40 deportes: atletismo, automovilismo, aviación, bádminton, baloncesto, balonmano, béisbol, boxeo, cámping, ciclismo, ciclocrós, cricket, esquí, fútbol, fútbol americano, fútbol sala, gimnasia, golf, halterofilia, hípica, hockey sobre hielo, hockey sobre hierba, hockey sobre patines, lucha, motociclismo, natación, pádel, piragüismo, puentismo, remo, rugby, squash,, tenis, tenis de mesa, tiro con arco, tiro olímpico, vela, voleibol, waterpolo y windsurf.

Todavía era posible encontrar afirmaciones que hacían a los periodistas responsables del deterioro o de la corrección del buen uso del idioma en público y la recomendación de evitar los anglicismos porque pervierten el lenguaje al no coincidir con sus equivalencias en castellano, sobre todo en la jerga deportiva del fútbol que fue descrita como una invasora plaga moderna.

Siglo XXI

Primeros decenios

De 2001 a 2020 se registraron varios hechos lingüísticos destacados, una vez que la «Declaración de Valladolid» en 2001 puso en marcha el Observatorio del

Neologismo para analizar el tratamiento de sus formas con gran éxito social, entre otros el deporte, antes de que llegasen a instalarse en el habla común. Y al mismo tiempo, se produjo un cambio de paradigma en las formas de expresión de la nueva comunicación en movilidad con la aceleración de tiempos y la reducción de espacios que trajeron las actualizaciones tecnológicas y las redes sociales (Abad, 2019).

En primer lugar, la transformación del Departamento de Español Urgente en Fundación del Español Urgente BBVA, que aplicó un patrón de trabajo basado en la búsqueda de expresiones en castellano, la incorporación de anglicismos necesarios acomodados a los rasgos gráficos y morfológicos propios del español y la escritura de voces extranjeras en letra cursiva o entre comillas. Contaba con cinco líneas generales de actuación: la búsqueda de equivalencias en español, con preferencia por la traducción; la españolización del extranjerismo, respetando su pronunciación y una grafía conforme a las reglas del español; el rechazo a las transliteraciones de alfabetos no latinos hechas desde el francés y el inglés; las advertencias sobre traducciones inexactas, cuando se han hecho de forma literal y errónea; y los avisos sobre construcciones erróneas en español por influencia de otros idiomas (Rodríguez Muñoz, 2019).

El tratamiento lingüístico del ámbito deportivo desplegó once líneas de actuación entre 2005 y 2020:

(1) La orientación sobre pronunciación de nombres extranjeros, imprecisiones léxicas, términos deportivos de carácter general, así como terminología específica de deportes olímpicos y paralímpicos de verano y expresiones deportivas coincidiendo con momentos de alta competición en Juegos Panamericanos y campeonatos continentales o mundiales de balonmano, fútbol e hípica.
(2) La aceptación de anglicismos necesarios en actividades dirigidas.
(3) El tratamiento de anglicismos innecesarios con alternativas de uso.
(4) Consejos ortográficos y tipográficos sobre extranjerismos tanto en su uso recto como figurado.
(5) Consejos sobre grafías, tipografía y formación de plurales en voces extranjeras, con especial atención a nombres de instituciones, campeonatos, deportes e instalaciones.
(6) Terminología de gimnasia, golf, hockey, natación, tiro con arco.
(7) Publicación de un número monográfico de la revista *Donde dice*.
(8) Información y memoria del *VII Seminario Internacional de Lengua y Periodismo: El español en el periodismo deportivo*, celebrado en 2012.

(9) Guías de redacción para los Juegos Olímpicos de verano de 2012, 2016 y 2020.
(10) Orientaciones gramaticales sobre la supresión injustificada de artículos, las preposiciones que rigen algunos verbos o la formación de plurales en términos foráneos.
(11) Edición de *La Liga del español urgente* sobre el campeonato español con 9 anglicismos: *balompié, chutazo, club, crac, fan zone, football, grogui, hat-trick* y *penalty* (Gallego, 2015).

También en 2005 apareció el *Diccionario panhispánico de dudas*, tras gestarse en el I Congreso Internacional de la Lengua Española, celebrado en Zacatecas (México), para favorecer el buen uso del idioma mediante orientaciones argumentadas y acordadas entre todas las academias de habla española. Con el aval de los principales medios informativos en la comunidad hispana, aportó 150 entradas deportivas con orientaciones sobre adaptaciones gráficas, uso del género, formación de plurales, equivalencias, uso de otros términos como sinónimos, recomendaciones ortográficas y comentario de dudas y errores más comunes. Para el tratamiento de anglicismos comentó 30 voces de carácter general y 95 expresiones de 24 deportes específicos: aeróbic, atletismo, automovilismo, aviación, baloncesto, béisbol, boxeo, campin, ciclismo, críquet, deporte extremo, esquí, fútbol, golf, hípica, hockey, lucha, montañismo, motociclismo, natación, pádel, rugby, surf, tenis, tenis de mesa, vela, voleibol, waterpolo y windsurf. Y propuso adaptaciones gráficas, recomendaciones ortográficas, equivalencias léxicas y alternativas a construcciones sintácticas con influencias extranjeras.

Trece años más tarde, con el objetivo de promover la responsabilidad institucional y colectiva con el idioma y su expresión clara y propia con un enfoque panhispánico, la Real Academia Española publicó *Libro de estilo de la lengua española, según la norma panhispánica*. Recogió dudas, variaciones, las voces y locuciones más vivas del léxico, así como recomendaciones basadas en la percepción de los hablantes cultos que elaboran juicios sobre el idioma. En él, el deporte proporcionó 69 términos de carácter general, pseudoanglicismos y relacionados con Juegos olímpicos y 19 deportes: aerobismo, atletismo, automovilismo, bádminton, baloncesto, béisbol, boxeo, camping, ciclismo, deporte extremo, esquí, fútbol, golf, hípica, hockey, pádel, piragüismo, rugby y surf (Real Academia Española, 2018).

Los libros de estilo de esta etapa, entre 2001 y 2022, mantuvieron el criterio de preferir las voces españolas a los términos foráneos, que deben escribirse en letra cursiva.

La información general contribuyó con 518 anglicismos diferentes procedentes de los manuales de la prensa escrita (ABC, 2001; El País, 2021; El Periódico, 2002; La Vanguardia, 2004; La Voz de Galicia, 2002 y diarios del Grupo Vocento, 2003), las agencias de noticias (Fundación del Español Urgente-Agencia Efe, 2015 y Servimedia, 2007), la radio (cadenas Cope, 2003 y Ser, 2017) y la televisión (Canal Sur, 2004 y Radio Televisión Canaria, 2021).

También contaban con normas internas o en fase de proyecto los rotativos Diario de León y La Razón, los diarios integrados en los grupos de comunicación El Día, El Progreso, Grupo de Medios de Prensa, Joly y Público; las agencias de noticias Colpisa; la cadena de emisoras Punto Radio; los canales de televisión Telecinco y La Sexta; las publicaciones de prensa gratuita Metro y 20 Minutos (Rojas, 2011a).

La información especializada analizó 907 anglicismos y sus posibles soluciones gracias a los libros de estilo de la prensa escrita a cargo de los diarios As y Marca, las guías de redacción para la alta competición de la Fundación del Español Urgente y el volumen *Periodismo deportivo de calidad.* (González-Palencia y Mendaña, 2012; Grijelmo, 2019; Rojas, 2011b).

Entre todos contribuyeron con 1.115 convenciones. De ellas, 71 fueron siglas relativas a organismos, federaciones, elementos deportivos, denominaciones de deportes y vida social de deportistas. Y las otras 1.044 eran voces de carácter general y específicas de olimpismo, industria y comercio del deporte, apodos de equipos y 63 deportes: actividades dirigidas, aerobismo, artes marciales, atletismo, automovilismo, aviación, bádminton, baile deportivo, baloncesto, balonmano, béisbol, biatlón, billar, bobsleigh, boxeo, camping, caza, ciclismo, críquet, cróquet, crossfit, decatlón, deporte extremo, escalada, esquí, fútbol, fútbol americano, fútbol sala, golf, halterofilia, heptatlón, hípica, hockey en línea, hockey sala, sobre hierba, hockey sobre patines, luge, montañismo, motociclismo, motonáutica, mushing, natación, pádel, patinaje, pentatlón, piragüismo, remo, rugby, snowboard, sóftbol, squash, submarinismo, surf, tenis, tenis de mesa, tiro con arco, tiro olímpico, triatlón, vela, videojuegos, voleibol, waterpolo y windsurf.

Años 20

En el decenio actual destacó la labor de Manual de redación de La Voz de Galicia con numerosas orientaciones léxicas, ortográficas y ortotipográficas. Y la Fundación del Español Urrgente BBVA se reorganizó en junio de 2020 como FundéuRAE desarrollando las siguientes líneas de acción:

(1) Orientación sobre imprecisiones léxicas, terminología específica de deportes olímpicos y paralímpicos de verano y de invierno. Es el caso de atletismo, bádminton, baloncesto, balonmano, béisbol y sóftbol, boxeo, ciclismo, escalada deportiva, esgrima, gimnasia, golf, halterofilia, hípica, hockey, judo, karate, lucha, natación, natación sincronizada, pentatlón moderno, remo, rugby, skateboarding, surf, taekwondo, tenis, tenis de mesa, tiro con arco, tiro olímpico, triatlón, vela, voleibol y waterpolo para los primeros. Y para los segundos, de 20 competiciones deportivas y sus practicantes, de las que 10 cuentan con nombre en español y 10 con nombre extranjero con una posible solución amoldada al castellano (FundeuRAE, 2021).
(2) Aceptación de anglicismos necesarios.
(3) Tratamiento de anglicismos innecesarios con alternativas de uso.

Conclusiones

Del estudio constante y de la observación detallada de los recursos del idioma del deporte en el lenguaje periodistico se pueden obtener varias conclusiones.

Primero, el crecimiento del deporte y su constante diversificación con novedades sociales y en comunicación ha supuesto su uso como fuente documental para el registro de usos idiomáticos.

Segundo, la preocupación histórica del periodismo deportivo por el buen uso del idioma se registra desde finales del siglo XIX tanto en el uso y abuso de extranjerismos como en la búsqueda de formación desde las escuelas de periodismo.

Tercero, la importancia de la comunicación ante el deterioro del idioma y su evolución en prensa, radio, televisión e Internet con los consiguientes reajustes. Una relevancia que ha sido destacada por las instituciones lingüísticas como la Asociación de Academias de la Lengua Española y la Real Academia Española, por las entidades deportivas así como por la puesta en marcha de 13 secciones específicas de orientación lingüística (Castañón, 2021 y 2022).

Cuarto, la evolución de los libros de estilo desde la información general a la atención dedicada a la información especializada.

Quinto, de su análisis se desprende una evolución de 66 orientaciones con 3 siglas y 63 recomendaciones sobre 18 deportes a una realidad compuesta por 1.115 orientaciones con informaciones sobre 71 siglas y 1.044 expresiones relacionadas con 63 deportes. Es decir, se han multiplicado un 16,8 % el número de recomendaciones, un 23,6 % los datos sobre siglas, un 16,5 % el número de términos y un 3,5 % los deportes atendidos.

Y sexto, la aplicación como criterios más comunes de actuación: la adaptación de extranjerismos, la presencia de terminología con dudas en su uso o en su grafía, la uniformidad en el uso de neologismos y la unificación de criterios de transcripción de nombres de personas, lugares y entidades.

Referencias bibliográficas

Abad, M. (2019): El lenguaje impaciente: cada vez más corto, cada vez más rápido, *Archiletras*, 5, 86–88.

Abc (1993): *Libro de estilo de Abc*. Barcelona: Ariel.

Abc (2001): *Libro de estilo de Abc*. Barcelona: Ariel.

Agencia Efe (1978): *Manual de estilo*. Madrid: Castalia.

Agencia Efe (1980): *Manual de estilo*. Madrid: Castalia.

Agencia Efe (1992): *Vademécum del español urgente (I)*. Madrid. Fundación Efe.

Agencia Efe (1996): *Vademécum del español urgente (II)*. Madrid: Fundación Efe.

Agencia Efe (1997): *Vademécum del español urgente*, Madrid, edición electrónica.

Agencia Efe (1998): *Manual de español urgente*. Madrid: Cátedra.

Agencia Efe (2000): *Diccionario de español urgente*. Madrid: SM.

Agencia Efe y Gobierno de La Rioja (1992a): *El neologismo necesario*. Madrid: Fundación Efe.

Agencia Efe y Gobierno de La Rioja (1992b): *El idioma español en el deporte. Guía práctica*. Logroño: Gobierno de La Rioja.

Agencia Efe y Gobierno de La Rioja (1994): *El idioma español en el deporte*. Madrid: Fundación Efe.

Agencia Efe-Fundación Germán Sánchez Rupérez (1990): *El idioma español en las agencias de prensa*. Madrid: Fundación Germán Sánchez Rupérez.

Ahumada, I. (2012): Ideología y corrección lingüística: los precedentes peninsulares de los diccionarios de dudas. En Rodríguez González, F. (Ed.), *Estudios de lingüística española. Homenaje a Manuel Seco* (pp. 55–67). Alicante: Universidad de Alicante.

Alonso Pascual, J. (1996): *Anglicismos deportivos: uso y abuso en la información española*. Valladolid: Junta de Castilla y León.

Álvarez Mellado, E. (2021): Radiografía del anglicismo en la prensa española, *Archiletras*, 10, 102–103.

Alzugaray, J. J. (1982): *Extranjerismos en el deporte*. Barcelona: Hispano-Europea.

Apezarena, J. (2003): *COPE: Libro de estilo*. La Rioja: Cadena COPE.

Asociación de Academias de la Lengua Española (1987): *Primera reunión de Academias de la Lengua Española sobre el lenguaje y los medios de comunicación*. Madrid: Real Academia Española.

Baralt, R. M. (1890): *Diccionario de galicismos*. Madrid: Sucesores de Rivadeneyra.

Benavente, J.: De sobremesa. *El Imparcial* [Madrid] 10 de agosto de 1908.

Bernárdez, J. (1998): *El deporte correctamente hablado*. Oviedo: Universidad de Oviedo.

Cadena Ser (1989): *Proyecto de Normas de estilo*. Madrid: Cadena Ser.

Cadena Ser (2017): *En antena. Libro de estilo del periodismo oral*. Madrid: Taurus.

Canal Sur Televisión (1991): *Libro de estilo*. Sevilla: Canal Sur Televisión.

Canal Sur Televisión (2004): *Libro de estilo*. Sevilla: Canal Sur Televisión.

Carriazo Ruiz, J. R. (2008): Libros de estilo y diccionarios de dudas: brújulas para orientar al profesional de la lengua en la norma policéntrica del español. En Fernández Martínez, P. y Blanco Alfonso, I. (Coords.): *Diccionarios y libros de estilo* (pp. 213–231). Madrid: Fragua.

Castañón Rodríguez, J. (2002): *Tendencias actuales del idioma del deporte*. Salamanca: edición del autor.

Castañón Rodríguez, J. (2011): *La comunicación deportiva y la lengua española*. Valladolid: edición de autor.

Castañón Rodríguez, J. (2019): De carrileros y piscinazos. En Merino, J. M. y Grijelmo, Á. (Coords.): *Más de 555 millones podemos leer este libro sin traducción* (pp. 263–278). Barcelona: Taurus-Penguin Random House.

Castañón Rodríguez, J. (2021): Guía del lenguaje deportivo 2021. Las instituciones deportivas y el idioma español. *Idiomaydeporte.com*, 234.

Castañón Rodríguez, J. (2022): El creciente valor del lenguaje periodístico del deporte. En *VII Congreso Internacional Comunicación y Pensamiento. El poder de la comunicación deportiva*, Sevilla.

Cavia, M. de: El balompié. *El Imparcial* [Madrid] 1 de agosto de 1908.

Cavia, M. de (1923): *Cháchara*s. Madrid: Renacimiento.

Cejador, J.: Y dale con el balompié. *El Imparcial* [Madrid] 8 de agosto de 1908.

Comisión Permanente del Congreso de Academias de la Lengua Española (1952): Resolución XXI Vigilancia para la conservación de la pureza de la lengua española. En *Memoria del Primer Congreso de Academias de la Lengua Española* (pp. 350–352). Ciudad de México.

Comisión Permanente del Congreso de Academias de la Lengua Española (1956): *Memoria del Segundo Congreso de Academias de la Lengua Española*. Madrid.

Diario 16 (1976): *Normas básicas de redacción*. Madrid: Diario 16.

Díaz-Retg, E. (1951): *Diccionario de dificultades de la lengua española*. Editorial: A. G. Martorell, Madrid.

Echeverri Mejía, Ó. (1964): Anglicismos, galicismos y barbarismos de frecuente uso en Colombia. En Oficina Internacional de Información y Observación del Español-OFINES: *Presente y futuro de la lengua española*, II (pp. 92–98). Madrid: Ediciones Cultura Hispánica.

El Correo Español-El Pueblo Vasco (1987): *Libro de estilo*. Madrid: SGEL.

El Mundo (1996): *Libro de estilo*. Madrid: Temas de Hoy.

El Mundo Deportivo (1995): *Libro de estilo*. Barcelona: El Mundo Deportivo.

El País (1980): *Libro de estilo*. Madrid: Pomotora de Informaciones S.A.

El País (1996): *Libro de estilo*. Madrid: El País.

El País (2021): *Libro de estilo de El País. Edición 2021*. Madrid: Aguilar.

El Periódico (2002): *Libro de estilo de El Periódico de Catalunya*. Barcelona: Primera Plana.

Ente Público Radio Televisión Madrid (1993): *Libro de estilo de Telemadrid*. Madrid: Ediciones Telemadrid.

Fernández Beaumont, J. (1987): *El lenguaje del periodismo moderno*. Madrid: SGEL.

Franquelo y Romero, R. (1910): *Frases impropias, barbarismos, solecismos y extranjerismos de uso más frecuente en la prensa y en la conversación*. Málaga: El Progreso.

Fundéu BBVA (2015): *Manual de español urgente*. Barcelona: Debate.

FundéuRAE (2021): *Guía de redacción. Juegos Olímpicos Tokyo 2020*. Madrid.

Gallardo, B.-García, I y Pons, S. (1992): Libros de estilo: norma, urgencia y gramática. En Laguna A. y López, A. (Eds.): *Dos-cents anys de prensa valenciana* (pp. 879–890). Valencia: Generalitat Valenciana.

Gallego Barbeyto, D. (2015): *La liga BBVA del español urgente*. Fundeu.es. Madrid.

García Escudero, J. M. (1983): *El pensamiento de «El Debate»*. Madrid: Biblioteca de Autores Cristianos.

García Mouton, P. (2012): Norma, uso y variación en el *Diccionario de dudas y dificultades de la lengua española*. En Rodríguez González, F. (Ed.): *Estudios de lingüística española. Homenaje a Manuel Seco* (pp. 561–568). Alicante: Universidad de Alicante.

Gómez Aparicio, P. (1971–1981): *Historia de periodismo español*. Madrid: Editora Nacional.

Gómez Capuz, J. (1992): El problema de los extranjerismos en los libros de estilo. Purismo y defensa del idioma. En Laguna A. y López, A. (Eds.): *Dos-cents anys de prensa valenciana* (pp. 879–890). Valencia: Generalitat Valenciana.

Gómez Font, A. (2014): *Español con estilo*. Gijón: Trea.

González Ruiz, N. (1940): *Curso práctico en el que se introducen algunas orientaciones sobre redacción periodística*. Madrid: Magisterio Español.

González-Palencia, R. y J. C. Mendaña (2012): *Marca: Libro de Estilo*. Madrid: La Esfera de los Libros.

Graña, M. (1930): *La escuela de periodismo: programas y métodos*. Madrid: Compañía Iberoamericana de Publicaciones SA.

Grijelmo, Á. (coord.) (2019): *As: Libro de estilo*. Madrid: Diario As.

Hernández, H. (2021): *Manual de estilo de Radiotelevisión Canaria*. Santa Cruz de Tenerife: Ente Público Radiotelevisión Canaria.

Hernández, M. J. (2008): Las traducciones periodísticas: entre la aceptabilidad y el trasvase lingüístico, *Herméneus*, 10, 1–12.

Huidobro, E. de (1915): *¡Pobre lengua!* Santander: La Propaganda Católica.

La Vanguardia (1986): *Libro de redacción*. Barcelona: La Vanguardia.

La Vanguardia (2004): *Libro de redacción*. Barcelona: La Vanguardia y Ariel.

La Verdad (1996): *Libro de estilo de La Verdad*. Murcia: La Verdad.

La Voz de Galicia (1992): *Libro de Estilo de La Voz de Galicia*. La Coruña: La Voz de Galicia.

La Voz de Galicia (2002): *Libro de Estilo de La Voz de Galicia*. La Coruña: La Voz de Galicia.

La Voz de Galicia (2022): *Libro de estilo. Manual de redaccion de La Voz de Galicia*. La Coruña: La Voz de Galicia.

Lázaro Carreter, F. (1993): *El lenguaje del periodismo y la Academia*. La Coruña: Editorial La Voz de Galicia.

Lázaro Carreter, Fernando (1997): *El dardo en la palabra*. Barcelona: Círculo de Lectores-Galaxia Gutenberg.

Lázaro Carreter, Fernando (2003): *El nuevo dardo en la palabra*. Madrid: Aguilar.

Loza, E. y Castañón Rodríguez, J. (2010): *Términos deportivos de origen extranjero*. Logroño: Universidad de La Rioja.

Luca de Tena, Torcuato. "El idioma y los deportes". *ABC* [Madrid] 17 de mayo de 1981.

Madero, F. et al. (1996): *Guía de estilo de Onda Cero Radio*, Madrid, Onda Cero.

Martínez Albertos, J. L. (2008): La responsabilidad lingüística de los periodistas. En Fernández Martínez, P. y Blanco Alfonso, I. (Coords.): *Diccionarios y libros de estilo* (pp. 21–38). Madrid: Fragua.

Martínez de Sousa, J. (2003): *Libro de estilo Vocento.* Gijón: Trea.

Medio para la defensa del idioma. *Ya* [Madrid] 20 de febrero de 1973.

Mendieta, S. (1993): *Manual de estilo de TVE.* Barcelona: Labor.

Menéndez Pidal, R. (1944): *La unidad del idioma.* Madrid: Instituto Nacional del Libro Español.

Mir y Noguera, P. J. (1907): *Rebusco de voces castizas.* Madrid: Sáenz de Jubera Hermanos.

Mir y Noguera, P. J. (1908): *Prontuario de Hispanismo y Barbarismo.* Madrid: Sáenz de Jubera Hermanos.

Moreno, V.: Polémica del año 1908: ¿ "Football", "fuboll" o balompié? *Nuevatribuna. es* [Madrid] 15 de febrero de 1922.

Nomdedeu Rull, A. (2019): Las aportaciones de Antonio Viada (1902) a la estrategia españolizadora del lenguaje deportivo anglosajón. Estudio a propósito del Diccionario Histórico de Términos del Fútbol, *Boletín de la Real Academia Española*, XCIX–CCCXX, 723–769.

Nomdedeu Rull, A. y Torrebadella, X. (2018): Antonio Viada: regeneracionismo, deporte y lengua española. La institucionalización de las primeras voces del fútbol en España en el *Manual del sport* (1903), *Arbor*, 194–789, a470.

Olmos, V. (1997): *Historia de la Agencia Efe*. Madrid: Espasa.

Pérez Calderón, M. (1985): *Libro de estilo de los Servicios Informativos.* Madrid: Ente Público RTVE.

Ramón y Cajal, S. (1934): *El mundo visto a los 80 años.* Madrid: Beltrán.

Real Academia Española (2018): *Libro de estilo de la lengua española.* Madrid: Espasa.

Real Academia Española y Asociación de Academias de la Lengua Española: *Diccionario Panhispánico de dudas.* Madrid: Santillana, 2005.

Rodríguez González, Félix y Castañón Rodríguez, Jesús (2021): *Diccionario de anglicismos del deporte*. Madrid: Arco/Libros.

Rodríguez Muñoz, S. (2019): *La Fundación del Español Urgente (Fundéu): norma e innovación para un buen uso del lenguaje periodístico (2005–2019).* Tesis doctoral, Madrid, Universidad Complutense de Madrid.

Rojas Torrijos, J. L. (2011a): *Libros de estilo y periodismo global en español*, Valencia, Tirant Humanidades.

Rojas Torrijos, J. L. (2011b): *Periodismo deportivo de calidad.* Madrid: Fragua.

Rosenblat, A. (1960): *Buenas y malas palabras II.* Madrid: Editorial Mediterráneo.

Rosenblat, A. (1969): *Buenas y malas palabras III.* Madrid: Editorial Mediterráneo.

RTVE-Radio Nacional de España (1980): *Manual de estilo para informadores de radio.* Madrid: RTVE-Radio Nacional de España.

Santamaría, A. (1956): *Diccionario de incorrecciones del lenguaje.* Madrid: Paraninfo.

Seco, M. (1966): *Diccionario de dudas de la lengua española.* Madrid: Aguilar.

Seco, M. (1979): *Diccionario breve de dudas de la lengua española.* Madrid: Ministerio de Cultura.

Servimedia (2007): *Periodismo social. El compromiso de la información.* Madrid: Servimedia.

Viada, A. "¿En qué quedamos?". *Los deportes*, 6–7 [Barcelona] 16 de febrero de 1902.

Viada, A. "Sobre el vocabulario deportivo". *Los deportes*, 10, 12, 16, 21, 24, 33, 35 y 51 [Barcelona] 16 y 30 de marzo, 27 de abril, 1 y 22 de junio, 24 de agosto, 7 de septiembre y 28 de diciembre de 1902.

Zamora Vicente, V. (1985): Prólogo. En Pérez Calderón, M.: *Libro de estilo de los Servicios Informativos* (pp. 7–17). Madrid, Ente Público RTVE.

David Giménez Folqués

Universidad de Valencia[1]

Presencia del inglés en las revistas gráficas satíricas actuales

Resumen: Durante la contracultura española de los años 70, las revistas gráficas, en su afán de encontrar un lenguaje subversivo e innovador, incluyen un gran número de anglicismos. Este fenómeno se refuerza con la influencia que Estados Unidos generaba en muchas temáticas notables para estas publicaciones, como la drogadicción, la apertura sexual y la música de los años 60. Muchos de estos anglicismos se instauraron en nuestra sociedad y fueron incluidos, principalmente a partir de los años 80, por los diccionarios académicos de la RAE. De este modo, el objetivo de este trabajo es observar las principales temáticas que incluyen anglicismos en las revistas gráficas de la contracultura de los años 70 y analizar la influencia que han tenido en el género de revistas gráficas satíricas en la actualidad, sobre todo a partir de los últimos números publicados.

Palabras clave: anglicismos, contracultura juvenil, revistas gráficas satíricas.

1. Introducción

En las últimas décadas del siglo XX, España ha recibido una gran cantidad de anglicismos, en parte debido a la influencia que ha ejercido Estados Unidos en nuestro país. En 1950, justo después de la II Guerra Mundial, Estados Unidos aparece como la máxima influencia lingüística en el español, ocupando el lugar que mantenía hasta entonces Gran Bretaña. Este posicionamiento del país norteamericano coincide con una etapa donde el franquismo se aleja, ligeramente, del aislamiento político al que había sometido a España en su primera etapa más conservadora. Este hecho, como señala Rodríguez (2019), lo podemos ver plasmado en la implantación de bases militares como las de Rota y Torrejón de Ardoz.

En los años 60, la influencia lingüística del inglés se acentúa con la apertura turística que experimenta el país. España se convierte en un destino

1 David.gimenez-folques@uv.es. Código ORCID: https://orcid.org/0000-0002-9059-5591

atrayente para países como Gran Bretaña, hecho que provoca el interés de diferentes sectores de nuestro país por incorporar términos de este idioma como el ocio, la moda y la restauración. Encontramos ejemplos en esta época como *snack bar*, *barman*, *gin tonic*, *bikini* o *miniskirt* (Rodríguez, 2019: 801). No hay que olvidar, en este sentido, la importancia del nacimiento y desarrollo de la música pop (sobre todo con grupos como los *Beatles* y los *Rolling Stones*).

En las décadas siguientes, el desarrollo tecnológico, el interés por el deporte y por la música, junto con el papel de los medios de comunicación y las revistas marginales, siguen estimulando la llegada de estas voces. Asimismo, en la década de los 70, con el fin de la dictadura próximo, algunos sectores de la juventud se vieron influidos por el movimiento *underground* norteamericano. De esta manera, se inicia en España un periodo de apertura en esferas culturales como las revistas, la música, el cine y la literatura que encuentran en el uso de voces inglesas un modo de lenguaje renovador y alternativo a lo establecido hasta ese momento. Las revistas con historietas gráficas icónicas de los años 70, en el contexto de la denominada contracultura juvenil, siguen este patrón, como veremos en los apartados siguientes.

Precisamente en este punto iniciaremos el presente trabajo, ya que nuestro objetivo es analizar, cualitativamente, qué tipo de anglicismos aparecían en este contexto contracultural, concretamente a partir de revistas gráficas notables para la época como *Star* o *El Víbora*. A partir de este parámetro observaremos, de modo aproximado, cómo estas incorporaciones anglófonas han influido a las revistas gráficas actuales como *El Jueves*, *Mongolia*, *Tmeo* o *El Batracio amarillo* entre otras[2].

2. Las revistas gráficas en la contracultura

La década de los años 70 resulta fundamental en el posicionamiento de las revistas gráficas alternativas en España. Como hemos comentado anteriormente, los jóvenes encuentran en las revistas gráficas *underground* un espacio donde evadirse de la realidad, una realidad que, pese al fin de la dictadura, reflejaba una situación de crisis económica y social. Con pocas perspectivas de futuro, como señala Rodríguez (2002), los jóvenes no quieren integrarse en la sociedad que

---

2 Entiéndase que este será un trabajo cualitativo donde pretendemos huir de los números y acercarnos a las tendencias.

estaban viviendo, ya que se presentaban unos valores que no compartían. Por lo tanto, anhelan una cultura alternativa diferente de la establecida, por lo que buscan la suya propia contraria a la establecida, de ahí al nombre de contracultura juvenil. Esta denominación también es utilizada por las revistas juveniles de historietas de la década, como señala Migoya (2008) en la entrevista que realiza a Juanjo Fernández, editor de la revista *Star* (Fig. 2), una de las más icónicas de la época que nace en 1974, cerca del fin de la dictadura. Junto a ella, Dopico (2011: 169) indica otras revistas influyentes como *El Rrollo Enmascarado* (1973), *La Piraña Divina* (1975), *Butifarra!* (1975), *Los Tebeos del Rrollo* (1976), *Rock Comix* (1976) o *El Víbora* (1979) (Fig. 1).

Fig. 1. N.º 1 de *El Víbora*[3]

3 Imagen extraída de *Tebeoesfera*: https://www.tebeosfera.com/

Fig. 2. N.º 11 de la revista *Star*[4]

Desde un punto de vista lingüístico, observamos cómo los jóvenes empiezan a emplear un lenguaje alternativo con carácter jergal que es estudiado y denominado por diferentes especialistas, como así indica Casado Velarde (1989) o Lázaro Carreter (1979), como "cheli" o "pasota". Asimismo, Hoyos González (1981) indica la recurrencia en el uso de voces foráneas en estas revistas como elemento innovador e identitario, por ejemplo, mediante "la deformación que se produce cuando se utilizan formas extranjeras como en 'monis' en lugar de 'money' o 'sexi' en lugar de 'sexy' [...]" (1981: 31). El objetivo, como señala Rodríguez (2002, 34), es el de encontrar voces novedosas que, además de modificar y deformar las acepciones establecidas, supongan una alternativa, como sería con el caso de los extranjerismos.

En este contexto contracultural, los ámbitos que generan un mayor número de anglicismos están relacionados con las drogas, la liberación sexual y la música, como veremos en los apartados siguientes cuando incluyamos ejemplos representativos de estas temáticas. De esta manera, los jóvenes encuentran esferas de evasión, ya que buscan en el pasotismo una manera de vivir. Entre los fenómenos lingüísticos predominantes en estas temáticas, Rodríguez (2002: 35) incluye algunos relevantes en la conformación de este léxico contracultural.

4 Imagen extraída de *Tebeoesfera*: https://www.tebeosfera.com/

En primer lugar, el empleo de cambios semánticos, especialmente de vertiente metafórica. De este modo, en voces como *trip* se tomará el significado de *viaje* para hablar del efecto producido por las drogas. En segundo lugar, encontramos el fenómeno del cambio de código, donde aparecen los extranjerismos en forma de voces o expresiones, principalmente bajo la influencia del inglés. Finalmente, el autor habla del cambio de registro, principalmente a partir de las formas lingüísticas más estigmatizadas. Encontramos, como mecanismo, el recurso de los vulgarismos, de los eufemismos y del tono informal e incluso humorístico, también en resultados deformados como *vicius* en lugar de *vicious*, o *beibi* en lugar de *baby*.

3. La herencia de la contracultura en las décadas siguientes

Es indudable la importancia que estas revistas tuvieron sobre el género, ya que marcaron el inicio de un movimiento cultural y de un tipo de lenguaje innovador que seguirían en los años 80 en revistas de historietas como *El Víbora* (diciembre de 1979), *Cairo* (1981) o *Makoki* (1982), como amplía Pérez (2013). Pese al periodo de declive que se vive a mediados de los años 80 y los años 90, donde se populariza el género de los superhéroes y el manga de importación, seguimos teniendo en este periodo, y en las décadas siguientes, revistas gráficas con sello nacional. Siguiendo con el hilo de los anglicismos, muchas de estas voces nacidas en la época de la contracultura seguirán siendo utilizadas por los jóvenes de las décadas siguientes en España, pero también por otros estratos de edad. Incluso algunos de ellos tendrán una extensión tan notable que serán recogidos por los diccionarios académicos. Según Andreva (2017), en el periodo que va desde 1956 hasta 2001 se incorporan en el *Diccionario* de la RAE 509 incorporaciones de anglicismos. Dentro de esta etapa, llaman la atención las 117 nuevas voces que incluye la 22.ª edición del *Diccionario*. Por otro lado, Giménez (2021) señala que se incluyen 124 nuevas incorporaciones de anglicismos en la última edición, es decir, la 23.ª edición.

De hecho, tanto el lenguaje como el contenido contracultural dejan una herencia importante en las revistas gráficas de las décadas siguientes. Como podremos observar en *El Jueves* (1977 – actualidad), que además nace en la época contracultural, *Tmeo* (1987 – actualidad), *Amaníaco* (1991 – actualidad), *El Batracio Amarillo* (1994 – actualidad) o *Mongoli*a (2012 – actualidad). Como hemos podido observar en los ejemplos que hemos citado, el género gráfico de humor y satírico encuentra su espacio en este ámbito, en algunos casos con mucha difusión, como los ejemplos de *El Jueves* o *Mongolia* (Figs. 3 y 4). Con el avance de la democracia en España, observamos cómo este tipo de revistas agudiza su crítica directa al sector político. Pese a ello, muchas veces han recibido denuncias procedentes de la persona o entidad caricaturizada, provocando la censura e, incluso, la eliminación de algún número, como ha sucedido con *El Jueves* en numerosas ocasiones, como señala Vilches (2014).

Fig. 3. Revista *El Jueves*. 2021

Fig. 4. Revista *Mongolia*. 2022[5]

5 Ambas imágenes extraídas de Tebeoesfera: https://www.tebeoesfera.com/

Tanto *El Jueves* como *Mongolia* son revistas gráficas críticas e irreverentes que cuentan con vigencia y tienen una divulgación y popularidad consumada. Precisamente, este contexto satírico provoca que se tomen como parámetro aquellos aspectos sociales más notables del momento como la política, las crisis, el amor o las innovaciones tecnológicas, entre otros temas. De esta manera, en el aspecto lingüístico también se siguen aquellas formas actuales o que están de moda, como sería el caso del uso de los anglicismos. En el punto del empleo de voces foráneas, además, sería interesante observar si existe una herencia lingüística de movimientos tan importantes como la contracultura juvenil, hecho que intentaremos analizar en los siguientes apartados. Asimismo, la revista *El Jueves* es una publicación semanal editada en Barcelona que nació a finales de los años 70, es decir, en el periodo posdictatorial y en plena etapa contracultural española, con lo cual, en este caso es fácil intuir la mencionada herencia *underground*. Representa, además, uno de los supervivientes del periodo denominado "boom del cómic adulto en España".

Por otro lado, la revista *Mongolia*, con clara influencia de las revistas satíricas españolas predecesoras, también de *El Jueves* (de donde han surgido algunos de sus dibujantes), y con menor historicidad que estas, nace en el 2012. La revista sigue el camino marcado por publicaciones que fueron importantes en el género satírico como *El Papus* o *Hermano Lobo*. Como señala Gascón (2020), ha ido evolucionando igual que lo ha hecho la política, la sociedad y el idioma, principalmente desde el punto de vista de su inclusión en el mundo digital y audiovisual. De este modo, su adaptación a este medio junto con su popularidad ha provocado que en el 2017 reciba un espacio en el canal La Sexta, concretamente en el programa Al Rojo Vivo.

En cuanto a otras revistas que cumplan con estos parámetros gráficos y satíricos y con una posible herencia lingüística de la contracultura, encontramos el caso de *El Batracio Amarillo*, principalmente centrada en temas sociopolíticos de Granada en particular y de España en general. Creada en Motril, distribuida en Granada y actualmente accesible para toda la Península. Nace en 1994, adquiriendo, progresivamente, un tono agresivo y sin complejos, hecho que le ha ido proporcionando popularidad fuera de su provincia. En cuanto a *Tmeo*, nos encontramos con una revista de historietas creada en 1987 en Vitoria. Su nombre procede de un juego de palabras entre *tebeo* y el verbo "mear", hecho que indica su carácter satírico marcado e incisivo. De hecho, destaca su humor escatológico y la agresividad. Su principal temática es la política de Euskadi y España. Finalmente, *Amaníaco* se edita desde 1991 en Barcelona y es el origen también de su propio sello editorial. De intención cómica y satírica, su temática es variada; además, aparecen muchos números especiales centrados en una temática en concreto, pero sin olvidar el aspecto social.

4. Temáticas de herencia contracultural en la actualidad

Después de haber analizado un amplio número de revistas de los títulos de la contracultura mencionados en este trabajo (con especial hincapié en *Star*, *El Rrollo Enmascarado, y El Víbora*) y habiendo hecho lo propio con las revistas gráficas satíricas con vigencia en la actualidad (con especial hincapié en los números actuales de *El Jueves*, *Mongolia*, *Tmeo* y *El Batracio amarillo*), podemos afirmar que existen no solo temáticas que se repiten, sino también los anglicismos usados en ellas. Estas temáticas tienen que ver con la música, las drogas y el sexo. Además, encontramos un gran número de interjecciones propias del formato gráfico que proceden del inglés y que continúan usándose en los formatos satíricos actuales.

Por ejemplo, en el ámbito de la música encontramos voces que han pervivido con el paso de las décadas y que han pasado del contexto contracultural de los 70 a los números actuales de revistas como *El Jueves, Tmeo, El Batracio amarillo* y *Mongolia*. Ponemos como ejemplo aquellas voces que hemos encontrado con una gran frecuencia: *blues, dance, dancing, dolby, folk, funky, gruppie, heavy, hit, jazz, LP (long play), playback, pop, punk, reggae, riff* (…de guitarra), *rock, rockero/a, soul* o *twist*. Como podemos observar, la influencia que generó el ámbito musical de Inglaterra y Estados Unidos de los años 60 en la contracultura española provocó la incorporación o el recurrente uso de muchas voces inglesas en las revistas gráficas del momento. De hecho, tal fue su importancia en la sociedad española que algunas de estas voces fueron incluidas, posteriormente, en el diccionario académico de la RAE en los años 80, como sería el caso de *rock* o *blues*. En los números actuales de las revistas satíricas analizadas, aparecen con mucha frecuencia las voces *blues, jazz, pop* y *rock*. Evidentemente, influye el hecho de que sean voces totalmente extendidas en nuestra sociedad y que pertenezcan a géneros musicales con gran extensión en el mundo. Observemos algunos ejemplos:

- *Contrataban a Ramoncín para que el punk se desfogara.* (*El Jueves*, n.º 2350).
- *Jaume Roures no tuvo nada que ver en la aparición de Villarejo en TV3 como si fuera una estrella del rock* (*Mongolia*, n.º 111).
- *Entrenado desde niño para ser todo un killer, supo usar todas sus armas, incluso la de ser una estrella del pop* (*Mongolia*, n.º 111).
- *Mi rollo es el rock* (*Tmeo*, n.º 163).

- *¡Qué gran invento esto del sonido dolby stéreo!* (*El Batracio amarillo*, n.º 233).
- *Sofío, el espíritu del pop* (*El Batracio amarillo*, n.º 233).

En cuanto al género de la drogadicción o el alcohol su uso en las revistas satíricas actuales sigue siendo muy alto, ya que pueden conllevar, entre otros efectos, polémica o mofa, según el escritor desee. Además, como observaremos, muchas de estas voces inglesas han logrado una gran extensión en la sociedad española. Algunos de los ejemplos que ya aparecían con cierta frecuencia en la contracultura juvenil de los años 70 serían los siguientes: *bloody mary, bourbon, cocktail, crack, dealer, güisqui, heroína, LSD, marihuana, smoking, speed, trip, vermouth, whisky*. Este campo temático en las revistas contraculturales encontró una gran acogida, ya que las drogas son utilizadas, sobre todo con la dictadura finalizada, como elemento desinhibidor. También, en este sentido, resulta notable la influencia estadounidense de los años 60 y 70 en la transmisión de estas voces y su posterior arraigo en la sociedad española, como podemos observar en las revistas gráficas satíricas actuales o en la alta frecuencia de aparición que tienen en los corpus académicos como el CREA o el CORPES XXI. De esta forma, encontramos ejemplos como los siguientes:

- *¿Desea un güisquito el señor?* (*El Jueves*, n.º 2351)
- *Te metiste medio pollo de speed* (*Tmeo*, n.º 165).
- *Si buscas entornos paradisíacos, heroína barata…* (*Tmeo*, n.º 166).
- *¿Un poco de coca o LSD?* (*Mongolia*, n.º 110).

Llama la atención, particularmente, el uso de *whisky*, en su formato original, y la adaptación *güisqui*, que se sigue manteniendo incluso en la última versión del *Diccionario de la lengua española* (2014, 23.ª edición). Aunque *marihuana* aparece en los años 50 en los diccionarios académicos de la RAE y *heroína* en los 70, es en los años 80 cuando muchos de estos ejemplos se suman a este diccionario, como es el caso de *whisky* y *güisqui*, tal como sucede con las voces que hemos visto en la temática de la música, quizás reforzados por el uso que se realizó de ellos en la mencionada contracultura de los años 70.

En relación al tema del sexo y la liberación sexual, del mismo modo que hemos visto con las temáticas anteriores, asistimos a un periodo de mayor desinhibición, principalmente con el final de la dictadura. De este modo, voces como *baby, bikini, dandy, fuck, fucking, gay, sex, sex-appeal, sex-symbol, sexy, striptease* o *unisex* empiezan a ser usadas con asiduidad en las páginas de las revistas contraculturales de los años 70. Asimismo, estas voces se mantienen en las décadas siguientes y llegan hasta la actualidad de las revistas satíricas gráficas analizadas, como podemos observar en los siguientes ejemplos:

- *¿Está familiarizado con el término first fucking?* (*El Jueves*, n.º 2351)
- *Los famosos despiden al fucking rey* (*Mongolia*, n.º 111)
- *¡Qué alegría, han vuelto los turistas! ¡Fuck you!* (*Tmeo*, n.º 165)
- *El rey sex-symbol por excelencia* (*Mongolia*, n.º 111)

De estas voces, entran en los diccionarios académicos de la RAE de los años 80 muchas formas representativas de este género como *bikini, gay, sexy* o *unisex*, reforzadas, como en los otros ámbitos comentados, por su uso frecuente en la contracultura de los años 70.

En último lugar, nos centramos en el ámbito de las interjecciones. Estos elementos suelen ser recurrentes en las revistas gráficas, principalmente en el apartado de las viñetas. Encontramos muchos recursos expresivos en lengua inglesa en las revistas contraculturales de los años 70, que aparecen también en las revistas satíricas actuales, como es el caso de *all right, bang, bitch, boom, click, cloc, clock, clok, crack, follow me, hey, let's go, oh shit, ok, okey, shit, too much, wow, yeah, yes*. En las nombradas revistas actuales encontramos ejemplos como los siguientes:

- *Ok, tú sabrás* (*Tmeo*, n.º 164).
- *Okey, ¿por dónde empezarás?* (*El Jueves*, n.º 2350).
- *Adiós Juanito, click (Mongolia,* n.º 111).
- *¡Espera niño, ya te explico! ¡Boom! (Mongolia, n.º 110).*

5. Temáticas novedosas en las revistas gráficas y satíricas actuales

Como hemos comentado en apartados anteriores, actualmente contamos con revistas gráficas con tintes satíricos que guardan un tono irreverente, como también ocurría en la época de la contracultura juvenil. Aunque revistas como *El Jueves*, *Tmeo*, *El Batracio amarillo* o *Mongolia* estén destinadas a un público más amplio, siguen manteniendo, además del tono irreverente, algunos aspectos de la década de los 70. Por ejemplo, el recurso del gráfico donde destaca la viñeta, algunas temáticas[6] representativas como la música, el sexo y la drogadicción y recursos inherentes de este género como el uso de las interjecciones. En este sentido, tenemos que matizar que las temáticas han evolucionado y se han adaptado a los nuevos tiempos. En primer lugar, en cuanto a las temáticas coincidentes del sexo y la drogadicción, estas ya no resultan tan novedosas como

6 Véanse los apartados anteriores.

en los años 70, ya que, con el avance de la democracia y el tipo de contenido al que estamos acostumbrados en los medios de comunicación y los medios de entretenimiento, hemos naturalizado muchos de estos términos y expresiones. Además, se utilizan con otros fines y perspectivas, principalmente con un objetivo cómico, satírico y crítico.

Por otro lado, aparecen nuevas temáticas como, por ejemplo, una sátira mucho más directa y constante hacia gobernantes y otros personajes populares, como podemos observar en la Fig. 5. De hecho, aparecen números especiales que se centran en la crítica a uno de estos personajes como, por ejemplo, el número 111 de *Mongolia* (Fig. 6) que se centra en la figura del rey emérito Juan Carlos de Borbón.

Fig. 5. *El Batracio amarillo.* N.º 233[7]

7 Imagen extraída de Tebeoesfera: https://www.tebeosfera.com/

Fig. 6. *Mongolia*. N.º 111[8]

Otra temática que inunda las páginas de estas revistas tiene que ver con los avances tecnológicos donde destacan las redes sociales. De hecho, vivimos en la era de la digitalización y los productos culturales no son ajenos a esta realidad. Con la apertura comunicativa, el fulgurante avance de la tecnología, la digitalización y la inclusión de las redes sociales en nuestras vidas, se genera una cantidad de léxico que en muchas ocasiones es difícil de asimilar, clasificar y analizar. En este punto, los anglicismos cuentan con un papel importante, ya que proceden de un idioma que se ha erigido como la lengua de comunicación por excelencia. Además, muchos de los nuevos instrumentos tecnológicos y digitales toman directamente el nombre en inglés y de esta manera llegan a otros idiomas.

En tercer lugar, otra temática cada vez más recurrente tiene que ver con la sátira sobre las frecuentes crisis económicas y otros desastres que van sucediendo. Es cierto que las revistas contraculturales aparecieron como alternativa de una sociedad sumida en una profunda crisis económica y poco esperanzadora para el futuro de los jóvenes, sin embargo, en las revistas actuales la crítica o sátira parece mucho más directa, mordaz y, sobre todo, recurrente, como podemos observar en la Fig. 7.

8 Imagen extraída de Tebeoesfera: https://www.tebeosfera.com/

Fig. 7. Revista *Tmeo.* N.º 166[9]

De este modo, se genera un gran número de anglicismo en torno a estas temáticas, que vamos a dividir en "tecnología y redes sociales" y "crítica política, social y crisis". En cuanto a la temática de la tecnología y redes sociales, incluimos algunos ejemplos recurrentes como los siguientes: *byte, chip, Facebook, Gmail, GPS, Instagram, influencer, instagramer, like, Linkedin, microchip, post, selfi, sensorround, smartphone, streaming, TikTok, terabyte, tuitero, Twitter, web, WhatsApp, youtuber, Youtube.* A diferencia de las temáticas de la contracultura, las voces que han sido recogidas por el diccionario académico de la RAE han sido incorporadas en la última década, como es el caso de *byte, GPS, microchip, selfi, terabyte, tuitero* o *web.* De hecho, existen muchas voces que todavía no aparecen por su reciente incorporación en la sociedad española, como *Facebook, Gmail, Instagram, influencer, instagramer, like, Linkedin, post, sensorround, Smartphone, streaming, TikTok, Twitter, WhatsApp, youtuber* o *Youtube.* Observemos algunos ejemplos en las páginas analizadas:

- *Sacó su móvil y se hizo un selfi. Lo subió a su cuenta de Instagram y fue el post que más likes ha conseguido* (*Mongolia*, n.º 110).

9 Imagen extraída de Tebeoesfera: https://www.tebeosfera.com/

- *Un nuevo proyecto en streaming para redes del que editorial Mong, SL, tiene el 20 %* (*Mongolia*, n.º 111).
- *Arrancar flores con forma de pene, la última moda de las influencers* (*El Jueves*, n.º 2351)
- *Ni te cuento ya cuando saqué la foto del abanico en Twitter* (*El Jueves*, n.º 2351).
- *Tengo 10 terabytes de porno en mi disco duro* (*El Jueves*, n.º 2351).
- *El quinto de la semana con el sabotaje del GPS* (*Tmeo*, n.º 165).
- *¡Qué gran invento esto del sonido dolby estéreo!* (*El Batracio amarillo*, n.º 233).

Por otro lado, la temática sobre la "crítica política, social y crisis" cada vez ocupa un mayor número de páginas. Estos términos en inglés suelen aparecer por la internacionalización de las crisis tratadas (pandemias, crisis económicas globales, guerras) que tienen un mayor acceso a diferentes idiomas mediante la apertura de los medios de comunicación. De este modo, encontramos algunos ejemplos como los siguientes: *bróker, COVID, crown, eslogan, gasolina, gel hydroalcoholic, King, mitin, Mr. President, power, Queen, security, stoling, tarjeta black*. La mayoría de estas voces, debido a su reciente aparición en nuestra sociedad, no suelen estar recogidas en los diccionarios académicos de la RAE, salvo algún ejemplo como *bróker, COVID* (incluidos en la 23.ª edición) o voces que sí estaban extendidas en el español con anterioridad como *eslogan, gasolina* (incluidas ambas en los años 80) o *mitin* (incluida a principios de los años 90). Veamos algunos contextos de los últimos números analizados:

- *Historias de the Crown* (*Mongolia*, n.º 110).
- *S.O.S, Save the Queen* (*Mongolia*, n.º 111).
- *O sea, desde que te fuiste nada es tan divertido como antes: nos quitaron las tarjetas "black", me prohibieron ir al bingo y papá no para de pedirme que le presente a mis amigas* (*Mongolia*, n.º 111).
- *Y efectivamente, la gasolina por las nubes* (*El Jueves*, n.º 2350).
- *Ermitaño lo abandona todo para hacerse bróker de Wall Street* (*El Jueves*, n.º 2351).
- *Se investigan los contratos COVID de Ayuso. Contratos COVID Madrid reguleros* (*El Jueves*, n.º 2351)
- *Se ha documentado para los mítines en Andalucía escuchando un casete de chistes de Chiquito* (*El Jueves*, n.º 2351).
- *¡Una motrileña embarazada que se contagió de COVID-19, solo una semana antes de dar a luz, bautizó a sus gemelos Corona y Virus!* (*El Batracio amarillo*, n.º 233).

6. Conclusiones

En el presente trabajo hemos podido comprobar la importancia que tuvo la contracultura juvenil de los años 70 no solo en el aspecto social y cultural, sino también en el lingüístico. En la búsqueda de un lenguaje novedoso, rompedor e irreverente, las revistas gráficas emplearon el recurso de las voces inglesas. Recordemos que durante la dictadura se produjo un cierre al exterior, también en lo que se refería al idioma, por lo tanto, empezar a recurrir a voces y expresiones de otros idiomas reforzaba este punto subversivo que se buscaba. Estas palabras se incluían principalmente en temáticas de influencia estadounidense de los años 60 y 70, como es el caso de la música, la liberación sexual y la drogadicción.

De este modo, se marcó una tendencia que provocó la introducción de muchas voces inglesas en la sociedad española. De hecho, algunas de estas palabras tuvieron tanto arraigo en nuestro idioma que fueron incluidas durante los años 80 en los diccionarios académicos de la RAE. Durante los años 90 y siguientes décadas seguimos encontrando rastros de esta influencia, como sucede en el caso de las revistas gráficas satíricas, que recogen no solo muchas temáticas de la contracultura, sino también muchos de los anglicismos analizados, como hemos comprobado en este trabajo. Inevitablemente, la sociedad avanza y se generan nuevos ámbitos de interés que genera un nuevo discurso y, por lo tanto, la inclusión de nuevas voces, también procedentes de otros idiomas. Encontramos, en este sentido, las temáticas de la crisis, la crítica política, la tecnología o las redes sociales. Teniendo en cuenta que son temáticas extendidas internacionalmente y que el inglés es el idioma de comunicación por excelencia, es normal que estas publicaciones recurran a voces inglesas, en alguna ocasión de manera forzada en búsqueda de un tono intencionado (sarcasmo, crítica, expresividad…).

En definitiva, una vez más comprobamos cómo el idioma suele avanzar de la mano de la sociedad modificando, eliminando o incluyendo nuevas voces según la necesidad del momento y de la intención de su interlocutor. Una sociedad donde el inglés aparece en una posición de poder y utilidad, por lo que su influencia sigue generando nuevos términos en el resto de idiomas.

7. Bibliografía

Andreva García, Fernando (2017): "Anglicismos no asimilados en el DRAE (23.ª ed.)". *Études romanes de Brno*, vol. 38, págs. 11–27. DOI: https://doi.org/10.5817/ERB2017-2-2

Casado Velarde, Manuel (1989): "Léxico e ideología en la lengua juvenil". En Félix Rodríguez González (coord.), *Comunicación y lenguaje juvenil* (pp. 167–178). Madrid: Fundamentos.

Dopico, Pablo (2011): "Esputos de papel. La historieta 'underground' española". En Antonio Altarriba (coord.), *La historieta española, 1857–2010. Historia, sociología y estética de la narrativa gráfica en España.* Madrid: Arbor. Ciencia, pensamiento y cultura, vol. 187, pp. 169–182.

Giménez Folqués, David (2021): *Análisis lingüístico en la adopción y adaptación de los nuevos extranjerismos de origen europeo y amerindio en el español actual.* Valencia: Tirant lo Blanch.

Hoyos González, Margarita de (1981): "Una variedad en el habla coloquial: la jerga cheli". *Cauce: Revista Internacional de Filología, Comunicación y sus Didácticas*, 4: 31–42.

Lázaro Carreter, Fernando (1979): "Una jerga juvenil: el cheli". En *Los domingos de ABC*, ABC, 16-octubre-1979: 6–7.

Migoya, Hernán (2008): "Cuando vivir no era consumir. Entrevista a Juanjo Fernández, editor de la revista *STAR*". Editorial Glénat. En línea: https://cualia.es/cuando-vivir-no-era-consumir-entrevista-a-juanjo-fernandez-editor-de-la-revista-star/

Pérez del Solar, Pedro (2013): *Imágenes del desencanto. Nueva historieta española 1980–1986.* adrid: Iberoamericana-Vervuert.

Real Academia Española: Banco de datos (CREA). *Corpus de Referencia del Español Actual.* En línea: https://www.rae.es/banco-de-datos/crea

Real Academia Española: Banco de datos (CORPES XXI). *Corpus del español del siglo XXI.* En línea: https://www.rae.es/banco-de-datos/corpes-xxi

Real Academia Española (2001): *Diccionario de la lengua española* (22.ª edición). Madrid: Espasa.

Real Academia Española (2014): *Diccionario de la lengua española* (23.ª edición). Madrid: Espasa.

Rodríguez González, Félix (2002): "Lenguaje y contracultura juvenil: anatomía de una generación". En Félix Rodríguez (coord.), *El lenguaje de los jóvenes* (pp. 29–56). Barcelona: Ariel.

Rodríguez González, Félix (2019). "La introducción de los anglicismos en español: historia, actitudes, registro". En por Ramón González Ruiz, Inés Olza y Óscar Loureda Lamas (ed.), *Lengua, cultura, discurso. Estudios ofrecidos al profesor Manuel Casado Velarde* (pp. 799–819). Navarra: Ediciones Universidad de Navarra, EUNSA.

Vilches, Gerardo (2014): "La primera etapa de El Jueves: un análisis de los primeros 26 números del semanario". *Cuco. Cuadernos de cómic*, n.º 2, pp. 137–158.

REVISTAS ANALIZADAS Y CITADAS

El Rrollo Enmascarado (1973). Barcelona: Producciones Editoriales.

Star (1974). Barcelona: Producciones Editoriales.

La Piraña Divina (1975). Barcelona: Autoedición.

Butifarra! (1975). Barcelona: A.N.C.H.E.

Los Tebeos del Rrollo (1976). Madrid, Barcelona: EDICIONES RECREATIVAS.

Rock Comix (1976). Barcelona: Luis Zanoletty.

El Jueves (1977). Barcelona: RBA Editores.

El Víbora (1979). Barcelona: La Cúpula.

Cairo (1981). Barcelona: Norma Editoral.

Makoki (1982). Barcelona: Ediciones populares.

Tmeo (1987). Vitoria: Ediciones populares.

El Batracio Amarillo (1994). Granada: Ediciones El Batracio Amarillo.

Mongolia (2012). Barcelona: Editorial Mong S.L.

María Jesús Rodríguez-Medina

Universidad de Las Palmas de Gran Canaria

Estudio de la presencia del inglés en las revistas para hombres en España: análisis comparativo

Resumen: Si bien es cierto que abundan los estudios sobre los anglicismos en las revistas de moda o las denominadas tradicionalmente revistas femeninas o revistas para mujeres (Fernández, 2016; Vega, 2017; Vázquez, 2018), las revistas para hombres en español apenas se han investigado (Iriarte, 2016; Ganzabal-Learreta y Meso-Ayerdi, 2022). Por ello, el objetivo de este trabajo es analizarlas y averiguar si la presencia del inglés en ellas es tan elevada como en las dirigidas al público femenino.

Dado que las tiradas en formato papel cada vez son más reducidas y este sector, como otros muchos, se dirige hacia la comercialización digital, el corpus se ha extraído de la publicación en la red social Facebook de *Men's Health España*, la revista de este perfil más leída de este país y la más importante del mundo en popularidad y ventas, lo que permite la comparación de los resultados con investigaciones previas muy recientes sobre las revistas femeninas en las redes (Rodríguez-Medina, 2022), análisis que revelará si la prensa en español especializada en el público masculino también recurre al inglés para los mismos fines o similares que las revistas para mujeres.

Palabras clave: sociolingüística, anglicismos, lexicografía, género, revistas masculinas.

1. Introducción

Mucho se ha hablado de las llamadas revistas femeninas o para mujeres y sus diferentes tipos (moda, prensa rosa, etc.) en el español europeo. Sin embargo, llama la atención que apenas existan publicaciones científicas sobre la prensa destinada al público masculino en España, a pesar de que forma parte de una industria potente de alcance internacional que consumen millones de personas. De hecho, de acuerdo con los datos del EGM a fecha de septiembre de 2022, las revistas para hombres cuentan con un público de 5.743.000 lectores en este país. No obstante, en uno de los pocos estudios al respecto (Ganzabal-Learreta y Meso-Ayerdi, 2022: 44), se afirma que “contrariamente a toda obviedad, no existen revistas masculinas. Ninguna editora de estas publicaciones, ni tampoco ninguna revista especializada en medios las define como tal”. Es más, se expresa con contundencia que ni siquiera se dispone de "una definición o clasificación mínimamente coherente que organice este sector".

Los autores citados documentan también que estas revistas nacieron como suplementos de las femeninas y, por tal motivo, están muy ligadas a ellas. Precisamente esto ha propiciado que, algunos especialistas, basándose en trabajos previos relativos a las revistas para mujeres, sí que hayan aportado alguna definición que ayude a contextualizar esta tipología textual. Así, Iriarte (2016: 96) define las revistas dirigidas a hombres como

> aquellas publicaciones seriadas especializadas, de periodicidad variable y superior a una semana; distribuidas bajo distintas fórmulas de difusión (de pago, gratuitas o mixtas), cuyo público objetivo es explícita o implícitamente de sexo masculino, ya sea adulto o juvenil (circunstancia verificable a través de sus editoriales, la temática, sus inserciones publicitarias y los estilos de comunicación); cuya audiencia está mayoritariamente integrada por hombres, entre el 60 y el 75 por ciento como mínimo, y que, en función de sus características formales, pueden formar parte o no de las publicaciones de alta gama. Las estrategias discursivas de estas revistas se apoyan en tres elementos: conseguir la complicidad de los lectores, instruir sobre determinados temas y fomentar la participación de la audiencia.

Diversos investigadores destacan que, a diferencia de las revistas femeninas, en el sector raramente se alude a ellas con el adjetivo *masculinas*, sino que se prefiere *para hombres* o, sobre todo, está muy extendida la etiqueta calcada del inglés *life style,* revistas *de estilo de vida* (Iriarte, 2016: 97), ya que se sobreentiende que "estas publicaciones venden estilos de vida y no pueden catalogarse en función del género al que se dirigen" (Marín et al., 2010: 273), visión cuestionada por autores especialistas en estudios de género como Iriarte (2016: 98) o Ganzabal-Learreta y Meso-Ayerdi (2022: 44), quienes, citando a Illera (2020: 180), resaltan que se trata de "una prensa nacida de la carencia de un discurso mediático que aborde la dimensión masculina en el ámbito privado, intencionalmente dirigida a los hombres, donde ellos son los protagonistas de la información". Esta polémica no se abordará en este trabajo (ni ninguna otra relativa a los estereotipos de roles de género o de índole similar), dado que es de corte lingüístico y no ideológico (se aludirá a estas indistintamente como revistas para hombres o revistas masculinas).

De este modo, teniendo en cuenta, de forma muy resumida, las características desgranadas por Iriarte y su clasificación (2016: 117–119; 365–367), las revistas para hombres publicadas en España, al igual que las femeninas, presentan rasgos propios del periodismo de servicio: ofrecen abundante información práctica redactada de manera atractiva y orientada al consumo, con temas recurrentes como el riesgo, la osadía y la aventura, el sexo, el motor, el deporte y la estética masculina (afeitado y calvicie), si bien, como apuntan Marín et al. (2010: 261), se trata de una clasificación revestida de complejidad por lo difuso del concepto de *revista para hombres*; se pueden establecer dos grupos diferenciados dentro de ellas (bastantes ya han desaparecido como se comentará posteriormente): (1) de información general con tono desenfadado y ligero tanto en el contenido como en la forma y con importante presencia de información sexual o erótica, destinadas a un público más bien joven (p. ej., *For Him Magazine* o *FHM*, *CQ*, *DT*, *Men's Health*); (2) especializadas en ocio, moda y cultura, de tono sobrio, dirigidas a hombres maduros con poder adquisitivo, por lo que la calidad formal es alta, así como la gama de las marcas reseñadas (*Gentleman, Esquire, ICON*) (Iriarte, 2026: 365–367). Marín et al. (2010: 261) añaden que se persigue, en general, el perfil de un hombre urbano joven a partir de unos 25 años hasta mediana edad, cuyo nivel cultural suele ser elevado, que busca entretenerse con los contenidos frívolos o de evasión que suelen caracterizar estas revistas. En general, "tienen como receptor a este nuevo estereotipo masculino [...] hombre heterosexual, consumista y especialmente interesado por su apariencia personal [...], una de las señas de identidad del neonarcisismo actual" (Marín et al., 2010: 280).

No obstante, no se puede obviar que este sector atraviesa una crisis importante desde el inicio de su declive a principios del siglo XXI, lo que ha supuesto, como ya se ha señalado, la desaparición de la mayoría de estas revistas (*FHM*, *Man*, *DT*, *Primera línea*, *Ego)*, al igual que otras que surgieron digitalmente como dejatetentar.com o dtlux.com, que tampoco existen ya, si bien sobrevive alguna digital como *MADMEN Magazine* u otras que se presentan como suplementos de periódicos de tirada nacional (*ICON*, de *El País*). Algunos estudiosos achacan esta caída en las ventas de este tipo de prensa para hombres a una supuesta carencia de identificación como grupo social (Lozano, 1995, citada por Marín et al., 2010: 262), en la que no indagaremos por alejarse del objeto de este trabajo. No obstante, aun en horas bajas, la historia de esta modalidad de prensa en este país ha tenido un corto pero peculiar recurrido digno de reseñar.

2. Breve esbozo de la historia de las revistas para hombres en España: auge y declive

Existe un consenso generalizado[1] en que las revistas para hombres en España vieron la luz una vez consolidadas las revistas femeninas internacionales que habían

1 Los datos de este epígrafe se han extraído de las pocas investigaciones que aportan información sobre la llegada y evolución de las revistas para hombres en España (Ganzabal-Learreta y Meso-Ayerdi, 2022: 46–54; Iriarte, 2016: 106 y ss.; Marín et al., 2010: 260–261).

lanzado versiones para su venta en España tras el fin del franquismo y el aperturismo hacia Europa[2]. Se considera que es "el momento idóneo de lanzar estas publicaciones dirigidas al hombre a modelo y semejanza de las femeninas, porque este como público objetivo lector era uno de los buscados desde hace tiempo por las editoriales" (Ganzabal-Learreta y Meso-Ayerdi, 2022: 46). Así, a mediados de los ochenta, la revista *Dunia* incluye primero una página y luego referencias "solo para hombres", con el fin de que las parejas de las lectoras vieran su contenido. En el primer cuatrimestre de 1986, nace *Hombres Dunia* como extra de la edición femenina, por lo que puede considerarse la primera publicación española exclusiva para hombres. *L'Uomo Vogue* aparece en español poco después en 1987, lo que no es de extrañar, ya que estas primeras ediciones se centraban sobre todo en moda, aunque trataban también otros temas como viajes y gastronomía. Les sucedieron otras revistas ya alejadas del mundo de la moda como *Hombres de Hoy* (Grupo Zeta) y *Varón*, ambas de vida efímera. El lanzamiento más destacado de esta época por su gran acogida y larga duración (desde noviembre de 1987 hasta 2012) es *Man*, de corte más revolucionario que sus antecesoras y más bien centrada en personajes de actualidad, con secciones de viajes, acontecimientos sociales y coches, además de moda, si bien ya a principios de los noventa dio un giro hacia el erotismo, fenómeno que afectó a casi todas las revistas para hombres de la época, pues las editoriales se percataban de que "es mucho más rentable incluir contenido cercano a la pornografía que seguir con el contenido clásico de la prensa masculina" (Ganzabal-Learreta y Meso-Ayerdi, 2022: 48).

Sin embargo, como ya se ha explicado, a principios del siglo XXI, el sector comienza a atravesar una grave crisis con la competencia de otras publicaciones y el éxito arrasador de Internet. El mismo destino corren otras como *DT*, que había nacido en 1992 para un segmento distinto del sector, con reportajes sobre interiorismo, arquitectura, naútica, tecnología, etc., aunque algunas multinacionales aprovechan para lanzar sus ediciones españolas, intentando diferenciarse de sus predecesoras recurriendo al humor, al descaro, los concursos y las polémicas. Así, *FHM* llegó a España en 2004 cosechando muy buenos resultados hasta su decadencia y cierre 10 años después. Pero para los fines de este trabajo interesa, en especial, otro perfil de revistas para hombres que, al igual que las reseñadas anteriormente, llegan a los quioscos a mediados de los noventa[3].

2 Según Iriarte (2016: 104) y Marín et al. (2010: 284), la primera revista femenina cuya publicación supuso un hito en España fue *Telva* (1963).

3 Surgen también en esta época diversas cabeceras para público LGTBI+ como *Shangay* (1994), *Zero* (1998) y, muy posteriormente, *Kink* (2006), aunque la precursora en España había sido *Party* (1977), nacida con la democracia española (Iriarte,

Se trata de ediciones que se centran en nuevos modelos de masculinidad, relacionados con lo que en su momento se denominó *el hombre metrosexual* o *übersexual*, preocupado, en especial, por el cuidado de su imagen personal y buena forma física. En esta línea, en 1994 se empieza a vender en España *GQ* (*Gentlemen's Quaterly*), donde se ensalza la belleza del cuerpo masculino con imágenes de torsos esculturales de hombres sometidos a dieta y deporte, contenidos muy similares a los de *Men's Health*, que llegó a este país en 2001 y es una de las pocas, al igual que *GQ*, que sigue publicándose en la actualidad (cf. epígrafe 3.2), aunque al principio "el concepto del cuidado del cuerpo tarda en calar en la sociedad española y no será hasta 2008 cuando despegue en los quioscos, con datos de audiencias y difusión más o menos estables hasta nuestros días" (Ganzabal-Learreta y Meso-Ayerdi, 2022: 52). Según datos del EGM y de la propia empresa, actualmente es la revista para hombres más leída en España. Posteriormente, llegaron *Gentleman* (2003), centrada en la elegancia y el estilo, que continúa publicándose con muchos problemas de "supervivencia"; *Esquire* (2007), orientada también a la moda y al buen gusto, y *Ego* (2015), una de las más recientes en ver la luz, especializada en públicos de hombres elegantes e inteligentes, pero desaparecida tan solo cuatro años después. En cuanto a las relacionadas con los diarios digitales, cabe destacar *Código Único* (2011, Grupo Vocento), el ya mencionado *ICON* (2013) de *El País* y *H Hombre de Vanguardia* (2016, Grupo Godó), a las que hay que sumar dos desvinculadas de los grupos editoriales, pero activas y publicadas también en formato exclusivamente digital: *MADMEN Magazine*, que se anuncia en su web como "revista digital para hombres que quieren estar a la última" y *Vidapremium* (*VP*), especializada en estilo de vida de lujo y artículos exclusivos de alta gama como relojes, con un *target* claramente masculino.

En resumen, a día de hoy, solo se publican en formato impreso en España *Gentleman*, *Esquire* y *Men's Health España* (propiedad de Hearst Magazines, editada por Motorpress Ibérica) que, al ser la de mayor tirada y alcance en popularidad, fue la escogida como fuente para este estudio[4].

2016: 108). De todas ellas, solo pervive *Shangay*. Se sale del ámbito de esta investigación profundizar en ellas, aunque destacamos el análisis de su léxico que llevó a cabo el lingüista F. Rodríguez González para su *Dicccionario gay-lésbico* (2008).

4 Debido a los límites de extensión del presente trabajo, no se ha podido incluir un estado de la cuestión del anglicismo en español, si bien hemos dado buena cuenta de ello en publicaciones previas (cf. Rodríguez-Medina, 2021, 2016, 2000).

3. Metodología y análisis de los resultados

3.1. Metodología

Como ya se ha explicado, las revistas masculinas impresas en español están desapareciendo, por lo que la tendencia del sector parece indicar que, en un futuro próximo, probablemente solo pervivan en formato digital. Por ello, dado que dicho formato sigue unas estrategias de captación y, por ende, un lenguaje algo diferente, se ha optado por analizar la versión digital de la revista masculina que cuenta con mayor número de seguidores en este país, *Men's Health España*. Según el EGM, a fecha de septiembre de 2022, cuenta con 201.000 lectores al mes y ocupa la posición decimoctava en el ránking del total de lectores españoles de revistas. Además, con el fin de comparar los resultados con los obtenidos en un estudio muy reciente de una revista femenina también muy seguida (*ELLE España*) en la red social Facebook/Meta[5] (Rodríguez-Medina, 2022), cuestión que resulta relevante, se analizó la página de *Men's Health España* en Facebook/Meta, que cuenta con más de 4 millones de seguidores, datos que se ampliarán en la contextualización del corpus (cf. 3.1.1). Hay que destacar que se trata del primer estudio lingüístico de estas características de las revistas para hombres, pues las pocas investigaciones previas son más bien de índole sociológica o periodística.

De este modo, el objetivo principal es recopilar y analizar los anglicismos puros, los semiadaptados (queda en ellos algún rasgo morfológico de su origen inglés) y los pseudoanglicismos o falsos anglicismos (términos "inventados" que parecen de origen anglosajón, pero, en realidad, resultan desconocidos en los países anglófonos o se usan de forma diferente o con otro significado), detectados en la página de Facebook/Meta de *Men's Health España* durante 21 días (tres semanas completas de diferentes meses del verano de 2022: 25–31 de julio; 18–24 de agosto; 1–7 de septiembre). Se leyeron, completa y detalladamente, todas las publicaciones y comentarios (solo de hablantes del español europeo si esto se podía verificar en sus perfiles), excluyendo los anuncios publicitarios y los vídeos (la página publica una media de uno a dos contenidos por hora al día durante las 24 horas de lunes a domingo).

5 Como se ha especificado en otros trabajos previos (Rodríguez-Medina, 2021, 2022), esta red resulta ideal para el objeto de estudio, ya que no cuenta con restricciones en cuanto a extensión de contenido, así que presenta muchas publicaciones con material escrito de una longitud adecuada para que su análisis resulte representativo, a diferencia de otras redes como Instagram o TikTok.

Al seleccionar una semana de cada uno de los tres meses y no tres semanas seguidas de un solo mes, se evita que los datos estén condicionados por publicaciones muy similares correspondientes a esos días concretos. La extensión habitual de cada una equivale aproximadamente a entre dos y tres páginas A4, incluyendo los titulares y todos los comentarios de los usuarios (una media de 3–4 por publicación de unas tres líneas como máximo, salvo alguna excepción). De esta manera, se observó que, en general, el perfil medio del seguidor de *Men's Health España* en Facebook/Meta suele ser hombre, hablante nativo de español europeo, de entre 30 a 50 años, con nivel cultural medio-bajo. Por otro lado, a diferencia de *ELLE*, *Men's Health España* sí repite, en ocasiones, algunos contenidos idénticos en días sucesivos. En dichos casos, solo se analizó el primer día de su publicación y se obviaron los posteriores para no desvirtuar los datos.

En cuanto a la muestra, se tomó como criterio de selección nuestra propia definición de anglicismo, aplicada en recopilaciones previas (Rodríguez-Medina, 2021, 2022): "términos ingleses o aquellos de otras lenguas llegados al español a través del inglés que se emplean en su forma original, o bien adaptados mediante cualquier tipo de procedimiento de asimilación". Hay que aclarar que no se recogieron los ya asimilados, pues los hablantes no especialistas no los perciben como voces inglesas. Por otra parte, tampoco se recopilaron los anglicismos que constituyen marcas registradas o nombres propios (p. ej., franquicias deportivas, eventos internacionales, etc.).

Por último, dada la valoración que había que realizar de cada término antes de su inclusión, no resultaba recomendable recurrir a una herramienta informática, por lo que se llevó a cabo de forma manual con un modelo de ficha que en investigaciones previas ha facilitado la obtención de datos (Rodríguez-Medina, 2021, 2022): fecha, titular de la publicación, contexto, tipo de anglicismo y observaciones relevantes.

3.2. Contextualización del corpus: *Men's Health*

Antes de presentar los resultados, resulta pertinente describir, de forma somera, las características principales de la revista *Men's Health*, pues buena parte del análisis del corpus va estar directamente relacionada con estas. La propia empresa se presenta en la red como "la revista de estilo masculina más leída del mundo" y, ciertamente, los datos avalan esta afirmación. En la página matriz en inglés (menshealth.com), se afirma que actualmente cuenta con 25 ediciones diferentes en 35 países y más de 21 millones de lectores en sus plataformas sociales y digitales. Presumen de ser la fuente número uno de información "for and about men". Describen así el perfil de sus lectores:

> active, successful, professional men who want greater control over their physical, mental, and emotional lives. We give men the tools they need to make their lives better through in-depth and expert-backed reporting, covering everything from fashion and grooming to health, nutrition, fitness, weight loss, as well as cutting-edge gear, the latest in entertainment, science, and more.

Ese parece ser también el perfil de lector en los inicios de la edición española según algunos autores (Ganzabal-Learreta y Meso-Ayerdi, 2022: 51), que la vinculan a un hombre urbanita de entre 25–45 años, de clase social media-alta y de gran preparación intelectual, perfil que parece haber cambiado para la edición digital, como se ha comentado anteriormente.

Por otro lado, además de ostentar 17 galardones desde su creación en Estados Unidos en 1986, aunque recordemos que la versión española no llegó hasta 2001, afirman recurrir a especialistas contrastados e incluso a revistas científicas para los temas que abordan (*fitness*, salud, nutrición, relaciones, etc.), con un riguroso proceso de edición y revisión, pese a tratarse de una revista divulgativa y de entretenimiento. No obstante, la edición española, al menos en su versión digital en Facebook/Meta, recurre también a menudo a contenidos frívolos sobre famosos sin camiseta o en el gimnasio, cotilleos de culturistas, actores, cantantes, presentadores de televisión e incluso de *youtubers* y *tiktokers*. En general, se detecta mucha publicidad encubierta, si bien no tanta como en *ELLE España*, pero relacionada principalmente con el mundo del *fitness* y los gimnasios[6] (material deportivo como esterillas y pesas, bandas elásticas); la estética masculina (depiladoras eléctricas, cremas hidratantes y productos para evitar la caída del pelo o protegerlo) y artículos de nutrición (vitaminas y suplementos). Los contenidos más recurrentes son relativos a lo que parece ser una obsesión con el culto al torso masculino y los brazos con musculatura desarrollada, de ahí que apenas se hable de los deportes de equipo y sí de los individuales donde esta cualidad sea muy apreciada como, por ejemplo, los deportes de contacto (boxeo, *MMA*). En este sentido, se puede afirmar que la revista sigue manteniendo vivo el mismo espíritu con que llegó a España y que Iriarte (2016: 202) resume de la siguiente manera:

> El concepto de salud y de lo saludable en *MH* se identifica con un cuerpo joven y musculoso, asociado a la imagen corporal potente y atractiva que a su vez se identifica

6 De hecho, en su análisis de los estereotipos en las revistas masculinas, Espés (2015, citado por Ganzabal-Learreta y Meso-Ayerdi, 2022: 44) identifica *Men's Health* con "el atleta".

con el éxito social y los valores de triunfo personal e individualismo y la superación personal.

Llama la atención la escasez de contenidos de moda masculina (solo zapatillas deportivas y algunos trajes, pero en proporción mucho menor que todo lo que tiene que ver con el culto al cuerpo físico), relojes, libros y algunos coches. En cuanto al resto de publicaciones, aunque se observan bastantes noticias sobre cine y series y, en menor grado, música, no cabe duda de que se llevan la palma los artículos divulgativos sobre rutinas deportivas de musculación y ejercicios para estar en forma (sentadillas, dominadas, pesas, etc.) y dietas de frutas, verduras o comida sana en general, además de consejos de nutrición; abundan también los contenidos sobre sexo (tanto heterosexual como homosexual, si bien las imágenes de sexo entre homosexuales son más frecuentes). En este sentido, cabe destacar que, aunque tanto Iriarte como Marín et al., cuyos estudios abarcan aproximadamente el período de 2010 a 2016, apenas detectaban contenidos destinados a lectores homosexuales, actualmente la revista parece dirigirse cada vez más a este público de acuerdo con nuestras observaciones y análisis de textos e imágenes, lo que se aprecia también en los comentarios de los lectores, que parecen desconcertados ante ciertas informaciones que no consideran propias de esta revista y preguntan, de forma abierta y sin tapujos, a qué se deben, de lo que se puede deducir que el perfil está más desdibujado hoy en día que hace 10 años, probablemente por tanteos de la editorial en distintos nichos de mercado del público masculino para intentar sortear la crisis del sector.

Por último, el tono del lenguaje con que se dirigen a los lectores no es tan edulcorado ni "empalagoso" como el detectado en *ELLE España*. Así, el estilo se percibe más frío, menos afectuoso y paternalista, sin pretensiones esnobistas, con frases breves que van al grano, carentes de las florituras tan típicas de *ELLE* (Rodríguez-Medina, 2022: 354). Para terminar y, en conclusión a modo de resumen, toda la temática de la revista gira en torno a un culto nada disimulado a la musculación y a los cuerpos atléticos, que llega a rozar la obsesión, con noticias sobre hombres que muestran en las redes sociales sus cuerpos musculados y sin vello (con especial énfasis en sus torsos, brazos y abdominales), publicidad y artículos divulgativos en torno a este mundo del *fitness* y de la búsqueda de la "perfección física" masculina. Todo ello tendrá una clara y lógica repercusión en el léxico empleado como se muestra en el análisis del corpus a continuación.

3.3. Análisis de los resultados

Se recopilaron un total de 635 anglicismos: 613 puros, 19 semiadaptados y 3 pseudoanglicismos. Hay que señalar que se incluyen aquí las repeticiones de los términos y que los anglicismos bimembres o formados por lexías complejas (p. ej., *power sprint*) se contabilizaron como uno solo. En comparación con los datos obtenidos en *ELLE España* en Facebook/Meta (Rodríguez-Medina, 2022: 355), se observa un uso significativamente menor (635 anglicismos frente a 1795, casi el triple) en todos los diferentes tipos de la taxonomía, en especial en el caso de los anglicismos puros (613/1699), pero también, aunque en menor medida, en los semiadaptados (50/ 19) y en los pseudoanglicismos (46/ 3). Esto puede deberse a que el estilo de *Men's Health España*, como ya se ha señalado, es más sobrio y austero, menos proclive al lenguaje almibarado y esnobista, cargado de anglicismos y frases en inglés que caracteriza dicha revista femenina. A continuación, se analiza el corpus recogido de acuerdo con su clasificación:

3.3.1. Anglicismos puros

(a) **Deporte, material, programas, máquinas y ejercicios para estar en forma, cuerpo/estado físico.** Siendo el culto a la musculación y a los cuerpos fuertes y atléticos un tema tan recurrente en esta fuente, no es de extrañar que, de todo el grupo de anglicismos puros, más de la mitad estén relacionados con este campo (326; 53,18 %), a diferencia de *ELLE España*, donde este apenas llegaba a un 2 % (Rodríguez-Medina, 2022: 367), pues es la moda y sus complementos el sector que casi monopoliza el empleo de anglicismos en dicha revista femenina (61 %). Como se demostró en una investigación sobre el léxico anglicado de los gimnasios españoles (Rodríguez-Medina, 2016), la terminología relativa al culturismo, los deportes de contacto, las máquinas, los ejercicios y las actividades dirigidas de gimnasio, así como el material utilizado e incluso las instalaciones, recibe una gran influencia de las franquicias internacionales y contiene, por tanto, numerosos anglicismos. De hecho, el anglicismo más usado de todo el corpus es *curl* (48[7]), tipo de movimiento o ejercicio muy frecuente en las rutinas de musculación, que cuenta, además, con variantes como *curl spiderman* (2). No es de extrañar que le siga en importancia *fitness* (34), que, si le sumamos los 11 usos como adjetivo invariable también detectados, alcanza un total de 45: atleta *fitness* (2), dieta *fitness*, vida *fitness*, mundo *fitness*, objetivos *fitness*, referente *fitness*, rutina *fitness*, tarea *fitness*, *youtubers fitness*, desde el punto de vista *fitness*.

Otro de los más usuales resultó ser *sixpack* (23) y su variante *6-pack*, nada sorprendente, dado que lucir así los abdominales o ejercitarse para lograrlo parece ser el objetivo principal de esta revista, apreciable claramente tanto en las imágenes como en los textos. En esta línea, se recogieron también 3 casos de *ab/*

7 Aparece entre paréntesis el número de repeticiones en el corpus. Los términos aparecen sin número cuando solo se ha detectado un solo caso

abs y 12 de *core*. En investigaciones previas (Rodríguez-Medina, 2016), se ha explicado también por qué *gym* (11) es tan frecuente actualmente en este sector e incluso en el habla cotidiana de los españoles más jóvenes. Otros anglicismos puros destacados que se han registrado son los siguientes: *MMA* (10), *sprint* (8), *kit* [de material de entrenamiento] (7), *box (5)*, *crunch* (5), *full body* (5), *pack* [de entrenamiento] (5), *ring* (5), *WOD* (5), *press* (4) y sus múltiples variantes *press-down*, *press* [de banca] (5), *press grip; coach* (4), *cross training* (4), *golf* (4), *running* (4) y su variante *runner* (2), *finisher* (4), *workout* (4), *burpee* (3) o *half burpee*, *goblet* (3), *kettlebell* (3), *mountain climber* (3) y su variante *spider mountain climber*, *paddle surf* (3), *pit shark* (3), *ring* (3) y *Russian twist* (3). Como puede observarse, casi todos tienen que ver con lo relativo al entrenamiento (material, ejercicios, etc.), instalaciones para entrenar, deportes (en especial los de contacto), al igual que ocurre con el resto del corpus de esta sección, aunque con un menor número de casos detectados:

animal flow, *barbell* (2), *bear crawl*, *bodybuilder* (2), *bodybuilding*, *bulking* (2), *challenger*, *chest fly*, *crush*, *curl deadlift*, *devil press*, *drop set* (2), *elevated bear walk*, *face pull*, *flutter kick*, *front squat*, *full-contact twist*, *gorilla walk*, [sentadilla] *hack* (2), *hip extern rotation*, *hip flexor extension walk*, *hip thrust*, *jack knife*, *jumping jack*, *jump squat kickboxing*, *kitesurf*, *K.O.*, *L-sit knee tuck*, *lateral hip move*, *lunge walk*, *mass gainer*, *mindfulness*, *minigolf*, [los] *muscle up*, *pallof press*, *plank thoracic rotation*, *power sprint*, *pre-workout*, *pull down*, *pull over* [en máquina], *pump* [de bíceps], *push-pull*, *relax*, *rock pull*, *rugby*, *round*, [remo] *seated*, *set* (2), *side bend*, *skipping*, *snatch*, [sentadilla] *split*, *sports*, *squat*, *strongman* (2), *surf*, *waiter curl*, *workshop*.

(b) Tecnología, Internet y redes sociales. Este grupo de anglicismos, el segundo en importancia con respecto al total del corpus, ha resultado ser más numeroso que en *ELLE España* (66 casos, esto es, un 10,76 % frente a 5,47 % en *ELLE)*, aunque los términos en sí son prácticamente los mismos (cf. Rodríguez-Medina, 2022: 363):

app (6), *blog*, *clickbait*, *cookies* (2), *e-commerce*, *feed*, *follower*, *gadget*, *hashtag*, *hater*, *influencer* (4), *like* (4), *link* (3), *online* (3), *podcast* (3), *post* (6), *selfie* (7), *smartphone*, *smartwatch* (2), *story* (4), *streamer*, *tiktoker* (3), *youtuber* (6) y *web* (3).

(c) Sexo. Resulta llamativo que de esta categoría no se detectara ningún caso en *ELLE* y aquí constituya el tercer grupo de anglicismos más frecuente con 57 lexías (9,3 %), dato coherente con la línea de la revista, que dedica, como mínimo, uno o dos artículos al día al sexo (posturas, juguetes eróticos, problemas de disfunción eréctil, masajes y juegos sexuales con la pareja, etc.) con imágenes de prácticas tanto heterosexuales como homosexuales:

BDSM (6), *blue cowgirl*, *bondage*, *child's pose*, *cosplay*, *dirty talk*, *edging* (2), *fingering* (2), *fisting*, *flogger*, *gooch*, *grundle*, *handjob*, *kink*, *milf*, *peek-a-boo* (2), *peep show* (3), *plug* [anal] (5), *role play*, *sex-appeal*, *sex shop*, *squirt* (14), *squirting* (2), *thigh fucking* (3), *twerk*, *twerking*, [vibrador] *wand*.

(d) **Cine, música y espectáculos.** Aunque no abundan los contenidos de este sector, aparecen bastantes reportajes sobre hombres famosos en todas las modalidades del artisteo, por lo que el porcentaje (57 casos: 9,3 %) es incluso ligeramente superior al observado en *ELLE* (6,29 %) y, de nuevo, es *fan* el anglicismo que más se repite (Rodríguez-Medina, 2022: 362):

all-stars, biopic, blockbuster, cliffhanger, fan (21), *flashback, flow, hip hop, jazz, LP, latin lover, mint, one-shot, playlist, plot-twist, pop* (2), *reboot, rock* (2), *rock-star, sex symbol, show* (4), *single* (3), *sketch, spin-off, thriller, trap, videoclip* (2), *zoom* (2).

(e) **Ropa, calzado y complementos.** Cabe destacar que el apartado con mayor número de anglicismos en *ELLE* (1039, es decir, el 61,10 % del total) aquí es casi testimonial, con tan solo 24 lexías (4 %): *jeans, look* (11), *outfit, sneakers, streetwear* (4), [camiseta] *tank, total look* (4), *urban fashion*. Resulta llamativo el caso de *look*, el anglicismo más empleado en *ELLE*, con múltiples variantes (Rodríguez-Medina, 2022: 359), mientras que apenas supera la decena en esta fuente y, además, solo se detectó la variante *total look*. Esto parece reforzar la idea de que es exclusivamente el culto al "cuerpo físico" el que interesa en *Men's Health* y otras cuestiones relativas a la imagen personal como la ropa o los complementos apenas se mencionan o, como mínimo, no se les concede el espacio que cabría esperar de una publicación donde el cuidado de la imagen del hombre ocupa el centro de atención de la mayoría de los textos.

(f) **Alimentación y bebidas.** Los datos arrojan resultados muy similares en las dos fuentes (12 casos: 1,95 % frente al 1,58 de *ELLE*), a pesar de que los artículos sobre la alimentación son muy superiores en frecuencia en *Men's Health España*, pues aparecen a diario consejos sobre dietas y nutrición en general: [espinaca] *baby, cheat meal, cheat meal day, detox, mix* [de frutas], *pulled jack fruit, smoothie* (2), *snack* (2), *wine, whisky*. Esto se debe probablemente a la tendencia ya comentada al lenguaje directo y sencillo de esta fuente, con menor apoyo en recursos superfluos como los extranjerismos que no cumplan una función textual.

(g) **Otros.** Se incluyen en este apartado 42 anglicismos (6,85 %) de distintos sectores con baja presencia en el corpus, o bien formas lingüísticas y expresiones que no pertenecen a ninguno en concreto:

aka (6), *body shaming, ¡boom!, CEO, club, daddy issues* [psicología] (5), *female gaze, feedback, fuel, good, hippy, marketing, must, next big thing, next generation, no way, ok, old school, power, pratfall, prepper, ranking* (2), *resort* (3), *shock, target, test* (3) *tip, wonder woman*.

De todos ellos, llama la atención, en especial, *aka* por su frecuencia, a pesar de ser una expresión bastante desconocida para el hablante medio del español europeo. Actualmente se ha puesto también de moda el uso de *next* en el habla informal y buena cuenta de ello es que aparece en dos expresiones distintas. *Ranking* sigue presentando una grafía inestable, que compite en su forma de anglicismo puro con la semiadaptada con tilde *ránking*, como se verá más adelante. Hay que destacar que esta tendencia se ha observado también en investigaciones de campos diferentes como el deporte y se detectó también en *ELLE* (Rodríguez-Medina, 2020: 133, 2022: 366). En general, se puede afirmar que es bastante bajo el uso de anglicismos aislados que no sean típicos de temáticas concretas propias de esta fuente, ya que solo 5 de estas lexías se repite más de una vez.

(h) **Adjetivos.** Además del destacado y peculiar uso de *fitness* como fruto de una transposición categorial a adjetivo ya tratado en el apartado (a) (11 casos), se recogieron otros 18 anglicismos en función adjetival (4,73 %): *cool* (3), *fake*, *gay* (4), *healthy* (3), *light* (3), *top* (2), *trendy*, *wearable*. Hay dos rasgos destacables: por un lado, se trata de cifras escasas en comparación con las obtenidas en *ELLE* (169; solo *top*, por ejemplo, aparecía en 21 ocasiones; cf. Rodríguez-Medina, 2022: 361). Como en casos anteriores, parece deberse al tono más seco y poco dado al empalago y a la exageración de *Men's Health España*, lo que origina enunciados con pocos adjetivos y, en general, poco proclives a presentar anglicismos sin una motivación clara. Por otro lado, sorprende el uso de *wearable*, que no habíamos observado hasta ahora en ninguna fuente escrita en español.

3.3.2. Anglicismos semiadaptados

Frente a los 50 de *ELLE*, se recopilaron solamente 19 (apenas el 3 % con respecto al total), lo que coincide con la tónica general de cifras más bajas también en este tipo de anglicismos en *Men's Health España*. Se dividen en varios grupos:

(a) Casi todos pertenecen a esta modalidad: se trata de lexías ya antiguas en español que cuentan con algún rasgo morfológico indicativo de su adaptación a esta lengua como la tilde, pero aún conservan su grafía inglesa, lo que indica un proceso de asimilación todavía inacabado: *gángster*, *póker*, *ránking* (2), *récord* (7), *sándwich* (2), *sánwich*, *wélter* (2). Excepto *ránking* y *récord*, en realidad no pertenecen a temas típicos de la revista. *Ránking*, al aparecer también utilizado como anglicismo puro sin tilde, denota que su escritura presenta dudas aún a los hablantes.

(b) Solo se recogieron 3 casos de anglicismos semiadaptados que conservan su forma original pero añadiendo, por derivación, sufijos propios del español como *–ero* ('seguidor de', 'el que se dedica a') o *-ado* (forma de participio): *crossfitero* (2) *photoshopeado*. La derivación de un extranjerismo es muestra de un estadío de madurez en la evolución de la presencia de una lengua extranjera en otra, pero suele ocurrir tras un proceso de adaptación morfológica en el que dicho término pierde todos los rasgos extranjerizantes y ya se encuentra totalmente adaptado a la lengua receptora, en este caso, al español, y no cuando todavía presenta rasgos morfológicos de la lexía original como la *-ss-* de *crossfitero* y la *ph-* y la *-sh-* de *photoshopeado*. En todo caso, su presencia es mínima en este corpus frente a los más de 40 casos de *ELLE* (Rodríguez-Medina, 2022: 366), donde esta vía de creación neológica parece ser muy prolífica.

3.3.3. Pseudoanglicismos

Solo se aprecian 3 pseudoanglicismos o falsos anglicismos, que constituyen apenas el 0,47 % del corpus, al igual que ocurría en *ELLE*, donde resultó también la modalidad menos empleada, con apenas un 2 % (Rodríguez-Medina, 2022: 367). En *Men's Health España*, parece deberse a la tendencia también observada en los otros dos tipos anteriores, ya analizados, a un menor gusto por el uso de anglicismos en general y al hecho de que las publicaciones presentan menos comentarios de seguidores que en *ELLE*, donde los lectores eran los principales creadores de falsos anglicismos en frases ingeniosas que servían para causar extrañeza y llamar la atención. *Caravaning* responde al procedimiento lexicogenésico ya relativamente antiguo en español (Rodríguez González, 2013), que consiste en añadir el sufijo *-ing* a un sustantivo español (*caravana*) y denominar así una práctica deportiva, afición o costumbre, sin ningún fin humorístico en este caso, que se refiere a "la actividad veraniega de pasar unos días viajando de un lado a otro en caravana". Por su parte, *realfooding* parece "colar" más como anglicismo y, sin embargo, solo se emplea en inglés el sustantivo *real-food*. En España, se denomina así al movimiento que defiende el hábito de no consumir nunca productos ultraprocesados y decantarse por alimentos en su estado natural, si acaso mínimamente procesados. Por último, nos encontramos con un solo pseudoanglicismo empleado con fines expresivos y humorísticos, detectado en el comentario de un lector con respecto a una publicación titulada *Schwarzenegger nunca dejará de entrenar*: "es el *exterminator* y nunca se detendrá", que mezcla el sustantivo español *exterminador* y el famoso título de la saga protagonizada por este actor, *Terminator*.

3.3.4. Funciones pragmáticas

En cuanto al análisis de las funciones pragmáticas del corpus de anglicismos puros, semiadaptados y pseudoanglicismos, los resultados han arrojado datos muy distintos e incluso contrapuestos a los obtenidos en *ELLE* (Rodríguez-Medina, 2022: 371–372). Resulta significativo que, además de presentar, en general, un porcentaje moderado de anglicismos, se aprecia, además, que estos, en su gran mayoría, designan conceptos provenientes de países anglófonos de productos o conceptos para los que no existe todavía un equivalente patrimonial consolidado en español, a pesar de que, en algunos casos, son ya relativamente antiguos en la cultura española. Esto se observa, de forma clara, en muchos de los términos del grupo más nutrido de terminología anglicada (cf. apartado a), relativa al deporte en general y a los ejercicios y material relativo a la musculación, etc. (p. ej., *curl deadlift, devil press, face pull, flutter kick, hack*), pero también en otros campos se recogieron anglicismos que han permanecido inalterados a lo largo de los años como en la música (*pop, jazz, hip hop*), o en el nombre de bebidas como el *whisky*, entre otros.

En este sentido, cabe también destacar que, en otros casos, existe una traducción descriptiva o incluso se emplean ya equivalentes en español, pero más largos que la lexía original inglesa, o bien se trata de conceptos que disponen en inglés de abreviaturas o siglas. En estas tres situaciones, el hablante, por economía lingüística, parece decantarse por la elección del anglicismo: *abs*, *core* (músculos abdominales, lumbares, pélvicos, de los glúteos y la musculatura profunda de la columna), *app* (aplicación de móvil), *e-commerce* (comercio electrónico), *smartwatch* (reloj inteligente), casi todos los de cine y espectáculos (p. ej, *biopic, blockbuster, cliffhanger*), y expresiones de diversos sectores: *mix, aka, tip, light, wearable, top, trendy, gym, crossfitero, photoshopeado, caravaning, realfooding.* En el caso del sexo, algunos anglicismos empleados por economía lingüística parecen responder también a fines eufemísticos, ya que sus equivalentes o traducciones descriptivas podrían resultar malsonantes o, cuando menos, incómodas para algunos hablantes (p. ej., *BDSM, dirty talk, handjob, milf, peep show, sex shop y fisting*).

Por otro lado, se observa que no abundan los anglicismos que respondan exclusivamente a la búsqueda del prestigio y de connotaciones de calidad, modernidad y sofisticación que suele conferir el inglés, a diferencia de *ELLE*, donde este se erige en un recurso casi permanente (Rodríguez-Medina, 2022: 373). Entre los pocos ejemplos de este tipo se encuentran todos los del corpus relativos a la moda, que aparecen, además, en artículos que son los únicos cuyo tono y estilo recuerdan bastante al de *ELLE* (*jeans, look, outfit, sneakers, streetwear, tank, total look, urban fashion*). Por otro lado, también se han recopilado algunos anglicismos que no parecen responder a otra finalidad que el mero esnobismo lingüístico, aunque rozan también el uso anterior, pues aquí las fronteras semánticas nunca están muy claras y la intención última podría ser también la misma que en los ejemplos antes señalados (*workshop, workout, running, runner, next generation, wine, healthy, fake):*

(1) *Así añades algo de cardio a tu workout.*
(2) *Rovira es un loco del running.*
(3) *Bastaba con pedir cualquier cosa con queso de cabra y vinagre de Módena (cero healthy*).

Otra función también detectada en el corpus es la expresiva, puesto que recurrir al inglés rompe con "lo esperado" y logra llamar la atención: *boom, shock, wonder woman, no way, exterminator:*

(4) *Eso solo es capaz de hacerlo una wonder woman.*
(5) *Cuando dejas en shock a todo el gimnasio.*

Por último, dada su relevancia en el corpus, merecen un comentario aparte los términos *fitness* y *six-pack*. En ambos casos, se podría achacar su uso a la economía lingüística, ya que *fitness* engloba todo un concepto y sector económico que va más allá de *estar en forma*, omnipresente en *Men's Health España*, y *six-pack/6-pack* designa 'un vientre plano con los músculos abdominales del recto bien marcados y definidos', imagen icónica del culto al cuerpo del canon de belleza masculino imperante, idolatrado hasta la saciedad en esta revista. Por analogía, se traduce al español por *tableta* [*de chocolate*], pero no se ha encontrado ni un solo caso traducido en esta fuente. En ambas lexías, además de las posibles causas señaladas, su empleo también podría responder a motivaciones más bien cercanas al esnobismo lingüístico y a la búsqueda de enunciados más prestigiosos y sofisticados, sobre todo en el caso de *fitness*, que se ha convertido en un gran negocio hoy en día, que cuenta con un gran márketing muy presente en este tipo de publicaciones.

4. Conclusiones

El análisis del corpus confirma que la presencia del inglés en la página de Facebook/Meta de *Men's Health España* es moderada en comparación con los altos porcentajes de anglicismos recogidos en revistas femeninas como *ELLE España* en el mismo medio (Rodríguez-Medina, 2022: 372). Aunque se recopiló un total de 636 anglicismos (96,5 % puros, 3 % semiadaptados y 0,5 % pseudoanglicismos), se trata de cifras bastante bajas con respecto a las obtenidas en el estudio de *ELLE España*, lo que parece deberse, en general, al tono más sobrio y con menor proporción de contenidos de publicidad encubierta de *Men's Health España*, donde apenas se tratan temas de moda y complementos, sector donde predomina el uso constante de anglicismos en dicha revista femenina por motivos de márketing y prestigio.

Así, si bien también se recopilaron casos en textos sobre cine y espectáculos, tecnología o alimentación y bebidas, son las publicaciones sobre entrenamientos, rutinas y ejercicios deportivos (y, en general, sobre la exaltación del cuerpo masculino musculado y atlético) en las que destaca la presencia de anglicismos, lo que no es de extrañar al tratarse de un tipo de textos que suele recibir mucha influencia del inglés (cf. Rodríguez-Medina, 2016). Por otro lado, si tenemos en cuenta las funciones pragmáticas dominantes en este corpus, llama la atención que apenas se empleen anglicismos por razones puramente esnobistas o para conferir al concepto descrito connotaciones de innovación y modernidad como sí ocurre, con mucha frecuencia, en las revistas femeninas. Excepto algún caso aislado (p. ej. *runner, workout*), casi todos los usos se deben a lagunas terminológicas en la lengua española, por lo que el anglicismo no es intercambiable por un equivalente en español, a la economía lingüística o a fines expresivos o, en menor grado, eufemísticos, sobre todo en los contenidos sobre sexo.

Por otro lado, la poca frecuencia de anglicismos semiadaptados (3 %) y la casi inexistencia de pseudoanglicismos (0,5 %) refuerzan también la idea de que parece existir preferencia por el empleo de léxico patrimonial español en esta fuente, pues apenas se detectaron anglicismos en los comentarios de los lectores, mientras que, en investigaciones previas en otros campos afines, estos resultaron ser los más proclives a las creaciones ideolectales de pseudoanglicismos y al uso de anglicismos puros (Rodríguez Medina, 2021, 2022).

Por último, al tratarse de la primera investigación de índole sociolingüística sobre revistas masculinas, dado que las pocas previas se han centrado hasta ahora en analizarlas desde el punto de vista exclusivo de los estudios de género, con una perspectiva más bien ideológica o sociológica, pero sin tratar el plano lingüístico y, mucho menos, la influencia del inglés en ellas, no existen datos comparativos de otras revistas masculinas, así que serían bienvenidas tanto las actualizaciones periódicas de estudios sobre esta misma fuente, siempre tan cambiante y con léxico de vida a veces efímera, como los análisis de otras revistas para hombres españolas de distinto perfil y contenido (p. ej., *Gentleman*). Otra línea de investigación de interés en este campo sería comparar estos resultados con fuentes similares en otras lenguas europeas como, por ejemplo, el francés y el italiano, puesto que se trata de revistas que se publican en multitud de países.

5. Referencias bibliográficas

EGM (Estudio General de Medios) (2022): *Audiencia general de medios de septiembre de 2022*. Madrid: Asociación para la investigación de Medios de Comunicación. Documento de Internet consultado en octubre de 2022 en https://www.aimc.es.

Fernández Martínez, Cristina (2016): "Homogeneización cultural, transferencia y diferenciación cultural en la terminología del mundo de la moda inglés- francés- español.Implicaciones para la traducción editorial de textos de moda". *Entreculturas*, 7–8: 307–343.

Ganzabal-Learreta, María & Koldobika Meso-Ayerdi (2022): "La prensa masculina contemporánea en España: de *Hombres Dunia* a *Hombres de*

Vanguardia. Una propuesta de periodización". *Historia y comunicación social*, 27 (1): 43–56.

Illera, Paula (2020): *Contenidos mediáticos en función del género: de la prensa segregada a los canales de televisión especializados*. Tesis doctoral. Burgos: Universidad de Burgos.

Iriarte Martín, Teresa (2016): *Las revistas dirigidas a hombres en España y sus contenidos: masculinidades, feminidades y violencia simbólica. Análisis de siete publicaciones de "estilo de vida para hombres" en el mercado actual*. Tesis doctoral. Universidad del País Vasco.

Marín Murillo, Flora et al. (2009): "Claves de la construcción de género en las revistas femeninas y masculinas: análisis cuantitativo". *Estudios sobre el mensaje periodístico*, 16: 259–289.

Rodríguez González, Félix (2008): *Diccionario gay-lésbico*. Madrid: Gredos.

Rodríguez González, Félix (2013): "Pseudoanglicismos en español actual. Revisión crítica y tratamiento lexicográfico". *Revista española de Lingüística*, 43 (1): 123–169.

Rodríguez-Medina, María Jesús (2022): "Los anglicismos en las redes sociales". *Enciclopedia del anglicismo. Volumen I: Anglicismos en el español contemporáneo. Una visión panorámica*. Ed. F. Rodríguez-González. Berlín: Peter Lang, 337–378.

Rodríguez-Medina, María Jesús (2021): "Este jugador está en el *top ten* de los *cracks*: anglicismos en la prensa deportiva en las redes". *Anglicismos en los nuevos medios de comunicación*. Ed. C. Luján-García. Granada: Comares. 121–139.

Rodríguez-Medina, María Jesús (2016): "An approach to the study of the use of English in the activities of Spanish Gyms". *Spanish in Context*, 13 (1): 128–148.

Rodríguez-Medina, María Jesús (2000): "El anglicismo en español: revisión crítica del estado de la cuestión". *Philologia Hispalensis*, 14 (1): 99–112.

Vázquez, María (2018): "Los anglicismos de la moda en la prensa rosa española". *Onomázein* 40: 49–55.

Vega Falcón, Nadia (2017): *Anglicismos en prensa de moda internacional y su uso a través de la TIC por parte de estudiantes universitarios*.Tesis doctoral. Las Palmas de Gran Canaria: Universidad de Las Palmas de Gran Canaria.

VV.AA. (2022): *Men's health. About us*. Documento de Internet consultado en septiembre de 2022 en www.menshealth.com.

VV.AA. (2022): Página de *Men's Health España* en Facebook/Meta. Documentos de Internet consultados de julio a septiembre de 2022 en https://m.faceb ook.com/ menshealth.es/?locale2=es.

Javier Medina López

Instituto Universitario de Estudios Medievales y Renacentistas

Instituto Universitario de Lingüística Andrés Bello

Universidad de La Laguna

Aspectos socioculturales del anglicismo en España durante el siglo XIX: de *high life* y sus adláteres semánticos

Resumen: A lo largo del siglo XIX se va consumando un cambio de rumbo en las influencias socioculturales que recibe el español en el contexto internacional de las lenguas y naciones. El paulatino desplazamiento del francés a lo largo de dicha centuria se debe al protagonismo adquirido en el mundo por los países de habla anglosajona, especialmente Gran Bretaña y EE. UU. En el caso español, comienzan a registrarse anglicismos en numerosos aspectos de la vida cotidiana, científica y cultural que con mejor o peor suerte unos acabaron incorporándose al acervo léxico del español y otros cayeron en desuso. La cultura española de finales del siglo XIX vive momentos de esplendor en contrapartida con la crisis económica y política en la que estaba sumida la sociedad finisecular. La adopción de anglicismos es constante, como muestra el auge de la forma *high life* (y formas cercanas a esta lexía), tal y como se recoge en numerosos contextos socioculturales. Algunos de estos aspectos serán tratados en el presente artículo.

Palabras clave: lexicología, anglicismos, historia, español.

I. Introducción

La configuración del léxico español corre paralela a los acontecimientos históricos y sociales que España ha vivido a lo largo de los siglos, reflejándose en este terreno la incorporación de préstamos (además de la base constitutiva del latín)[1], primero del árabe, luego del italiano con la asunción de numerosos cultismos, para llegar al siglo XVIII en el que el francés adquirió un gran protagonismo, hecho que coincide con la rama borbónica en el trono

1 Está también el componente griego, bien a través del propio latín, bien en forma de cultismos a lo largo de distintas etapas en la historia del idioma.

español. La influencia de los galicismos, como bien señala Rodríguez González (2019: 799), se prolongó a lo largo de todo el siglo XIX, estando presente, si bien no con la misma fuerza, hasta nuestros días. El francés es, por tanto, la primera gran lengua moderna de cultura con la que el español entra en contacto desde el siglo XVIII, aunque su incidencia es menor a partir de la segunda guerra mundial, ya en el siglo XX. El francés ha jugado, además, un papel de enlace entre el español y el inglés al menos en las primeras épocas, lo que ha redundado en la presencia de numerosos calcos. Así, contamos con voces como *camping*, *dancing*, *leasing*, *pressing* o *smoking*, entre otras muchas, que han llegado al español por vía gala (Pratt, 1980; Fuster, 1995; Lorenzo, 1996).

Será a partir del siglo XIX también cuando de forma creciente se dé un cambio de rumbo en las dinámicas del préstamo en las lenguas y empiecen, de manera notoria en numerosas sociedades y culturas, los contactos del inglés a escala mundial, especialmente en las lenguas europeas como el alemán, francés, italiano... (Carstensen & Busse, 1993; Fischer & Pulaczewska, 2008; Furiasi, Pulcini & Rodríguez González, 2012; Görlach, 2001 y 2002; Gusmani, 1981 y 1983; Onysko, 2007; Picone, 1996; Pogarell & Schröder, 1999; Rey-Debove & Gagnon, 1984, entre otros). La aparición de los denominados anglicismos se vinculará, desde estos momentos, con el auge del Imperio británico, lo que significó un desplazamiento del francés en favor de la lengua inglesa[2]. La Europa afrancesada[3] poco a poco irá perdiendo presencia hacia finales del siglo XIX y principios del XX, mientras numerosos países entran de lleno en la órbita anglosajona. En el caso español, desde entonces, ya no será una lengua románica la preferida por los ambientes cultos y selectos, sino que una lengua con otra génesis estructural se encargará de ofrecer préstamos léxicos en numerosos terrenos e influir, aunque en menor medida, en otros ámbitos como la morfosintaxis o la propia pronunciación o adaptación de muchas voces. En el

2 No hay que perder de vista, no obstante, que el francés sirvió en muchas ocasiones de *préstamo inmediato* para el español, según la terminología de Pratt (1980: 44 y ss.), pues algunos anglicismos fueron incorporados a esta lengua vía francés. Según esto, la palabra *té* tiene como étimo inmediato al francés, quien la suministra al español, pero es el chino su *étimo último*, pues es este el que la ha exportado al inglés bajo la forma *tea*, al francés *thé*, al alemán *tee* o al español *té*.

3 Un magnífico ejemplo de las dinámicas culturales de buena parte de Europa, el nacimiento del concepto de "cosmopolitismo" y el auge de la industria cultural (en la que Francia y el desarrollo del ferrocarril tienen un gran protagonismo), puede verse en la obra del historiador Figes (2020).

"Prólogo" del diccionario de Alfaro (1950/1970[3]: 9), este abogado panameño escribe que:

> En el español hablado y escrito de nuestros tiempos la influencia del idioma inglés tiene preponderancia mucho mayor que la del francés. La intensidad de esta influencia tiene su razón de ser. El galicismo tenía el libro como vehículo casi único. El anglicismo tiene varios conductos de penetración por donde se cuela como corriente ora impetuosa, ora sutil, siempre efectiva.

Las referencias de Alfaro (1950/1970[3]), uno de los pocos diccionarios disponibles sobre anglicismos durante mucho tiempo en el siglo XX -aunque luego ya desfasado-, ponía de relieve dos maneras muy diferentes de abordar la huella extranjera en español. Por un lado, los mecanismos de contacto a través de la escritura, fundamentalmente y, por otro, los hechos derivados de los vínculos externos o de tipo social que han propiciado la introducción de anglicismos por parte de numerosas lenguas. Entre estos se destaca, por parte de la amplia literatura científica, el papel jugado por los EE. UU. en las dos guerras mundiales (especialmente en la segunda), la importancia creciente de las agencias de noticias internacionales y la notoriedad de la prensa escrita, el desarrollo de la industria y el comercio en los países de habla inglesa, la influencia de los medios de comunicación de masas, el mundo de la moda, el cine, la televisión, el auge de la informática y el extraordinario desarrollo de las redes sociales de comunicación[4], además de las relaciones internacionales que tienen en el inglés el idioma predilecto para sus interacciones y un largo etcétera de factores y hechos coyunturales que podrían argumentarse para explicar la preponderancia del inglés al convertirse en *lingua franca* a lo largo de todo el siglo XX (Medina López, 2004[2]: 9–12), tal y como se muestra en el resumen de las tres primeras lenguas[5] más usadas en la Web, con datos de marzo de 2020:

4 Recientemente se ha editado un conjunto de trabajos sobre la presencia de los anglicismos en los medios de comunicación. Cfr. Luján-García (2021).

5 Aparece la tabla completa en Medina López (2021: 24).

Top ten Languages Used in the Web – March 31, 2020

Top ten languages in the Internet	World Population for this Language (2020 estimate)	Internet Users by Language	Internet penetration (% Population)	Internet Users Growth (2000–2020)	Interntet Users % of World (Participation)
English	1,531,179,460	1,186,451,052	77.5 %	742.9 %	25.9 %
Chinese	1,477,137,209	888,453,068	60.1 %	2,650.4 %	19.4 %
Spanish	516,655,099	363,684,593	70.4 %	1,511.0 %	7.9 %

Fuente: https://www.internetworldstats.com/stats7.htm. Internet World Stats. Copyright © 2020, Miniwatts Marketing Group. All rights reserved worldwide.

En una visión histórica que lleva a cabo Rodríguez González (2019: 800–803), este pone de relieve cómo el peso del inglés anterior al siglo XVIII fue más bien escaso, aunque ya en esa misma centuria el conocimiento por parte de intelectuales españoles de la literatura inglesa empieza a ser notorio, además de la huella que ejerce la vida cultural y social de Gran Bretaña[6]. Pero fue hacia finales del siglo XIX cuando se dio una mayor presencia de todo lo inglés en la vida española, auspiciada, sin duda, por el propio desarrollo generado por la revolución industrial, el auge de los viajes y la denominada "vida social".

En efecto, en los últimos decenios del siglo XIX y principios del XX se asiste a una destacada entrada de préstamos léxicos que tiene que ver con la vida social y que tendrá su reflejo en ámbitos que caracterizan, de alguna manera, los hechos y manifestaciones culturales y sociales propios de esta época finisecular[7]. La

6 Señala Rodríguez González (2019: 800) que a partir de la segunda mitad del siglo XVIII comienza a impartirse el inglés en algunas escuelas, se publica la primera gramática inglesa y el primer diccionario bilingüe inglés-español, junto con las primeras traducciones del inglés al español en autores como Cadalso, Moratín o Jovellanos. Todo ello sin descartar las relaciones personales que se establecieron con la cultura británica en escritores como Blanco White, José de Espronceda o el Duque de Rivas, que emigraron a Inglaterra como exiliados políticos como consecuencia del régimen absolutista de Fernando VII. Cfr. para una visión histórica, desde la Edad Media hasta el siglo XIX, a Martín-Gamero (1961) y a Rodríguez Medina (2003) para los factores que han incidido en la expansión del inglés en España.

7 Tal es el caso, por ejemplo, de la influencia que ejerció en las clases altas españolas (realeza, aristocracia y burguesía), luego con imitaciones en las más populares, la llegada de la princesa británica, nieta de la reina Victoria y del príncipe Alberto de Sajonia-Coburgo-Gotha, Victoria Eugenia de Battenberg, quien al contraer matrimonio con el rey español Alfonso XIII el 31 de mayo de 1906 se convirtió en reina

presencia de anglicismos en terrenos como la música, la danza, la bebida, la crianza de perros, los automóviles, los vestidos o los deportes, entre otros, hace que los lazos con la cultura inglesa o norteamericana se vuelvan aún más estrechos. En este sentido, dice Rodríguez González (2019: 800) que:

> La sociedad española permaneció relativamente abierta a las influencias extranjeras hasta la Guerra Civil (1936–1939), cuando el país experimentó un período de nacionalismo lingüístico y asilamiento político que duró hasta principios de los años 50 durante la primera etapa de la dictadura franquista.

Será precisamente de estos últimos aspectos sobre los que me centraré en los párrafos siguientes, en los que pondré de relieve cómo la vida cultural española irá impregnándose de formas y modos anglosajones que tendrán su correlato en la adopción de anglicismos, algunos de los cuales tuvieron una gran vitalidad pero que con el transcurrir de los años, y la entrada de otras formas de expresión, fueron olvidándose o bien sustituidos por otras unidades léxicas. Tal es el caso del anglicismo *high life*, que tuvo una notable acogida en los ambientes sociales y culturales de la época, en competencia con otras formas, y que poco a poco fue siendo sustituido por otras formas a lo largo de los años. Para este estudio se tomarán como referencia algunas bases de datos disponibles para el español como son el *Corpus diacrónico del español* (*CORDE*), el *Corpus de Referencia del Español Actual* (*CREA*), el *Corpus del Español del Siglo XXI* (*CORPES XXI*) o la información suministrada por algunos periódicos del siglo XIX como son *Blanco y Negro* o *La Época*.

2. La vida social en España hacia finales del siglo XIX y la influencia del inglés

Una de las vías de penetración del anglicismo es a través de la prensa escrita, especialmente a partir del siglo XVIII, si bien el auténtico desarrollo de esta no se producirá hasta el XIX. Entonces surgen multitud de publicaciones en las que se da cuenta del transcurrir de la vida política nacional e internacional, y también en las que se incluyen secciones, anuncios publicitarios, pasatiempos o folletines (novelas por entregas). Entre toda esta efervescencia destacan las crónicas de salón, como han puesto de relieve algunos trabajos que se ocupan de este sector, como es el caso de Ezama Gil (2007), citado por Vázquez Amador

---

consorte de España. El estilo de vida "moderno" que imprimió a la corte madrileña contrasta con la austeridad marcada por su suegra, la reina regente María Cristina de Habsburgo-Lorena.

y Lario de Oñate (2014: 254). En ellas, igual que en la actualidad, se cuentan los entresijos de los nobles y la burguesía que recorrían los salones de la alta sociedad, particularmente la madrileña[8], al ser el centro de la Corte. En muchas de estas revistas o diarios se contaban los aconteceres de la vida social parisina[9] o londinense, que pronto serían imitados por la sociedad española y en los que con frecuencia se deslizaban galicismos o anglicismos. Así, por ejemplo, en el estudio llevado a cabo por Vázquez Amador y Lario de Oñate (2014: 257–258) fueron localizados 41 anglicismos vinculados con la crónica social para el período 1700–1900 en distintos periódicos como el *Mercurio de España* (1784–1830), *Eco del Comercio* (1834–1849) o *La Época* (1848–1936), entre otros. Se trata de voces como, *clown*, *dandysmo*, *drawing room*, *fashionable*, *flirt*, *gentleman*, *high life*, *lady*, *lord*, *lunch*, *music-hall*, *party*, *public house* o *pick-nick*. En otro trabajo de Vázquez Amador (2014) se inventaría, para el período 1800–1850, un total de 63 anglicismos procedentes de 57 voces inglesas, cuya aparición se aprecia (por orden de mayor frecuencia) en campos como los del comercio, transporte, vida social, política, generales, administración, alimentación y deporte. En lo que a la vida social se refiere, se encuentran voces como *whist* (1838), *baronet* (1838), *gentleman* (1835), *dandy* (1846) o *toast* (1843).

8 Por ejemplo, el periódico *La Época* (publicado entre 1849–1936) contaba con una sección titulada "Diversiones públicas", en la que se daba a conocer todo tipo de noticias breves sobre escritores, artistas, presentaciones de libros, lecturas públicas, obras teatrales, etc. A modo de ejemplo, véase el que aparece el 14 de mayo de 1896, p. 3: "El estreno en Apolo del sainete lírico *Las mujeres*, se verificará á principios dé la semana próxima", "La compañía que actúa en la Zarzuela, pondrá fin á sus tareas el día 30 del actual". En la sección "Noticias generales" del mismo día se informa también que "El Sr. García Alix, que se encuentra en cama, á consecuencia de un ataque de *grippe*, ha experimentado esta tarde notable alivio. Celebraremos que en breve se restablezca nuestro distinguido amigo". Adviértase el galicismo *grippe* que, según el *Diccionario Histórico de la Lengua Española* (*s.v.*: *grippe*), se documenta desde el año 1775 en el *Mercurio Histórico y Político (Madrid)*, donde se toma como un galicismo crudo. Desde 1831 aparece con regularidad.

9 Véase, a modo de ejemplo, el texto del anuncio donde se destaca la importancia de la moda de París y su impacto en el resto de Europa. "Les Modes Parisiennes. Diario de la buena sociedad de París". Las Modas parisiennes están reconocidas hace doce años como el mas bello periódico de modas de París, el mas elegante, el mas variado y como el que mejor sabe representar el tocador, el gusto y las maneras de la buena socieda parisiense Se le considera como el guia entre el mundo elegante, y cuenta entre sus suscritores todas las jóvenes reinas, las princesas y toda la aristocracia de los grandes estados". *La Época* (1/2/1856, nº 2.112, p. 4).

La España de finales del XIX observa al cambio de siglo en medio de una crisis política y de identidad (el llamado Desastre del 98)[10], que culminaría con la pérdida de los últimos vestigios del Imperio español en contraposición con el auge que representaban los países de la órbita anglosajona, especialmente Gran Bretaña y EE. UU. Como contrapartida a toda esta desazón política y moral del país, se comprueba el auge de la vida social y, particularmente, del espectáculo, con la apertura de nuevas salas y con una gran variedad de oferta cultural para el entretenimiento y goce de los ciudadanos, desde las selectas veladas de ópera en los teatros madrileños[11] (destaca por encima de todos el Teatro Real), o conciertos en los salones aristocráticos a modo de *soirée* (< fr. *soirée*), hasta las tardes de toros o la asistencia a las representaciones de zarzuelas[12]. El teatro es, sin duda, el epicentro de la vida social. Al mismo se acude para ver y ser visto[13]

10 El acontecimiento histórico señala que el 3 de julio de 1898 fue el punto de inflexión por el cual la escuadra del almirante Pascual Cervera fue hundida en la bocana del puerto de Santiago de Cuba por parte de la marina norteamericana. Este episodio se considera el fin de la guerra hispano-estadounidense que se había declarado el 20 de abril de ese mismo año. De esta forma, se pone fin a la presencia administrativa española en América, episodio conocido como el "Desastre del 98".

11 Además del Teatro Real, epicentro de la vida social de la corte madrileña, destacan los populares Teatro de la Zarzuela, Apolo, Felipe, Eslava, Circo, Lope de Vega, Maravillas, de la Comedia, de Variedades, del Príncipe (Teatro Español), de la Princesa (luego María Guerrero), El Recreo (café-teatro), Novedades, Lara, Romea, todos en Madrid. En Barcelona sobresale el Gran Teatro del Liceo desde 1847, símbolo del poder, la nobleza y burguesía catalanas.

12 Un análisis sociocultural y lingüístico de este género teatral-musical tan español en este período es el que lleva a cabo Calderón Campos (1995). Hacia mediados del siglo XIX se había impuesto la moda parisina del *café-concert*, *café-teatro* o *salones*, lugares donde se oían fragmentos o pequeñas obras teatrales, dando lugar, a partir de 1868, al nacimiento del llamado "género chico". Esta voz aludía, entonces, a la duración de las obras (no más de una hora, habitualmente) y podían ir acompañadas de música, algunas con carácter satírico, social, costumbrista, amoroso, etc. Solo posteriormente se asoció el término *chico* a 'inferior calidad', enfrentándolo a la ópera como 'género grande'. Se trataba, por tanto, de un teatro por horas (Calderón Campos, 1995: 12–14). Para Mendoza Martín (2019: 1339): "La denominación de género chico proviene del nombre otorgado por los hermanos Álvarez Quintero a una de sus zarzuelas y se basaba en un espectáculo ligero, o ínfimo, que se creó como oposición a las obras más extensas. A pesar de esta designación, con el paso del tiempo, la historiografía ha mantenido este apelativo de manera que toda actuación de corta duración y con número musical se acabó llamando *género chico* o *ínfimo*".

13 A este respecto, escribe Mendoza Martín (2019: 1344) que "un día en que se intentaron apagar las luces del Liceo barcelonés durante una función de ópera, la burguesía

y alternar con lo más granado de la sociedad, como bien narra Benito Peréz Galdós en algunas de sus célebres novelas como *La de Bringas*.

El intervalo del cambio de siglo XIX al XX propicia también el auge de géneros musicales considerados frívolos como el *music-hall*, espectáculos de varietés (< fr. *variété*) interpretados por famosas artistas que deleitaban a un público con cuplés (< fr. *couplét*) y canción española, acompañados por bailes, cuadros flamencos y todo tipo de ritmos del que disfrutaban tanto las clases más acomodadas como el pueblo llano.

La aparición también del *cinematógrafo* fue todo un acontecimiento social y cultural de primer orden. La posibilidad de ver las imágenes en movimiento que desde París habían lanzado al mundo los hermanos Lumière pronto revolucionó el espacio escénico y, por extensión, la visión de la realidad presente y la imaginaria. Nacen al amparo de este nuevo arte-industria algunos anglicismos. Desde 1896 se tienen noticias de las primeras proyecciones en España, tal y como recoge el diario *La Época* (14 de mayo de 1896, p. 3):

> Desde anoche cuenta Madrid con un espectáculo de tanta novedad como atractivo.
> El *Cinematógrafo*, ó sea la fotografía animada, es verdaderamente notable, y constituye uno de los adelantos más maravillosos alcanzados por la ciencia en el siglo actual.
> La exhibición de cuadros y vistas panorámicas, reproducidas por medio del Cinematógrafo, se hace en un espacioso local (Carrera de San Jerónimo, 34), que anoche estuvo muy concurrido por las muchas y distinguidas personas invitadas a la inauguración.
> La proyección de la fotografía animada sobre un telón blanco, no puede hacerse con más perfección que la que vimos anoche, estando reproducidos todos los movimientos de personas y objetos que atraviesan la escena.

El café era otro de los lugares indispensables en la vida social decimonónica española, pues los había populares, pero también para las gentes elegantes y de postín, en los que se hacían tertulias de todo tipo, destacando las literarias, las de los toreros o las de los cómicos. Junto a estos establecimientos, muchos de ellos privados al pertenecer a clubes (< ing. *club*), se promocionaron los encuentros en los que se escuchaban los fonógrafos y se podían bailar los ritmos como el *cake-walk*, además de las piezas populares regionales y castizas como el chotis (< al. *schottisch*).

Otra parte destacable es la afición por los deportes, terreno abonado a las influencias anglosajonas, tal y como ha demostrado Rodríguez González (2012: 289) al comentar voces que pronto se hicieron relativamente frecuentes en la prensa española de finales del XIX, como son los casos de *foot-ball*, *base-ball*, *golf*, *cricket*, *yaughting*, *team*, *match* o *sport*… además de las denominaciones de los equipos deportivos que llegan hasta la actualidad: *Sporting* de Gijón,

Athletic de Bilbao o *Racing* de Santander. Entre las clases más selectas se ponen de moda el *polo* y el *lawn tennis*, pero también la yincana (< ing. *gymkhana*). Destaca también, por último, el gran desarrolló que adquirió la bicicleta, llamada entonces velocípedo, con sus modelos como *safetyrudge*, *royal crescent*, *four-in-hand*, *tándem*, etc.

3. Un anglicismo (casi) olvidado: del *high life* > *gilí* y otros

Entre las voces inglesas que entraron en español hacia finales del siglo XIX resulta interesante el análisis de la expresión *high life* literalmente 'vida alta', para referirse al *modus vivendi* de lujo que llevaban algunos personajes de la alta sociedad de la época. Así lo atestigua Rodríguez González (2017, *s.v.*: *high life*) cuando señala que "En español, el término se empleó con frecuencia a finales del siglo XIX y en la primera mitad del XX. Muchos lo pronunciaban 'gilí', con un tono peyorativo, evocando el significado de 'tonto, estúpido', que esta voz tiene en caló"[14]. En efecto, los límites semánticos entre ambos sentidos no siempre aparecen de forma nítida, a juzgar por los ejemplos que deslizan sutilezas irónicas y descalificativos poco favorables para quien es denominado como un "gilí" o con comportamientos de *la gilí*. Las etimologías, sin embargo, parecen estar claras. Por un lado, tenemos *gilí* como voz procedente del gitano español *jilí* 'inocente, cándido', como indican Corominas-Pascual (1980, *s.v.*: *gilí*), quienes señalan la primera documentación en 1882–1883. Por otro, la adaptación fónica que a lo largo del XIX se emprendió con la introducción del anglicismo *high life* > [χi'li] > *gilí*, que en ocasiones aparecía[15], incluso, con la abreviatura "Hi-Li". Así se recoge en algunos números del diario *Blanco y Negro*:

---

asistente se negó rotundamente dado que ir al teatro significaba «ver y dejarse ver» y nunca pasar inadvertido. En la misma idea de espacios para la ostentación y la relación social podemos identificar la existencia, por ejemplo, en el Teatro Real, de numerosas salas de encuentro e, incluso, una peluquería de señoras".

14 Wagner (1941: 167–168), citado por Calderón Campos (1995: 458), señala la procedencia gitana de *gilí* 'tonto, cándido, inocente', registrándose esta voz tanto en catalán *gil*, como en español *gilí* o *jilé*. El término *gilí* o *gili* aparece integrado ya en la lengua española desde mediados del siglo XIX.

15 En la actualidad *high life* ha sido desplazado (término obsoleto) por su correlato semántico, *high society*. Cfr. Rodríguez González (2017, *s.v.*: *high life*). Pero aunque no son muchos tampoco los ejemplos que recoge el *CORPES XXI*, su presencia está atestiguada en varios países del mundo hispano. Así, el ejemplo venezolano de Rosanna di Turi: "Cuando comenzamos, aquí venía la *high society* de Caracas. El

(1) Huevos «High life», (*Blanco y Negro*, 7/6/1891).
(2) Papelería *High life*, 14, calle de Sevilla (*Blanco y Negro*, 30/1/1897).
(3) Bien es cierto que todos los chicos de la *high-life* la estaban contemplando (*Blanco y Negro*, 3/7/1897).

Si nos adentramos en la información que suministran algunos de los corpus lingüísticos disponibles para el español como es el *CORDE*[16], se observa que la mayoría de los casos responde al sentido de *gilí* "tonto, estúpido". Así se ve comprueba en las siguientes muestras:

(4) Al bajar de la visita, echaba siempre una parrafada con los memorialistas a fin de sonsacarles mil menudencias sobre los del cuarto segundo; si pagaban o no la casa, si debían mucho en la tienda (aunque este conocimiento lo solía beber en más limpias fuentes), si volvían tarde del teatro, si la sosa se casaba al fin con el *gilí* de Ponce, si había entrado el zapatero con calzado nuevo… (Benito Pérez Galdós, *Miau*, 1888. *CORDE*).
(5) Mírale la cara de "gilí" que tiene. Menos mal que estará conmigo unos días y yo le espabilaré -dice mi abuela. (Arturo Barea, *La forja de rebelde*, 1951. *CORDE*).
(6) Si está visto que eres anormal, o sea, vamos, *gilí*, que eso es lo que quiere decir lo de subnormal cuando la tía Vicenta… (Alonso Zamora Vicente, *A traque barraque*, 1972. *CORDE*).

Pero volviendo al caso del anglicismo *gilí*, su popularidad en el XIX debió ser muy alta, a juzgar por su presencia en una de las obras musicales más famosas de finales del siglo, como fue la zarzuela *La Gran Vía* (género tan dado a conectar con el público y a empatizar con el mismo a través de sus diálogos[17] y

antiguo dueño abrió este lugar porque cerca estaba la embajada de Estados Unidos y la Creole". (*El Nacional. Todo en domingo*, 20/4/2003).

16 Los datos del *CORDE* son, no obstante, muy limitados en este empleo, posiblemente por el tipo de documentación seleccionada. Un solo ejemplo del siglo XIX en Galdós (ejemplo 4), y luego, hasta un total de 67 casos en 7 documentos en autores del XX como Miguel Delibes, Arturo Barea, Camilo José Cela, Joaquín Calvo Sotelo, Alonso Zamora Vicente y Juan García Hortelano.

17 En la edición consultada por mí de la *La Gran Vía* (Cortizo y Sobrino, 1997) se observa tanto en los diálogos como en las letras cantadas la indicación del habla popular y castiza mediante el recurso de la letra en cursiva, como guía para los actores/cantantes del estilo de habla popular madrileña que debe caracterizar a sus personajes. Así, por ejemplo, *tóos/toas* (todos/todas), *misté* (mire usted), *estituto* (instituto), *catredal* (catedral), *señá* (señora), *señó* (señor), *usté* (usted), *salío* (salido), *melitar* (militar), *figurao* (figurado), *parné* (< 'dinero', caló), *pus* (pues), *cercunstancias* (circunstancias), *presopopeya* (prosopopeya), *destinguir* (distinguir), *naide* (nadie), *menistro* (ministro), *escogío* (escogido), *paece* (parece), *lu-menos* (lo menos),

letras cantadas). En efecto, durante la década de 1880 se produjo en Madrid una controversia sobre la conveniencia o no de crear una gran avenida que ayudara a descongestionar y modernizar el centro de la ciudad, tan condicionado por su trazado antiguo, lleno de plazas y callejuelas[18]. Surge así el gran proyecto de trazar una gran calle que, con el transcurrir de los años, dará nombre y fisonomía a la conocida "Gran Vía". Los acontecimientos sociales y políticos en torno a la propuesta de construcción de la arteria viaria de Madrid dieron lugar a la creación de la "Revista madrileña cómico-lírica, fantástico-callejera en un acto" (Cortizo y Sobrino, 1997)[19].

La Gran Vía fue estrenada con rotundo éxito el 2 de julio de 1886 en el popular teatro Felipe de Madrid, convirtiéndose, desde entonces, en una de las obras musicales más conocidas dentro de su género y pieza fundamental del repertorio zarzuelista de las orquestas nacionales y extranjeras cuando interpretan música española. Habría que esperar, no obstante, hasta 1910 para que se iniciaran las obras de demolición y el nuevo trazado de la arteria madrileña.

En el conocido "Chotis del Eliseo", escena V de la obra, es donde aparece la forma castiza de pronunciar el anglicismo *high life*, adaptado a *lai gilí*. La estrofa en cuestión dice así:

---

lu que es el talentu (lo que es el talento), *pasao* (pasado), *lao* (lado), *ustez* (usted), *Valladolí* (Valladolid), etc., donde observamos fenómenos de metátesis, cierre de vocales, disimilaciones, analogías y apócopes… todos rasgos considerados propios del habla popular.

18 En la zarzuela *La Gran Vía* aparecen numerosas calles encarnadas en personajes. Así, las calles de Sevilla, Ancha, Candil, Toledo, Cebada, Libertad, Sartén, Mayor, Ave María, Válgame Dios, Afligidos, Primavera, Paloma, Soldado, Baño, Tesoro, Oso, Rosa, Clavel, Reloj y la Luna. También los callejones del Perro y el Gato. Luego otros personajes como los Ratas, el petróleo, el barrio del Pacífico y de la Prosperidad, soldados, criadas, guardias, la Fuente, doña Sinceridad, marineritos-yernos, el Eliseo madrileño, la lidia o el tío Jindama, entre otros.

19 La revista lírica es un género dentro de la zarzuela en el que se tocaban temas de actualidad social, política o cultural que sucedían en un determinado año y que normalmente se representaban en un solo acto (género chico), sobre todo con un cariz satírico y crítico. Naturalmente, este tipo de espectáculo conectaba con gran facilidad con el público, pues este veía reflejados en escena los aconteceres de la vida cotidiana. Véase: Zarzuela para una nueva vía (fotomadrid.com). Desde el punto de vista lingüístico, sus variopintos personajes hablan en escena con los rasgos del habla popular del XIX y en función de su condición sociolingüística, como bien ha descrito Calderón Campos (1995) y puede observarse en la nota 17 precedente.

(7) Chotis del Eliseo. Número 10

Eliseo.- Yo soy un baile de criadas
y de horteras.A mí me buscan las cocineras;
a mis salones se disputan por venirlo más *seleto*[20] de *lai gilí*.

Coro.- *¡Gilí!*

En los ambientes madrileños de los últimos decenios del siglo XIX, el gusto por llevar una vida de lujo y esplendor era muy comentado entre las clases sociales. Y para ello se fue introduciendo el anglicismo *high life*, literalmente traducido como 'vida alta' y más específicamente como 'alta sociedad', si bien para esta última acepción también contamos con *high society*, aunque los registros del *CORDE* dan para este compuesto dos escasas frecuencias de 1936 y 1972 (ya en el siglo XX)[21]. Escasos son, también, las concurrencias del *CREA* (4 ejemplos entre 1976 y 2001). La forma, a pesar de estas cifras, sabemos que tiene una mayor vitalidad que lo que estos dos corpus ofrecen. Algo más representado está en los ejemplos del *CORPES XXI*.

Junto a *high life* también aparece otro término que semánticamente está en la misma esfera designativa. Me refiero a *fashionable* 'de moda', "moderno", 'a la moda', 'de buen tono' *CORDE* lo recoge desde la década de los años treinta del siglo XIX:

(8) [...] las damas más bellas de Zaragoza se disputaban los favores del señorito; los jóvenes imitaban sus modales y vestido; las modas de París y de Londres, los coches de Bruselas, los caballos normandos, todo le era presentado por diestros corredores, que hallaban el secreto de cuadruplicar su valor; y sin haber salido de Zaragoza, afectaba ya los usos de un *fashionable* de Londres, y hablaba mal de nuestras cosas, con lo cual, y fiándose de mercaderes extranjeros, muy pronto se vio asaltado de acreedores y chalanes. (Ramón de Mesonero Romanos, *Escenas de 1832*, 1832. *CORDE*).

---

20 Cantado con énfasis para exagerar la pronunciación simplificada del grupo culto [-k't-]: *selecto* > *seleto*.

21 Son los siguientes: "El Club Montezuma, lugar de reunión habitual de la *high society*, era frecuentemente visitado por altos dignatarios [...]". (Rafael Nogales Méndez, *Memorias*, a 1936, *CORDE*) y "Y por eso te pirras por las muchachas de la *high society*, bien limpitas, bien depiladas y envirgadas". (Juan García Hortelano, *El gran momento de Mary Tribune*, 1972. *CORDE*). En *CREA* se duplica el número de casos. Por ejemplo: "Y la "*high society*" de Washington se quedó totalmente fascinada". (Prensa: *El Mundo*, 11/11/1996: Música. Ópera. Plácido Domingo triunfa en Washington con "Il Guarany". España).

Otro claro ejemplo de su significado ligado a la moda se advierte en el comentario que hace Valera alternando el inglés y el francés (chic y *comme il faut*)[22]:

(9) Unos miraban la religión como una reserva sobrenatural de la Guardia Civil veterana, o como un complemento de la Policía; otros, como un asunto de moda, asegurando que ya es rococó, poco *fashionable*, falto de *comme il faut* y de chic el ser incrédulo. (Juan Valera, *La revolución y la libertad religiosa en España*, 1869. *CORDE*).

Pérez Galdós, por su parte, se refiere a que vestir a la manera inglesa conlleva un estilo *fashionable*:

(10) Pero se creía necesario un simulacro de parlamentarismo, por aquello de que era *fashionable* vestir a la inglesa, imitando los debates políticos, como se imitaban los fraques. (Benito Pérez Galdós, *De Oñate a la Granja*, 1876. *CORDE*).

(11) [...] Reapareció entonces el dandy, paquete, lion, *fashionable*, o como nombrársele quiera, D. Esteban Ordóñez de Castro [...]. (Benito Pérez Galdós, *Bodas Reales*, 1900. *CORDE*).

Así lo explican también Vázquez Amador y Lario de Oñate (2014: 262): "El adjetivo *fashionable* se encuentra tanto en contextos relacionados con la moda en los anuncios publicitarios como para hacer referencia a personas (e.g. el mundo *fashionable*, la gente *fashionable* y la sociedad *fashionable*) con un significado muy similar al del anglicismo *high life*, traducido como alta sociedad, como se expresa con sorna en el siguiente comentario:

(12) Pues penetremos en ese gran mundo, en esa alta sociedad hoy bautizada por todos los cronistas con el mal sonante y manoseado sustantivo adjetivo de *High-Life*. Puesto que vivís en *Alta Sociedad*, poned alta la mira y el pensamiento. (*La Época*, 2/3/1883, p. 3)".

En *CORDE* encuentro un ejemplo en el que alternan ambos anglicismos en contextos similares:

---

22 *Comme il faut* aparece en 9 concurrencias en *CORDE* para este galicismo en el siglo XIX. En el ejemplo de referencia (9) tiene el sentido de 'falto de buen gusto' o 'poco glamuroso' (según *DLE*, *s.v.*: *glamur*, < fr. *glamour*, y este del ingl. *glamour*). Es también expresión que aparece en *La Gran Vía* ya referida, en el vals que canta el Caballero de Gracia (escena IV, núm. 2). "Yo soy el caballero que con más finura baila en los salones *comm'il faut*", pero ahora con el sentido de 'como Dios manda', 'como debe ser'. Este mismo personaje en su vals dirá que "soy un *milord*, soy un *dandy*".

(13) La que con más modestia que justicia se llama á sí propia la buena sociedad, siempre dispuesta á buscar y recoger el mérito cuando éste se halla ya en disposición de servirla de adorno, encontró un nuevo motivo para solicitarle y atraerle, y Cervántes llegó á ser un pollo[23] verdaderamente *fashionable*, un gomoso con ménos goma que otros, no lo niego, pero digno de figurar á la cabeza de nuestra *high life*. (Carlos Coello, *Cuentos inverosímiles*, 1872–1878. *CORDE*).

Así pues, tenemos en el siglo XIX dos formas de origen inglés que compiten en la vida social para referirse a lo que está de moda, representa la elegancia y el buen tono o que está a la orden del día (*fashionable*) y perteneciente o relativo a la alta sociedad *high life*.

El propio Galdós es consciente de su uso anglosajón y así lo muestra en el fragmento de 1874:

(14) Pero, sin renunciar a ser cronista de los saraos de aquella matritense *high life* (¿por qué no decirlo en inglés?) seré muy breve por ahora, señores míos. (Benito Pérez Galdós, *Napoleón en Chamartín*, 1874. *CORDE*).

Algo más tarde, Clarín también usará el mismo término para referirse a la alta sociedad de la provinciana Vetusta:

(15) ¡Programa! -gritó don Víctor-: al teatro dos veces a la semana por lo menos; a la tertulia de la Marquesa cada cinco o seis días, al Espolón todas las tardes que haga bueno; a las reuniones de confianza del Casino en cuanto se inauguren este año; a las meriendas de la Marquesa, a las excursiones de la *high life* vetustense, y a la catedral cuando predique don Fermín y repiquen gordo. (Clarín (Leopoldo Alas), *La Regenta*, 1884–1885. *CORDE*).

Y con ironía expresa Juan Valera en las postrimerías del siglo XIX el gusto todavía por todo lo parisino, tal y como se aprecia en la siguiente referencia:

(16) No es de extrañar, en atención a lo expuesto, que los aspirantes a *high life*, en todos sentidos, vayan en peregrinación a París como van a la Meca los musulmanes. (Juan Valera, *Genio y figura*, 1897. *CORDE*)[24].

El progresivo abandono que se advierte en *high life* (y su castizo *gilí*) fue reemplazado en España en la década de los años ochenta y noventa del siglo XX por otra construcción de origen inglés como es *jet-set*. Según Rodríguez González

---

23 En más de una ocasión estos adjetivos acompañan al *pollo* 'hombre joven', con cierto matiz despectivo.

24 El último ejemplo que trae *CORDE* de *high life* pertenece a Francisco Ayala, *El fondo del vaso*, 1962: "Como periodista, Luis Erre tiene vara alta en los ambientes artísticos tanto como en la *high life* que ocasionalmente se mezcla con ellos en esta velada".

(2017, *s. v.*: *jet-set*), el término alude al "grupo social internacional integrado por personas acaudaladas y elegantes que disponen de tiempo y medios para desplazarse con frecuencia a los lugares de moda"[25]. En el diccionario de Rodríguez González (2017) se comprueba, además, la derivación que el término ha generado en el propio español, con voces como *jetsetero*, *jetsetter* o *jet-setter* o formaciones creadas sobre la base de *jet*-como *jet-sociedad* o *jet society*. El uso en España es claramente en femenino (*la jet set*), a juzgar por los registros que aparecen en *CREA* y *CORPES XXI*; sin embargo, para Hispanoamérica predomina[26] el empleo en masculino, quizá influenciado por el género de *jet* "reactor":

(17) Estaban invitados a la imponente casa del empresario italiano Giorgio Nocella en la zona norte de Cerdeña, donde tomaban sol en Porto Rotondo, uno de los lugares preferidos *del jet jet* internacional [...]. (Pablo Ibáñez y Walter Schmidt: *Scioli secreto. De Menem a Kirchner. De motonauta a presidente.* Buenos Aires: Sudamericana, 2015. *CORPES XXI*).

(18) [...] la zona de Punta del Este, que es conocida también como la pequeña Mónaco, por la afluencia de turistas y *del jet set* del mundo, que vienen a vacacionar a Punta del Este durante el verano [...]. (Guillermo García: «La Suiza de Latinoamérica». *El Universal.* Caracas: eluniversal.com, 2/10/2009. *CORPES XXI*).

(19) la página de sociedad que estaba llena *del jet set* peninsular, los deportesy hasta los clasificados [...]. (Álvarez, Sergio: *35 muertos.* Bogotá: Alfaguara, 2011. *CORPES XXI*).

Si bien *CORDE* no recoge casos de estas formas, en *CREA* sí que aparecen cinco referencias en cuatro documentos. Véase el siguiente ejemplo a modo de definición:

(20) *Jet set* es una categoría estrellizante en el mismo sentido en que, centrada en los actores de la industria del cine, la infraestructura promocional de Hollywood ubicaba individuos en el inaccesible y admirado olimpo de lo "glamoroso".

---

25 Dice Rodríguez González (2017, *s.v.*: *jet-set*) que el término aparece en los años cincuenta del siglo XX. En España se hizo muy popular en las décadas de los ochenta y noventa del siglo XX, fundamentalmente, donde destacó la *jet* internacional que recalaba en los veranos de Marbella y Puerto Banús (Málaga), dando lugar a todo un despliegue de fiestas, lujo y dinero nunca vistos antes en la sociedad española. Véase el siguiente ejemplo: "En Marbella, luego tenemos seis semanas en Afganistán. Nos vamos a Marbella con la *jet set*, a ver si los corregimos un poco, que están como locos, y a decirles se pongan supositorios normales" («" En Marbella vamos a corregir a la jet"». *Cambio 16.* Madrid: Grupo 16, 3/9/1990. *CREA*).

26 Así se observa en países como Bolivia, Colombia, Chile, Ecuador, México, Paraguay, Perú, Puerto Rico, República Dominicana, Uruguay, Venezuela...

(Tomás López-Pumarejo, *Aproximación a la telenovela: Dallas / Dinasty / Falcon Crest*, 1987. *CREA*).

Será en *CORPES XXI* donde encontremos el mayor número de frecuencias de *jet set*, reflejado en un variado número de documentos que representa a casi todos los países de habla hispana (142 ejemplos).

(21) Capri es sinónimo de lujo, sofisticación, glamour; destino de peregrinaje del *jet set* internacional y de clase, mucha clase. (Capri prohíbe los plásticos para siempre, *Horizontes, Bogotá: aviatura.com/contenidos/revista-horizontes*. 01/2020. *CORPES XXI*).

(22) [...] Mariachis, bailanteros, folcloristas y hasta el mismísimo Julio Iglesias rendirían tributo a los tórtolos, apretujados entre miles de sudoroso e incondicionales seguidores de los entretelones del mundo del *jet set* y la farándula. (Olga Wornat, *Menem-Bolocco*, Buenos Aires: Ediciones B Argentina, 2001. *CORPES XXI*).

Aunque *high life* y *jet set* se refieran a la misma realidad ("alta sociedad"), sin embargo parece que el segundo tiene la especificación de "alta sociedad internacional", y así aparece recogida esta locución inglesa en el *Diccionario de la Lengua Española* (*s. v.*: *jet set*) "clase social internacional, rica y ostentosa".

Emparentado semánticamente con estas formas que apuntan hacia la calidad y el elitismo, especialmente lanzado desde el mundo de la publicidad (modelo de marca), nos encontramos con *high elite*, donde se aúna una forma anglo-francesa[27]. Lo cierto es que el adjetivo *high* aparece en numerosos elementos compositivos con mayor o menor fortuna dentro del español. En el "Observatorio Lázaro", disponible en la red (https://observatoriolazaro.es/) se comprueba la alta productividad de compuestos del tipo *high school, high fashion, high-street, highlight, high concept, high class, high energy, high style, high efficiency, high level, high technology*..., ejemplos todos recogidos de la prensa española.

4. Conclusiones

La influencia ejercida por el inglés en la vida social y cultural española adquiere especial relevancia a lo largo del siglo XIX, afianzándose durante el XX como una de las manifestaciones más evidentes de la internacionalización en la que

27 El *DLE* prefiere la forma esdrújula (*élite*), aunque también propone *elite* (< ambas del fr. *élite*) 'minoría selecta o rectora'. La primera documentación en el corpus diacrónico aparece en "pero un Coronel halló que le quitaban el mejor cuerpo; el general López, que se comprometían al principio las tropas de *élite* que debían formar la reserva según todas las reglas [...]". (Domingo Faustino Sarmiento, *Facundo. Civilización y barbarie*, 1845–1874. *CORDE*).

se han desarrollado los procesos de globalización, en especial después de la segunda mitad del siglo XX. Algunas formas adoptadas por la sociedad española en su contacto con la cultura anglosajona así parecen demostrarlo ya desde el XIX en el que, en particular, las clases altas españolas emulaban las costumbres y actitudes tanto de Francia, primero, como de Gran Bretaña, después. El ejemplo del anglicismo *high life* y sus adláteres semánticos que giran en torno al mismo (*fashionable*, *jet-set*, *jet society…*), al igual que su propio uso en el ambiente castizo del siglo XIX (*gilí*), muestran cómo estamos ante un terreno muy permeable a entradas y salidas de voces que corren desigual suerte en el engranaje léxico, en los vaivenes de la moda y las dinámicas socioculturales de cada momento, lo que, en definitiva, tiene su correlato en la historia de las palabras. Estas páginas así lo han querido poner de relieve.

Bibliografía

Alfaro, Ricardo J. (1950), *Diccionario de anglicismos: enumeración, análisis y equivalencias castizas de los barbarismos, extranjerismos, neologismos y solecismos, de origen inglés que se han introducido en el castellano contemporáneo, y advertencias a traductores*, Panamá: Imprenta Nacional. [2.ª ed., 1964. Reedit., en 1970, Madrid: Gredos].

Calderón Campos, Miguel (1995), *Análisis lingüístico del género chico andaluz y rioplatense (1870–1920)*, Granada: Universidad de Granada. URL: https://digibug.ugr.es/handle/10481/14447?locale-attribute=en

Carstensen, B. & Busse, U. (1993), *Anglizismen Wörterbuch*, Berlin/New York, De Gruyter.

Corominas, J. & Pacual, J. A. (1980), *Diccionario crítico etimológico castellano e hispánico*, Gredos: Madrid.

Cortizo, M.ª Encina y Sobrino, Ramón (1997), *La Gran Vía. Revista madrileña cómico-lírica, fantástico-callejera en un acto*, música de Federico Chueca y Joaquín Valverde, con libreto de Felipe Pérez y González, Madrid: Instituto Complutense de Ciencias Musicales.

Ezama Gil, M.ª de los Ángeles (2007), "Emilia Pardo Bazán revistera de salones: datos para una historia de la crónica de sociedad", *Espéculo*, 37, pp. 1–23. Disponible en: http://webs.ucm.es/info/especulo/numero37/epbazan.html

Fischer, R. & Pulaczewska, H. (2008), *Anglicisms in Europe. Linguistic diversity in a global context*, Newcastle upon Tyne: Cambridge Scholars Publishing.

Figes, Orlando (2020), *Los europeos. Tres vidas y el nacimiento de la cultura cosmopolita*, Madrid: Taurus.

Furiassi, C., Pulcini, V. y Rodríguez González, F. (eds.). (2012), *The anglicization of European Lexis,* The Hague: John Benjamins.

Fuster, Miguel (1995), "La romanización del inglés y la anglización del español peninsular", en M.ª Teresa Echenique Elizondo, Milagros Aleza Izquierdo y M.ª José Martínez (eds.), *Historia de la lengua española en América y España*, Valencia: Tirant lo Blanch, pp. 245–259.

Görlach, Manfred (2001), *A dictionary of European anglicisms. A usage dictionary of anglicisms in sixteen European languages*, Oxford: Oxford University Press.

Görlach, Manfred (2002), *An annotated bibliography of European anglicisms*, Oxford: Oxford University Press.

Gusmani, R. (1981), *Saggi sull'interferenza lingüística: volumen primo*, Florencia: Casa Editrice.

Gusmani, R. (1983), *Saggi sull'interferenza lingüística: volumen secondo*, Florencia: Casa Editrice.

Lorenzo, Emilio (1996), *Anglicismos hispánicos*, Madrid: Gredos.

Luján-García, Carmen (ed.) (2021), *Anglicismos en los nuevos medios de comunicación*, Granada: Comares.

Martín-Gamero, Sofía (1961), *La enseñanza del inglés en España. (Desde la Edad Media hasta el siglo XIX)*, Madrid: Gredos.

Medina López, Javier (2004²), *El anglicismo en el español actual*, Madrid: Arco/Libros.

Medina López, Javier (2021), "El inglés y el español ante la globalización: una muestra de anglicismos en el ámbito de la economía", en Carmen Luján-García (ed.), *Anglicismos en los nuevos medios de comunicación. Tendencias actuales*, Granada: Comares, pp. 13–44.

Mendoza Martín, Irene (2019), "Las *varietés* y sus públicos en los teatros madrileños a finales del siglo XIX y primeros años del XX", en Mónica Moreno Seco (coord.) y Rafael Fernández Sirvent y Rosa Ana Gutiérrez Loret (eds.), *Del siglo XIX al XXI. Tendencias y debates: XIV Congreso de la Asociación de Historia Contemporánea, Universidad de Alicante 20–22 de septiembre de 2018*, Alicante: Biblioteca Virtual Miguel de Cervantes, pp. 1339–1348. Disponible en: http://rua.ua.es/dspace/handle/10045/96214

Onysko, A. (2007), *Anglicisms in German: Borrowing, lexical productivity, and written codeswitching*, Berlin/New York: De Gruyter.

Picone, M. (1996), *Anglicisms, neologisms and dynamic French*, Amsterdam/Philadelphia: John Benjamins.

Pogarell, R. & Schröder, M. (1999), *Wörterbuch überflüssiger Anglizismen*, Paderborn: IFB Verlag.

Pratt, Chris (1980), *El anglicismo en el español peninsular contemporáneo*, Madrid: Gredos.

Real Academia Española: Banco de datos (CORDE) [en línea]. *Corpus diacrónico del español.* <http://www.rae.es> [junio-julio de 2022].

Real Academia Española: Banco de datos (CORPES XXI) [en línea]. *Corpus del Español del Siglo XXI (CORPES).* <http://www.rae.es> [junio-julio de 2022].

Real Academia Española: Banco de datos (CREA. Versión anotada) [en línea]. *Corpus de referencia del español actual.* <http://www.rae.es> [juno-julio de 2022].

Rey-Debove, J. & Gagnon, G. (1984), *Dictionaire des anglicisms*, Paris: Le Robert.

Rodríguez González, Félix (2012), "Anglicismos en el mundo del deporte: variación lingüística y sociolingüística", *Boletín de la Real Academia Española*, t. XCII, cuad. CCCVI, pp. 285–309. Disponible en: http://rua.ua.es/dspace/handle/10045/36000

Rodríguez González, Félix (2017), *Gran diccionario de anglicismos*, Madrid: Arco/Libros.

Rodríguez González, Félix (2019), "La introducción de los anglicismos en español: historia, actitudes, registro", en Ramón González Ruiz, Inés Olza y Óscar Loureda Lamas (eds.), *Lengua, cultura, discurso. Estudios ofrecidos al profesor Manuel Casado Velarde*, Navarra: EUNSA, pp. 799–819. Disponible en: https://rua.ua.es/dspace/bitstream/10045/98387/1/HMC-Felix-Rodriguez.pdf

Rodríguez Medina, María Jesús (2003), "La presencia del inglés en España: antecedentes y panorama actual", *Analecta Malacitana*, n. 13. En línea: http://www.anmal.uma.es/numero13/Medina.htm

Vázquez Amador, María (2014), "Los anglicismos en la lengua española a través de la prensa en la primera mitad del siglo XIX", *Revista de Investigación Lingüística*, 17, pp. 1139–1146. Disponible en: https://revistas.um.es/ril/article/view/224031

Vázquez Amador, María y Lario de Oñate, M.ª Carmen (2014), "La influencia de la lengua inglesa en la crónica social del siglo XIX", *Verbum. Analecta Neolatina*, 15, pp. 251–270. Disponible en: http://www.verbum-analectaneolatina.hu/pdf/verbum15-1-2-2014.pdf

Wagner, Max Leopold (1941), "Sobre algunas palabras gitano-españolas y otras jergales", *Revista de Filología Española*, XXV, pp. 161–181.

Martín Jamieson

Investigador independiente

Re-visión del *Diccionario de anglicismos* de Ricardo J. Alfaro en el siglo XXI

Retornar a las páginas del *Diccionario de anglicismos. Enumeración, análisis y equivalencias castizas de los barbarismos, extranjerismos, neologismos y solecismos de origen inglés que se han introducido en el castellano contemporáneo, y advertencia a traductores* (Panamá, Imprenta Nacional, 1950, 850 pp.), de Ricardo J. Alfaro, obliga a un reajuste temporal, intelectual y hasta emocional. En el siglo XXI, próximos a una centuria de su primera salida, encontramos en el *Diccionario de anglicismos* de Alfaro una voz de alerta que se elevaba ante la notoria infusión de un caudal de léxico foráneo al español y en el que se proponía, unas veces, la aceptación sin más de los elementos extranjeros o con sus adecuadas modificaciones o bien el pleno rechazo de ellos cuando, a juicio del autor, las nuevas formas descoyuntaban lo patrimonial. La obra, aún hoy, conserva méritos y es útil, lo que no es poco admitir acerca de un libro sobre el cual el tiempo ha hecho labor depuradora.

La dualidad – aceptación, negación – frente al cambio, un constante en la lengua, se nota en el volumen, y se extiende a los lectores a los que se orientaba, ya el hombre culto, ya el profesional, y, en este caso, especialmente el que manejaba la lengua para los grandes grupos, hoy llamado comunicador, y específicamente al intermediario que es el traductor, a quien se le ponía sobre aviso en cuanto a los matices de su propio idioma.

Lo que experimentaba el español de los siglos XIX y XX (y presenta el actual) no era fenómeno reducido a sólo estas dos lenguas en contacto (el español y el inglés) sino fenómeno generalizado a muchos idiomas del mundo, pues la preponderancia de los países de habla inglesa se cierne sobre un gran número de los existentes, entre otras causas, debido a la mundialización.

Alfaro reparaba que el cambio que sobrevenía no se limitaba a lo lingüístico sino que estaba englobado en otro más amplio, cultural, o, dicho en los términos que Antonio de Nebrija aplicó al español en el prólogo a su *Gramática de la lengua castellana*, tomando una expresión con prosapia: "que siempre la lengua fue compañera del imperio; y de tal manera lo siguió, que junta mente començaron, crecieron y florecieron, y después junta fue la caida de entrambos". La densa erudición del libro de Nicholas Ostler, *Empires of the Word. A Language History of the World* (2005), documenta la serpenteante singladura de varias lenguas a través de territorios, tiempo y circunstancias y releva de aducir testimonios.

El *Diccionario de anglicismos* se imprimió por primera vez en Panamá en 1950, pero recibió su mayor difusión a partir de la "segunda edición aumentada" (Madrid, 1970), aligerada de su extenso título primero, y es la que aquí se toma en cuenta. El prólogo del *Diccionario de anglicismos*, en cambio, se publicó inicialmente en el *Boletín del Instituto Caro y Cuervo* en 1948 con el título "El anglicismo en el español contemporáneo". En él se hallan, *in nuce*, muchos elementos que, de manera científica o un poco menos, después se han seguido debatiendo en cuanto al contacto entre el inglés y el español: la amplitud léxica de éste (considérese el vocabulario sobre juegos de naipes o palabras relativas al automóvil, p. 11, o a la industria del cine, p. 12), los parónimos (p. 17), una tipología del anglicismo (pp. 17–19), los pseudoanglicismos (p. 19), lo que el inglés le debe al español (pp. 20–21), la necesidad de conservar el idioma (p. 24), y, aparte del influjo extranjero, tanto la unidad dentro de la variedad de una lengua tan extendida por el orbe como las deficiencias de algunas acepciones de la Real Academia en su diccionario (p. 23).

El pensamiento que sustenta el diccionario de Alfaro es claramente del siglo XIX. (El autor nació en 1882 y falleció en 1971. Para 1950 tendría cristalizada su visión del mundo y su norma lingüística individual). Los diccionarios de provincialismos que consultó (p. 15) son todos del siglo XIX, y el total de la bibliografía es de entre los años 1840 y 1947, con preponderancia de las obras del siglo XIX. Los extremos se encuentran demostrados por la *Gramática de la lengua castellana*, de Vicente Salvá, de 1840, y el *Thesaurus of Words and Phrases*, de Peter Mark Roget, de 1947, edición corregida, pero de concepción anterior. Alfaro defendía la norma del español que no había empezado a absorber rauda y masivamente el anglicismo léxico y sintáctico.

En Panamá el *Diccionario de anglicismos* se inserta dentro de una tradición lexicográfica incipiente, de historia aún no documentada, pues sus antecedentes fueron, casi unánimemente, repertorios limitados, prácticamente sólo nomenclaturas, es decir, listas, que sólo con dificultad servirían de apoyo seguro para un volumen de la extensión y conocimientos que vierte Alfaro. El de Alfaro fue el primer *diccionario* compuesto en el país. El precedente de algún sustento de estudio léxico panameño que conoció el autor fue el libro de Luisita Aguilera Patiño, *El panameño visto a través de su lenguaje* (1947?), luego rehecho como "Diccionario de panameñismos" (1951), que no enfoca en particular anglicismos aunque los incluya y, que si bien se había saludado en su día, merecía revisión. Alfaro acudió a otros diccionarios de regionalismos americanos para ampliar su indagación léxica, ya que prefería tratar el español del continente nuevo enlazado con el inglés estadounidense, no el británico, según también se constata por la bibliografía.

Dentro del clima intelectual en que se concibió y redactó el diccionario del internacionalista Alfaro se encuentra otro investigador, este sí especializado en temas de lenguaje, el germanista español Emilio Lorenzo, cuyo "El anglicismo en la España de hoy" inauguraba el estudio del anglicismo al otro lado del Atlántico. (Se encuentra primero en la revista española *Arbor* (1955) y se recoge en *El español de hoy, lengua en ebullición*, hasta la tercera edición, volumen del mismo autor, para pasar finalmente a sus *Anglicismos hispánicos* – 1996 –). Lorenzo conoció el diccionario de Alfaro, sobre el cual hizo anotaciones, y después, explorando la veta del anglicismo, en la que el panameño había hecho cumbre, publicó artículos, notas y recensiones que quedaron, a los años, plasmados en su minucioso *Anglicismos hispánicos*, cúmulo de observaciones referidas propiamente a la influencia léxica y sintáctica anglo sobre la lengua española y, en forma de atisbos, a la influencia cultural de los países anglohablantes.

Lorenzo comunicó sus limitaciones para considerar lo no verbal, "modas y costumbres como el silbido de admiración a la mujer hermosa, difundido por las películas norteamericanas, y menos original que el piropo" según escribía en 1955. Lo suyo era lo lingüístico. Pese a ello, años después volvía a mencionar cambios en las "predilecciones sartoriales o alimentarias {…} como en otras manifestaciones del trato social – silbidos por piropos, cumpleaños cantados a coro – u omisiones (abandono de la comunicación epistolar), antes desconocidas o inusitadas" que se daban en la Península (en "Anglicismos", M. Seco y G. Salvador, coordinadores, *La lengua española, hoy*, 1995, p. 171).

De pareja mudanza de costumbres se han hecho registros en otros países, Panamá es ejemplo, donde "en la mayoría de nuestros hogares no se celebra ya una *fiesta de cumpleaños*, se ignora la *fecha de nacimiento*, el *natalicio*, el *onomástico*, se ha abandonado la vieja costumbre de mandar a preparar, como acontecía en algunos pueblos de nuestras provincias, una gran rosca, cuidadosamente elaborada, en homenaje a la persona que ajustaba un año más de vida". (B. Isaza Calderón, *Correcciones de lenguaje*, 1965, p. 77).

La primera aparición del *Diccionario de anglicismos* obtuvo entre los hispanohablantes juicios celebratorios. Menudearon las enhorabuenas y aprobaciones de parte de varones ilustres. En el Congreso de las Academias de la Lengua Española, de 1951, en México, una resolución lo recomendó. (Se añadió esta información en la sobrecubierta en la edición del tomo madrileño).

A los que elogiaban el diccionario, casi siempre hablistas y profesionales de lengua española, los atrajo que fuera, cronológicamente, si no el primero, uno de los primeros de su tipo en cuanto repertorio de anglicismos, que tenía amonestaciones para los usuarios (lectores en general o profesionales de distinto orden) y que hacía una defensa del español, que consideraban atacado, desatendido o indefenso.

Dos campos semánticos se distinguían claramente en el léxico de los que escribían en esa vena refiriéndose a anglicismos: el de la higiene (*profilaxis*, *terapéutica*, etc.), por una parte, y el bélico (*enemigo*, *invasión*, *guerra*, etc.), por otra, que hoy se mantienen. La actitud que de ahí surge se justifica por la voluntad de oponerse a lo que Lorenzo proponía como "lo que pudiéramos llamar agravios a la lengua patria", de raíz política o, acaso, misoneísta. Esto se nota particularmente entre los reseñadores de Panamá, lugar de nacimiento de Alfaro y de la primera edición del diccionario. Los de mayor talante para las ciencias del lenguaje coincidieron en destacar el conocimiento de las dos lenguas de Alfaro – aunque también manejaba el francés – que le permitía discernir estupendamente y discurrir sobre voces patrimoniales; su actitud no necesariamente purista sino de defensa de lo patrimonial junto con su independencia de criterio frente a la consideración de los fenómenos del lenguaje, postura que lo llevaba a la aceptación de lo neológico siempre que no violentara la sintaxis expresiva o los matices léxicos del español; el idioma como representación de la nacionalidad que, debido a la presencia estadounidense como difusora principal de anglicismos en Panamá – véase E. Alvarado de Ricord, "El español en contacto con el inglés" *Homenaje a Ambrosio Rabanales*, BFUCh XXXI (1980–1981) – justificaba que Alfaro compusiera su diccionario y la mayor resistencia cultural de la Península al influjo ánglico, lo que, andando el tiempo, de algún modo se modificó, ya que E. Lorenzo mismo finalmente recurrió a un título que remite a esto: "El anglicismo, *problema* hispánico" (BFUCh XXV – 1995–1996 –). (Destacado añadido).

Pero también hubo comentaristas desafectos. Los menos atentos a lo político y a lo afectivo, más alejados del temeroso Rubén Darío de "¿Tantos millones de hombres hablaremos inglés?" (interrogación intuida en muchos de los que aprobaban la obra de Alfaro) y más severos en cuanto a exigencias de la ciencia del lenguaje, prefirieron señalar la localización del diccionario dentro de lo que se ha llamado "lingüística pre-científica". Es decir, la de los conocedores del lenguaje, de percepciones o afirmaciones certeras pero no desarrolladas con el rigor metódico que la ciencia reclama. Para resumirlos en uno solo, el profesor inglés Chris Pratt, meticuloso y perspicaz, en una valoración de varios años de después de la primera salida del diccionario, encontró que "la obra en sí constituye una muestra a la vez que una continuación de la escuela hispanoamericana fundada por Bello y Cuervo en el siglo XIX: normativista, prescriptiva y proscriptiva" (p. 91) "cuya meta principal consiste en erradicar los errores y vicios de dicción" (p. 95). (C. Pratt, *El anglicismo en el español peninsular contemporáneo*, 1980).

El Diccionario de Alfaro acicateó, no obstante, para seguir considerando la influencia del inglés sobre el español contemporáneo de América o de la Península. Hoy miles de artículos, notas, ensayos y libros – acaso mucho más que miles – tratan el tema desde distintas perspectivas, y repetidamente toman en cuenta a Alfaro, con aceptación o con rechazo respetuoso, pero nunca total. Resultado de ello, y dedicados específicamente al español europeo, aparecieron el *Nuevo diccionario de anglicismos* (1997) y el copioso *Gran diccionario de anglicismos* (2017), inventarios de autores de una lexicografía más profesionalizada, que iba ganando espacio y perfilándose entre las disciplinas lingüísticas. Aquel era de F. Rodríguez G. y A. Lillo, y éste, compilado por cuenta y riesgo del criterioso Félix Rodríguez González, de quien los investigadores agradecen los aportes teóricos y prácticos aparecidos en sus libros o artículos de revistas.

De todos modos, del diccionario de Alfaro todavía hoy puede rescatarse su aporte valioso, y por ello sigue considerándosele un hito. Sirve, por ejemplo, para discernir entre los parónimos del inglés y del español, algunos de los cuales finalmente se encuentran incorporados con el significado que le ha infiltrado el inglés a la forma española. O bien cumple para entender diferencias que gobiernan la sintaxis de ambas lenguas. Asimismo, y de manera más general, lo que les conviene mucho a los historiadores del español, consigna el estado de lengua previo a la inclusión de los anglicismos léxico-semánticos que empezaron a asentarse a partir del siglo XIX.

Cuando en un texto de antes de aquel siglo se incluye una palabra como *reportar*, no en tanto "transmitir, comunicar, dar noticia", significado tan común a partir de la segunda parte del siglo XX, sino con el de "refrenar, reprimir o moderar una pasión o ánimo o a quien la tiene", hay que valerse del significado patrimonial, desplazado por contacto con el inglés, aunque "dar noticia", arrolladoramente frecuente en el uso cotidiano, sea la última de las siete acepciones del diccionario académico de hoy para la voz *reportar*. Este tipo de enseñanza es el que permanece del *Diccionario de anglicismos*.

Al presentar su traducción ya clásica del *Curso de lingüística general* de Ferdinand de Saussure, Amado Alonso reflexionó que "Con este prólogo quisiera hacer ver al lector cómo la ciencia es tarea que se va cumpliendo sin detenerse nunca, y cómo puede un sabio ser tan ilustre por los problemas que se plantea y resuelve como por los que obliga a sus colegas y sucesores a replantear y resolver". Proporciones guardadas, mención parecida se merece el *Diccionario de Anglicismos* de Ricardo J. Alfaro por la ahora larga estela de estudios sobre el anglicismo en el español surgidos a raíz de su volumen inicial.

Juan Gómez Capuz

Grupo VAL.ES.CO.

Universitat de València

Anglicismos en el español oral y coloquial: uso real de anglicismos y distribución sociolingüística en el habla urbana

1. El estudio del anglicismo en el registro coloquial. problemas metodológicos

En este artículo abordaremos la cuestión del anglicismo en el español coloquial a partir de los materiales suministrados por nuestra Tesis Doctoral *Anglicismos en español actual: su estudio en el registro coloquial* (1997) y obtenidos a partir de grabaciones coloquiales de hablantes en la zona metropolitana de Valencia entre 1993 y 1996. No obstante, en la primera parte del trabajo también tendremos en cuenta los resultados obtenidos entre 1971 y 1988 a partir de un proyecto sobre el conocimiento y uso de los anglicismos en la norma lingüística culta de las principales ciudades de España e Hispanoamérica, con estudios de destacados lingüista como Quilis, Lope Blanch y López Morales.

2. Método de encuesta sobre el habla urbana culta de acuerdo con el cuestionario del PILEI. valoración y crítica

Uno de los principales métodos de encuesta empleados para la cuantificación de la densidad y frecuencia de uso de los anglicismos léxicos fue el desarrollado por el "Proyecto de estudio coordinado de la norma lingüística culta de las principales ciudades de Iberoamérica y de la Península Ibérica".

El estudio del anglicismo se basa, en principio, en un cuestionario léxico (Departamento de Geografía Lingüística, 1971), constituido por 4.452 preguntas organizadas en 21 áreas temáticas; este cuestionario debería ser aplicado a un mínimo de 12 informantes, representativos de las diversas variables sociales (edad, sexo y nivel sociocultural).

Esta metodología ha sido puesta en práctica en diversos trabajos, los cuales se extienden en un amplio lapso de tiempo; ahora bien, constituyen en conjunto el primer estudio del anglicismo en diversas ciudades del mundo hispanohablante, con un rigor metodológico aceptable y con datos comparables entre sí. En este trabajo nos limitaremos a los estudios que analizan el léxico global, es decir, los que aplican todas las preguntas de los 21 campos léxicos:

- H. López Morales (1971) para el habla de La Habana;
- J.M. Lope Blanch (1972) para el habla de Ciudad de México;
- A. Quilis (1984) para el habla de Madrid;
- Z.Pérez de González (1984) para el habla de Caracas;
- H. López Morales (1987) para el habla de San Juan de Puerto Rico;
- L. Contreras (1988) para el habla de Santiago de Chile.

Seguidamente, comentaremos los aspectos cuantitativos más relevantes de todos estos trabajos y las deducciones comparativas que de ellos podamos inferir:

2.1. Datos sociolingüísticos

En primer lugar, todos estos trabajos se inician con una descripción rigurosa de la metodología empleada (de acuerdo con el proyecto del PILEI):

(a) Se ha aplicado el volumen III del Cuestionario, relativo al léxico, el cual consta de 4.452 preguntas repartidas en 21 campos léxicos o áreas temáticas.
(b) Los informantes han sido seleccionados de modo que aparezcan representadas todas las variables sociales (sexo, edad y nivel sociocultural): el Proyecto prevee un mínimo de 12 informantes (como hacen H. López Morales, 1971 y Z. Pérez de González 1984), pero algunos estudios presentan cantidades superiores: L. Contreras (1988) trabaja con 13 informantes, A. Quilis con 16 y J.M. Lope Blanch (1972) con 24.

2.2. Densidad absoluta y densidad relativa

El dato cuantitativo más importante es la **densidad absoluta** de los anglicismos en el corpus recogido. Tomamos como base las 4.452 preguntas del Cuestionario; pero a causa de las diferencias en el número de informantes de cada trabajo de campo y otros factores menores de distorsión (algunas preguntas quedan sin respuesta, otras obtienen respuestas múltiples), se obtiene entre todos los informantes un **universo léxico** que oscila entre 12.000 y 60.000 unidades. De este total, un determinado tanto por ciento – entre el 1 % y el 7 % – lo constituyen **anglicismos**, y dicho tanto por ciento recibe el nombre de **densidad absoluta**.

La **densidad absoluta** del anglicismo en las diferentes ciudades del mundo hispánico es la siguiente:

La Habana	0,75 %
Ciudad de México:	≈ 3 %
Madrid:	1,73 %
Caracas:	3,47 %
San Juan de Puerto Rico:	≈5 %
Santiago de Chile:	4,11 %

Así pues, es comprensible la baja densidad de anglicismos en el español peninsular, pero sorprenden algunos de los datos relativos a las capitales americanas: la baja densidad de Ciudad de México y La Habana y la alta de Santiago de Chile contrastan de manera radical con las opiniones impresionistas de los autores que, por un lado consideran México y Cuba zonas de fuerte influencia inglesa – como comenta críticamente H. López Morales (1971: 86) – y por otro subordinan la influencia anglicista a la proximidad geográfica con Estados Unidos (el caso de Santiago de Chile lo desmiente).

La **densidad absoluta** es también un dato fiable desde otra perspectiva: como se mide el total de empleos de anglicismos por relación al total de empleos de unidades léxicas, se tiene presente la **frecuencia de uso** de los anglicismos, aunque no se mida directamente. En otras palabras, si en una determinada ciudad se registran numerosos anglicismos base, pero la mayoría son esporádicos, la densidad absoluta será menor que en una ciudad donde haya pocos anglicismos base pero de uso general entre los informantes.

La **densidad relativa**, en cambio, consiste precisamente en el tanto por ciento de **anglicismos base** ("lexemas diferenciados") respecto del total teórico de las 4.452 preguntas del Cuestionario. Por ello, la densidad relativa es un dato menos significativo, ya que no tiene en cuenta el factor de la frecuencia de uso. Así pues, los datos sobre la **densidad relativa** en los trabajos citados pueden resultar engañosos, ya que al no tener presente en el cómputo que gran parte de los anglicismos son de uso esporádico entre los informantes, los porcentajes suelen ser muy elevados:

La Habana	1,4 %
Ciudad de México:	4 %
Madrid:	5,2 %
Caracas:	6,3 %
San Juan de Puerto Rico:	6,5 %
Santiago de Chile:	4,1 %

2.3. Vitalidad de uso y frecuencia de los anglicismos

Ocurre que no todos los anglicismos gozan de la misma **vitalidad de uso** o **frecuencia**. Algunos, muy pocos, son empleados por el total de los informantes, lo cual constituye una frecuencia del 100 %; en cambio, otros anglicismos sólo son elicitados por un informante (lo cual supone una frecuencia del 4 % al 8 %, según el número de informantes de cada estudio). Siendo los anglicismos -y los extranjerismos en general- una categoría léxica inestable en la lengua receptora, cuyo conocimiento se limita frecuentemente a determinados grupos sociales y profesionales, es de suponer que buena parte de los anglicismos registrados serán de uso esporádico, y que los anglicismos "de uso general" (Lope Blanch, 1972: 193) o de uso frecuente constituyan una exigua minoría. Esta opinión se confirma en los datos de las encuestas, donde se observa una cierta homogeneidad en las seis ciudades, ya que el porcentaje de anglicismos de uso esporádico es muy superior al porcentaje de anglicismos de uso general; el único caso particular es el de ciudad de México, donde los anglicismos "de uso general" son muy frecuentes (llegan al 40 % del total de anglicismos base).

Así pues, podemos distinguir cinco categorías de anglicismos según su **frecuencia de uso** entre los informantes, siguiendo las clasificaciones de J.M. Lope Blanch (1972), A. Quilis (1984) y H. López Morales (1987):

CIUDAD	GENERALES	MUY USUALES	USO MEDIO	POCO USADOS	ESPORADICOS
México D.F.:	40 %	16 %	13 %	18 %	16 %
Madrid:	9 %	21 %	9 %	21 %	35 %
Caracas:	11 %	-----	-----	-----	39 %
San Juan:	5,6 %	19 %	18 %	21 %	35 %
Santiago:	10 %	-----	-----	-----	28 %

2.4. Frecuencia de uso de los anglicismos y alternancia con equivalentes españoles

Los autores que siguen esta metodología -en especial, A. Quilis (1984) y H. López Morales (1987) – dan a continuación del **anglicismo** el número de informantes que lo han empleado, y tras él, el signo "::" que introduce las restantes voces españolas que alternan con dicho anglicismo como respuesta a una misma pregunta. Ilustraremos esta cuestión con ejemplos tomados de A .Quilis (1984) para el habla de Madrid:

"*barman* (10; :: "camarero" 10, "coctelero" 2 y "chaval", "tabernero", "vinatero")";
"*suéter* (8; :: "jersey" 8, "chaqueta" 2 y "rebeca")";
"*spray* (4; :: "pulverizador" 7, "perfumador", "rociador" y "atomizador"; sin respuesta en 1) ".

Este análisis comparativo de los **anglicismos** y sus **equivalentes** castellanos resulta muy útil, a nuestro entender, para determinar el grado de **integración léxico-semántica** del anglicismo. En efecto, este análisis nos permite saber si el anglicismo es el único término empleado para designar un concepto u objeto y, si no es así, con qué términos españoles alterna, lo cual constituye un amplio banco de datos para posteriores estudios sobre la semántica de los anglicismos.

2.5. Diferencias en el empleo del anglicismo en función de las variables sociales

Aunque los informantes seleccionados para estas encuestas son representativos de las diversas variables sociales, los autores extraen escasas conclusiones sobre la posible covariación entre los datos lingüísticos (preferencia por el anglicismo o por los equivalentes españoles) y las variables sociales:

(a) J.M. Lope Blanch (1972: 193) pone de relieve que el corpus corresponde al habla urbana de individuos de nivel cultural superior y que viajan por el extranjero. Por tanto, como apunta H. López Morales (1971: 87), es de suponer que la densidad de anglicismos será menor en informantes de nivel sociocultural inferior y en zonas rurales.
(b) A. Quilis (1984: 420) pone en relación el uso de anglicismos con la variable edad: aunque, como era previsible, es la generación de más edad la menos proclive al empleo de anglicismos en Madrid, los porcentajes de los otros tres estratos de edad están bastante igualados, lo cual parece contradecir la idea apriorística de que el uso del anglicismo es casi exclusivo de los jóvenes españoles.

2.6. Problemas que suscita la metodología del PILEI. Propuestas alternativas

(a) Reconoce J.M. Lope Blanch (1972: 193) el hecho de que las respuestas a las preguntas del cuestionario "léxico" del PILEI suelen ser sustantivos, categoría a la que pertenecen la inmensa mayoría de los anglicismos. Por ello, sospecha que en la cadena hablada, la proporción de anglicismos será mucho menor. En ese sentido, H. López Morales (1971: 80–81) ya realizó un doble estudio para el español de La Habana: frente a un 1,42 % de anglicismos de acuerdo con el cuestionario léxico del PILEI, obtiene tan sólo un 0,05 % de anglicismos en discurso libre (conversación grabada).

(b) Sin embargo, los autores que han aplicado el método del PILEI, como J.M. Lope Blanch (1972: 200), A .Quilis (1984: 421), Z. Pérez de González (1984: 146) y H. López Morales (1987: 303) reconocen que el **discurso libre** (conversación libre grabada o técnica de serie abierta), pese a arrojar una densidad de anglicismos mucho menor, podría dar cuenta de ciertos elementos foráneos que no se elicitan nunca en una encuesta.

(c) En esta cuestión incide J. López Chávez (1991: 777–780) en su crítica de conjunto a la metodología del PILEI. Este autor se centra en las cuestiones de **conocimiento** y **uso**: el cuestionario del PILEI se limita a analizar el **conocimiento** de una realidad, normalmente un conocimiento pasivo; por ello, aparecen con bajas frecuencias -o ni siquiera aparecen- ciertos anglicismos que, aunque no encajen bien en las preguntas de la encuesta, pertenecen claramente al uso activo de los hispanohablantes urbanos. En suma, J. López Chávez pone en duda que el cuestionario del PILEI responda a criterios funcionales y dinámicos de **uso** y propone la **lexicometría** -en especial, el **coeficiente de disponibilidad**- como método alternativo para ofrecer una visión más exacta del uso de los extranjerismos en español.

3. Estudio sobre un corpus coloquial de habla urbana en 1993–1997

El aspecto más novedoso de nuestra Tesis Doctoral ha sido el de estudiar un fenómeno característico de los lenguajes técnicos -el préstamo- en la variedad diafásica más alejada de ellos, el lenguaje coloquial. Según Meillet y otros autores, los préstamos culturales se producen entre tecnolectos homólogos de dos lenguas históricas (p. ej. lenguaje deportivo inglés y español) y tardan bastante en llegar -por intermedio de otros agentes, como los medios de comunicación de masas- al lenguaje coloquial, donde presentan curiosas alteraciones semánticas (generalización, usos figurados, etc.). Para poder analizar este proceso, hemos dividido el corpus en unas áreas temáticas amplias (clasificación onomasiológica) que suelen corresponderse con tecnolectos especialmente permeables a la influencia angloamericana: deporte, música moderna, espectáculos, tecnología e informática.

De todas maneras, por las razones indicadas, supongo que suena extraño oír hablar del anglicismo en el lenguaje coloquial. De hecho, mi propósito inicial era estudiar el anglicismo conforme mandan los cánones, tratando los principales problemas (asimilación fónica, gramatical y semántica) en un corpus extraído de algún lenguaje técnico o, como mucho, de los medios de comunicación de masas, como así hice en mi Tesis de Licenciatura.

Sin embargo, mi pertenencia al grupo de investigación VAL.ES.CO. (Valencia Español Coloquial) de la Universidad de Valencia, centrado en el estudio del español coloquial, me empujaba de manera natural hacia otros temas más propios de esta variedad diafásica, hasta que en un momento dado decidí plantear el matrimonio imposible: seguir estudiando el anglicismo pero trabajando sobre un amplio corpus de lenguaje coloquial.

Tras solventar diversos problemas metodológicos (en especial, la dificultad de extraer muestras de habla oral espontánea y, sobre todo, la escasísima frecuencia de aparición de los anglicismos en el español coloquial), a partir del análisis de unas 100 horas de grabación pude obtener un corpus representativo: más bien pequeño con relación a los parámetros de una Tesis Doctoral, pero susceptible de permitir un completo análisis de las estrategias de asimilación del préstamo en diversos niveles (fónico, gramatical y semántico).

Así pues, el corpus de esta Tesis Doctoral consta de 922 usos de anglicismos (u *ocurrencias*), los cuales corresponden a 223 anglicismos base. Además de los anglicismos propiamente dichos, también hemos tenido en cuenta los equivalentes españoles empleados por los informantes (p.ej. *póster/cartel, ticket/billete, basket/baloncesto*) con el objeto de determinar el grado de frecuencia y vitalidad de los anglicismos en cada área temática: así pues, hemos registrado 370 ocurrencias de equivalentes españoles, correspondientes a 98 equivalentes base. En conclusión, los datos cuantitativos de nuestro corpus quedan como sigue:

	TIPOS/BASE	**OCURRENCIAS/EMPLEOS**
ANGLICISMOS	223	922
EQUIVALENTES	98	370
TOTAL	321	1292

Por tanto, este trabajo se centrará en la distribución sociológica de anglicismos y de su concurrencia con los equivalentes castellanos, teniendo muy en cuenta la estratificación social de los informantes (con las variables sociales "nivel sociocultural", "edad" y "sexo") y las áreas temáticas consideradas. En función de estos elementos y mediante la aplicación de la metodología sociolingüística, podremos confirmar (o rebatir) opiniones intuitivas y apriorísticas e impresionistas como el predominio de los anglicismos en los informantes de nivel sociocultural alto y edad joven frente a la ausencia de anglicismos o abundancia de equivalentes castellanos en el habla de los informantes nivel sociocultural bajo y edad avanzada, así como el supuesto predominio de los informantes de uno u otro sexo en ciertas áreas temáticas (mujeres en "vestuario" y "casa", hombres en "deportes" e "informática ").

3.1. Problemas metodológicos

En las fichas técnicas de las grabaciones que constituyen el corpus de español coloquial del área metropolitana de Valencia de que dispone el grupo VAL. ES.CO, se registra el nivel sociocultural, edad, sexo y lengua materna de los informantes (*cf.* Briz et al., 1995: 18–19).

Por tanto, sería posible estudiar posibles casos de **covariación** entre estas **variables sociales o sociológicas** registradas en la ficha técnica y algunas **variables léxicas** (p. ej. distribución de los anglicismos y equivalentes en determinadas áreas onomasiológicas), con el objeto de enriquecer con consideraciones sociolingüísticas el análisis lingüístico descriptivo que ofrecimos en nuestra Tesis Doctoral y, por tanto, poder acercarnos al ideal de enfoque mixto -lingüístico y sociológico- que propusieron Haugen y Weinreich, pioneros en el estudio de la interferencia lingüística y de la propia sociolingüística.

Sin embargo, este propósito tropieza con algunas deficiencias metodológicas, derivadas del carácter provisional del corpus citado y de nuestro particular objeto de estudio en este trabajo (*vid.* Moreno Fernández, 1990):

1. El amplio corpus de lengua oral de que dispone el grupo VAL.ESCO. evidencia de momento un cierto predominio de informantes jóvenes y de nivel sociocultural medio.
2. Otro problema ha sido el reducido número de empleos con que operamos en cada caso; por tanto, nuestras conclusiones tienen en la práctica un mero valor indicativo.

En suma, estas dos deficiencias metodológicas limitan nuestros objetivos en el presente trabajo. No pretendemos, por tanto, descubrir clarísimas y estrictas situaciones de **covariación** entre las variables sociales y las variables lingüísticas (aspectos lexico-semánticos y onomasiológicos del anglicismo). Tan sólo pretendemos verificar algunas **tendencias** generales, muchas de ellas obvias (p. ej. predominio de informantes jóvenes en el ámbito de la "música moderna y tribus urbanas", predominio de informantes de sexo femenino en áreas como "alimentación", "vestuario" y "la casa"), pero formuladas hasta ahora desde una perspectiva puramente intuitiva e "impresionista" (como ha criticado, entre otros, López Morales, 1979 y 1987), sin haber extraído previamente un corpus estratificado de datos reales, orales y espontáneos, como el que sustenta nuestro análisis, pese a las deficiencias indicadas.

3.2. Distribución sociológica del corpus total

En primer lugar, ofreceremos los datos globales de la distribución de los **anglicismos** y **equivalentes** de nuestro corpus en función de las diversas variables sociales, teniendo presente el claro predominio de ciertos sectores sociales, como hemos indicado (estrato de edad más joven; estratos socioculturales medio y alto).

3.2.1. Variable "edad"

En efecto, esta variable ofrece un predominio relativo del estrato menor de 25 años, aunque también es reseñable el importante porcentaje del estrato de edad intermedio: no obstante, cabría matizar que la frontera generacional es relativa, ya que buena parte de los 417 empleos del estrato de edad intermedio corresponden a estudiantes de postgrado, profesores de instituto y universidad menores de 40 años, edad que -a nuestro entender- puede marcar la frontera entre el **uso** de anglicismos y su mero **conocimiento** pasivo. Por su parte, como era previsible, el número de empleos que corresponden al estrato de edad más avanzado (mayores de 55 años) es muy reducido, ya que constituyen una generación ajena a este tipo de influencia foránea sobre el español.

Por tanto, el reparto de los anglicismos según estratos de edad es el siguiente:

menores de 25 años: 447 empleos (48,48 %)
entre 26 y 55 años: 417 empleos (45,22 %)
mayores de 55 años: 58 empleos (6,29 %).

Curiosamente, la distribución de los **equivalentes** castellanos entre los diversos estratos de edad ofrece unos porcentajes similares a los de los **anglicismos**: esto podría ser un indicio de que tanto anglicismos como equivalentes verbalizan realidades propias de la sociedad urbana moderna, las cuales quedan fuera del vocabulario "consolidado" y "cerrado" de los informantes mayores de 55 años:

menores de 25 años: 178 empleos (48,10 %)
entre 26 y 55 años: 162 empleos (43,78 %)
mayores de 55 años: 30 empleos (8,10 %).

3.2.2. Variable "sexo"

Esta variable arroja un porcentaje mayor de anglicismos correspondientes a informantes de sexo masculino, en concreto un 58,78 % (542 empleos) frente al 41,21 % (380 empleos) de los informantes de sexo femenino. Sin embargo, no creemos que estos datos correspondan a una mayor inclinación de los hombres hacia el empleo de anglicismos. Al contrario, estos datos se deben al carácter aleatorio de esta muestra de lengua oral coloquial: en este sentido, debemos indicar que las grabaciones con mayor número de anglicismos correspondían siempre a conversaciones entre hombres:

- [S 1 A.1], [H 5 B.1] y [H 19 B.1] para la música moderna y "tribus urbanas";
- [XP 48 A.1] y [H 38 A.1] para la informática;
- [H 11 A.1+B.1], [H 54 A.1], [G 92 A.1], [G 93 + G 94 A.1], [LR 110 A.1] y [G 206 A.1] para el deporte.

En cambio, en cuanto a los **equivalentes** castellanos, se produce una completa igualdad entre los porcentajes de ambos sexos: 50,27 % (186 empleos) para los informantes de sexo masculino y 49,73 % (184 empleos) para los de sexo femenino.

3.2.3. Variable "estrato sociocultural"

Esta variable confirma el predominio de los informantes del estrato medio:

estrato alto: 270 empleos (29,28 %)
estrato medio: 565 empleos (61,27 %)
estrato bajo: 87 empleos (9,43 %)

Ahora bien, el porcentaje de los informantes de estrato alto es muy importante en términos relativos, ya que, constituyendo una exigua porción del total de informantes de nuestras grabaciones, dan lugar al 29,28 % de los empleos de anglicismos en nuestro corpus. En otras palabras, las conversaciones en las que la mayoría de los informantes son de estrato alto ([XP 48 A.1], [G 92 A.1], [G 93 + G 94 A.1], [AA 81 A.1+B.1]) registran una elevada densidad de anglicismos (desde los más técnicos de la informática a los más usuales del deporte, la música moderna y la política).

Otra prueba de la elevada densidad de anglicismos en el habla de los informantes de estrato sociocultural alto es el hecho de que, en la distribución sociológica de los **equivalentes** castellanos el predominio del estrato medio es casi absoluto, mientras que el porcentaje del estrato alto no es muy superior al del estrato bajo: en otras palabras, no son los **equivalentes** castellanos, sino los **anglicismos** (por su aura de modernidad, tecnicismo, cosmopolitismo, esnobismo y afectación) los que atraen la atención -y el uso- de los hablantes de estrato alto. En efecto, la distribución de los **equivalentes** castellanos por estratos sociales es la siguiente:

estrato alto: 75 empleos (20,27 %)
estrato medio: 249 empleos (67,29 %)
estrato bajo: 46 empleos (12,43 %)

3.3. Distribución por áreas temáticas

A la hora de emprender el análisis semántico y sociolingüístico de los **anglicismos** y **equivalentes** castellanos que conforman nuestro corpus de lengua coloquial, necesitamos algún tipo de clasificación que vertebre en grupos homogéneos un nivel tan escasamente estructurado como es el léxico. Por ello, creemos conveniente partir de una clasificación del corpus por **áreas temáticas**. Se trata, pues, de una **clasificación onomasiológica**, recurso ya utilizado por los propios pioneros en el estudio del préstamo lingüístico (Salverda, Vidos) .

En nuestra opinión, el modelo más completo de clasificación onomasiológica del léxico español actual corresponde al "Proyecto de estudio coordinado de la norma lingüística culta de las principales ciudades de Iberoamérica y de la Península Ibérica", desarrollado por el PILEI y estudiado en el apartado anterior. Así pues, la clasificación onomasiológica del proyecto del PILEI -con ciertos retoques- constituirá nuestro modelo de organización temática del corpus de **anglicismos** y **equivalentes**.

Por lo que respecta a las diversas **áreas temáticas** surgidas de esta clasificación onomasiológica, señalaremos algunos aspectos relevantes:

(a) La proporción entre anglicismos base y número de empleos (lo que podríamos denominar "concentración léxica").
(b) La relación que se establece entre los anglicismos y los equivalentes/sinónimos españoles.
(c) El carácter denotativo, técnico o afectivo de los anglicismos. Los anglicismos denotativos o necesarios designan una realidad nueva o al menos no cubierta previamente por un sinónimo o equivalente de la lengua receptora, por lo cual actúan en el plano denotativo (un caso extremo de ellos son los **xenismos**, los cuales designan una realidad exclusiva de la cultura extranjera y desconocida en la nuestra). En cambio, los préstamos connotativos o innecesarios ya tienen sinónimos o equivalentes en la lengua receptora, y por tanto se suelen emplear con valores afectivos (esnobismo, humor, parodia).

3.3.1. Área temática "alimentación"

DATOS GLOBALES

	tipos/base	**ocurrencias/empleos**
anglicismos	15	69
equivalentes	1	5

En el área temática **alimentación** se observa una clara distinción entre ciertos anglicismos de uso frecuente, perfectamente aclimatados a la vida cotidiana española (*cocacola, güisqui*), y otros anglicismos de empleo esporádico que revelan su "aura de exotismo" y su condición de **xenismos** (*maltesers, M&Ms, after eight, after six*). Ahora bien, todos ellos son préstamos denotativos que verbalizan comidas y bebidas procedentes del mundo anglosajón.

En cuanto a la distribución sociológica de los anglicismos, hemos advertido estas tendencias:

a) La hipótesis "impresionista" del predominio de los informantes de sexo femenino en este ámbito no concuerda con los datos obtenidos: 37 empleos por parte de mujeres (53,62 %), 32 empleos por parte de hombres (46,37 %).
b) Pese al predominio cuantitativo de los empleos correspondientes a los informantes del estrato de edad más joven, debemos destacar los elevados porcentajes alcanzados por los informantes de los estratos de edad intermedio y avanzado. En efecto, el reparto por estratos de edad es el siguiente:
   menores de 25 años: 38 empleos (55,07 %)
   entre 26 y 55 años: 22 empleos (31,88 %)
   mayores de 55 años: 9 empleos (13,63 %).
c) En cuanto a la distribución por estratos sociales, hemos constatado el abrumador predominio de empleos de informantes de estrato sociocultural medio (72,46 %).

3.3.2. Área temática "vestuario"

DATOS GLOBALES

	tipos/base	**ocurrencias/empleos**
anglicismos	8	34
equivalentes	2	24

En el área temática **vestuario** advertimos una fuerte "concentración léxica": consta de pocos anglicismos base, pero éstos son de uso muy frecuente. Como la alta frecuencia de uso afecta tanto a los **anglicismos** como a los **equivalentes** españoles, también podemos concluir que nuestros informantes se han decantado claramente por unos o por otros en función de criterios difíciles de determinar: así, *jersey, suéter* y *biquini* no sufren la concurrencia de posibles equivalentes nativos, mientras que *vaquero(s)/pantalón vaquero* y *calzoncillo* han desplazado por completo del uso hablado espontáneo a *blue jeans/jeans* y *slip* .

En cuanto a la distribución sociológica de los anglicismos del área temática del **vestuario**, ahora sí hemos constatado el esperable predominio de informantes femeninos o de los informantes de los estratos de edad intermedia y avanzada:

a) El predominio de los informantes de sexo femenino es evidente: 27 empleos (79,41 %) frente a 7 de los informantes masculinos (20,58 %), limitados además a los anglicismos *suéter* y *jersey* .
b) La importancia cuantitativa de los empleos correspondientes a los estratos de edad intermedio y mayor de 55 años es muy clara en esta área temática, una de las pocas donde los empleos correspondientes a informantes de edad inferior a 25 años son minoritarios:
   menores de 25 años: 7 empleos (20,58 %)
   entre 26 y 55 años: 19 empleos (55,88 %)
   mayores de 55 años: 8 empleos (23,52 %)
c) Si tenemos en cuenta que los anglicismos relativos al vestuario suelen ser préstamos relativamente antiguos (*jersey, suéter, nylon, biquini*) ampliamente difundidos entre informantes de sexo femenino y estrato sociocultural medio y bajo, podemos afirmar que nos encontramos ante una de las escasas áreas temáticas donde el predominio corresponde al estrato sociocultural bajo, escasamente representado en el conjunto de nuestro corpus:
   estrato alto: 4 empleos (11,46 %)
   estrato medio: 15 empleos (44,11 %)
   estrato bajo: 15 empleos (44,11 %)

En suma, los anglicismos tradicionales y domésticos correspondientes al área temática del "vestuario" confirman su perfecta aclimatación en sectores sociales poco propicios al empleo de extranjerismos, en particular, las mujeres de edad intermedia o avanzada y estrato sociocultural medio y bajo.

3.3.3. *Área temática "la casa"*

DATOS GLOBALES

	tipos/base	**ocurrencias/empleos**
anglicismos	9	55
equivalentes	4	20

En el área temática **la casa** advertimos nuevamente una fuerte "concentración léxica": los anglicismos base son escasos, pero de uso muy frecuente en el habla cotidiana, ya que la mayoría de ellos lexicalizan nuevas realidades domésticas (*spray, póster, váter, grill*).

En cuanto a la distribución sociológica de estos anglicismos, hemos constatado de nuevo un cierto predominio informantes femeninos o de informantes del estrato de edad intermedio, aunque con menor claridad que en las dos áreas temáticas anteriores.

a) De nuevo, registramos un claro predominio de los informantes de sexo femenino: 37 empleos (67,27 %) frente a 18 de informantes masculinos (33,72 %).
b) Pese al elevado número de empleos correspondientes a los informantes del estrato de edad más joven, debemos destacar el alto porcentaje alcanzado por los informantes del estrato de edad intermedio:
   menores de 25 años: 30 empleos (54,54 %)
   entre 26 y 55 años: 20 empleos (36,36 %)
   mayores de 55 años: 1 empleo (1,81 %)
c) En cuanto a su distribución sociológica, hemos obtenido estos datos:
   estrato alto: 6 empleos (10,90 %)
   estrato medio: 39 empleos (70,90 %)
   estrato bajo: 10 empleos (18,18 %)

Por tanto, los anglicismos relativos al área temática de "la casa" presentarían una distribución sociológica similar a la del área "alimentación": predominio de informantes de sexo femenino; ligero predominio de los informantes menores de 25 años sobre los del estrato de edad intermedio; claro predominio de los informantes de estrato sociocultural medio. Así pues, se trata de la distribución sociológica esperable en dos áreas temáticas que comprenden anglicismos designadores de realidades cotidianas y domésticas (de ahí la superioridad de informantes de sexo femenino), aunque sin perder un ligero matiz de modernidad y "americanización" (visible en *cocacola, póster, light*) que justifica el predominio del estrato de edad más joven y el estrato social intermedio.

3.3.4. *Area temática "vida amorosa y sexualidad".*

DATOS GLOBALES

	tipos/base	**ocurrencias/empleos**
anglicismos	8	11
equivalentes	5	25

El área temática **vida amorosa y sexualidad** es cuantitativamente limitada (tanto en anglicismos base como en número de empleos), pero muy representativa de las nuevas actitudes y valores de inspiración anglosajona. En este campo se observa una clara "concentración lexicogenésica": 5 de los 8 anglicismos corresponden a dos familias léxicas, *flirteo* y *flirtear* por un lado, y *sexy*, *sex-shop* y *sex-appeal* por otro.

Los 11 empleos de anglicismos correspondientes al área temática de **vida amorosa y sexualidad** presentan un perfil sociológico muy definido:

a) La variable sexo no es relevante en este caso: 5 empleos de informantes de sexo femenino y 6 de sexo masculino.
b) La edad sí es determinante: 10 empleos (90,90 %) corresponden al estrato de edad intermedio (más bien, 26–40), quizá porque pertenecen a una generación que necesita "relexicalizar" sus concepciones sobre la vida amorosa y la sexualidad.
c) El estrato sociocultural se convierte también en una variable determinante, ya que los empleos correspondientes a informantes de estrato alto constituyen el 81,81 %, lo cual confirma el carácter eufemístico, cosmopolita y sofisticado de los anglicismos correspondientes a esta área temática (*sex-shop, sexy, look, glamour, sex-appeal*).

En cambio, los numerosos empleos de **equivalentes** castellanos (25) se concentran en el estrato sociocultural medio (76 %) y, en menor proporción, en el bajo (25 %), niveles sociales donde se prefiere llamar a las cosas por su nombre tradicional (p. ej. los equivalentes de *gay*), aunque se incurra en el disfemismo y la grosería.

3.3.5. *Área temática "salud y drogas"*

DATOS GLOBALES

	tipos/base	**ocurrencias/empleos**
anglicismos	9	27
equivalentes	7	9

El área temática **salud y drogas** presenta una interesante similitud con el área anterior: cuantitativamente limitada, consta de anglicismos muy representativos de las nuevas actitudes y realidades procedentes de la civilización urbana anglosajona.

Por lo que respecta a la distribución sociológica de los anglicismos de esta área temática, se hace imprescindible separar los ámbitos de la salud y de las drogas.

A) En cuanto a la **salud**, el anglicismo *estrés* predomina en informantes mayores de 40 años, para quienes designa, a modo de término genérico, una especie de enfermedad o trastorno provocado por la sociedad urbana moderna, inexistente cuando ellos eran jóvenes pero omnipresente hoy en día, como si fuera uno de los males de fin de siglo. En efecto, de los 7 empleos de *estrés*, 4 corresponden al estrato de edad intermedio y 3 a los mayores de 55 años.

B) Los anglicismos pertenecientes al ámbito de las **drogas** presentan también una distribución sociológica interesante, en función de las dos principales fuentes de origen de estos términos en nuestro corpus: los drogadictos de clase baja en proceso de desintoxicación ([AP 80 A.1+B.1]) y los jóvenes de clase media conocedores de las drogas blandas y de diseño (sobre todo en el contexto de la "ruta del bakalao"):
   1. Los anglicismos relativos a los usuarios (*junky*) y las formas de administración (*chutarse, esnifar*) predominan entre los drogadictos de clase baja y estrato de edad intermedio, con 7 empleos (38,88 %).
   2. Los anglicismos relativos a drogas blandas/de diseño (*speed, trippy*) predominan entre jóvenes de estrato medio menores de 25 años (9 empleos, 50 %).

3.3.6. Área temática "sensaciones y actitudes"

DATOS GLOBALES

	tipos/base	**ocurrencias/empleos**
anglicismos	21	42
equivalentes	7	13

Con esta peculiar área temática hemos pretendido subsanar algunas de las deficiencias que estudiosos como Ch. Pratt (1980: 105) atribuían a las clasificaciones onomasiológicas tradicionales: su incapacidad de dar cuenta de partes de la oración que no fuesen sustantivos concretos y verbos. En efecto, este campo de "sensaciones y actitudes" comprende anglicismos afectivos y valorativos con potencial pragmático, repartidos en los siguientes grupos:

a) Sustantivos deverbales, verbos y adjetivos que verbalizan sensaciones y actitudes aplicables a cualquier tipo de realidad: *flipar, flipante, flipe, flipazo, estar flaseado, (estar) up-to-date* .
b) Adverbios y expresiones de claro contenido elativo y valorativo: *too much, for ever, number one* .
c) Diversos anglicismos empleados con valor figurado y funcionalidad pragmática: *off the record* , *cóctel molotov* ; *va que chuta* y *es un show* .
d) Anglicismos pragmáticos: *please, okey, good bye, miss, míster* .

Esta área se caracteriza por la nula "concentración léxica": consta de numerosos anglicismos base, pero de escaso uso por su carácter idiolectal, esnobista y efímero, exceptuando no obstante la elevada frecuencia de uso del verbo *flipar* entre los jóvenes (16 empleos).

En la medida en que buena parte de estos anglicismos son "palabras-clave" del léxico juvenil (*flipar* y derivados), podemos predecir el predominio de este sector, generalmente vinculado al estrato sociocultural medio.

a) En cuanto a los estratos de edad, la distribución es la siguiente:
   menores de 25 años: 29 empleos (69,04 %)
   entre 26 y 55 años: 11 empleos (26,19 %)
   mayores de 55 años: 2 empleos (4,76 %)
b) En cuanto a su distribución por estratos socioculturales, tenemos los siguientes datos:
   estrato alto: 4 empleos (9,52 %)
   estrato medio: 31 empleos (73,80 %)
   estrato bajo: 7 empleos (16,66 %)

3.3.7. Área temática "lugares de ocio"

DATOS GLOBALES

	tipos/base	**ocurrencias/empleos**
anglicismos	8	101
equivalentes	11	25

En el área temática **lugares de ocio**, el fenómeno de la "concentración léxica" llega al extremo: con sólo 8 anglicismos base, alcanzamos un total de 101 empleos a causa de la elevada frecuencia de uso de los anglicismos *bar* y *pub*, los cuales han generado a su vez los derivados *pafeto, pafete* y *bareto* . Así pues, también se registra en esta área una poderosa "concentración lexicogenésica", ya que 6 de los 8 anglicismos base (con un total de 88 empleos), corresponden a dos familias léxicas.

Esta área temática presenta un perfil sociológico muy definido: predominio del estrato sociocultural medio y de los informantes menores de 25 años, público asiduo de estos locales.

Por tanto, la distribución sociológica de esta área temática es la siguiente:

a) En cuanto a los estratos de edad:
menores de 25 años: 71 empleos (70,29 %)
entre 26 y 55 años: 30 empleos (29,70 %)
mayores de 55 años: 0 empleos (0 %)
b) En cuanto a su distribución por estratos socioculturales:
estrato alto: 17 empleos (16,83 %)
estrato medio: 78 empleos (77,22 %)
estrato bajo: 6 empleos (5,94 %)

3.3.8. Área temática “deportes y juegos”

DATOS GLOBALES

	tipos/base	**ocurrencias/empleos**
anglicismos	43	197
equivalentes	10	26

El área temática **deportes y juegos** es la más numerosa, tanto en anglicismos base (43) como en número de empleos (197). Sin embargo, la “concentración léxica” resulta bastante desigual: los anglicismos que designan los nombres de los deportes son empleados con gran frecuencia (*fútbol, tenis, basket, squash, footing, aerobic* y *surf* suman por sí solos 91 empleos); en cambio, los anglicismos que designan lances del juego (*córner, gol, chut* y derivados) propios de un determinado deporte presentan menor frecuencia de uso, pues se trata de términos más técnicos que sólo se actualizan en ocasiones muy concretas. En cuanto a la concurrencia con los **equivalentes** españoles, parece no confirmarse la tradicional hipótesis del predominio de los anglicismos en los deportes elitistas y el triunfo de los equivalentes españoles, más expresivos y comprensibles, en deportes populares como el fútbol. A nuestro entender, la inestable concurrencia entre **anglicismos** y **equivalentes** en esta área temática está motivada por la “eficacia lingüística comparativa” de unos y otros (factores tales como la brevedad, la capacidad derivativa y la expresividad) .

Hemos dividido en el corpus de esta área en dos grupos por lo que respecta a la distribución por estratos socioculturales:

a) Por un lado, los anglicismos que verbalizan deportes no marcados como elitistas, en especial fútbol, baloncesto y tenis, con un total de 162 empleos. Pese a tratarse de deportes no elitistas, el porcentaje de empleos correspondientes al estrato alto es importante:
   estrato alto: 40 empleos (24,69 %)
   estrato medio: 102 empleos (62,96 %)
   estrato bajo: 20 empleos (12,34 %)
b) Por otro lado, los anglicismos que verbalizan deportes elitistas como golf y squash (29 empleos) también presentan un resultado sorprendente: el porcentaje de empleos correspondientes a informantes de estrato alto es sensiblemente inferior al del grupo anterior, aunque por otro lado también es significativa la completa ausencia de empleos correspondientes a informantes de estrato bajo.
   estrato alto: 3 empleos (10,34 %)
   estrato medio: 26 empleos (89,65 %)
   estrato bajo: 0 empleos (0 %)

En cuanto a la variable edad, la abundancia en nuestro corpus de conversaciones sobre fútbol entre hablantes cuya edad oscila entre 26 y 35 años determina el relativo predominio del estrato de edad intermedio:

menores de 25 años: 82 empleos (41,83 %)
entre 26 y 55 años: 88 empleos (44,89 %)
mayores de 55 años: 19 empleos (9,69 %)

En cuanto a la variable sexo, el elevado número de anglicismos relativos al fútbol determina el claro predominio de los informantes de sexo masculino: 138 empleos (70,41 %) frente a sólo 54 de informantes de sexo femenino (27,56 %).

3.3.9. *Área temática "vida social y tipos humanos"*

DATOS GLOBALES

	tipos/base	**ocurrencias/empleos**
anglicismos	26	77
equivalentes	16	33

El área temática **vida social y tipos humanos** se divide en dos grandes bloques.

a) Por un lado, los anglicismos relativos a diversos aspectos de la "vida social", incluyendo la política. Se trata de una sección en la que predominan anglicismos ya antiguos en español, todavía vigentes porque las nuevas realidades sociales que verbalizan siguen siendo básicas en la sociedad urbana capitalista (*mitin, líder, club*).

b) Por otro, la sección de "tipos humanos" constituye una de las principales novedades de la sociedad urbana moderna verbalizadas por anglicismos, aunque observamos una inestable concurrencia con los equivalentes españoles:
   - algunos anglicismos, sentidos como **xenismos**, han desplazado por completo a los imperfectos equivalentes castellanos: *marines, yanqui* ;
   - otros, pese a poder ser catalogados como **xenismos**, sufren en el registro coloquial la presión de equivalentes españoles más "transparentes" o "populares": *sheriff/guardia, cow-boy/vaquero, jet set/famosos de la tele, gángster/matón* y *mafioso* ;
   - otros, finalmente, son desplazados del uso oral espontáneo por equivalentes españoles más comprensibles y expresivos: así, *canguro, niñera* y *chica que le cuida* ocupan en el uso hablado el lugar que corresponde a *baby-sitter* y *nurse* en otros registros.

Aunque se trata de un área temática bastante heterogénea, la distribución sociológica de los datos ofrece un relativo predominio del estrato de edad intermedio y del estrato sociocultural medio; en cuanto a los dos estratos socioculturales extremos, destaca el importante porcentaje del estrato alto y la representación prácticamente nula del estrato bajo, ya que designan realidades sociales prestigiosas (*VIP, jet, jet-set, role, club*).

a) Distribución por estratos de edad:
   menores de 25 años: 20 empleos (25,97 %)
   entre 26 y 55 años: 35 empleos (45,45 %)
   mayores de 55 años: 9 empleos (4,68 %)
b) Distribución por estratos socioculturales:
   estrato alto: 25 empleos (32,46 %)
   estrato medio: 38 empleos (49,35 %)
   estrato bajo: 2 empleos (2,59 %)

De todo ello, podemos concluir que los anglicismos incluidos en esta área temática son propios de los estratos socioculturales medio y alto,

3.3.10. Área temática "tribus urbanas y música moderna"

DATOS GLOBALES

	tipos/base	**ocurrencias/empleos**
anglicismos	17	77
equivalentes	0	0

El área temática **tribus urbanas y música moderna** es la única que carece por completo de **equivalentes** españoles: se trata, pues, de un área donde la necesidad de verbalizar nuevas realidades de origen anglosajón -las llamadas "tribus urbanas" y los estilos de música moderna a ellas asociados- domina sobre cualquier intento de hispanización.

En virtud de su homogeneidad, esta área temática presenta uno de los perfiles sociológicos más claros, definidos y previsibles.

a) En cuanto al estrato sociocultural, predomina el estrato medio, pero no podemos olvidar la presencia de un 20 % de empleos correspondientes al estrato bajo, acorde con el carácter marginal de muchas de estas "tribus urbanas" (*heavies, punks*):
estrato alto: 3 empleos (3,89 %)
estrato medio: 56 empleos (72,72 %)
estrato bajo: 16 empleos (20,77 %)
b) En cuanto a la edad, el predominio del estrato de edad más joven (menores de 25 años) es total (92,20 %) y resulta perfectamente comprensible por la vinculación directa de estos anglicismos con ciertos sectores juveniles.
c) La variable sexo también presenta un claro desfase a favor de los informantes de sexo masculino, quizá por el carácter machista y patriarcal de determinadas "tribus urbanas" marginales y violentas como *heavies, punks* y *rockers*: los empleos correspondientes a informantes masculinos constituyen un 79,22 %, mientras que los de informantes de sexo femenino tan sólo alcanzan un 18,18 %.

3.3.11. Área temática "transportes y viajes"

DATOS GLOBALES

	tipos/base	**ocurrencias/empleos**
anglicismos	10	27
equivalentes	2	8

En el área temática **transportes y viajes** destaca también la escasa proporción de **equivalentes** españoles: nos encontramos de nuevo ante **préstamos denotativos** cuya función es verbalizar nuevas realidades de la vida urbana y la circulación vial, como *land-rover, stop* y *buga/buggy*.

Esta área temática presenta un perfil sociológico con predominio absoluto de los informantes de estrato sociocultural medio y alto y del estrato de edad intermedio: es decir, las personas que por su edad y nivel económico mejor conocen este tipo de anglicismos técnicos.

a) Distribución por estratos de edad:
menores de 25 años: 12 empleos (44,44 %)
entre 26 y 55 años: 11 empleos (40,74 %)
mayores de 55 años: 4 empleos (14,81 %)
b) Distribución por estratos socioculturales:
estrato alto: 7 empleos (29,92 %)
estrato medio: 19 empleos (70,37 %)
estrato bajo: 1 empleo (3,70 %)

3.3.12. ´Área temática "medios de comunicación y espectáculos"

DATOS GLOBALES

	tipos/base	**ocurrencias/empleos**
anglicismos	25	72
equivalentes	10	87

El área temática medios de comunicación y espectáculos se desdobla en dos grandes bloques:

a) Los anglicismos relativos al cine, televisión y espectáculos constan de 14 lexemas base, pero son de uso esporádico (30 empleos) y sufren la fuerte presión de los **equivalentes** españoles, incluso en el caso de los anglicismos más recientes y de mayor éxito como *zapping* (el cual alterna con *cambiar de cadenas* y *lo del mando*).
b) Por contra, los anglicismos relativos a la los medios de difusión de música moderna (*compact disc, duet, playback, videoclip*) constan de un menor número de lexemas base (8), pero alcanzan un número similar de empleos (28). La mayor frecuencia de uso y la escasa concurrencia con equivalentes españoles se justifica por su condición de **préstamos denotativos** que verbalizan realidades de tipo técnico.

Advertimos aquí un perfil sociológico similar al del área anterior: como buena parte de los anglicismos que la integran aún conservan un cierto colorido técnico (televisión, cine y espectáculos), son de uso frecuente en informantes de estrato sociocultural medio y alto y en el estrato de edad intermedio; el porcentaje relativamente alto de los informantes menores de 25 años se explica por la frecuencia de uso de algunos anglicismos técnicos estrechamente vinculados al mundo de la música moderna, como *compact disc* y *play-back* .

a) Distribución por estratos de edad:
menores de 25 años: 34 empleos (47,22 %)
entre 26 y 55 años: 37 empleos (51,38 %)
mayores de 55 años: 1 empleo (1,38 %)

b) Distribución por estratos socioculturales:
estrato alto: 21 empleos (29,16 %)
estrato medio: 50 empleos (69,44 %)
estrato bajo: 1 empleo (1,38 %)

Los numerosos equivalentes castellanos de esta área temática (debidos a la elevadísima frecuencia de uso de *película*) se decantan hacia el estrato sociocultural medio:

estrato alto: 23 empleos (26,43 %)
estrato medio: 53 empleos (60,92 %)
estrato bajo: 8 empleos (9,19 %)

3.3.13. Área temática "economía y comercio"

DATOS GLOBALES

	tipos/base	**ocurrencias/empleos**
anglicismos	6	17
equivalentes	7	13

En el área temática **economía y comercio** destaca el limitado número de anglicismos base (6) y empleos (17), a pesar de la indiscutible influencia angloamericana en el vocabulario de la economía. El evidente carácter técnico de este campo y la inexistencia en nuestro corpus de conversaciones entre especialistas en la materia (a diferencia de lo que ocurre con la informática, como veremos) no sólo determina la escasa proporción de anglicismos, sino también la concurrencia en el uso con **equivalentes** españoles más breves, expresivos, comprensibles y "transparentes" (*ticket/entrada*, *stand/puesto*, *boom/explosión* y, sobre todo, la necesidad de explicar el contenido del anglicismo *marketing* mediante giros como *de empresas*, *de contabilidad*, *(de) empresariales*).

En consecuencia, el carácter moderno, técnico -y esnobista- de los escasos anglicismos de esta área temática también determina un un perfil sociológico similar al de las dos áreas temáticas anteriores, con total predominio del estrato sociocultural medio/alto y del estrato de edad intermedio:

a) Distribución por estratos de edad:
menores de 25 años: 6 empleos (35,29 %)
entre 26 y 55 años: 11 empleos (64,70 %)
mayores de 55 años: 0 empleos (0 %)

b) Distribución por estratos socioculturales:
estrato alto: 9 empleos (52,94 %)
estrato medio: 8 empleos (47,05 %)
estrato bajo: 0 empleos (0 %)

3.3.14. *Área temática "enseñanza"*

DATOS GLOBALES

	tipos/base	ocurrencias/empleos
anglicismos	3	24
equivalentes	7	35

La **enseñanza** sólo nos proporciona 3 anglicismos base (*test, máster* y *coffee break*), los cuales sufren la concurrencia de numerosos equivalentes nativos, prueba de su deficiente asimilación semántica.

Estos escasos anglicismos tienen también un perfil sociológico claramente definido, en función del tipo de informantes que se sirve de estos términos: estudiantes universitarios de nivel sociocultural medio en un 100 %.

3.3.15. *Área temática "avances técnicos"*

DATOS GLOBALES

	tipos/base	ocurrencias/empleos
anglicismos	30	95
equivalentes	6	42

El área temática **avances técnicos** consta de 30 anglicismos base, con un total de 95 empleos, entre los que destacan en el uso anglicismos tecnológicos ya antiguos hoy en día como *MS-DOS, walkman, replay* y *window.* Responde a las novedades tecnológicas de principios de los 90 y es por tanto el área temática más caduca. Su distribución sociológica se halla condicionada por el elevado número de empleos procedentes de la conversación [XP 48 A.1+B.1], entre profesores de informática de estrato alto y grupo de edad intermedio (pues de hecho el empleo de este tipo de anglicismos técnicos corresponde a este perfil sociológico, ya que suelen ser profesionales cualificados con cierta experiencia):

a) Distribución por estratos de edad:
menores de 25 años: 20 empleos (21,05 %)
entre 26 y 55 años: 75 empleos (78,94 %)
mayores de 55 años: 0 empleos (0 %)
b) Distribución por estratos socioculturales:
estrato alto: 70 empleos (73,68 %)
estrato medio: 20 empleos (21,05 %)
estrato bajo: 5 empleos (5,26 %)

En cambio, los **equivalentes** españoles ofrecen un perfil sociológico más variado, donde destaca el predominio del estrato sociocultural medio mientras que el estrato de edad más joven alcanza un porcentaje similar al del estrato de edad intermedio; de hecho, los informantes que optan por los **equivalentes** españoles (*ordenador*) suelen ser jóvenes estudiantes universitarios, cuyo conocimiento de la informática se limita a su condición de usuarios:

a) Distribución por estratos de edad:
menores de 25 años: 16 empleos (38,09 %)
entre 26 y 55 años: 19 empleos (45,23 %)
mayores de 55 años: 7 empleos (16,68 %)
b) Distribución por estratos socioculturales:
estrato alto: 12 empleos (28,57 %)
estrato medio: 28 empleos (66,66 %)
estrato bajo: 2 empleos (4,76 %)

3.4. Conclusiones del estudio sobre anglicismos en el habla coloquial de Valencia

En conclusión, la distribución sociológica de nuestro corpus de anglicismos en el registro coloquial confirma una serie de ideas obvias, ya apuntadas por los estudiosos del fenómeno desde una perspectiva impresionista e intuitiva. El avance que supone nuestro análisis es el de apoyar estas intuiciones en un corpus real y representativo, pese a las deficiencias metodológicas indicadas al comienzo esta exposición:

a) En cuanto al **corpus total**, podemos destacar los siguientes fenómenos:
- la escasa participación de los informantes de edad más avanzada y el predominio de los estratos de edad joven e intermedio;
- la escasa representatividad de la variable sexo;
- el predominio cuantativo de informantes de estrato sociocultural medio junto a una importante presencia cualitativa de informantes de estrato alto.

b) En cuanto a la distribución sociológica de anglicismos y equivalentes por las distintas **áreas temáticas**, resulta difícil agrupar estas áreas temáticas en grupos sociolingüísticamente homogéneos. En todo caso podríamos apuntar tres grupos principales:
   1. El relativo predominio de las mujeres de estrato de edad intermedio y nivel sociocultural medio o bajo en áreas temáticas cercanas a sus intereses, como las de "alimentación", "vestuario" y "la casa".
   2. El claro predominio del sector social constituido por informantes de nivel sociocultural alto y estrato de edad intermedio en las áreas temáticas más claramente vinculadas a los anglicismos técnicos, indispensables en determinadas esferas profesionales: economía, espectáculos, medios de comunicación, transportes.
   3. El previsible predominio de los informantes jóvenes y estrato de edad intermedio en una serie de áreas temáticas muy concretas, pero importantes desde el punto de vista cuantitativo (en especial, "lugares de ocio" y "tribus urbanas y música moderna"), lo cual influye en los procentajes del corpus global.

Finalmente, podemos concluir señalando, respecto del corpus total, los anglicismos más usados en el español coloquial actual (aquéllos que tienen una frecuencia de uso igual o superior a 8 empleos):

a) Anglicismos antiguos, asimilados y difundidos, convertidos en préstamos cuyo carácter inglés comienza a olvidarse en la consciencia lingüística de los hispanohablantes (p.ej. *gol, mitin, jersey, póquer*).
b) Anglicismos relativos al mundo del deporte, unos más antiguos (*fútbol, gol, tenis*) y otros más recientes (*squash, aerobic, basket*).
c) Anglicismos relativamente antiguos referidos a realidades domésticas: *jersey, spray, suéter, grill, cocacola, sándwich* .
d) Anglicismos recientes, que lexicalizan realidades básicas del modo de vida de los jóvenes: *pub, flipar, hippy, rocker, cómic, póster, compact disc* ;
e) Algunos anglicismos técnicos recientes: *PC, marketing, estrés, test* .

4. Estudios posteriores sobre los anglicismos en un corpus oral

Aunque con posterioridad a nuestra Tesis Doctoral, se han seguido publicando innumerables trabajos sobre el anglñicismo en español, en pocos de ellos se ha documentado su uso en un corpus de habla oral y se ha preferido seguir pescando en los caladeros más fáciles de la prensa escrita, complementada hoy en día con periódicos online, blogs y demás fuentes escritas digitales, como hacen los diversos trabajos recogidos en la compilación editada por Luján-García (2021), muy interesante por otra parte en cuanto a las áreas temáticas y medios modernos de comunicación (revistas digitales para adolescentes, prensa deportiva online, foros de internet).

Es cierto que hoy en día hay más recursos tecnológicos para investigar el habla oral coloquial, pero a la vez hay más restricciones legales a la hora de grabar conversaciones ajenas sin consentimiento (porque cuando los hablantes saben que se les está grabando, los rasgos de coloquialidad disminuyen).

Tan solo Giménez Folqués (2021) intenta registrar la frecuencia de uso de los anglicismos aceptados por la Real Academia en 2014 a partir de los datos del CORPES XXI (Corpus del Español del Siglo XXI), que recoge tanto textos escritos como orales. Así, en su trabajo, Giménez Folqués destaca la elevada frecuencia de uso de anglicismos actuales como *performance, pub, thriller, jeep, spam, coach, country, wifi, stop, parking, swing,* todos ellos con más de 500 usos.

Referencias bibliográficas

Alvar, M. (1992): "Los diccionarios académicos y el problema de los neologismos", en Fundación EF*E El neologismo necesario*, Madrid: Agencia EFE, pp. 51–70.

Briz, Antonio et al. [Grupo Val.Es.Co.] (1995): *La conversación coloquial. Materiales para su estudio*, Valencia: Universitat.

Contreras, Lidia (1988): "Los anglicismos en el léxico del habla culta de Santiago de Chile", *Actas del VI Congreso de la ALFAL (Phoenix, Arizona, septiembre de 1981)*, México: UNAM, pp. 593–654.

Giménez Folqués, David (2021): "Análisis de los nuevos anglicismos léxicos en la lengua española en el contexto de las obras y corpus académicos digitales", en *Texto Livre. Linguagem e Tecnologia,* 14 (1), Belo Horizonte [fecha de consulta 5/12/2021].

Gómez Capuz, J. (1998): *El préstamo lingüístico (conceptos, problemas y métodos)*, Anejo XXIX de la Revista Cuadernos de Filología, Valencia: Dpto.Filología Española/Facultad de Filología/Universitat de València.

Gómez Capuz, J. (1999): "Vitalidad y frecuencia de uso de los anglicismos en el español coloquial actual", *Quaderns de Filologia V: Estudis Lingüístics. El contacto lingüístico en el desarrollo de las lenguas occidentales*, Valencia: Universitat, pp. 127–137.

Lope Blanch, J. M. (1972): "Anglicismos en la norma linguistica culta de México", en *Romanica V*, Buenos Aires, pp. 191–200.

López Chávez, Juan (1991): "Préstamos, extranjerismos y anglicismos en el español de México. Valores lexicométricos (Planteamientos previos)", en C. Henández et al. (eds.), *"El español de América". Actas del III Congreso Internacional de El Español de América, vol II*, Valladolid: Junta de Castilla y León, 775–784.

López Morales, H. (1971): "Tres calas léxicas en el español de la Habana (indigenismos, afronegrismos, anglicismos)", en *Estudios sobre el español de Cuba*, La Habana: Las Américas Publishing Company-Anaya, pp. 72–87.

López Morales, H. (1974)(1979): "Anglicismos en Puerto Rico. En busca de los índices de permeabilización del diasistema: diseño de investigación", en *Dialectología y sociolingüística: temas puertorriqueños*, Madrid: Playor-Hispanova, pp. 101–106.

López Morales, H. (1979): *Dialectología y sociolingüística: temas puertorriqueños*, Madrid, Playor-Hispanova.

López Morales, H. (1987): "Anglicismos léxicos en el habla culta de San Juan de Puerto Rico", *Lingüística Española Actual, IX/2*, Madrid: Instituto de Cooperación Iberoamericana, pp. 285–303.

López Morales, H. (1993, 2ª): *Sociolingüística*, Madrid: Gredos.

Luján-García, Carmen (ed.) (2021): *Anglicismos en los nuevos medios de comunicación. Tendencias actuales*, Granada: Comares.

Moreno Fernández, Francisco (1990): *Metodología sociolingüística*, Madrid: Gredos.

Pérez Goznález, Zaida (1984): "Anglicismos en el léxico de la norma culta de Caracas", *Actas del VII Congreso de la ALFAL: Homenaje a Pedro Henríquez Ureña, tomo II*, Santo Domingo: ALFAL, pp. 143–157.

Pratt, Ch. (1980): *El anglicismo en el español peninsular contemporáneo*, Madrid: Gredos.

Quilis, A. (1984): "Anglicismos en el español de Madrid" en *Athlon, Satura Grammatica in honorem Francisci R. Adrados*, Madrid: Gredos, pp. 413–423.

Goretti García-Morales

Universidad de Las Palmas de Gran Canaria

Tratamiento del anglicismo en traducciones automáticas español-inglés

Abstract: Developments in machine translation engines have shown that a high degree of accuracy can be reached automatically, as long as there is a large pool of source and target texts from which the tool can "learn". Conveying denotative meaning entails little difficulty for computer programmes or human translators alike. It is when utterances hide connotative meaning that translation problems arise. Studies show that, outside technical languages, pragmatics is often behind the users' choice of Anglicisms. Our objective is to examine if the intention of writers who include Anglicisms in source texts in Spanish is maintained in target texts in English, which are provided by the automatic translation tool *Deepl*.

Keywords: Anglicism, machine translation, *DeepL*, connotative meaning, pragmatics.

Palabras clave: anglicismo, traducción automática, *DeepL*, significado connotativo, pragmática.

1. Introducción

Desde los tiempos en los que los primeros motores de inteligencia artificial causaban risa con sus propuestas de traducción automática ha llovido mucho. La tecnología se ha desarrollado hasta el punto de que tanto el ámbito académico como la sociedad en general se preguntan si en el futuro desaparecerá la profesión del traductor como la conocemos hoy, al menos para las combinaciones lingüísticas más frecuentes (Hofstader, 2018).

Entre los denominados traductores automáticos más eficientes destaca *DeepL*, basado en redes neuronales que, como se señala en su sitio web, "son capaces de captar hasta los matices más sutiles de las frases y […] trasladar con mayor precisión el significado de las frases traducidas, superando con gran éxito hasta el reto que suponen los textos con jerga profesional específica" (https://www.DeepL.com/es/whyDeepL).

Es cierto que los motores de traducción automática se basan en corpus textuales de textos traducidos por seres humanos. De igual forma, al intentar "trasladar con mayor precisión el significado de las frases traducidas", necesitan de modelos realizados por personas para poder imitarlos. Ello revela que evidentemente dichos motores de traducción dependen de la inteligencia humana, pero, dado que los corpus paralelos no dejan de aumentar, cada vez es menos frecuente que los textos traducidos automáticamente tengan errores sintácticos o léxicos graves (Grass, 2022).

Sin embargo, no cabe duda de que traducir es mucho más que trasladar significados, del modo en que lo hacen las fuentes lexicográficas. El buen traductor humano interpreta el sentido profundo de los textos originales, ahonda en la intención de su autor, dota al texto meta de coherencia y cohesión, tiene en cuenta el encargo de traducción y el público al que se dirige. En ocasiones, incluso corrige errores del texto original. La fascinación que producen los sistemas de traducción automática, que sin duda suponen un avance en el terreno de la comunicación para determinados fines, pierde de vista que la inteligencia humana no funciona exclusivamente comparando los datos que la memoria o los sentidos le proporcionan. Si fuera así, desde luego que estaríamos en desventaja con respecto a los superordenadores. No obstante, a diferencia de *Deepl* que, como hemos dicho, identifica los retos para la traducción en la jerga profesional específica, Flöter-Durr (2022: 14) opina que las mayores limitaciones de los corpus paralelos de traducción son el carácter limitado del contexto y que no pueden analizar las relaciones entre frases:

> Les corpusparallèles en traduction se heurtent aux mêmes limites que les big data dans d'autres domaines. À titre d'exemple, on citera l'hétérogénéité des données, l'impossibilité d'analyser les relations entre les phrases qui conduit à des contresens ou des passages totalement incompréhensibles et le caractère très limité du contexte pris en compte par la méthode statistique et ce malgré les tentatives d'élargissement du contexte linguistique et extralinguistique (Maruf, Saleh, Haffari, 2019).

Es por ello por lo que esta autora afirma que ciertos mecanismos cognitivos superan la capacidad de las máquinas (Flöter-Durr, 2022: 3). Melby (2019: 25) sostiene que lo que diferencia a los seres humanos de los sistemas de traducción automática es "their ability to organize a collection of instances of language, such as idioms, into a coherent semantic system without a pre-existing framework". Grass (2022), por su parte, señala que los motores de traducción son incapaces de detectar errores de significado relacionados con el conocimiento del mundo y las relaciones causales. Entre los fallos comunes que este autor comenta están las interjecciones, los errores ortográficos, los neologismos, las expresiones o giros, las abreviaturas, la modalidad y las ambigüedades acerca del referente. De fondo, subyace la imposibilidad de la traducción automática de intuir las causas que llevan a una persona a expresarse de una determinada manera.

En efecto, cuando se redacta un texto, su autor pone en funcionamiento toda una serie de herramientas lingüísticas y extralingüísticas que el traductor ha de tener en cuenta a la hora de elaborar un texto meta en otra lengua. Cualquier decisión acerca del empleo de una u otra estrategia de traducción, incluyendo el empleo de préstamos léxicos, debe estar basada en una intención concreta. De ahí que sea pertinente preguntarnos acerca de los motivos que llevan a los autores a incluir voces extranjeras en sus textos.

2. Motivaciones para el empleo de anglicismos

Como telón de fondo del escenario en el que los hablantes se expresan, Lorenzo (1998: 21) establece que "la penetración de usos extranjeros – palabras o expresiones más amplias – en un idioma no es otra cosa que una manifestación más del predominio político, cultural o económico de una potencia sobre otras". En ese sentido, González Cruz y Rodríguez Medina (2011: 265) dan por sentado que la presencia creciente de anglicismos en el español continuará mientras que los Estados Unidos mantengan su liderazgo económico, político y cultural en el mundo. Lógicamente, este influjo subyace en las elecciones que los hablantes hacen de los anglicismos.

El que muchos de los avances en distintos ámbitos nazcan en inglés predispone a que se adopte una denominación prestada de esa lengua en los países donde se difunden dichos avances. Indudablemente este es el caso de los préstamos técnicos, que tienen una función básicamente denotativa. Sin embargo, en la era de las comunicaciones instantáneas, es frecuente que los tecnicismos abandonen la jerga donde se originaron y se empiecen a difundir en la lengua común. El fácil acceso a la información del que gozamos en la actualidad difumina los contornos de los lenguajes especializados y, como resultado, muchos de los anglicismos procedentes de estos ámbitos adquieren en la lengua común un valor connotativo que trasciende las necesidades lingüísticas de la lengua receptora. Por ello, Gómez Capuz (1998: 276) concede que, aunque la función mayoritaria de este tipo de anglicismos es la denotativa, al emplearse fuera del lenguaje que las importó en primera instancia, desempeñan nuevos oficios.

Por su parte, Pratt (1980: 213) confirma la opinión difundida de que los anglicismos surgen para lexicalizar realidades o conceptos nuevos, pero añade que, entre ellos también se incluyen actitudes, posturas y valores sociales. En efecto, las lagunas o ineficacias lingüísticas responsables de que la lexía anglosajona se imponga en español no se reducen solo a objetos materiales o realidades tangibles. Rodríguez González (1996: 109) afirma incluso que los hablantes pueden decidirse por una lexía prestada por causas, "which may be relevant from a stylistic point of view". En este grupo se incluyen la función referencial y expresiva, que como veremos, difícilmente pueden conservarse en un TM traducido automáticamente.

Siendo importantes las causas lingüísticas, es indudable que hay factores extralingüísticos que favorecen la importación de anglicismos. Pratt (1980) destaca el esnobismo lingüístico; la función argótica, que es más responsable del origen de anglicismos que de su difusión; los factores materiales, que motivan el empleo de anglicismos en busca de un beneficio económico; y, por último, el lugar y el tema. Autores como Rodríguez Segura (1999) y Lillo (2022) también apuntan a la ostentación, la ironía, la complicidad, etc. como causas extrínsecas para el empleo de anglicismos. Una de estas motivaciones, que Rodríguez Segura (1999: 132) recoge, diferenciada del esnobismo, es que el anglicismo a veces actúa como núcleo de ciertas licencias expresivas en los medios de comunicación para lograr un efecto concreto en el oyente o lector:

> Al ser el anglicismo patente aquél cuya morfología extranjera o sucesión inusual de sonidos en nuestra lengua son evidentes para los receptores del mensaje que lo incluye, el profesional de la comunicación que juega con los anglicismos aprovecha su fisonomía y sonoridad extrañas para dotar de contundencia a su discurso y, en muchas ocasiones, para exagerar o corromper conscientemente su escritura o pronunciación [...] La mayoría de estas frases combinan el inglés y el español, son esporádicas y pertenecen al dominio de la expresión individual.

En el análisis de nuestro corpus, veremos algunos ejemplos de usos que aparentemente buscan transmitir al lector este efecto o complicidad. Morales de Walters (2001: 19) también señala esta causa cuando dice que "en ocasiones, el hablante se vale del anglicismo para pasar a un discurso afectivo y metafórico para el cual el préstamo le provee la voz más idónea".

Las consideraciones anteriores reflejan que la necesidad mayor o menor de emplear un anglicismo con valor eufemístico o para evitar la homonimia, entre otros motivos posibles, depende en gran medida de la subjetividad de la persona que lo emplea. En última instancia, "podemos considerar un axioma que todas y cada una de las palabras prestadas se toman por alguna razón que se considera buena y suficiente para el prestatario" (Gray en Gómez Capuz, 1998: 255).

En este artículo, nos proponemos explorar cómo aborda *DeepL* la conversión al inglés de textos escritos originalmente en español donde se emplean anglicismos léxicos, teniendo en cuenta que optar por un préstamo, sobre todo en el caso de los lenguajes no especializados, apunta a algún tipo de motivación que normalmente se halla en un nivel supraoracional y responde a una elección subjetiva, no forzada por la ausencia de mecanismos semánticos en español.

3. Metodología

Con el fin de averiguar cómo aborda *DeepL* el empleo de anglicismos en la combinación español-inglés, partimos de un corpus de textos originales en español en los que aparecen anglicismos. Como se ha puesto de manifiesto, los lenguajes especializados que se emplean en el ámbito técnico favorecen el empleo de préstamos léxicos por causas lingüísticas intrínsecas, con una función mayoritariamente denotativa. En este estudio nos centramos en anglicismos que no estuviesen restringidos a jergas técnicas.

Para obtener las lexías que tomaríamos como referencia, partimos de un artículo de Luján-García (2020), que analiza el empleo de anglicismos relacionados con el ocio en fuentes periodísticas. Esta autora analiza las secciones denominadas "deporte", "vida y estilo", y "cultura, ocio y sociedad". De estas tres, seleccionamos "vida y estilo", que, entre las letras A y Z, aporta 135 préstamos diferentes. La extensión del presente artículo impide que expongamos el análisis completo del listado de Luján-García (2020: 122–123). Por ello, presentamos por orden alfabético y analizamos los anglicismos comprendidos entre las letras A y E.

Una vez obtenida una muestra de anglicismos que los hablantes de español emplean en la actualidad para referirse a cuestiones de la vida cotidiana, necesitábamos poner estas lexías sueltas en el contexto de una oración, susceptible de ser traducida. Para ello, nos servimos de la versión actual del *Corpus del Español del Siglo XXI (Corpes XXI)*, publicada en abierto desde julio de 2021 en la página web de la Real Academia Española (https://apps2.rae.es/CORPES/view/inicioExterno.view).

En el espacio "lema" introdujimos, uno por uno, todos los anglicismos sin establecer ningún tipo de filtro. La herramienta muestra concordancias desde el año 2001 hasta el 2021 en España y los países de Latinoamérica, en todas las categorías gramaticales y en todo tipo de fuentes. De todos los ejemplos de oraciones en los que aparecían los anglicismos, seleccionamos algunos y obtuvimos el contexto en el que dicha palabra aparecía. El recurso permite acceder al texto completo, pero la mayoría de las veces no necesitamos recurrir a un contexto superior a la frase para entender el significado del préstamo empleado.

Después de obtener resultados de frases completas en español que contuvieran los anglicismos de la lista contextualizados, recabamos la información relativa al autor, fecha, fuente y título del texto completo. Seguidamente, introdujimos los enunciados en el motor de traducción automática *DeepL* en la combinación de español a inglés, con el fin de analizar cómo gestionaba cada caso en el texto meta que esta herramienta informática ofrecía.

Algunos anglicismos, incluidos en el listado de referencia compilado por Luján-García, no obtuvieron concordancias en el *Corpes XXI*, quizás por tratarse de combinaciones poco frecuentes o idiolectales. En el apartado de análisis especificaremos cuáles son estas voces, que, lógicamente, no tendremos en cuenta para este estudio.

Finalmente, cuando se emplea, prestamos atención también al resalte tipográfico mediante cursiva o comillas, ya que "ambos recursos constituyen signos visibles del grado de integración léxica del anglicismo" (Rodríguez González, 2019: 443), por lo que cuando se usan en español, de alguna manera el redactor manifiesta que es consciente de que se trata de una voz foránea.

4. Análisis

La extensión del presente artículo impide que expongamos el análisis completo del listado de Luján-García que hemos tomado como referencia. Por ello, a continuación, presentamos por orden alfabético los anglicismos comprendidos entre las letras A y E. Como veremos más adelante, esta selección resulta suficiente para extraer conclusiones relevantes sobre el tratamiento que dan a los anglicismos los motores de traducción.

Para cada entrada, incluimos un enunciado en español donde se recoge el préstamo con los datos acerca del autor y la fuente en la que apareció publicado, la opción de traducción que ofrece *DeepL* y un comentario analítico sobre dicha propuesta. En el caso de *beauty* aportamos dos extractos distintos, pues observamos diferencias en el comportamiento del motor de traducción en función del género del artículo que precedía a la voz.

Los siguientes anglicismos aparecen en el artículo de Luján-García, pero no muestran coincidencias en *Corpes XXI* o, si lo hacen, se refieren a nombres propios: *airless*, *anti frizz*, *baby blond*, *baby lights*, *beauty freaks*, *beauty victim*, *chunky sneakers*, *cushion*, *cut out*, *dad sandals*, *dermaroller*, *dry brushing*, *eco-green*, *eyecat* y *eyeliner*.

4.1. Adware

> O el NeoAudio, un freeware para digitalizar CD de audio, financiado con avisos en nuestra pantalla, es decir, un adware (por ad, aviso en inglés) (Sametband, Ricardo: "Spyware: alguien te está mirando". La Nación. Buenos Aires: lanacion.com.ar, 2002-08-12)
>
> Or NeoAudio, a freeware for digitising audio CDs, financed with ads on our screen, i.e. adware

Al tratarse de una palabra técnica que se emplea de manera idéntica en español y en inglés, sin uso connotativo, la traducción debe ser y es literal. Sin embargo, en este ejemplo el TO explica de dónde proviene la palabra y en el TM se omite porque para el lector de lengua inglesa es evidente y, en todo caso, queda explicado en el pretexto.

4.2. After Sun

Después del sol aplique productos After Sun para refrescar la piel, suavizarla y prolongar el bronceado (Quintero, Carolina: "De cara al sol". El Universal. Estampas. Caracas: estampas.com, 2003-07-20)
After the sun, apply After Sun products to refresh the skin, soothe it and prolong the tan

En este ejemplo, el TM pierde variación estilística y se incurre en una repetición fácilmente evitable mediante una estrategia de traducción simple, como la omisión o la reformulación.

4.3. Animal print

Ella bajó vestida con una minifalda ajustadísima *animal print*, botas al tono y una camisa blanca anudada a la cintura (Wornat, Olga: Menem-Bolocco, S.A. Buenos Aires: Ediciones B Argentina, 2001)
She came down dressed in a very tight *animal print* mini skirt, matching boots and a white shirt tied at the waist, boots and a white shirt tied at the waist

En el TO se emplea el anglicismo en cursiva, lo cual denota la conciencia por parte de su autor de que se está haciendo uso de una palabra extranjera. En textos cortos, *DeepL* no permite introducir cursiva por lo que, incluso en el caso de que se identificara una intención para usarla por parte del autor del TO, se perdería en el TM. Sin embargo, *DeepL* sí mantiene la cursiva si, en lugar de teclear oraciones sueltas en el motor de búsqueda, se sube el texto como documento. En este caso, *DeepL* deja *animal print* en cursiva en el TM, lo cual carece de sentido.

4.4. Antiaging/anti aging

El futuro idealizado del "antiaging" es la mayor felicidad posible del ser humano: prevención de la enfermedad, el sufrimiento, el dolor, la discapacidad y la tristeza por el paso de los años ("13 CLAVES PARA SER FELIZ Y ENVEJECER MEJOR". La Guía. Sarasota: revistalaguia.com, 2006–05)
The idealised future of "anti-aging" is the greatest possible human happiness: prevention of illness, suffering, pain, disability and the sadness of ageing

En el TO se emplea el anglicismo entre comillas para marcar que se trata de una voz perteneciente a otra lengua (Fundéu, https://www.fundeu.es/recomendacion/comillas-uso-de-este-signo-ortografico/). Sin embargo, según el diccionario Merriam-Webster, la palabra *antiaging* se usa en inglés desde 1917. Por ello, no se comprende que se mantengan las comillas en el TM.

4.5. App

> Este es el caso de www.cappaces.com, No es una aplicación, sino un blog en donde se analizan aplicaciones para niños. [...] El nombre pretende jugar con las palabras app y capacidad (en contraposición a todo lo negativo que implica la palabra discapacidad). (Martín, Javier: "Análisis de aplis para niños". Aplilandia. http://blogs.elpais.com/aplilandia: blogs.elpais.com/aplilandia, 2012-06-04)
> This is the case of www.cappaces.com, not an app, but a blog where apps for kids are reviewed. [...] the name is meant to play on the words app and ability (as opposed to all the negative things that the word disability implies)

Es bien sabido que los juegos de palabras suponen un gran reto para el traductor. En este ejemplo nos encontramos con uno, que combina las palabras capacidad-discapacidad, con el anglicismo *app*. Para referirse a estas situaciones, en inglés se emplean las palabras *ability-disability*. Esta es la opción que elige *DeepL*, a pesar de que en inglés existe la palabra *capacity*, con un significado similar, que habría servido para mantener, al menos en parte, el juego de palabras.

4.6. Baby shower

> "baby shower" con 29 infectados, entre ellos el hijo de una embarazada que parió unos días después (Lewkowicz, J. F.: "Covid-19: consideraciones para la planificación de una estrategia". La Prensa. Buenos Aires: laprensa.com.ar, 2020-06-14)
> "baby shower" with 29 infected, including child of pregnant woman who gave birth a few days later

Según el diccionario Merriam-Webster, *baby shower* es un uso de Estados Unidos. Mantener las comillas en el TM podría justificarse si este fuera dirigido a un público meta de otra variedad dialectal del inglés, que podría desconocer su significado. Sin embargo, *DeepL* permite especificar si se quiere traducir el texto a inglés británico o americano y, tanto en un caso como en el otro, mantiene las comillas.

4.7. Back-up

> La mayoría de los usuarios no nos preocupamos en lo más mínimo por contar o crear una copia de seguridad o back-up de los archivos ("RESGUARDANDO LA

INFORMACIÓN". El Diario. Ciencia & Computación. La Paz: eldiario.net/computacion, 2008-03-03)
Most of us do not bother in the least to have or create a backup or back-up copy of our files

El autor del TO emplea en este caso la lexía en español (copia de seguridad), pero añade la denominación común en argot informático. Resulta absurdo que se mantenga ese añadido en el TM, empleando dos veces la misma palabra, con una ligera variación estilística.

4.8. Batch cooking

Cocción por lotes: También conocido en las redes como *Batch cooking*, es hacer grandes lotes de una receta específica, luego dividirla en porciones para congelar y comer en los próximos meses (Paolini, Mariángel: "Cocinar en la nueva normalidad". El Universal. Estampas. Caracas: estampas.com, 2020-07-19)
Batch cooking: Also known on the interwebs as batch cooking, this is making large batches of a specific recipe, then dividing it into portions to be frozen and eaten over the next few months

Lo que un traductor humano habría resuelto fácilmente omitiendo la información redundante ("What is know on the Internet as batch cooking is making [...]", por ejemplo) se convierte en un sinsentido en la propuesta de traducción automática.

4.9. Beauty

Finalmente la legendaria beauty apareció, sin edad y sonriente, del brazo de Arocena padre (Cozarinsky, Edgardo: "Sidra en el Tortoni". Página 12. Radar libros. Buenos Aires: pagina12.com.ar, 2003-02-02)
Finally the legendary beauty appeared, ageless and smiling, on the arm of Arocena Sr.
Pero Chanta, no más que por fastidiarlo, se ofreció a acompañarlo a comprar la batida primero, de manera que luego pudieran ir juntos al beauty (Font Acevedo, Francisco: "Mundillo". Caleidoscopio. San Juan: Isla Negra, 2004)
But Chanta just to annoy him, he offered to go with him to buy the milkshake first, so that they could then go to the beauty parlour together

En estos ejemplos se pone de manifiesto que el motor de traducción reconoce que cuando *beauty* va precedido de un artículo masculino, debe traducir *beauty parlour* en inglés; mientras que, si el artículo es femenino, se refiere a una mujer bella. En ninguno de los casos se mantiene en la versión inglesa la intencionalidad del autor del TO al emplear el anglicismo.

4.10. Beauty look

> Toma nota, pues estos beauty looks son todo lo que necesitas durante esta temporada de sol (Rocha, Fer: "Tintes de pelo que te hacen ver más joven". El Universal. Ciudad de México: eluniversal.com.mx, 2021-06-14)
> Take note because these beauty looks are all you need this sunny season

El Diccionario de la Real Academia de la Lengua Española (DLE) recoge *look* entre los anglicismos que se emplean en nuestra lengua, por lo que se trata de una palabra frecuente "especialmente si responde a un propósito de distinción". Este hecho facilita que *DeepL* pueda comparar diversísimos textos traducidos en los que, al menos en el nivel oracional, no se ven diferencias entre el inglés y el español en lo referente al empleo de la palabra *look*, lo cual da como resultado una traducción palabra por palabra coherente.

4.11. Biker

> Un biker mira de reojo a una mascota que traen en una mochila (Riva Palacio Alatriste, Rodolfo; Riva Palacio Alatriste, Gabriel: Un gallo con muchos huevos. s. l.: s. n., 2015)
> A biker looks sideways at a pet in a backpack

El repositorio de *Corpes XXI* solo contiene cuatro ejemplos de *biker.* Uno de ellos forma parte de una descripción en lengua inglesa. Los otros tres ejemplos se emplean en contextos relacionados con la denominada "cultura biker", ámbito al que se circunscribe el empleo de este anglicismo en español. Este matiz pragmático, que trasciende la oración e incluso el texto en el que se emplea el anglicismo, pasa desapercibido en la traducción propuesta.

4.12. Bluetooth

> Dos tecnologías serán las protagonistas absolutas: Bluetooth, un estándar para conectar dispositivos cercanos, y WiFi –también conocida como 802.11b–, un sistema de conexión inalámbrico para redes Ethernet (Jiménez, Ángel: "Permanentemente conectado". El Mundo. Ariadn@. Madrid: elmundo.es, 2001-12-06)
> Two technologies will be the absolute protagonists: Bluetooth, a standard for connecting nearby devices, and WiFi – also known as 802.11b – a wireless connection system for Ethernet networks

Alcalde y Cano (2013: 64) reconocen que el uso extendido de anglicismos en el ámbito de la tecnología se debe, entre otras razones, "a la falta de tiempo que existe para la búsqueda de equivalente en español en un área que está en continuo cambio". El ejemplo que hemos seleccionado, publicado en 2001, lo refleja claramente, pues se mencionan como novedosas las tecnología bluetooth y WiFi, hoy ampliamente conocidas y casi desfasadas. El caso de wifi es especialmente llamativo pues lo recoge el *DLE* sin ningún tipo de marca. Por tanto, la traducción literal al inglés que *DeepL* ofrece transmite el sentido del TO

4.13. Blush

> Se finaliza con un colorete pure blush en tono rosa que resalta y marca los pómulos dándoles un aspecto saludable (Parrilla, Ana: "Maquíllese como una modelo". El Mundo. Magazine. Madrid: elmundo.es, 2003-12-21)
> It is finished off with a pure blush in a pink shade that highlights and highlights the cheekbones for a healthy look

Cuando un hablante ve la necesidad de explicar mediante paráfrasis el significado del anglicismo que ha empleado, de alguna manera expresa su incertidumbre acerca de lo extendido del término en español. Con todo, algún motivo le conduce a mantener la voz inglesa. Esta intencionalidad por la que decide reiterar una lexía se pierde en la traducción automática.

4.14. Body milk

> Todo su organismo emanaba un aroma saludable, en el que hallaban acomodo el jabón, el desodorante y el body milk (Mendoza, Eduardo: La aventura del tocador de señoras. Barcelona: Seix Barral, 2001)
> His whole organism emanated a healthy scent, in which soap, deodorant and body milk found their place

Quienes estén familiarizados con la pluma irónica de Eduardo Mendoza, sin duda, verán en el TO una intención humorística detrás del empleo del anglicismo, que se obvia en el TM.

4.15. Bronzer

> [...] marcas como Smashbox han agregado un tercer tono, bronzer, para esculpir de manera más natural el rostro he integrar los tonos (Convers, Adriana: "Contouring, consejos de un experto" Revista Infashion. Bogotá: infashion.com.co, 2016-02-03)
> [...] brands like Smashbox have added a third shade, bronzer, to sculpt the face in a more natural way and integrate the tones

En el ámbito de la estética, el anglicismo *bronzer* forma parte del lenguaje jergal internacional. La traducción literal funciona bien al tratarse de un término técnico.

4.16. Business intelligence

> SAS Intelligence Platform puede incluso extenderse y ser adaptada para crear nuevas aplicaciones de *Business Intelligence* (Ramos, Fátima: PRIMERA PARTE.

Tecnologías o Hardware. Adquisición y Uso en la Administración Pública Nacional. Caracas: Ministerio de Ciencia y Tecnología, 2006)
SAS Intelligence Platform can even be extended and adapted to create new Business Intelligence applications.

Se trata de un ejemplo más de que "los expertos se rigen a la hora de utilizar los anglicismos por la necesidad de sentar las bases de una comunicación homogénea en el área en el que desempeñan su labor" (Alcalde y Cano, 2013: 64). No presenta dificultades a la hora de la traducción porque el anglicismo se emplea con esta intención práctica.

4.17. Casual

A la vuelta de una columna se lleva un tremendo susto al dar de sopetón con un maniquí vestido con ropa casual, que no logra disimular su aspecto de marica sonriente (Schlesinger, Guillermo: Yo nunca me olvidaré de ti. San Salvador: Editorial del Oso, 2001)
At the turn of a column, he is startled by a mannequin dressed in casual clothes, which fails to disguise its appearance as a smiling faggot

Este anglicismo que designa la ropa diseñada para uso informal carece ya de significado connotativo en español, por lo que ni siquiera se marca tipográficamente en el TO. No ofrece dificultades de traducción.

4.18. Cat eye

Hay reediciones cat eyes que supieron lucir Marilyn Monroe o Grace Kelly ("Pasó, pasa, pasará". Lanacion.com. Buenos Aires: lanacion.com.ar, 2011-03-10)
There are cat-eye reissues that Marilyn Monroe or Grace Kelly wore

El anglicismo que aparece en el TO es un sustantivo en función adjetiva y lleva marca de plural por analogía con los adjetivos en español. El traductor automático, indudablemente por la gran cantidad de textos parecidos que contienen esta o similares estructuras, identifica que se trata de un adjetivo y en el TM lo adelanta al sustantivo y añade guion entre los dos sustantivos que conforman el adjetivo.

4.19. Celebrity/ celebrities

Me he pasado la mayor parte de mi vida evitando ser una 'celebrity' (Hernández, Virginia: "DONALD TRUMP JR, HIJO MAYOR DEL MAGNATE. El verdadero 'aprendiz' de Trump". Elmundo.es. Madrid: elmundo.es, 2008-04-07)
I have spent most of my life avoiding being a celebrity

A diferencia de lo que suele hacer *DeepL*, en este caso, omite en el TM las comillas del TO. Parece una decisión acertada, pues podría entenderse que el anglicismo se entrecomilla en español, precisamente para marcar su carácter de extranjerismo necesario pues hacer referencia a una realidad foránea (entendiendo que una *celebrity* no es exactamente lo mismo que una persona famosa).

4.20. Check point

Los residentes sólo podían entrar y salir por el check point de la avenida Jaffo, blanco de furibundos ataques (Gamboa, Santiago: Necrópolis. Bogotá: Norma, 2009)
Residents could only enter and exit through the checkpoint on Jaffo Avenue, the target of furious attacks

A veces, los hablantes no emplean los anglicismos correctamente, como se observa en este ejemplo, en el que el redactor escribe el sustantivo *checkpoint* en dos palabras, basándose en su origen compuesto. *DeepL* lo corrige en la versión inglesa.

4.21. Chill out

Había compartido con ella medio gramo de coca en un chill out (Etxebarria, Lucía: De Todo lo Visible y lo Invisible. Una novela sobre el amor y otras mentiras. Madrid: Espasa Calpe, 2001)
I had shared half a gram of coke with her in a chill out

Las lenguas evolucionan al ritmo de los hablantes y, aunque *chill out* en inglés no se ha empleado tradicionalmente con valor sustantivo, algunos diccionarios on-line ya recogen este uso, más bien referido a un tipo de música, no un local de copas, con sillones y música relajante (www.macmillandictionary.com). Por si el público meta no estuviera familiarizado con este empleo, quizás un traductor humano habría optado por una paráfrasis explicativa. Sin embargo, *DeepL* mantiene la voz en el TM con la misma categoría gramatical y el significado que tiene en español.

4.22. Coach

El término "coach" va ligado usualmente al mundo deportivo; su traducción literal es "entrenador", de ahí su asociación con el deporte. Hacer "coaching" significa "entrenar a otros". (Menéndez, José L.; Worth, Cristian: Abre el melón. Cómo te puede ayudar el Coaching a conseguir tus metas. Madrid: Santillana, 2002)
The term "coach" is usually linked to the world of sport; its literal translation is "trainer", hence its association with sport. To coach means "to train others"

Corpes XXI ofrece muchas coincidencias para *coach*, ya que se trata de un término que ha visto multiplicado su empleo en los últimos años. No en vano, el *DLE* lo recoge ya entre los anglicismos que se han introducido en español, aunque recomienda su uso en cursiva. En el ejemplo que hemos seleccionado, *DeepL* explica en el TM el significado de coach, recurriendo a un sinónimo.

4.23. Contouring

> Kim Kardashian y otras 'celebrities', a través de las redes sociales, han puesto en boca de todos términos como 'contouring', 'strobbing' o 'baking' (Sotillo, Marta: "Cómo dar con la base perfecta de maquillaje". Yo Dona. El Mundo. España: elmundo.es/yodona, 2016-05-08)
> Kim Kardashian and other 'celebrities', through social networks, have put on everyone's lips terms like 'contouring', 'strobing' or 'baking'

Según el diccionario Merriam Webster, el italiano es el étimo último y el francés, el étimo inmediato (Cf. Pratt, 1980) de la palabra *contour*. Se trata de un galicismo en inglés. En el caso de *contouring* estaríamos ante un derivado híbrido en inglés, al incorporar un sufijo propio de esta lengua. El TO añade comillas, tanto en *celebrities*, que se resalta por su condición de extranjerismo, como en *contouring*, *strobbing* y *baking*, que se resaltan por ser extranjeras y por la función metalingüística. *DeepL* las mantiene en el TM en todos los casos, sin distinguir entre una función que existe también en el TM y otra, que no.

4.24. Cookie

> [...] entra en su sistema y lo almacena en el ordenador del mismo por medio de una cookie (o galleta de información que recoge en su interior el código de usuario) (Royo, Javier: Diseño digital. Barcelona: Paidós, 2004)
> [...] enters your system and stores it on your computer by means of a cookie (or information cookie that collects the user code inside)

A pesar de tratarse de un vocablo muy común en español hoy en día, el motor de traducción ofrece un TM que carece de sentido, al repetir la palabra *cookie* en la explicación de lo que este término significa en lenguaje informático.

4.25. Cool

> Evidente *win-win*. Dejan espacio para el *afterwork*, eso sí, una cervecita en un garito *random*, una *app* donde hacerle *match* al *crush*. Si Cavia levantara la cabeza, se encontraría con que ese exotismo lingüístico que denunciaba cien años atrás dejó de ser asaz bajuno y excesivamente cursi; ahora es *mainstream*, *cool* y *friendly*. Salve, don

Mariano; el idioma que va a morir te saluda (Mayoral, Carlos: El prestigio del "webinar". Zenda. Autores, libros y compañía. Madrid: zendalibros.com, 2020-06-04)
Obvious win-win. They leave room for afterwork, yes, a beer in a random bar, an app where you can match up with your crush. If Cavia were to raise his head, he would find that the linguistic exoticism that he denounced a hundred years ago is no longer so low and excessively cheesy; it is now mainstream, cool and friendly. Salve, don Mariano; the language that is going to die salutes you

En este ejemplo, hemos extraído algo más de texto para mostrar la ironía con la que, en el TO, se emplean los anglicismos, entre los que se encuentra *cool* y algún otro que hemos comentado en este artículo. Al margen de la imposibilidad de mantener la cursiva en el TM por las razones comentadas (véase anteriormente *animal print*), la traducción no refleja en absoluto la actitud del hablante, que se manifiesta en el TO, precisamente mediante la selección de palabras en inglés que desplazan a las españolas.

4.26. Cow boy

Tengo para mí que es improbable que los heroicos *cow boys* que conquistaron incontables leguas de terreno para la civilización, lo hayan hecho comiendo únicamente judías (Vázquez Rial, Horacio: El cuñado de Nietzsche y otros viajes. Sevilla: Fundación José Manuel Lara, 2007)
I think it unlikely that the heroic cow boys who conquered countless leagues of land for civilisation did so by eating only beans

Gómez Capuz (1998: 276) menciona que uno de los motivos por los que se emplean anglicismos es mantener el colorido local de una realidad extranjera. Sin duda, esa es la causa por la que se emplea *cow boy* en este ejemplo, que se refiere a los personajes reflejados en las películas del Oeste. Este matiz se pierde en el TM.

4.27. Crop top

El crochet tiene aplicaciones diversas que van desde sexies crop tops en blanco, azul, verde, rosa hasta vestidos combinados con satén, bikinis y múltiples accesorios (Costa, Paulina; Orellano, Sofía: "Las tendencias de la moda en la gran pasarela de Punta". El País. Montevideo: tvshow.com.uy/tendencias-moda-gran-pasarela-punta.html, 2016-01-07)
Crochet has diverse applications ranging from sexy crop tops in white, blue, green, pink to dresses combined with satin, bikinis and multiple accessories

Estamos ante un ejemplo más de cuánto han evolucionado los motores de traducción automática. En el TO se añade una terminación de sustantivo plural a lo que en realidad es un adjetivo, que no lleva marca de número en inglés (*sexies*). Eso lo corrige *DeepL* en el TM que ofrece.

4.28. DIY

> El contenido se enfoca en verticales lifestyle (estilo de vida) como Belleza, Cocina, Manualidades (DIY), Hogar y Salud ("COMPAÑÍA LÍDER DE MEDIOS HISPANOS SE ASOCIA CON LA PRINCIPAL RED DIGITAL LATINA". La Opinión. Los Ángeles: laopinion.com, 2013-12-16)
> The content focuses on lifestyle verticals such as Beauty, Cooking, DIY, Home and Health

El TO alterna el español y el inglés de forma algo arbitraria. En la propuesta para el TM, a diferencia de lo que se ha hecho en otros casos, se omiten las voces que en un texto escrito totalmente en inglés serían meras repeticiones o aclaraciones innecesarias.

4.29. Expertise

> Cumplimos bastante bien las normas básicas que comentaba Ramón y Cajal como necesarias para una buena tertulia: principalmente, hablar de lo que no se sabe. De lo que no es su expertise que dicen los finos (Armentia, Javier: "Dioses Y Tibiezas". Por La Boca Muere El Pez. www.javarm.blogalia.com: javarm.blogalia.com, 2002-01-29)
> We comply quite well with the basic rules that Ramón y Cajal mentioned as necessary for a good get-together: mainly, talk about what you don't know. Of what is not your expertise, as the finos say

Una manera de compensar la carga pragmática que se pierde al omitir un anglicismo en la traducción de un texto de español a inglés podría ser emplear un préstamo del español en el TM. A simple vista, parece que eso es lo que ha hecho *DeepL* en este caso, al usar la palabra *fino*, después de que se haya perdido la ironía que el anglicismo *expertise* aportaba al TO. Sin embargo, no es ese el propósito que persigue pues, en efecto, en inglés se emplea el préstamo *fino*, pero para referirse a un tipo de vino español, sentido muy alejado del TO. *As the finos say* es una cláusula carente de sentido en inglés.

4.30. Express

> La ciudad cuenta con una oferta gastronómica inmensa, que he decidido descubrir hace unas semanas en un viaje express ("La mejor gastronomía de Valencia: Marina Beach y Apicius". La Razón. Madrid: larazon.es, 2019-01-29)
> The city has an immense gastronomic offer, which I decided to discover a few weeks ago on an express trip

Luján-García incluye *express* en el listado de anglicismos, pero el *DLE*, aunque reconoce el inglés como étimo último, considera que el francés es el étimo inmediato. Sea como sea, no es un préstamo reciente y hoy en día no aporta connotaciones significativas, por lo que una traducción literal como la que ofrece *DeepL* refleja bien el sentido del TO.

5. Conclusiones

Los ejemplos de frases reales en las que aparecen anglicismos, extraídos de un corpus de español general, nos han permitido constatar las distintas funciones con las que los anglicismos se emplean, desde la meramente referencial en lenguajes técnicos o jergales hasta la estilística, cuando se prefieren voces foráneas en lugar de sus equivalentes semánticos en español. La validez de las traducciones automáticas propuestas por el motor de traducción *DeepL* en las oraciones analizadas varía en función de la combinación de lenguas y el papel que desempeñan los anglicismos en cada caso. Por un lado, en el par de lenguas español-inglés, indudablemente existe un gran corpus de textos traducidos de los que la máquina puede nutrirse y aprender. Como se ha puesto de manifiesto en ejemplos como *look*, empleados habitualmente en el ámbito de la moda y otros afines, la traducción literal funciona bastante bien. En otros casos, como el de *beauty*, el motor de traducción ha aprendido que la palabra tiene significados diversos si va precedida de artículo femenino o masculino, por lo que ofrece variantes distintas en cada caso. Por otro lado, el motor aporta traducciones muy acertadas cuando se trata de contextos especializados, donde se emplean anglicismos con un significado denotativo. Sería lo que ocurre con *bluetooth* o *business intelligence*.

Sin embargo, las connotaciones que se infieren de los anglicismos en algunos empleos de nuestro corpus, como *biker*, *body milk* o *blush*, se pierden en las variantes en inglés de *DeepL*. Esta ineficacia manifestada por la herramienta para reflejar aspectos pragmáticos en textos traducidos por ordenador no es sorprendente puesto que los mecanismos de comprensión, inferencia y selección que aplica el ser humano exceden las capacidades de la inteligencia artificial (Flöter-Durr, 2022). Por ello, *DeepL* tampoco acierta con las marcas tipográficas empleadas para resaltar los anglicismos en los textos en español. La cursiva no se puede usar directamente desde la interfaz de Internet, por lo que es necesario abandonar la intención de marcar el anglicismo con este resalte, tal y como se recomienda hacer en español (Real Academia de la Lengua Española, 2010: 601; Instituto Cervantes, 2012: 194).

En el caso de las comillas, *DeepL* se comporta de forma irregular. En algún caso, como hemos observado en el ejemplo de *celebrity*, las omite. En otros, las conserva en la traducción al inglés, sin que exista un motivo para entrecomillar los anglicismos en un texto escrito completamente en inglés. Además de los casos ya comentados de *anti-aging*, *baby shower* o *contouring*, en *Corpes XXI* identificamos otra muestra del empleo de las comillas para reflejar ortográficamente la pronunciación inglesa de la palabra. Para la frase "[…] a costa de su ensoñación artística quisieron hacerse un 'bisnes' (business)" (https://apps2.rae.es/CORPES/org/publico/pages/consulta/entradaCompleja.view), *DeepL* ofrece la versión *at the expense of their artistic reverie wanted to make themselves a "bisnes" (business)*. Esta opción no aporta ninguna clave al lector del TM acerca de las dificultades que los hablantes de español tienen ante sistemas de pronunciación no ortográfica. Por el mismo motivo, se diluye la necesidad de aclarar entre paréntesis a qué término en inglés se está haciendo referencia.

De forma similar, como hemos visto con *after sun*, *batch cooking*, *blush*, *back-up* o *cookie*, cuando en el TO se aporta el anglicismo y su traducción al español, en la versión del TM que propone el motor de traducción automática, es habitual que se repita la misma palabra en inglés. Sin embargo, en algunos casos, *DeepL* busca un sinónimo. Es lo que refleja el ejemplo antes comentado de *coach*. Además, cuando el TO en español dice explícitamente que la palabra responde a una sigla o expresión en inglés, tal y como hemos visto en el caso de *adware*, en la traducción propuesta se omite dicha acotación. Sin duda, como también se observa en nuestro corpus en el caso de *cat eye*, *check point* o *crop top* el hecho de que los motores de traducción hagan generalizaciones basándose en cómo se han resuelto problemas similares en otros textos, facilita que se sistematicen algunas operaciones y se obtengan traducciones acertadas.

No obstante, la creatividad de los usuarios de la lengua no puede sistematizarse. Esto se pone de manifiesto en la traducción de juegos de palabras, para los que hay que buscar soluciones *ad hoc*. En este estudio hemos visto cómo *DeepL* no acierta a la hora de traducir la combinación paronomástica *app-cappacidad*, pero, más allá de estas estructuras, constantemente se acuñan palabras nuevas o se añaden significados distintos a voces ya existentes. Los sistemas de traducción automática, que se basan en corpus paralelos de traducciones humanas, no pueden actualizarse al mismo ritmo que avanza la lengua y necesariamente van a la zaga de los usos del momento. A modo de ejemplo, el *DLE* (2022) recoge una acepción de pescar en el sentido de *entender, captar con rapidez el significado de algo*. Sin embargo, mucha gente joven emplea hoy en día ese verbo para afirmar todo lo contrario. Con la intención de aumentar la carga coloquial de la expresión, también es común decir el verbo en inglés, aunque en dicha lengua no exista con ese significado. En ese sentido y al menos en lo que respecta a la traducción automática de textos que contienen anglicismos por razones pragmáticas, *DeepL* está *fishing*.

6. Referencias bibliográficas

Alcalde, Elena y Cano, Ana Gregorio (2012): "Implicaciones didácticas en la traducción especializada: los anglicismos y su (no) traducción en el ámbito profesional del desarrollo de softwares", en *Íkala, Revista de Lenguaje y Cultura*, 18(2): 59–67.

Flöter-Durr, Margarete (2022): "Les limites épistémologiques des techniques numériques actuelles de l'intelligence artificielle en traduction", en *Lebende Sprachen*, 67(1), pp. 1–41

Fundéu (Fundación del Español Urgente). https://www.fundeu.es/

Gómez Capuz, Juan (1998): *El préstamo lingüístico: conceptos, problemas y métodos*. Valencia: Departamento de Filología Española, Universitat de València.

González Cruz, Isabel y Rodríguez Medina, Mª Jesús. (2011). "La función pragmática de los anglicismos: algunos ejemplos en el habla juvenil de Las Palmas de Gran Canaria", en *Miscelánea: A Journal of English and American Studies*, 43, pp. 13–32

Grass, Thierry (2022): "L'erreur n'est pas humaine" en *Traduire*, 246, pp. 10–23.

Hofstadter, Douglas (2018): "The Shallowness of Google Translate", en *The Atlantic. Online*. www.theatlantic.com/technology/archive/2018/01/the-shallowness-of-google-translate/551570/, January 30, 2018.

Instituto Cervantes (2012): *El libro del español correcto. Claves para hablar y escribir bien en español*. Barcelona: Espasa.

Lillo Buades, Antonio (2022): "Anglicismos coloquiales en la toponimia española", en *Lebende Sprachen*, 67–1, pp. 133–167.

Lorenzo Criado, Emilio (1998): "Neologismo y Anglicismo", en *V Jornadas de Metodología y Didáctica de la Lengua Española*, 19–30. Cáceres: Universidad de Extremadura.

Luján-García, Carmen (2020): "Contacto lingüístico: anglicismos en la sección de ocio de la edición digital de *La Provincia*" en *ELIA, Estudios de Lingüística Inglesa Aplicada*, 20, pp. 113–146.

Macmillan Dictionary. https://www.macmillandictionary.com/

Melby, Alan K. (2019): *Human and machine translation quality: Definable? Achievable? Desirable?* Based on the presidential lecture delivered on August 10, 2012, at the occasion of LACUS XXXIX, York University, Toronto, Canada. Disponible en 2018-12-17-LACUS2012-melby-formatted-v9h.pdf (ttt.org).

Merriam Webster Dictionary and Thesaurus. https://www.merriam-webster.com/

Morales de Walters, Amparo (2001): *Anglicismos puertorriqueños.* San Juan de Puerto Rico: Plaza Mayor.

Pratt, Chris (1980): *El anglicismo en el español peninsular contemporáneo.* Madrid: Gredos.

Real Academia de la Lengua Española. (2010): *Ortografía de la lengua española.* Madrid: Espasa.

———. (2014): *Diccionario de la lengua española.* https://www.rae.es/

Rodríguez González, Félix (1996): "Functions of anglicisms in contemporary Spanish" en *Cahiers de lexicologie,* LXVIII: 107–128. París: Didier Erudition.

———. (2019): "Aspectos tipográficos del anglicismo" en *Zeitschrift für romanische Philologie,* 135(2): 442–468. https://doi.org/10.1515/zrp-2019-0026.

Rodríguez Segura, Delia (1999): *Panorama del anglicismo en español: presencia y uso en los medios.* Almería: Universidad de Almería.

David L. Gold

The polysemous Spanish noun *safacón* ~ *zafacón*: A borrowing from English or a native Spanish coinage?

Abstract: This article is the first study of any breadth and depth of the polysemous Spanish count noun *safacón* ~ *zafacón*, which has appeared in every edition of the *Diccionario de la Lengua Española* of the Royal Spanish Academy since 1970 and which at least in Puerto Rico and the Dominican Republic has often been considered to be of American English origin.

The author begins with the known (*safacón* ~ *zafacón* has been used at least in Cuba, the Dominican Republic, Panama, Puerto Rico, and Venezuela; it has at least ten meanings, at least five derivatives, and two spellings), proceeds to the unknown (the origin of the word), weighs two suggested etymologies ([1] < English *safety can*? [2] = Spanish *zafa* + *-aco* + *-ón*?), and concludes that the available evidence is too weak to allow us to accept or to reject either one. Nonetheless, the present article lays the foundation for any future treatment of the word.

Keywords: English, etymology, lexicology, lexicography, *safacón* ~ *zafacón*, Spanish.

1. Introduction[1]

The Royal Spanish Academy, founded in Madrid in 1713, has since 1726 published twenty-four editions of its *Diccionario de la lengua española* (an unabridged general dictionary, hereinafter referred to as DLE). Ever since the appearance of the first one (DLE 1726–1739), it has included (1) lexemes that arose in Western Hemispheric Spanish and (2) meanings acquired in that topolect by lexemes that had arisen in Peninsular Spanish. Since the founding of the academies of the Spanish language outside Spain (the first to be established, in 1871, was the Colombian Academy of the Spanish Language), the compilers of the DLE have been paying ever closer attention to Western Hemispheric Spanish.

---

1 I thank Michael J. Flory, José Rafael Hernández Fereira, María Julia Labrador, José Antonio Sánchez Fajardo, José Antonio Sánchez Gil, Miriam Ticoll, Sheila N. Torres Negrón, the staff of the Department of References at the Central Archives of the Indies, and the publisher's anonymous copy-editor for their help of many kinds.

As will be shown below, abundant information can still be collected about the noun *safacón ~ zafacón* (hereinafter *s~z*) and its derivatives.

*

At least one and maybe two linguistic myths have been circulating chiefly in Puerto Rico since the early-twentieth century: the myth is that the place name *Porto Rico* is an American English coinage and the possible myth is that the noun *safacón ~ zafacón* (hereinafter *s~z*) dates to the time just after the end of the Spanish-American War and comes from the American English noun *safety can*. In point of fact, *Porto Rico* was coined in native Spanish under no alloglossal influence and has a well-documented history in native Spanish going back at least to 1562 (Gold, 2012). With respect to *s~z*, our knowledge about the word is still scanty enough to justify neither acceptance nor rejection of the suggestion that it derives from *safety can* or the suggestion that it is a native Spanish coinage consisting of the Spanish elements *safa ~ zafa*, *-aco*, and *-ón*.

I follow here the usual method in all sciences by beginning with the known (Sects. 2.1, 2.2, and 2.3 deal with synchronic aspects of the word) and on the basis of the known I try to reconstruct as much of the unknown as possible (Sects. 3.1, 3.2, 3.3, and 3.4 deal with diachronic aspects).

Having gathered as much synchronic and diachronic information as possible, I then look at how the Royal Spanish Academy has treated the word for the last fifty years (*s ~ z* first appeared in the DLE in 1970) and find that significant improvements can be made (Sect. 4).

2. Synchronic aspects

2.1. The known forms and present-day spatial distribution of *safacón ~ zafacón*

Cuba

S ~ z is now less than universal in Cuban Spanish. Here is evidence for occasional use of the word in eastern Cuba and sometimes elsewhere in the country:[2]"[Yo]

2 In the present article, if understanding a quotation in Spanish is essential for following my line of reasoning, it is translated and/or summarized in English (for instance, the sentences beginning "*S ~ z* is now [...]" and "Here is evidence [...]" are a summary of the quotation in Spanish that begins "[Yo] personalmente [...]"). The other quotations in Spanish are not translated or summarized because their purpose is only to document use of the word (or a derivative thereof) in specific Spanish topolects.

personalmente nunca había escuchado (o usado) la palabra en ninguno de los sentidos que comentas. He revisado el *Diccionario de cubanismos* de Gisela Cárdenas (2000) y tampoco aparece registrada. Les he preguntado a mi padre, José Antonio Sánchez Gil (nacido en 1943 en Melena del Sur en la Provincia de Mayabeque), y a una filóloga cubana, María Julia Labrador (nacida en 1978). Ella me ha confirmado que se usa (no con mucha frecuencia) en la región oriental de Cuba con el significado de 'basurero' o 'recipiente para la basura'. Mi padre, además, me confirma que le suena que se usara hace mucho tiempo la frase *echar* (algo) *al zafacón*, que significa algo así como 'desperdiciar una oportunidad', tal vez en poblaciones colindantes con La Habana" (José Antonio Sánchez Fajardo, email, 2 June 2021).

Dominican Republic

S ~ *z* is now universal in Dominican Spanish. Section 2.3 has two Dominican quotations (from unsigned 2010 and Cruz Triffolio, 2020).

Panama

S ~ *z* is now less than universal in Panamanian Spanish. Examples of recent use are:

"Geo. F. Novey Inc Inc. [sic], baldes para agua y **zafacones** 7 bultos de Nueva York por . . . . 723" (an entry in a list made by Panamanian customs officials of merchandise imported from outside Panama, published in unsigned 1948: 16; leaders in original). Geo F. Novey Inc. is a Panamanian importing company with headquarters in Panama City.

"El panameño está acostumbrado a tirar cuanta basura sea a la calle, playas o ríos. No les interesa lo que signifique tal acción. […]. Otro dato educativo que debemos practicar es colocar bien la tapa a todo antes de botarlo. Bote la basura en una bolsa plástica, amárrela bien y métala dentro de un **zafacón**" (Redacción 2003).

"Reclaman por la mala colocación de **zafacones** por la Autoridad de Aseo" (unsigned 2017).

"El Pacto de Estado por la Justicia ha hecho una labor encomiable con el examen de las credenciales de los abogados que tienen aspiraciones para ocupar dos vacantes en la Corte Suprema de Justicia, una vez que se concreten las salidas de Oydén Ortega y Jerónimo Mejía. […]. Y, a pesar de que es una labor concienzuda, no pocas veces la selección que hacen termina en el **zafacón**, porque los políticos prefieren que esos cargos los ocupen amigos fieles, cuyo criterio no responda a su deber de impartir justicia, sino el de garantizarse impunidad" (unsigned 2018a).

Puerto Rico

S ~ *z* is now universal in Puerto Rican Spanish.

Singular *safacón* occurs four times and plural *safacones* once in Raul 1903, all five times with initial <s>.[3] An examination of the Puerto Rican Spanish-language newspapers viewable at *Chronicling America* on 23 May 2021 showed that between 11 January 1903 and 31 December 1915 the <s>- and <z>-variants, whether the noun is in the singular or the plural, were about equally frequent (see LC in References in the present article). In all those occurrences (including the ones in Raul 1903) it means 'garbage can, garbage pail, trash can'. Sections 2.2 and 2.3 each have one more Puerto Rican quotation (from Martes Pedraza, 2010 and Roque Rivera, 1999).

Venezuela

S ~ z is now less than universal in Venezuelan Spanish.

In his blog *Maracucholario Plus*, which deals with Maracaiban Spanish, José Rafael Hernández Fereira gives some details about use of the word in the state of Zulia:

"Esta palabra ya no se escucha pero fue algo popular en la época de la explotación petrolera en los campos donde vivían trabajadores y gringos. Se le llamaba así a las pipas o envases que se destinaban para almacenar los desechos o desperdicios, para su posterior recolección y bote por parte de vehículos destinado a esto. 'Echá esos papeles en el safacón'" (Hernández Fereira, 2013; double quotation marks in original).[4] On 21 September 2014, he answered my questions about the foregoing passage:

---

3 The oldest evidence that research for the present article has found for *s* ~ *z* in any country is in Raul 1903. See section 3.1 on the importance of earliest-known uses in etymological investigations.

4 "José Rafael Hernández Fereira nació en Maracaibo, Venezuela, el 20 de mayo de 1956. Escritor desde su adolescencia, ha incursionado en diversos géneros de la literatura tales como el cuento, la novela, el ensayo, el teatro, la literatura infantil, la prosa y la poesía, con un número de obras escritas que sobrepasan la media centena" (from the author's blog, in which he gives details about himself; https://www.xinxii.com/jos%C3 %A9-rafael-hern%C3 %A1ndez-fereira-45590).

Question 1: Usted hace mención de «la explotación petrolera». ¿Puede precisar los años (al menos aproximadamente)?

Answer: La explotación petrolera en Venezuela se inicia a principios del siglo 20 y es en los años 20 aproximadamente en que el país es invadido por extranjeros para realizar esta. En el Zulia los más representativos fueron los ingleses quienes se asentaron en la costa oriental.

Question 2: No entiendo «trabajadores y gringos». ¿Quiere decir 'trabajadores venezolanos y extranjeros' ¿O 'trabajadores venezolanos y gerentes extranjeros'? Es decir, no me es claro el contraste que usted hace entre «trabajadores [¿que no fueron gringos?]» y «gringos [¿que no fueron trabajadores?]».

Answer: La mano de obra traída por los ingleses era trinitaria, jamaiquina y haitiana y a la misma se le mezcló la nacional, pero el término *gringo* se hace popular años después para señalar a cualquier persona de otra nacionalidad sin importar si eran nativos de Estados Unidos. En otras regiones también se hizo popular el término *musiú*.

Question 3: Si se trata de extranjeros, supongo que todos fueron dominicanos o puertorriqueños (porque al menos durante el siglo veinte dicha palabra se empleaba solamente en el español dominicano y puertorriqueño, además del maracaibero) [I did not know in 2014 that the word has been used in Cuban and Panamanian Spanish too (D. L. G.)]. ¿Sabe usted de dónde vinieron los extranjeros?

Answer: Los puertorriqueños y dominicanos no fueron mano de obra en la industria petrolera zuliana, pero eso no indica que no haya podido haber alguna minoría, por lo tanto la palabra no es heredada de ellos así como tampoco la de *guachimán*. En el dialecto maracucho existen muchas palabras que terminaron convirtiéndose en neologismos, nacidos de la homofonía.

Question 4: ¿Tengo razón en suponer que en Venezuela *safacón* se empleaba (o sigue empleándose hoy, aunque menos) solo en la municipalidad de Maracaibo?

Answer: "*Safacón* se empleaba en la región zuliana, sobre todo en la costa oriental y donde existía influencia petrolera. No tengo conocimiento que se empleara en otros lugares."

Question 5: "De la frase de ejemplo «Echá esos papeles en el safacón» deduzco que en Maracaibo *safacón* significa o significaba 'papelera' (p.ej. en los despachos). ¿Se empleaba también para denominar el recipiente para los desperdicios de [1] la industria petrolera, [2] las cocinas, [3] la calle o [4] los parques?"

Answer: "En el dialecto maracucho las palabras terminan generalizándose y no puntualizando, por lo tanto cualquier recipiente que sirva para botar la basura se le llama igual, o sea papeleras, pipas, botes, etc. por lo cual envases para diferentes fines toman el mismo nombre."*

Zafacón has survived into the twenty-first century in Venezuela. The authors of the following passages are Venezuelans writing on Venezuelan topics in Venezuelan electronic publications:

> "Para 'los 'ladrones', la faena consistía en dispersarse por las calles aledañas del barrio para colectar 'prendas' que se definían de antemano: Una piedra… un objeto descuidado… y a falta de éstos, las camisas de 'los policías', ubicadas en vallados, árboles y **zafacones**" (Moreno Arreche 2009; single quotation marks in original).
> "Lo del diputado de Primero Justicia Juan Carlos Caldera no sorprendió a ningún bolivariano y no tenía porque sorprenderlo, incluso en su[s] declaraciones donde no hallaba como [sic] tapar su extorsión, ya nos tienen acostumbrado que todo hecho que hagan en contra de la ética y la moral lo niegan de manera descarada, para ellos no hay ningún principio ético donde acepten su responsabilidad, su famoso autobús del progreso donde van todos los dirigentes de Primero Justicia conducido por su candidato [a la] presidencia lo que van es: Pa' el **Zafacón**" (Camacaro, 2012; the bracketed material is mine).

"[…] muy bien acotaba gabo marquez, en una de sus obras literarias,, cuando la mierda coja valor,los pobres naceran sin culos.incluso existe por ahi en un **zafacon** de la historia una expresion de un pundonoroso presidente de norte america que reza mas o menos PARA NUESTRO PAÍS,ES MUY IMPORTANTE QUE SUS CIUDADANOS HAGAN DINERO HONRADAMENTE,PERO SI NO PUEDES HACERLO HONRADAMENTE, HAGA DINERO" (3a cual club o club 2014, quoted here verbatim et literatim et punctuatim).

2.2. A stemma suggested for the known current meanings of *safacón* ~ *zafacón*

Reconstructing a semantic stemma has been a procedure in etymological research at least since 1828 (see Facciolati and Forcellini with Bailey 1828: 855, s.v. *uindex*, as well as the discussion and the significant improvements in Szemerényi, 1981). Depending on the nature of the etymological problem to be solved, a stemma is indispensable, helpful, or unnecessary. It being indispensable for *s* ~ *z* because the word has at least ten meanings (attested by quotations in the present article), I suggest this stemma for the currently known ones:

Sense **1**. '(very large?) container for anything that one wants to keep clean and undamaged' (see Sect. 3.4 and the second paragraph of the comment on sense 2.1.2 below).

Sense **2.** '(very large?) container for anything that is to be disposed of' (see that paragraph).
Sense **2.1.** '(very large?) container for anything dirty' (see that paragraph).
Sense **2.1.1.** '(very large?) container for dirty laundry' (used at least in Dominican Spanish).
Sense **2.1.2.** 'garbage can, garbage pail, trash can'. Where *s* ~ *z* has that meaning (at least in the Spanish of the Dominican Republic, Panama, Puerto Rico, andVenezuela), *zafacón de reciclaje* 'recycling bin, recycling can', a recently coined hyponym, is possibly used too. At least Dominican Spanish also has *zafacón de basura*, used if the speaker or writer believes that unmodified *zafacón* is, may, or would be ambiguous.

Whether this Puerto Rican quotation is evidence for *zafacón* in sense 1, 2, and/or 2.1 remains to be determined: "Tan pronto como el maíz esté completamente seco se debe poner en un receptáculo herméticamente cerrado y fumigarlo con sulfuro de carbono. Si es poca cantidad de maíz se puede usar una lata o un 'zafacón' […]" (Wolcott, 1922: 6–7; double quotation marks in original). If sense 2.1.2 was intended, an absolutely clean can is understood.

Sense **2.1.2.1** = figurative use of sense 2.1.2.

This passage in a Dominican text shows the word in several of the foregoing senses (the *unidad* under discussion is an *unidad de cólera* 'cholera ward' in a hospital): "Es una unidad provista de **zafacones** para ropa sucia [sense 2.1.1] y contaminada [sense 2.1] y **zafacones** para material contaminado [sense 2.1] como también **zafacones** para material limpio [sense 1] […]" (unsigned 2010).

This passage in a Dominican text shows the word in sense 2.1.2.1: "El rechazo ejemplarizante de nuestra nieta adorada, Mila Marie, no lo echaremos al **zafacón** del olvido, su reacción ha sido y será un mandato de valoración permanente y de agradecimiento eterno" (Cruz Triffolio, 2020).

Sense **2.2.** 'wastepaper basket', which probably derives from sense 2.1.2.[5] Sense **3.** 'filthy person' (used at least in Puerto Rican Spanish), which derives from sense 2.1.2.
Sense **4.** 'large amount or number [of anything], that is, enough to fill a large container' (used at least in Puerto Rican Spanish), as here: "Se quedó con todas sus astronómicas ganas de decirles que no creía en la patraña aquélla de un **zafacón** de ideas escondido en sitio alguno, que él era un poeta y punto, muy capaz de soñar despierto y escribir dormido lo que por mero gusto hacía al revés" (Martes Pedraza, 2010: 15). The word has that sense in these Puerto Rican examplesentences too (sent to me by Sheila

5 At least in Venezuelan Spanish, the noun *pipote*, which DLE 2014 defines as 'pipa pequeña que sirve para encerrar y transportar licores, pescados y otras cosas' and to which it assigns no spatial label, has acquired sense 2.1.2 (*pipote de basura* is used to convey that sense if unmodified *pipote* may be ambiguous). The semantic history of the word is thus identical to part of that of *s* ~ *z*.

N. Torres Negrón): "mi vecino tiene un **zafacón** de libros" and "había un **zafacón** de gente." See below for more on that sense. Does sense 4 come from sense 1?

Sense **5**. 'large amount of knowledge' (used at least in Puerto Rican Spanish), which seems to occur just in the idiom *saber un zafacón* 'be extremely knowledgeable, know a great deal, know a whole lot'. The oldest evidence that research for the present article has turned up for the idiom is in Claudio de la Torre 1989 (where it is defined as 'saber mucho'). Sense 5 is a narrowing of sense 4.

If *s* ~ *z* has or had more meanings, they remain to be discovered.

The discussion of the meaning of *s-z* will be concluded in Sect. 3.4.

2.3. Derivatives of *safacón* ~ *zafacón unrecorded in the* DLE

No edition of the DLE lists any of these derivatives:

Section 3.4 will suggest the possibility that *s* ~ *z* was originally an augmentative form. If so, the diminutive form *safaconcito* ~ *zafaconcito* (with the diminutive suffix *-cito*), used at least in Puerto Rican Spanish, arose after *s* ~ *z* was no longer felt to be an augmentative form because had it arisen before, the diminutive suffix would in all likelihood have been added to the base form (*zafa* ~ *safa* + *-ita* = **zafita* ~ **safita*). The word, which appears in the following passage, was therefore coined presumably after *s* ~ *z* was no longer felt to be a diminutive (see the analogous remark about *camisetaca* in Sect. 3.4).

"Mi madre fue la primera persona 'eco-amigable' que conocí. Desde pequeña, no entendía por qué nunca podía depositar el sobrante de mi comida en el **zafacón**, como el resto de las personas normales. Ella imponía su propio orden y proceso: los pedazos de carne serían para las mascotas, el residuo de arroz iría al **zafaconcito** donde le haría compañía a la hoja de pastel, la cáscara de plátano y la borra de café" (Roque Rivera, 1999).

*

Safaconero ~ *zafaconero* has several meanings:

Sense **A**. 'garbage collector, garbage man, sanitation worker' (used at least in Dominican and Puerto Rican Spanish). In the Department of Sanitation of the National District (= the city of Santo Domingo) and presumably in such departments elsewhere in the Dominican Republic, *obrero zafaconero* 'sanitation worker' is the official designation of a sanitation worker.

This is a Puerto Rican example: "ZAFACONERO / POR FAVOR NO TIRE, NI DENTRO O FUERA, / ESCOMBROS. NI DE LA CASA NI VEGETATIVOS." (sign for the sanitation workers, posted outside an apartment house by the Asociación Condomines Cluster 8 Río Cristal, Inc. La Original [Asociación n. d.]).

Sense **B**. *'garbage digger, garbage scavenger, trashmonger, waste picker' (used at least in Dominican Spanish). In that sense the word is applied at least to birds and dogs (as well as to cats, humans, mice, and rats?):

"Palomas cagonas, Gorriones safaconeros" (Pantaleón Inoa n. d.) 'shitting pigeons. garbage-scavenging sparrows'.
"Perro paramedico del dario safaconero" (the caption, likely not proofread, of a photograph that accompanies Féliz, 2016 and shows a dog foraging in a garbage dump; is "dario safaconero" a misprint for *vertedero* 'garbage dump'?).[6] "los perros eran verdaderos analfabetos, un tanto callejeros por naturaleza, zafaconeros por instinto [...]" (Forcadell, 2016).

Sense **C** (used at least in Dominican Spanish). In the following passage, the noun phrase "perros zafaconeros" ('garbage-picking dogs', etc.) is applied to human beings: "A la jauría de perros zafaconeros o viralatas, portadores de las más degradantes patologías contagiosas [...] no le falta ninguna infamia denigratoria por llevar a cabo ni ignominia por practicar [...]" (unsigned 2018b).

Neither the following passage nor its cotext or its context makes clear whether the writer meant 'garbage-digging dog' in a transferred sense or '[human] garbage digger': "No soy un safaconero" (González Beltré, 2014).

Sense **D**. 'person whose occupation involves garbage cans in one or more ways" (used at least in Puerto Rican Spanish). Expertos Zafaconeros, a Puerto Rican company, offers these services: "Limpieza y mantenimiento de zafacones soterrados y comerciales. Tenemos tapas y liners de plástico para el interior. No sólo limpiamos zafacones y recogemos basura sino que le damos personalidad a cada unidad. Convertimos cada zafacón en un atractivo tanto para su hogar como para su local comercial. No hay límites para nosotros [...]" (unsigned 2023).

Sense **E**. In this Puerto Rican text, the word seems to be a noun meaning 'stealer of garbage cans': "Según dice un diario ponceño, no hay zafacón que se salve en aquella población, habiendo familias que han perdido hasta cuatro de ellos sin que se haya podido dar con el autor de tales hazañas. ¶ Sin duda es un buen negocio el que tienen el o los autores de esos robos. ¶ No puede la policía atrapar uno de esos pillos zafaconeros?" (unsigned 1918). If the word is a noun here, it and the noun *pillo* are in apposition to each other. Alternately, it could be an adjective, in which case it would mean *'garbage-can-stealing'.

6 By 6 September 2021 the caption, including the word *safaconero*, had been replaced by one not containing it, though the original caption could still be found on that day through Google's advanced search.

In these three passages (the first is Puerto Rican and the other two are Dominican), the meaning of *zafaconero* is not clear and the cotexts do not help to disambiguate the word:

> "Allí, a Tipo de Noche, con su melena tropical, toda empapada de aceite, melena de don Juan zafaconero" (Miraflores, 1919).
> "Lo que sucede es que los tiempos han cambiado mucho. El arte popular dominicano se ha convertido en un negocio zafaconero, luego de la aparición de los llamados mamberos, reguetoneros. Algunas orquestas les han caído atrás bajando a niveles ridículos su tarifa, y por ello han descendido de categoría. Entonces quieren criticar a los que se mantienen, como El Torito, buscando con ello encontrar compañeros, pues es duro no tener compañía en el 'zafacón del arte'. Y ya se sabe que el que está en el zafacón, su destino final será un 'viajecito' en un camión compactador, hacia el vertedero de Duquesa" (Caceres, 2012; double quotation marks in original).
> "[Marino] Ramírez, quien no es cronista de arte, y que toda la vida se ha desempeñado como zafaconero de programas de radio de comentarios políticos [...]" (Caceres, 2017).

The Dominican Academy of the Spanish Language ignored my request for a definition of *zafaconero* in the second and third passages, as did Joseph Caceres with respect to the third.

To the extent that *safaconero* ~ *zafaconero* refers to a female, as the word may at least in sense B, it unsurprizingly takes the form *safaconera* ~ *zafaconera*.

*

"Una de las grandes características de nosotros los Dominicanos es la de ser muy trabajadores, joceadores y gran zafaconeador del peso donde quiera que esté, pero también somos famosos en inventarnos cosas para dar nuestra barajita en el trabajo y así las horas pasan mas [sic] suaves" (Moronta, 2009; "gran zafaconeador" should be *grandes zafaconeadores*).)

What does the noun *zafaconeador* mean? It implies the existence of the verb *zafaconear* '?', which occurs at least in Dominican Spanish:

> "[...] se quedó sin empleo, lo que lo llevó a 'zafaconear el peso' y, por ende, se agravó su enfermedad, la diabetes" (Jiménez, 2019).
> "Y los que nos fajamos a safaconear el voto, pa cuando" (Ramoncastro, 2020).

*

It appears that at least in recent times *s* ~ *z* has had more meanings and more derivatives in Dominican Spanish than in any other Spanish topolect. If so, and in light of the fact that meanings and derivatives take time to develop, it may be reasonable to assume that the word arose in that topolect or, if it arose in Peninsular Spanish, that it reached that topolect before it did other Western

Hemispheric ones. In connection with the first possibility, let it be notd that the first Spanish settlement in the Western Hemisphere was the Captaincy General of Santo Domingo, founded in 1492.

3. Diachronic aspects

3.1. The mistaken report that *safacón* appears in a document dated 31 December 1787

In etymological research, ascertaining the date of the earliest-known use of the lexeme or of a meaning of the lexeme under scrutiny, even if it is just approximate, is essential if the fallacy of anachronism is to be avoided (Gold, 2005). Thus, if *s* ~ *z* were attested, say, for 1830, any suggestion that the word arose after the Spanish-American War (see Sect. 3.2) would be wrong (see the of footnote 9).

By no later than 2014 a claim had been posted on the Internet that María Teresa Vaquero de Ramírez (1937–2008), known for short as *María Vaquero*, an accomplished linguist who specialized in Caribbean, especially Puerto Rican, Spanish (López Morales, 2009), had uncovered occurrences of *safacón* in a document written in Spanish in Amsterdam and dated 31 December 1787.[7] The document is a 35-page invoice for goods bought and to be delivered (*factura de géneros*) once in file 2489 and now in file 2489A of the Records of the Royal Audiencia of Santo Domingo (*Fondo de la Real Audiencia de Santo Domingo*), which is part of the General Archives of the Indies (*Archivo General de Indias*). It is headed "Amsterdam 31 de Diciembre de 1787," following which is this

7 The full text of the claim is "Quiero hacer referencia a un recorte que tengo sobre idioma de la profesora María Vaquero. Lamentablemente lo recibí de segunda mano y no he podido determinar a qué revista corresponde ni de qué fecha es. Pero el dato que aporta es el siguiente, que espero poder corroborar más tarde: 'En un documento del Archivo General de Indias, Audiencia de Sto. Domingo, Legajo 2489, fechado en Amsterdam, Diciembre 31 (de) 1787, […] aparecen repartidas las cerámicas españolas en dos tipos de recipientes: cajas y safacones. La tabla núm. 4, por ejemplo, consigna que '1 safacón (sic) contiene, entre otros, 12 platos grandes, a 6 placas' [o sea, a 6 monedas cada uno, con el precio total por safacón]". La conclusión a la que llega la profesora Vaquero es que cien años antes de la llamada 'operación limpieza' del 1898, la palabra 'safacón' ya existía en el idioma. Y que el hecho de que se distinguiera entre safacón y caja demuestra que debían diferenciarse por la forma o el material con el que estaban hechos" (http://etimologias.dechile.net/?zafaco.n; double quotation marks in original).Might María Vaquero have reported her discovery in her weekly column on Spanish ("Idioma") in *El Nuevo Día*, a newspaper published in San Juan?

title: "Factura de los Generos Siguientes Comprados y Cargados a bordo del navio nombrado El Marques de Sonora, Su Cap: Juan Angel de Musquiz, con destino de [the last word is an inadvertence for *à*, *á*, or *a*] Puertorico, de orden del Excelmo Señor Dn Antonio Valdes, del despacho Universal de Indias: por Cuenta de La Real Hacienda y a la Consignacion de la Real factoria de dha Isla. á Saber" (the bracketed addition is mine). The invoice then specifies all the merchandise sent to Puerto Rico at that time by Couriau Echenique Sanchez y Ca, a trading house in Amsterdam.

We will now analyze and compare three passages in the invoice to show that María Vaquero misread at least one of them (they are reproduced here by permission of the Spanish Ministry of Culture and Sport).

As may be expected in a document written with a quill by someone who was not a calligrapher, the invoice shows that the writer often lifted it from the paper for redipping because he saw that it was running out of ink (quills do not hold much). If he lifted it before finishing an orthographic word, after redipping he should have left no space before adding the letter or letters needed to complete the word, but many times he did leave one, so that one orthographic word now appeared as two in the document, the result being passages that make no sense if we take (1) each space as necessarily marking the end of one orthographic word and (2) each absence of a space as necessarily marking the middle of a word.

Figure 1 shows a phrase fully in accord with the rules of Spanish spacing in 1789, thus, with no unjustified addition or omission of spaces:

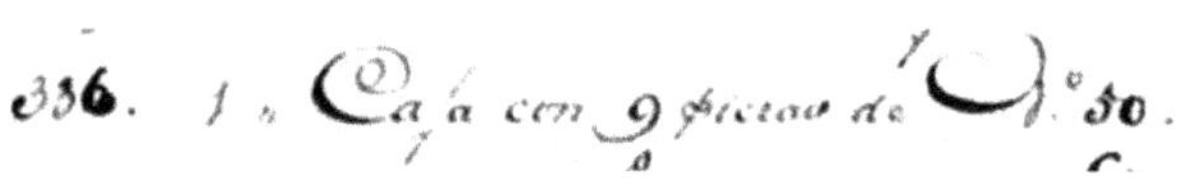

Fig. 1. 1 Caʃa con 9 piezas […]
ESPAÑA. MINISTERIO DE CULTURA Y DEPORTE
Archivo General de Indias. Santo_Domingo 2489A / 452/V
SRD_C_00592_0502.jpg (the second line of the page on the left)

The only letter requiring comment is the third one of the first word, <ʃ> (called *equis* in Spanish, the shape of which is now <x>), which in Old Spanish represented the phoneme that linguists represent by /ʃ/ (if they follow the International Phonetic Alphabet) or by /š/. By the 1780s, that phoneme had evolved into /x/, realized as [x] or [χ]. The first word is thus *Caʃa* 'Box, Case, Crate', which is now spelled <caja> and pronounced /ˈkaxa/ or /ˈkaχa/. The passage is easily interpreted as meaning '1 Box ~ Case ~ Crate with 9 pieces of [the rest is illegible but must designate some kind of merchandise]'.

Figures 2 and 3 show the phrases which María Vaquero presumably read and misunderstood:

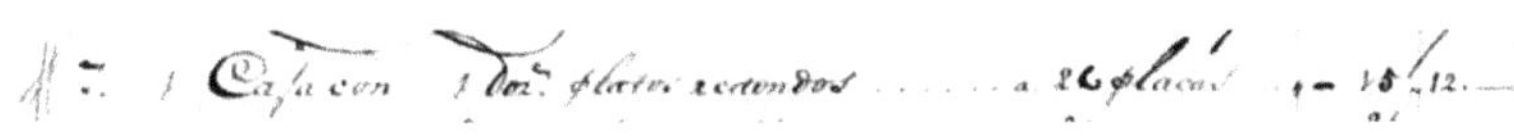

Fig. 2. 1 Ca ʃa con 1 Doz. platos redondos . . . . . . a 26 placas [...]
ESPAÑA. MINISTERIO DE CULTURA Y DEPORTE
Archivo General de Indias. Santo_Domingo 2489A / 460/V
SRD_C_00592_0510.jpg (the second line of the page on the left)

The spacing departs a bit from the norm because it contains a half space where there should be none, namely between the second and third letters of the word after the first instance of the numeral *1*. Once the half space is recognized as unjustified, the four letters are easily interpreted as constituting the word *caʃa*, mentioned above. The passage therefore reads *1 Caʃa con 1 doz. de platos redondos . . . . . . a 26 placas*, that is, '1 Box ~ Case ~ Crate with 1 dz. ['dozen' (D. L. G.)] round plates . . . . . . at 26 placas'.[8] Figure 3 shows the unjustified absence of a space between the noun *Caʃa* 'Box ~ Case ~ Crate' and the preposition *con* 'with':

Fig. 3. 1 Caʃacon 8 ...8 o
ESPAÑA. MINISTERIO DE CULTURA Y DEPORTE
Archivo General de Indias. Santo_Domingo 2489A / 452/V
SRD_C_00592_0502.jpg (the fifth line of the page on the left)

The sequence of letters *Caʃacon*, preceded and followed by a space but with no space between the fourth and fifth letters, thus suggests the existence of a single word, in which case the entire passage is *1 Caʃacon 8*, but since that does not

8 DLE 2014 defines *placa* as 'moneda de los Países Bajos, que circulaba en los demás dominios españoles y valía aproximadamente la cuarta parte de un real de plata vieja' and Varela Merino 2009, vol. 1, pp. 1778–1783, treats the word in detail.

make sense (‘1 Box ~ Case ~ Crate 8”’the rest of the passage, which is illegible, must designate some kind of merchandise]). We therefore assume the unjustified omission of a space, in which case the right interpretation is *1 Caſa con 8* ‘1 Box ~ Case ~ Crate with 8’.

*

None of those three passages thus contains *s ~ z*; the same may be said of the rest of the invoice; and if anyone finds a distinction between *s ~ z* and *caja* in that document (see “el hecho de que se distinguiera entre safacón y caja” above), it is a distinction between *caja* wrongly identified and caja rightly identified

In conclusion:

1. María Vaquero mistook the letter <ʃ> for the letter <f> (called *efe* in Spanish) and therefore mistook <caʃacon> to be a slip of the quill for <çaʃacon>, which she mistook to be an older spelling of *s ~ z.*
2. The fact that in no edition of Vaquero and Morales 2005 does the entry for *s ~ z* mention or quote the invoice of 31 December 1787 tells us that María Vaquero later became aware of her mistake.
3. The invoice is irrelevant to the history of *s ~ z.*
4. As of this writing (221 March 2024), the earliest-known use of *s ~ z* in any sense and in any topolect is dated 11 January 1903 (Raul 1903).

3.2. The unproven but not impossible suggestion that *safacón ~ zafacón* comes from American English *safety can*

“When United States citizens arrived in Puerto Rico to examine the new territory that had been ceded by Spain in the Treaty of Paris in 1898, they found an island in ruin. Spanish neglect, the ravages of war, and a recent major hurricane had combined to leave many Puerto Ricans impoverished. Even worse, the population seemed completely disease-ridden. Smallpox was epidemic throughout the island; dysentery, typhoid fever, malaria, hookworm infestations, and tuberculosis were all widespread in different areas. Doctors and health officials from the United States initially responded with measures to directly treat these maladies as they occurred, but soon concluded that such efforts were doomed to failure if unaccompanied by wholesale health and sanitation reforms” (Espinosa, 2000: [1]; see also Carroll, 1899, Hernandez et al., 1901, and Rigau-Pérez, 2017).

`As one of the measures taken to reduce the spread of disease, John Van Rensselaer Hoff, a member of the Medical Corps of the United States army then stationed on the island, where he served as the Chief Surgeon of Puerto Rico from 25 September 1898 to 7 August 1900 (unsigned 1918: 12) ordered lidded brass cans from the United States for the disposal of garbage. The cans were distributed free of charge in San Juan (and elsewhere on the island too?). According to Hernández Aquino, 1955, Robert H. Todd Wells (1862–1955), who served as Mayor of San Juan from 1903 to 1907, 1911 to 1920, and 1925 to 1931, claimed that the cans bore the words SAFETY CAN, which, he claimed further, constituted the etymon of Puerto Rican Spanish *s* ~ *z* 'garbage can, garbage pail, trash can'.

In 1936, after completing a course of study at the School of Tropical Medicine in San Juan, Luis Hernández Aquino (1907–1988) became an inspector of sanitation in the municipality of Caguas. Later he held the same position in the municipality of Humacao and finally in the municipality of Ponce. At the University of Madrid he earned a doctorate in philosophy and literature. He wrote for newspapers and published novels, poetry, literary criticism, and a dictionary of Puerto Rican Spanish usages derived from Puerto Rican Eastern Taino. In light of those diverse activities, a couple of which are related to the subject of the present article, it is not surprizing that the origin of *s* ~ *z* drew his attention.

Skeptical of Todd's etymology, on 6 July 1955 Hernández Aquino wrote to the United States Department of Defense asking whether the American army in Puerto Rico had ever called the garbage cans handed out to civilians just after the Spanish-American War *safety cans* and about a month later I. H. Ahfeld responded that a search of official reports, army manuals, and other possibly relevant documents had turned up no instances of *safety can* (it did find several of *garbage container*). In Hernández Aquino, 1955, he therefore concluded that the suggested etymology *safety can* > *s* ~ *z* was untenable.

Indeed,

1. as just noted, the Department of Defense could find no evidence in its records that the American army in Puerto Rico had called garbage cans *safety cans*;
2. no material evidence, such as a garbage can bearing words SAFETY CAN impressed into it or a photograph of such a can, has ever been found in Puerto Rico (or anyplace else where *s* ~ *z* has been used).
3. because safety cans are containers used for the safe storage and transport of hazardous materials, such as flammable liquids, whereas garbage cans are for holding refuse pending its disposal, manufacturers or anyone else would not call garbage cans *safety cans*.[9]

---

9 Eagle Manufacturing Company (of Appleton, Wisconsin) began manufacturing welded steel cans for the use in factories, quarries, and railroads in 1907 (Eagle 2021)."Since

4. one would have to assume that from Puerto Rico *s ~ z* in one way or another spread to Cuba, the Dominican Republic, Panama, and Venezuela, which might be unlikely.

The suggested etymology "American English *safety can* > Puerto Rican Spanish *s ~ z*" would thus seem to be without foundation, but at this early stage in the investigation of the Spanish word it cannot be dismissed inasmuch as Todd was probably an eyewitness to the distribution of American garbage cans in Puerto Rico, he presumably had no reason to lie about its origin, and he may therefore have had relevant information unknown to us (possibly, public health was so bad [see the first paragraph of this section] that John Van Rensselaer Hoff ordered not garbage cans but safety cans). The first thing we need is a bibliography of Todd's relevant publications and any unpublished ones that may be pertinent.

3.3. The suggestion that *safacón ~ zafacón* and Spanish *zafarrancho* are etymologically related

"Tiene más sentido pensar que el origen de la palabra *zafacón* proviene de *zafarrancho*, cuya segunda acepción según el DRAE es 'limpieza general'. Además, cobra más sentido porque parte de una raíz común y tiene una clara relación semántica" (Vaquero de Ramírez & Morales, 2005, s. v. *zafacón*), that is, '[Rather than thinking that *zafacón* comes from *safety can*,] it makes more sense to derive the word from *zafarrancho*, the second meaning of which is 'general cleaning' in the dictionary of the Royal Spanish Academy. It makes even more sense because the two words go back to the same root and are clearly similar to each other semantically'.

1906 customers have looked to Justrite [Manufacturing Company] for innovative solutions to help protect workers, reduce fire risks, and improve productivity. Faithfully tested for unsurpassed quality and compliance to applicable codes and regulations, Justrite safety cabinets, safety cans, specialty containers and storage products and drum handling equipment are available through authorized distributors worldwide" (Justrite 2021; the bracketed addition is mine).

If the word *safety-can ~ safety can* was coined after 11 January 1903 (see the last paragraph of section 3.1) or after whatever the date of its earliest-known use may one day be, *s ~ z* could not possibly derive from it. Unfortunately, not even the largest English dictionaries list safety can, much less provide information about its history, so that at the moment it is impossible to say whether it ~ *z* predates the distribution of the cans in Puerto Rico.

It is hard to see, at least now, (1) how *zafarrancho* '[a] general cleaning' can help elucidate the origin of *s* ~ *z* or (2) how "*zafarrancho* > s- ~ z" could be defended phonologically, morphologically, or semantically.

3.4. A possibly right etymology: *safacón* ~ *zafacón* = Spanish *safa* ~ *zafa* + *-ac*[*a*] + *-ón*

Inasmuch as certain Spanish nouns and adjectives contain two diminutive suffixes (for instance, the adjective and noun *chiquitillo* = *chic-* (the stem of *chico*-small') + *it-* (the stem of the diminutive suffix *-ito*) + the diminutive suffix *-illo),* it is possible that other Spanish nouns have two augmentative suffixes, which may be the case here: *s* ~ *z* could consist of three Spanish elements, namely, one free morpheme (*safa* ~ *zafa*) and two bound ones (the augmentative suffixes -*aca* and *-ón*) (suggested by Helena at https://etimologias.dechile.net/?zafaco.n).[10] If so, *s* ~ *z* is a Spanish coinage (which may or may not be calqued on a word in some other language). Let us look at those elements more closely:Federico Corriente treated Spanish *safa* ~ *zafa* as follows:

> "**safa** (ar., val. e ib. con la var. men. **safra**, contaminada) y *zafa* (ar. y cs.) 'palangana': del and. *ṣáḥfa* < cl. *ṣaḥfah* 'lebrillo'. Del mismo origen, por metonimia, es el ar. *zafa* 'piedra inferior a base de la almazara; orinal' y 'copa de árbol' (bab.). V. **safar**" (Corriente, 2003: 430), that is,
> **safa** (Aragon, Valencia, and Ibiza) ~ **safra** (Minorca; a contaminated form) ~ **zafa** (Aragon and Castile) [see footnote 11 for definitions (D. L. G.)] < Hispanic Arabic *ṣáhfa* < Classical Arabic *ṣaḥfah* 'glazed earthenware bowl' and/or 'earthenware pot'. Aragonese **zafa** 'lower stone at the base of an oil mill; urinal' and Asturian **zafa** 'tree top' are of the same origin (by metonymy). See **safar**.[11]

*

10 The DLE has defined and labeled *zafa* as follows: 'aljofayna, albornía' Andalusia, Murcia (1738, 1780, 1783, 1791, 1803), 'aljofaina' Andalusia, Murcia (1817, 1822, 1832, 1837, 1843), 'aljofaina' (1852, 1869, 1884, with no labels), jofaina (1899, 1914, with no labels), 'jofaina' Albacete, Murcia (1925, 1936, 1939, 1947), 'jofaina' Albacete, Granada, Murcia (1956, 1970, 1984, 1992, 2001, 2014), that is, 'washbasin, washbowl'. The omission of spatial labels is puzzling. No edition of the DLE has listed *safa* (or *safacón*).

11 *Cruce* 'amalgam, blend, cross, merger' (as in "*patata* es un cruce de *papa* y *batata*" '*patata* is a blend of *papa* and *batata*'), *cruzarse* (as in "*papa* y *batata* se han cruzado en *patata*" '*papa* and *batata* have been blended to form *patata*'), and *cruzado* (as in "una palabra cruzada con otra" 'one word blended with another') are objective, descriptive terms, hence preferable to "contaminación," "contaminarse," and "contaminado," which are judgmental, hence unscientific, hence to be avoided.

Most often, the suffix *-aco* ~ *-aca* denotes contempt, as in *hombraco*, *libraco*, *mujeraca*, *negraca*, *negraco*, and *paraco* 'paramilitary soldier [in Colombia]' (= *para* [a clipping of *paramilitar* (a shortening of *soldado paramilitar*)] + *-aco*). Sometimes, it denotes large size, as in these three augmentative nouns:

berraco 'big wild boar' (= Spanish **berr*[*o*] 'wild boar' [(< ?) < Latin *verrem* 'idem'] + Spanish *-aco*). In response to a request for an example of *-aco* as an augmentative suffix, Frías, 2014 notes *-ac*[*a*] + *-ón*"berraco (jabalí de 139 kilos) abatido por Sito Lozano. Con 80 kilos seria un simple guarro. Con 40, un jabato." Spanish also has *verraco* 'adult, uncastrated pig', likewise with the augmentative suffix *-aco*.
camisetaca 'oversized T-shirt' (= *camiseta* 'T-shirt, undershirt' [= *camisa* 'shirt' + diminutive suffix *-eta*] + *-aca*). The word was coined presumably after *camiseta* was no longer felt to be a diminutive form (see the analogous remark about *safaconcito* ~ *zafaconcito* in the second paragraph of Sect. 2.3).
rabaco 1. 'large behind [buttocks]'. 2. 'large dick, huge prick [penis]' (= *rabo* 1. 'behind [buttocks]'. 2. 'dick, prick [penis]' + *-aco*).

*

The suffix *-ón* ~ *-ona* is in some words a diminutive (as in *carreta* 'cart' + *-ón* = *carretón* 'small cart', *rata* 'rat' + *-ón* = *ratón* 'mouse', and *torre* 'tower' + *-ón* = *torreón* "turret") and in most an augmentative, as here:

camisa 'shirt' + *-ón* = *camisón* 'nightgown'.
cuchara 'spoon' + *-ón* = *cucharón* 'ladle'.
lámpara 1. 'lamp' '. 2. 'grease stain' + *-ón* = *lamparón* 1. 'large lamp'. 2. 'large grease stain'.
silla 'chair' + *-ón* = *sillón* 'armchair, easy chair'.

Hence the possibilities that *safa* ~ *zafa* in one or more senses + *-aca* yielded the first-degree augmentative **safaca* ~ **zafaca* in one or more senses and that **safaca* ~ **zafaca* in one or more senses

+ *-ón* yielded the second-degree augmentative *safacón* ~ *zafacón* in one or more senses.[12]

12 Whether *-ón* ~ *-ona* is used to form diminutives or augmentatives, its masculine form (*-ón*) is added not only to masculine stems (as expected) but also to feminine ones if they are marked [- human] (as in the text), a semi-exception being the feminine noun *casa* 'house', the augmentative form of which is feminine *caserona* 'big rambling house' in certain topolects and masculine *caserón* 'idem' in others.If the stem is marked [+ human], *-ón* is added (as expected) to masculine ones and *-ona* to feminine ones, as in masculine *hombre* 'man' → masculine *hombrón* 'big, strong man' and feminine *mujer* 'woman' → feminine *mujerona* 'big, strong woman'.

Italian too has examples of the addition of a masculine augmentative suffix to feminine stems marked [- human]: at least feminine *porta* 'door' → masculine *portone* 'large door' and feminine *strada* 'street' → masculine *stradone* 'big street',

4. Improving the treatment of *safacón* ~ *zafacón* in the *Diccionario de la lengua española* of the Royal Spanish Academy

In 1967, the Royal Spanish Academy approved this entry for the next edition of the DLE (which appeared in 1970):

> "**zafacón** m. *P. Rico y Sto. Dom.* Recipiente hecho comúnmente de hoja de lata, que se usa en las casas para recoger las basuras" (Enmiendas 1967: 199).

The later editions have these definitions:

1984 = 1970
1985: "Recipiente de hoja de lata para recoger basuras". The omission of "se usa en las casas" "used in houses" was justified because by that time (actually, earlier) garbage cans were also being used elsewhere.
1989 = 1985
1992 = 1970. Reversion in 1992 to the definition of 1970 is inexplicable because by that time (actually, earlier) garbage cans were being manufactured of rubber and of plastic too and they were being used not only in residences.
2001: "Recipiente para recoger las basuras". Omission of references to houses and to tin was justified because the word had by that time acquired a broader meaning.
2022 = 2014 = 2001.

As we have seen, (1) the word has also been spelled with <s> rather than <z>, (2) it has been used not just in Puerto Rico and the Dominican Republic but also in Cuba, Panama, and Venezuela, and (c) it has at least ten senses and subsenses.

Whereas the Royal Spanish Academy has done well to give no etymology (because no obviously or likely right one had been proposed by 2014), the other omissions noted earlier in the present article (of one spelling, of nine meanings, and of all derivatives) suggest that all the academies – within and without Spain – need to expand their reading and listening programs.

---

a semi-exception being feminine *donna* 'woman' → feminine *donnona* 'big, strong woman' ~ masculine *donnone* 'idem'.

Does such a change in gender occur in other Romance languages? To what extent is the phenomenon an independent innovation and to what extent did it result from alloglossal influence? Why does it occur at all?

5. Conclusions

Although not exhaustive, the present article is by far the broadest and deepest treatment of *s ~ z* published to date. It has (1) cleared up several misunderstandings about the word, (2) demonstrated that the document of 31 December 1787 is irrelevant to its history, (3) shown that the *zafarrancho* etymology is unlikely, and (4) shown that all four parts of the entry for *s ~ z* in the DLE can be improved.

Although this article has answered a few questions, for lack of information it has left others unanswered, such as how many times, when, and where was *s ~ z* coined (see the last paragraph of Sect. 2.3) and how did the word spread? Believing that it is found only in Puerto Rican Spanish, many Puerto Ricans have believed that it originated in Puerto Rico, but in light of its presence elsewhere too, those questions are still open.

6. References

Asociación n. d. = Asociación Condomines Cluster 8 Río Cristal, Inc. La Original [outdoor sign]. *Facebook.* https://ar-ar.facebook.com/1450787945057084/posts/2315819008553969/ (accessed 2 September 2021).

Caceres [sic], Joseph (2012): Chivateando. *Las Noticias Locas.* 11 October. https://merengala.blogspot.com/2012/10/se-solto-el-chivo.html (accessed 30 September 2021) [reprinted, with attribution, in Zabaleón 2012].

Caceres [sic], Joseph (2017): Elecciones en Acroarte. 23 May. https://merengala.blogspot.com/2017/05/elecciones-en-acroarte_23.html (accessed 4 August 2021).

Camacaro, Orlando (2012): Pa' el Zafacón. 15 September. www.aporrea.org/oposicion/a150275.html (accessed 4 August 2021).

Carroll, Henry K. (1899): *Report on the Island of Porto Rico; its population, civil government, commerce, industries, productions, roads, tariff, and currency, with recommendations.* Washington: Government Printing Office.

Claudio de la Torre, Josefina A. (1989): *Diccionario de la jerga del estudiante universitario puertorriqueño.* With a foreword by Humberto López Morales. Río Piedras: Editorial de la Universidad de Puerto Rico.

Corriente, Federico (2003): *Diccionario de arabismos y voces afines en iberorromance.* 2 ed., expanded. Madrid: Gredos.

Cruz Triffolio, Juan (2020): Un Rechazo Ejemplarizante. *Periódico Digital.* 14 July. https://lomejordelasemanasde.com/un-rechazo-ejemplarizante-por-juan-cruz-triffolio-sociologo-comunicador-dominicano/ (accessed 4 August 2021).

DLE = the unabridged general dictionary of the Royal Spanish Academy, which began appearing in 1726 as either *Diccionario de la lengua española* or *Diccionario de la lengua castellana.*

Eagle 2021 = the website of Eagle Manufacturing Company. https://www.eagle-mfg.com/eagle-oil-can-history (accessed 30 September 2021).

Enmiendas 1967 = Enmiendas y adiciones a los diccionarios de la Academia aprobadas por la Corporación (Mayo-agosto de 1967). *Boletín de la Real Academia Española*. Vol. XLVII. No. CLI. May–August. Pp. 187–199.

Espinosa, Mariola (2000): Sanitary and American: Disease eradication efforts and the transformation of Puerto Rico After 1898 [a talk given at the Latin American Studies Association International Congress, Miami, Florida]. https://scholar.google.com/citations?view_op=view_citation&hl=en&user=RNPbSZ8AAAAJ&citation_for_view=RNPbSZ8AAAAJ:zYLM7Y9cAGgC (accessed 10 August 2021).

Facciolati, Jacobo & Egidio Forcellini (1828): *Totius Latinitatis Lexicon*. Vol. II. With contributions by James Bailey. London: Baldwin & Cradock [and] Gugliemo Pickering.

Féliz, Yanet (2016): ADN creará clínica veterinaria municipal. *El Día*. 8 February. https://eldia.com.do/adn-creara-clinica-veterinaria-municipal/ (accessed 31 August 2021).

Forcadell, Sergio (2016): Los perros de ahora. *El Jaya*. 18 April. https://www.eljaya.com/36519/los-perros-de-ahora/ (accessed 13 December 2021).

Frías, Ignacio (2014): [untitled comment, 25 August]. Comment board for unsigned, Asunto: Terminaciones *-aco, -aca*, Centro Virtual Cervantes: Archivo del Foro del español. https://cvc.cervantes.es/foros/leer_asunto1.asp?vCodigo=46748 (accessed 19 March 2020).

Gold, David L. (2005): An aspect of lexicography still not fully professionalized: The search for antedatings and postdatings (with examples mostly from English and some from other languages). *Revista Alicantina de Estudios Ingleses*. No. 18. Pp. 25–69. https://rua.ua.es/dspace/bitstream/10045/5210/1/RAEI_18_02.pdf.

Gold, David L. (2012): The politicization of a monophthong: A refutation of all the Puerto Rican myths about the native Spanish Place Name *Porto Rico*. In Félix Rodríguez González (ed.), *Estudios de Lingüística Española: Homenaje a Manuel Seco* (pp. 215–268). Alicante: Publicaciones de la Universidad de Alicante.

Gold, David L. in preparation. More on the etymology of the Spanish noun *safacón ~ zafacón*.

González Beltré & Sandy Natanael (2014): El turismo en Barahona nunca se impulsa por los funcionarios de nuestra amada provincia, que son indolentes, corruptos, ineptos e hipócritas. *La verdadera realidad de Barahona y Pedernales.* 9 August. http://barahonapedernales.blogspot.com/2014/08/el-turismo-en-barahona-nunca-se-impulsa.html (accessed 13 December 2021).

Hernandez [sic], R. M., Wm. Faucett Smith, & W. H. Elliott (1901): Exhibit C. In Charles H. Allen, *Report of the Governor of Porto Rico, Covering the Period from May 1, 1900, to May 1, 1901: Respectfully Submitted to Hon. William McKinley, President of the United States, Through the Hon. John Hay, Secretary of State, May 1, 1901*, 335–343. Washington: Government Printing Office [Hernandez and Smith, each holding the degree of Medicinae Doctor, were practicing physicians at the time and Elliott was then the Commissioner of the Interior in the Puerto Rican government].

Hernández Aquino, Luis (1955): Sobre la Voz Zafacón: El Mito del Safety Can. *El Mundo*. San Juan. 15 October. Unpaginated.

Hernández Fereira & José Rafael (2013): Safacón. *Maracucholario Plus: Uso, significado y raíz de palabras y expresiones del dialecto maracucho*. 25 March. www.maracucholario.blogspot.com/2013 (accessed 14 September 2014).

Jiménez, Karina (2019): Margaro "Guzbay Nueva York me viene a catapultar ya como protagonista." *pressreader*. 27 September. https://www.pressreader.com/dominican-republic/el-caribe/20190927/282123523237692 (accessed 12 March 2020).

Justrite 2021 = the website of Justrite Manufacturing Company. www.justritemfg.com/utility-pages/about-us1/ (accessed 30 September 2021).

LC = Library of Congress. *Chronicling America*: Historic American Newspapers site. https://chroniclingamerica.loc.gov/.

López Morales, Humberto (2009): Necrología: María Vaquero (1937–2008). *Revista de Filología Española*. Vol. LXXXIX. No. 1. Pp. 187–190.

Martes Pedraza, Daniel (2010): El Soñador Literario. *Revista Surco Sur*. Vol. 1. No. 2. October–December. Pp. 14–17 [the author is Puerto Rican].

Miraflores, Luis (1919): Zaguanes de San Juan. *El Imparcial*. San Juan. 10 June. P. 1.

Moreno Areche & Andrés Simón (2009): Guarimbas, maniobras y sitios. *Analítica*. 1 September. https://www.analitica.com/opinion/opinion-nacional/guarimbas-maniobras-y-sitios/ (accessed 14 May 2019).

Moronta, R. (2009): La Baraja. *La Columna de Angel Vargas*. 14 February. http://15y30.blogspot.com/2009/02/ (accessed 16 November 2015).

Pantaleón Inoa & José Miguel. [untitled, undated comment]. *flickr. https://www.* flickr. flickr.https://www.com/photos/cimarronmayor/3535557930 (accessed 16 December 2021).

Ramoncastro (2020): Untitled tweet. 20 August. https://twitter.com/reynon151/status/1296599485049638913 (accessed 23 January 2020).

Raul (1903): Revista Cómica. *La Correspondencia de Puerto-Rico*. San Juan, Puerto Rico. Vol. XII. Whole no. 4390. 11 January. P. 1.

Redacción (2003): Creo ser un buen ciudadano: Sin embargo, hago daño a los animales. *Crítica en línea*. 19 September. https://portal.critica.com.pa/archivo/09192003/opi02.html#TOP (accessed 1 June 2021).

Rigau-Pérez, José G. (2017): The work of US Public Health Service officers in Puerto Rico, 1898–1919. *Puerto Rico Health Sciences Journal*. 36. No. 3. September. Pp. 130–139.

Roque Rivera & Paula E. (1999): Mirar para atrás y para adentro. *Archivos del Caribe*. https://archivosdelcaribe.org/mirar-para-atras-y-para-adentro/ (accessed 30 June 2021) [the author is Puerto Rican].

Szemerényi, Oswald (1981): Etyma Latina III (19–23): Latin *uindex*, *uindicit*, *uindicta*, *prouincia*, Greek *(w)anaks*, and West European *Veneti* from the point of view of semasiology. In Wolf Dietrich & Horst Geckeler (eds.), *Logos Semantikos: Semantik Semántica Sémantique Semantics* [= *Logos Semantikos: Studia Linguistica in Honorem Eugenio Coseriu 1921–1981*, vol. III], 303–323. Berlin/New York: Walter de Gruyter. Madrid: Editorial Gredos.

unsigned (1918): Esos zafacones. *La Correspondencia de Puerto-Rico*. San Juan. 17 May. P. 2.

unsigned ([1918]): *Military Record of Col. John Van Rennselaer Hoff, Medical Corps, U. S. A., Retired, 1872–1918*. [Washington, DC]. https://collections.nlm.nih.gov/bookviewer?PID=nlm:nlmuid-101604048-bk#page/1/mode/2up.

unsigned (1948): Alcance a la Gaceta Oficial: Administración de Aduana de Panamá: Relación general de la mercadería examinada y liquidada para Panamá. *Gaceta Oficial: Organo del Estado*. Vol. XLV. Whole no. 10,520. 12 February. Pp. 15–16. http://gacetas.procuraduria-admon.gob.pa/10520_1948.pdf.

umsigned (2010): Navidad en tiempos de Cólera. *Barco Amapola: Espacio para toda Información Social: Literatura, Arte y Ciencia*. 30 November. https://amapolaparaelmundo.blogspot.com/2010/11/navidad-en-tiempos-de-colera.html (accessed 22 October 2020).

unsigned (2017): Residentes de Santa Ana cierran calles en protesta. *TVN Noticias*. 20 September. https://www.tvn-2.com/videos/noticias/Residentes-Santa-Ana-cierran-protesta_2_4853534673.htm (accessed 13 October 2020).

unsigned (2018a): Hoy por hoy. *La Prensa*. Panama City. 28 June. https://www.prensa.com/opinion/Hoyporhoy_0_5063493706.html (accessed 23 May 2021).

unsigned (2018b): Jauría mercenarios contra sandinistas; descripción. 28 July. https://www.ivoox.com/en/jauria-mercenarios-contra-sandinistas-audios-mp3_rf_27274235_1.html (accessed 14 December 2021) [*La Voz del PACOREDO* is the name of the radio program of the Communist Party of the Dominican Republic; *PACOREDO* is one of the two acronyms, the other being *PORD*, of the Spanish name of the party, *Partido Comunista de la República Dominicana*].

unsigned (2023 [sic]): Safacones Plus +. www.expertoszafaconeros.com (accessed 30 June 2021).

Vaquero de Ramírez, María T. & Amparo Morales (2005): *Tesoro lexicográfico del español de Puerto Rico*. San Juan: Plaza Mayor & Academia Puertorriqueña de la Lengua Española [now incorporated into a continuously updated version at https://tesoro.pr; accessed 5 September 2021].

Varela Merino, Elena. (2009): *Los galicismos en el español de los siglos XVI y XVII* [= Anejos de la *Revista de filología española* 100]. 2 vols. Madrid: Consejo Superior de Investigaciones Científicas.

Wolcott, G. N. (1922): *Insectos que atacan los productos almacenados* [= Circular No. 65, Gobierno de Puerto Rico, Departamento de Agricultura y Trabajo, Estación Experimental Insular, Río Piedras, P. R.]. San Juan, P. R.: Negociado de Materiales, Imprenta y Transporte.

Zabaleón, José (2012): Ay chivo, chivo, chivo, chivo de la loma, quien ha visto un chivo, haciendo maroma. *Z@D Zabala al Día*. 11 October. https://zabalaaldia.com/ay-chivo-chivo-chivo-chivo-de-la-loma-quien-ha-visto-un-chivo-haciendo-maroma/ (accessed 15 May 2019).

3a cual club o club (2014): [untitled comment]. Comment board for Juan Luis Francia, Inseguridad y el "homo shopping" (Opinión). *Correo de Orinoco*. 29 January. http://www.correodelorinoco.gob.ve/inseguridad-y-%E2%80%9Chomo-shopping%E2%80%9D-opinion/ (accessed 9 December 2021).

Overseas Areas

María Isabel González Cruz

Universidad de Las Palmas de Gran Canaria

Pervivencia y mortandad léxicas: el caso de los anglicismos canarios

Resumen: Este capítulo ofrece los resultados de una pequeña investigación realizada recientemente entre un grupo de 154 jóvenes canarios universitarios. El objetivo fue recabar datos preliminares sobre su conocimiento de los "antiguos" anglicismos canarios que figuran en el *Diccionario ejemplificado de canarismos* (Corrales y Corbella, 2009). Las dudas planteadas en un trabajo anterior (González Cruz, 2022a), acerca de la vitalidad real de esos términos entre los hablantes jóvenes de hoy, motivaron esta primera aproximación a la cuestión de su pervivencia. Los datos obtenidos parecen sugerir que buena parte de esas voces han caído en el desuso y se enfrentan ya a un proceso de sustitución o de mortandad léxica.

Palabras clave: anglicismos, español de Canarias, pervivencia y mortandad léxicas, habla juvenil.

1. Introducción

Es bien sabido que el nivel lingüístico que más rápidamente experimenta cambios es el del léxico. Esto es lógico en tanto que el vocabulario es el aspecto que mayor vinculación presenta con la realidad en la que vivimos y en la que usamos el lenguaje. Por ello nuestro léxico refleja todos los conceptos y objetos que utilizamos, así como todos los cambios que acontecen en el mundo, como prueban los numerosos estudios sobre neologismos y préstamos, especialmente del inglés. Obviamente, los sustantivos son el tipo de palabras que más a menudo suelen cambiar, porque constantemente se incorporan nuevas voces para designar las novedades que surgen en nuestro entorno sociocultural, siguiéndoles en orden decreciente los adjetivos y los verbos[1] (Van Hout y Muysken, 1994: 401).

1 Del resto de categorías gramaticales puede decirse que apenas sufren cambios perceptibles a lo largo del periodo de vida media de los hablantes. Las locuciones adverbiales constituyen quizá una excepción puesto que, ocasionalmente, sobre todo en los ámbitos juveniles, se forman nuevas expresiones con función adverbial que permanecen en uso durante algún tiempo, por ejemplo, *por un tubo,* para indicar cantidad, o bien una de las locuciones temporales más recientes: *en un cero coma.*

Quienes tenemos ya cierta edad somos muy conscientes del aluvión de nuevas palabras que hemos ido incorporando en las últimas décadas a nuestro repertorio léxico; en su mayoría son anglicismos que, día a día, se siguen filtrando en nuestra lengua desde múltiples campos, sobre todo a través de la tecnología, el deporte, la cultura y las nuevas costumbres, etc. El papel que juegan los medios de comunicación y las redes sociales para su difusión y normalización es fundamental. Es cierto que muchas de esas nuevas palabras ganan prestigio y consiguen que a los hablantes les guste utilizarlas; pero también sucede que algunas palabras nuevas no llegan realmente a arraigar en la lengua y solo tienen un uso efímero: se ponen de moda durante un tiempo y luego pasan al olvido. Debido al continuo proceso de cambios en el que están inmersos tanto nuestra sociedad como el lenguaje que empleamos en nuestras relaciones sociales, sucede que a menudo percibimos que ciertas palabras nos resultan anticuadas mientras que otras nos suenan más nuevas y modernas. Y es que, como comentan García Mouton y Grijelmo (2011: 16),

> [...] en la lengua también hay modas. Y los hablantes tienden a incorporar a su vocabulario las palabras que les parecen nuevas e interesantes, porque les gusta usar términos con prestigio. Esa dinámica provoca unos cambios que son siempre paulatinos y no impiden la comunicación, ya que las palabras tradicionales suelen convivir, al menos durante un tiempo, con las nuevas.

Si bien la lengua "avanza implacable [...] creando nuevas palabras y nuevos significados", como señala Álvarez Mellado (2016: 201), no hay que olvidar que "como en la vida misma, el nacimiento de unas formas está estrechamente ligado a la muerte y desaparición de otras". Como bien explica esta autora, "a la misma velocidad a la que creamos términos nuevos, hacemos desaparecer otros; forma parte del ciclo vital léxico" (201). De hecho, en su libro *Palabras moribundas,* García Mouton y Grijelmo (2011) demuestran que son ya numerosas las voces del idioma que, con el paso de los años, han ido cayendo en el desuso. Esto puede ocurrir, como apunta Álvarez Mellado (2016: 201), porque sean "experimentos morfológicos abortados nada más nacer" o bien porque el nombre "autóctono" de un objeto o concepto pasa a ser reemplazado por motivos socioculturales por otro foráneo;[2] incluso se ha dado el caso de "palabras centenarias que dejan de usarse", algo que con frecuencia se debe simplemente al hecho de que "la realidad que denominan deja de estar en vigor". Esto es algo

2 Álvarez Mellado (2016: 2002) ilustra este caso con lo sucedido con "el noble arte de correr, que devino en *footing*, que ahora llamamos *running*, y veremos qué nuevas sorpresas léxicas nos da la vida".

que se comprueba fácilmente en las "novelas de época", donde se hace referencia a "enseres que hacían furor en tiempos pasados" (Álvarez Mellado, 2016: 201), y también en los diccionarios, que esta autora compara, no sin razón, con anticuarios donde podemos encontrar "magníficos ejemplares hoy olvidados que viven a la espera de ser redescubiertos o rehabilitados [...] [pues esconden] todo tipo de antiguallas léxicas y otras rarezas que no se encuentran en el circuito *mainstream*" (Álvarez Mellado, 2016: 202). Según Hoffer (2002: 18), para que una palabra nueva figure en un diccionario de prestigio debe haber estado en uso activo durante unos 25 años. Otra cuestión es la permanencia en el tiempo de ese uso, pues, como venimos comentando y bien señala García Mouton (2007: 81), "el léxico es el campo más propenso a experimentar sustituciones de unas formas y abandono de otras". De ahí la importancia de que los diccionarios incluyan en sus registros no solo información acerca de la distribución dialectal en cuanto al uso de cada palabra sino también datos actualizados acerca de su vitalidad o frecuencia de uso.

Desde esa perspectiva de la pervivencia y la mortandad léxicas, este capítulo se centra en el caso de los 29 anglicismos que figuran registrados en el *Diccionario ejemplificado de canarismos* de Corrales y Corbella (2009, en adelante *DEC*). Son voces anglicadas que se incorporaron al habla insular por la importancia que tuvo la presencia británica en las islas capitalinas a partir de las últimas décadas del siglo XIX. El estudio se concibe como una pequeña aproximación que solo pretende recabar algunos datos preliminares que nos puedan dar una idea acerca del uso actual de esas palabras entre los jóvenes universitarios canarios. La elección de este segmento poblacional responde al hecho de que se les supone un nivel educativo alto y, además, son los hablantes de cuyos usos lingüísticos dependerá el futuro del español de Canarias.[3]

2. El español de Canarias y su patrimonio léxico

El español de Canarias es actualmente una de las variedades más estudiadas del ámbito hispánico (Corbella y Medina, 1996; Álvarez, 1996: 67; Corrales, Álvarez y Corbella, 2007). Pertenece al denominado *español atlántico*, término

3 Ya en un trabajo anterior (González-Cruz, 2014), tras pasar una encuesta a un grupo de 100 universitarios grancanarios, aporté datos que indicaban que la gran mayoría de los canarismos seleccionados como muestra (a partir del amplio repertorio léxico que registra el *DEC*) les resultaban desconocidos o eran raramente usados, con unas pocas excepciones.

acuñado por el filólogo Diego Catalán en 1958 y que "aglutina variedades similares y al mismo tiempo diferentes", como señala Corujo (2019). Estas modalidades atlánticas, que comparten varias similitudes fonéticas y gramaticales, incluyen "por lo general, tres conjuntos de variedades geográficas o diatópicas más o menos próximas entre sí, desde perspectivas históricas y lingüísticas, como son las diversas hablas andaluzas, de las Islas Canarias y solo algunas variedades hispanoamericanas, las costeras e insulares" (Rodríguez Muñoz, 2012: 24). Sin embargo, lingüistas canarios como Almeida y Díaz Alayón prefieren hacer referencia a las "hablas canarias" de modo que de una manera más amplia y precisa se respete "la identidad lingüística canaria en su unidad y la rica diferencia insular en su fragmentariedad" (Corujo, 2019)[4].

Si bien los rasgos diferenciadores del español de Canarias son numerosos (Alvar, 1975; Almeida y Diaz Alayon, 1988; Morera, 1990), en este trabajo nos interesa destacar especialmente los del nivel léxico, que podemos resumir en los tres aspectos siguientes:

(a) un cierto número de arcaísmos del castellano que se utilizó durante la conquista,
(b) un mayor número de préstamos del portugués, del gallego-portugués, del español de América y del inglés que en el español peninsular,
(c) algunos términos prehispánicos, que se han conservado de la lengua hablada por los aborígenes guanches.

Algunas investigaciones publicadas en los últimos años (Morín y Castellano, 1990; González-Cruz, 2006; Morgenthaler, 2008) sugieren que el español de Canarias ha pasado de ser una variedad que sus hablantes percibían como no prestigiosa (Ortega, 1981) a adquirir cierto prestigio (Morín, 1993; Almeida, 1994, Morera, 2002; Hernandez, 2003). De hecho, el interés por su estudio, y particularmente por los canarismos, es palpable en la cantidad de compilaciones que se han ido publicando[5], además de la valiosa aportación de los dos

4 Como señala este mismo autor, "las particularidades lingüísticas del canario no son exclusivas, pero su mestizaje sí lo es" (Corujo, 2019). Esa personalidad mestiza de las hablas canarias tiene que ver con sus características fónicas, pronominales, verbales y léxicas.

5 Véanse el *Diccionario básico de canarismos*, publicado en 2010 por la Academia Canaria de la Lengua, disponible para consultas en línea en https://www.academiacanarialengua.org/diccionario/ donde "cada día sugerimos una palabra de nuestro vocabulario", y el *Diccionario de canarismos* de Antonio Lorenzo, Marcial Morera y Gonzalo Ortega, publicado en 1994. También Hernández y Samper (2003).

volúmenes del ya mencionado DEC. Es en este trabajo donde se pone de manifiesto la enorme riqueza y variedad del vocabulario de la variedad lingüística canaria. Sus 19000 entradas y 25000 significados y expresiones típicas del léxico insular están ilustradas mediante referencias a unos 1300 documentos. Este tesoro lexicográfico ha reunido todas las palabras que representan la historia, los recursos naturales y la sabiduría popular, así como el pasado y el presente de la variedad canaria del español. Incluye términos utilizados tanto en el habla popular como en la culta, así como las voces antiguas y nuevas que se emplean tanto en zonas rurales como urbanas. Se trata de palabras que pertenecen al ámbito de las tradiciones canarias (ya sea en los deportes locales como en los contextos agrícolas y marítimos), además de las nuevas creaciones léxicas propias, fruto de la influencia de los medios de comunicación. Dado que todo este vocabulario constituye una parte importante de nuestro legado cultural intangible, es importante mantenerlo vivo, pues representa, en palabras de Dalby, "a different way of looking at, mapping and classifying the world" (2002: 216), en tanto que ofrece su propia clasificación de los seres vivos, de los fenómenos naturales y de los conceptos culturales.

El siguiente epígrafe presentará brevemente el pequeño número de canarismos incluidos en el *DEC* que además son anglicismos. Son 29 voces anglicadas que evidencian la importante huella que la presencia británica dejó en el patrimonio léxico insular.

3. Los anglicismos canarios en el *DEC*

Mucho se ha investigado en las últimas décadas sobre la influencia británica en Canarias a lo largo de la historia, así como sobre las tempranas e intensas relaciones comerciales y turísticas de las islas con el mundo anglosajón (Morales Lezcano, 1970; Guimerá Ravina, 1985; Iglesias, 1985; Martín Hernández, 1990; Bethencourt Massieu, 1991; Fernández-Armesto, 1995; González Cruz, 1995; García Pérez, 2007, entre otros). Los esfuerzos por recopilar datos sobre todo lo relativo al rico patrimonio anglo-canario, tanto a nivel arquitectónico (Hernández Gutiérrez, 1988, 1995; Quintana Navarro, 1985) como documental y bibliográfico (Quintana Navarro, 1992; González Cruz, 2002, 2003), han derivado en numerosas publicaciones que dan testimonio del relevante papel desempeñado por los "hijos de Albión" en la evolución económica y sociocultural de las islas, principalmente de Gran Canaria y Tenerife. No menos importante fue el enriquecimiento léxico del habla insular como consecuencia de la situación de contacto sociocultural y lingüístico que se vivió en algunas zonas, especialmente en Las Palmas de Gran Canaria, así como en La Orotava y su puerto, hoy Puerto de La Cruz, en Tenerife[6] (Armistead, 1996, 1997; Castillo, 1991, 2003, 2005; Corbella, 1991–92; González-Cruz, 1993, 1995, 2012). El torrente de palabras inglesas que aparecen en la prensa local de la época nos da una idea del furor que estaban causando todas las novedades y modas que llegaban a las islas de la mano de *los ingleses*, como se les denominaba popularmente, aunque en realidad muchos de ellos eran de origen irlandés o escocés. Una pequeña parte de ese vocabulario llegó a consolidarse y permanecer en el tiempo, integrándose en el repertorio léxico del español de Canarias, como se demuestra con su inclusión en el DEC y otros diccionarios. Se trata de los 29 anglicismos siguientes, que enumeramos por orden alfabético con sus variantes entre paréntesis: *autodate, belmontina, breque, brete, cherche (chercha, chirche,) choni (chone), concreto, concretera, fao, fati, flis (flit), fotingo, fulo, guachimán, guagua, guanijay, guinche (winche), insay (linsay), naife, paipa, piche (pichi), pichicoma, pimpe, queque (quequi), quinegua (chinegua), quini, rambana (rambane), tifar (tifiar), trinque.*

La siguiente sección describirá el pequeño estudio realizado para indagar acerca de la vitalidad actual de estos anglicismos canarios que recoge el DEC. En ella se aportarán datos sobre la encuesta, los informantes y los resultados obtenidos.

4. El estudio

La curiosidad por obtener indicios acerca del conocimiento y uso real actual de 28 de los 29 anglicimos[7] arriba mencionados, me llevó a elaborar un formulario de Google que conseguí distribuir entre un total de 154 informantes. El formulario se abrió el 14 de abril de 2022 y estuvo operativo hasta el 14 de junio. En su primera sección se pedían datos personales relativos a la edad, el género, el lugar de procedencia, la isla de residencia y la titulación que el informante había cursado o estaba cursando. La segunda sección, titulada ¿CONOCES ESTAS PALABRAS?, planteaba la siguiente solicitud: *Para cada una de estas palabras*

---

6 Esa situación de contacto también dejó su huella en los residentes y visitantes británicos, como demuestran varios trabajos de González Cruz (2011a, 2011b, 2013, 2022b) que estudian los hispanismos y canarismos usados en los distintos textos publicados por autores de habla inglesa.

7 Para evitar que la encuesta se hiciera demasiado larga, eliminamos el anglicismo *concreto* y solo incluimos su derivado, *concretera*. Con este mismo fin, los cuatro anglicismos que nombran distintas variedades de papas (patatas) se incluyeron en una sola pregunta final, como señalamos más adelante.

indica tu grado de conocimiento y, en caso de que sepas con seguridad su significado, escríbelo en la opción "OTRO". A continuación, se iban desplegando de manera individual los primeros 24 anglicismos, por orden alfabético. Para cada uno de ellos, se pedía al informante que marcara una de las tres opciones siguientes:

→ *Ni idea, no la he oído nunca*
→ *Me suena, pero no sé lo que significa*
→ *OTRO: ....*

Finalmente, los cuatro anglicismos restantes *(autodate, quinegua, quini, rambana),* al hacer referencia a cuatro variedades distintas de papas (patatas) se agruparon en una sola pregunta, en la que se pedía al informante marcar una respuesta para cada palabra, eligiendo en cada caso entre las siguientes opciones:

→ *No la conozco*
→ *Me suena, pero no sé el significado*
→ *Tiene algo en común con las otras*
→ *Sé lo que significa: ......*

4.1 Descripción de los informantes

Las 154 personas que participaron voluntariamente en la encuesta eran jóvenes canarios, todos universitarios, de edades comprendidas entre los 18 y los 30 años y en su mayoría mujeres (92, frente a 62 hombres). Los datos en la Tabla 1 confirman su juventud, ya que solo 6 de ellos llegaban a los 30 años.

Tabla 1: Número de informantes según edades

EDAD	N informantes	EDAD	N informantes
18	40	24	4
19	21	26	3
20	27	28	3
21	28	29	1
22	11	30	6
23	10		

En cuanto a su lugar de procedencia, solo 18 habían nacido fuera de las islas, mientras que 75 eran originarios de la isla de Gran Canaria, 40 de Tenerife, 11 de La Palma, 4 de Lanzarote, 2 de Fuerteventura, 2 de La Gomera y 2 de la isla de El Hierro. En relación al lugar de residencia, la mayoría afirmó vivir actualmente en Gran Canaria (95) o en Tenerife (53), que son las dos islas con instituciones universitarias completas, 2 en La Palma, 2 en El Hierro, 1 en Lanzarote y 1 en La Gomera. En cuanto a las titulaciones cursadas por los informantes fueron muy variadas, algo que queríamos conseguir para evitar el sesgo que supondría el alumnado de las facultades de Filología. Concretamente se trataba de estudiantes (o titulados) de los grados que enumeramos a continuación: Economía, Educación Primaria, Geografía y Ordenación del Territorio, Ingeniería Civil, Ingeniería de Diseño Industrial y Desarrollo del Producto, Ingeniería en Tecnologías de la Telecomunicación, Lengua Española y Literaturas Hispánicas, Lenguas Modernas, Pedagogía, Psicología, Título Superior en Arte Dramático, Trabajo Social, Traducción e Interpretación.

4.2 Los resultados

En esta sección ofreceré los datos obtenidos a partir de las respuestas de los 154 informantes a las cuestiones del formulario. En un primer apartado (4.2.1) me centraré en el análisis cuantitativo de las respuestas a la pregunta que indagaba en el grado de (des)conocimiento de cada uno de los anglicismos. En el segundo (4.2.2) realizaré un análisis cualitativo, dando primero el significado real de cada palabra y comentando luego los aciertos y errores en los distintos significados aportados por los informantes.

4.2.1 Análisis cuantitativo

Una ojeada a las gráficas que ofrece el formulario Google con el resumen de los resultados no hizo más que confirmar nuestras sospechas: la tendencia generalizada entre los informantes al desconocimiento del significado de la mayoría de los 28 anglicismos seleccionados. A continuación, en la Tabla 2 recopilaré los datos relativos al número de informantes (N) que reconocían desconocer el significado de cada uno de los 28 anglicismos estudiados en la encuesta, ya sea porque (A) nunca habían oído esas palabras o bien porque (B) aunque "les suenan" no saben su significado.

Tabla 2: Número total de informantes que dicen desconocer los anglicismos (A: no los han oído nunca; B: les suena, pero no saben su significado)

ANGLICISMOS	(A)	(B)	ANGLICISMOS	(A)	(B)
BELMONTINA	132	13	GUINCHE	91	48
BREQUE	117	33	INSAI (LINSAY)	133	17
BRETE	130	20	NAIFE	61	20
CHERCHA	118	26	PAIPA	126	26
CHONI (CHONE)	16	47	PICHE (PICHI)	80	21
CONCRETERA	84	50	PICHICOMA	144	10
FAO	134	19	PIMPE	141	11
FATI	132	16	QUEQUE (QUEQUI)	14	21
FLIS	32	30	TIFAR (TIFIAR)	109	25
FOTINGO	85	38	TRINQUE	89	36
FULO	120	29	AUTODATE	80	25
GUACHIMAN	92	46	QUINEGUA	63	31
GUAGUA	0	0	QUINI	125	20
GUANIJAI	103	33	RAMBANA	132	14

Obviamente, convendría sumar los datos recogidos arriba en las dos columnas A y B, para obtener la cifra total de informantes que confirman abiertamente su desconocimiento de los anglicismos, y ordenar esa lista de anglicismos según el grado de desconocimiento que reconocen los propios informantes. Al hacerlo, se obtiene la clasificación que refleja la Tabla 3, donde presentamos los anglicismos en orden creciente, de menos a más desconocidos, si bien a estas cifras habría que añadir las de los encuestados que aportaron significados erróneos, algo que haremos en el siguiente apartado (4.2.2) en el análisis cualitativo.

Tabla 3: Relación ordenada de los anglicismos desconocidos según declaraciones de los 154 informantes

ANGLICISMOS	No lo conocen (N)	ANGLICISMOS	No lo conocen (N)
GUAGUA	0	GUINCHE	139
QUEQUE	35	CHERCHA	144
FLIS	62	BELMONTINA	145
CHONI	63	QUINI	145
NAIFE	81	RAMBANA	146
QUINEGUA	94	FATI	148
PICHE	101	FULO	149
AUTODATE	105	BREQUE	150
FOTINGO	123	BRETE	150
TRINQUE	125	INSAI	150
CONCRETERA	134	PAIPA	152
TIFAR	134	PIMPE	152
GUANIJAI	136	FAO	153
GUACHIMÁN	138	PICHICOMA	154

En definitiva, como observamos arriba en la Tabla 3, los anglicismos con los que nuestros informantes parecen estar, en principio, menos familiarizados son *breque, brete, insai, paipa, pimpe, fao* y *pichicoma,* pues casi la totalidad de los informantes (entre 150 y 154) declara abiertamente no haberlos oído nunca ni conocer su significado; mientras que los más conocidos parecen ser *guagua, queque, flis* y *choni,* que son reconocidos por bastante más de la mitad de los encuestados (o por todos en el caso de *guagua*). No obstante, el análisis pormenorizado de las respuestas aportadas en cada caso hizo que nos llevásemos algunas sorpresas, como veremos a continuación.

4.2.2 Análisis cualitativo

En los siguientes párrafos comentaré brevemente lo que las respuestas de los informantes revelaron acerca de sus ideas sobre los significados de los 28 anglicismos seleccionados, frente a lo que señalan el DEC y los lexicógrafos. Seguiré el orden alfabético, tal y como aparecían en el formulario:

BELMONTINA: Corbella (1991–92: 64) explica que esta palabra, usada por el gran escritor grancanario Benito Pérez Galdós, fue recogida por "los primeros lexicógrafos de las Islas […] con el significado de 'petróleo'". Según el

DEC proviene posiblemente de "*Belmont*, la marca impresa en las etiquetas de las latas de combustible". Solo cuatro informantes mencionaron su vinculación con el petróleo, mientras que otros cuatro lo consideraron "una marca de tabaco" y uno apuntó que creía que era un lugar.

BREQUE (de *break,* en el sentido de "freno"): El DEC registra su uso en la isla de Fuerteventura en la expresión "echar(le) el breque a una cabra", es decir, "mantenerle una de las patas traseras con la corva para ordeñarla". Dos informantes identificaron esta voz como "un interruptor" y otro señaló erróneamente que "viene de la palabra *brake* [sic] en inglés que habla de tomar un descanso cuando se está realizando una tarea".

BRETE: El reconocido investigador canario Pancho Guerra (1965: 99) en su *Léxico popular de Gran Canaria* incluye esta voz con el significado de "pan" y explica que es una adaptación de *bread.* Según sus palabras: "Pertenece el término a la jerga creada por el contacto del familiar lenguaje inglés. El "brear" [sic] británico lo ha convertido el isleño en *brete*, con adopción semejante a la de *naife*". Por su parte, el DEC la considera una variante de *breque,* de uso no frecuente en Fuerteventura, pero también aporta como segunda acepción la propuesta por Guerra, que se usa en Gran Canaria. Por otro lado, el DLE señala que esta palabra significa "Aprieto sin efugio o evasiva" y aporta como ejemplos las conocidas expresiones *Estar en un brete,* y *Poner en un brete.* Tres informantes dieron a esta palabra su significado general de "apuro, aprieto, situación comprometida", mientras que para otro equivalía a "chisme, habladuría". Es obvio, pues, que ninguno de los 154 informantes reconoce esta palabra como anglicismo.

CHERCHA: Con este sustantivo se hace referencia al cementerio protestante más antiguo de España, el cementerio inglés del Puerto de la Cruz (Tenerife), conocido en la localidad como la *chercha.* Probablemente se deriva del inglés *churchyard* y es el anglicismo de uso más temprano del que tenemos noticias en Canarias (Castillo, 2003: 521). El DEC lo registra junto con sus variantes *cherche* y *chirche,* además de la expresión *irse (alguien) para la cherche,* con el significado de "morirse". Solo dos informantes apuntaron su significado de cementerio y otro señaló "patio de iglesia", mientras que dos personas la relacionaron con "una especie de broma". Otros significados erróneos aportados individualmente por sendos informantes fueron los de "zona muy sucia" y "lugar desordenado".

CHONI (CHONE): El DLE en su versión en línea reconoce dos acepciones para esté término. La primera corresponde al anglicismo procedente de *Johnny,* de uso reconocido en Canarias y con el significado coloquial de "turista extranjero, especialmente de habla inglesa", mientras que, según la segunda acepción, se usa para referirse a una "mujer joven que pretende ser elegante e ir a la moda, aunque resulta vulgar", o bien puede ser usado como adjetivo informal con el significado de "chabacano, vulgar". Curiosamente, del porcentaje de informantes que declararon conocer este anglicismo, solo 17 reconocieron en la voz *choni* el significado "tradicional" más extendido en las islas ("turista, extranjero") y el resto (74 respuestas) señaló la relación de este término con la idea de "persona vulgar, barriobajera, poligonera".

CONCRETERA: Este derivado de la voz *concreto* ("hormigón") es otro anglicismo que el DEC define como "hormigonera (máquina que sirve para mezclar los componentes del hormigón)". Solo 20 informantes aportaron significados correctos relacionados con "amasadora del cemento, hormigonera".

FAO: El DEC incluye el canarismo *fao* e indica su procedencia del inglés *fault*, "falta". Castillo (2003: 531) solo lo menciona, pero en comunicación personal nos ha confirmado su idea de que *fao* proviene más bien del inglés *foul*, anglicismo que el DLE sí registra con la forma adaptada *faul*, de uso en muchos países de Hispanoamérica, con el significado de "infracción del reglamento consistente en una entrada brusca de un jugador contra un rival" en una competición deportiva. Es una de las palabras más desconocidas entre nuestros informantes; solo uno escribió erróneamente "una discoteca, me parece".

FATI (de *fatty*): Adjetivo utilizado por hablantes de Tenerife que el DEC define como "gordo u obeso" e indica que es de poco uso. De hecho, es también otro de los anglicismos más desconocidos. Tres informantes dieron significados tan dispares como "gordo", "diminutivo de Fátima", y "fatiga"; mientras que otros tres relacionaron este término con el apellido de un jugador de fútbol, y uno de ellos especificó que se trataba de "un jugador del F.C. Barcelona que está lesionado".

FLIS: El DEC recoge dos variantes, *flit* y *flis*, para este anglicismo que proviene de FLIT, nombre comercial de un insecticida líquido o ambientador, "que se echaba con un pulverizador de émbolo", designando también "el aparato mismo". Aunque 62 informantes declararon desconocer esta palabra, la mayoría de las respuestas identificaron su significado, mayormente como "producto para matar insectos" y también como "pulverizador" o *spray*, término que muchos aportaron como sinónimo. Dos personas incluso dieron un nombre comercial, Baigón. Un informante lo consideró adjetivo, al darle el significado de "rápido"; dos lo identificaron erróneamente como "producto de limpieza" y otros dos con "limpiacristales". Por último, dos respuestas fueron muy vagas al escribir: "cuando rocías a alguien con líquido" y "agua que viene en un envase y se echa a un objeto", por lo que contabilizamos un total de 7 respuestas erróneas.

FOTINGO: Según el DEC, hace referencia a un "coche, especialmente el muy usado y algo desvencijado" y procede del "eslogan *foot it and go*, literalmente 'pisa y arranca', con que se publicitó uno de los modelos de la casa Ford". Otra acepción de este término, por extensión, es la de "cosa de poco valor", registrada en Gran Canaria, aunque ya un tanto en desuso. Fueron muchos los informantes que declararon no haber oído nunca este término (85) o bien que les sonaba la palabra, pero desconocían su significado. Hubo 18 que sí acertaron al describirlo como "coche viejo, antiguo o en mal estado", mientras que 5 indicaron su significado general de "coche" y 2 lo catalogaron como "coche pequeño". Un informante lo definió como "coche de hora" (los antiguos transportes de línea), en tanto que varios ofrecieron significados dispares y sorprendentes, además de erróneos, como "embrollo", "potaje", "foto" e incluso "asqueroso".

FULO (de *full*): El DEC documenta su empleo como adjetivo de uso registrado en La Palma, con el significado de "lleno o completo", y como adverbio, para designar "totalmente o por completo". Al parecer, se usa también "como intensificador de *negro, negra* aplicado al pelaje de los animales". Aunque la gran mayoría de nuestros informantes reconocían desconocer esta palabra, algunos significados curiosos que se propusieron fueron "el macho de la fula" (un pez local), 'una mentira' o bien calificativos como 'malo', 'irritado, enfadado'.

GUACHIMAN: Según el DEC este anglicismo, de mayor uso en Tenerife y La Gomera, se utiliza para nombrar a un "vigilante o guardián". Si bien esta palabra resultó ser desconocida para la mayoría de los informantes (92 no la habían oído nunca y a 46 les sonaba, pero no sabían su significado) hubo 13 respuestas acertadas o parcialmente relacionadas, como "guardaespaldas". Otros significados erróneos y curiosos que nos dieron fueron "persona guay", "orquesta folclórica guanche" y "hombre que va mucho de guachinche".

GUAGUA: Este popular término, de uso extendido tanto en Canarias[8] como en Cuba para referirse al "autobús", podría proceder de una lectura dificultosa del inglés *waggon*, tal y como señalaron en su día Corbella (1991–92: 65)

8 Al parecer, también es usado en alguna zona de Alicante. Guerra (1965: 274) así lo indica también.

y González Cruz (1995: 576). Sin embargo, hoy existe otra teoría que defiende que la voz pudo surgir del nombre abreviado de la primera fábrica estadounidense que exportó autobuses a Cuba: *Wa & Wa Co. Inc.*, es decir la *Washington, Walton and Company Incorporated*. Todos los informantes la reconocieron correctamente.

GUANIJAI: Esta voz (también con las formas *guanijay* y *guonijei*) la recoge el DEC indicando su procedencia del inglés, concretamente de la marca de whisky *John Haig*. Se dice que viene "del modismo *One John Haig* que se le pegó al isleño, bien por mimetismo o por guasa". Designa una "copa de bebida alcohólica, especialmente whisky". Solo 6 informantes indicaron este significado concreto y otras dos respuestas vincularon esta palabra con significados relacionados como "pizco" o "ir a beber". Algunas respuestas curiosas fueron las siguientes: dos informantes dieron como sinónimo "machango", significado que parece relacionado con otros propuestos como "tolete", "tonto, un don nadie", "un cualquiera, también *guelisnai*" (este último término nos resultó totalmente desconocido); un informante señaló haber escuchado la expresión "¡Qué pasa, guanijei!"; otros dos dieron como significados "porro" y "piti", respectivamente, mientras que un último informante (pensamos que con obvias conexiones con hablantes del español peninsular) identificó *guanijai* como sinónimo de "tontolaba".

GUINCHE (de *winch)*: El DEC define este sustantivo como "cabrestante, o torno de eje vertical, que se emplea para mover grandes pesos por medio de un cable que se va enrollando en él. Se usa especialmente para extraer las embarcaciones del mar". Corbella (1991–92: 66) señala que es de uso general en todo el archipiélago y cita a Alfaro, que destaca cómo este término "ha ascendido así de la jerga de los muelles al vocabulario de los escritores". La gran mayoría de nuestros informantes (91) declaró desconocer el significado de esta palabra, o bien que solo les sonaba (48), y únicamente 11 aportaron significados correctos o aproximados, mientras que dos respuestas se limitaron a indicar que conocían su significado, pero sin especificarlo. Dos informantes debieron confundir este término con el canarismo *guirre*, pues propusieron "buitre" y "ave" como significados de *guinche,* y otro señaló como significado, también erróneamente, "lugar de comida".

INSAI (de *inside;* también *linsay*): El DEC define este anglicismo como "[e]spacio del barco entre el banco de popa y el de proa, donde se almacena el pescado capturado". Solamente un informante aportó este significado. Una persona escribió que tenía "una amiga que se llama así pero no sé realmente su significado", mientras que dos respuestas vincularon esta palabra con la voz inglesa *inside,* matizándose en una de ellas "en inglés malo".

NAIFE (de *knife*): Esta voz designa una navaja singular, el típico "cuchillo canario" que usan los campesinos, sobre todo en Gran Canaria y el norte de Tenerife, y que "en algunos casos, aparte de bella obra de artesanía puede considerarse una joya, si atendemos al empleo ocasional de la plata y algún que otro metal noble", como señala el DEC. Es relativamente conocido, ya que algo menos de la mitad de los informantes (73) declararon conocer su significado y lo aportaron correctamente.

PAIPA (de *pipe*): el DEC describe este sustantivo como "cachimba para fumar". Es uno de los anglicismos más desconocidos, según declaran 152 de los informantes. Además, los dos informantes restantes propusieron significados erróneos, "abanico" y "una fruta", respectivamente.

PICHE (PICHI) (de *pitch)*: El DEC recoge esta voz junto con su variante, señalando su transmisión directa o bien a través del habla portuaria, así como su significado de "asfalto o alquitrán". Solo 53 informantes declararon conocer la palabra, que relacionaron con el alquitrán, el asfalto, la carretera, o el petróleo, si bien hubo 5 respuestas erróneas que aportaron significados tan dispares como "rofe" (sic), "fino", "embudo", "poco", "tipo de ropa de tirantes con falda" y otras 3 que se aproximaron parcialmente al indicar "carretera asfaltada, pero sin marcar líneas de tráfico", "suelo" y "crudo".

PICHICOMA (de *beach-comber,* literalmente "peinaplayas"). Esta voz designa, según Corbella (1991–92: 66), "a los vagos que pululan por los puertos". El DEC lo define como "ratero de muelle", señalando su uso documentado también en varios países latinoamericanos, con ligeras variantes, "aunque no siempre con el mismo significado canario". Ninguno de nuestros informantes aportó el posible significado de este anglicismo, que resultó totalmente desconocido.

PIMPE (de *pimp,* alcahuete). Este término se usaba, según Corbella (1991–92: 64), para referirse a quienes ejercían de intérpretes en los muelles canarios. La gran mayoría de respuestas (152) confirmaron el desconocimiento de esta voz. Únicamente dos informantes aportaron significados, si bien solo uno de ellos coincide con el que señala el DEC: "Guía procedente del Puerto de Santa Cruz". La otra respuesta explicaba que era un "nombre de mujer". Casualmente, puedo corroborar este último uso, pues hace unos años tuve una compañera de trabajo, profesora de inglés, que se hacía llamar Pimpe, como hipocorístico del popular nombre canario de mujer Pino.

QUEQUE (QUEQUI): De uso muy extendido en Gran Canaria, este anglicismo hace referencia a un bizcocho de harina, huevos, azúcar y a veces pasas, que se cuece en un molde. Surge "de la castellanización de *cake*" (Castillo, 1991: 360). Solo 14 informantes dijeron no tener ni idea del significado de este anglicismo, que también desconocían otros 21, si bien "les sonaba" la palabra. El resto (119 informantes) aportó definiciones correctas o sinónimos como "bizcochón", "dulce" o "pastel".

TIFAR (TIFIAR): El DEC registra ambas formas con el significado de "hurtar o robar", mencionando además su empleo en Cuba y su procedencia "del inglés *to thieve*". Solo 20 informantes aportaron respuestas para este término, ya que el resto (un total de 134) confesó desconocerlo. Únicamente 15 de esas respuestas fueron correctas, en tanto que las restantes sugirieron significados erróneos como "liarla", "fastidiar", "arruinar algo", o bien el combinado "arruinar, fastidiar"; un informante se expresó así: "que algo te salga mal".

TRINQUE (de *drink):* Al parecer, en las islas esta voz "se registra ampliamente con el significado de 'bebida alcohólica' y, por extensión, 'borrachera'" (Corbella, 1991–92: 67). El DEC señala que también se usa para referirse al acto de beber y menciona su variante *trinqui*. Esta voz, abiertamente desconocida para 125 de nuestros informantes, fue reconocida por el resto, si bien solamente 6 respuestas coincidieron con el significado que le da el DEC. Una de ellas explicaba: "Darle al trinque es como beber alcohol, viene del inglés *drink* pero en canario". En once respuestas se observa que se ha relacionado esta voz con el verbo trincar y sus significados de "coger", "agarrar", "pillar", "lo cogió por sorpresa", "pillé a alguien haciendo algo". Otro informante propuso "apretar", que guardaría cierta relación, pero seis respuestas fueron totalmente erróneas, al aportar significados tan dispares como "nuevo", "robo", "palo de una vela", "algo que te suena, pero no sabes qué es", y alguien respondió "creo que tiene varios significados, enfado, apuro".

QUINEGUA / QUINI / RAMBANA /AUTODATE: Estos cuatro términos, con algunas variantes (*rambane, artodate*) son adaptaciones, respectivamente, de las siguientes voces inglesas: *King Edward, Kidney, Arran Banner* y *Up-to-date*. Todas ellas están incluidas en el DEC y se corresponden con distintas variedades de papas (patatas). Solo 25 informantes señalaron que estas cuatro palabras tenían algo en común, siendo *rambana* las más desconocida (146), seguida de *quini* (145), *autodate* (105) y *quinegua* (94), que resultó ser la más popular.

Por último, teniendo en cuenta los errores cometidos por diversos informantes al aportar el significado de varios anglicismos, debemos ajustar la información ofrecida arriba en la Tabla 3 incluyendo los errores que muchos de ellos cometieron. La Tabla 4 ofrece los datos tanto del desconocimiento de sus significados, declarado abiertamente por parte de los 154 informantes, como del número de respuestas erróneas. También se contabilizan aquí aquellas respuestas en las que se dio a la palabra otro significado correcto pero diferente al esperado como anglicismo, como fueron los casos de los términos *brete* y *choni*.

Tabla 4: Relación de los anglicismos por orden de conocimiento según los informantes y con sus errores

ANGLICISMO	No lo conocen (N)	errores / otro sign (N)	Total	ANGLICISMO	No lo conocen (N)	errores / otro sign (N)	Total
GUAGUA	0	-	0	GUINCHE	139	3	142
QUEQUE	35	-	35	CHERCHA	144	4	148
FLIS	62	7	55	BELMONTINA	145	5	150
CHONI	63	74	137	QUINI	145	-	145
NAIFE	81	-	81	RAMBANA	146	-	146
QUINEGUA	94	-	94	FATI	148	6	154
PICHE	101	5	106	FULO	149	4	153
AUTODATE	105	-	105	BREQUE	150	3	153
FOTINGO	123	4	127	BRETE	150	4	154
TRINQUE	125	18	143	INSAI	150	3	153
CONCRETERA	134	-	134	PAIPA	152	2	154
TIFAR	134	5	139	PIMPE	152	1	153
GUANIJAI	136	9	145	FAO	153	1	154
GUACHIMÁN	138	3	141	PICHICOMA	154	-	154

En general observamos que los 154 informantes muestran un notable desconocimiento de los antiguos anglicismos canarios. Los menos desconocidos son *guagua, queque, flis* y *choni,* que constituyen notables excepciones al ser reconocidos por al menos la mitad (o más) de los encuestados. Sin embargo, la voz *choni* es un caso especial, pues parece ser más conocido como término de la jerga coloquial ("mujer vulgar", "chabacano") que por su significado como anglicismo ("turista extranjero"). Algo similar ocurre con *brete,* si bien esta palabra es mucho más desconocida (150 informantes no saben su significado); solo tres personas la reconocieron por su significado general de "aprieto" o "apuro". Teniendo en cuenta estos detalles, debemos reorganizar la relación de anglicismos ordenándolos de acuerdo al mayor o menor conocimiento de sus significados (anglicados) que han demostrado los informantes con sus respuestas. A continuación, la Tabla 5 ofrece esos datos finales:

Tabla 5: Relación final de los anglicismos por orden creciente de desconocimiento

ANGLICISMO	No lo conocen (N)	ANGLICISMO	No lo conocen (N)
GUAGUA	0	GUANIJAI	145
QUEQUE	35	QUINI	145
FLIS	55	RAMBANA	146
NAIFE	81	CHERCHA	148
QUINEGUA	94	BELMONTINA	150
AUTODATE	105	BREQUE	153
PICHE	106	FULO	153
FOTINGO	127	INSAI	153
CONCRETERA	134	PIMPE	153
CHONI	137	BRETE	154
TIFAR	139	FAO	154
GUACHIMÁN	141	FATI	154
GUINCHE	142	PAIPA	154
TRINQUE	143	PICHICOMA	154

5. Comentario final

Los datos obtenidos evidencian que los jóvenes universitarios canarios que participaron en esta encuesta desconocen la mayoría de los anglicismos antiguos que atesora el DEC. Las únicas excepciones, como ya señalamos, serían las voces *guagua, queque* y *flis.* Hay que destacar también el caso del anglicismo *choni,* para el que solo 17 respuestas aportaron su significado "tradicional" en las islas de "turista, extranjero", mientras que la gran mayoría (74 respuestas) lo vinculó con los significados que le otorga el DLE, es decir, "mujer joven que pretende ser elegante e ir a la moda, aunque resulta vulgar", o bien "chabacano, vulgar". Puede decirse que esta voz parece estar perdiendo su valor local como anglicismo y está siendo más usada por los jóvenes con su significado en la jerga coloquial. Lo mismo sucede con *brete*, que solo 3 informantes reconocieron con su significado general, pero no como anglicismo.

Obviamente esta investigación tiene sus limitaciones y sus resultados no deben generalizarse hasta que se contrasten con los de otros estudios futuros que utilicen una muestra mayor, que sea más representativa. No obstante, creo que las respuestas a nuestro formulario constituyen un indicio que va en la misma línea de los resultados obtenidos en el estudio ya mencionado (González Cruz, 2014) sobre el conocimiento y uso de un pequeño corpus de canarismos. En mi opinión no resultaría descabellado afirmar que buena parte de este patrimonio léxico canario tenderá irremediablemente a perderse con el paso del tiempo, como ya ha ocurrido con el listado de palabras moribundas que recogieron en su día García Mouton y Grijalbo (2011) o las que recopiló la Biblioteca Pública de Burgos en sendos *Diccionarios de Palabras Olvidadas* (vol. I: 2008; vol. II: 2009) un interesante trabajo que comenta Perdiguero Villareal (2017). Otros investigadores canarios (Almeida y Vidal, 1996–1997; Medina López, 2003; Samper Padilla y Hernández Cabrera, 2003) también han hecho aportaciones muy relevantes sobre este tema de la mortandad léxica en el español canario.

Como conclusión quizá cabría preguntarse: ¿hay algo que podamos hacer para evitar que se pierdan estas y otras tantas palabras de nuestro patrimonio léxico? Me temo que no podría dar ninguna respuesta. Como reconoce David Crystal (2000: 127) existen múltiples factores de gran complejidad que parecen interactuar para que los hablantes se impliquen en la conservación de su lengua; sabemos por qué algunos usan otras palabras o incluso llegan a cambiar de idioma, pero realmente desconocemos qué es exactamente lo que hace que algunas comunidades se mantengan leales a sus hablas.

Referencias:

Academia Canaria de la Lengua (2010): *Diccionario Básico de Canarismos*. La Laguna: Academia Canaria de la Lengua. Disponible en https://www.academiacanarialengua.org/diccionario/

Almeida, Manuel y Carmelo Vidal (1996–1997): "Mortandad léxica en el español canario". *Anuario de Lingüística Hispánica*, 12–13 (2), 883–897.

Almeida, Manuel y Carmen Díaz Alayón (1988): *El español de Canarias*. Santa Cruz de Tenerife: Litografía A. Romero.

Alvar, Manuel (1975): *Atlas lingüístico y etnográfico de las Islas Canarias*. Las Palmas de Gran Canaria: Cabildo Insular de Gran Canaria.

Álvarez, Mª Ángeles: (1996): "Sobre algunas construcciones sintácticas en el español de Canarias", en Javier Medina y Dolores Corbella (eds.), *El español de Canarias hoy: análisis y perspectivas*. Frankfurt and Main: Vervuert / Madrid: Iberoamericana, 67–82.

Álvarez Mellado, Elena (2016): *Anatomía de la lengua. Historias, curiosidades y porqués del idioma.* Barcelona: Larousse Editorial.

Armistead, Samuel G. (1996): "Pichingli: An English-Spanish Pidgin from the Canary Islands." *Journal of Pidgins and Creole Languages*, 11, 85–87.

Armistead, Samuel G. (1997): "Sobre la lengua de los cambulloneros: El Pichingli." *Revista de Filología de la Universidad de La Laguna*, 14, 245–252.

Bethencourt-Massieu, Antonio (1991): *Canarias e Inglaterra: el comercio de vinos, 1650–1800.* Las Palmas de Gran Canaria: Cabildo Insular de Gran Canaria.

Biblioteca Pública de Burgos (2008): *Diccionario de palabras olvidadas I.* Burgos: Amabar.

Biblioteca Pública de Burgos (2009): *Diccionario de palabras olvidadas II.* Burgos: Amabar.

Castillo, Francisco Javier (1991): "El vocabulario de una modalidad del español. Algunas notas sobre los anglicismos en las hablas canarias", en *Actas del Congreso de la Sociedad Española de Lingüística.* XX aniversario. Madrid: Gredos, 354–362.

Castillo, Francisco Javier (2003): "A propósito de los anglicismos de las hablas canarias. Cuestiones históricas, léxicas y etimológicas", en Carmen Díaz Alayón, Marcial Morera Perez, y Gonzalo Ortega Ojeda (eds.), *Estudios sobre el español de Canarias.* Editorial Islas Canarias, vol. 2, 517–541.

Castillo, Francisco Javier (2005): "Sobre anglicismos y canarismos: a vueltas con varias proposiciones etimológicas", en *Con quien tanto quería: estudios en homenaje a María del Prado Escobar Bonilla.* Servicio de Publicaciones de la Universidad de Las Palmas de Gran Canaria, 93–100.

Corbella Díaz, Dolores (1991–1992): "Los anglicismos en el español de Canarias: Interferencias lingüísticas". *Cauce. Revista de Filología y su Didáctica*, 14–15, 61–69.

Corbella, Dolores y Javier Medina (coords.) (1996): *El español de Canarias hoy: Análisis y perspectivas.* Madrid: Vervuert Iberoamericana.

Corrales, Cristóbal, Dolores Corbella y Mª Ángeles Álvarez (1996): *Diccionario diferencial del español de Canarias.* Madrid: Arco Libros, S. L.

Corrales, Cristóbal y Dolores Corbella (2001): *Diccionario histórico del español de Canarias.* La Laguna: Instituto de Estudios Canarios.

Corrales, Cristóbal y Dolores Corbella (2009): *Diccionario ejemplificado de canarismos.* La Laguna: Instituto de Estudios Canarios, 2 vols.

Corrales, Cristóbal, Mª Ángeles Álvarez y Dolores Corbella (2007): *El español de Canarias. Guía bibliográfica.* Tenerife: Instituto de Estudios Canarios.

Corujo, Arturo (2019). "El español de Canarias: origen, diferencia e identidad". *Alegando! Magazine. Revista Digital sobre Cultura Canaria.* https://alegando.com/el-espanol-de-canarias/ (4 marzo).

Crystal, David (2000): *Language death.* Cambridge: Cambridge University Press.

Dalby, Andrew (2002): *Language in danger.* Londres: Allen Lane.

Fernández-Armesto, Felipe (1995): *Canarias e Inglaterra a través de la historia.* Las Palmas de Gran Canaria: Cabildo Insular de Gran Canaria.

García Mouton, Pilar (2007): "Vitalidad y mortandad léxica en las hablas rurales de Madrid." En Josefa Dorta Luis (ed.), *Temas de dialectología.* Tenerife: Instituto de Estudios Canarios, 81–94.

García Mouton, Pilar y Alex Grijelmo (2011): *Palabras moribundas.* Madrid: Santillana. Ediciones Generales.

García Pérez, José Luis (2007/1988): *Viajeros ingleses en las Islas Canarias durante el siglo XIX.* Santa Cruz de Tenerife: Ediciones Idea.

González Cruz, Mª Isabel (1993): "El contacto lingüístico anglocanario: algunas consideraciones para su estudio". *Revista canaria de estudios ingleses,* 26–27, 131–48.

González Cruz, Mª Isabel (1995): *La convivencia anglocanaria. Estudio sociocultural y lingüístico, 1880–1914.* Las Palmas de Gran Canaria: Cabildo Insular de Gran Canaria.

González Cruz, Mª Isabel (2002): *Notas para una bibliografía inglesa sobre Canarias. Primer repertorio bibliográfico y análisis de su estructura y contenido.* La Laguna: Instituto de Estudios Canarios.

González Cruz, Mª Isabel (2003): *"The Canary Islands Review" (1903–04). Textos sobre Canarias y la colonia británica en el periódico inglés de Las Palmas.* Las Palmas de Gran Canaria: Cabildo Insular de Gran Canaria.

González Cruz, Mª Isabel (2011a): "Hispanismos y canarismos en los textos de dos viajeras británicas decimonónicas". *Revista de Filología de la Universidad de La Laguna,* 29, 81–99.

González Cruz, Mª Isabel (2011b): "Exploring the Canarian contribution to Hispanicisms in English". *Revista Alicantina de Estudios Ingleses,* 24, 131–152.

González Cruz, Mª Isabel (2012): "English in the Canaries: Past and present". *English Today. The International Review of the English Language,* 109/1, 20–28.

González Cruz, Mª Isabel (2013): "Hispanismos y canarismos en un corpus de textos ingleses sobre Canarias". *LEXIS. Revista de Lingüística y Literatura,* 37 (2): 229–267.

González Cruz, Mª Isabel (2014): "Approaching lexical loss in Canarian Spanish: A preliminary study". *Revista de Lingüística y Lenguas Aplicadas,* 9, 33–44.

González Cruz, Mª Isabel (2022a): "Anglicismos en el español de Canarias." En Félix Rodríguez González (ed.), *Anglicismos en el español contemporáneo: una visión panorámica.* Peter Lang, 379–412.

González Cruz, Mª Isabel (2022b): *Hispanicisms in Romance Fiction. An Annotated Glossary.* Lewiston, New York: The Edwin Mellen Press.

Guimerá Ravina, Agustín (1985): *Burguesía extranjera y comercio atlántico. La empresa comercial irlandesa en Canarias.* Santa Cruz de Tenerife: C.S.I.C.

Guerra, Pancho (1965): *Contribución al léxico popular de Gran Canaria.* Madrid: Mancomunidad de Cabildos/ Ayuntamiento de San Bartolomé de Tirajana, vol. 3.

Hernández, Clara Eugenia y José Antonio Samper (2003): *Voces canarias recopiladas por Galdós.* Las Palmas de Gran Canaria: Cabildo de Gran Canaria.

Hernández, Humberto (2003): "Dialectalismos, medios de comunicación y enseñanza de la lengua", *Estudios sobre el español de Canarias. Actas del I Congreso Internacional sobre el español de Canarias,* vol. 2. Islas Canarias: Litografía Romero. pp. 895–909.

Hernández Gutiérrez, A. Sebastián (1988): "Arquitectura inglesa en Canarias: pautas de comportamiento", en *Actas del VII CEHA* (Congreso Español de Historia del Arte), 633–638.

Hernández Gutiérrez, A. Sebastián (1995): "Arquitectos e ingenieros ingleses en las islas Canarias." En *Canarias e Inglaterra a través de la historia.* Las Palmas de Gran Canaria: Cabildo Insular de Gran Canaria, 193–216.

Hoffer, Bates L. (2002): "Language borrowing and language diffusion: An overview". *Intercultural Communication Studies,* 11 (4), 1–37.

Iglesias Hernández, Mª Luisa (1985): *Extranjeros en Gran Canaria.* Las Palmas de Gran Canaria: Gobierno de Canarias.

Lorenzo, Antonio, Marcial Morera y Gonzalo Ortega (1994): *Diccionario de canarismos.* La Laguna: Francisco Lemus ed.

Martín Hernández, Ulises (1990): *La presencia extranjera en Tenerife.* Santa Cruz de Tenerife: Cabildo Insular de Tenerife.

Medina, Javier (1997): "Los prehispanismos canarios: quinientos años después", en José Luis Otal, Inmaculada Fortanet y Victoria Codina (eds.), *Estudios de lingüística aplicada.* Castelló de la Plana: Universitat Jaume I, 793–799.

Medina López, Javier (2003): "Léxico canario: pervivencia y mortandad léxicas". En *Lexicografía y lexicología en Europa y América. Homenaje a Günter Haensch en su 80 aniversario,* Madrid: Gredos, 493–508.

Morales Lezcano, Víctor (1970): *Relaciones mercantiles entre Inglaterra y los archipiélagos del Atlántico Ibérico: su estructura y su historia (1530–1783)*. La Laguna: Instituto de Estudios Canarios.

Morales Lezcano, Victor (1986): *Los ingleses en Canarias*. Las Palmas de Gran Canaria: Edirca.

Morera, Marcial (1990): *Lengua y colonia en Canarias*. La Laguna: Editorial Globo.

Morera, Marcial (2006): *Diccionario histórico-etimológico del habla canaria*. Cabildo de Fuerteventura. Servicio de Publicaciones.

Morgenthaler, Laura (2002): "Globalización lingüística y pérdida de identidad". *Disenso. Revista canaria de análisis y opinión*, 38, 7–9.

Morgenthaler, Laura (2008): *Identidad y pluricentrismo lingüístico. Hablantes canarios frente a la estandarización*. Madrid/Frankfurt and Main: Vervuert/Iberoamericana.

Morín, Adela y Ángeles Castellano (1990): "Creencias y actitudes del docente canario hacia su modalidad de habla". *El Guiniguada*, 1, 257–261.

Morín, Adela (1993): *Actitudes sociolingüísticas en el léxico de Vegueta*. Servicio de Publicaciones de la Universidad de Las Palmas de Gran Canaria.

Ortega, Gonzalo (1981): "El español hablado en Canarias: visión sociolingüística". *Revista de Filología de la Universidad de La Laguna*, 0, 11–115.

Perdiguero Villareal, Hermógenes (2017): "Voces de la vida cotidiana en el Diccionario de palabras olvidadas" en *El diccionario en la encrucijada, de la sintaxis y la cultura al desafío digital. Actas del VII Congreso Internacional de Lexicografía Hispánica*. Santander: Escuela Universitaria de Turismo Altamira, 1019–1027.

Quintana Navarro, Francisco (1985): *Barcos, negocios y burgueses en el Puerto de La Luz*. Las Palmas de Gran Canaria: C.I.A.C.

Quintana Navarro, Francisco (1992): *Informes consulares británicos sobre Canarias (1856–1914)*. Las Palmas de Gran Canaria: Seminario de Estudios Históricos Canarios del Centro Asociado de la UNED.

Rodríguez Muñoz, Francisco J. (2012): "El español atlántico: revitalización de un concepto metodológico desde la dialectologia". *Sintagma*, 24, 23–32.

Samper Padilla, José A. y Clara E. Hernández Cabrera (2002). "Condicionantes sociales y mortandad léxica", en *Sprachgeschichte als Varietätengeschichte. Historia de las variedades lingüísticas. Anläbich des 60. Geburtstages von Jens Lüdtke* (coordinadores: Andreas Wesch, Waltraud Weidenbusch, Rolf Kailuweit y Brenda Laca). Tubinga: Stauffenburg Verlag, 167–176.

Van Hout, Roeland y Peter Muysken (1994): "Modelling lexical borrowability". *Language Variation and Change*, 6, 39–62.

Silvia Betti

Università di Bologna y ANLE

El español y spanglish en los Estados Unidos. Una reflexión desde Europa

Introducción[1]

El español en los Estados Unidos fue durante mucho tiempo una lengua que carecía de aprecio social, era, sobre todo, un "idioma de color", pero con el tiempo se ha convertido en la lengua extranjera que en este país ha operado como mediación cultural, forjando alianzas y accesos, ocupando escenarios públicos y enriqueciendo la vida cotidiana. Como se sabe, el español ha tenido una presencia antigua en los territorios del Sur de los actuales Estados Unidos. A este respecto, Ortega (1999: web) observa que las nuevas formas culturales bilingües, "las tesis de la hibridación y del multiculturalismo, son parte de este espacio de reflexión sobre las nuevas identidades políticas y sus discursos de mediación". Y agrega que "Más allá de la perpetuación institucional de las 'minorías' y de la victimización post-colonial, hay un espacio de creatividad, respuestas, y negociaciones cuyos procesos cognitivos, expresiones heteróclitas, y prácticas fluidas, exceden la autoridad académica de las teorías al uso, y demandan más radicales formas de lectura".

Se trata, como es sabido, de una sociedad, la latina[2], muy polifacética, de un mosaico multicultural extraordinario[3]. Y nada califica, o une más, a los latinos en los Estados Unidos que la lengua española. Muchos hablan español en el hogar y muchos lo emplean en sus momentos de ocio, mientras que, en el mundo laboral, se suele utilizar el inglés. Del encuentro entre estas dos lenguas surge el fenómeno del cambio de código, fenómeno común entre bilingües en

---

1 Este capítulo presenta algunos fundamentos teóricos, investigaciones y parte de los resultados de los estudios llevados a cabo durante años sobre el tema del español *en* y *de* los Estados Unidos y el fenómeno relacionado con el tema del spanglish.

2 En este estudio utilizaremos los términos latino e hispano, o hispanounidense como sinónimos, pero advirtiendo que tienen matices diferentes.

3 En realidad, se trata de grupos nacionales heterogéneos por culturas, etnias, etc. En este trabajo, de todos modos, optamos por usar el término "minoría", usual en muchos estudios sobre estos temas.

muchas partes del mundo, y que puede ocurrir a nivel intraoracional (dentro de la misma oración) o interoracional (entre una oración y otra).

Para numerosos sociolingüistas el fenómeno bilingüe representa un aspecto relevante del estudio de las actitudes lingüísticas. Los propios hablantes han creado definiciones peculiares para referirse a ciertas variedades en las que el cambio de código o el préstamo léxico ocupan un lugar prominente (Blas Arroyo 2005). *Tex-mex*, por ejemplo, se usa entre los chicanos de Texas, mientras que *pachuco* designa el dialecto original de la ciudad fronteriza de El Paso (Texas). Otra forma es *cubonics*, que se refiere a los hablantes de origen cubano que residen en Florida.

Y, naturalmente, el término *spanglish* que indica lo que popularmente se considera como una modalidad comunicacional peculiar de los Estados Unidos.

Otros estudiosos prefieren hablar de "español popular de los Estados Unidos" (Otheguy 2009), que reflejaría la cultura anglo presente en ese país. Este investigador (2009: 222), efectivamente, subraya que se trata de aquella habla que todos los hispanos utilizan en los momentos más informales y populares, es decir, el habla de la familia, de la tienda, de la iglesia, de la calle. Otheguy (2013: 133–134) ve el español en los Estados Unidos como:

> un habla sumamente variada, estructurada por una lengua heterogénea también, caracterizada por sus muchos rasgos divergentes, importados de los distintos países desde donde han emigrado los hispanounidenses. Sería una exageración decir que en EE.UU. no ha habido ningún desarrollo de comunidad lingüística y que cada cual 'habla a su manera'; los préstamos léxicos de origen inglés, por ejemplo, al ser compartidos por todos, sirven de elemento cohesionador.

Lipski en un trabajo fechado 2010 escribe: "no existen criterios dialectológicos aceptados que justifiquen el rechazo a priori del concepto de un español estadounidense, matizado según parámetros geográficos, socioculturales y étnicos". Y en otro estudio de 2013 (121), observa que "la lengua española en Estados Unidos ha logrado una autonomía lingüística tanto en términos de una masa crítica de hablantes como en su propia naturaleza dialectal". Por eso, muchos estudiosos hablan ya de español estadounidense como resultado de la "reproducción y diversificación natural de una lengua de inmigración en tierras nuevas" (Lipski, 2016). López García-Molins (2014: 131) nota la necesidad de una "norma culta lo suficientemente flexible" en este país para que el español pueda convertirse en español *de* los Estados Unidos. Un "español *de* los Estados Unidos" que refleja, como hemos mencionado, la realidad en la que se gesta, la necesitad de comunicarse de forma cotidiana en un ambiente que acoge estas prácticas lingüísticas y las hace suyas.

El spanglish

El término *spanglish* puede dar una idea de la comunicación que caracteriza a las comunidades de origen hispano que viven en los Estados Unidos. Se trata, según algunos investigadores, del resultado de la simbiosis de la lengua española y de la lengua inglesa o, según otros, de la conmutación de código, o cambio de código, entre el español y el inglés. El término, en cierto sentido, muestra, de forma metafórica, la multiplicidad cultural de los hablantes latinos y, además, da una idea de la identidad que quieren reivindicar algunos de estos hablantes.

El *spanglish*[4], de *span- (spanish)* y *-glish (english)* se puede en cierta manera considerar como el producto del encuentro (o, en otros casos, del choque) entre dos universos, dos sensibilidades, dos culturas y dos idiomas: el hispánico y el anglosajón, y representa una práctica interesante en la comunicación entre los latinos bilingües, como alternativa a la comunicación en un solo idioma. El *spanglish* puede llegar a ser un medio de comunicación provechoso en determinados contextos, y signo también, según los latinos que lo practican, de una nueva identidad *in-between*. Y acaso sea símbolo de una identidad para negociar la integración de los latinos en los Estados Unidos, ya que supone mucho más que saber dos idiomas, es una "forma de vida" y es expresión de diferentes culturas, ricas y variadas.

Torres (2004: web) cree que el *spanglish* no procede, únicamente, de una actitud individual, sino:

> del entorno familiar en el que crecen los latinos y, a la vez, del contexto social en el que están inmersos. Por otro lado, este código híbrido, de orígenes populares, tiene mucho de actitud contracultural, de desapego a las "normas de conducta". Y lo destacable es que estas manifestaciones expresivas se documentan, se recogen, ya sea en pintadas, en letras de canciones, en películas, en la prensa, en la literatura, o también en estudios y recopilaciones de interesados y especialistas en el tema.

Ofelia García (2013: 353), por su parte, rechaza el término *spanglish*, que lo considera despectivo, y, en cambio, observa: "para que se deje de considerar al

4 *Spanglish* es el término más generalizado, que también aparece como *espanglis*. Además se conocen las formas *slanglish, casteyanqui, ingleñol, bilingo, Tex-Mex, pocho, caló, pachuco, papiamento gringo, español bastardo, español mixtureado, spanglés, angliparla*, etc. (*vid.* A. Torres 2004 y F. Moreno Fernández 2006). Se ha propuesto también el término *gringañol*. En nuestro estudio usaremos el término *spanglish*.

español como presencia extranjera en los EE.UU. a adoptarlo como un español de los EE.UU., hablado por ciudadanos bilingües, tendríamos que aceptar las prácticas comunicativas que he denominado "translanguaging" [...] y adoptar una metodología en la enseñanza que utilizara esas prácticas del translenguar bilingüe". (Énfasis de la autora)

El cambio de códigos y la mezcla de códigos

Aclaramos que el significado que se da a las expresiones cambio de codigos[5]. conmutación de códigos (en inglés *code-switching*), alternancia de códigos (en

5 J. Lipski (2004a: web), a propósito del cambio de códigos, subraya: "Para dar cuenta de algunas de las restricciones gramaticales que circunscriben el cambio de lenguas, notamos que son inaceptables los cambios: **(1)** Entre un sujeto pronominal y el predicado: **Él IS COMING TOMORROW; *He VIENE MAÑANA.* **(2)** Entre un clítico pronominal y el verbo: **Juan lo SAID / *Juan quiere decir IT; *John wants to say LO.* **(3)** Entre una palabra interrogativa desplazada a la posición inicial y el resto de la oración: **¿Cuándo WILL YOU COME?; *¿When VAS A HACERLO?* **(4)** Entre un verbo auxiliar (sobre todo *haber*) y el verbo principal: **María ha FINISHED THE JOB; *We had ACABADO DE COMER.* Son menos extrañas las oraciones que contienen un cambio de lengua entre el verbo auxiliar estar/be y el gerundio: María está CHECKING HER ANSWERS. Mary is REVISANDO SU INFORME. Porque ella está GOING TO HAVE A BABY. El gerundio puede ocurrir en la porción de la oración realizada en inglés aun cuando el gerundio no sería aceptable si la misma frase ocurriera en español; igualmente un gerundio en español puede asumir la función nominal que retiene en inglés: *Estoy por LOWERING THE STANDARD. I'm talking about CONOCIÉNDONOS.* **(5)** Los adverbios de negación tienen que estar en la misma lengua que los verbos que modifican: **El médico no WANTS THAT. *The doctor does not QUIERE ESO*". Y agrega que: "Existen muchas otras restricciones absolutas, así como configuraciones parcialmente aceptables de acuerdo a la selección léxica, el entorno pragmático y el registro sociolingüístico. En la mayoría de los casos las restricciones reflejan la necesidad de respetar las reglas gramaticales de cada lengua, siguiendo el orden lineal de las oraciones tanto en inglés como en español. Así es por ejemplo que una configuración prohibida tal como **El médico no WANTS THAT* antepone un solo adverbio de negación al verbo inglés, sin añadir el verbo de apoyo *do/does*, creando una violación sintáctica lineal. En otros casos las restricciones gramaticales surgen de las relaciones jerárquicas postuladas por los modelos sintácticos generativos, rompiendo los enlaces de rección o ligamiento al oscilar entre configuraciones incompatibles (DiSciullo, Muysken y Singh 1986). Como contrapartida de las restricciones gramaticales hay configuraciones que favorecen el cambio

inglés *code alternativo*), mezcla de códigos (en inglés *code-mixing*)[6] y al término popular *spanglish*, tiene diferentes interpretaciones según los estudiosos del tema. Por lo que se refiere a estas estrategias lingüísticas no hay una terminología generalmente aceptada, y las investigaciones sobre esta práctica de comunicación a menudo no son idénticas. El cambio (y la mezcla) de códigos representa una parte central del discurso bilingüe; es por eso, por lo que *no* se puede considerar una práctica lingüística del hispanohablante que aparece de una forma caótica, sino que resulta gobernada por requisitos funcionales y pragmáticos, y desempeña un papel único en la comunicación entre los hispanos que viven en los Estados Unidos, precisamente como alternativa a la comunicación en un solo idioma. Efectivamente, la convivencia de lenguas es una situación natural en el mundo, y diferentes estudios han demostrado que el fenómeno resulta afectado por la etnicidad del interlocutor y por la formalidad de la situación comunicativa.

José Luis Blas Arroyo (2005: 642–643) observa que el cambio *interoracional* exige ya una relevante competencia activa por parte de los hablantes bilingües, ya que los cambios deben respetar la gramática de ambos idiomas. A este respecto, este sociolingüista (2005: 642) añade: "Por ello no son previsibles en la actuación lingüística de los monolingües, salvo en los contextos formulares y bajo una función estética o lúdica del lenguaje". Mientras que los cambios de código *intraoracionales*, según ese mismo autor, presuponen un riesgo sintáctico más alto que los anteriores, lo que demuestra el hecho de que estén presentes solamente en el habla de los bilingües más equilibrados y fluidos (*apud* Betti 2008).

Investigaciones realizadas en comunidades de hablantes de inglés-español en los Estados Unidos sugieren toda la complejidad de esta forma lingüística, y muestran que la alternancia de códigos se rige sobre una serie de elementos que permite practicar este cambio de código solo a quien conoce bien ambas lenguas (Scannavini, 1994; Medina López, 1996, 1997). Medina López (1997: 16)

---

de lenguas en el discurso bilingüe. La presencia anticipada de un nombre propio en la otra lengua puede estimular un cambio antes de la articulación de la palabra clave [...], etc. (*vid.* Lipski 2004a)" (*apud* Betti 2008).

6 Con la denominación *mezcla de códigos (code-mixing)* algunos investigadores designan ciertas clases de cambio de códigos, como ocurre con el llamado *cambio intraoracional*. Otros, como McClure (1977), distinguen, por el contrario, entre *cambio de código –code changing-*, cuando el intercambio está motivado por restricciones situacionales y/o estilísticas, y *mezcla de código –code-mixing-* cuando el cambio de lengua obedece a razones puramente referenciales, debido, por ejemplo, a las dificultades para acceder a un vocablo o expresión en una lengua que el hablante no domina bien (*vid.* Blas Arroyo 2005).

sobre este tema aclara que los estudios que se han llevado a cabo en comunidades de hablantes inglés-español en los Estados Unidos, prueban que el cambio de código está regido por una serie de factores y que son los bilingües más equilibrados (es decir, quienes mejor conocen cada una de las dos lenguas) los que más practican la alternancia de códigos. Gimeno Menéndez (2001), por su parte, escribe que muchos cambios han surgido gracias a la convivencia continua con la lengua inglesa, y se denominan con los términos de sobregeneralización, simplificación y convergencia. Pero los más estudiados, al principio, fueron los léxicos.

El cambio de códigos ha sido estudiado ampliamente y a través de diferentes enfoques. Su estudio se remonta a finales de 1970, cuando divergieron dos líneas de investigación en torno a este fenómeno, una que estudiaba las motivaciones sociales y el uso del cambio de código en comunidades bilingües, y otra que analizaba los aspectos gramaticales del cambio de código (MacSwan & MacAlister 2010). En un trabajo pionero sobre el cambio de código, Poplack (1980) propone que los bilingües pueden combinar sus lenguas en la misma oración si la yuxtaposición de elementos de las dos lenguas no viola ninguna regla sintáctica de las dos lenguas, condición que se conoce como la *restricción de equivalencia* (*equivalence constraint*) (Munarriz /Parafita Couto, 2014).

Recordamos, entonces, de forma no exhaustiva, solo algunos trabajos como los de Poplack (1982), Myer- Scotton (1993a, 1993b), Appel y Muysken (1996), Auer (1998), Zentella (1997, 1998, 2016, entre otros), Lipski (1982, 2004a, 2008), Toribio (2000), entre muchos otros. Carol Myers-Scotton (1993), por lo que concierne a ese comportamiento lingüístico, observa que el *Markedness Model* (Modelo de marcadez) indica que los hablantes cambian de lengua o introducen elementos de otra lengua en su discurso cuando hay una determinada situación, cuando quieren comunicar ciertos significados, o la pertenencia a determinados grupos sociales. Para Myers-Scotton (1990, 1992) el cambio de códigos es un fenómeno, sobre todo, social. Según los principios de la Teoría sobre la lengua matriz (*Matrix Language Frame Model -MLF-* Myers-Scotton, 1993), cuando los bilingües comunican entre ellos, pueden decidir cambiar de códigos. Su elección depende de distintos factores sociolingüísticos, como los significados que quieren vehicular, su consideración de las lenguas utilizadas y del mismo *code-switching*.

Así, a estos cambios se le da en muchos casos el nombre popular de *spanglish*, porque el *spanglish* encierra y cuenta una historia que el cambio de código, como "expresión técnica", no logra contar. El *spanglish* creemos que se puede describir como un sistema de comunicación familiar, una estrategia expresiva natural que da la posibilidad de comunicarse pasando simultáneamente de un código a otro, del inglés al español o viceversa, o de mezclar estas dos lenguas en los discursos dialógicos espontáneos e intrafamiliares (Betti, 2013, 2015a, 2015b, 2016, 2018).

De hecho, Rojas Marcos (2003) ve en el alternar los idiomas un elemento de fraternidad y de confianza. Insertar en el diálogo [en inglés, *N.d.la A.*] una o dos palabras en español es siempre un gesto de aproximación, de familiaridad y tiene en los debates tensos un efecto consolador. Asimismo, en las discusiones, puede ser la invitación a encontrar una solución pacífica. Se usa esta estrategia, según autores como René Appel y Pieter Muysken ([1987] 1996: 177-180), cuando, por ejemplo, se desea incorporar a un nuevo participante que habla otra lengua o, contrariamente, se desea excluir de la conversación a una persona que no conoce una de las dos lenguas, usando durante la interacción frases o palabras de la lengua desconocida, o se recurre a esa conducta verbal para manifestar la identidad mixta, como en el caso de los latinos bilingües español/inglés.

Ana Celia Zentella que se ha ocupado del bilingüismo en la ciudad de Nueva York en su conocido libro *Growing Up Bilingual: Puerto Rican Children in New York* (1997), advierte: "En contra de lo que muchos creen, el *spanglish* es un signo de destreza lingüística" y añade que "El *code switching* lo utilizan no sólo los inmigrantes de clase baja de *El Barrio*, sino también sus hijos acomodados que trabajan en Wall Street" (apud Fresneda, 1999: web). Además, Zentella observa que "Las nuevas generaciones de latinos, los nacidos aquí, se manejan mejor en inglés que en español, pero antes que resignarse a perder su segunda lengua materna, la incorporan espontáneamente a su discurso. Es un modo de reafirmar su identidad". Según Gutiérrez-Rivas (2006), este fenómeno es el modo y el medio de comunicación de ciertas comunidades y es característico de los hablantes que tienen control de dos lenguas. Y sustenta también la teoría de Zentella (1997) de que el cambio de códigos es un fenómeno que responde a complejas variables sociales y lingüísticas, y es, sin duda, una competencia.

El *spanglish* se puede considerar también una manera de vivir entre dos mundos culturales, lingüísticos, sociales, económicos, políticos, diferentes, que posee sus propias reglas de desarrollo y constituye algo "transgresor", que ha surgido de la experiencia común del exilio, la discriminación y el acceso limitado a los derechos sociales, civiles, políticos y culturales (Pastor, 2000).

Spanglish: práctica lingüística e identidad

Poblaciones, las latinas, heterogéneas y amplias que no quieren abrazar -aunque no todos los latinos, sí muchos de ellos-, como único idioma el inglés, y desean mantener su propia identidad dentro de un país que no es el de origen. Porque la identidad latina es multifacética y compleja, y no todos la viven de la misma forma. Silvina Chmiel (1996: 88) escribe que "Tener un código común refuerza la identidad, a la vez que diferencia a una comunidad del resto".

Cabe destacar también la actitud de los hispanohablantes con respecto a su lengua materna: a pesar del progresivo retroceso por lo que concierne a la tercera generación, los hispanos no olvidan la importancia de hablar español e intentan preservar su idioma. Lo confirma una encuesta realizada por Taylor, Lopez, Martínez y Velasco del Pew Research Center (2012), *Language Use among Latinos*, en la que los hispanos tuvieron que responder sobre la importancia que pueda tener el hecho de hablar español para las futuras generaciones. La encuesta constató que, aunque se está experimentando una disminución general de la competencia en español en los de la tercera generación, la misma población hispana considera que es fundamental la transmisión del español a las generaciones futuras. De hecho, tres de cada cuatro encuestados respondieron que es imprescindible que las generaciones futuras sigan hablando español. El mismo Observatorio del Instituto Cervantes en Harvard afirmó, hace algunos años, que "la tasa de bilingüismo de los hispanos, incluso en la tercera generación, sigue siendo superior a la de otros grupos étnicos y raciales" (Martínez et al., 2016: web), ya que casi un tercio de la población de tercera generación tiene el español como "idioma de uso primario". La mayor parte de esta cifra se debe a la proporción de hispanos nacidos en el extranjero que hablan español en el hogar, cuyo porcentaje no solo sigue manteniéndose alto, sin cambios significativos desde hace más de treinta años, sino también aumentará mientras la población hispana en los Estados Unidos siga creciendo (Krogstad et al., 2015; Krogstad y López, 2015).

La lengua española lleva unos años experimentando un proceso de cambio dentro de los Estados Unidos, debido al crecimiento extraordinario de la población hispana durante las últimas décadas. Estados Unidos representan no solo el destino de muchos inmigrantes, sino también el lugar de nacimiento de nuevas generaciones de hispanos, así el país "juega un papel muy importante en el mundo hispánico" (Jenkins, 2013: 43). La preservación de la lengua especialmente en la zona del suroeste se relaciona con la densidad y la lealtad de los hablantes. Esto justifica la importancia que los hispanos quieren dar a la lengua española, frente a la presencia de la lengua inglesa, especialmente en una perspectiva futura. Además, no habría que olvidar la popularidad que ejerce el español entre los demás idiomas dentro del panorama educativo de los Estados Unidos. Por todo ello, también debido a las barreras sociales en la competencia del inglés, se producen situaciones de estrecho contacto, influencia y, al mismo tiempo, choque entre las dos lenguas y, por consiguiente, entre las dos culturas.

El *spanglish* nace, así, como estrategia expresiva propia de una parte de estas comunidades que expresan a través de esta práctica su identidad en el medio de dos mundos, creando un tercer espacio (Bhabha, 2002). Sin embargo, muchos latinos que viven en los Estados Unidos tienen el deseo de que sus hijos aprendan bien el inglés, considerado *clave* del éxito en este país, y se integren en la sociedad estadounidense. Es por esto que los latinos de las últimas generaciones, nacidos en los Estados Unidos, casi no hablan español, sino inglés, y prefieren expresarse en este idioma. Por esto, en los Estados Unidos existen en muchos departamentos universitarios programas para los llamados "hablantes de herencia", "Heritage Speakers", como el de la Universidad de Santa Barbara (https://www.spanport.ucsb.edu/undergrad/language-program/heritage-native-speakers), solo por poner un ejemplo de los muchos que se encuentran.

La lealtad absoluta al verbo materno a costa de la lengua inglesa, precisaba hace algunos años Rojas Marcos (2003), puede producir retrasos académicos, limitar las oportunidades en el mundo laboral y reducir las posibilidades de participar e influir en los grandes temas que conciernen al país. Existen estudios, según este especialista, que han demostrado que los hispanos que hablan con dificultad en inglés tienden a ser percibidos por sus interlocutores como individuos menos inteligentes de lo que realmente son. Pero, al mismo tiempo, es llamativo lo que señalaba en otro estudio Criado (2004: 147), o sea que el inglés es cierto condición necesaria "para desenvolverse en la sociedad y acceder a mejor posición y empleo, pero es evidente también que su mayor dominio no garantiza estos logros: ahí están los datos de pobreza de los puertorriqueños, por ejemplo, sin olvidar los de los afroamericanos".

El Pew Research Center llevó a cabo una encuesta "A majority of English-speaking Hispanics in the U.S. are bilingual" publicada el 24 de marzo de 2015 (web), donde se observaba que: "*Fully 87 % said Latino immigrants need to learn English to succeed. At the same time, nearly all (95 %) said it is important for future generations of U.S. Hispanics to speak Spanish*". En la misma encuesta se podía leer que: "*Due in part to bilingualism, in 2013 Spanish was the most spoken non-English language in the U.S., used by 35.8 million Hispanics in the U.S. plus an additional 2.6 million non-Hispanics. Overall, three- in-four Hispanics (73 %) ages 5 and older speak Spanish in their homes, when including those who are bilingual.*" Y sobre el *spanglish* los autores de esta encuesta, Krogstad y Gonzalez-Barrera, notaron que: "*And as a sign of the times, Spanglish, an informal hybrid of both languages, is widely used among Hispanics ages 16 to 25. Among these young Hispanics, 70 % report using Spanglish, according to an analysis we did in 2009*".

Se ha escrito, y se puede leer todavía hoy, que el *spanglish* es fruto de la ignorancia, de los que no tienen cultura o recursos suficientes para aprender bien el inglés y, en algunos casos, incluso el mismo español. Cabe recordar, entonces, a los escritores chicanos o *nuyorican*, entre otros, que han experimentado con estos dos idiomas y culturas. Es en la literatura, en efecto, donde el *Spanglish* adquiere su sello de legitimidad, dando a esa estrategia verbal autoridad y verosimilitud, gracias a escritores chicanos, puertorriqueños, cubano-americanos y dominicanos, entre otros. La fuerza de estos autores reside en su literatura y su identidad se refugia en la lengua, una lengua algunas veces mestiza, híbrida, a veces rebelde, pero siempre expresión de una vida *in-between*, que les hace únicos (Betti, 2008a, 2009). Baste recordar tan solo un libro icónico como el de Giannina Braschi, *Yo-Yo Boing!* (1998), que se considera la primera novela escrita, en parte, también en *spanglish*.

Hay intelectuales que ven en el *spanglish* una renovada muestra del vigor del español, como elementos que pueden llevar no a una corrupción de este idioma, sino a su consolidación en los Estados Unidos. Por ejemplo, Armando Alonso Piñeiro (2001: web), se preguntaba durante el II Congreso Internacional de la Lengua Española de Valladolid:

> ¿Y si alteráramos la carga de la prueba y dijéramos que el *spanglish* es una renovada muestra del vigor de nuestra lengua, porque es capaz de contribuir a la formación de otras? [...] De allí que deberíamos aprovechar la fuerza centrífuga de algunos idiomas o dialectos, y en vez de rechazarlos, convertirlos en modelos centrípetos. Nos guste o no, el *spanglish* es, precisamente un dato de la realidad cotidiana en gran parte de los Estados Unidos. [...] Creo que el *spanglish* y el *chicano* son elementos conductores que finalmente pueden llevar a la consolidación del español en los Estados Unidos.

Y, además, precisaba (2001: web): "Lo mismo está ocurriendo en el sur de los Estados Unidos, con la aparición e intensa difusión del *chicano*, una lengua nacida en los mexicanos residentes en esa región norteamericana y en el norte del país azteca. En el territorio estadounidense, las regiones de mayor influencia son, naturalmente, Texas, Nuevo México y Arizona". También el conocido periodista Jorge Ramos Ávalos (2001) opina que antes las nuevas convergencias en las comunicaciones, los embates de la Internet y el *spanglish*, la lengua española no puede más que fortalecerse. Han sido los medios de comunicación como la radio, la televisión, la prensa escrita, la música, así como el cine y la literatura e Internet que han permitido al popular *spanglish* difundirse y, en cierto sentido, "uniformarse" y pasar de ser un fenómeno oral a una manera de expresarse también escrita.

Juan Flores (1999, *apud* Dagnino, s.p.) sobre el *spanglish* observaba:

> Vista desde afuera, esa mezcla parece fortuita, pero no lo es. Estudios sociolingüísticos encuentran que hay una gramática del *spanglish*, ciertas reglas que permiten el paso de un idioma al otro. Eso no ocurre al azar. Hay puntos en una oración donde hay un cambio de un código lingüístico a otro, y hay razones para eso. Hay que llegar donde está la gente, hablar con ellos y hacer el estudio con la grabadora. El *spanglish* es un fenómeno de Estados Unidos, [...]. No es que porque usted quiera poner una palabra en inglés en el medio, está hablando *spanglish*.

A propósito de una "gramática del *spanglish*", Enghels et al. (2020: 76) ponen de relieve: "[...] los datos empíricos confirman que, en este punto, la gramática del spanglish no es diferente a la de las otras lenguas: por un lado, persigue la economía en su sistema, y por tanto se caracteriza por reglas y recursividad; por otro lado, las reglas son más bien de índole prototípica en vez de impermeable (Betti y Enghels, 2018)" y agregan sobre una posible gramática:

> Además, los datos empíricos parecen sugerir que la morfosintaxis del spanglish no parece ser el resultado de una simple mezcla o combinación de dos sistemas separados: no es la gramática de la lengua matriz (el español) la que se impone y que deja al inglés un papel secundario consistente en rellenar algunos vacíos; la sintaxis no depende de manera unívoca de la lengua (o del léxico) ni del elemento lingüístico observado. Al contrario, se observa un sistema con regularidades –eso sí– que ante todo tienden a integrar la gramática de las dos lenguas en contacto (Enghels et al., 2020: 76–77).

El *spanglish,* por su peculiaridad, a pesar de ser criticado por muchos entre estudiosos, gente común e intelectuales, da voz a toda una parte de sociedad que expresa su identidad a través de estas dos lenguas y culturas. Bravo Raidi (1997) durante el I Congreso Internacional de la Lengua Española de Zacatecas, a propósito de esta práctica lingüística en la música *rap* y en el merengue *hip-hop*, aclaraba:

> Si revisamos los segmentos más populares, el *rap* y el merengue *hip-hop* son dueños de un *spanglish* con pronunciaciones y significados a veces herméticos. Pero en esas canciones de Proyecto Uno, El General o Zona 7 está contenida la realidad y el discurso social o amoroso de la gran mayoría de los habitantes pobres de las urbes. Negarles un espacio, y más aún, una penetración altísima, es estar de espaldas a lo que sucede entre la gente sencilla, la que ni siquiera tiene tiempo de pensar en el idioma como objeto de estudio.

El *spanglish* en este tipo de música encarna la realidad de muchas personas que se identifican con esta cultura mixta.

Los mismos periodistas intervinieron en el debate sobre el *spanglish*. El periodista Roberto Guareschi (2001), ex secretario general de redacción del diario *Clarín*, veía en el *spanglish* algo que se debía aceptar. Y durante el II Congreso Internacional de la Lengua Española de Valladolid, él mismo observaba (2001: web):

> El español está de moda, pero admitamos que está de moda por razones cuantitativas. Se expande en Internet pero con insuficientes contenidos de calidad, y a través de tecnologías que llevan la marca del inglés. Y se expande con millones de migrantes latinos -muchos de ellos pobres y subeducados- inmersos en el mundo del inglés. Darse cuenta de esto equivale a reconocer límites concretos. En esos territorios privilegiados no podrá crecer impoluto. El *spanglish* es uno de los precios que ha de pagar, y *tal vez no sea un precio sino un beneficio mutuo para el español y para el inglés*[7], si se modificaran las condiciones actuales. Por el contrario, habría un empobrecimiento del español si ese hibridaje se realizara entre un inglés sólido y un español enclenque. El problema es, sobre todo, una cuestión económica y política. [...] Quizá por eso hay quienes denigran al *spanglish*. Me parece que no es una actitud inteligente, aunque hoy sea apenas una jerga.

Efectivamente, es una forma de expresión que ha permitido y permite a estas comunidades expresarse a su manera, dar voz a dos mundos que conviven, una forma de identificarse también para algunos latinos cultos que hacen del *spanglish* un modelo cultural, además de una herramienta lingüística (piénsese, como se ha dicho, en los muchos escritores latinos que se sirven de esta estrategia en sus novelas y poemas). Mientras que los jóvenes latinos, y no solo ellos, han encontrado un medio para dar voz a su identidad *"en el medio"*, peculiar y compleja. Es una práctica comunicacional que podría resultar útil, como mencionamos, en algunos contextos, en particular en los informales. Como nos hace notar el profesor Eduardo Márceles Daconte (2008: web): "Sería ridículo y confuso para un inmigrante en Nueva York decir 'préstame una ficha metálica para abordar el tren subterráneo', para ganar tiempo en su lugar diría 'préstame un *tóken* para tomar el *subway*'". Así, es también un principio de *economía lingüística* que hace que numerosas personas utilicen esta modalidad expresiva.

Antonio Muñoz Molina, por ejemplo, en un artículo titulado "Una provincia del idioma" (1998: web) contaba el atractivo que tenía para él la mezcla de lenguas en la Gran Manzana, con personas que: "saltan del español

7 La cursiva es nuestra.

al inglés y del inglés al español con una agilidad deslumbrante, sembrando cada uno con palabras del otro, contagiándole su música con una desenvoltura y un descaro que resaltan la belleza de los dos idiomas". Cada modalidad es adecuada a las diferentes situaciones comunicativas, y en ellas se justifica. Naturalmente, no se puede considerar todo igual, hay modelos de prestigio que deben utilizarse en determinados contextos, si no se corre el riesgo de incentivar la pobreza expresiva. Pero al mismo tiempo ningún hablante se sirve de la lengua en contra de sus intereses (Moreno Fernández, 2006). El futuro de la lengua española y del inglés en los Estados Unidos dependerá, según él, de la escuela y de los medios de comunicación. Guareschi (2001: web), por su parte, opinaba:

> [...] sobre todo el *spanglish* va a progresar gracias a la creciente integración entre EE.UU. y México, es decir, por la política y la economía. [...], porque las condiciones son propicias. Hay intereses políticos y económicos que quieren verlos como una comunidad homogénea, aunque no lo sean. Desde fuera de su comunidad se les otorga valor y entidad social como hispanos y se los induce a reconocerse como tales. No tiene sentido subestimar al *spanglish*.

La utilidad del *spanglish* la comprobamos también en muchos anuncios de trabajo de los Estados Unidos, en los que se emplean términos en *spanglish* porque, de otra forma, sería más difícil comprenderse y podría ser más complicado trabajar, por ejemplo, en el sector de la construcción, por citar un solo caso de los muchos que existen. En la ciudad de Nueva York[8], en el sector que acabamos de mencionar, los latinos no utilizan la palabra *tejado* (o *techo*), sino *rufo* o *rufa* (modificación del inglés *roof*), ni *edificio*, sino *bildin* (modificación del inglés *building*), o usan el término *factoría* (modificación del inglés *factory*) y no *fábrica*. Y muchos puertorriqueños que viven en los Estados Unidos, por ejemplo, lavan el piso con un *mapo*, compran un *tique pa'l* cine, leen *panfletos*, *dan el OK* y *llaman pa'atrás* cuando están muy *busi pa'hablar* por teléfono, como recuerda Esmeralda Santiago (1994). Pero no se encuentran solamente nuevas creaciones, como las citadas, o calcos; se asiste también a una sintaxis "calcada" del inglés pero pronunciada en español. La frase *vacunar la carpeta* (de *to vacuum the carpet*, es decir *pasar la aspiradora a la alfombra*) es uno de los ejemplos más conocidos (y, al mismo tiempo, criticado porque se supone que, en realidad, tal expresión no se oye), así como las expresiones: *see you, brodel*[9] (de *brother*, hermano, en el sentido de amigo, colega), *cuesta una cuora*

8 En Nueva York existe una amplia comunidad puertorriqueña y latinos de otro origen.
9 Existen también las formas *broder*, o *bróder*.

(de *quarter*, moneda estadounidense de 25 centavos), *va a correr para presidente* (de *He's going to run for President*, va a lanzar su candidatura a la presidencia), *necesitamos una josa para rociar la yarda* (de *We need a hose to water the yard*, necesitamos una manguera para regar el césped), *forwardéame* este *email* (de *to forward an email*, enviar a un tercero un correo electrónico), o verbos como *baquiar* (de *to go back*, retroceder), *aplicar* (de *to apply for*, solicitar, presentar una solicitud) y muchos otros términos como: *muvi* (de *movie*, película), *guaifa* (de *wife*, mujer), *bisne* (de *business*, negocio), *díler* (de *dealer*, concesionario de carros, coches; el lugar y el vendedor), *Néibi* (de *Navy*, la marina, en especial la de guerra), etc. Se hace hincapié una vez más en la utilidad comunicacional que podría ofrecer el *spanglish*, dado que dondequiera que dos idiomas estén en contacto en comunidades bilingües, existe la posibilidad de que los hablantes se sirvan también de nuevas formas en la comunicación informal.

Se encuentra también un supuesto *ciberspanglish*, creado por Yolanda M. Rivas en 1996 y muy criticado, formado por centenares de términos que se utilizan en computación, con formaciones (que se crean por medio de afijos en español como *-ear*, *-iar*) como *chatear* (de *to chat*, charlar), *emiliar* (o *imailiar* o *emailiar*, enviar un correo electrónico), *linkear* (enlazar), *printear* o *printiar* (de *to print*, imprimir), *dragear* (de *to drag*, arrastrar), *deletear* (de *to delete*, cancelar, borrar), *efetepear* (hacer un FTP, de *FTP -File Transfer Protocol-* o protocolo de intercambio de archivos por modem), *downlondear* (de *to download*, "bajar" un archivo de la Internet), *surfear* (de *to surf*, navegar por el ciberespacio), *zapear* (de *to zap*, cancelar, modificar un programa, cambiar), *backupear* (de *backup copy*, hacer un archivo de respaldo), *browsear* (la acción de buscar, rastrear u hojear); con términos como *e-mail, email* (correo electrónico), *links* (enlaces), *maus* (ratón, elemento del ordenador), *exit* (de *to exit*, salir), *blog* (de *weblog*, bitácora), y con neologismos con afijos en *-dor* (*navegador, explorador, visualizador, direccionador*), en *-ero /-era* (*disquetera, listero, netero, bloguero*), etc. Esta forma de comunicación creció gracias también al uso de los ordenadores y de la Internet, y la gran mayoría de los cibernautas usaba y usa, en su discurso en español, muchos términos en inglés porque, a menudo, es más rápido y conciso que en español. Según Rivas (*apud* Trejo Delarbre, 1997), en este nuevo espacio, los diferentes grupos latinos, inconscientemente, han creado nuevos paradigmas para la perpetuación de su identidad en la época de la información. El llamado *cyberspanglish* no representa solamente un signo de la evolución de la lengua, sino también de su gente que se conecta a través de un medio como el ordenador.

Muchos autores han analizado este tema con diferentes enfoques; entre ellos, y sin querer ser exhaustivos, se encuentra a Ana Celia Zentella, en un trabajo ya clásico fechado en 1997 (y también 1998, 2016, entre muchos otros), Ed Morales (2002), Marta Fairclough (2003), Ilan Stavans (2000, 2003, entre muchos otros), John Lipski (2008, 2010, 2016, entre muchos otros), Alfredo Ardila (2005), Ricardo Otheguy (2009, 2013, entre muchos otros), Francisco Moreno Fernández (2009, 2013, 2014, 2015, entre otros), Ángel López García-Molins (en particular 2014, 2015a, 2015b y el último bosquejo sobre el tema de 2022), Humberto López Morales (2009), Domnita Dumitrescu (2010, 2015 y muchos otros), Silvia Betti (2008a y 2008b, 2013, 2015a, 2015b, 2016, entre otros), Maricel Mayor Marsán (2008), Antonio Torres (2004, 2015, 2016 y otros), etc.

Y hay que mencionar también una copiosa y, en muchos casos, interesante literatura escrita en estos dos idiomas, muy atenta a las diversidades y a los problemas culturales, una literatura fruto también de las reivindicaciones latinas. Efectivamente, en los años 60 y 70 del siglo XX y los movimientos políticos y culturales como, en el sur del país, el surgimiento de la *conciencia chicana* (entre inmigrantes de origen mexicano) y la gran promoción de poetas y dramaturgos *nuyorriqueños* en la ciudad de Nueva York, otorgaron una nueva posición al *spanglish*, considerado y despreciado, hasta aquel momento, por ser expresión callejera y marginal de gentes pobres. Estos movimientos lo convirtieron en símbolo de identidad de sus propuestas ideológicas y estéticas. El *spanglish* representaba, entonces y en muchos casos ahora, también una actitud de rebeldía ante lo anglosajón dominante, un lenguaje casi "secreto y mítico" (Prieto Osorno, 2004), que otorgaba y otorga identidad, orgullo y unidad como nuevo modelo cultural híbrido. Guillermo Gómez Peña ha afirmado en varias ocasiones que "El *spanglish* es nuestra única patria". La profesora Luz Mercedes Hincapié (2008)[10], a este propósito, escribía:

> Pues a mí el *Spanglish* me parece un fenómeno muy interesante. Puedo decir que entre mi familia es un lenguaje vivo. Mi madre llegó a USA de 40 años [...] a trabajar como obrera y nunca tuvo el tiempo para aprender inglés y ahora mis sobrinos y hasta sobrinos nietos nacidos allá, ya han perdido el español. Luego muchas veces el lenguaje que circula entre abuela / bisabuela y nietos / bisnietos es el *Spanglish*. Esto me parece bien, pues no soy una purista del lenguaje. Me parece que los lenguajes son cosas vivas que evolucionan, cambian, incorporan otros lenguajes, palabras de la nueva tecnología y del lenguaje de los jóvenes que inventan.

Así, a medida que la influencia social y el poder adquisitivo de los latinos aumentan, las clases profesional, política y económica intentan, también, captar

10 Comunicación personal enviada el 19 de febrero de 2008.

los votos latinos y recursos facilitando el acceso a los servicios y bienes privados y públicos en español. Esta estrategia ha revalorizado la cultura hispana y la identidad bilingüe de la nación (Rojas Marcos 2003).

López García-Molins (2015: 110) pone en evidencia que: "Las dos lenguas se mezclan, pero no de forma caótica", porque, según él, el *spanglish* responde sea a normas sistemáticas internas como a normas sociales externas. Ana Roca y José Gonzalo García de León (2013: 263-264) destacan, por ejemplo, como en los bancos de Miami las conversaciones entre los empleados y sus clientes se desarrollan en español y además "con un pizca de *spanglish* o cambio de códigos de un idioma a otro", usando ambos idiomas:

> [...] con todas sus variantes normativas o no, y entendiéndose los unos a los otros perfectamente cuando hablan de "balance" para referirse al "saldo de la cuenta," o cuando llega otro cliente y pide enviar un "transfer" por medio del "oficial del banco," que es el que puede aprobar la gestión, después que le hayan aprobado el "loan" para un nuevo "mortgage". Estos autores explican que muchas de esas personas, si bien conocen las palabras "hipoteca" y "saldo", prefieren utilizar las formas "locales" para comunicarse, y los que quizás no las conocen prefieren comunicarse según el contexto donde viven y trabajan. El cambio de código efectivamente, lejos de ser una práctica aislada, se usa frecuentemente en los medios de comunicación y en la vida diaria estadounidense.

Y Domnita Dumitrescu en en estudio de 2016 (60) escribía sobre el *spanglish*:

> [...] se trata de tres fenómenos diferentes, que no se deben confundir. En primer lugar, el Spanglish– con sus dos facetas, la "más prestigiosa" (el cambio de código) y también la "menos prestigiosa" (la que contiene muchos préstamos del inglés innecesarios)- es simplemente una manera típica de comunicarse entre sí de los bilingües (más o menos equilibrados), que, en interacciones verbales intracomunitarias, cambian de código (o sea de lengua, en este caso de español a inglés y viceversa) o acuden a préstamos del inglés, principalmente como una forma de expresar su identidad híbrida, resultado de su pertenencia a dos culturas y a dos códigos lingüísticos diferentes, con los que están en contacto permanente. El Spanglish no es, por lo tanto, ninguna lengua propia del país, ni mucho menos (como hemos visto que tratan de presentarla algunos), sino una variedad del español hablado en los Estados Unidos, al lado de otras variedades.

Según Ricardo Navas Ruiz (2004: 103) la denominación más apropiada quizá sea la de *lengua franca* por su mezcla entre los dos idiomas que puede facilitar la comprensión entre latinos y estadounidenses que conviven en el mismo territorio. Son significativas las palabras del escritor y artista Guillermo Gómez-Peña (*apud* Prieto Osorno, 2004: web) que reivindica: "Sólo el *spanglish* y su cultura híbrida me han otorgado la plena ciudadanía que ambos países me negaban".

Roxana Rodríguez Ortiz (2008: 107) considera el *spanglish* algo más que el resultado de la hibridación de dos culturas y lo ve como "un sistema institucionalizado de símbolos que requieren una traducción filosófica, estética y cultural". Rodríguez Ortiz explica: "[...] traducción que al cambiar un elemento cultural por otro, cambia al lenguaje mismo, eliminando aquellos elementos culturales que ya no son necesarios. Es decir, al cambiar el español por el inglés, pero al mantener ciertas palabras en español, se enriquecen dos lenguas y se crea una".

Carmen Silva-Corvalán (2000: web) explica que la situación sea social que lingüística de las comunidades latinas bilingües español-inglés es de una gran diversidad, de una complejidad que evidencia la complicada situación demográfica y social típica de estas comunidades. Debido a los movimientos migratorios desde zonas rurales a zonas urbanas, y a las continuas olas de migrantes (por razones políticas o económicas), asistimos a cambios demográficos que transforman la estructura familiar y que modifican el contacto con variedades funcionalmente completas del idioma español. En el aspecto lingüístico, aclara Silva-Corvalán (2000: web), se reproduce el típico *continuum* de competencia bilingüe y en el ámbito social se evidencia también una vasta gama de niveles socioeconómicos. Este abanico "se extiende desde el nivel más bajo de trabajador indocumentado hasta las esferas más altas, donde encontramos hispanos desempeñando quehaceres de importancia en círculos políticos, educativos, comerciales, industriales, artísticos, etcétera".

López García Molins y Morant Marco (2015: 153), por su lado, interpretan el valor del término *spanglish* con estas palabras "[...] el término *Spanish in the United States* carece del valor simbólico de la palabra *Spanglish* con la que se expresa una intermediación cultural inequívoca. Como fenómeno, el llamado *spanglish* es ciertamente español popular de los EE. UU. Pero como expresión de valores, apunta a algo más, apunta a una dimensión nacionalista" y añaden que "El *spanglish*, como valor simbólico, apunta a la nación, aunque sin llegar a alcanzarla porque es bien sabido que en última instancia responde a un deseo de los hispanos de integrarse en los EE. UU.".

Reflexiones finales

En el marco de los Estados Unidos el *spanglish* se declina en los varios niveles de lengua y también a nivel pragmático, y es importante, a este propósito, tener en cuenta la tendencia demográfica que ve los hispanos como la "minoría" étnica más numerosa, que va aumentando su poder adquisitivo y que tiene rasgos culturales y tradicionales específicos. No lo podemos considerar una lengua, ni un pídgin, tampoco un criollo: se trata de una modalidad comunicativa, más o menos intencional, que ya varios escritores han usado en sus novelas y poemas o cantantes en sus canciones, de la cual existen también hablantes que se declaran usuarios, aunque hay estudiosos que la tachan de peligrosa, dañina para el inglés y el español, o índice de ignorancia lingüística.

Los hispanos que viven en los Estados Unidos, que hablan español, se identifican con su parte latina, guardan un bagaje cultural que los conecta, y al mismo tiempo formando también parte de la comunidad anglosajona, cogen de esa cultura lo que necesitan.

Los contactos con otras culturas y formas de vida, la hibridación de lenguas, culturas, estilos de vida sirven para confrontarse con las diferencias, para poder comprenderlas, aceptarlas, vivirlas.

El mundo latino y el anglosajón son complejos y diferentes por visión de la vida, sensibilidad, culturas, forma de vivir y lenguas. Pero mantener las raíces, para muchos latinos, no implica cerrarse a la integración. La conservación del idioma y de las culturas latinas en los estados Unidos sirve también para un bilingüismo y un biculturalismo que, sin lugar a dudas, son enriquecedores, y el expresarse en momentos de ocio e informales en *spanglish* puede representar una estrategia ulterior a través de la cual numerosos latinos perciben su mundo y se expresan a su manera, pasando de un espacio a otro para formar una nueva identidad de *panlatino* (Zentella, 1995: 63), y al mismo tiempo una identidad que les transforme en "únicos", distintos de los *otros* americanos (Guibernau 2008). El *spanglish*, de hecho, no existe sin el español ni el inglés y nace de ese contacto. López García-Molins (2015) a este propósito nota que: "Los hablantes de *spanglish* tienen que hablar, mejor o peor, español e inglés para poder hablar *spanglish*. No existe un sistema lingüístico del *spanglish* independiente de los del español y del inglés: por eso se puede afirmar que el *spanglish* no es, tan solo se practica" (83–84).

De todos modos, creemos que es más que una hibridación lingüística, para algunos latinos es una especie de barrera protectora, de autodefensa contra un mundo ajeno, pero sobre todo es una señal de identidad y, por lo tanto, se trata de un fenómeno más complejo de lo que se cree.

El multilingüismo es una riqueza, una ventaja. Y el *spanglish* es una práctica se podría decir "simbólica", por todo lo que representa y que encierra en su denominación, que a menudo se utiliza como un registro y cuyo uso no significa necesariamente un desconocimiento del español y del inglés.

En un mundo globalizado hecho de hibridaciones e interferencias, el *spanglish* encaja como una forma de comunicación familiar, que no quiere representar ni el español *en* los Estados Unidos ni el español *de* los Estados Unidos, sino una práctica expresiva natural, reflejo de una sociedad y de las personas que viven en ella, y que da la posibilidad de comunicarse pasando simultáneamente de un código a otro, del inglés al español o viceversa, o de mezclar estas dos lenguas en los discursos dialógicos espontáneos, o incluso de crear nuevos términos. Los cambios que se reconocen en esa sociedad, responden también a los cambios sociales que ocurren a diario.

Referencias

Appel, R. y Muysken, P. 1996 [1987]: *Bilingüismo y contacto de lenguas.* Barcelona: Ariel.

Ardila, A. (2005): "Spanglish: An anglicized Spanish dialect". *Hispanic Journal of Behavioral Sciences*, 27 (1), 60–81.

Auer, P. (ed.) (1998): *Code-switching in conversation: Language, interaction and identity.* London: Routledge.

Betti, S. (2008a): *El spanglish. ¿Medio eficaz de comunicación?* Bologna: Pitagora.

———. (2008b): "Convivencia lingüística en los Estados Unidos. Utilidad y creatividad del *span- glish*". *Cuadernos del Lazarillo*, (35): 56–69.

———. (2009): "*Spanglish* en los Estados Unidos: Apuntes sobre lengua, cultura e identidad". *Confluenze. Rivista in Studi Iberoamericani.* Lingua e identità, 1 (2): 101–121.

———. (2009–2010): "La vida entre dos lenguas y culturas: reflexiones sobre el fenómeno del *spanglish*". *Boletín de la Academia Norteamericana de la Lengua Española* (BANLE), 12/13: 131–180.

———. (2010a): "Simbiosi di lingue, culture e sensibilità negli Stati Uniti: il fenomeno dello *Spanglish*". *Trickster, Rivista del Master in Studi Interculturali. Lingue future*, 8. Consulta: junio de 2010 en http://www.trickster.lettere.unipd.it/doku.php?id= lingue_future:betti_simbiosi.

———. (2010b): "Viaje a través del *spanglish*: ¿fenómeno útil y creativo?". *Suplemento especial de HispanicLA*, serie *Spanglish.* Consulta: 19 de abril de 2010 en http:// www.hispanicla.com/viaje-a-traves-del-spanglish-%C2%BFfenomeno-util-y-creativo-2-8536/silvia-betti.

———. (2011): "*See you, brodel*: Utilità e creatività dello *spanglish*". En G. De Rosa y A. De Laurentiis (eds.), *Atti dell'Incontro di Studi Interdisciplinare 'Lingua MaternaVs Lingua Matrigna Vs Lingua Letteraria: Tra Diglossia, Bilinguismo Sociale e Literacy'* (pp. 147–157). Lecce, Franco Angeli: Università del Salento, Facoltà di Lingue.

———. (2013): "La ilusión de una lengua: el *spanglish* entre realidad y utopía". En D. Dumitrescu y G. Piña-Rosales (eds.), *El español en Estados Unidos: E*

Pluribus Unum? Enfoques multidisciplinarios (pp. 189–216). Academia Norteamericana de la Lengua Española. New York: Ediciones ANLE (USA).

———. (2015a): "Español en/de los Estados Unidos: ¿español estadounidense o *spanglish*?". En S. Betti y D. Jorques (eds.), *Visiones europeas del spanglish* (pp. 12–25). Valencia: Uno y Cero Ediciones.

———. (2015b): "La definición del Spanglish en la última edición del *Diccionario de la Real Academia* (2014)". *Glosas* (Academia Norteamericana de la Lengua Española), 8 (8), 5–14.

———. (2016): "*Spanglish* imaginativo y sugerente. Entre práctica lingüística e identidad". En S. Betti y E. Serra Alegre (eds.), *Nuevas voces sobre el spanglish. Una investigación polifónica*, New York: Academia Norteamericana de la Lengua Española y Universidad de Valencia.

Betti S. y Enghels R. (2018): *Spanglish: Current issues, future perspectives and linguistic insights*. En I. Stavans (ed.), *Oxford handbook of Latino Studies*. New York: Oxford University Press.

Bhabha, H. (2002): *El lugar de la cultura*. Buenos Aires: Manantial.

Blas Arroyo, J. L. (2005): *Sociolingüística del español*. Madrid: Cátedra.

Braschi, G. (1998): *Yo-Yo Boing!*. Pittsburgh: Latin American Literary Review Press.

Chmiel, S. (1996): "El milagro de la eterna juventud". En M. Margulis (ed.), *La juventud es más que una palabra: Ensayos sobre cultura y juventud* (pp. 85–101). Buenos Aires: Biblos.

Criado, M. J. (2004): "Percepeciones y actitudes en torno la lengua española en Estados Unidos". *Migraciones Internacionales*, vol. 2, n.°004, Tijuana, México, Colegio de la Frontera Norte, 123–158.

Dagnino, M. (1999): "El spanglish no es universal". *El Universal*, 18 de noviembre.

DiSciullo, A., Muysken, P., y Singh, R. (1986): "Government and code-mixing". *Journal of Linguistics*, 22, 1–24.

Dumitrescu, D. (2015): "Spanglish, estadounidismos y bilingüismo vestigial: ¿Qué es qué?". En S. Betti y D. Jorques (eds.), *Visiones europeas del spanglish* (pp. 26–40). Valencia: Uno y Cero Ediciones.

———. (2016):"Español y rumano en contacto con inglés en los Estados Unidos, o *spanglish* versus *romglish*". En S. Betti y E. Serra Alegre (eds.), *Nuevas voces sobre el spanglish. Una investigación polifónica*. New York: Academia Norteamericana de la Lengua Española y Universidad de Valencia.

Enghels, R., Van Belleghem, L., y A. Vande Casteele (2020): "¿Existe una gramática del spanglish? Estudio de caso de la posición del adjetivo en *Killer*

Crónicas (2004)". En S. Betti y R. Enghels (Eds.), *El inglés y el español en contacto en los Estados Unidos. Reflexiones acerca de los retos, dilemas y complejidad de la situación sociolingüística estadounidense* (pp. 57–81). Roma: Aracne.

Fresneda, C. (2005): "Hablar español ha dejado de ser un estigma en Estados Unidos". *El Mundo: Cultura*, 8 de julio.

Fairclough, M. (2003): "El (denominado) Spanglish en Estados Unidos: Polémicas y realidades". *Revista Internacional de Lingüística Iberoamericana*, 1(2), 185–204.

García, O. (2013): "El papel de translenguar en la enseñanza del español en los Estados Unidos", Domnita Dumitrescu y Gerardo Piña-Rosales (eds.), *El español en los Estados Unidos: E pluribus unum? Enfoques multidisciplinarios* (pp. 353–373). New York: Academia Norteamericana de la Lengua Española.

Gómez-Peña, G., Chagoya, E., y Rice, F. (2000): *Codex Espanglienses: From Columbus to the Border Patrol.* San Francisco: City Lights Books.

Guibernau, M. (2008): "¿Qué significa 'ser americano'?". *La Vanguardia*, 8 de marzo.

Lipski, J. M. (1982): "Spanish-English language switching in speech and literature: Theories and models". *The Bilingual Review/La Revista Bilingüe*, 9 (3), pp. 191–212.

———. (2004a): "La lengua española en los Estados Unidos: avanza a la vez que retrocede". En http://www.personal.psu.edu/. (consulta 6/03/2020).

———. (2008): *Varieties of Spanish in the United States.* Washington, DC: Georgetown UP.

———. (2010): "¿Existe un dialecto estadounidense del español?". *La proyección internacional de la lengua española*, Congreso Internacional de Valparaíso (CILE). En en http://congresosdelalengua.es/valparaiso/ponencias/america_lengua_espanola/lipski_john_m.htm (consulta 10/09/2016).

———. (2013): "Hacia una dialectología del español estadounidense". En D. Dumitrescu y G. Piña- Rosales (eds.), *El español en Estados Unidos: E Pluribus Unum? Enfoques multidisciplinarios* (pp. 107–127). New York: Academia Norteamericana de la Lengua Española.

———. (2016): "El español en Estados Unidos: lo que es y lo que no es". *El español en el mundo. Unidad y diversidad*, Congreso Internacional de Puerto Rico (CILE). En en http://congresosdelalengua.es/puertorico/mesas/lipski-john.htm (consulta 10/09/2016).

Jenkins, D. L. (2013): "El suroeste creciente: un breve análisis sociodemográfico de la población hispanohablante de los Estados Unidos". En D. Dumitrescu y G. Piña-Rosales (eds.), *El español en Estados Unidos: E Pluribus Unum?*

Enfoques multidisciplinarios (pp. 31–45). New York: Academia Norteamericana de la Lengua Española.

Krogstad, J. M. y Lopez, M. H. (2015): "Hispanic population reaches record 55 million, but growth has cooled". *Pew Research*. 21 de junio. En en http://www.pewresearch.org/fact-tank/2015/06/25/u-s-hispanic-population-growth-surge-cools/ (consulta 30/07/2015).

Krogstad, J. M. y Ana G. B. (2015): "A majority of English-speaking hispanics in the U.S. are bilingual". *Pew Research*. 24 de marzo. En http://www.pewresearch.org/fact-tank/2015/03/24/a-majority-of-english-speaking-hispanics-in-the-u-s-are-bilingual/ (consulta 30/07/2015).

Krogstad, J. M., Stepler, R., y López, M. H. (2015): "English proficiency on the rise among Latinos". *Pew Research*. 12 de mayo. En https://www.pewresearch.org/hispanic/2015/05/12/english-proficiency-on-the-rise-among-latinos/ (consulta 24/01/2023).

López García-Molins, Á. (2014): *El español de Estados Unidos y el problema de la norma lingüística*. New York: Academia Norteamericana de la Lengua Española.

———. (2015a): *Teoría del Spanglish*. Valencia: Tirant Humanidades.

López García-Molins, Á. y R. Morant-Marco (2015): "El *spanglish* como fundamento del nacionalismo latino en EE.UU.". S. Betti y D. Jorques (eds.), *Visiones europeas del spanglish*. Valencia: Uno y Cero Ediciones, pp. 86–95.

López García-Molins, Á. (2022). "Reflexiones multidisciplinares sobre el espanglish". *Estudios del Observatorio Observatorio Studies*, 77: 1–98. En https://cervantesobservatorio.fas.harvard.edu/es/informe

López Morales, H. (2009) (coord.), *Enciclopedia del español en los Estados Unidos, Anuario del Instituto Cervantes 2008*. Madrid, Santillana.

Martínez, D., Mueller, A., & Hernández Nieto, R. (2016): *Mapa hispano de los Estados Unidos 2016 / Hispanic Map of the United States* (En español: 024-10/2016SP; in English: 024-10/2016EN). Octubre/October.

McClure, E. (1977): "Aspects of code-switching in the discourse of bilingual Mexican-American Children". *Georgetown University Round Table on Languages and Linguistics*, 93–115.

MacSwan, J. y K. T. McAlister (2010): Naturalistic and elicited data in grammatical studies of codeswitching. *Studies in Hispanic and Lusophone Linguistics*, 3: 521–532.

Medina López, J. (1996): *El anglicismo en el español actual*. Madrid: Arco Libros.

Medina López, J. (1997): *Lenguas en contacto*. Madrid: Arco Libros.

Morales, E. (2002): *Living in Spanglish. The search for Latino identity in America*. New York: St. Martin's Press.

Moreno-Fernández, F. (2006): "Sociolingüística del español en los EE.UU.". *E-Excellence*. En: http://www.liceus.com[http://www.liceus.com] (consulta el 15 de abril de 2008).

———. (2013): "Panorama interdisciplinario del español en los Estados Unidos". *Tribuna Norteamericana*. Instituto Franklin, 14, octubre, 1–6.

———. (2014): "El español en los Estados Unidos y el Instituto Cervantes en Harvard". *Anuario del Instituto Cervantes 2014*, 375–392.

———. (2015a): "La estandarización del español estadounidense". *Diálogo Atlántico*, Instituto Franklin (UAH), 17 de junio. En http://dialogoatlantico.com/2015/06/la-estandarizacion-del-espanol-estadounidense/ (consulta 20/06/2015).

———. (2015b): "Lexicografía del español estadounidense. Propuesta de diccionario de anglicismos". *Glosas* (Academia Norteamericana de la Lengua Española), 8 (8), 39–54. En http://www.anle.us/usr/docs/glosas_vol9_num1.pdf. (consulta 20.09.2015).

Moreno-Fernández, F. y Dumitrescu, D. (dirs.) (2016): *Bibliografía lingüística del español en los Estados Unidos / Linguistic bibliography of Spanish in the United States*. Cambridge: Instituto Cervantes at Harvard University - ANLE.

Munarriz A. y Parafita Couto, M. C. (2014): "¿Cómo estudiar el cambio de código? Incorporación de diferentes metodologías en el caso de varias comunidades bilingües", *Lapurdum. Basque Studies Review*, XVIII: 43–73.

Muñoz Molina, A. (1998): "Una provincia del idioma", *El País Semanal*, 8 de marzo, 122.

Myers-Scotton, C. (1993a): *Social motivations for code-switching: Evidence from Africa*. Oxford: Clarendon Press.

———. (1993b): *Duelling languages: Grammatical structure in code-switching*. Oxford: Clarendon.

Navas Ruiz, R. (2004): *Los signos del cuervo: entorno al 2003*. Salamanca: Editorial Ambos Mundos.

Ortega, J. (2001): "El español, una lengua diversa". *El País- Babelia*, 13 de octubre.

Ortega, J. (2002): "Desafíos para Hispanoamérica". *Identidades*, suplemento de *El Peruano*, n.° 22, 7 de octubre, 5–7.

Otheguy, R. (2009):"El llamado *espanglish*". En H. López Morales (Coord.), *Enciclopedia del español en los Estados Unidos, Anuario del Instituto Cervantes 2008* (pp. 222–243). Madrid: Santillana.

Otheguy, R. (2013):"Convergencia conceptual y la sobrestimación de la presenciade elementos estructurales ingleses en el español estadounidense". En D. Dumitrescu y G. Piña-Rosales (Eds.), *El español en Estados Unidos: E Pluribus Unum? Enfoques multidisciplinarios* (pp. 129–149). Academia Norteamericana de la Lengua Española. NewYork: Ediciones ANLE (USA).

Poplack, S. (1980): "Sometimes I'll start a sentence in Spanish y *termino en español*: Towards a typology of code-switching". *Linguistics*, 18 (7/8), 581–618.

———. (1982): "Bilingualism and the vernacular". En Valdman, A. y Hartford, B. (eds.), *Issues in International bilingual education: The role of the vernacular* (pp. 1–24). New York: Plenum Publishing Co.

Roca, A. y J. Á Gonzalo García de León (2013): "El español en Miami: expansión y desarrollo". En Domnita Dumitrescu y Gerardo Piña-Rosales (eds.), *El español en Estados Unidos: E Pluribus Unum? Enfoques multidisciplinarios* (pp. 251–267). New York: Academia Norteamericana de la Lengua Española.

Rodríguez, Ortiz, R. (2008): "Disidencia literaria en la frontera México-Estados Unidos". *Andamios. Revista de Investigación Social*, vol. 5, núm. 9, diciembre, 113-137.

Rojas Marcos, L. (2003): "Hispanos en EE.UU.: una convivencia en peligro". *El País*, 17 de febrero.

Santiago, E. (1994): *Cuando era puertorriqueña*. New York: Vintage Books.

Silva-Corvalán, C. (2000): "La situación del español en Estados Unidos". *Centro Virtual Cervantes*. En https://cvc.cervantes.es/lengua/anuario/anuario_00/silva/p01.htm (consulta 20/02/2021).

Stavans, I. (2000): *Spanglish para millones*. Madrid: Casa de América.

Stavans, I. (2003): *Spanglish: The making of a new American Language*. New York: Harper Collins.

Taylor, P., Lopez, M. H., Martínez, J., & Velasco, G. (2012): "Language Use among Latinos". *Pew Research Center*. 4 de abril. En: https://www.pewresearch.org/hispanic/2012/04/04/iv-language-use-among-latinos/

Toribio, A. J.: "*Nosotros somos dominicanos*: Language and self-definition among Dominicans". En A. Roca (ed.), *Research on Spanish in the United States: Linguistic issues and challenges*. Somerville, MA, USA: Cascadilla Press.

Torres Torres, A. (2004): "El Spanglish, un proceso especial de contacto de lenguas". 1*st International Conference on Spanglish*, Amherst (USA). En www.amherst.edu/~spanglish/Torres.htm (consulta 21.03.2014).

———. (2015): "Sobre el spanglish en los Estados Unidos: implicaciones de un caleidoscopio de perspectivas". En S. Betti y D. Jorques (Eds.), *Visiones europeas del spanglish* (pp. 96–109). Valencia: Uno y Cero Ediciones.

———. (2016): "El español estadounidense, entre el spanglish y el español internacional". En S. Betti y E. Serra Alegre (Eds.), *Nuevas voces sobre el spanglish. Una investigación polifónica.* New York: Academia Norteamericana de la Lengua Española y Universidad de Valencia.

Zentella, A. C.: "La hispanofobia del movimiento 'Inglés oficial' en los Estados Unidos por la oficialización del inglés". *Alteridades*, 5 (10), 55–65.

———. (1997): *Growing up bilingual: Puerto Rican children in New York.* Malden: Blackwell Publishers.

———. (1998): "Would you like your children to speak English and Spanish?" / "¿Quieren que sus hijos hablen el inglés y el español?". En vhttp://www.spanishdict.com/answers/170367/would-you-raise-your-children-to-speak-spanish-if-that-language-isnt-part-of-your-family-heritage (consulta 22/11/2011).

———. (2016): "Spanglish: Language Politics vs el habla del pueblo". En R.E. Guzzardo Tamargo et al. (Eds.), *Spanish-English codeswitching in the Caribbean and the U.S.* John Benjamins series Issues in Hispanic and Lusophone Linguistics, 12–35.

Fuentes de Internet Páginas, sitios

- *CyberSpanglish WebSite*: www.actlab.utexas.edu/~seagull/spanglish.html
- *Cuadernos Cervantes*: www.cuadernoscervantes.com
- *La Vanguardia*: www.lavanguardia.es
- La Página del Idioma Español: http://www.el-castellano.com
- Real Academia Española: www.rae.es

Estudios y artículos

Alonso Piñeiro, A. (2001): "Pobreza y riqueza del español en el tercer milenio". *Centro Virtual Cervantes. Congreso de Valladolid.* En: cvc.cervantes.es (consulta diciembre 2007).

Betti, S. (2005): "*Spanglish on-line*: Lengua y opinión en un foro de debate en Internet". *Cultura e Intercultura en la enseñanza del español como lengua extranjera*, Facultat de Filologia, Universitat de Barcelona. Nueva edición actualizada. En: http://www.ub.es/filhis/culturele (consulta marzo 2006).

Bravo Raidi, J. E. (1997): "La programación juvenil: ¿desfiguración del lenguaje?", *Centro Virtual Cervantes. Congreso de Zacatecas.* En: cvc.cervantes.es (consulta marzo 2006).

Criado, M. J. (2005): "La orografía de la lengua española en los EE.UU. Primera parte: la variable demográfica (DT)", nº. 46, Documentos, *Real Instituto Elcano*. En: http://www.realinstitutoelcano.org (consulta enero 2007).

Fresneda, C. (1999): "Livin' hablando spanglish". *La Revista de "El Mundo"*, n.º191. En: http://www.elmundo.es/larevista (consulta marzo 2006).

Gimeno Menéndez, F. (2001): "El desplazamiento lingüístico del español por el inglés en la prensa hispana de Estados Unidos". *Centro Virtual Cervantes. Congreso de Valladolid*. En: cvc.cervantes.es (consulta marzo 2007).

Guareschi, R. (2001): "El español: economía y cultura". *Centro Virtual Cervantes. Congreso de Valladolid*. En: cvc.cervantes.es (consulta marzo 2007).

Gutiérrez Rivas, C. (2006): "Perfil sociolingüístico de un bilingüe: Actitudes, uso y patrones lingüísticos". *LLJournal*, Vol. 1, n.º 1. En: http://ojs.gc.cuny.edu/index (consulta marzo 2007).

Lipski, J. M. (2004): "La lengua española en los Estados Unidos: avanza a la vez que retrocede". En: http://www.personal.psu.edu/ (consulta marzo 2007).

Lipski, J. M. (2004b): "Is "Spanglish" the third language of the South? Truth and fantasy about U. S. Spanish", *LAVIS-III*, University of Alabama, Tuscaloosa, inédito. En: http://www.personal.psu.edu/ (consulta marzo 2007).

López Morales, H. (2000): "El español en la Florida: Los cubanos de Miami", *Anuario 2000, Centro Virtual Cervantes*. En: cvc.cervantes.es (consulta enero 2002).

Márceles Daconte, E. (2008): "Spanglish: puente entre dos culturas". En: http://www.elpelao.com (consulta enero 2008)

Moreno Fernández, F. (2004): "El futuro de la lengua española en los EEUU", *ARI* n.º 69, *Real Instituto Elcano*. En: http://www.realinstitutoelcano.org (consulta web 2007).

Moreno Fernández, F. (2006): "Sociolingüística del español en los EE.UU.", *E-Excellence*. En: http:// www.liceus.com (consulta web abril 2008).

Ortega, J. (1999): "Introducción", *Foro sobre Memoria, Comunicación y Futuro, Proyecto Trans- Atlántico de Brown University*. En: http://www.brown.edu/Departments/Hispanic_Studies (consulta 19 de marzo 2008, actualmente no disponible).

Otheguy, R. (2001): "Simplificación y adaptación en el español de Nueva York", *Centro Virtual Cervantes. Congreso de Valladolid*. En: cvc.cervantes.es (consulta enero 2002).

Pastor, B. (2000): *Vid*. "Estados Unidos: El castellano a debate", *Unidad en la diversidad*. En: http://www.unidadenladiversidad.com (consulta marzo 2006).

Prieto Osorno, A. (2004): "Spanglish: una patria, una identidad", En: cvc.cervantes.es/elrinconete (consulta marzo 2007).

Ramos Ávalos, J. (2000): "El profesor de espanglish". En: http://www.jorgeramos.com (consulta marzo 2004).

Ramos Ávalos, J. (2001): "En defensa del español mal hablado. El periodista en la era de las convergencias", *Centro Virtual Cervantes. Congreso de Valladolid*. En: cvc.cervantes.es (consulta marzo 2007).

Scannavini, A. (1994): "Le frontiere della lingua. La commutazione di codice nella letteratura portoricana in inglese", *Ácoma*. En: www.esterni.unibg.it (consulta el 4 de marzo de 2004).

Silva-Corvalán, C. (2000): "La situación del español en Estados Unidos", *Anuario 2000, Centro Virtual Cervantes*. En: cvc.cervantes.es (consulta marzo 2004).

Stavans, I. (2004): "La imaginación restaurada", *Anuario 2004, Centro Virtual Cervantes*. En: cvc.cervantes.es (consulta febrero 2007).

Stavans, I. (2005): "¿Es el spanglish una lengua?". En: http://sapere_aude.blogspot.com (consulta enero 2008).

Torres, A. (2001): "Culturas latinas en Estados Unidos", *Cultura e Intercultura en la enseñanza del español como lengua extranjera*. En: <http://www.ub.es/filhis/culturele.html> (consulta marzo 2006).

Torres, A. (2004): "El Spanglish, un proceso especial de contacto de lenguas". En: http://www.amherst.edu (consulta el 15 de marzo de 2005).

Trejo Delarbre, R. (1997): "Lengua y periodismo en el kiosco electrónico (prensa digital)", *Ponencia para el tema "La Prensa", Primer Congreso Internacional de la Lengua Española Zacatecas, México*. En: www.monografias.com (consulta marzo 2008).

Isabel Álvarez

University of Wisconsin Oshkosh

El léxico del fútbol en la prensa estadounidense en español

Resumen: Es creencia bastante generalizada que el español hablado en los Estados Unidos está plagado de anglicismos y errores gramaticales debido a la influencia del inglés, la lengua dominante. Sin embargo, estudio tras estudio demuestra que esa no es la realidad. Para poder probar lo erróneo de esa creencia es necesario llevar a cabo estudios que muestren que el español de los EE. UU. no está, en realidad, tan influido por el inglés como pudiera pensarse. El presente estudio analiza la lengua usada en las crónicas del fútbol. Este campo es particularmente interesante debido al elevado número de anglicismos presentes en el léxico general del fútbol. A pesar de esto, los artículos analizados muestran una preferencia por el término en español, en algunas ocasiones con una frecuencia superior a la encontrada en países hispanohablantes.

Palabras clave: léxico futbolístico, anglicismos, corpus lingüísticos, español en los Estados Unidos.

1. Introducción

La población hispana en los Estados Unidos ha experimentado un crecimiento exponencial en las últimas décadas. Según los datos de Krogstad & Noe-Bustamante (2021), en 2020 había 62.1 millones de latinos, que constituyen el 19% del total de la población estadounidense. Esta mayor presencia de hispanos en los Estados Unidos ha traído consigo un aumento del uso del español en todas las esferas de la vida pública.

A pesar de que el español se usa a lo largo y ancho del país, cuando se menciona el asunto del español en los Estados Unidos, con frecuencia se traen a colación términos como el *spanglish* y es bastante generalizada la idea de que el español aquí hablado es una lengua mezclada o híbrida que está sufriendo un proceso de degeneración debido a la influencia del inglés. Las creencias populares quedan bien reflejadas en el artículo de Cabrera (2011) publicado en la revista *Siempre mujer*, donde se afirma que "el nivel del español que se escribe y se habla hoy en los Estados Unidos deja mucho que desear" y además se añade que "la ensalada del spanglish empobrece el lenguaje y hace que las personas terminen siendo incapaces de expresarse con coherencia y claridad en ambos idiomas". Es decir, al gran público frecuentemente se le transmite la imagen de que la comunidad hispanohablante en los Estados Unidos, debido a la influencia del inglés, no sólo habla un español empobrecido sino que también tiene problemas para expresarse en inglés.

Sin embargo, la realidad es muy distinta y estudio tras estudio ha demostrado que el nivel de transferencia es bajo y, en muchos casos, comparable al que se da en comunidades monolingües. Entre estos estudios destaca el de Mrak (2011), quien comparó el nivel de transferencia en la prensa en español en comunidades monolingües y bilingües y concluyó que el nivel de transferencia en el español de los Estados Unidos era bajo. En sus conclusiones, la citada Mrak anima a realizar futuras investigaciones que corroboren sus datos, ayuden a desterrar la idea de la degeneración del español de los Estados Unidos y pongan de manifiesto la legitimidad de esta variedad.

El presente estudio, que analiza el léxico de las crónicas futbolísticas escritas en español en los Estados Unidos, busca demostrar que el nivel de transferencia léxica es bajo, que el español aquí hablado es un español rico y cuidado y que está muy lejos de esa degeneración que se le presupone. En este sentido, el estudio también servirá para corroborar la preocupación por la lengua que se observa en las publicaciones en español y que ya habían puesto de manifiesto Gómez Font (2008) y sucesivos anuarios del Instituto Cervantes.

El léxico del fútbol en cualquier país hispanohablante ha estado muy influido por el inglés desde siempre. Bergh & Ohlander (2012) hacen referencia al doble impacto del inglés en el fútbol dada la propia historia del deporte así como el papel del inglés como lengua franca actualmente. En Estados Unidos, a este doble impacto hay que añadir el estatus del español como lengua minoritaria y la influencia que la lengua mayoritaria, el inglés, tiene. Es por esto que las crónicas futbolísticas ofrecen grandes posibilidades ya que nos permitirán ver si esa estrecha relación con el inglés puede abrir la puerta a una mayor presencia de anglicismos en el discurso futbolístico de los Estados Unidos. Para llevar a cabo la comparación del léxico de las crónicas estadounidenses con el de otras comunidades monolingües se utilizaron el Corpus de Referencia del Español Actual (CREA) y el Corpus del Español del Siglo XXI (CORPES).

El estudio pondrá de manifiesto que el nivel de anglicismos es comparable, cuando no inferior, al de las comunidades monolingües y que el léxico futbolístico es rico.

2. Antecedentes y situación actual del fútbol en los Estados Unidos

Antes de proceder con los detalles y los resultados del estudio, es necesario hacer un breve repaso a la historia de este deporte, de origen inglés, que primero llega a los países hispanohablantes y muy posteriormente a los Estados Unidos. Tal como pone de manifiesto Goldblatt (2006)[1] el fútbol llega a los países hispanohablantes de la mano de emigrantes británicos a finales del siglo XIX, en medio de una ola de anglofilia en la que tanto latinoamericanos como españoles abrazaron las costumbres inglesas. En los comienzos, el español carecía del léxico necesario para hablar del juego y un abundante número de anglicismos pasaron a ser parte de la lengua vernácula.

La historia del fútbol en los Estados Unidos ha sido, sin embargo, muy diferente. Como explica el mencionado Goldblatt (2006), el fútbol, tal como se conocía en Europa, fue excluido de las universidades y otros centros educativos. Aunque tuvo cierta popularidad en zonas industriales donde había comunidades de trabajadores británicos, las distintas propuestas de una liga profesional fallaron de forma bastante estrepitosa hasta la Major League Soccer (MLS), que arrancó en 1996.

A pesar de los comienzos inciertos del fútbol en los Estados Unidos actualmente el deporte goza de un buen estado de salud. Según los datos aportados por Johnson (2015), hay más de 24 millones de personas que practican este deporte y unos tres millones de jóvenes están oficialmente registrados en alguno de los programas de US Soccer Programs. La popularidad es tal que, entre los más jóvenes, el fútbol es hoy más popular que el béisbol, tal como apunta Neil (2016). Todo esto hace pensar que el fútbol ha llegado para quedarse.

En este aumento de la popularidad del fútbol, la comunidad hispana de los Estados Unidos ha jugado un papel clave. El mencionado Johnson (2015) indica que una cuarta parte, 25.5 %, de los que se identifican como hispanos o latinos reconocen que el fútbol profesional es su deporte favorito. La comunidad hispana se interesa tanto por las grandes ligas hispanohablantes – ligas de México, España, Argentina, etc. – así como por la MLS. Ante este interés, las compañías editoriales han hecho un esfuerzo por llegar a esa comunidad con publicaciones en español. Gómez Font (2008) ya indicaba que "las empresas en inglés contratan editores y periodistas en español para sus nuevos productos con la intención

1 Toda la información referente a la historia del fútbol usada en este estudio procede de Goldblatt (2006), quien estudia la evolución de este deporte alrededor del mundo.

de que las noticias se redacten en esa lengua y no se limiten a meras traducciones". Esto es exactamente lo que ocurre en el fútbol. Muchas de las publicaciones en español incluyen crónicas de AP u otras agencias de prensa para dar información sobre las ligas de fútbol extranjeras y contratan a periodistas para que escriban crónicas en español sobre los equipos de la MLS. Actualmente equipos como Los Angeles Galaxy, Chicago Fire, Colorado Rapids o New York City FC ofrecen crónicas y noticias en español. Además, hay emisoras de radio como la 1270AM en Dallas, que transmite los partidos del FC Dallas, y publicaciones y periódicos que incluyen crónicas de los equipos locales en español.

3. Metodología

El presente estudio analiza en profundidad las crónicas futbolísticas estadounidenses escritas en español con el objetivo de establecer el nivel de transferencia del inglés al español.

El objeto de estudio fueron sesenta y seis crónicas escritas en español de varias publicaciones digitales (*La Estrella Digital*, *Vívelo hoy*, *La Prensa de Houston*, *Hoy Los Ángeles* y *Univisión Deportes*) así como las páginas web de cinco equipos de la MLS (LA Galaxy, New York City FC, Chicago Fire, Colorado Rapids y Orlando City SC). Cabe destacar que no todos los equipos están representados con el mismo número de crónicas, pero esto no supuso un problema puesto que la localización geográfica o la variante lingüística no se tuvieron en consideración.

Cada una de las sesenta y seis crónicas fue analizada minuciosamente con el objetivo de identificar los anglicismos más frecuentes, así como las voces españolas que aparecen con más regularidad. El resultado de este análisis fue una larga lista de anglicismos así como de voces españolas. El estudio se centró en siete pares de anglicismos y su equivalente español. Se escogieron estos siete pares por dos razones: se trata de voces muy frecuentes tanto en los Estados Unidos como en el resto de los países hispanohablantes y la alta frecuencia tanto del anglicismo como de la voz española equivalente permite determinar fácilmente cuál de las dos voces es más común.

Una vez escogidas las voces objeto de estudio, se procedió a su análisis usando dos de los corpus electrónicos elaborados por la RAE: el Corpus de Referencia del Español Actual (CREA) y el Corpus del Español del siglo XXI (CORPES). Ambos corpus, disponibles a través de la página web de la RAE, permiten realizar búsquedas fijando distintos parámetros. En el caso del CREA, las búsquedas se limitaron al tema de los deportes en la prensa escrita en los EE.UU. En el caso del CORPES las búsquedas realizadas se hicieron bajo los siguientes parámetros: documentos escritos de no ficción tanto de internet como escritos con los temas de actualidad, ocio y vida cotidiana. El CORPES tiene la ventaja de que aporta frecuencias normalizadas o número de ocurrencias por millón de palabras, lo que permite determinar con facilidad si la frecuencia de una voz es superior en un país o en otro.

4. Estudio del léxico: Resultados

Como ya se mencionó, se estudiaron siete pares de anglicismos y su equivalente español para contrastar las frecuencias que ofrecen el CREA y el COPRES. Además de estos pares también se estudió la presencia de otros anglicismos así como calcos y extensiones semánticas.

El primero de los pares analizado es *liguilla* y *playoff(s)*. Según la RAE, uno de los significados de la palabra *liguilla* es "fase de competición en la cual un número reducido de equipos se disputa el pase a otra fase o categoría". El Diccionario Merriam Webster reconoce el mismo significado para el anglicismo *playoff*, que con frecuencia se usa en plural. Los ejemplos recogidos en 1 ilustran el uso que de estas dos voces se hace en algunas de las crónicas estudiadas, donde también se encontró *postemporada* para aludir a la fase que sigue la competición oficial.

(1) a. y de paso colocaron otro clavo en el ataúd de los Revs cuyas aspiraciones de ir a la liguilla penden de un hilo muy fino. (*Chicago Fire*, 16 Oct. 2016)
b. quedan matemáticamente sin posibilidades de ir a la liguilla. (*Chicago Fire*, 16 Sept. 2016)
c. Rapids clasifican a los Playoffs tras vencer a Portland 1–0 en casa. (*Colorado Rapids*, 2 Oct. 2016)
d. Pero de nada sirvió para evitar los partidos de eliminación directa de los playoffs. (*LA Galaxy*, 17 Oct. 2016)

Si bien es cierto que las dos voces aparecen en las crónicas analizadas, tanto los resultados del CREA como del CORPES ponen de manifiesto cierta predilección por la voz española. El CREA recoge siete casos de la voz *liguilla* frente a cinco del término *playoff*[2]. La popularidad de *liguilla* en los Estados Unidos queda también confirmada por los datos del CORPES. La frecuencia

2 Los cinco casos a los que aquí se alude se refieren todos al fútbol. El CREA recoge muchos más casos de esta misma voz, pero aparecen en crónicas de otros deportes como el baloncesto o el béisbol.

normalizada de esta voz, 8.16, que sólo es superada por México, cuya frecuencia normalizada es de 11,85, está muy por encima de las frecuencias de Chile, 4.06, o de la región del Río de la Plata, 2,47.

Uno de los casos más reveladores es tal vez el par *saque/tiro de esquina* y *córner*. El anglicismo es bastante popular en los países de habla hispana y en Argentina, por ejemplo, tiene una frecuencia normalizada de 4.42, en España de 3.39 y en Paraguay de 2.56. Sorprendentemente, el anglicismo *córner* es mucho menos frecuente en los Estados Unidos. El CREA no recoge ningún caso del anglicismo, mientras que el CORDE indica una frecuencia normalizada de 1.57, muy por debajo de las frecuencias indicadas anteriormente. Nuestro estudio corrobora esta tendencia. En las sesenta y seis crónicas analizadas, sólo se encontraron tres casos de la voz *córner*, que se recogen en 2.

(2) a. Andrea Pirlo jugó un córner a Ronald Matarrita. (*New York City FC*, 24 Sept. 2016)
b. Jugó en corto el córner. (*New York City FC*, 30 Sept. 2016)
c. Su disparo fue despejado a córner. (*Vívelo hoy*, 11 Mar. 2017)

En el caso de la alternancia *penal* y *penalti*, los resultados siguen la línea del caso anterior. Las crónicas estadounidenses, tal como ponen de manifiesto los ejemplos incluidos en 3, usan tanto el anglicismo *penalti* como otras voces españolas como *pena máxima*, *manchón* o *tiro penal*. Los datos aportados por el CREA y el CORPES muestran con rotundidad la mayor popularidad de la voz española. El CREA sólo recoge dos casos del anglicismo *penalti*, ambos en el año 1997, frente a veintidós ejemplos de la voz *penal*. Las frecuencias normalizadas del CORPES corroboran esta tendencia. El anglicismo tiene una frecuencia normalizada de 2.82 mientras que el equivalente español *penal* presenta una frecuencia de 10.99. Es decir, la voz española es casi cuatro veces más frecuente que el anglicismo.

(3) a. En una segunda jugada tras uno de los interminables servicios, tuvieron su premio en forma de un penalti. (*Colorado Rapids*, 17 Oct. 2016)
b. Pero en este, Tim Howard tuvo su revancha ante el nigeriano, atajándole la pena máxima. (*Colorado Rapids*, 17 Oct. 2016)
c. El mismo se encargó de convertir en gol el disparo desde el manchón penal. (*Colorado Rapids*, 14 Oct. 2016)
d. Pero dos minutos más tarde Xolos empató vía tiro penal. (*Univisión*, 13 Feb. 2017)

Otro par ilustrativo es el de *árbitro* frente a *réferi* o *referí*. El anglicismo en sus dos versiones, esdrújula o aguda, se utiliza en Latinoamérica para referirse a la persona que aplica el reglamento en algunas competiciones. El CREA refleja casos de *referí* en Argentina, Guatemala, Perú y Venezuela, mientras que *réferi* aparece en México, Argentina, Honduras y Venezuela. Las frecuencias normalizadas que indica el CORPES para estos países son bajas, pero no queda duda de que el anglicismo sigue vigente. En las crónicas estadounidenses, sin embargo, no se encontró ningún ejemplo del anglicismo, lo que encaja con los resultados del CORPES, que no recoge ningún caso. No deja de ser sorprendente que el anglicismo siga vigente en los países hispanohablantes y, sin embargo, no se use en los Estados Unidos. Otra de las personas encargadas de aplicar el reglamento es el juez de línea o linier. Este par se incluyó por presentar un aspecto único, ya que la voz *linier* no es un anglicismo en sí, sino lo que Campos Pardillos (2015) cataloga como derivativo autónomo, es decir, una voz que parece inglesa, pero que no existe en esa lengua. En este sentido estaría en la misma categoría que la voz *footing*. *Linier* es relativamente frecuente en el Río de la Plata, donde tiene una frecuencia de 3.30 así como en España y México. En las crónicas analizadas sólo se encontró un caso de *linier*, recogido en 4. La baja o casi nula frecuencia del falso anglicismo queda probada por los resultados del CORDE y el CREA, que no identifican ningún caso. Lo interesante de la presencia de la voz *linier* en los Estados Unidos es el hecho de que procede necesariamente del español puesto que la voz no existe en inglés.

(4) El gol fue protestado por el equipo de Utah debido a que el linier levantó el banderín marcando fuera de juego. (*Vívelo Hoy*, 11 Mar. 2017)

Otro par que presenta características especiales es el de *seguidor/hincha* frente a *fanático* pues en este caso no estamos ante un anglicismo patente sino ante una extensión semántica. Las extensiones semánticas son palabras que adoptan un significado que procede de una palabra similar en otra lengua. En inglés *fanatic* designa a una persona excesivamente entusiasta y dedicada a una actividad. En este sentido, el equivalente español de *fanatic* sería *hincha* o *aficionado*. La RAE no recoge *fanático* como sinónimo de *seguidor* o *hincha*, pero sí indica que *fanaticada* significa hinchada en Cuba, Ecuador, El Salvador, Honduras y República Dominicana, aunque no lo cataloga como anglicismo. Morales (2009), sin embargo, indica que *fanaticada* es un anglicismo. Siguiendo el criterio de Morales, aquí se ha catalogado *fanático* como anglicismo. En 5 se recogen los casos donde *fanático* se usó con el significado de *hincha* o *aficionado*. Una vez más, en los Estados Unidos el anglicismo presenta una frecuencia más baja que en otros países hispanohablantes: 8.16 frente a 19.22 en Panamá o 22.84 en República Dominicana. Cabe destacar que la frecuencia más alta de esta extensión semántica se observa en Puerto Rico (32.21).

(5) a. enfrente de 30.374 fanáticos en el Yankee Stadium. (*New York City FC*, 24 Oct. 2016)
b. 40.000 fanáticos descendieron sobre el estadio en el centro de Guayaquil. (*New York City FC*, 8 Feb. 2017)

El último de los pares analizados, *fútbol* frente a *balompié*, presenta un enfrentamiento tan antiguo como la práctica del deporte mismo y refleja una de las luchas más enconadas en lo que a los anglicismos del fútbol se refiere. En 1908, el periodista español Mariano de Cavia publicaba un artículo en el diario *El Imparcial* y allí proponía la voz *balompié* como alternativa ya que se trata de "un vocablo español de la más clara significación y de la más castiza estructura". Días más tarde, el dramaturgo Jacinto Benavente defendía el anglicismo *fúboll* porque "suena dulcemente y desentonaría menos en cualquier composición poética que el balompié ó el piebalón académicos". En este debate, el anglicismo resultó ganador y el balompié de Cavia nunca disfrutó de demasiada popularidad. Lo sorprendente es que al otro lado del Atlántico *balompié* siga vigente más de un siglo después. Que se usa en los Estados Unidos lo deja patente el ejemplo recogido en 6 y los datos que aportan el CREA y el CORPES. El primero registra tres casos en 1998, 2000 y 2004 mientras que el segundo indica una frecuencia normalizada de 2.19, algo inferior a la de México[3], 3.88, pero muy superior a la de España, 0.84.

(6) El exarquero de la selección mexicana Jorge Campos lanzó varias críticas a los representantes del balompié azteca. (*Hoy Los Ángeles*, 24 Ene. 2017)

Lo hasta aquí expuesto pone de manifiesto que en los casos de términos futbolísticos para los que hay un anglicismo y una voz española se usan los dos, pero las voces españolas parecen ser más populares. Sin embargo, estos datos no son suficientes para determinar de forma concluyente el nivel de influencia del inglés en el léxico. Bergh & Ohlander (2012) indican que el discurso del fútbol muy probablemente incluirá tanto voces específicas del fútbol como otros anglicismos de uso general. Es por esto que el presente estudio analizó también la presencia de otros anglicismos, calcos y extensiones semánticas. En las crónicas analizadas el anglicismo que más se repite es *líder* y sus derivados, tal como muestras los ejemplos en 7. Se trata de un anglicismo de uso común en todos los países hispanohablantes y, por tanto, no sorprende su uso en los

---

3 La popularidad de la voz *balompié* es considerable en países como Ecuador (9.66), Bolivia (5.84) y Costa Rica (6.99). Esta voz originaria de España ha logrado mayor popularidad en las Américas que en el país de origen.

Estados Unidos. Además de *líder*, también se encontraron otros anglicismos igualmente frecuentes en los países hispanohablantes. *Hat trick*, que el Diccionario Merriam Webster define como el hecho de que el mismo jugador marque tres tantos en un solo partido, es uno de los anglicismos futbolísticos más comunes y así lo reflejan los ejemplos recogidos en 8. Si bien es de uso bastante generalizado, la RAE todavía no lo recoge en su diccionario.

(7) a. Primer gol de Goossens lidera victoria del Fire sobre San Jose. (*Chicago Fire*, 3 Jul. 2016)
b. Colorado se pone a dos puntos del superliderato. (*Colorado Rapids*, 9 Oct. 2016)
c. Los tres puntos colocan a Colorado firme como sublíder. (*Colorado Rapids*, 9. Oct. 2016)
d. eran los encargados de liderar el ataque angelino. (*LA Galaxy*, 26 Oct. 2016)
e. Estados Unidos llegó a siete puntos de 12 posibles, tres menos que el líder Trinidad y Tobago. (*La Prensa de Houston*, 30 Mar. 2016)

(8) a. Giovinco tuvo su hat trick en el primer minuto de tiempo añadido. (*New York City FC*, 7 Nov. 2016)
b. Badji de hecho pudo haber terminado con un hat trick. (*Colorado Rapids*, 9 Oct. 2016)

Anglicismos como *indoor*, *noquear*, *cameo* y *slalom*, recogidos en 9, no son exclusivos del fútbol y también se observaron en las crónicas analizadas. La RAE ya incluye estas voces en su diccionario, lo que pone de manifiesto que su uso no es exclusivo de los Estados Unidos. Cabe destacar que los anglicismos recogidos de 7 a 9 son los únicos anglicismos de uso común que se encontraron en las sesenta y seis crónicas analizadas. Este es un dato muy importante ya que corrobora la tesis de que el nivel de anglicismos es menor de lo que comúnmente se piensa.

(9) a. en su instalación indoor de The Private Bank Fire Pitch. (*Vívelo hoy*, 22 ene. 2017)
b. cuando noqueó un centro de Lloyd Sam. (*New York City FC*, 17 Oct. 2016)
c. tuvo un impacto en su cameo de 30 minutos. (*New York City FC*, 8 Feb. 2017)
d. Poku hizo su slalom a un defensa. (*New York City FC,* 11 Dic. 2015)

La investigación, sin embargo, también reveló algunos anglicismos que no son de uso generalizado en los países hispanohablantes monolingües. En las crónicas analizadas, se encontraron cuatro anglicismos de este tipo, recogidos en 10. Tres de ellos, *script*, *sub* y *staff*, podrían catalogarse como anglicismos innecesarios puesto que el español tiene términos equivalentes: *guion*, *sustituto* y *personal* respectivamente. El cuarto de estos anglicismos, *draft*, designa el sistema en el que los derechos sobre nuevos jugadores se asignan o distribuyen entre los equipos profesionales. En este caso el anglicismo estaría justificado al no existir un término en español que designe de una manera precisa y económica este proceso. De cualquier forma, vuelve a quedar patente que el uso de anglicismos es bajo.

(10) a. gracias a una jugada fuera del script. (*Colorado Rapids*, 27 Ago. 2016)
b. Harrison fue el primer sub de Vieira. (*New York City FC*, 24 Sep. 2016)
c. El "staff", ellos realmente me han ayudado a llegar aquí. (*Hoy Los Ángeles*, 29 Ene. 2017)
d. Las ausencias de jugadores como [...] y algunos del draft son notorias. (*La Estrella*, 10 Feb. 2017)

La influencia del inglés puede pasar desapercibida en los calcos y las extensiones semánticas puesto que se trata de palabras españolas que sencillamente han adquirido un nuevo significado. Los calcos, según López Morales (2008) son "traducciones literales de una lengua a otra" y pone como ejemplos *rascacielos* o *salón de belleza*, que son traducciones de *skyscraper* y *beauty parlor* respectivamente. En las crónicas estudiadas se encontraron varios calcos, algunos de los cuales aparecen en 11. En 11a se puede ver que *llevar en mente* es una traducción literal de la frase verbal inglesa *to keep in mind*, cuyo equivalente español es *tener en cuenta* o *considerar*. Otro calco bastante frecuente es *agente libre*, 11b, una traducción literal de *free agent*, que designa a un jugador que tiene libertad para negociar contrato con cualquier equipo. Morales (2009) lo identifica como anglicismo adaptado de uso frecuente. Los otros dos calcos encontrados son *caja de 6 yardas* y *caja de 18 yardas*, 11 c-d, que son traducciones literales del inglés para designar el área pequeña o chica y el área grande.

(11) a. El FC Dallas llevó en mente la participación de cada uno de los viajeros. (*La Estrella*, 10 Feb. 2017)
b. después de que éste se convirtiera en agente libre al final de la temporada. (*La Estrella*, 24 Feb. 2017)
c. adentro de la caja de seis yardas. (*New York City FC*, 24 Sep. 2016)
d. desde el borde de la caja de 18 yardas. (*LA Galaxy*, 15 Nov. 2016)

Las extensiones semánticas, o desvíos semánticos según la terminología de Morales (2009), son palabras españolas que adquieren un nuevo significado por influencia de una palabra similar en inglés. *Fanático*, como ya se discutió anteriormente, es un claro ejemplo de extensión semántica. Las crónicas analizadas sólo incluyen otro caso de extensión semántica: *reportarse*. Según la RAE, el verbo español *reportar* no tiene el significado de "presentarse en un sitio como estaba establecido", significado que sí tiene el verbo inglés *to report*. Morales (2009) cataloga este uso como desvío semántico. En 12, el verbo *reportarse* se usa claramente con el significado inglés. La incidencia baja de calcos y extensiones semánticas refuerza los resultados del estudio de anglicismos patentes o crudos y vuelve a poner de manifiesto que la influencia del inglés es baja.

(12) hasta que el Galaxy se reporte para la pretemporada en enero. (*LA Galaxy*, 15 Nov. 2016)

Teniendo en cuenta el estrecho contacto entre el inglés y el español que afecta tanto a los periodistas y redactores como a los lectores, una salida fácil sería recurrir al anglicismo, pero ya se ha visto que este no es el caso. Es más, el estudio demostró que los periodistas hacen un esfuerzo claro por evitar el anglicismo, tal como ilustran los ejemplos incluidos en 13. El equipo de San José, California, se llama San Jose Earthquakes y en algunos casos, 13 a-b, su nombre aparece traducido y se habla de los Terremotos. Así mismo, en algunas crónicas se busca un nombre en español para la Major League Soccer (MLS) y no una traducción literal, tal como se puede ver en 13 c. Uno de los ejemplos más claros de ese interés por evitar el anglicismo es el uso de *punta* y sus derivados, 13 d-e, que se usan como alternativas al anglicismo *líder*.

(13) a. derrotó en casa a los Terremotos de San José. (*Hoy Los Ángeles*, 19 Mar. 2016)
b. ocurrió en 2004 cuando Kansas enfrentó a los terremotos de San José. (*New York City FC*, 2 Nov. 2016)
c. que milita en la Liga Profesional de Fútbol (MLS). (*La Prensa de Houston*, 20 Sept. 2016)
d. Los dos punteros empatan a uno en Colorado. (*Colorado Rapids*, 24 Jul. 2016)
e. en la pelea por la punta del Oeste. (*Colorado Rapids*, 21 Ago. 2016)

Más allá de la influencia del inglés, para determinar la calidad del español de las crónicas futbolísticas es necesario considerar otros aspectos como la riqueza del léxico. Todas las crónicas estudiadas reflejan una variedad y sofisticación en el léxico semejante, sino superior, a la que se observa en los países hispanohablantes. Los ejemplos encontrados que ponen de manifiesto la riqueza del léxico futbolístico son demasiados para poder incluirlos todos, pero basta fijarse en los sinónimos de *poste*, *portero* y *portería* para demostrar este aspecto. En el caso de *poste*, como se ve en 14, se usan también *travesaño*, *palo*, *barra* o *larguero*. El jugador encargado de guardar la portería es uno de los que más sinónimos presenta y así lo mismo nos encontramos *portero* que *arquero*, *guardameta* o *cancerbero*. Todos estos ejemplos se recogen en 15. El área que defiende el portero también presenta un buen número de posibilidades: desde *meta* o *arco* hasta *portería* o *red* (16). La riqueza léxica de las crónicas futbolísticas es similar a la que Chaston (2017) y Smead (2017) observaron en el léxico del béisbol. Esto demuestra que los redactores no se conforman con una voz española sino que buscan constantemente sinónimos y alternativas que den variedad y sofisticación al discurso.

(14) a. mandando el balón a la red cerca al poste izquierdo. (*New York City FC*, 16 Sep. 2016)
b. saldría apenas rosando [sic] el travesaño. (*Chicago Fire*, 23 Jul. 2016)
c. Villa disparó en el larguero. (*New York City FC*, 11 Dic. 2015)
d. su disparo desde el borde de la caja de 18 yardas fue a dar a la barra. (*New York City FC*, 31 Oct. 2016)
e. desviado por Antonio Nocerino al palo izquierdo. (*Colorado Rapids*, 21 Ago. 2016)

(15) a. fuera del portero de Chicago. (*New York City FC*, 24 Sep. 2016)
b. la estirada del arquero Monarca. (*Univisión*, 13 Feb. 2017)
c. sin que el guardameta pudiera evitar el gol. (*Chicago Fire*, 10 Jul. 2016)
d. para fortuna del cancerbero Jake Gleeson. (*Colorado Rapids*, 2 Oct. 2016)

(16) a. Los protagonistas buscaron con insistencia la portería rival. (*Chicago Fire*, 23 Jul. 2016)
b. Su cobro entró en la red. (*Chicago Fire*, 16 Jul. 2016)
c. el defensor galáctico Jelle Van Damme cabeceó en contra de su propio arco. (*Hoy Los Ángeles*, 25 Sep. 2016)
d. se adelantó al defensa y encajó el balón en la meta contraria. (*New York City* FC, 11 Dic. 2015)
e. se escapa solo hacia el marco del Real Salt Lake. (*Vívelo hoy*, 11 Mar. 2017)
f. dispara a puerta para batir con cierta fortuna. (*Vívelo hoy*, 11 Mar. 2017)

g. quien hizo su parte para mantener su vaya[4] invicta. (*Chicago Fire*, 21 Ago. 2016)

Un aspecto que también debe mencionarse es que el léxico de las crónicas futbolísticas presenta influencias del español de América. Esto no debería sorprender a nadie dada la proximidad de Estados Unidos a la América hispanohablante y la procedencia o ascendencia hispanoamericana de muchos de los periodistas que escriben estas crónicas. Algunos de los ejemplos del español de América encontrados son el nombre *gambeta* y sus derivados, recogidos en 17, que según la RAE en América significa *regate*. También se usa con bastante frecuencia el nombre *onceno*, tal como se refleja en 18, que en Chile, Ecuador, Guatemala, México, Perú y Uruguay designa a un equipo de once jugadores. *Catracho*, que aparece en un par de crónicas, 19, es una voz coloquial para referirse a alguien de Honduras.

(17) a. tras gambetear desde fuera del área y rematar un disparo. (*Orlando* City, 25 Abr. 2016)
b. mostró su habilidad gambetera en línea de fondo. (*LA Galaxy*, 30 Oct. 2016)

(18) a. El onceno galáctico perdía cuando entró Landon Donovan. (*Hoy Los Ángeles*, 25 Sep. 2016)
b. con lo que el onceno angelino derrotó a los de Utah. (*LA Galaxy*, 26 Oct. 2016)

(19) a. Los catrachos han demostrado un buen juego de conjunto. (*La Prensa de Houston*, 27 Sep. 2016)
b. Pero el catracho Víctor Bernárdez salvó el intento de manera dramática. (*Colorado Rapids*, 14 Oct. 2016)

5. Conclusión

El propósito del presente estudio era demostrar el nivel de influencia del inglés en las crónicas futbolísticas de los Estados Unidos con el objetivo último de demostrar que el español aquí hablado no es un lenguaje híbrido, sino un lenguaje rico y de calidad que se ajusta a la norma de la variante estándar. En el

4 En este ejemplo no está muy claro el uso de la voz *vaya*, pero creemos que se trata de una falta de ortografía y que la palabra que se quiere usar es *valla*, con el significado de límite defensivo que se debe sobrepasar.

léxico, quedó demostrado que el anglicismo no es la norma. Al contrario, las voces españolas suelen ser la norma y no la excepción. Además, su frecuencia es en muchas ocasiones superior a la de los países monolingües. También se demostró que el vocabulario es rico y que el discurso busca la variedad. Este estudio, como el de Mrak (2011) y otros antes, vuelve a demostrar que el español de los Estados Unidos es una variedad legítima y que no se trata de una lengua híbrida resultado de una mezcla con el inglés. Es nuestra esperanza que estudios como este contribuyan a que se acepte el español de los Estados Unidos como una variante de prestigio. No estamos, ni mucho menos, ante un proceso de degeneración de la lengua y todo indica que entre los periodistas se está haciendo un gran esfuerzo por mostrar el español como una lengua de prestigio. Es necesario desterrar de una vez por todas la idea de que los hispanohablantes de los Estados Unidos hablan algo que no es español.

Referencias

Benavente, J. (1908, 10 de agosto). De sobremesa. *El Imparcial.*

Bergh, G. & Ohlander, S. (2012): English direct loans in European football lexis. En C. Furiasi, V. Pulcini, & F. Rodríguez González (Eds.), *The anglicization of European lexis.* Amsterdam/Philadelphia: John Benjamins Publishing Company, 281–304.

Cabrera, R. (2011, Agosto–Septiembre). ABCD…¡Español! *Siempre Mujer*, 94–98.

Campos-Pardillos, M. A. (2015): All is not English that glitters: False Anglicisms in the Spanish language of sports, *Journal of the Spanish Association of Anglo-American Studies*, 37(2), 155–174.

Cavia, M. de. (1908, 1 de Agosto): El balompié, *El Imparcial*, 1.

Chastom, J. (2017, 7 de abril): *Hits o incogibles, innings o capítulos: Variety, Style, and Anglicisms in Baseball Terminology.* Presentación en la 26th Conference on Spanish in the US, Brigham Young University, Provo, UT.

Goldblatt, D. (2006): *The ball is round. A global history of soccer.* New York: Penguin.

Gómez Font, A. (2008): La prensa escrita. En H. López Morales (Coord.), *Enciclopedia del español en los Estados Unidos* (473–481). Madrid: Instituto Cervantes-Santillana.

Johnson, A. (2015, Mayo): *Soccer by the numbers: A look at the game in the US.* Extraído de la página web NBC News: www.nbcnews.com/storyline/fifa-corruption-scandal/soccer-numbers-look-game-u-s-n365601

Krogstad, J. M. & Noe-Bustamante, L. (2021). *Key facts about US Latinos for National Hispanic Heritage Month*. Extraído de la página web Pew Research Center: https://www.pewresearch.org/fact-tank/2021/09/09/key-facts-about-u-s-latinos-for-national-hispanic-heritage-month/

López Morales, H. Cubanos. En H. López Morales (Coord.), *Enciclopedia del español en los Estados Unidos* Madrid: Instituto Cervantes-Santillana, 311–356.

Merriam-Webster. (2018): *English Dictionary*: www.merriam-webster.com

Morales, A. (2009). *Diccionario de anglicismos actuales. Fotografía desde la Internet*. Castaño, PR: Academia Puertorriqueña de la Lengua.

Mrak, A. (2011): Lexical transfer from English to Spanish: How do bilingual and monolingual communities compare?, *Southwest Journal of Linguistics*, 30(1), 95–115.

Neil, S. P. (2016, 20 de abril): *Soccer is here, for real this time*. Extraído de la página web Huffington Post: www.huffingtonpost.com/shane-paul-neil/soccer-is-here-for-real-t_b_9730440.html

Real Academia Española. (2014). *Diccionario de la lengua española* (23ª ed.). www.rae.es/diccionario-de-la-lengua-espanola/la-23a-edicion-2014

Real Academia Española. (2017). *Corpus de referencia del español actual (CREA)*. http://corpus.rae.es/creanet.html

Real Academia Española. (2017). *Corpus del Español del Siglo XXI (CORPES)*.

Smead, R. (2017, 7 de abril): *Sobre los hits o batacazos en el vocabulario beisbolístico*. Presentación en la 26th Conference on Spanish in the US, Brigham Young University, Provo, UT.

Group II: Other lexical relations Spanish / English / French

John Humbley

Université Paris Cité

Peer-produced encyclopaedias disseminating loan neology: *Crowdsourcing* and *crowdfunding* in French and Spanish

Abstract: The aim of the study is to exemplify contrastively how commons-based peer produced/collaborative encyclopaedias dessiminate neology, both directly borrowed and adapted. The example chosen is a qualitative study of the treatment of the related concepts of *crowdsourcing* and *crowdfunding* in French and Spanish *Wikipedias*. A close study of the wording of the relevant entries shows differing tendencies on several levels. It will be argued that collaborative dictionaries and encyclopedias give a more comprehensive perception of language contact, reflecting as they do not only linguistic but also cultural and conceptual influence. In addition, as these new tools also allow users and contributors to express themselves, in particular in the "Talk" section, it is possible to gain insight into language awareness.

Keywords: lexicology, anglicisms, neology, French, Spanish.

The article contains the following sections. As an introduction, the role of *Wikipedia* as a source and field of study for neologisms is discussed, as is a programme initiated by the late Jean-François Sablayrolles (*Empnéo*, see Hildenbrand et al. (eds.) (2016)) comparing the incorporation of direct loans or calques in various European languages. The main section of the article is devoted to comparing the presentation of *crowdsourcing* and *crowdfunding* in French and Spanish *Wikipedia* with particular attention paid to:

- the history of the coining of both expressions in English and their equivalents in French and Spanish;
- initiatives to officialize certain expressions;
- differences in adapting in the French and Spanish-speaking worlds;
- the sources used to back up the entry – (bibliography): which languages are used?
- the names given to more specific concepts derived from *crowdsourcing/ crowdfunding;*
- the talk page containing metalinguistic considerations from contributors or users.

It will be shown that the collaborative encyclopaedias give a balanced view of the phenomenon but with varying orientations. French *Wikipédia*, as has been shown on previous occasions (Humbley, 2019), tends to adopt an assimilatory strategy, giving preference to native forms or calques, whereas the Spanish pages are more mixed. But examining the details reveals many cases of direct borrowing in French and adaptation in Spanish. All the articles bring out the relative nature of the novelty of a concept: practices of *crowdsourcing/crowdfunding* existed before the words were coined in 2006 and previous words used to designate them can be pressed back into service. Cultural and conceptual influence can be measured indirectly, for example by examining the proportion of documents in English on the one hand and French and Spanish on the other, as quoted in the reference section/bibliography of the article. This feature underlines the advantages of working with peer-produced encyclopaedias as linguistic innovation can be correlated with cultural influence.

1. Introduction

Félix Rodríguez González has had a remarkable career in several areas of applied linguistics, in the noblest sense of the term. He is the author of an incredible number of dictionaries, most of which have a neological or otherwise specialised dimension. He is also one of the foremost specialists in loanword studies on the international scene, in particular on Anglicisms in Spanish. For this particular hommage to his work, the choice has been made to try to combine these features by focusing on the role that dictionaries and encyclopaedias can play in disseminating either direct loanwords or adaptations in the native tongue. The nature of dictionaries and encyclopaedias has however changed radically over the last twenty years, an additional justification for broaching the subject. Twenty years ago *Wikipedia* was launched, to become the world's by-default encyclopaedia. Contrary to traditional dictionaries and encyclopaedias, *Wikipedia* is a participative or collaborative enterprise, with no Mr Webster or M. Robert to decide on what goes in or how it is presented. It may be felt that metalexicography has taken its time to examine how these participative reference works are produced and received, though a considerable body of research has been constituted, presented for French and Italian in the comprehensive study by Eiber (2020). The role of participative dictionaries and encyclopaedias[1] in language contact study is a new field just opening up.

1 Though there is a difference that can tendentially be made between dictionaries, which focus on language, and encyclopaedias, which deal with the world as language reflects it, the two overlap considerably and will not be considered separately in this article.

This research has quite logically encompassed other less known participative resources apart from *Wikipedia*. It has notably examined how new or specific lexical items are reflected. In French-speaking metalexicography, for example, attention has been paid to how French outside France is represented in these dictionaries (c.f. Molinari & Vincent eds. 2019). Other work has been done on neologisms – and on loans in particular – and how they are represented. Sajous et al (2022) even claim that these participative dictionaries are not just vectors but also major producers of neology.

The question posed in this study concerns how imported neologisms are reflected lexicographically. It is well known that emerging concepts can be rendered in another language by a direct loan or by a translated expression, often referred to as a calque. It has been suggested, by comparing traditional French and German dictionaries (Humbley, 2011), that translations are favoured in the first and direct loans in the second. Is this also the case in participative dictionaries, where there is no one to mastermind this sort of policy?

The survey takes it that, in principle, *Wikipedia* entries are written independently. In other words, a French or Spanish language *Wikipedia* article is written by anonymous contributors without copying what has been written in other languages. If the content has indeed been translated, this is indicated explicitly. The bottom-up approach of this type of project could be expected to reflect social attitudes in the language community concerned.

The languages of the study are Spanish and French, both communities that have language authorities which tend to favour translated neologisms rather than direct loans. It is moreover intended to extend this survey to other languages, namely Italian and German on one hand and to Polish and Czech on the other. The second pair of languages has been the focus of an international research group formed around the late Jean-François Sablayrolles to investigate why these languages use – for example *whistleblower* – whereas French has been generally content to talk about *lanceur d'alerte*. The research methods used in this project (see Cartier et al., 2020) can therefore be brought to bear on the current project.

The neologisms chosen for this study are *crowdsourcing* and *crowdfunding*. Both are well documented, the date and circumstances of their coining, in English, being readily accessible though not uncontroversial. They are also representative of several trends in society, in particular peer production and the sharing economy; they have been widely adopted and have spawned many similar initiatives, which may also be expressed by direct loans or by translated expressions. Like all innovations, however, they are not completely new, and the novelty may be seen as simply a minor variation of a well-known phenomenon. In other words, the originality of the neologism can be called into question.

Finally, *crowdsourcing* was chosen as a starting point since *Wikipedia* itself is precisely a stereotypical example of this very concept. In addition, the present author is currently engaged in a study of the reception of *crowd-* compounds in French, Czeck and Polish (Sablaryolles et al., 2023), and some of the preliminary work can shed light on the current issues.

2. The coining of *crowdsourcing, crowdfinancing*

Many neologisms come into being by various speakers using a particular turn of phrase which eventually goes mainstream but some are well documented events, in particular when they concern an innovation, especially a technical one. Our two terms, *crowdsourcing* and *crowdfunding,* are closely related as they are both good examples of the concept of affordance set in the early Internet era. The possibilities opened up by the web were just being explored, in particular ways of mobilising large numbers of people to take part in certain projects. The emergence of *crowdsourcing*, both the word and the phenomenon, is dealt with in some detail by mainstream English-language dictionary Merriam-Webster:

> The term "crowdsourcing" was coined in 2005 by Jeff Howe and Mark Robinson, editors at Wired, to describe how businesses were using the Internet to "outsource work to the crowd", which quickly led to the *portmanteau* "crowdsourcing". However, first published a definition for the term crowdsourcing in a companion blog post to his June 2006 *Wired* article, "The Rise of Crowdsourcing", which came out in print just days later.
> *Crowdsourcing* and *crowdfunding* are two words that have recently found their way into the crowded pool of English. *Crowdsourcing,* which typically refers to the practice of soliciting services, ideas, or content from a large group of people online, was coined by Jeff Howe in a 2006 article in Wired, and *crowdfunding* was created by entrepreneur Michael Sullivan in that same year. Both words conceptualize "the crowd" as a vast online community from which something needed may be obtained. In crowdsourcing, the crowd is called upon for needed assistance or information. A well-known use of crowdsourcing is Wikipedia, whose content is the result of various contributors. Crowdfunding, on the other hand, involves a more specific request: the crowd is solicited for financial contributions to a particular venture or cause, such as a film project or cancer research.
> https://www.merriam-webster.com/dictionary/crowdfunding Merriam-Webster

From the neological point of view it is noteworthy that the model on which the word and the concept of *crowdsourcing* is based is mentioned quite explicitly both in the dictionary and in the founding publication, i.e. *outsourcing.* The motivation of the neologism is thus to distinguish this new practice, tapping in to the resources of the Internet, to do the job better than by subcontracting out (i.e. *outsourcing*). This is how it was put in what is claimed to be the original article by Jeff Howe, the online journalist who is credited with coining the expression:

> The rise of crowdsourcing
> Remember outsourcing? Sending jobs to India or China is so 2003. The new pool of cheap labor: everyday people using their spare cycles to create content, solve problems, even do corporate R&D.
> Hobbyists, part-timers, and dabblers suddenly have a market for their efforts, as smart companies in industries as disparate as pharmaceuticals and television discover ways to tap the latent talent of the crowd. The labor isn't always free, but it costs a lot less than paying traditional employees. It's not outsourcing; it's crowdsourcing. https://www.wired.com/2006/06/crowds/

Similarly, *crowdfunding* was created to stress the financial dimension of this shared work. The IT expert Michael Sullivan, credited as the coiner of the term, stated in an interview:

> During early development of fundavlog, I wanted a better term to use to describe what fundavlog was for. I came up with Crowdfunding and registered crowdfunding.com … I decided that 'Crowdfunding' was the obvious choice especially since 'Crowd' and 'Crowdsourcing' were recently becoming common goto terms.

Sullivan was the author of the *Wikipedia* page: " […] the Crowdfunding Wikipedia article that I created at that time", an example of personal promotion discouraged by *Wikipedia* principles.

In fact, closer examination reveals that the situation is more complicated than it would seem at first blush. Firstly, other contenders for the coining of the neologisms have been suggested. Secondly and more importantly, it has been suggested that these two innovations are less revolutionary than one may think and are in fact simply modern examples of practices that have existed over long periods of time. There is nothing new about this, it is well known that the concept of neologism is a relative one, which depends on both the speaker (or writer) and the listener in a particular setting.

3. Adapting to French and Spanish : What the dictionaries say

In France, the official website FranceTerme has recommended *financement participatif* for *crowdfunding* since 18.05.2013 and *production participative* for *crowdsourcing* since 05.03.2014. As far as paper dictionaries are concerned, it is significant that the best-selling French dictionary, *Le Petit Robert* in its 2019 edition, has no entry for either *crowdsourcing* or *crowdfunding*. In Spain, there is no entry for either term in the Real Academia Dictionary, though as we shall see, government initiative has given official recognition of one form.

Wikipedia[2], all languages included, on the other hand, has many substantial articles on the two concepts: 45 articles on *crowdsourcing* (i.e. entries on the subject in 45 different languages) and 50 on *crowdfunding*. The articles in the languages examined here are generally long. Table 1 presents the number of words per article per language, showing a tendency for English to go into more detail than the other languages, in particular for *crowdsourcing*, by quoting many examples.

Table 1: Number of words per *Wikipedia* article and related talk page (28.03.2021).

	Crowdsourcing: **article**	*Crowdsourcing:* **talk**	*Crowdfunding:* **article**	*Crowdfunding:* **talk**
English	14422 words	1147	9015	3878
French	3263	1118	8210	1357
Spanish	4230	247	2494	665
Italian	4522	694	2165	490
German	2624	1944	1996	4355

4. Metalexicographical analysis

4.1 Entry structure

The structure of the entry is comparable for the three languages for *crowdsourcing* with the number of subsections in brackets. This shows that the main difference between the English-language article and the two others is that the number of examples in the latter, past and present, is much higher.

2 The relevant *Wikipedia* articles were all downloaded on 28 March 2021 and all references in this article refer to the version available on this date.

Table 2: Structure of article *crowdsourcing* per language.

English	French	Spanish
• Definitions	– Origin of the term	– The problem of the definition
• Historical examples (14)	– History	– History
• Modern methods	– Ethical issues, limits and controversies	– General description
• Examples (17)	– Crowdsourcing and the economy (2)	– Users (2)
• Crowdsourcers (4)	– Context, challenges	– The first examples
• Limitations and controversies (5)	– Difficulties in communitary production	– Recent examples
• See also	– Close neologisms	– Advantages of crowdsourcing
• References	– See also (2)	– Applications
• External links	– External links	– Controversies
		– Marketing
		– Historical examples
		– References
		– See also
		– External links

It will be noted that only the French article devotes a separate section to distinguishing between closely related synonyms, including borrowed and supposedly equivalent native forms.

4.2 Choice of term and definition

In both French entries, the headword is an adapted form: *Production participative* and *Financement participatif*. If the query is made in the French *Wikipédia* dialogue box for either *crowdsourcing* or *crowdfunding*, the user is automatically redirected to the adapted forms (with the mention *Redirigé depuis crowdsourcing)*, or the Spanish entries, the headwords are *Crowdsourcing* and *Micromecenazgo* respectively. In the second case, a request for *crowdfunding* entered into the Spanish *Wikipedia* dialogue box leads directly to *Micromecenazgo* but there is no explicit mention of the redirection, as there is for French.

From this presentation it would seem safe for the user to assume that *production participative* and *financement participative* are the normal, unmarked forms used in French and that in Spanish the loanword is regularly used for *crowdsourcing* and a loan creation or semantic loan for *crowdfunding*. Reading the content of the relevant entries however shows a rather different situation.

As shown in Table 3 below, the definition usually comprises the term itself and various synonyms. For *crowdsourcing* the French entry presents the headword first, followed by a synonym (no mention is given of how it is used) and the direct loan as a third (and presumably less common) form. In Spanish however the direct loan is given. *Crowdfunding* is similar for French, as two adapted forms are given, one of which is marked as Canadian. Only later in the history of the word is the English-language neologism mentioned and even then in relation to…*crowdfunding*! In Spanish the headword is a loan creation or semantic loan but no less than eight possible translations are indicated. Mention is also made in the Spanish article of an official related term, *plataformas de financiación participativa,* official it should be pointed out, in that it is the name of a legal device intended to allow crowdfunding. It thus has a different status to the French, which is given by the language authority, though this is not mentioned in the corresponding *Wikipédia* article.

Table 3: Naming the concepts.

	French	Spanish
crowdsourcing	La **production participative**, l'**externalisation ouverte** ou le ***crowdsourcing***, est l'utilisation du *travail*, de la *créativité*, de l'*intelligence* et du *savoir-faire* d'un grand nombre de personnes, en *sous-traitance*, pour réaliser certaines tâches traditionnellement effectuées par un *employé* ou un *entrepreneur*.	**Crowdsourcing** (del inglés *crowd* –multitud– y *outsourcing* –recursos externos–) se podría traducir al español como ***colaboración abierta distribuida*** o ***externalización abierta de tareas***, y consiste en externalizar tareas que, tradicionalmente, realizaban empleados o contratistas, dejándolas a cargo de un grupo numeroso de personas o de una comunidad, a través de una convocatoria abierta.
crowdfunding	Le **financement participatif**, ou **sociofinancement** au *Canada*, est un outil de collecte de fonds fonctionnant sur une plateforme internet et permettant à un ensemble de contributeurs de choisir collectivement de financer directement et de manière traçable des projets identifiés […] Il s'est diversifié avec l'apparition d'*Internet*, dès le milieu des années 1990. Le terme anglais *crowdfunding* est issu du néologisme *crowdsourcing* inventé et popularisé par Howe dans le magazine *Wired* en 2006[6]	El término proviene del inglés ***crowdfunding***, que se traduce al español como *financiación de masas*. El micromecenazgo también recibe los siguientes nombres: **micromecenaje**[23], **financiación masiva**, **financiación en masa** o **por suscripción**, **cuestación popular**[4], **financiación colectiva**[5] y **microfinanciación colectiva**.[6] El micromecenazgo en España recibe formal y legalmente el nombre de **plataformas de financiación participativa**, regulado por el Título V de la Ley 5/2015, de 27 de abril, de fomento de la financiación empresarial

4.3 Effective name use

The two French entries under discussion and the Spanish for *crowdfunding* lead the reader to believe that the direct loan is not the normal form of the relevant word. A wordcount of the entries concerned, however, show that this is not indeed the case and that there is a significant distinction between the two concepts.

Table 4: Occurrences in entries (excluding bibliography, external links), more than 1.

	French	Spanish
Crowdsourcing	Production participative : 3 Externalisation ouverte : 2 Crowdsourcing : 33	Crowdsourcing 71
Crowdfunding	Financement participatif :95 Sociofinancement :6 Crowdfunding : 7	Micromecenaje 5 Crowdfunding 7

A wordcount of the four different entries shows a significant difference between *crowdsourcing* and *crowdfunding*. It is the (slightly) more recent term that has been most effectively adapted. This is most striking in French, where *crowdfunding* is in fact used in the course of the entry but far less than *financement participatif*, which scores near to one hundred occurrences. The Spanish article offers a different picture, but one that shows direct loan and loan creation almost equal. The real difference is with *crowdsourcing*, where no other expression is used more than once in the Spanish article. This also corresponds to the French entry, where, in spite of a pro-active use of headwords, the direct borrowing dominates the texts.

4.4 Talk… and metatalk

The talk and history sections of *Wikipedia* articles are the most innovative parts of the encyclopaedia since they insure two-way communication between users and contributors (not distinguished) over issues of content and presentation. In this chapter only the metalinguistic comments will be noted.

These are particularly prominent in French. In *financement participatif* (*crowdfunding*) a discussion took place in 2014 between five Wikipedists on the semantic scope of *crowdfunding*, which at the time was given as *production communautaire*. The possibly diverging semantic extension of *finance participative*, *financement participatif* and *production communautaire* is discussed, as is the relationship in English between *crowdfunding* and *collective finance*.

For *production participative* (*crowdsourcing*) the discussion is more varied, the bulk being devoted to the definition. There are two proposals for a different French equivalent: *démopégie* (2009) and *collaborat* (2013), neither of which are followed up. Another contributor in 2019 suggested a distinction between active and passive crowdsourcing (using the English *crowdsourcing*), whereas yet another in 2020 suggested to amalgamate *production participative* and *production communautaire*.

A similar discussion took place in Spanish in 2011 to present *financiación en masa* or *crowdfunding* as a subcategory of *crowdsourcing*.

These discussions can lead to the change of headword for both French and Spanish. In 2013 the Spanish term *Micromecenazgo* was suggested to replace the Anglicism.

4.5 Cultural aspects

So far attention has been paid to the linguistic forms of expression, as made manifest in the two *Wikipedias*. We now propose to take a step towards determining not just the linguistic influence of English but also the cultural. It has been argued that English is increasingly exerting an influence over other languages which is not only linguistic – this has been documented for many years, but also from a cultural and a conceptive level. This latter aspect has been examined by Joaquin García Palacios and his colleagues in terms of terminological dependency (García Palacios & Humbley (2012), Sánchez Ibáñez, García Palacios (2014)). More and more in the sciences, the terminology used in languages such as French or Spanish is derived from English. It is the English terminology which represents the reference and terminologies in other languages are simply derivatives of this. Thus, when clarification is needed, reference is made systematically to English terminology. Similarly, in countries where English is changing status from a foreign language to a second language attention is being paid to the cultural impact. Gottlieb (2020) considers that most neology in Danish now comes directly or indirectly from English.

From one point of view, *Wikipedia* could be held up as an example of cultural autonomy, since individual entries are made in principal without reference to other – especially English-language sources. But is this really case? Reading our *Wikipedia* entries – starting from the most adapted one, *financement participatif*, the first examples given are the funding of the construction of the Statue of Liberty (admittedly made by a French engineer), then business angels in America, a French botanical network, the English rock group Marillon and so on. French sources are indeed quoted but then so are many English-language documents too.

In order to gain an impression of what proportion of the sources are English-language, a count was made of the languages in which the sources quoted in the Reference/bibliography section were written (Table 5).

Table 5: Language of references quoted.

	French	Spanish
Crowdsourcing	References in French 17 References in English 13	References in Spanish 0 References in English 30 But links to blogs and similar resources in Spanish.
Crowdfunding	References in French around 100 References in English less than 20	References in Spanish 14 References in English 06

It will be noted that the proportions vary enormously. No Spanish-language source is given for *crowdsourcing* whereas almost 100 are given in French for *financement participatif.* Compared with the degree of English-language influence on the terms themselves, there is only a limited amount of overlap between use of adapted terms and reliance on native-language sources. This very much proves to be the case for crowdfunding (*financement participatif*) in French where native-language sources are overwhelmingly used. Similarly in Spanish, more native sources are used. For the less adapted *crowdsourcing*, there are no references in Spanish, though there are links to blogs and other similar resources in that language. For French, native-language documentation predominates, but not by much.

4.6 Further term coinages

Another way to measure the degree of English influence on coining new specialised terms is to compare the new words derived or compounded on the original neologism. In other words, when French or Spanish-speaking people want to further refine new categories of crowdsourcing or crowdfunding, do they simply use forms already used in English, do they coin new forms based on English or do they take the adapted form and create a new word based on this ? To find out, a count was made of derived or compound forms in the four articles (Table 6).

Table 6: Naming derived concepts.

	French	Spanish
Crowd-sourcing	Crowdinnovation *Crowdsourcé* *crowdworkers* « *perverted crowdsourcing* » ou « travail spéculatif » Pronétariat	crowdsourced testing *Crowdfunding* (financiación colectiva) *Crowdcreation* (creación colectiva) *Crowdvoting* (votación colectiva) *Crowd wisdom* (sabiduría colectiva) *Crowdlearning* (aprendizaje colectivo) Collaboratition Collaborapetitive Crowdshipping Crowdspeaking Crowdranking Crowdlearning proyecto "crowdsourced"
Crowd-funding	financement participatif par titres (*equity crowdfunding* en *anglais*) Financement participatif en échange de redevances Mécénat participatif *Financement participatif de la transition énergétique* *Financement participatif pour la croissance verte* système de financement participatif avec rétribution financement participatif de documents patrimoniaux financement participatif immobilier plateformes de financement participatif site de financement participatif	Micromecenazgo empresarial. Micromecenazgo solidario Micromecenazgo musical Micromecenazgo personal **Micromecenazgo especializado** - Micromecenazgos basados en donaciones/recompensas/acciones/préstamos/*royalties*

Once again, a clear distinction is made in both Spanish and French between *crowdsourcing*, the derivatives of which are overwhelmingly expressed in English, and *crowdfunding*, where both languages derived concepts are systematically named in French or in Spanish respectively. In the Spanish-language *crowdsourcing* entry the typology suggested by J. Howe is quoted in English with equivalents suggested in Spanish, which could become terms in their own right. In both French and Spanish there are also occasional desinential derivations made from *crowdsource*: (*journalisme*) *crowdsourcé* and *projectos crowdsourced*

5. Discussion

The results of the analysis of *Wikipedia* entries in French and Spanish for closely related neologisms are encouraging for fine-grained appraisal of English influence. It emerges that the two concepts studied are integrated into both French and Spanish in very different ways: *crowdfunding* is generally rendered by a calque, whereas for *crowdsourcing*, the original concept, is overwhelmingly expressed as a direct loan. How can this discrepancy be explained? Part of the reason may be the greater prominence that *crowdfunding* has in society since it implies money, whereas *crowdsourcing* on the contrary implies none. In the study comparing French, Czech and Polish (Sablayrolles et al. 2023) the press corpora showed many more occurrences of *crowdfunding*, which appeared significantly sooner than its in fact earlier counterpart. Another factor may be the relative nature of both the phenomenon and the words that designate it. In all three *Wikipedia* articles (English, French and Spanish) the phenomenon of *crowdfunding* is presented as a practice going back in time. The linguistic formulation of both *financement participatif* and *micromecenaje* is not particularly innovative either – both certainly appeared when the necessity arose and were only institutionalized when the phenomenon took hold with the rise in use of the Internet. In addition, when new concepts are added to the paradigm, it is French or Spanish that is resorted to for the first and English for the second. Analysing the languages of the sources quoted confirms the difference: there is a direct relationship between the dominant language of the entries and that of the sources on which it is based.

Using *Wikipedia* thus presents some advantages in evaluating neology and language contact in a broad perspective. It has it over a primary corpus in that it is the result of collective work carried out in a communicative context, i.e. placing the emphasis on the extralinguistic rather than being language orientated and could well be used for analysis of specialised English-influenced neology.

Further work is scheduled to compare *Wikipedia* pages at various stages of development to see how language changes over the years, in particular substitution of direct loans.

6. Conclusion

Collaborative encyclopaedias – *Wikipedia* in particular – provide opportunities for research into language contact which go beyond the usual methods of detecting English-language influence by examining corpora – generally large, often newspaper based. This primary corpus method is still perfectly relevant, but *Wikipedia* allows for focusing on more specialised areas, i.e. where neology, including borrowing, very often starts and provides the material for the linguist to follow the evolution of the borrowed term. As these encyclopaedias are being constantly updated, they also give insight into how the borrowed forms develop. Moreover, as opposed to other resources, participative encyclopaedias with their "talk" facility, give some idea of the reception of new (and in this case borrowed) terms. Contrary to our expectations, the users (and/or contributors) did not comment on borrowings or forms of borrowings as such, but were much more concerned with defining the semantic scope of the new concepts – a linguistic feature indeed, though not the one which was expected. Investigating the lexicographical evidence it is possible to measure cultural influence by examining the language of the sources – the more sources are quoted in the national language, the less English influence may be attested.

Bibliographic references

Cartier, Emmanuel, Kacprzak, Alicja, & Mudrochova, Radka (eds.). (2021): *AUC Philologica – Romanistica Pragensia*. Prague.

Crowdfunding.de (2015): Crowdfunding-Wortschöpfer Michael Sullivan im Interview https://www.crowdfunding.de/magazin/crowdfunding-wortschoepfer-michael-sullivan-im-interview/

Eiber, Bettina (2020): *Wikipedia und der Wandel der Enzyklopädiesprache: Ein französisch-italienisch Vergleich*. Tübingen: Narr Francke Attempto.

García Palacios, Joaquín & Humbley John (2012): En torno a la dependencia terminológica. *Hermeneus,* 14: 133–165.

Hildenbrand, Zuzana, Kacprzak, Alicja, Sablayrolles, & Jean-François (eds.) (2016): *Emprunts néologiques et équivalents autochtones en français, en polonais et en tchèque*. Limoges: Lambert Lucas.

Humbley, John (2011): Le traitement des anglicismes dans un dictionnaire français et allemand. in Steuckardt, Agnès, O. Leclercq, A. Niklas-Salminen, & M. Thorel (dir.), *Les dictionnaires et l'emprunt (16è-21è siècle)*. Publications de l'Université de Provence, pp. 219–233.

Humbley, John (2019): Vedettariat militant des dictionnaires collaboratifs? in Molinari, Chiara & Nadine Vincent (eds.), *Dictionnaire et culture numérique dans l'espace francophone Éla. Études de linguistique appliquée* 2019/2 (N°194), pp. 165–176. https://www.cairn.info/revue-la-2019-2-page-165.htm

Molinari, Chiara & Nadine Vincent (eds.) (2019): *Dictionnaire et culture numérique dans l'espace francophone Éla. Études de linguistique appliquée* 2019/2 (N°194).

Sablayrolles, Jean-François, Bobińska, Anna, Podhorná-Polická, Alena, & Humbley, John (2023): Paradigmes et créations analogiques : composés en *crowd-* empruntés ou allogéniques. 113-135.

Sánchez Ibáñez, Miguel & García Palacios, Joaquín (2014): Semantic characterization of terms as a trace of terminological dependency. *Terminology*, 20 (2): 171–197.

Sajous, Franck & Jocelyn-Leray, Amélie (2022): Issues in collaborative and crowdsourced lexicography. in *Bloomsbury Handbook of Lexicography.* 343-358.

Alicia Roffé Gómez

Universidad de Granada

Créativité lexicale et anglicisme dans l'argot de la drogue français

Abstract: This article is focused on French drug slang. English slang has flooded the present language. The main aim of this article is to analyse the anglicisms that are collected by dictionaries and Internet vocabularies. After examining the motivations of borrowings, their etymology, the article studies the lexical creativity of drug "argot" by means of anglicisms and their phonetics, graphics, morphosyntactic and semantic adaptation to this language.

KEY WORDS: slang, drugs, dictionaries, lexical creativity, anglicisms.

L'argot des toxicomanes c'est le parler de groupe qui adopte le plus d'emprunts au slang anglo-américain mais aussi à l'anglais pour remplir une fonction crypto-ludique, conniventielle et identitaire, ainsi que pour accroître l'économie linguistique, l'expressivité et l'esthétique de ce langage. Les usagers de drogue parlent la langue française tout en utilisant un registre argotique identitaire, qui les relie aux membres du même groupe, c'est aussi un sociolecte qui était au début volontairement ou accidentellement cryptique, et en même temps ludique, humoristique. "Les termes du jargon utilisés pour les drogues peuvent aller d'humour à des avertissements intelligents ou graves" (SN, SD, "Un glossaire...", en ligne), ils révèlent l'angoisse et la peur parfois.

Il faut voir également dans l'argot, comme dans tout langage informel, une recherche de l'expressivité, et ceci nous semble très important, car elle s'efface suite à l'usage fréquent de ce langage:

> En ce qui concerne l'emploi du terme «argot», l'argotologie actuelle comprend le lexique argotique dans un sens large, c'est-à-dire comme un stock lexical utilisé / créé par un réseau de communication cohérent et chargé d'expressivité. Dans cette acception moderne du terme argot, qui est sinon très polysémique, ce type de lexique remplit notamment les fonctions conniventielle et identitaire (Podhorná-Polická, 2007: 379-385). L'argotologie pourrait donc être rapprochée de la socio-lexicologie. Malgré de nombreuses remarques sur les effets expressifs ou affectifs dans les travaux des argotologues ou des sociolinguistes, l'expressivité ne semble pas avoir gagné une autonomie définitoire. (Podhorná-Polická, 2010: 214).

Les membres d'une comunauté partagent la même vision du monde et ils ont parfois besoin de rendre leur message obscur. Comme le dira Napieralski (2007: 228): "Certaines occupations des jeunes surtout celles qui ont un caractère illicite comme: le vol ou le braquage, la revente ou la consommation de drogue possèdent des champs lexicaux très variés et adaptés pour constituer un code connu seulement par les personnes concernées. C'est une nécessité pour eux, car cela leur permet de ne pas être compris par les représentants de la justice." Les expressions dont ils se servent devenant à la mode moyennant la culture de masses, la littérature, la bande dessinée, le cinéma, la musique, ou bien par le biais des réseaux sociaux, elles vont alors avoir besoin de se renouveler; du fait de la dynamique changeante du monde de la drogue aussi.

Un argot est un sociolecte spécifique à un groupe social ou socio-professionnel. Il faut le distinguer du jargon, qui est propre aux membres d'une profession ou d'une activité. L'utilisation du lexique argotique est aussi une façon de contourner les tabous concernant la drogue. L'existence de dictionnaires d'argot annule l'opacité des mots, ce qui incite à renouveler son lexique. Haramburu et al. (1998: 102) diront: "La plupart des termes sont anglais, rarement français (il ne faut pas oublier que la plupart de l'argot des toxicomanes, y compris en France, est dérivé de l'américain, voire de l'hispano-américain, du Sud-Ouest des États-Unis)."

L'argot des toxicomanes c'est le langage qui présente le plus d'emprunts anglo-américains. Rodríguez González (2022: 301) ajoute que:

> "Conviene recordar que buena parte del narcotráfico tiene lugar en el área norteamericana, y, aunque la droga consumida en Norteamérica es mayormente de procedencia hispanoamericana, lo que produce cierta ósmosis entre el inglés y el español, es el inglés el que se erige en una especie de lingua franca para "correos" y narcotraficantes".

Le langage de la drogue se concentre, en France comme ailleurs, autour de plusieurs aires sémantiques: les dénominations des divers stupéfiants, leur apparence, leur origine, leurs effets, la consommation des produits narcotiques, les substances qui les composent, leur couleur, la dose et les types de toxicomanes et de toxicomanies, enfin le trafic et les trafiquants de stupéfiants et leur emballage, la forme de l'emballage, la prise de la drogue, les effets de celle-ci et l'achat de drogue. Les principaux usagers et créateurs de ce parler sont les jeunes des cités, mais pas uniquement, les dealers sont de différents milieux socioculturels qui vont de certains vieillards aux trafiquanst de drogue jeunes en passant par des gens qui arrondissent leur fin du mois. Cependant, "plus des trois quarts des consommateurs de drogue en France ont entre 16 et 25 ans, un âge où on est encore dépendant de ses parents" (Cahoreau et Tyson, 2006, *Introduction*). "Les emprunts dans le langage des jeunes proviennent principalement de l'anglais. Cela s'explique par le fait que la culture jeune des pays anglophones, surtout des États-Unis, a servi d'exemple pour les jeunes Européens depuis la fin de la Deuxième Guerre Mondiale. (…) Il s'agit à la fois d'emprunts pour des objets auparavant inconnus et d'emprunts qui permettent d'économiser linguistiquement" (Bedijs, 2015: 305).

Haramburu et al. ajouteront (1998: 102):

> L'origine des termes est très variée. Certains datent des années 60-70 et ont été popularisés par des chansons: par exemple girl (cocaïne) (…); la liste est longue et il faudrait citer également les contributions d'Elvis Presley, Bob Dylan, etc. Dans la plupart des cas, l'origine est beaucoup plus obscure: mots adoptés dans certains quartiers d'une ville ou certaines régions, parfois abrégés, transformés à l'exportation, etc., ce qui traduit bien l'évolution permanente du langage oral.

Le corpus utilisé est issu de l'ouvrage argotographique français le plus important publié par des chercheurs français sur l'argot, Colin, Mével et Leclère (2019), du riche dictionnaire de la drogue de Rodríguez González (2014), du célèbre dictionnaire de *slang* américain de la drogue de Richard A. Spears (1986), du dictionnaire de *slang* de Thorne (2014), ainsi que de nombreux dictionnaires et lexiques français et anglais en ligne cités dans notre webographie.

Analyse du vocabulaire de la drogue.

Nous focaliserons notre travail sur les anglicismes, étant donné que ce sont les emprunts les plus nombreux à une langue étrangère. Le vocabulaire de la drogue est en évolution constante, et comme Mátételki Holló (2013: 108) l'explique, parmi d'autres linguistes, hormis ces emprunts, les nouveaux mots peuvent provenir de la langue commune, des langages professionnels, de vieux mots, ainsi que de mots déjà existants. "Après l'invasion de l'anglais dans le vocabulaire de la musique, du sport, de la technique etc. au début du XXe siècle (Fidelius 2009, [en ligne]), les anglicismes se sont de plus en plus propagés dans d'autres secteurs de l'activité humaine", comme l'exprime Mudrochová (2017: 50).

I. Niveau paradigmatique.

1. Variantes de registres.

A. Les noms des drogues:

les séries synonymiques sont très importantes, les unes en français standard, d'autres en argot des toxicomanes. "Cette diversification permet aux jeunes de se repérer dans leur communauté et bien sûr la fonction cryptique y est décisive" (Napieralski, 2007: 230):

> Français standard: marijuana, haschisch, amphétamine, LSD, ecstasy, héroïne
> Argot de la drogue: *chocolat, dope, foin, grass, herbe, marie-jeanne, noir(e), speed, acide, XTC, brown sugar (Colin et al., 2019)*

"La multitude des associations imagées de ce langage s'explique avant tout par l'effet hallucinogène visuel des stupéfiants rattaché toujours à des situations particulières." Ce sont en partie des calques de l'anglais, des traductions, comme l'explique Rodríguez González (1994a: 185). Pour cette linguiste, "les locuteurs ne créent pas, en général, de métaphores (…), mais utilisent de préférence une forme de la métonymie, la synecdoque, figure qui met directement en relation le produit indispensable consommé et la matière (poudre, herbe, sucre, shit/merde, coca, etc.) dont il est constitué (acide) ou sa couleur (blanche, neige, etc.), la forme de l'emballage et le mode de conditionnement dans lesquels il est livré (paquet)." Elle ajoutera:

> Ce n'est qu'à propos des modes de consommation et des effets qu'on peut constater des créations métaphoriques en particulier utilisant les formes verbales, empruntées de l'anglo-américain. On a déjà mentionné pour d'autres raisons la série de transpositions métaphoriques désignant l'évolution physique et psychique du toxicomane; comme p. ex: se fixer, flasher, avoir un flash, flipper, planer, faire un trip, avoir le ticket, se défoncer, être stone, se speeder, se destroyer, être dans le cosmos, sevrer, etc.

a) de couleur ou de resemblance formelle:

barrette, morceau de 5 grammes de cannabis provenant d'une savonnette de 250g de résine (Rodríguez González, 1994a: 192), (Carcel, SD, en ligne);
black, du slang anglais *black,* marijuana brune (Johnson *et al.*, 2005); variété puissante de marijuana provenant d'Afrique (Spears, 1986);
black acid/tabs, du slang anglais *black acid/tabs*, cristal; LSD (Spears, 1986);
blanc (le), *reine blanche, dame blanche,* du slang angl. *white lady,* cocaïne;
chocolat, du slang anglais *chocolate* (*Thai*), haschish (Spears, 1986);
foin, cannabis sativa, marijuana de qualité médiocre, qui correspond au slang *weed,* et surtout à *ragweed* (Spears, 2000: 334) qui possède les mêmes acceptions;
grass, du slang angl. fam. *id.*, marijuana (Spears, 1986);
gazon, cannabis, calque du slang anglais *grass, id.*;
herbe, cannabis, du slang anglais *erb, herb,* marijuana (Spears, 2000: 201); verlan (par inversion des syllabes) *beu*(*h*);

ice, du slang angl. *id.*, cocaïne, par allusion à la transparence (Spears, 1986);
neige, du slang angl. *snow*, cocaïne;
marron, du slang anglais, *brown,* héroïne, syn. *brune;*
noir/e, du slang anglais *black,* LSD (Spears,1986: 46);
sugar (*yellow, black, brown…*), *sucre,* du slang anglais de la drogue *sugar,* héroïne de basse qualité;
thé, du slang de la drogue *tea,* thé préparé à partir du cannabis ou du pavot (Mátételki Holló, 2013); cannabis; marijuana (Spears, 2000: 417).

b) de matière:

huile, du slang angl. *oil,* distillat huileux du hasch qui est habituellement plus puissant que le haschisch (Carcel, SD, en ligne); (Thorne, 2014); (Colin *et al.*, 2019), (Spears, 1986);
poudre (*à canon*), drogue blanche, cocaïne (slang angl. *powder*) (SN, SD, "The online slang dictionary", en ligne);
papier, du slang anglais (*blotter*) *paper,* LSD;
paquets, doses de stupéfiants, de l'angl. *packet;*
talc, de l'angl. *talcum*, cocaïne.

c) d'effet produit:

cheval, héroïne. D'après Colin *et al.* (2019), il s'agit d'un calque du slang *horse* (*La horse,* titre d'un film de Granier-Deferre, en 1969). Il y a une association avec l'animal.

C. *Emprunts à l'anglais.*

Ils se répartissent en trois aires sémantiques, comme l'explique Brunet (1990: 232): les appellations des divers stupéfiants, les types de toxicomanes et de toxicomanies, enfin les fournisseurs de stupéfiants:

business (*faire du…*), de l'ang. *id.*, trafiquer avec de la drogue;
chit, shit, haschisch, du slang américain, et avec inversion des syllabes, donc verlanisé, en: *le teuch, le teuchi, le teush;*
dross, résidu des pipes d'opium, en anglais déchets, impuretés;
joint, slang anglais *id.* cigarette de haschisch;
pétard, ang. *id.*, cigarette de haschisch;

poppers, ang. *id.*, nitrite d'amyle;
pusher, du slang anglais *pusher*, trafiquant de drogue;
Les emprunts aux noms désignant l'argent en anglais font allusion aux différentes doses de drogue (*cf.* SN, SD, "Le dico des drogues", en ligne);
halfapound, 225 g;
once (le), 290 g;
pound (le), 450 g;
plaque (la), 500 g.

Dans l'*Argot de drogue…* (SN, SD, en ligne), on explique qu'il existe des termes couramment utilisés associés à différents types de drogues:

> Quelqu'un surfant sur la vague ou sur le signe de tête est sous l'influence de drogues. Injecter de la drogue avec une seringue, c'est tirer, piquer, amorcer ou claquer la drogue. Quelqu'un qui bip sniffe de la drogue, tandis qu'un tweaker est une personne en mission pour trouver du crack (mais tweek est une substance semblable à la méthamphétamine). Les personnes qui dirigent, font sauter ou participent à une cuisson de palourdes fument de la marijuana.

Nous constatons que les mêmes faits que l'auteur de "Argot de drogue…" (SN, SD, en ligne), énonce sur la marijuana, se reproduisent pour le reste des noms des drogues:

> Il existe littéralement des centaines de termes d'argot ou de noms de rue pour la marijuana ou le cannabis, la drogue la plus consommée aux États-Unis. De nombreux termes ont été dérivés de la source de la drogue, de l'effet de la marijuana sur les utilisateurs ou de l'apparence de la plante transformée. Mais certains noms de rue sont utilisés simplement pour masquer le sujet de la conversation. (…) Certains termes d'argot pour la marijuana combinent l'emplacement géographique avec l'apparence de la plante transformée. Certains des noms de marijuana (…) ont atteint le niveau de « noms de marque » pour la drogue illégale.

Les dénominations des drogues sont en grande partie des emprunts à l'anglais ou au slang anglo-américain sous leur graphie originale. Il s'agit pour la plupart de mots composés. Dans "Le Dico des drogues" (SN, SD, en ligne) nous avons repéré, parmi certains monosyllabes: *bath salts,* cathinones; *bombe A,* cannabis de qualité supérieure; *Jack Herrer* et *White Widow,* désignant une variété spécifique ou un mode de culture du cannabis; *magic mushrooms,* champignons hallucinogènes; *black Bombay,* haschish; *twenty five, purple haze,* LSD; *homegrown*, marijuana; *China white, China girl, Dance fever, Drop Dead, Lollipops, Murder 8, Perc-o-Pops*, fentanyloïdes; *black tar,* heroïne; *Great Bear,* héroïne de synthèse; *free base,* crack; *Lady Sally* et *Sally-D,* salvia divinorum; *Lucy in the Sky with Diamonds, mellow yellow,* LSD; ('*herbal*') *party pills,* pipérazines; *Lady Sally,* salvia divinorum.

Le calque anglais et l'anglicisme jouent un rôle important dans la créativité lexicale de l'argot des toxicomanes, et leur assimilation lexicale dans ce langage peut être: phonétique, graphique, morphosyntaxique et sémantique.

a) Assimilation phonétique.

Elle a lieu lorsqu'un lexème anglais passe dans le vocabulaire de la drogue français sans changer sa forme, seulement sa prononciation, il s'adapte phonétiquement en utilisant un son français similaire pour substituer le son absent dans le répertoire français. Le terme *helen* qui désigne l'héroïne en anglais, est imité dans le français avec *helène* sans aspiration du phonème initial comme en anglais.

Lexème ou locution emprunté(e) - Prononciation anglaise et française

crack [kræk] (anglais)/ [krak] (français), cocaïne cristallisée qui se fume, d'une grande toxicité, de l'anglais *crack*, coup de fouet;

junk, junky, junkie, ['dʒʌŋ.ki] [ʌ] (anglais) face à [d͡ʒœ̃ki] avec [oe] nasalisé (français), héroïnomane, toxicomane;

smaké, [smake], infinitif argotique qui signifie "ressentir les effets d'une certaine drogue", angl. *smack,* ['smæk], héroïne et *smackhead* ['smæk.hed], nom, héroïnomane.

On trouve le même phénomène en espagnol par rapport aux voyelles anglaises: "Las mayores variaciones encontradas en los anglicismos en el nivel fonológico afectan a las vocales y combinaciones de vocales, cuya pronunciación con frecuencia difiere del sistema español." (Rodríguez González, 2017a: 101).

b) Assimilation graphique.

Au niveau graphique, l'intégration voit le jour sous plusieurs versions du même mot car le langage informel ne suit pas de normes et comme il est surtout utilisé à l'oral, les graphies diffèrent suivant les auteurs des livres, des magazines ou selon les usagers. Certains mots ont été adoptés à la graphie française. Voici quelques exemples d'assimilation graphique:

poffer (se), fumer du cannabis, ang. *to puff*; une *pof* est une bouffée de fumée (voir Carcel SD, en ligne).

c) Assimilation morphosyntaxique.

Elle fait référence aux mots adaptés au français avec une variation de leur valeur morphologique et/ou syntaxique. Le mot emprunté s'adaptera graphiquement et phonétiquement à la langue cible, et il subira les modifications nécessaires à son assimilation. Voir ci-dessus le mot argotique *cheval* qui coexiste en argot face à *horse* pour dénommer l'héroïne, l'un étant un calque, l'autre un emprunt.

Les mots empruntés de l'anglais sans modification donnent de nouvelles unités lexicales après être parfois complétés d'affixes français (préfixes, suffixes, affixes, dérivatifs et flexions). La formation de l'infinitif se fait avec le suffixe verbal le plus usité dans la langue de Molière, "-er", qu'on trouve dans des verbes désignant une action ou un résultat de l'action:

s'accrocher, s'intoxiquer avec une drogue dure, de *accro,* apocope d'*accroché,* avec influence de l'américain *hooked,* "qui est dépendant d'une drogue";
bogarter un joint, refuser de le partager (ang. *to bogart a join*), par allusion humoristique à la façon de fumer de Humphrey Bogart;
se destroyer, se droguer, de l'angl. *id,* (dér. avec suff. -er du verbe *to destroy* «détruire ») attesté dep. 1894, qui fut à l'origine le nom propre d'un torpilleur américain (1882) et qui caractérisa par la suite certains torpilleurs (torpedo-boat(-)destroyer 1893, également torpedo[boat]-catcher) pour devenir le nom générique de ce type de bateau de guerre (Thorne, 2014), (Colin *et al.*, 2019);
se doper, se droguer, de l'anglais *to dope*; voir le déverbal *dope* en argot de la drogue français;
poudrer (*se… le pif*), dér. de *poudre,* se droguer à l'héroïne ou à la cocaïne (Mátételki Holló, 2013: 114);
shooter (*se*), de l'argot français *shoot,* qui vient du mot anglais de même sens, s'injecter une drogue par voie intraveineuse, syn. *se faire un shoot*;
smoker, de l'anglais *smoke,* fumer;
snif(fe), prise de cocaïne, d'héroïne ou de colle par le nez, de l'ang. *snif,* reniflement;
sniffer, se faire un sniff, absorber un stupéfiant pulvérulent par voie nasale, de l'anglais *sniff,* sentir, syn. *se faire un sniff;*
speeder (*se*), se droguer aux amphétamines, de l'argot anglais *speed,* même sens, amphétamines utilisées comme drogue;
triper, de *trip* dans *faire un …*, absorber des substances hallucinogènes, de l'anglo-américain qui signifie faire un "voyage"; en verlan, *trip* devient *treupi.*

Il existe un cas de composition, à partir de deux mots anglais dans:

shitman, fumeur de haschich, pseudo-anglicisme, de *shit,* haschisch et de *man,* homme.

d) Assimilation sémantique.

Il faut souligner que les procédés de néologie de sens sont très rares en ce qui concerne les emprunts anglais dans la langue des toxicomanes.

Certains mots possèdent un sens intéressant et en même temps compliqué à emprunter, dans ces cas là, nous nous servons d'un calque, c'est-à-dire de l'adaptation du signifiant en français pour donner un signifié identique à celui représenté par le mot de base. On utilise des calques lexicaux formés à base de termes anglo-américains ainsi que moyennant des termes anglais originaux.

Brunet (1990: 230) signale certains substantifs francisés calqués sur l'anglais:

> La *shooteuse* ou le *fix*, séringue hypodermique; le *sniffage*, prise d'un rail de cocaïne par de cette liste de calques de l'anglais: *acid(e)*, drogue, LSD; *artillerie*, seringue hypodermique, angl. *artillery*; *buvard*, morceau de buvard avec du LSD pour être sucé; *chanvre*, cannabis; *cheval*, héroïne; *connection*, trafiquant de drogue. *Cf. pizza connection*, livraison d'un stupéfiant à domicile ou dans un lieu convenu entre l'acheteur et le vendeur; *douce* (drogue), marijuana; *dure* (drogue), toutes les autres; *foin, gazon, herbe, thé*, cannabis; *guenon*, besoin de drogue, angl. *monkey; marie-jeanne*, marijuana; *merde*, haschisch; *neige*, cocaïne; *propre*, désintoxiqué, angl. *clean; poulet froid*, sevrage total, angl. *cold turkey; speed*, amphétamines; *sucre*, LSD, angl. *sugar; voyage*, expérience d'une prise de drogue. Les noms des toxicomanes aussi: *junkie*. Le toxicomane et ses activités: *pot, tea party*, réunion d'amateurs de haschisch; *hot shot*, injection fatale.

Pot, marijuana, est un anglicisme passé dans la langue espagnole et française d'après Rodríguez González (1917: 398).

Le même auteur (Brunet, 1990: 203-1) ajoutera des verbes francisés suivant le même procédé:

chipper (ang. *to chippy*), se droguer occasionnellement; *crasher*, s'endormir sous l'effet d'un stupéfiant; *dealer; droper, se fixer, se faire un fix*, s'injecter une drogue par voie intraveineuse; *flasher, flipper, poffer*, fumer du cannabis (ang. *to puff*).

Rodríguez González (1994b: 148) explique ainsi l'importance du sème qui se repète dans des séries synonymiques face au signifiant des mots qui entreprennent entre eux des relations métaphoriques:

> En ce qui concerne leur configuration sémantique spécifique, les associations de type métaphorique ne sont pas un fait isolé; dans certains cas, un même sème est répété dans une série de lexies qui, comme des "chaînes isotopiques", renforcent et rendent plus frappante l'association supposée. Le mot caballo lui-même, pour désigner l'héroïne, illustre très bien ce que nous disons. On en déduit qu'en anglais horse provient d'une extension du H de heroin, répondant ainsi, pourrions-nous ajouter, à une raison

> crypto-ludique qui est essentielle dans l'argot. Ensuite le terme aurait été traduit dans d'autres langues moyennant un calque. C'est-à-dire que l'important c'est l'identité du sème qu'il faut faire ressortir, dans ce cas, "force", plus que le signifiant, qui peut être different (…).

D'ailleurs *tigre,* comme *cheval,* désigne aussi l'héroïne dans l'argot français; et *dada,* en langage enfantin, cheval, désigne un mélange d'héroïne et de cocaïne.

Les expressions passées dans le langage informel sont nombreuses, d'après Rodríguez González (1994b: 151):

> En français, le verbe *flipper* ("planer, délirer"), qui doit aussi son origine à l'anglais, a l'acception de 'faire un mauvais voyage' (Fckaut et Schaetzen, 1988: 35); à partir de cette acception il a développé un sens métaphorique dans la langue parlée avec un signifié négatif évident: 'avoir mauvais moral, éprouver une vive déception' (Caradec, 1989), qui se répète aussi dans d'autres membres de la serie (…). Au contraire et très curieusement, le verbe se shooter a développé un sens positif ("se faire plaisir") (…). Cf. aussi *trip, passion, intérêt*" et tripper "avoir une passion pour quelque chose" (Walter, 1984: 84). 10 Cf. fr. *flasher* 'avoir un très vif intérêt' (Walter, 1984: 80).

Comme le dira aussi Rodríguez González (1994 b: 149), il existe des axes notionnels très productifs du point de vue du lexique. Et ceci se produit dans plusieurs langues, par exemple, autour de viaje (argot espagnol des toxicomanes) "apparaissent plusieurs expressions. Le consommateur de LSD qui entreprend un "voyage" hallucinogène (angl.: tri; fr: voyage, ticket) devient un viajero ou viajante (angl.: tripper, …) mais pour volar (angl.: *fly;* fr: planer) (…). Pendant le voyage on peut pasarse et rester colgado (angl.: get hooked; fr: accroché)."

II. Niveau syntagmatique.

1. *Dérivation par un suffixe:*

camé, héroïnomane, de came(lote), terme tronqué qui traduit le mot anglais *junk,* auquel on lui ajoute -é, héroïne. Pour Carrère (1976): c'est un 'drogué, drogué d'habitude, qui consomme des drogues en excès (junkie), qui prend de la drogue (ou des médicaments); être consommateur de drogue, être sous l'effet de la drogue'.

dealer, usager-revendeur de drogue, de *deal;*
sniffage, prise d'un rail de cocaïne, de *snif;*
sniffeur, cocaïnomane, de *snif;*
speedé, speedy, adjectif qui provient de l'argot anglais *speed,* qui se drogue aux amphétamines;

être stone(d), qui subit l'effet violent de la drogue (héroïne ou haschisch), de l'anglo-américain "soûl, défoncé", littéralement "lapidé", issu de *stone,* pierre;

tripeur, individu qui se drogue aux hallucinogènes, de l'anglo-américain *trip,* état hallucinatoire procuré par le LSD, cf. *triper;*

a) suffixes diminutifs:

sniffette, cocaïne, dérivé de *snif,* prise de drogue par le nez, de l'ang. *id.*, reniflement.

b) suffixation parasitaire:

Pour Mandelbaum-Reiner (1991: 112), il s'agit d'un emploi intensif de la suffixation. Ses utilisateurs se signalaient branchés, qu'ils soient des jeunes, des politiciens, ou des professionnels des média. "Simultanément marqueur d'argot et marque de compétence argotique, la suffixation par allongement qui ne change pas le sens du mot déformé, acquiert une valeur d'un autre type, celle d'une fonction de signalisation dans le texte oral ou écrit."

- *ard*: suffixe péjoratif, *camard,* de *came* (voir ce mot ci-dessus), drogué;
- *ingue*: suffixe familier, *camelingue,* de *came,* drogué;
- *man*: emprunté à l'anglais, *bagman,* trafiquant de drogue;
- *os*: suffixe du parler jeune, demodé actuellemet, *matos,* cannabis, de l'anglais *material,* stupéfiants, forme calqué dans matériel, avec resuffixation argotique (Mátételki Holló, 2013: 114).

2. Troncation.

a) apocope:

accro, apocope d'accroché, avec influence de l'américain *hooked,* du même sens;

coca, coke, coco, formes hypocoristiques de l'anglais *coke,* cocaïne; *coco* signifie aussi vendeur de cocaïne, dealer, selon Olivenstein (1970, en ligne);

héro, de l'anglais, héroïne. Dans l'argot de la drogue espagnol, on trouve la même apocope (voir Rodríguez González, 2014);

b) apocope + aphérèse:

feta, amphetamine, du slang angl.;

c) aphérèse:

cotics, pour *narcotics;*
ludes, pour *Quaaludes,* un anxiolitique;
shrooms, pour *mushrooms,* champignons hallucinogènes.

3. Ellipse.

ball, (angl. *goof balls*) séance collective où l'on consomme des drogues;
dealer, prononcé [di.loeʁ], abrègement de l'anglais *drug dealer,* vendeur de drogue, de stupéfiants, en anglais *dealer* [ˈdiː.lər];
pompe, angl. *pump,* instrument qui envoie ou aspire un liquide, un gaz.

4. Emploi des sigles.

Il s'agit d'anglicismes dans tous les cas.

AD, toxicomane;
C, CC, cocaïne; dans l'*Argot de drogue…* (SN, SD), on donne aussi la variante *Big C* qui est tirée du slang;
D, prononcé à l'anglaise (di:), LSD;
G.B., barbituriques (angl. *goof balls*);
H, héroïne, du slang anglais *H,* héroïne, par siglaison;
K, kétamine, du slang angl., de même que ses variantes: *spécial K, Vitamine K, Super K;*
O.D., surdose (ang. overdose, qui devient un calque dans l'argot des toxicomanes);
XTC, du slang ang. *id.*, ecstasy (Patterson, 2022, en ligne). Var. *E* prononcé à l'anglaise (i:), *Ex, X, MD.*

5. Verlan.

C'est un procédé de formation lexicale très productif dans l'argot des jeunes. Il consiste à inverser les syllabes. On verlanise ici à partir d'anglicismes et de calques:

tarpé, de pétard;
teuch, de shit;
zonga, de gazon, marijuana.

Conclusion

Le langage de la drogue français adopte de plus en plus d'emprunts anglo-américains. Ces emprunts vont d'un pays à l'autre, comme les stupéfiants. Comme la prononciation française diffère de l'anglaise, lorsqu'un lexème anglais passe dans le vocabulaire de la drogue français, il ne change pas sa forme, seulement sa prononciation, il s'adapte phonétiquement en utilisant un son français similaire. Il existe des changements nécessaires de phonèmes à cause de l'absence en français de certaines voyelles anglaises principalement. Les mots anglais sont prononcés avec les règles phonétiques du français, sauf en ce qui concerne les sigles. L'intérêt de maintenir un langage secret provoque l'apparition de nouveaux lexèmes et la disparition d'autres mots. Le vocabulaire des toxicomanes, y compris en France, est internationalement dérivé en grande partie de l'anglo-américain, et ces formes étrangères sont surtout adaptées sans modification mais il existe également des calques lexicaux. Les mots empruntés de l'anglais sans modification sont souvent des dérivés, complétés par des affixes français. L'emprise britannique pour les monosyllabes est présente dans ces emprunts à l'anglais ou au slang. Puis il existe nombre de mots composés tirés du slang anglais pour dénommer les appellations des stupéfiants principalemenet. Les mots obtenus par dérivation sont nombreux aussi: par exemple, *sniffage, sniffeur, speedé, être stone(d), tripeur, sniffette.* Une grande partie de ce lexique est passé dans le registre familier, voire dans le langage courant. Les emprunts à l'anglais ou à l'anglo-américain concernent tous les registres de la langue et tous les pays. La créativité lexicale de cette forme langagière est évidente dans des figures telles que la métaphore et la métonymie, comme dans les suites synonymiques. Les inventions lexicales utilisent les affixes propres à l'argot, ou bien et surtout, ceux qui existent dans la langue commune. Et on n'introduit pas d'éléments grammaticaux qui n'existent pas en français.

Références bibliographiques.

Bedijs, Kristina (2015). "Langue et générations: le langage des jeunes", *Manuel de linguistique française*, 293–313. De Gruyter. Eds.: Claudia Polzin-Haumann, Wolfgang Schweickard. En ligne: //www.researchgate.net/publication/312026541_Langue_et_generations_lelangage_des_jeunes

Brunet, Jean-Paul (1990). "L'argot des toxicomanes en français et en anglais", *Meta,* vol. 35 (1), 230–235. En: //www.erudit.org/fr/revues/meta/1990-v35-n1-meta327/002152ar/

Cahoreau, Gilles et Tyson, Cristophe (2006 [1987]). La *drogue expliquée aux parents,* Paris: Balland.

Carrère, Jean, Dessaignes, Jacques (1976). "Termes d'argot utilisés par les usagers de la drogue", en *Lexique des termes usuels de psychiatrie.* En ligne: //www.languefrancaise.net/Source/2079

Colin, Jean-Paul; Mével, Jean-Pierre et Leclère, Christian (2019 [1990]). *Dictionnaire de l'argot et du français populaire,* Paris: Larousse.

Haramburu, F., Neveu, D., Jouglard, J., Moulin, M., Lagier, G. (1998). "Lexique argotique de la drogue", *La Lettre du Pharmacologue,* vol. 12 (5), mai. En ligne: //www.edimark.fr/Front/frontpost/getfiles/9809.pdf

Johnson, Bruce D., Bardi, Flutura, Sifaneck, Stephen J., Siphanec, Dunlap, Eloise (2006). "Marijuana Argot as Subculture Threads: Social Construction by Users in New York City", *British Journal of Criminology,* 46 (1), 46–77. En ligne: //www.researchgate.net/publication/31208179_Marijuana_Argot_As_Subculture_Threads_Social_Constructions_by_Users_in_New_York_City

Kuzmina, Olga (2021). "Couche synchronique la plus récente de l'argot français des jeunes (2010–2021): systématisation de mécanismes de création lexicale", *Synergies Europe,* 16, 211–222.

Lazar, J. (2012): «Les anglicismes dans le discours électronique médié». *Studia Romanica Posnaniensia,* 39/4, 61–69.

Mandelbaum-Reiner, Françoise (1991). "Suffixation gratuite et signalétique textuelle d'argot", *Langue française,* 106–112. Fait partie du numéro thématique: *Parlures argotiques.*

Mátételki Holló, Magdolna (2013): «Étude de la langue parlée: Aspects sociolinguistiques de l'argot des toxicomanes et influences de l'anglo-américain ». *Synergies Espagne,* 6, 105-120. En ligne: //dialnet.unirioja.es/servlet/articulo?codigo=4664367

Mudrochová, R. (2017). « Des « fashion » anglicismes en français contemporain provenant d'un corpus oral – une hybridation voulue ou un métissage necessaire ». *Annales de l'Université de Craïova. Langues et littératures romanes,* 49–64. En ligne: www.researchgate.net/publication/323572732_Des_fashion_anglicismes_en_francais_contemporain_provenant_d'un_corpus_oral_-_une_hybridation_voulue_ou_un_metissage_necessaire

Napieralski, Andrzej Jr (2007). "Le vocabulaire de la drogue dans la langue des jeunes en tant qu'exemple de l'expansion de la langue", *Romanica Olomucensia XVIIIe,* Grandeur et décadence de la parole au XXème siècle, Univerzita Palackého v Olomuci, Olomouc: Slamovír Míca, Radim Zaméc, 225–235. En ligne: //www.academia.edu/2652620/Le_vocabulaire_de_la_drogue_dans_la_langue_des_jeunes_en_tant_qu_exemple_de_l_expansion_de_la_langue

Napieralski, Andrzej Jr (2010). "L'emprunt et l´argot: assimilation du lexique anglais dans la culture hip-hop en Pologne", *Études romanes de Brno,* 1,177-184. En ligne: file:///C:/Users/Usuario/Downloads/Dialnet-LempruntEtLargot-4362332.pdf [consulté le 15 octobre 2022].

Podhorná-Polická, Alena (2007). *Peut-on parler d'un argot des jeunes? Analyse lexicale des universaux argotiques du parler de jeunes en lycées professionnels en France (Paris, Yzeure) et en République tchèque (Brno).* Thèse en cotutelle sous la direction de Jean-Pierre Goudaillier et Marie Krcmovâ. Paris-Brno, Université René Descartes-Université Masaryk. En ligne: //is.muni.cz/th/yl3iy/Teze_PD.pdf

Podhorná-Polická, Alena (2010). "Expressivité des mots identitaires dans l'argot des jeunes", *XXVème CILPR Congrès International de Linguistique et de Philologie Romanes,* p. 213-221.

Rodríguez González, Félix (1994a): "Anglicismos en el argot de la droga", *Atlantis,* 16, 1/2, 179-216. En ligne: file:///C:/Users/Usuario/Downloads/Dialnet-AnglicismosEnElArgotDeLaDroga-637519%20(1).pdf

Rodríguez González, Félix (1994b): "Remarques sur les glisements de sens dans l'argot. A propos du langage de la drogue et les anglicismes en espagnol", *Cahiers de Lexicologie,* 64, 1, 147-154.

Rodríguez González, Félix (2014): *Diccionario de la droga: vocabulario técnico y argot*, Madrid: Arco/Libros.

Rodríguez González, Félix (2017a): *Gran diccionario de anglicismos,* Madrid: Arco/Libros.

Rodríguez González, F. (2017b): "Variaciones fonológicas en el uso del anglicismo: panorama y revisión crítica" *Revista Española de Lingüística,* 47(2), 99-134.

Rodríguez González, F. (2022): "Anglicismos en el argot de la droga", in Rodríguez González, F. (éd.). *Enciclopedia del anglicismo.* Vol I*: Anglicismos en el español contemporáneo. Una visión panorámica.* Berlin: Peter Lang, 297-316.

Spears, Richard, A. (2000: 1995). *NTC's Dictionary of American Slang and Colloquial Expressions,* NTC Publishing Group, En ligne: //www.academia.edu/35040693/Dictionary_of_American_Slang_and_Colloquial_Expressions

Spears, Richard, A (1986). *The Slang and Jargon of Drugs and Drink,* Metuchen, New Jersey-Londres: The Scarecrow Press Inc. En ligne: //archive.org/details/slangjargonofdru0000spea/page/n9/mode/1up

Thorne, Tony (2014): *Dictionnary of Contemporary Slang,* Londres-New Dely-New York-Sidney: Bloomsbury Publishing Pic.

Webographie

Olivenstein, Claude & Aron, Michel (1970). "Lexique, dans La drogue. Drogues et toxicomanes". En ligne: www.languefrancaise.net/Source/3604.

Patterson, Eric (2022). "List of Street Names for Drugs. American Addiction Center Drug Abuse.com". En ligne: //drugabuse.com/addiction/list-street-names-drugs/#mdma

(SN)(SD). "Argot de drogue et termes de rue pour les drogues illicites (googlawi.com)". En ligne: www.googlawi.com/fr/blog/mental/a-z/drug-use/Drug-Slang-and-Street-Terms-for-Illicit-Drugs/

(SN)(SD). "Un glossaire des termes du jargon lié à la drogue (pflegeboard.ch)". En ligne: //pflegeboard.ch/fr/un-glossaire-des-termes-du-jargon-lie-a-la-drogue/Glossaire.

Carcel, Jean Paul (SD): "Drogues et toxicomanies Glossaire ABC - (online.fr)". En ligne: www.caat.online.fr/glossaire/abc.htm

(SN)(SD). "Observatoire français des drogues et des substances addictives. Produits et addictions". En ligne: www.ofdt.fr/glossaire/

(SN)(SD). "Le dico des drogues - Drogues Info Service.fr". En ligne: www.drogues-info-service.fr/Tout-savoir-sur-les-drogues/Le-dico-des-drogues)

(SN) (2011-2015): "The Online Slang Dictionary (American, English, and Urban slang). The Online Slang Dictionary | Real definitions. Real slang". En ligne: //onlineslangdictionary.com/

(SN) (2017): "Drug Slang Code Words (dea.gov)". En ligne: www.dea.gov/documents/2017/2017-05/2017-05-01/drug-slang-code-words

(SN) (2021): "Drogue: douce, dure, liste, types, effets, dépendance (journaldesfemmes.fr)". En ligne: //sante.journaldesfemmes.fr/quotidien/2698935-drogue-douce-dure-liste-noms-effets-secondaires-dependance/

Pedro Mogorrón Huerta

Universidad de Alicante

Analyse lexicale des expressions figées avec des zoonymes en espagnol et en français

0. Introduction

Les séquences figées (SFS) sont des séquences linguistiques pluriverbales[1] utilisées dans toutes les langues comme des instruments visant à créer un sentiment de communauté qui possède des codes linguistiques, culturels et conceptuels communs ainsi qu'à produire une économie discursive dans les productions linguistiques utilisées pour la représentation conceptuelle de situations stéréotypées fréquentes dans la vie quotidienne. La répétition de ces séquences identiques de mots préfabriquées qui vont réapparaître spontanément lors des mêmes situations contextuelles de communication va être l'élément catalyseur qui assurera la survie de ces formes.

La phraséologie, est devenue à la fin du XXe siècle l'un des sujets de recherche les plus étudiés et analysés dans de nombreuses langues. La connaissance d'une langue se mesure généralement par la maîtrise et l'aisance avec laquelle un locuteur utilise les unités phraséologiques propres et caractéristiques de cette langue. Chez les utilisateurs natifs, ces séquences figées représentent une connaissance linguistique culturelle et sociale commune déposée dans leur mémoire par l'expérience. Pour les utilisateurs non natifs apprenant une langue seconde, les unités phraséologiques représentent généralement un défi, car elles représentent la plus grande difficulté qu'ils rencontreront, en raison de la complexité et de la grande quantité d'informations linguistiques, sociales et culturelles qu'ils ont reçues pour apprendre à utiliser et différencier les caractéristiques de leur langue maternelle.

1 Les séquences figées posent de nombreux problèmes théoriques et pratiques qui sont traités exhaustivement depuis la fin du XXème siècle dans de nombreuses langues: (classification syntaxique, traitement lexicographique, degré de figement, fixité syntaxique, variantes paradigmatiques, créations diatopiques, interprétation du sens, traduction des phraséologismes, transparence, opacité, etc.).

1. Délimitation de l'étude

Il existe des dizaines de milliers de séquences figées appartenant à une ample typologie linguistique : proverbes, collocations, locutions, pragmatèmes ou formules conversationnelles ou routinières, etc. qui vont s'utiliser par les différentes tranches de la population et par les différents groupes sociaux dans les mêmes situations communicationnelles. L'étendue de ce phénomène linguistique est telle qu'il est impossible de mémoriser et de connaître toutes les formes figées, ce qui revient à dire que la compétence linguistique des usagers est limitée, d'autant plus qu'une très grande partie de ces séquences figées sont opaques.

Chacune des typologies d'EF/UF contient des exemples avec des zoonymes. Ex :

- Proverbes.
  muerto el perro se acabó la rabia; morte la bête, mort le venin;
  Perro ladrador poco mordedor; perro que ladra no muerde; Chien qui aboie ne mords pas;
- Pragmatèmes,
  A otro perro con ese hueso ; à d'autres
  ¡*Menuda* vaca !; *Quelle vache* !:
  etc.

Nous ne pouvons pas dans le cadre de ce travail analyser le contenu et la présence lexicale des zoonymes dans tous les types d'EF, aussi, dans le cadre de cette étude, nous désirons examiner :

- pour l'espagnol, les constructions verbales figées (CVF[2]) à contenu zoonymique, présentes dans la Base de Données, (BD) élaborée par le groupe de recherche Frasytram[3].
- Pour le français une Base de Données d'expressions figées élaborée par M.Gross que nous avons pu consulter à l'I.Gaspard Monge[4].

Ces expressions contiennent un ou plusieurs noms d'animaux et sont généralement employées pour parler de, définir le comportement des êtres humains dans leurs activités quotidiennes[5]. Cette analyse nous permettra d'observer si l'utilisation des noms d'animaux est la même dans les deux langues. Cependant il convient de signaler que la BD française contient non seulement des expressions figées (EF), mais également des milliers de pragmatèmes (c'est du beau, c'est du joli, attention chien méchant, etc.), ainsi que des proverbes qui contiennent très peu de noms d'animaux. Nous partirons donc de l'analyse de la BD espagnole que nous comparerons par la suite avec la BD française tout en

2 Pour voir les bases théoriques des constructions incluses dans les constructions verbales figées, voir Mogorrón 2010 (88–90). Dans cette base de données nous traitons :

Les « locutions verbales » qui ont pour principale propriété l'idiomaticité. Leur sens ne peut se déduire de la somme de la signification individuelle de chacun de leur composants: *coger el toro por los cuernos* (DUE), (prendre le taureau par les cornes) (GR).

Les « collocations verbales » combinaisons syntagmatiques dans lesquelles il s'établit une relation de solidarité lexicale entre leurs composantes: *guiñar un ojo* (DUE), (faire un clin d'œil) (GR).

Les « constructions à verbes support »: *dar un paseo* (RAE), (faire une promenade) (GR).

Les constructions verbales comparatives: *dormir como un tronco* (DEA), (dormir comme une souche) (GR); etc.

Les constructions V + loc adverbiale qui ont un paradigme fermé avec un ou plusieurs verbes avec lesquel(s) ils forment une combinaison interdépendante à usage fréquent ou à caractère préférentiel. *Llover a cántaros* (DUE), (pleuvoir à verses).

Nous sommes conscients que les cinq types de constructions que nous venons d'énumérer n'appartiennent pas à une même catégorie de constructions verbales. Elles ont des propriétés différentes, par exemple l'idiomaticité ou la compositionnalité, mais elles ont en commun le fait de se construire avec un verbe + un complément ainsi que de présenter un certain degré de figement.

3 Fraseología y traducción multilingüe. (https://dti.ua.es/es/frasytram/grupo-de-investigacion-frasytram.html).

4 Université Gustave Eiffel, actuellement Université Paris Est-Créteil, Val de Marne.

5 Dans de nombreuses cultures, les animaux peuvent même exercer des fonctions symboliques.

sachant que la BD française n'est pas aussi représentative que l'espagnole quant au nombre de CVF et quant à la représentativité des zoonymes..

Les deux Bases de données contiennent environ 40.000 entrées chacune, mais une autre grande différence est que dans le cas de la BD espagnole elle contient environ 24.000 entrées appartenant à l'espagnol péninsulaire et ou commun en hispano Amérique et 14.400 entrées appartenant à l'espagnol hispanoaméricain.

2. Importance numérique des EF avec un nom d'animal

Le monde animal offre un système très productif pour la conceptualisation transmise par les CVF / EF. Ainsi, l'analyse de la BD espagnole nous a permis d'observer que les deux grands champs lexicaux les plus présents dans la formation des CVF sont par ordre d'importance, les noms du corps humain avec environ 7000 entrées et les zoonymes avec environ 2500 CVF. En ce qui concerne les EF avec des composantes zoonymes, elles sont généralement liées à des caractérisations de l'aspect physiques des êtres humains, voir même à leurs qualités psychiques.

L'extraction des CVF contenant un ou plusieurs termes d'animaux dans leurs composantes nous offre les résultats suivants.

2.1. CVF espagnoles avec des zoonymes

Tableau n° 1: Noms d'animaux dans les EF espagnoles.

Zoonyme	Tot EF	Diat	Zoonyme	Tot EF	Diat	Zoonyme	Tot EF	Diat	Zoonyme	Tot EF	Diat
Abeja	9	3	abejón	5	3	abejorro	1	-	águila	5	2
alacrán	8	8	alcatraz	1	1	almeja	3	-	ameba	1	1
anguila	6	2	animal	12	2	apipizca	1	1	araña	12	7
Ardilla	6	1	asno	9	2	atún	2	-	aura	4	4
Ave	12	3	avestruz	3	1	avispa	8	4	babosa	2	2
bacalao	19	8	bagre	6	6	baifa	1	-	ballena	3	-
becerro/a	5	1	berraco	2	1	bestia	12	1 1	besugo	6	-
bibijagua	3	3	bicha/o	5	-	bicharraco	1	-	bigornia	1	1
Boa	2	2	borrego	5	3	borrico	5	-	buey	42	200
buitre	7	3	burro	88	15	caballito	6	3	caballo	103	32
cabestro	5	-	cabra	27	7	cabrillas	4	-	cabrón	3	-
cacatúa	1	1	cacho	1	-	caguama	1	1	caimán	2	1
camaleón	2	2	camarón	6	6	camaroncito	1	1	camello	4	-
Can	2	2	canario	6	-	cangrejo	21	5	canguamo	1	1

Tableau n° 1: Suite

Zoonyme	Tot EF	Diat	Zoonyme	Tot EF	Diat	Zoonyme	Tot EF	Diat	Zoonyme	Tot EF	Diat
capón	1	-	caracol	12	7	caracolito	2	2	caraira	1	1
carapacho	2	2	carnero	8	2	carrao	1	1	cebón	1	-
cerdo	20	5	cermeño	1	1	cernícalo	2	-	chachito	2	2
chahuiscle	1	1	chahuistle	3	3	chahuiztle	2	2	chanchita	2	2
chanchito	2	2	chancho	35	35	charal	1	1	chicharra	8	6
chiche	1	1	chichicúa	1	1	chimango	2	2	chinche	17	8
chita	2	-	chiva/o	35	31	chivito	1	-	chompipe	1	1
chorlito	6	3	chota	1	-	chotuno	1	-	chucha	2	1
chucho	9	9	chuncho	1	1	churra	4	-	cigueña	6	2
cisne	2	2	cochino	5	2	cochinito	2	2	cocodrilo	7	3
cocuyito	1	1	colibrí	1	1	concha	6	2	cóndor	2	2
conejo	17	9	conejillo	1	-	conejito	1	-	coral	1	-
corderito	1	-	cordero	7	2	corvina	1	1	cotorra	15	6
coyol	1	1	coyote	1	1	criatura	2	-	cucaracha	12	10
cucarachita	1	-	cucarachón	1	-	cucho	2	2	cuco	1	-
cuerno	14	12	cuervo	4	-	culebra	11	8	culebrilla	1	1
cuyo	1	1	elefante	11	3	erizo	7	3	escarabajo	2	1
faisán	2	2	fiera	13	7	foca	6	4	galápago	2	1
galgo	10	3	gallina	55	17	gallito	6	4	gallo	55	31
gamba	14	3	gamo	3	-	gamusino	1	1	ganado	3	2
ganso	8	3	garrapata	4	3	garrobo	3	3	garza	9	9
gato	127	40	gatazo	2	1	gaviota	1	-	gocho	1	-
gofio	4	4	golondrinaa	1	1	gorgojo	1	1	gorila	1	-
gorrión	2	-	grillo	10	3	grulla	4	1	guá	2	2
guabina	3	1	guacamaya	1	1	guacharaca	1	1	guajalote	1	1
guanacaste	1	1	guanaja	1	1	guate	1	1	guayabito	1	1
güevo	1	1	gusanillo	3	1	gusano	8	2	haca	3	1
hiena	1	-	hipopótamoo	1	1	hormiga	25	11	hormiguita	7	7
huilota	1	1	iguana	3	3	jaba	2	2	jaca	1	-
jején	1	-	jilguero	4	-	jiquillo	1	1	jirafa	2	2
jobillo	1	1	jobo	1	1	jolote	2	2	jutía	1	1
ladilla	3	2	lagartija	6	6	lagarto	4	4	langosta	2	2
lapa	2	-	lechón	1	1	lechuza	3	-	león	10	4
leonesa	1	1	liebre	12	1	liendre	3	3	lince	4	4
lobo	14	-	lombriz	2	-	loro	17	4	lorito	4	-
macaco	1	1	machito	2	-	macho	7	-	manso	2	-
mariposa	1	-	marrano	5	-	merluza	1	1	*merluzo	3	3
mero	1	1	mica	2	-	mico	15	10	mime	2	2

(*suite*)

Tableau nº 1: Suite

Zoonyme	Tot EF	Diat	Zoonyme	Tot EF	Diat	Zoonyme	Tot EF	Diat	Zoonyme	Tot EF	Diat
mirlo	5	-	mochuelo	10	-	mono	69	48	monstruo	2	-
mosca	64	12	moscardónn	1	-	moscón	2	-	mosquita	3	-
mosquito	8	-	mula	41	15	murciélago	2	1	musaraña	3	-
nigua	6	6	novillo	4	-	oca	2	-	ocote	2	2
oso	11	5	ostra	1	-	oveja	7	-	pájara	11	
pajaríco	1	-	pajarilla	6	3	pajarita	3	3	pajarito	14	7
pájaro	50	15	pajarón	1	1	paloma/o	13	10	palomita	1	1
pantera	1	1	papagayo	7	-	papalote	5	5	pargo	1	1
pato	20	8	patito	1	-	pavo/a	34	15	pavita	1	1
pavote	1	1	perdiz	7	4	perico	12	12	periquito	2	2
perro/a	188	90	pescadilla	1	1	pescado	9	4	pez	23	6
piche	2		pichón	4	4	pingüino	2	-	piojillo	1	-
piojito	1	1	piojo	10	8	polilla	3	2	polla	2	1
pollito	3	3	pollo	36	12	puerco	13	9	puerquito	3	3
pulga	22	10	pulpo	8	-	rana	6	3	rata	14	6
ratón	18	8	res	1	1	rocín	1	-	ruiseñor	1	-
sabandija	1	-	sanguijuelaa	1	-	sapillo	1	1	sapito	1	1
sapo	21	9	sardina	5	2	serpiente	2	-	suri	2	2
tarántula	5	1	tigre	20	18	tilingo	1	-	tití	2	2
tlaconet	2	2	topillo	1	1	topo	6	3	torito	1	1
toro*	64	11	tortuga	7	3	trucha	3	2	tusa	10	10
urraca	2	-	vaca	30	16	vaquita	1	1	venadito	1	1
venado	7	5	vencejo	1	-	verraco	1	-	víbora	7	5
yagua	1	1	yegua	7	6	yegüita	1	1	zanate	4	4
zope	8	8	zopilote	4	4	zorillo	1	1	zorro	13	3

Dans le cas des EF espagnoles, les chiffres des zoonymes doivent s'analyser de la forme suivante :

> La première colonne contient le zoonyme, la seconde colonne le nombre total d'entrées relevé dans la BD de Frasytram, la troisième colonne indique la quantité d'EF qui contiennent le zoonyme cataloguées comme hispanoaméricaine. Ainsi, comme exemple, dans le cas de *abeja* (abeille), les chiffres de la première colonne indiquent que la BD contient 9 EF et la deuxième colonne signale que 3 des EF appartiennent à l'espagnol d'hispanoamérique.

Les EF qui contiennent le zoonyme *abeja* son les suivantes : (voir capture écran nº 1).

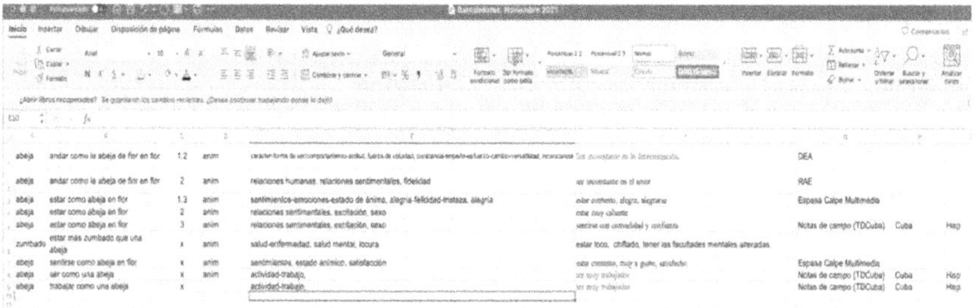

Capture d'écran nº 1. EF avec abeja.

La colonne C indique qu'il y polysémie (1.2 signifie qu'il y a deux sens, 1.3 trois sens et x qu'il n'y a pas de polysémie. À la colonne F, nous trouvons le sens et à la colonne G figure le dictionnaire ou bien la source où nous l'avons recueillie. Lorsqu'il n'y a pas de source l'EF est utilisée également et indiquera VV).

Dans le cas de *besugo* (daurade) nous trouvons les données suivantes : besugo 6 / -, qui indique qu'il y a six EF en espagnol et qu'aucune d'entre elles appartient à l'espagnol d'Amérique. (Voir capture d'écran nº 2).

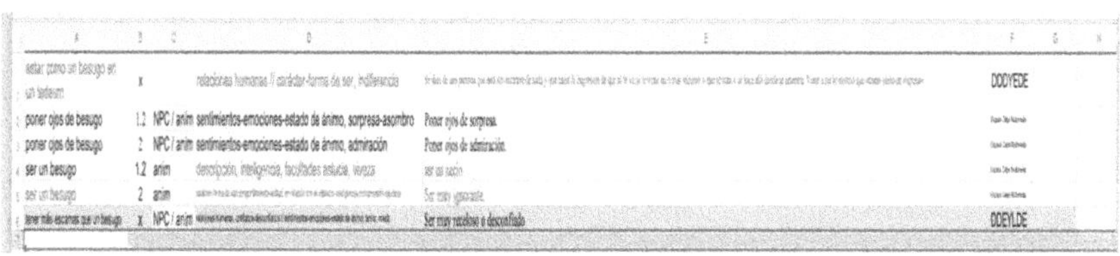

Capture d'écran nº 2 . EF avec besugo.

2.2. Expressions figées françaises avec des zoonymes[6]

Tableau nº 2: Noms d'animaux dans les EF françaises.

Zoonyme	Tot	Zoonyme	Tot	Zoonyme	Tot	Zoonyme	Tot
agneau	2	aigle	2	âne	9	anguille	2
baleine	1	bête	1	biche	2	bique	1
boeuf	9	bouc	4	brebis	1	cafard	1

(suite)

6 La BD de M.Gross n'inclus que des EF appartenant au français de l'hexagone.

Tableau nº 2: Suite

Zoonyme	Tot	Zoonyme	Tot	Zoonyme	Tot	Zoonyme	Tot
caille	1	canard	5	chacal	1	chameau	1
chat	26	cheval	38	chèvre	4	chien	27
chouette	2	cigale	1	cloporte	1	cobaye	1
cochon	20	cocotte	1	colombe	1	coq	2
corbeau	2	coucou	3	crapaud	1	crocodile	1
dahut	1	dinde	1	dindon	2	dinosaure	1
dragon	1	éléphant	4	faisan	1	faucon	1
fauve	1	fourmi	5	gazelle	1	gibier	2
girafe	1	gorille	2	goujon	1	grenouille	2
grue	1	gueunon	1	guêpe	1	hareng	1
hibou	1	hirondelle	1	hyène	1	jument	1
lapin	9	larve	1	lièvre	2	limace	1
linotte	3	lion	7	loup	13	lynx	1
mammouth	1	maquereau	1	maquerelle	1	mérinos	1
merlan	2	merle	1	moineau	1	mollusque	1
morue	2	mouche	9	mouton	14	mule	1
œuf	1	oie	2	oiseau	10	orfraie	1
ours	2	pachyderme	1	paon	1	papillon	8
patte	1	perroquet	1	phénix	1	pie	1
pigeon	3	poisson	6	poule	2	poulet	3
pouliche	1	poulette	1	pourceau	2	puce	4
rapace	1	rat	4	renard	2	requin	1
sanglier	1	sangsue	1	sauterelle	1	serpent	4
souris	2	sphynx	1	taupe	2	taureau	4
tigre	1	truie	1	vache	15	vampire	1
vautour	1	veau	3	ver	1	vif	1
vipère	2	zèbre	2				

Dans le cas des EF françaises, les colonnes sont différentes et les chiffres des zoonymes doivent s'analyser de la forme suivante :

> La première colonne contient le zoonyme, la seconde colonne le nombre total d'entrées.

3. Polysémie

La BD française que nous utilisons dans ce travail, ne contient pas d' EF diatopiques et ne contient pas non plus de cas de polysémie[7], contrairement à la BD espagnole ce qui diminue considérablement le nombre d'entrées et change considérablement, les résultats d'usage des EF. Il s'agit cependant d'un phénomène de grande envergure.

Comme preuve à l'appui de la phrase antérieure, nous trouvons, par exemple, dans le TLFI[8] les expressions figées *manger du cheval* et *avoir du chien* avec les suivantes définitions :

- *manger du cheval*: 1. Manger de la viande très dure ; 2. Avoir une force décuplée.
- *avoir du chien* : 1.[En parlant d'une femme] Avoir un charme quelque peu provocant, être attirante; **2.** *P. ext.* [En parlant d'une chose] *C'est aussi la chapelle nocturne que je connais le mieux (...) Elle a plus de chien, plus d'âme et plus de résonance* (FARGUE, *Le Piéton de Paris,* 1939, p. 25). **3.** *Vx.* [En parlant d'un artiste et, en partic. d'un comédien] Faire preuve d'un talent brillant.

Cependant en espagnol, l'analyse minutieuse des CVF de la BD de Frasytram nous a permis de dénombrer 14.348 cas de CVF polysémiques[9]. L'examen minutieux de ces 14.348 cas et le classement des CVF qui sous une même forme[10] présentent des sens différents, nous a permis de relever des CVF polysémiques avec, deux, trois, quatre, cinq, six, sept, huit, neuf, et jusqu'à 10 sens différents (Voir tableau nº x).

---

7 La polysémie est un phénomène d'économie du langage de grande envergure dans toutes les langues et également en phraséologie. Dans Mogorron 2020, nous avons montré que l'analyse actuelle de la BD espagnole qui n'est pas encore terminée a relevé déjà plus de 14.348 EF polysémiques.

8 Les sigles des dictionnaires dans lesquels nous avons trouvé les CVF ou les informations pertinentes sur ces CVF sont indiquées dans la partie dictionnaire de la bibliographie.

9 Cette recherche n'analyse que les CVF polysémiques et laisse de côté les sens littéraux qui peuvent apparaître dans de nombreux cas. Par ex: *estar en la luna*, (être dans la lune; 1. être réellement dans la lune; 2. être distrait, rêveur); *estar en el ajo*, (être dans l'ail; 1. être dans un endroit qui a pour toponyme el ajo; 2. être au courant, dans le coup). Les sens marqués avec un 1 ne sont pas inclus dans la BD et dans la recherche.

10 Dans la BD de 40.400 entrées, chaque entrée correspond à un sens bien différentié. C'est-à-dire que les CVF polysémiques ont une entrée pour chacun de leur sens..

Tableau nº 3: Cas de polysémie dans les CVF espagnoles.

CVF polysémiques		
1 sens	1	26652
Deux sens	2	4335
Trois sens	3	1006
Quatre sens	4	328
Cinq sens	5	120
Six sens	6	31
Sept sens	7	19
Huit sens	8	6
Neuf sens	9	1
Dix sens	10	4

Exemples :

- *Coger las vueltas* (1. Eludir, esquivar, buscar rodeos, RAE, esquiver qq chose, tourner autour du pot ; 2. Adivinar los planes y propósitos de alguien, RAE, deviner les intentions de qq'un; 3. llegar a conocer su carácter o sus mañas y saber cómo tratarle, RAE, Cuba, arriver à connaître la façon d'être de qq'un);
- *No tener abuela (1. Se dice irónicamente de la persona que se alaba a sí misma, DUE, se dit ironiquement de la personne que se fait des éloges; 2. Mantener una costumbre o conducta incorregible, DdAm, México, conserver une habitude négative; 3. Ser algo muy bueno o muy malo, DRLE, México, se dit d'une chose très bonne ou mauvaise; 4. Ser alguien malo, AoMex, México, être méchant).*
- *meter caña* (1. Aumentar la velocidad, intensidad de algo, RAE, augmenter la vitesse, intensité; 2.Hostigar presionar , DUE, faire pression sur qq'un; 3. pegar, golpear, RAE, frapper qq'un; 4.provocar, recriminar, DUE, provoquer, récriminer; 5. Comenzar un trabajo, DdAm, Cuba, Puerto Rico, commencer un travail).
- etc.

3.1. Typologies d'usage géographique des CVF/EF polysémiques.

Nous avons relevé trois grandes typologies polysémiques d'utilisation géographiques dans les CVF/EF espagnoles qui se retrouvent également dans les CVF/EF avec des zoonymes[11].

11 La délimitation géolinguistique des zones d'utilisation des EF est très compliquée à établir. Encore plus lorsqu'une langue est utilisée comme langue officielle dans de nombreux pays. Nous avons déjà souligné cette option dans (Mogorrón Huerta 2014) « También observamos que los diccionarios pertenecientes a cada país hispanoamericano se limitan generalmente a recopilar algunas expresiones y a señalarlas como pertenecientes a esa variedad del español hispanoamericano sin informar si esas expresiones son usuales en otros países de Hispanoamérica.

3.1.1. CVF polysémiques qui appartiennent à l'espagnol péninsulaire et commun (EspPC). Ex : *cascar las liendres* (1. Golpear, pegar a alguien, DUE; 2. Regañar, reñir, reprender duramente a alguien, RAE).
3.1.2. CVF polysémiques aves des sens qui appartiennent à l'EspPC et d'autres qui appartiennent simultanément à l'EspDiat. Ex : *hacer la gamba* (1. Detener a alguien, DFDEA ; 2. Adular, alabar con exageración para agradar, DdAm, Chile ; 3. Ayudar en alguna tarea o situación, DdAm, Argentina).
3.1.3. CVF polysémiques avec des sens qui n'appartiennent qu'à l'EspDiat. Ex : *comer gallina* (1. Practicar el acto sexual, DdAm, Honduras, República Dominicana; 2. Conversar y hacerse gestos de cariño una pareja de enamorados, generalmente vigilados por la madre de la novia, DdAm, Honduras, República Dominicana; 3. Tenerle miedo a alguien, DdAm, Costa Rica).

4. Zoonymes les plus fréquents dans les CVF/EF

Nous avons indiqué pour chaque zoonyme en espagnol et en français, dans les tableaux 1 et 2 le nombre d'expressions figées recueillies dans les deux Bases de Données utilisées à l'appui. L'analyse de la fréquence des 20 zoonymes les plus employés dans chacune des deux langues offre les chiffres suivants[12]:

4.1. Dans le cas de l'espagnol : perro (chien) 188/90; gato (chat) 127/40; caballo (cheval) 103/ 32; burro (bourrique) 88/15; toro (taureau) 77/10; mosca (mouche) 72/18; mono (singe) 69/30; pájaro (oiseau) 64/14; gallina 56/22; **chancho** (porc) 0/54; mula 44/27; buey (boeuf) 43/22; pollo (poulet) 36/1; chivo (bouc) 35/10; pavo (dindon) 34/16; cabra (chèvre) 28/13; cangrejo (crabe) 21/8 ; loro (perroquet) 26/11; vaca (vache) 28/19 ; sapo (crapaud) 21/6 ; etc.
4.2. Dans le cas du français : cheval 38 ; chien 27 ; chat 26 ; cochon 20 ; vache 15 ; bête 14 ; loup 13 ; oiseau 10, âne 10 ; bœuf 9; lapin 9 ; mouche 9; papillon 9; papillon 8; poisson 6; canard 5 ; fourmi 5 ; bouc 4 ; chèvre 4 ; taureau 4 ; etc.

La première conclusion qui surgit si nous comparons les résultats des zoonymes les plus fréquents dans les EF des deux langues (voir tableaux 1 et 2) est que les animaux les plus fréquents sont les mêmes, mais dans le désordre. En espagnol : *perro* (chien) 188/90; *gato* (chat) 127/40; *caballo* (cheval) 103/ 32; en

Así por ejemplo el DDMexicanismos señala que la CVF *comer gente* (Censurar o hablar mal de las personas) se usa en México y el DdAm indica que se usa en Nicaragua y en Costa Rica. Lo mismo sucede con la CVF *ganarse los fríjoles* (Ganarse la vida) señalada también por el DDmexicanismos como mexicanismo mientras que el DdAm señala que su zona de influencia es Nicaragua, Cuba y Ecuador.

12 Nous indiquons dans chaque cas d'abord le nombre total de CVF et +a continuation le nombre de CVF hispanoaméricaines.

français : *cheval* 38 ; *chien* 27 ; *chat* 26. Si nous continuons à analyser les 20 zoonymes les plus fréquents dans les deux langues, nous observons :

5. que dans les deux langues les zoonymes les plus fréquents dans les BD sont dans le désordre: **perro** (chien); **gato** (chat); **caballo** (cheval); **burro** (bourrique); **toro** (taureau); **mosca** (mouche); **pájaro** (oiseau); **buey** (boeuf); **chivo** (bouc); **chancho** (porc); **cabra** (chèvre); **vaca** (vache) ; etc.
6. que les zoonymes espagnols qui suivent à continuation, n'apparaissent pas dans les 20 plus fréquents français : *mono* (singe); *gallina* (poule); *mula* (mule); *pollo* (poulet) ; **chancho** (porc); *pavo* (dindon); *cangrejo* (crabe); *loro* (perroquet); *sapo* (crapaud); etc.
7. que les zoonymes français qui suivent à continuation n'apparaissent pas dans les 20 plus fréquents en espagnol: *bête*; *loup*; *lapin*; *papillon*; *poisson* ; *canard* ; fourmi ; etc.

Il convient également de signaler qu'un même animal peut avoir plusieurs dénominations différentes.

C'est le cas par exemple de *cerdo* (cochon), *asno* (âne) en espagnol qui apparaissent sous les formes suivantes dans la BD espagnole.

8. cerdo : cerdo/a, chanchito/a, cochino/a, marrano/a, verraco.
9. asno : asno/a, borrico/a, burro/a.

Ce qui expliquerait pourquoi ces zoonymes n'apparaissent pas dans les plus fréquents en espagnol alors qu'ils apparaissent dans les zoonymes les plus fréquents en français.

5. Usages diatopique des EF

Nous voulons rappeler que la BD espagnole contient également des EF diatopiques. Il est important de le signaler, car par exemple le zoonyme *chancho* (dénomination hispanoaméricaine pour porc) apparaît dans 54 EF espagnole d'Amérique du Sud et n'apparaît dans aucune CVF de l'espagnol péninsulaire et ou commun..

L'analyse des 2500 EF espagnoles qui contiennent des zoonymes dans la BD de Frasytram, dévoile que 1200 EF ont une origine hispanoaméricaine (voir tableau nº 1), c'est donc dire l'ampleur du phénomène diatopique phraséologique.

Nous avons trouvés différentes possibilités d'usage géographique des zoonynmes dans les EF espagnoles.

5.1. Les zoonymes n'apparaissent que dans des EF appartenant à l'espagnol péninsulaire et/ou commun[13]. C'est le cas de: *almeja, animal, araña, ardilla, asno, atún, ave, avestruz, avispa, bacalao, ballena, besugo, borrego, borrico, cabestro, canario, cernícalo, chicharra, chinche, churra, cisne, cuervo, gorrión, jilguero, lapa, lechuza, lobo, lombriz, lorito, manso, marrano, mica, mirlo, mochuelo, moscón, mosquita, mosquito, musaraña, novillo, oca, oveja,* papagayo, *pingüino, pulpo, serpiente, urraca.*

5.2. Les zoonymes apparaissent avec des EF qui peuvent appartenir soit à l'espagnol péninsulaire soit à l'espagnol d'Amérique. *Abeja, águila, anguila, becerro, berraco, bestia, buey, buitre, burro/*a, *caballo, cabra, caimán, cangrejo, caracol, carnero, cerdo/*a, *chivo/*a, *chorlito, cigüeña, cochino, cocodrilo, cocodrilo, concha, conejo, cordero, cotorra, cucaracha, cucho, cuerno, culebra, elefante, erizo, escarabajo, fiera, foca, galápago, galgo, gallina, gallito, gallo, gamba, ganado, ganso, garrapata, garrobo, gatazo, grillo, grulla, guabina, gusanillo, gusano, haca, hormiga, ladilla, león, liebre, loro/*a, *mico, mono, mosca, mula, oso, pajarilla, pajarito, pájaro/*a, *paloma, pato/*a, *pavo/*a, *perdiz, perro/*a, *pescado, pez, piojo, polilla, pollo, puerco/*a, *pulga, rana, rata, ratón, sapo, sardina, tarántula, tigre, topo, toro*[14], *tortuga, trucha, vaca, venado,* víbora, *yegua, zorro/*a.

5.3. Les zoonymes n'apparaissent que dans des EF appartenant à l'espagnol d'Amérique.

Nous pouvons observer dans ce dernier cas, des zoonymes appartenant:

5.3.1. à l'espagnol[15]. *Alacrán, aura, babosa, bagre, bibijagua, bicho/a, boa, caball**ito**, cabr**illas**, cabr**ón**, camaléon, camarón, camaron**cito**, can, caracol**ito**, chanch**ito**, chanch**ita**, chancho, chimango, chita, chucho, cochin**ito**, culebrilla, gamo, garza, gato, gofio, guá, hormigu**ita**, iguana, jaba, jirafa, lagartija, lagarto, langosta, liendre, lince, loro, machito, macho, mime, pájar**ita**, perico, periqu**ito**, pichón, poll**ito**, puerqu**ito**, tití, tusa,.*

5.3.2. à des langues précolombines. *Chahuistle, chahuistle, cóndor, coyol, coyote, guajalote, guacama, huilota, jolote, nigua, ocote, papagote, surí, tlaconet, zanate, zope, zopilote.*

5.4. dans le cas du français la BD ne contient pas d'EF francophones, utilisées ou crées dans les territoires ou pays francophones.

---

13 Nous n'incluons dans ce relevé que les zoonymes avec au moins deux EF.

14 L'analyse des EF de l¡espagnol hispanoaméricain permet de trouver des usages féminins non admis dans les autres pays qui utilisent l'espagnol comme langue officielle.

15 Nous pouvons observer une certaine tendance, dans les EF de l'espagnol d'hispanoamérique, avec l'utilisation plus fréquente de suffixes dans les zoonymes. Peut-être pour rehausser l'expressivité des EF ? Par ex : caballito, cabrillas, camaroncito, caracolito, chanchito, cochinito, etc. Nous avons souligné en gras les zoonymes qui utilisent les suffixes.

Il faudrait comme nous avons montré dans le cas de l'espagnol réaliser une recherche visant à inclure dans une grande BD toutes les EF appartenant au monde de la francophonie linguistique. C'est le cas du projet BFQS qui analyse l'usage des UF dans 4 pays francophones (Belgique, France, Québec, Suisse) (voir Ladmiroy, 2010). Dans le cas du français de Côte d'Ivoire, la thèse de P.H Anoy: *Estudio sintáctico y semántico de las construcciones verbales fijas en francés de Costa de Marfil. Sus equivalencias en español y en francés*, contient quelques EF de Côte d'Ivoire, contenant des zoonymes. Par exemple: être un cabri mort (49, capII, IV), préparer un canari à qq'un (126, capIII), être un corbeau (au) beau corps (134, cap III, VIIII, IX); faire caiman (171, capIV, V); Voir le chat avaler la lune (183, Cap IV, VIII); avoir un canari (250, cap V); laisser pisser le cabri (374, cap VIII); avoir un rire d'hyène (391, cap VIII); vivre rienard (414, cap VIII); finir rienard (415, cap`VIII).

Dans le cas de langues comme l'espagnol, le français, l'anglais, etc, utilisées comme langues (co) officielles dans de nombreux pays, il faudrait donc signaler et ne pas oublier l'importance d'inclure dans les BD/dictionnaires les usages diatopiques.

6. Phénomènes à analyser

Nous sommes actuellement en train d'analyser la variation dans les EF de l'espagnol péninsulaire et de l'espagnol hispanoaméricain. (Mogorrón, 2020a, 2020b, 2020c).

Un des phénomènes qu'il convient d'analyser avec l'appui de la linguistique de corpus est celui de la variation en genre et en nombre des EF. L'analyse des termes utilisés dans les EF hispanoamericaines, a permis de trouver des variations très intéressantes en ce qui concerne le genre masculin ou féminin qui ne se produisent pas ou ne sont pas acceptées actuellement en Espagne.

Il s'agit de formes féminines du genre *estar como una tora*, *como una caballa, (*utilisées à Cuba*)* qui se sont formées à partir des formes canoniques des EF :

10. *estar como un toro* (RAE) / *être (fort) comme un bœuf.*
11. *estar como un caballo* (Cuba) / *être fort comme un bœuf.*

La tendance actuelle d'utiliser un langage plus féminisé est en train de faire apparaître des combinaisons qui transforme des mots épicènes masculins du genre (animal/animala, tipo/tipa). Dans les CVF espagnoles, le féminin de *toro* en espagnol est *vaca* est non *tora*. De même le féminin de *caballo* en espagnol est *Yegua*. Cependant la population cubaine dans la conversation parlée familière est en train d'utiliser ce genre de transformation plus égalitaires.

7. Conclusion

L'analyse de deux grandes bases de données de CVF espagnoles et françaises afin d'étudier et de comparer et de comparer le contenu zoonymique de chacune d'entre elles montre que les deux langues utilisent fréquemment les noms d'animaux dans le contenu lexical des CVF/EF. L'analyse de ce contenu zoonymique permet d'observer que les noms d'animaux les plus fréquents dans les deux langues sont les mêmes, quoique dans le désordre : à savoir chien, chat et cheval. Nous avons montré l'importance de relever, dans le cas des langues cofficielles dans de nombreux pays, les CVF/EF diatopiques étant donné l'ampleur du phénomène. Nous nous proposons dans une prochaine étude d'analyser la possibilité de variation en genre de nombreuses CVF/EF afin de permettre une utilisation actualisée et qui permette grâce à la linguistique de corpus et les nombreux exemples contextualisés qu'elle offre d'utiliser les expressions correctement.

Bibliographie

Anoy, Pierre Henri (2013): *Estudio sintáctico y semántico de las construcciones verbales fijas en francés de Costa de Marfil. Sus equivalencias en español y en francés*. Tesis doctoral. U. de Alicante.

Ladmiroy, B. (2010): Les expressions verbales figées de la francophonie. Gap-Paris: Ophrys.

Mogorrón Huerta, P. (2014): "Importancia (numérica) de las variantes diatópicas españolas y su tratamiento en los diccionarios", *Year Book of phraseology*, 5, pp. 123–144.

Mogorrón Huerta, P. (2020): "La polysémie dans les constructions verbales figées de l'espagnol", *LingVisticae Investigationes*, 43–2, pp. 241–264.

Mogorrón Huerta, P. (2020): "Análisis multidisciplinar del fenómeno de la variación fraseológica en traducción en interpretación", MONTI, SP 36–64.

Dictionnaires

AoMex. *Diccionario breve de mexicanismos* (2001): Guido Gómez de Silva. México: Academia Mexicana – Fondo de Cultura Económica.

DdAm. *Diccionario de americanismos* (2010): Asociación de Academias de la Lengua Española. Madrid: Santillana.

DRLE. *Diccionario de regionalismos de la lengua española* (1997): Cristina Echegoyen y Pablo Grosschmid. Barcelona: Editorial Juventud.

DUE. Moliner, M. (1999 [1977]): *Diccionario de uso del español, 2 tomos.* Madrid: Gredos.

Espasa. *Diccion@ario Espasa 2.0 Diccionario de la lengua española.* Diccionario de sinónimos y antónimos.

RAE. *Diccionario de la Real Academia.* Española (1992): (vigésimo primera edición), Madrid: Espasa-Calpe.

TLFI. *Trésor de la langue française informatisée*: http://atilf.atilf.fr/.

English / Italian

Virginia Pulcini

Università di Torino

The ordinal superlative in Italian and English: A morphosyntactic calque?[1]

Abstract: The article carries out a contrastive analysis between the morphosyntactic structure of the ordinal superlative form in Italian and in English. This pattern is considered an example of a morphosyntactic calque of English origin, imported into the Italian language. This study is based on descriptions and data provided by grammars, dictionaries and language corpora, in particular English Web 2020 and Italian Web 2020. The aim of this analysis is to observe the differences between these two languages in the syntactic construction of the complex noun phrase that characterises the ordinal superlative form, as well as the different semantic relations that are established among the elements of the phrases in the two languages.

Keywords: Language contact, morphosyntactic borrowing, Ordinal superlative.

1. Introduction

English is currently the main donor language for Italian, especially as regards the numerous lexical borrowings and, to a limited extent, phraseologisms and morphosyntactic calques. While lexical borrowings can be easily accepted and integrated into the context of the target language and often have a transitory nature (Pulcini, 2023), morphosyntactic calques can modify the norms of a language in a more profound and lasting way, so they are much more resistant to integration and rare as a phenomenon (Berruto, 2017). As a result of the interlinguistic contact at the morphosyntactic level, exogenous influence can introduce new structures into the target language (*innovation*) or more commonly reinforce ongoing changes within a linguistic system (*exploitation*) (Carlucci, 2017). According to Cerruti (2015), the new patterns that are recorded in contemporary

1 This paper is an adapted version of a paper published in Italian and entitled *La seconda montagna più alta del mondo.* Il superlativo relativo ordinale in inglese e in italiano (2022) In: Mollica Anthony, Onesti Cristina (eds.), *Studi in onore di Carla Marello*, Corciano (PG): GLU Distribuzione / Welland (ON): éditions Soleil publishing. inc., pp. 225–238.

Italian contribute to filling structural "gaps", or to reinforcing trends already underway, such as for example the prenominal placement of the adjective (which will be discussed below in relation to the pattern under investigation). Morphosyntactic calques, as well as lexical calques, can arise from "hasty" translations from English, the lingua franca par excellence of international communication. In any case, exogenous influence is part of the normal dynamics of change and modernization of every living language and represents an enrichment of its expressive potential, as we intend to demonstrate in this case study. The morphosyntactic structure analysed in this essay concerns the ordinal superlative. This structure involves the use of an ordinal with the function of pre-modifier of a superlative, as shown in the example *the second highest mountain in the world*. This pattern is often cited as an innovation of an exogenous nature in the Italian language, imported as a morphosyntactic calque from the English language (Cerruti, 2015).[2] The use of the ordinal superlative in Italian has increased in recent times, especially in specific registers like journalism, but is considered a new norm characterising neo-standard Italian (Berruto, 2013).

In this essay, examples of ordinal superlatives in English and in Italian will be compared, based on descriptions provided by grammars (Sect. 2) and on data extracted from dictionaries and corpora – in particular English Web 2020 and Italian Web 2020 (Sects. 3 and 4).[3] The goal of this analysis is to observe the differences between the two languages not only in the syntactic construction of the complex noun phrase that characterises the ordinal superlative, but also in the semantic relationships that are established between the constituents of the superlative phrases in the two languages.

---

2 Among other phenomena of morphosyntactic interference, Cerruti (2015: 398) mentions multiple interrogatives (e.g. *chi è chi, chi fa cosa*, ecc. / *who's who, who does what*, etc.), the phrase *grazie di/per / thank you for+* simple infinitive (e.g. *grazie di inviarmi i campioni richiesti / thank you for sending me the requested samples*), the double preposition attached to the same nominal phrase (e.g. *affascinato dalla, e invischiato nella, regola / fascinated by, and involved into, the rule*), the coordination of prepositions with the ellipsis of the related noun (e.g. *trasferire files da e verso il cellulare / transfer files from and to a mobile phone*); more generally, the presence of prepositions without the explicitly related element (eg. *vediamo chi vota per / let's see who votes for whom*).

3 Italian Web 2020 (itTenTen) and English Web 2020 (enTenTen) belong to the same family of text corpora retrieved from the web and available on the SketchEngine platform. Italian Web 2020 contains 12 billion words collected online between November 2019 and December 2020. English Web 2020 contains 36 billion words collected online between 2019 and 2021.

2. The superlative and the ordinal superlative

The superlative is a syntactic structure, whose function is to denote the quality (greater or lesser) of the referent with respect to a larger group of similar referents, as illustrated in example (1):

(1) Everest is *the highest mountain in the world* / L'Everest è *la montagna più alta del mondo*

In the definition given by Serianni (2000: 150),

> Il grado superlativo esprime il massimo livello possibile di intensificazione della qualità posseduta, in relazione ad altre grandezze, persone, cose (superlativo *relativo*), oppure in senso assoluto (superlativo *assoluto*).
> [The superlative degree expresses the highest possible level of intensification of the possessed quality, in relation to other dimentions, people, things (*relative* superlative), or in an absolute sense (*absolute* superlative).]

With reference to the Italian language, Serianni adds that in the relative superlative it is essential to compare a referent with a set of similar elements, which must necessarily be more than two. In the absence of a broader term of comparison, a sentence can be ambiguous, as in the case of example (2) which can be interpreted both as a comparative, i.e. "Everest is the higher mountain (between two)" and as a superlative, i.e. "Everest is the highest mountain of all".

(2) L'Everest è *la montagna più alta* [Everest is *the higher / highest mountain*]

In Italian the noun phrase containing the superlative (*la montagna più alta / the highest mountain*) is composed of "article+noun+superlative" and is generally followed by a prepositional phrase that indicates the term of comparison (*nel mondo / in the world*). The latter, when expressed, contains the preposition "di" (of) in simple or complex form ("del" / of the) according to the gender and number of the nominal element. Other simple or complex prepositions can be "in" (in), "a" (of), "fra" (among), depending on the context of the sentence and on the term of reference.

In English the model is similar, with a few morphosyntactic differences, as shown in example (3):

(3) Everest is *the highest mountain in the world*

First of all, the superlative adjective (*highest*) is placed in prenominal position, since English is a language that tends to pre-modify, so that the structure is "article + superlative + noun" (*the highest mountain*). Furthermore, while in Italian the superlative degree is obtained by adding a definite article before the comparative adjective (*più alta < la più alta*), in English the superlative adjective (*highest)* is morphologically different from the comparative (*higher*). Owing to this difference, in English the comparative and the superlative forms cannot be confused (as noted in example 2 in Italian). Hence example (4) is a superlative form, not a comparative one, though lacking a term of reference.

(4) Everest is *the highest mountain*

Finally, the prepositional phrase indicating the broader group of referents, when it is expressed, is introduced by "in", or in other cases by "on" or "of", depending on the context of the sentence and the specific terms.

The ordinal superlative in English is obtained by introducing an ordinal number in pre-modifying position. In this way, a superlative quality is attributed to the referent and ordered with respect to a broader range of referents; for example, when talking about the highest peaks in the world, after the highest one of all, we could list the other peaks that appear to be in second, third, etc. position, as in examples (4) and (5):

(4) K2 is *the second highest mountain in the world*
(5) Kangchenjunga is *the third highest mountain in the world*

In the description of the superlative form in English provided by Huddleston and Pullum (2002), its interpretation is conceived in a scalar way, i.e. comparing the members of a category (e.g. high mountains) and focusing on the "first" element in the ranking (or the "last" in the case of a minority superlative). This cognitive aspect is very important to understand the difference between the two languages. In fact, in English the use of an ordinal number does not clash with the hierarchical vision of all the elements involved in the comparison; in fact, it is logical and complementary. As Huddleston and Pullum (2002: 1169–1170) state: "The ordinal numerals indicate position in a rank ordering, counting from the top or from the bottom, in the case of comparison of inferiority, as in *the third least expensive model*".

The order of the elements of the ordinal structure in English is "article+ ordinal+superlative+noun". The superlative can be formed synthetically (*highest*) or analytically for the adjectives that require it (e.g. *least/most expensive*). In minority superlatives, the adjective is always analytically modified by *least* (e.g. *the least important*), as happens in Italian (e.g. *il/la meno importa*nte).

In the English language the massive presence of pre-modifiers in a noun phrase is very common. In a sequence of pre-modifiers of the noun head of a phrase, the norm imposes a hierarchical order which places the definite article in first position (deictic function in the utterance), followed by the numeral (quantity indicator), one or more epithets (indicators of quality) and a classifier (indicator of subtype) (Halliday, 2014). For greater clarity, if the noun phrase in example (5) contained the adjective *volcanic*, this should be placed immediately before the nominal head as a classifier, and the order of the elements would therefore be the following: *the* (deictic) *third* (numeral) *highest* (qualifier) *volcanic* (classifier) *mountain* (head). In the experiential model of the English noun phrase, the quantity indicator (numeral) is more specific and "definitive" than the quality indicator (qualifier), and for this reason it is placed before it. In fact, "An ordinal is a kind of superlative cardinal: *third* = 'three-est', i.e. identified by being at number three." (Halliday, 2014: 381).[4]

The use of the ordinal numeral in the superlative structure is a rather common phenomenon in the English language and probably a very old one, too. Performing a full-text search in the *Oxford English Dictionary*, it is possible to find numerous instances of this pattern in the formulation of definitions, as in examples (6), (7) and (8) and in quotations (9) and (10), respectively of the entries *salutatory* and *overtrawl*. In examples (8) and (10) the ordinal and the superlative (*second-highest*) are graphically linked by a hyphen, confirming the mutual relationship and the strong semantic link between these two elements.

(6) **alto**, *n.*[2] and *adj.* **1.** In polyphonic music: the *second highest* of the four parts, occupying a range below the soprano and above the tenor

(7) **junior varsity**, *n.* and *adj.* The *second highest* classification of school or university sport, ranking after first or varsity; a team having this classification.

(8) **simple majority** *n. (a)* (originally) a majority comprising more than half of all votes cast; an absolute majority; *(b)* (in later use also) a majority in which the highest number of votes cast for any one candidate, issue, etc., exceeds the *second-highest* number, while not comprising more than half of all votes cast; a plurality.

(9) 1947 E. A. Kaump *High School Commencement Bk.* (rev. ed.) 93 The Salutatory address is another honor speech..given by the student who makes the *second highest* average during the high school years.

4 The hierarchical order of the elements of a noun phrase is the object of very careful analysis in the English language, given its complexity. Starting from the concept that greater proximity to the head of the phrase implies greater specificity of the modifier element, Huddleston and Pullum (2002: 453) quote a case of complex pre-modification: "an attractive tight-fitting brand-new pink Italian lycra women's swimsuit", based on the following order: "evaluative > general property > age > colour > provenance > manufacture > type."

(10) 1994 *Sunday Times* (Nexis) 31 July The Italian market has been over-trawled in the past few months. Italians are the *second-highest* saving people on earth..but even they look close to being swamped by the issuing of corporate paper worth 26,000 billion lire..this year.

Checking back throughout the centuries in the English Historical Book Collection (1473–1800) corpus, available on the SketchEngine platform, it is possible to find combinations of ordinal superlatives such as *the second highest*, *the second greatest*, *the third greatest*, etc.. Numerous cases can be observed dating back to Early Modern English and later centuries, a small sample of which are quoted in (11), (12), (13), (14) and (15). It can be noted that already in the past the superlative form of the adjective could be formed both in a synthetic way (adjective + -est) or in an analytical one (most + adjective). The element indicating the wider reference is often missing, since it can be guessed from the context of the sentence, and sometimes is introduced by the preposition "of".

(11) then came to embrase him swéetly the infant Philocrista and Esquiuela her companion, who could not tell what countenance to make for the extreame ioy shée felt in her mind, hauing before her eies *the second highest hope of her heart*: and albeit she did all she might to dissemble it, she was constrained notwithstanding in the end to fill the eares of the assistants with these spéeches: (*The deligtful [sic] history of Celestina the faire*. English Historical Book Collection)

(12) To him that putteth in *the third greatest* number, 300 Crownes.

(13) Oswestre, named thus, and occasioned from Oswald, *the second most Christian king of Northumberland*, slaine here in a blooddy battaile by Penda, king of the Mercians, reputed a Saint, & Martyr by the people of that devouter age, honouring the place with their frequent pilgrimages.

(14) *The third most Southerne River in comp ssing Guiana*, is that of Amazon, so called (not as some have conjectured, for that the Women have killed, or expelled the Males, not admitting any society with t em, but onely for one moneth, in the yeare, for the continuance of Procreation, but because both Male and Female, usually go in long hair hanging downe below their .)

(15) *The second most important object*, for the good of Society, is those rules for the regulation of mankind in their relative situation, which, in their operation, will tend to harmonize the conduct of mankind towards each other.

Surprisingly for an English speaker, the use of the ordinal numeral in the construct with the superlative is new in contemporary Italian.[5] Furthermore, as Berruto (2013: 54) explains, the ordinal superlative represents an "anomalous" use from a logical point of view, as "in italiano un superlativo relativo dovrebbe identificare per definizione un'entità unica, in quanto quella che presenta in massimo grado la proprietà superlativizzata" [in Italian a relative superlative should by definition identify a single entity, i.e. the one presenting the highest degree of the superlative property]. The presence of an ordinal associated with a superlative is in conflict with this rule, as it implies that the property indicated by the superlative does not have a single referent, but more than one or many.

However, it can be argued that the alleged anomaly of the ordinal superlative in Italian concerns only the grammatical norm, but not the logic of the concept expressed. In fact, in Italian it is possible to place the referent on a scale (for example, in second place) with respect to a certain quality, as for example in sentence (16), which represents the "standard" form, in which the superlative is not used, in compliance with the grammatical rule, but is implicit with respect to the logical content of the sentence itself.

(16) Il K2 è *la seconda montagna* del mondo in altezza (see [20] below)

Examples (17) e (18), which are also grammatically acceptable in standard Italian, imply a ranking order in the altitude of the mountains that are compared.

(17) Il K2 è *la seconda tra le montagne più alte* del mondo (see [21] below)
(18) Il K2 è *la montagna più alta del mondo* dopo l'Everest (see [22] below)

In example (18) the grammatical norm of Italian is respected but not the logic of the superlative, which should refer to a "single entity". On the contrary, the clause indeed indicates that the highest mountain of all is Everest, followed by K2 in second position.

The new "English-inspired" pattern (example 19), which combines an ordinal with a superlative, expresses exactly the same content as (16), (17) and (18), although it is considered "anomalous" in Italian grammar and is labelled as a morphosyntactic calque.

(19) Il K2 è *la seconda montagna più alta* del mondo

---

5 A search in Google Books allowed us to antedate the occurrence of the phrase *la seconda montagna più alta del mondo* to 1893, in an entry of *Supplemento alla sesta edizione dell'Enciclopedia italiana* by S. Pagliani (Torino, Unione Tipografico-editrice Milano-Roma-Napoli). Further 19th century results always relate to geographic contexts.

Observing this "new" structure carefully, it can be noted that, in contrast to English, in the Italian construct the superlative is placed after the noun, in compliance with the tendency to place an adjective of the [+predicative] and [+ intersective] type (Cerruti, 2015) like *alto* in postnominal position (*la montagna è alta / una montagna alta*),[6] whereas the ordinal is placed in prenominal position. Word order appears to indicate that in Italian there is a syntactic attraction between the ordinal and the noun (*seconda montagna*), whereas in English there is a syntactic attraction between the ordinal and the superlative (*the second highest*), a tendency that is further confirmed by the fact that the elements can be orthographically linked with a hyphen (*second-highest*), as noted above.[7] It can be argued that the different syntactic order in the two languages may lead to a different cognitive representation of the referential content of the utterance. In Italian the focus of the ordinal appears to be on the referent (la seconda *montagna*), while in English the focus is placed on the superlative quality (the second *highest*). As will be shown later, the use of the superlative placed before the noun in the Italian language (modelled on English word order) is anyway quite frequent, but less common.

Turning to English, we may say that its fixed word order does not exclude the use of forms that are similar to Italian examples (16), (17) and (18), as shown in examples (20), (21) e (22), which are grammaticaly acceptable:

(20) K2 is *the second mountain in the world in altitude*
(21) K2 is *the second among the highest mountains in the word*
(22) K2 is *the highest mountain in the world* after Everest

However, placing an adjective after a noun cannot be considered acceptable in English from a grammatical point of view:

(23) *K2 is the second mountain highest in the world

6 The [+intersective] value of an adjective concerns its semantic property. Indeed, the adjective *alto* (high) denotes a quality that is shared by a mountain as well as by many other referents. In this specific case, with the prenominal collocation (*alta montagna*) the adjective would acquire a semantically different value, that is, it would denote an area geographically located at high altitudes.

7 According to Huddleston and Pullum (2002) ordinals and superlatives are "early pre-head modifiers" and are mandatorily placed in that order before any other modifier. In Italian, instead, the rule applies only to the ordinal, which is always placed before the noun, but not to the superlative, which is usually postponed.

Finally in English it is possible to add a possessive "genitive" (*the world's*) to the complex pre-modifying pattern (example 24), creating an even more compact phrasal structure, an option that is not grammatically acceptable in Italian (example 25):

(24) K2 is *the world's second highest mountain*
(25) *Il K2 è la del mondo seconda più alta montagna.

3. Contrastive analysis

The discussion so far has been largely based on the information provided by grammars and on personal expertise in the use of the superlative construct in the two languages. In order to carry out an analysis based on authentic and recent data, we extracted concordances of the patterns *K2 is the second* and *K2 è la seconda* from the English Web 2020 and Italian Web 2020 language corpora, respectively. These corpora are large enough to provide results for such specific searches. The choice was dictated by the need to find occurrences of ordinal superlatives with a feminine gender referent, since the options for Italian could be between *montagna*, *vetta* or *cima*.[8] Despite the limited number of results (7 for English and 11 for Italian), these allowed us to observe some important differences between the two languages, supporting what grammars describe.

The 7 occurrences of *K2 is the second* (Fig. 1) confirm the rigid syntactic order of the English noun phrase, namely "article+ ordinal+superlative+noun". The recurrent use of the word mountain (as opposed to the possible synonym *peak*) and the alternation between the adjectives *high* and *tall* can be noted. In English *high* and *tall* are almost synonymous, but the adjective *high*, in addition to the extension in height, expresses importance and authority, and is probably preferable in this context, while the adjective *tall* also indicates height in people and things.

---

8 The same structure in the masculine gender *il K2 è il secondo* (*monte*) did not yield any results.

Left context	KWIC	Right context
out of the yards and did everything it could do to get away.'</s><s>(	K2 is the second	highest mountain in the world).</s><s>In the early part of his career Not
s out on.</s><s>Located between the border of china and Pakistan,	K2 is the second	tallest mountain in the world.</s><s>'Mountain of mountains' is what Re
l ski descents of K2 died</s><s>At 8,611 meters, or 28,251 feet tall,	K2 is the second	highest mountain in the world, just below Everest.</s><s>Only 417 peop
us structures apart from the Eiffel Tower in Paris."</s><s>At 8611m,	K2 is the second	tallest mountain in the world and widely regarded as a much more daunt
the most dangerous with 41 per cent mortality.</s><s>3.</s><s>K2	K2 is the second	highest mountain in the world.</s><s>It's easy to climb Kilimanjaro, but
died this month trying to climb it.</s><s>At 28,251 ft (8,611 meters),	K2 is the second	highest mountain on this planet, and is technically a much more difficult
ntinue reading →</s><s>Standing 8611 meters (28,251 ft) in height,	K2 is the second	tallest mountain on the planet, but it just might be the toughest to climb.

Fig. 1. Concordances of the phrase *K2 is the second* followed by a superlative

Among the 11 occurrences of *K2 è la seconda*, 7 cases contain the superlative, including 6 with the order "article+ ordinal+ noun+superlative" (Fig. 2). Only in one case does the order of the items mirror that of English, with the ordinal and superlative preceding the head (*K2 è la seconda più alta montagna sulla Terra dopo l'Everest*). A greater lexical variety to indicate the referent is worth noting – *summit*, *mountain*, *peak* – while the adjective *high* remains constant.

Left context	KWIC	Right context
Tue, 10 Jan 2017 00:00:00 +0100	K2 è La seconda	montagna più alta del mondo dopo l'Everest.</s><s>Di una bellezza ac
>Nessuno prima di loro era riuscito in una impresa del genere.</s><s>Il	K2 è la seconda	cima più alta del mondo, dopo l'Everest, ma è la più difficile da scalare).
sti trecento metri sotto la vetta della montagna venerdì mattina.</s><s>Il	K2 è la seconda	vetta più alta del mondo (8.611 metri) dopo l'Everest, si trova nel grupp
i giorno la vita, e grazie perché fate cultura.</s><s>Prodotti K2</s><s>Il	K2 è la seconda	vetta più alta sulla faccia della terrà con i suoi oltre 8.600 metri di altitud
isite da parte delle associazioni umanitarie.</s><s>Con i suoi 8611 m, il	K2 è la seconda	montagna più alta della Terra dopo l'Everest, ma tenendo conto di altez
pia che contrappone la Sterlina... leggi tutto →</s><s>Ambientazione "Il	K2 è la seconda	vetta più alta del mondo (dopo il Monte Everest) con un'altitudine di 861
stato il peggior singolo incidente nella storia del K2 alpinistico.</s><s>Il	K2 è la seconda	più alta montagna sulla Terra dopo l'Everest con una quota massima di

Fig. 2. Concordances of the phrase *il K2 è la seconda* followed by a superlative

The 4 remaining cases express the same concept without the use of a superlative (Fig. 3):

Left context	KWIC	Right context
e e, qualora... _OMISSIS_ ......</s><s>Abstract: Con i suoi 8611 metri il	K2 è la seconda	montagna della Terra, nonché la più irraggiungibile.</s><s>Quattro
<s>La spedizione guidata da Ardito Desio era giunta vicina alla meta : il	K2 è la seconda	cima del mondo dopo l'Everest ma è certamente al primo posto per
ti salendo per lo Sperone degli Abruzzi.</s><s>Con i suoi 8611 metri, il	K2 è la seconda	vetta del mondo.</s><s>Dopo settimane di attesa forzata per il brutt
classifiche internazionali (ora è sceso al secondo posto, proprio come il	K2 è la seconda	montagna della terra) richiede perseveranza, preparazione e determ

Fig. 3. Concordances of *il K2 è la seconda* without the superlative

4. Use and frequency of the ordinal superlative in Italian and English

A further interesting finding in the comparison between Italian and English with respect to the ordinal superlative is its use and frequency. For this purpose, the phrases *is the second* for English and *è il secondo / è la seconda* for Italian have been extracted from the two reference corpora. In order to obtain occurrences of ordinal superlatives, a positive filter was applied: for English the search was limited to phrases containing *in the world*; for Italian the search was run including the words *più* (to retrieve a superlative), *al*, *del*, *nel* and *mondo*, to retrieve all possibile options with prepositional phrases. The data show that the frequency order of the prepositional patterns are *al mondo*, *del mondo* and *nel mondo*. The overall data for the masculine gender (*è il secondo*) are slightly more frequent than the feminine ones (*è la seconda*).

The most surprising finding of this specific search concerns the frequency of the ordinal superlative in the two languages, which turns out to be almost the same: for English we obtained the frequency of 0.14/million, while for Italian, adding up all the masculine and feminine occurrences with the various prepositions, the value was 0.13/million. Since Italian scholars consider the ordinal superlative structure a novelty in contemporary Italian, we may claim that its spread has been extremely fast, reaching the frequency of the same pattern in a language where the ordinal superlative has existed for al least five centuries.[9] The assimilation of the ordinal superlative in Italian that emerges from our data is also corroborated by surveys of perceptions by educated speakers of

9 In an article published in the special web section entitled "Consulenza linguistica" [Linguistic Consulting] of the *Accademia della Crusca*, the Italian Language Academy, the alleged 'unstoppable' use of the relative superlative is discussed in connection with the Italian phrase *di sempre*, with the meaning of 'of all time/ever', especially in advertising and newspaper headlines; an example is "Temo l'elezione più caotica di sempre" [I fear the most chaotic election of all time/ever] (Repubblica.it, 19.12.2014). The phrase *di sempre* is considered to be modelled on English *ever* which, in comparatives and superlatives, emphasises the comparison with the past and the future (e.g. *better than ever* corresponding to *migliore di prima*; *the best ever* corresponding to *il migliore in assoluto*). This article also meantions the recent introduction of an ordinal with the phrase *di sempre*, in particular in the context of sports news (e.g. "terza prestazione mondiale *di sempre*" [the third world performance ever] Repubblica 24.7.1988), spreading to other contexts beyond sport where rankings are referred to. <https://accademiadellacrusca.it/it/consulenza/la-crusca-%C3 %A8-laccademia-italiana-pi%C3 %B9-longeva-di-sempre/1174>

Italian, who find it entirely acceptable and even preferable to the "standard" one (Berruto, 2017: 48–49).

With respect to the frequency of the pattern "il secondo+nome+più+aggettivo" / "la seconda+nome+più+aggettivo", which is considered more in line with the syntactic order of Italian than the pattern "il secondo più+aggettivo+nome" / "la seconda più+aggettivo+nome", the data indicate that the latter structure is used in 23.5 % of the concordance strings analysed. The influence of the "Anglicizing" order is therefore incipient but already relevant.

Another point of interest concerns the domains of use (Table 1). Considering that the reference corpora contain texts taken from the web, the domains mainly reflect geographic/tourist, economic and computer contexts, as can be inferred from the most frequent referents: *country*, *producer*, *market*, *city*, *language*, *company*, *exporter*, *cause* etc. for English; *paese*, *sito*, *produttore*, *motore di ricerca*, *lingua*, *città*, *bevanda*, *industria*, etc. for Italian. The superlative adjectives are also very similar in the two languages: *largest*, *biggest*, *highest*, *oldest*, *longest*, *most popular*, *most populous*, *most spoken*, etc. in English; *più grande*, *più vecchio*, *più visitato*, *più alto*, etc. for the masculine adjectives, *più grande*, *più inquinante*, *più parlata*, *più diffusa*, etc. for the feminine adjectives in Italian.

In this article no examples containing both the ordinal and the superlative are given. However, a search in the Italian Web 2020 yielded 63 occurrences of the pattern *seconda migliore … di sempre*, in which the word *prestazione* appears to be the most common collocate (e.g. "La finale di Parigi fu la 14a finale vinta consecutivamente da Nadal, seconda migliore prestazione di sempre dopo le 24 finali di Federer." [The Paris final was the 14th consecutive final won by Nadal, the second performance ever after the 24 finals won by Federer])

Table 1: Frequency of the patterns with an ordinal superlative in English and Italian.

search phrase	**English Web 2020**	**superlative adjectives**	**referents**	**examples**
is the second… in the world	6.180 0,14/m.	largest, biggest, highest, oldest, longest, most popular, most populous, most spoken, tallest, leading, fastest, most common, most populated, best, smallest, richest, most traded, busiest	country, producer, market, city, language, company, exporter, cause, economy, language, religion, manufacturer, consumer, lake, building, industry, nation	Canada is the second largest country in the world. India is the second biggest producer of fruits and vegetables in the world. Beer is the second most popular drink in the world – right after water and tea.
search phrase	Italian Web 2020	superlative adjectives	referents	examples
è il secondo… più… al/del/nel/mondo	al mondo 542 0,04/m. del mondo 357 0,02/m. nel mondo 69 0,01/m.	grande, vecchio, visitato, alto, diffuso, ricco, esteso, popoloso, antico, lungo, importante, venduto	paese, sito, produttore, motore di ricerca, edificio, pesce, parco, lago, mestiere, vulcano	Il Canada è il secondo paese più grande del mondo, solo dietro la Russia. Youtube è il secondo sito più visitato al mondo, proprio dopo Google. L'Italia è il secondo Paese più vecchio nel mondo, dopo il Giappone e il primo in Europa.

(continued)

Table 1: Continued

search phrase	English Web 2020	superlative adjectives	referents	examples
è la seconda... più... al/del/ nel/mondo	al mondo 421 0,03/m. del mondo 254 0,02/m. nel mondo 83 0,01	grande, inquinante, parlata, diffusa, consumata, alta, bevuta, utilizzata, antica, lunga, bella, comune, diffusa, importante, popolare	lingua, città, bevanda, industria, forma, nazione, spezia, economia, capitale, isola, montagna, causa, lingua, forma, malattia, compagnia	La moda è la seconda industria più inquinante al mondo. Tokyo, letteralmente la capitale orientale, è la seconda capitale più grande del mondo dopo Pechino. Secondo un rapporto pubblicato dall'Istituto Cervantes lo spagnolo è la seconda lingua più parlata del mondo dopo il cinese.

5. Conclusion

Mountain lovers are generally well acquainted with the characteristics of the major peaks conquered by great mountaineers and certainly possess in their expressive repertoire the resources to talk not only about the highest peak of all, but also about the other peaks that are less high but no less challenging and risky to reach. In addition to the mountain context, there are innumerable areas in which it is useful to be able to attribute qualities of superlative degree to specific referents and place them in scalar order.

In the English language, the interpretation of the superlative arises from the comparison between members of a category; moreover, the use of an ordinal together with a superlative is logical, as well as grammatically acceptable. In contrast, the Italian language does not allow for the use of an ordinal with a relative superlative, although it has alternative forms for expressing a superlative property in relation to other referents. The increasing use of the ordinal superlative in Italian is a case of *exploitation* of a morphosyntactic construct that is very common in the English language and particularly useful for its compactness and economy, which certainly enriches the expressive potential of the Italian language.

As for its novelty, it has been verified that the ordinal superlative was already used in Italian texts in the past centuries, although whether or not these sporadic attestations were modelled on translations from English needs to be verified. What emerges from the comparable data extracted from the reference corpora is that the use of the ordinal superlative appears to be rapidly increasing in contemporary Italian and it can now be considered fully assimilated. Another interesting finding is that the ordinal superlative is used in specific areas of discourse, preferably in texts of a geographic and tourist nature for the description of towns, cities, lakes, parks, mountains, buildings, etc. Starting from this privileged domain, the use of the ordinal superlative has extended to scientific popularization to journalism and finally to everyday language to describe and compare the "superlative" qualities of our contemporary reality.

References

Accademia della Crusca <https://accademiadellacrusca.it/> (December 2022).

Berruto, Gaetano (2013): "Che lingua fa? Alcune riflessioni sullo standard e sul neo-standard" In Raffaella Bombi (a cura di) *Manuale di comunicazione istituzionale e internazionale*. Roma: Il Calamo, pp. 45–67.

Berruto, Gaetano (2017): "What is changing in Italian today? Phenomena of restandardization in syntax and morphology: An overview." In Massimo Cerruti, Claudia Crocco & Stefania Marzo (eds.), *Towards a new standard. Theoretical and empirical studies on the restandardization of Italian*. Berlin: De Gruyter Mouton, pp. 31–60.

Carlucci, Alessandro (2017): "English influences in contemporary Italian: Innovation or exploitation?". *Modern Language Review*, 112: 381–396.

Cerruti, Massimo (2015): "La collocazione prenominale dei sintagmi aggettivali complessi nell'italiano contemporaneo. Il contatto linguistico come 'rinforzo' di una possibilità del sistema" In Carlo Consani (a cura di) *Contatto interlinguistico tra presente e passato*. Milano: LED, pp. 397–420.

English Historical Book Collection. <www.sketchengine.eu> (December 2022).

English Web 2020 (EnTenTen2020). <www.sketchengine.eu> (December 2022).

Italian Web 2020 (itTenTen2020). <www.sketchengine.eu> (December 2022).

Halliday Michael, A. K. (2014): *Halliday's introduction to functional grammar*. Revised by Christian M.I.M. Matthiessen. London: Routledge.

Huddleston, Rodney & Geoffrey K. Pullum (2002): *The Cambridge grammar of the English language*. Cambridge: Cambridge University Press.

Oxford English Dictionary <www.oed.com> (December 2022).

Pulcini, Virginia (2023): *The influence of English on Italian. Lexical and cultural features.* Berlin: Mouton De Gruyter.

Serianni, Luca (2000): *Italiano: grammatica, sintassi, dubbi.* Milano: Garzanti.

Latin / French / English

Amanda Roig-Marín

Universidad de Alicante

Nueva aproximación al uso de palabras inglesas en textos administrativos en latín medieval

Resumen: Este capítulo ahondará en el estudio de las palabras procedentes del inglés medio en documentos producidos en latín medieval, en particular, en textos administrativos como cuentas o inventarios. Ofreceremos una visión panorámica sobre los rasgos lingüísticos más distintivos de este tipo de producción que aquí clasificaremos como *transligue* y entre los que cabe destacar el uso del artículo definido de origen francés, no existente en latín, la presencia de morfemas que se pueden interpretar como pertenecientes a varias lenguas de forma simultánea y el uso de abreviaturas o marcas de suspensión que permiten una ambigüedad taxonómica del material al que acompaña. Concluiremos haciendo alusión a un área todavía poco explorada como es la dimensión dialectal de este tipo de producción textual híbrida.

Palabras clave: multilingüismo, Inglaterra medieval, lexicología, lexicografía, préstamos

1. Introducción. El estudio de textos multilingües históricos y contemporáneos

Una pregunta recurrente en el estudio de textos en latín medieval pero con una notable presencia de voces cuyo origen son las lenguas vernáculas es taxonómica: cómo clasificar tipológicamente este material y a qué lengua o lenguas adscribirlo. Como intentaremos demostrar a lo largo de este capítulo, los escribas encargados de la producción de estos textos tenían un amplio repertorio híbrido en el cual las barreras lingüísticas que hoy rigen nuestra concepción de las lenguas como entidades independientes no son extrapolables. El contexto que aquí nos ocupa, la Inglaterra tardomedieval, viene marcado por la presencia de, al menos, tres lenguas: el inglés medio, el anglonormando (o anglofrancés como actualmente se hace alusión a la variedad de francés empleada en Inglaterra) y el latín medieval o postclásico (si lo consideramos de forma amplia para englobar el periodo moderno temprano). Es preciso señalar que a menudo se prefiere referirse al vocabulario de las lenguas vernáculas como "vernáculo" (*vernacular*), sin hacer distinciones entre si es inglés medio o anglo-francés. Ello, se debe a que, como indica Rothwell (1991: 174), "la relación entre el anglo-francés y el inglés medio era de fusión, no de préstamo" y en ocasiones resulta complejo determinar si el vocabulario en cuestión es francés o inglés. En esta línea, Durkin (2014) apunta cómo muchos académicos que han pasado tiempo trabajando con documentos como los que aquí nos ocupan han adoptado la postura de pensar que los propios hablantes no siempre distinguían claramente lo que constituía vocabulario en "inglés" y "francés" como entidades separadas. La pregunta es ahora, pues, desde cuándo los investigadores se han interesado por la lengua de este tipo de textos.

Ya a principios del siglo XX, algunos historiadores advirtieron en sus publicaciones la presencia de palabras inglesas en documentación administrativa escrita en latín medieval. Hone (1906), unos de primeros estudiosos de estos textos, señalaría que "el repertorio en latín del contable le había fallado" (1906: 203).[1] Hone (1906), como historiador, tenía un propósito radicalmente distinto al de los filólogos, lo que puede ayudarnos a comprender esta explicación reduccionista. El uso de la lengua estaba alejado de su área de trabajo, centrada en el contenido histórico o socioeconómico: la información que estos documentos nos proporcionan sobre la maquinaria administrativa del país en tiempos pre-modernos. No obstante, más allá de la investigación de tipo histórico, las connotaciones negativas tradicionalmente asociadas al término *macarrónico*, de uso extendido, reflejaban una posición sesgada al clasificar y tratar textos que combinaban el latín con lenguas vernáculas como el francés o el inglés.

Treinta años después de la publicación de Hone, encontramos el primer estudio, de carácter filológico, acometido por Hulbert (1936). Hulbert publicó un artículo con un extenso glosario que recogía las palabras en inglés presentes en registros señoriales (*manorial records*) de los siglos XIII y XIV de la colección archivística de la Universidad de Chicago. En su estudio, señalaba cómo el *Diccionario de Oxford* (la primera versión del *Oxford English Dictionary* (*OED*)) o bien no incluía registros de muchas de las palabras halladas en los documentos administrativos medievales que escrudiñó, o bien las primeras citas databan del siglo XVIII o XIX (cf. Hulbert, 1936: 38). Ello se debe a que estas palabras no aparecían en los textos literarios coetáneos que el *OED* usó como base y, por tanto, no había ejemplos de las mismas hasta siglos después. El corpus que subyace al *OED* no ha dejado de crecer desde entonces, un proceso que sigue todavía en marcha como parte de la tercera edición de este diccionario (*OED3*).

1 Todas las traducciones del inglés citadas en este capítulo son propias.

En línea con el valor que se les otorgó a estos textos en la publicación del pionero Hulbert (1936), aquella visión simplista a la que hemos hecho alusión progresivamente dio paso a un reconocimiento, prácticamente unánime, sobre la importancia de todo tipo de evidencia textual para mejorar nuestra comprensión del multilingüismo medieval en el tramado social y cultural de la época. En consonancia con ello, nació un creciente interés por textos que combinan más de una lengua en su producción, analizados como testimonios de las realidades políglotas de la época. En el contexto de la Inglaterra medieval, así lo demuestran monografías como las editadas por Trotter (2000), Schendl y Wright (2011), y Pahta, Skaffari y Wright (2018), en las que se analiza una gran variedad de géneros textuales, desde textos administrativos, como los que constituyen el principal objeto de estudio del presente capítulo, a médicos.

Autores como Wright (1994, 1996, 1998, 2002) y Alcolado Carnicero (2013, 2015, 2017, 2018, 2019) se centraron en material administrativo y estudiaron los archivos de *the London Bridge Accounts* (entre otros) y *the Wardens' Accounts of the Mercers' Company*, respectivamente. Concluyeron que el sistema de escritura híbrido al que se refieren como "*mixed-language system*" habría empezado a sufrir un deterioro a partir de la década de 1370, proceso que habría culminado con una anglización completa de la lengua alrededor del año 1480, coincidiendo con el auge del inglés estándar (cf. Wright, 2018: 339). No obstante, hay cuentas que conservan el latín de forma consistente: por ejemplo, *the Inventories and Account Rolls of the Benedictine House or Cell of Jarrow* (tratados en Roig-Marín, 2018) demuestran que el latín postclásico se siguió empleando hasta bien entrado el siglo XVI, momento en el que acaban los registros. De no haberse dado esta interrupción (en 1536 se disolvieron las casas monásticas cuyas ganancias anuales fueran menores a 200 libras), podría ser que el uso del latín hubiera pervivido en este ámbito más allá de esta fecha, lo que daría indicios de una tradición arraigada de la propia comunidad religiosa, no sujeta a los devenires de las estructuras gubernamentales centrales.

El tomar como punto de partida textos escritos en latín, en lugar de en inglés o en francés como se ha hecho en estudios filológicos clásicos, nos permite comprender mejor las posibles rutas de entrada al inglés de un gran número de lexías que, tal y como se indica en el *OED*, su origen sólo se puede clasificar como "múltiple". En los casos relativamente menos complejos (implicando dos lenguas), a menudo los étimos directos se encuentran tanto en anglo-francés como en latín medieval, y precisamente estos textos reflejan la variación morfo-ortográfica que a menudo es empleada para decantarse taxonómicamente por una lengua u otra. Esta determinación del punto de acceso directo a la lengua inglesa (a menudo, a través del francés o del latín medieval), pese a ser una cuestión pertinente, no es central al presente estudio.

Otra clasificación que ha preocupado a los investigadores es la distinción entre préstamos y cambios de código. El marco teórico de la lengua matriz (el *Matrix Language Frame* de Myers-Scotton (véanse, entre otras, 1993, 2001)) es el que ha gobernado el análisis de este tipo de textos y permite determinar la función del latín como lengua matriz. No obstante, como defiendo en Roig-Marín (2019), encontramos algunas deficiencias a la hora de dar cuenta de textos premodernos que no se corresponden al tipo de discurso que se tenía en mente cuando se diseñó este modelo. En textos como los aquí considerados, la libre circulación léxica entre las lenguas vernáculas y el latín, con una integración morfológica en latín a menudo oscilante o ambigua, dificulta los esfuerzos taxonómicos que pueden dar más frutos con textos producidos en lenguas vernáculas. Incluso trabajando con lenguas vernáculas contemporáneas, Poplack y Meechan (1998: 130) ponen de relieve que "es importante tener una idea, lo más explícita posible, de la naturaleza de las vernáculas antes de concluir que un elemento de cambio de código toma aspectos de una o de otra o de ambas". Por ello a menudo se establece un continuo entre cambios de código y préstamos (véanse, por ejemplo, Myers-Scotton, 2002: 153–163; Gardner-Chloros, 2009: 30–33; Matras, 2009: 110–114; Schendl, 2013: 48) ya que estos fenómenos no son tan fácilmente distinguibles. Recientemente, se ha recurrido a la neurociencia para medir el tiempo de respuesta de los hablantes y, en principio, determinar si se trata de un cambio de código único o un préstamo. Sin embargo, aparte de no ser una opción viable para fuentes históricas, la fiabilidad de este parámetro puede ser debatida.

Picone (1994: 271) sugirió la existencia de una tercera alternativa distinta al préstamo o cambio de código, la creación de un código neutralizado ("*intercode*" o "*buffer code*") que él aplicó a formas híbridas entre el francés de Luisiana y el inglés norte-americano, y que, tiempo más tarde, Wright traspasaría al estudio de *bare forms* medievales (Wright, 2002: 485). De acuerdo con Picone (1994: 272), "no está claro que las categorías de préstamo y cambio de código a una segunda lengua sean las únicas dos alternativas adecuadas para la clasificación de material importado"; así añade que, en algunas situaciones, "el estatus de un préstamo o un cambio de código se deja en suspensión y se crea un 'buffer code' (código mediador)". Por esta razón, mi investigación no pretende clasificar los términos recogidos como cambios de código o préstamos, sino examinar, y a menudo problematizar, su tratamiento en los siguientes diccionarios: el *Middle English Dictionary* (*MED*), el *Dictionary of Medieval Latin from British Sources* (*DMLBS*), el *Anglo-Norman Dictionary* (*AND*), y el citado *OED*.

El latín medieval es sustancialmente distinto al latín clásico y tiene una gran capacidad de acomodación de material léxico procedente de las lenguas vernáculas, lo que a menudo me ha llevado a defender que verdaderamente no podemos considerar que textos como con los que trabajo están escritos en una lengua mixta (*mixed-language*), como a menudo se clasifican, dado que esta observación implicaría que es posible demarcar claramente las fronteras léxicas entre lo que constituye el latín medieval y las lenguas vernáculas. Por este motivo, más recientemente he propuesto el uso del concepto, en mi opinión menos problemático, transligüe (*translingual*). *Translingüe* va más allá de la dicotomía monolingüe/multilingüe y es un término de uso relativamente extendido en la actualidad en campos como la lingüística aplicada y los estudios literarios. El translingüismo precisamente reconoce la naturaleza fluida de las lenguas y analiza la competencia del usuario de forma transversal en varias lenguas. De ahí que pueda ser una formulación relevante en contextos multilingües tanto del presente como de épocas pretéritas (véase, por ejemplo, Hsy, 2013).

Aunque la investigación del homenajeado Profesor Félix Rodríguez González y la aquí descrita parecen distantes tanto cronológica como temáticamente, ambas comparten un aspecto clave: el estudio de los efectos del contacto de lenguas a nivel léxico. Si bien acostumbramos a encontrar e identificar, con relativa facilidad, palabras de origen inglés en las lenguas modernas actuales, al remontarse al estudio del periodo medieval, nuestra concepción sobre la lengua, basada en un estándar en mayor o menor medida homogéneo, entra en conflicto con la gran variabilidad y tolerancia hacia la hibridad lingüística que encontramos. En este sentido, al igual que hoy en día los puristas de la lengua defienden que el uso de anglicismos se debe, en algunos casos, a la ignorancia del equivalente en la lengua receptora, los primeros estudiosos de los textos en latín medieval con palabras en inglés vieron una lengua imperfecta, resultado de un conocimiento deficiente del latín. No obstante, en ambos contextos, dilucidar las razones detrás del uso de lexías procedentes de otra lengua es complejo.

A continuación, pasaremos revista a los principales rasgos lingüísticos encontrados en estos textos y que dan muestra de su complejidad. Toda la producción científica de esta área está escrita en inglés, por lo que con la presente publicación pretendemos dar visibilidad a este tipo de investigación, en sí misma multilingüe, a una audiencia más amplia, más allá del contexto anglófono.

2. Lexías neutras y abreviaturas

Dos de los rasgos más visibles de la lengua de estos textos administrativos son dos: está basada en fórmulas fijas, donde prima el contenido léxico, y el uso de abreviaturas y signos de suspensión es mucho más acusado que en otros géneros textuales. Si se trabaja con ediciones, el hecho de que los editores hayan podido expandir silenciosamente abreviaturas y no lo hayan indicado explícitamente puede tener consecuencias si se quiere clasificar y medir con precisión, a nivel cuantitativo, las formas desprovistas de inflexiones (*bare forms*) y las declinadas. No obstante, a menudo los propios editores se muestran reacios a expandir estas marcas de abreviación/suspensión en palabras vernáculas, precisamente porque se desconoce hasta qué punto el escriba prefería utilizar una marca ambigua al final de la palabra (representada convencionalmente en ediciones por la comilla simple «'» o un punto «.»), al no estar claro qué declinación o declinaciones podrían corresponder a un gran número de palabras que no necesariamente descienden directamente del latín clásico. Por ejemplo, encontramos *tunakyll'* "una vestimenta (en un contexto eclesiástico)" (compárense con las formas en francés antiguo *tunicle*, *tonicle* y *tenicle* y en latín clásico, *tunicula*), *argent'* "plata" (francés *argent* y latín *argentum*) o *vernag.* "un tipo de vino blanco fuerte y dulce de Italia" (anglo-francés *vernage* < italiano *vernaccia*).

3. Uso del artículo de origen francés

Los artículos definidos *le*, *les* y *lez* se encuentran en textos administrativos escritos en latín medieval precediendo, de forma regular, lexías procedentes de las lenguas vernáculas: hay variación en el uso de este artículo de origen francés incluso dentro del mismo texto, lo que puede estar condicionado por las estructuras sintácticas empleadas (véanse, por ejemplo, "le Straynyo^{r}clath" (Rott. Celer. 1460–61, 90) y "14 streynowrcloþs" (Rott. Celer. 1505–6, 104)).[2] Dentro de la gran variabilidad encontrada, hay ciertos grupos de lexemas que suelen aparecer precedidos del artículo (por ejemplo, "le Stankart" and "del Stankart" en Rott. Bursar. c. 1357, 560). El uso del artículo de origen francés, también en

2 Citamos aquí ejemplos de las cuentas de la Abadía de Durham que editó Fowler (1898–1901), siguiendo el mismo sistema de abreviaturas en latín que se utiliza para referirse a los distintos lugares en los que los rollos manuscritos se produjeron dentro de la abadía: Rott. Celer. (*Rotuli Celerariorum*), Rott. Hostill. (*Rotuli Hostillariorum*), Rott. Camer. (*Rotuli Camerariorum*), Rotuli Elemos. (*Rotuli Elemosinariorum*), Rott. Terrar. (*Rotuli Terrariorum*), Rott. Sacrist. (*Rotuli Sacristarum*), Rott. Feretrar. (*Rotuli Feretrariorum*) y Rott. Bursar. (*Rotuli Bursariorum*). Tras esta referencia, proporcionamos el número de página en el texto editado en la que se encuentran las citadas palabras.

combinación con *de*, continuó siendo sistemático hasta mediados del siglo XV, cuando este artículo empezaría a funcionar como un marcador textual que indicaba un cambio a la lengua vernácula (función descrita por Trotter, 2007; véase también Ingham, 2009) en contextos sintácticos imprevisibles: por ejemplo, en conjunción con lo que sería el partitivo en francés a pesar de que no haya concordancia de número ("purgacione del kirvyngknyffes", Rott. Bursar. 1492–3, 652) y con adjetivos o numerales en latín (por ejemplo, "2^{bus} le hekkys", Rott. Feretrar. 1501–2, 481). Estas transformaciones después del año 1450 se produjeron en paralelo a la decadencia en el uso del francés como lengua de comunicación en contextos señoriales (Ingham, 2009: 93).

Tradicionalmente, se asumía que el artículo francés bloqueaba la latinización de las lexías que precedía (Trotter, 2007; Ingham, 2009, 2013; Wright, 2010, 2013). Solo pesos y medidas habrían constituido una categoría especial (véase Wright, 2013: 14). No obstante, en textos como los *Durham Account Rolls* encontramos sintagmas como "le fleshlardar." (Rott. Celer. 1459–60, 89), "le buttriciam Infirmarii" (Rott. Bursar. 1493–4, 652) o "les bayngoxinstallis" (Rott. Celer. 1512–3, 105).[3] Esta pequeña muestra es un reflejo de cómo la supuesta correlación entre la ausencia de declinaciones latinas en lexías procedentes de las lenguas vernáculas y el uso del artículo de origen francés a veces falla.[4]

El uso de este artículo se puede examinar en relación con 1) términos para referirse a entidades físicas que no forman parte de nombres propios o 2) epítetos/descriptores. En Roig-Marín (2018), se refinó una de las premisas formuladas en la literatura (véanse, entre otros, Trotter, 2010; Ingham, 2013; Wright, 2010, 2013, 2018) y se expuso cómo la afirmación de Britnell (2009), que atribuye su uso a un conocimiento lingüístico deficiente por parte del escriba, está empíricamente infundada. En general, *le(s/z)* precede a un término en la lengua vernácula (aunque no siempre) y sus usos parecen alinearse con los que tiene en francés. Así pues, un uso prototípico se encuentra cuando el referente es compartido o ya se ha aludido al mismo con anterioridad. Ello explicaría la oscilación en la aparición de dicho artículo en algunos casos. Asimismo, hallamos ejemplos en los que *le* sistemáticamente precede a sustantivos cuyo origen es el

3 En este último ejemplo, "les bayngoxinstallis" (Rott. Celer. 1512–3, 105), encontramos también el sufijo *-is*, usado tanto en latín como en inglés medio norteño (véase la siguiente sección sobre cuestiones dialectales).

4 Véase el *DMLBS* para más ejemplos del uso del artículo de origen francés precediendo léxico latinizado, entre ellos, "la barella" (v. *barellus*, 1, 2).

inglés antiguo (e.g. *le gryndystan*), lo que, de nuevo, demuestra su apropiación y empleo con lexías que no son de origen francés.

El estudio de la onomástica ha recibido un tratamiento menos exhaustivo si se compara con nombres comunes u otras categorías gramaticales en general, pero en el caso que nos ocupa, resulta conveniente trazar el uso de nombres latinizados frente a otros procedentes del francés o del inglés antiguo sin adaptar. Anexos a estos nombres, encontramos epítetos o descriptores. Las fronteras entre lo que hoy en día conocemos como apellidos *per se* y epítetos generales son problemáticas. De ahí el uso generalizado de la categoría *descriptor* o término equivalente. Generalmente, pueden denotar profesiones, origen geográfico o incluso cualidades y, pese a que en muchos casos existan equivalentes en latín, el uso entre la palabra vernácula y la latina puede alternarse o coexistir, como ocurre con el léxico general. No se puede saber a ciencia cierta si estos descriptores se utilizaban con fines puramente identificativos en contextos burocráticos o profesionales, o si eran ampliamente conocidos así en sus comunidades (en cuyo caso, por ejemplo, *Roberto le engles* tendría relevancia en Inglaterra si los otros trabajadores tuvieran una procedencia distinta, lo que es difícil de determinar con el escaso volumen de datos disponibles en el texto). Un patrón común es el de nombre + el artículo *le* + la profesión o, más esporádicamente, un adjetivo (por ejemplo, *long*' in "Thome le long'"; para más detalles, véase Roig-Marín, 2018).

Por último, cabe mencionar una variante del citado artículo definido de origen francés que se encuentra en textos norteños como los *Durham Account Rolls*, a saber, *ly*. Como se expone en Roig-Marín (2021), la única información sobre esta variante acabada en <y>, la encontramos en el *Dictionary of the Older Scottish Tongue* (s.v. *le, lie,* art.), que describe *ly* y *lie* como variantes ortográficas escocesas tardías de la forma más antigua *le*. El escocés distintivamente adaptó préstamos del francés como *ulyie* para *oil* "aceite" o *cunyie* para *coin* "moneda" (véase Aitken, 2015: 2) y, pese a que no exista una descripción formal de los cambios fonológicos de la vocal en este artículo de origen francés (en teoría una vocal cercana a una schwa), podría haber dado paso a la misma variación alográfica (<ie>/<y>) que en préstamos integrados, independiente de si es producto de un cambio fonológico o no.

4. Componente dialectal

Trabajo preliminar basado en *the Inventories and Account Rolls of the Benedictine Houses of Jarrow and Monk-Wearmouth, in the County of Durham* me llevó a reflexionar sobre otro elemento que merecía ser investigado aparte de la compleja interrelación entre el latín medieval y las lenguas vernáculas: la dimensión dialectal del vocabulario procedente de las lenguas vernáculas en estos textos. Después de llevar a cabo una revisión de la literatura sobre estos textos híbridos, se descubrió que no se habían tratado cuestiones dialectales en profundidad. Hubo que remontarse a una nota de la investigación de Hulbert (1936: 40) de principios del siglo XX, en la cual indicaba lo siguiente:

> It may be possible eventually, when someone has studied all extant manorial records, to obtain from the English words in them evidence as to the dialect of the places where the rolls were written. If in general the scribes who wrote them, however, were not residents of the manors, the value of this evidence would be limited. In any event, the data which I have been able to collect are not sufficient to be of value for that purpose.

Hulbert (1936) trajo a colación dos cuestiones centrales a la empresa que proponía: si se marca como objetivo el estudio del dialecto de estos registros señoriales, haría falta llevar a cabo un estudio completo de toda evidencia existente, incluyendo los escribas involucrados en su producción. Ciertamente, todavía estamos lejos de llegar a dicho estado de la cuestión. Hay limitaciones prácticas: no contamos con transcripciones de los extensos repositorios de documentos administrativos medievales que se conservan y su estado de conservación, en ocasiones pobre, complica esta tarea. Estos objetos textuales funcionales fueron ignorados durante mucho tiempo y, en consecuencia, su almacenamiento se llevaba a cabo en entornos poco óptimos. Otro problema que Hulbert ya señaló se debe a la identidad incierta de los escribas que redactaron estos documentos administrativos en lugares como pudieran ser conventos o monasterios a lo largo de todo el territorio. Se ha asumido que escribas locales produjeron estos documentos, y esta parece ser la tendencia general a juzgar por la escasa información disponible en los registros. No obstante, la posibilidad de la movilidad geográfica de los escribas no debe ser completamente descartada. Asimismo, en contextos monásticos como los aquí examinados, clérigos en vez de escribas profesionales podrían haber sido los responsables de la producción de dichos textos. Si bien todavía no disponemos de suficientes datos como a los que tenemos acceso sobre otro tipo de producciones (como manuscritos literarios más elaborados), es posible utilizar el material léxico hallado en estos textos (sobre todo sustantivos y, en menor medida, adjetivos y algunos verbos) como punto de partida para rastrear los dialectos de los escribas en dichas cuentas. Así, en base al extenso trabajo previo sobre dialectos del inglés medio y moderno temprano, así como la información dialectal disponible en trabajos lexicográficos de referencia como el *English Dialect Dictionary*, *MED* y *OED*, propuse una clasificación basada en el tipo de evidencia lingüística que se podía utilizar para determinar la naturaleza dialectal del vocabulario procedente de las lenguas vernáculas (véase Roig-Marín, 2022). A continuación, describiremos dicha taxonomía en relación con el repertorio léxico norteño: la Clase 1a engloba vocabulario con vocales o consonantes norteñas descritas en la literatura previa, que se sirve de textos monolingües en inglés medio norteño y escocés;

la Clase 1b comprende vocabulario clasificado como norteño desde un punto de vista textual o semántico, es decir, palabras etiquetadas como norteñas en uno o varios diccionarios, una aserción asentada en los registros escritos, que son exclusivamente norteños, o conceptos específicamente norteños;

la Clase 2 trata palabras halladas en textos del norte, pero que no necesariamente son norteñas. Esta categoría precisamente recoge vocabulario que no tiene por qué ser norteño, teniendo en cuenta que solo hay registros del mismo en muy pocos textos editados (incluso exclusivamente en uno);

la Clase 3 está reservada para lexías que son norteñas o "dialectales" solo en periodos posteriores de la lengua, es decir, en el inglés moderno temprano o tardío; por último, la Clase 4 se refiere a formas que no son norteñas. Diccionarios como el *OED* y el *MED* pueden haberlas etiquetados como "escocesas" o "norteñas" y el *Dictionary of the Older Scottish Tongue* como "inglés medio norteño", pero no hay prueba fehaciente que permita corroborar esa adscripción geográfica. Al margen del vocabulario, también encontramos rasgos morfológicos como el morfema de plural *-is*, que se puede interpretar como latín pero también como inglés medio norteño, o el citado artículo *ly*. Esta área, por tanto, ofrece mucho potencial investigador y espero poder seguir desarrollándola en el futuro.

5. Conclusiones

La producción textual en el campo de los negocios y la administración no había atraído tanta atención de filólogos como textos literarios o de otra índole, ya que su contenido, *a priori*, parece de relevancia solo para historiadores, pero ofrece una perspectiva única en el estudio de los efectos del contacto de lenguas en la Inglaterra tardomedieval. Por lo general, este tipo de texto es reflejo de transacciones cotidianas orales, preservadas de forma escrita sin ninguna pretensión estilística elevada. En documentos administrativos como inventarios y cuentas, el contenido semántico tiene prevalencia sobre su marcación morfológica: los sufijos a menudo se abrevian y el grado de integración de las lexías procedentes de las lenguas vernáculas es muy variable. De esta forma, la dicotomía entre lenguas vernáculas y no vernáculas se difumina. Los escribas de estos textos no están, pues, constreñidos por una supuesta noción de la *pureza* de la lengua, que yace en un constructo llamado *estándar*.

El análisis de los principales rasgos lingüísticos se ha centrado en el uso de descriptores en nombres propios, el uso de formas lingüísticamente ambivalentes y del artículo definido de origen francés como marcador que, en su mayoría, precede a una lexía vernácula. Esta es la percepción general en la literatura, aunque también se encuentra precediendo a voces latinas, lo que, de nuevo, podría mostrar cómo replica los usos del artículo francés en un texto en latín, pero sin necesariamente concordar en género o número. Si bien la lengua matriz o base es el latín, cuyas fronteras con las vernáculas no estás claramente delineadas, los escribas de textos administrativos han de tomar decisiones a la hora de utilizar material léxico tomado de las lenguas vernáculas; entran así en juego algunos marcadores lingüísticos que se emplean para introducir material de origen vernáculo no adaptado al latín más allá del citado *le/-s/-z/ly*.

Los mecanismos internos de textos producidos, en principio, en latín medieval, han revelado cómo los hablantes pueden internalizar varios códigos lingüísticos y crear un repertorio léxico común, con patrones y funciones idiosincráticas. Clasificar el latín de estos textos como "defectuoso" o "empobrecido" es, por tanto, una falacia. Más bien sería muestra de lo contrario: nos encontramos ante una lengua flexible, rica y eficaz, que transmite, como pocas otras, la realidad transligüe de la época.

Referencias

Aitken, Adam J. [1954] 2015. "Sources of the vocabulary of Older Scots." En *Collected Writings on the Scots Language*, editado por Caroline Macafee. Scots Language Centre <d3lmsxlb5aor5x.cloudfront.net/library/document/aitken/Sources_of_the_vocabulary_of_Older_Scots.pdf>_.

Alcolado Carnicero, José Miguel. 2013. "Social networks and mixed-language business writing: Latin/French/English in the Wardens' accounts of the Mercers' Company of London, 1390–1464." Tesis doctoral no publicada, Universidad de Castilla-La Mancha.

Alcolado Carnicero, José Miguel. 2015. "Dating the shift to English in the financial accounts of some London livery companies: A reappraisal." *Multilingua* 34 (3): 373–404.

Alcolado Carnicero, José Miguel. 2017. "Bridges of innovation and change: The English language around the networks of the Mercery of London." En *Merchants of Innovation: The Languages of Traders*. Studies in Language Change

Series 15, editado por Esther-Miriam Wagner, Bettina Beinhoff, y Ben Outhwaite, 40–67. Berlin/New York: Mouton de Gruyter.

Alcolado Carnicero, José Miguel. 2018. "Merchant taylors of London's shift to business English: New insights on the languages of record in their Master and Wardens' accounts." *Journal of Historical Sociolinguistics* 4 (1): 1–32.

Alcolado Carnicero, José Miguel. 2019. "Diachrony of code-switching stages in medieval business accounts: The Mercers' livery company of London." *Journal of Historical Linguistics* 9 (3): 378–416.

Britnell, Richard. 2009. "Uses of French language in medieval English towns." En *Language and Culture in Medieval Britain: The French of England c.1100–c.1500*, editado por Jocelyn Wogan-Browne et al., 81–89. York: York Medieval Press.

Craigie, William A., et al. 1937–2002. *Dictionary of the Older Scots Tongue*, 12 vols. Oxford: OUP. <www.dsl.ac.uk>.

Durkin, Philip. 2014. *Borrowed Words: A History of Loanwords in English*. Oxford: OUP.

Fowler, Joseph Th. 1898–1901. *Extracts from The Account Rolls of the Abbey of Durham, from the Original MSS.*, 3 vols. Durham: Surtees Society.

Gardner-Chloros, Penelope. 2009. *Code-Switching*. Cambridge: CUP.

Hone, Nathaniel J. 1906. *The Manor and Manorial Records*. London: Methuen.

Hsy, Jonathan. 2013. *Trading Tongues: Merchants, Multilingualism, and Medieval Literature*. Columbus: Ohio State University Press.

Hulbert, James R. 1936. "English in manorial documents of the thirteenth and fourteenth centuries." *Modern Philology* 34 (1): 37–61.

Ingham, Richard. 2009. "Mixing languages on the manor." *Medium Ævum* 78 (1): 80–97.

Ingham, Richard. 2013. "Language-mixing in medieval Latin documents: Vernacular articles and nouns." En *Multilingualism in medieval Britain (c. 1066–1520): Sources and Analysis* (Medieval Texts and Cultures of Northern Europe 15), editado por Judith A. Jefferson y Ad Putter, 105–121. Turnhout: Brepols.

Kurath, Hans, Kuhn, Sherman M., y Lewis, Robert E. (eds.). 1952–2001. *Middle English Dictionary* [*MED*]. Ann Arbor: University of Michigan Press. <quod.lib.umich.edu/m/med/>.

Latham, Ronald E., Howlett, David R., y Ashdowne, Richard K. 1975–2013. *Dictionary of Medieval Latin from British Sources* [*DMLBS*]. Oxford: British Academy. <http://www.dmlbs.ox.ac.uk/>.

Matras, Yaron. 2009. *Language Contact*. Cambridge: CUP.

Myers-Scotton, Carol. 1993. *Duelling Languages: Grammatical Structure in Codeswitching.* Oxford: Clarendon Press.

Myers-Scotton, Carol. 2001. "The matrix language frame model: Development and responses." En *Codeswitching Worldwide II*, editado por Rodolfo Jacobson, 23–58. Berlin: Mouton de Gruyter.

Myers-Scotton, Carol. 2002. *Contact Linguistics: Bilingual Encounters and Grammatical Outcomes*. Oxford: OUP.

Pahta, Päivi, Skaffari, Janne, y Wright, Laura (eds.). 2018. *Multilingual Practices in Language History.* Berlin: Mouton de Gruyter.

Picone, Michael D. 1994. "Lexicogenesis and language vitality." *Word* 45 (3): 261–285.

Poplack, Shana y Meechan, Marjory. 1998. "How languages fit together in codemixing." *International Journal of Bilingualism* 2 (2): 127–138.

Raine, James. 1854. *The Inventories and Account Rolls of the Benedictine Houses or Cells of Jarrow and Monkwearmouth in the County of Durham*. London: Surtees Society.

Roig-Marín, Amanda. 2018. "When the vernaculars (Anglo-Norman and Middle English) and Medieval Latin fuse into a functional variety." *Studia Neophilologica* 90 (2): 176–194.

Roig-Marín, Amanda. 2019. "Towards a multilingual approach to the history of English." *Atlantis* 41(1): 185–194.

Roig-Marín, Amanda. 2021. "The French-origin definite article *ly* in English records." *Notes and Queries* 68(1): 11–12.

Roig-Marín, Amanda. 2022. "A study of Northern Middle and Early Modern English vocabulary in medieval Latin texts: The case of the *Durham Account Rolls*." *Anglia* 140(2), 163–189.

Rothwell, William, Gregory, Stewart, Trotter, David, De Wilde, Geert, Derrien, Virginie, y Pagan, Heather (eds.). (1977–). *Anglo-Norman Dictionary* [*AND*]. <www.anglo-norman.net/>.

Rothwell, William. 1991. "The missing link in English etymology: Anglo-French." *Medium Aevum* 60: 173–196.

Schendl, Herbert y Wright, Laura. 2011. *Code-Switching in Early English*. Berlin: Mouton de Gruyter.

Schendl, Herbert. 2013. "Multilingualism and code-switching as mechanisms of contact-induced lexical change in late Middle English." En *English as a Contact Language*, editado por Daniel Schreier y Marianne Hundt, 41–57. Cambridge: CUP.

Simpson, John A. y Proffitt, Michael. 1990-en progreso. *The Oxford English Dictionary* [*OED*], 3rd edn. <http://www.oed.com/>.

Trotter, David (ed.) 2000. *Multilingualism in Later Medieval Britain*. Cambridge: D. S. Brewer.

Trotter, David. 2007. "Building bridges in Anglo-Norman: The lexical evidence." Trabajo presentado en el *Symposium on Middle English and Anglo-Norman*, University of Central England, febrero de 2007.

Trotter, D. 2010. "Bridging the gap: The (socio)-linguistic evidence of some medieval English bridge accounts." En *The Anglo-Norman Language and its Contexts*, editado por Richard Ingham, 52–63. Woodbridge: York Medieval Press.

Wright, Laura. 1994. "Early Modern London business English." En *Studies in Early Modern English*, editado por Dieter Kastovsky, 449–465. Berlin: Mouton de Gruyter.

Wright, Laura. 1996. *Sources of London English: Medieval Thames Vocabulary*. Oxford: Clarendon Press.

Wright, Laura. 1998. "Mixed-language business writing. Five hundred years of code-switching." En *Language Change: Advances in Historical Sociolinguistics*, editado por Ernst Håkon Jahr, 99–118. Berlin: Mouton de Gruyter.

Wright, Laura. 2002. "Code-intermediate phenomena in medieval mixed-language business texts." *Language Sciences* 24 (3–4): 471–489.

Wright, Laura. 2010. "A pilot study on the singular definite articles le and la in fifteenth-century London mixed-language business writing." En *The Anglo-Norman Language and its Contexts*, editado por Richard Ingham, 130–142. Woodbridge: York Medieval Press.

Wright, Laura. 2013. "On historical language dictionaries and language boundaries." En *Evur Happie & Glorious, ffor I Hafe at Will Grete Riches (Medieval English Mirror 9)*, editado por Liliana Sikorska y Marcin Krygier, 11–26. Frankfurt: Peter Lang.

Wright, Laura. 2018. "A multilingual approach to the history of standard English." En *Multilingual Practices in Language History*, editado por Päivi Pahta, Janne Skaffari, y Laura Wright, 339–358. Berlin: Mouton de Gruyter.

Andreu van Hooft, Iclal Yildiz, Mustafa Akpinar, and Frank van Meurs

Radboud University Nijmegen

Andreu van Hooft: Department of Language and Communication / Centre for Language Studies, Radboud University, Erasmusplein 1, 6525 HT Nijmegen, the Netherlands, e-mail: andreu.vanhooft@ru.nl

Iclal Yildiz: Department of Gender & Diversity Studies, Radboud Social Cultural Research, Radboud University, Thomas van Aquinostraat 4, 6525 GD Nijmegen, the Netherlands, e-mail: iclal.yildiz@ru.nl

Mustafa Akpinar: Communication Science, Behavioral Science Institute, Communication & Media, Radboud University, Thomas van Aquinostraat 4, 6525 GD Nijmegen, the Netherlands, e-mail: mustafa.akpinar@ru.nl

Frank van Meurs: Department of Language and Communication / Centre for Language Studies, Radboud University, Erasmusplein 1, 6525 HT Nijmegen, the Netherlands, e-mail: frank.vanmeurs@ru.nl

The use of English in job advertisements in Turkey

Abstract: Relatively few studies have investigated the use of English in job advertisements in countries where English is not the first language and factors on which this use may depend. Countries studied earlier are Belgium, the Netherlands and Spain. This study is the first to study English in job ads in Turkey, thereby expanding evidence on the presence of English in job ads to a different linguistic context. The purpose of this study was to quantify the use of English in job advertisements in Turkey and to investigate two factors on which this use may depend: the sector and the national/international nature of the organisations with the vacancy. A corpus analysis of 120 job advertisements on the job site

Kariyer.net revealed that 80.8 % of the job advertisements contained one or more English words. Organisations from the Tourism sector used a larger concentration of English words than organisations from the Retail, Manufacturing and Healthcare sectors. Multinational organisations used a larger concentration of English words than local and national firms. It can be concluded that English words were relatively frequently used and that the extent to which English was used depended on the sector and the multinational nature of the organisation with the vacancy. These findings confirm findings regarding the use of English in job ads in other linguistic contexts, Belgium, the Netherlands, and Spain.

Keywords: Anglicisms, Turkish, job advertisements, quantitative corpus analysis, sector, internationality.

A Félix con quien compartimos el encantamiento por las lenguas en contacto

1. Introduction

English is widely present across the world, also in countries where it is not an official language, in two main ways (Zenner et al., 2013). Firstly, English can be used as a language of communication in professional and informal situations, for example as a lingua franca between speakers who do not share a common first language. Secondly, English words and phrases are used in communication in other languages, for instance as loanwords (Görlach, 2002; Pulcini et al., 2012). One of the domains in which English is used in countries in which it is not the first language is advertising. While much scholarly attention has been paid to the presence and effects of English in product advertising in such countries (for overviews, see Hornikx & van Meurs, 2020, chapter 4; Piller, 2003), much less attention has been paid to English in job advertisements.

There are a small number of studies that have quantified the use of English in job ads in countries where English is not the first language nor an official language, both in all-English job ads and in job ads that combine the national language with English. For Belgium and the Netherlands, Zenner et al. (2013) showed that of circa 13,000 ads published in two vacancy magazines (the Belgian magazine *Vacature* and the Dutch magazine *Intermediair*) between 1989 and 2008, 8.1 % were completely in English and 36.4 % contained English job titles. For the Netherlands, Korzilius van Meurs and Hermans (2006) found that 2.4 % of 679 ads published in the Dutch quality newspaper *de Volkskrant* in 2001 were completely in English and 39 % of 120 ads contained at least one English word, and van Meurs, Korzilius, and den Hollander (2006) demonstrated that

4 % of 120 ads published on the Dutch job site Monsterboard.nl in 2004 were completely in English and 88.5 % contained at least one English word. For Spain, van Hooft (2015) established that 11.1 % of 208 ads published on the Spanish job site www.monster.es in 2011 were completely in English and 87.5 % contained at least one English word.

These quantitative studies have identified factors that can determine the extent to which English is used in job advertisements. The main factors evidenced in these studies are the economic sector in which the organisation advertising the vacancy operates, and whether the organisation offering the vacancy is national or international. For each of these factors, we will first discuss some evidence from the genre of product ads, followed by a comprehensive discussion of the relevant job ad studies.

One factor that may affect the use of English in job advertisements is the sector of the organisation advertising the vacancy. For product ads, Cheshire and Moser (1994: 459–463) and Griffin (1997: 37) established that English in advertising in Switzerland and Poland was used more for particular types of products, such as cigarettes and computers, than for others. In relation to job advertising, job ad makers in the Netherlands remarked that they used certain English terms because they were common in the sector in which their organisations were active (van Meurs et al., 2015b: 98). Generally, corpus analyses show that the use of English in job ads is related to the sector of activity of the organisation that placed the advertisement. While Korzilius et al. (2006) found no significant differences in the concentration of English in job ads from the Dutch national newspaper *de Volkskrant* among different sectors of the economy, van Meurs et al. (2006) showed that advertisements on the Dutch job site Monsterboard.nl for jobs in the "Transport, Storage and Communications" and "Commercial Services" sectors contained more English than ads for jobs in the "Financial Institutions" sector. For print-medium job ads from job ad magazines in Belgium and the Netherlands, Zenner et al. (2013) demonstrated that job ads placed by companies in the IT sector contained more English than ads from eleven other sectors (Media & IT; Service, HR & Consultancy; Pharmaceutical Industry; Finance; Retail & Distribution; Energy & Safety; Education & Research; Industry; Food & Agriculture; Healthcare & Hospitals; Government, Culture & Social Profit; Unknown activities). Similarly, for job ads on the Spanish Monster job site, van Hooft (2015) found that more English was used in ads from organisations in the ICT sector than in five other sectors (Financial and Insurance; Wholesale and Retail; Hospitality; Scientific, Professional and Technical Activities; Administrative and Auxiliary Activities).

A second factor that has been found to determine the use of English in job ads is whether the organisation offering the vacancy is national or international. For product ads, Cheshire and Moser (1994) and Gerritsen et al. (2007) showed that ads for consumer goods distributed by multinational corporations contain English more frequently than ads placed by local companies. This may be because multinational organisations wish to create international consistency and therefore, for instance, use the same English brand names or slogans (Alm, 2003: 150; Gerritsen et al., 2000: 20). For job ads, a similar rationale has been given for the use of English terms. Specifically, Larson (1990: 368) posits that multinationals use the same English job titles in job advertising in different countries to create international consistency. In line with this argument, corpus analyses in the Netherlands and Spain have shown that English words were used more frequently in job advertisements placed by multinational organisations than by domestic organisations (Korzilius et al., 2006 for print-medium job ads in the Dutch newspaper d*e Volkskrant*; van Hooft, 2015 for online job ads on the Spanish Monster platform; van Meurs et al., 2006 for online job ads on the Dutch Monsterboard platform).

We aimed to establish whether these findings are robust and more widely applicable. We chose to investigate this for job ads in a country, Turkey, with an official language that belongs to a different language family than the countries investigated earlier. While Dutch is a Germanic language and Spanish is a Romance language, Turkish belongs to the Turkic language family. Turkey can be placed in the Expanding Circle in Kachru's (1986) model of World Englishes, indicating that English is not an official language (Doğançay-Aktuna & Kiziltepe, 2005). Doğançay-Aktuna (1998) showed that 21.7 % of 419 job advertisements published in two Turkish newspapers were fully in English. However, to our knowledge, no study has investigated how much English is used in job advertisements that are largely in Turkish nor what factors determine the extent to which English is used in job ads in Turkey. We wished to gain insights into the extent to which English is used, not just in fully English communication but also in the use of English words in basically Turkish communication. Therefore, our research questions relating to the extent to which English is used were the following:

1. How many words in the job advertisements are in English, Turkish or other languages?
2. How many job advertisements contain English?
3. How many of the advertisements are entirely in English and how many are partly in English?

On the basis of earlier quantitative corpus analyses of job ads in Belgium, the Netherlands and Spain, we formulated the following research questions relating to factors that may determine the extent to which English is used:

4. Does the use of English in job ads depend on the sector of the organisation with the vacancy?
5. Is English used more in job ads placed by multinationals than by domestic organisations?

2. Methodology

2.1 Materials

In order to answer the research questions, a corpus study was carried out in which 120 job advertisements from the Turkish job site Kariyer.net were analysed. The job site Kariyer.net was chosen because this website is most frequently used by Turkish applicants when looking for a job (Genç, 2012). The 120 advertisements were selected from 3236 advertisements found on Kariyer.net on 11 February 2014, using the "iş ara" (search job) option. Location, key words and sector of the organisation were not specified. A random selection of 120 advertisements was made by using the Random Integer Generator option on the website Random.org.

2.2 Procedure

For all ads, we coded the following: (1) the number of English words, Turkish words, hybrid words and words in another language; (2) the sector of the organisation offering the vacancy; (3) the national or multinational nature of the organisation offering the vacancy. In our analysis, we counted all of the words of the ad, including the text of the banner and the information at the bottom added by the organisation. The rationale behind this choice is that all this information is relevant to potential applicants, and all this information is seen by the reader as pertaining to the job ad as presented on screen. Figure 1 shows an example of a job ad from the corpus, in which the words we classified as English are underlined.

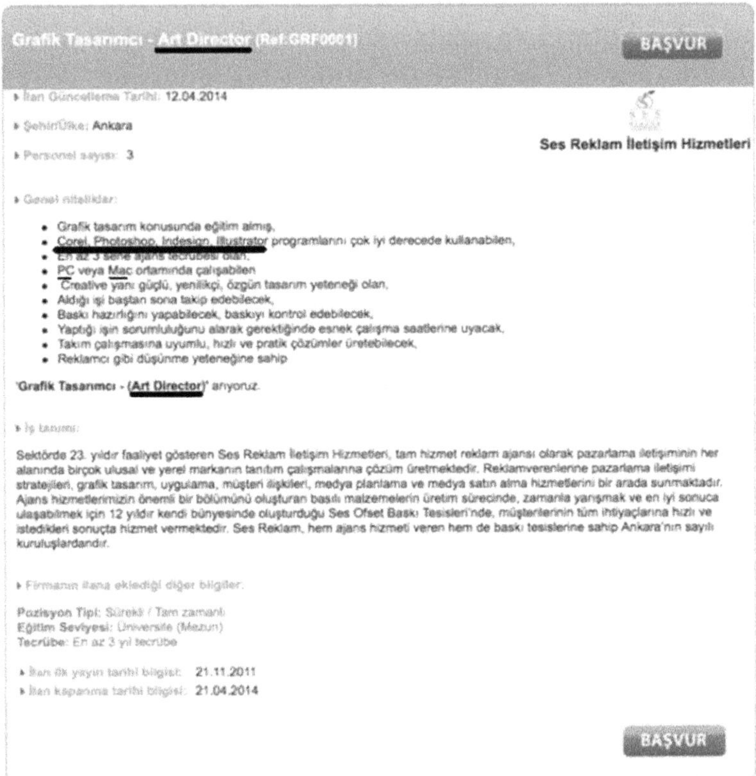

Fig. 1. Example of a job advertisement found on Kariyer.net on 11 February 2014. Note: words we classified as English are underlined.

The advertisements were independently coded in two rounds: first by two coders who were native speakers of Turkish (and Dutch) and highly proficient in English (mean Krippendorff's alpha was .73; range .53–.87, with "0 indicating the absence of reliability" and "1 indicating perfect reliability"; Krippendorff, 2004: 222), and subsequently by two non-Turkish-speaking coders who checked the status of English words determined by the first two coders. Disagreements between the coders regarding particular cases were discussed until they reached mutual agreement.

We counted the absolute numbers of English words, Turkish words, hybrid words and other-language words per advertisement. We also calculated the concentration of English by dividing the number of English words by the total number of words per advertisement, which gives a more precise indication of the use of English relative to the total advertisement. We did this for all 120 ads in the corpus, and also for 97 ads that contained at least one English word.

Below we present definitions and operationalisations of the key concepts in our study.

2.2.1 Definition of "word"

A word was defined as "any segment of written or printed discourse ordinarily appearing between spaces or between a space and a punctuation mark" (Merriam-Webster Online Dictionary, 2021). Based on this definition and on the operationalisations in Korzilius et al. (2006: 150) and van Hooft (2015: 256–257), we made the following decisions regarding word status:

- An abbreviation that was written with or without dots was counted as one word, regardless of the number of words the abbreviation stood for. For example, the abbreviation "MS" ("Microsoft") in "MS Office", "Ltd." ("Limited"), "HVAC" ("Heating, Ventilation and Air Conditioning"), "HRS" ("Health Research Systems"), "TS" ("Technical Standard"), "APQP" ("Advance Product Quality Plan") and "MYO" ("Meslek Yüksek Okulu", Vocational School of Higher Education) were regarded as one word each.
- URLs were regarded as one word: "www.gulaylar.com"; facebook.com/çagdasholding
- Hyphenated words, such as "part-time" were counted as one word.
- Words with a slash, such as "bay/bayan" ("male/female"), were regarded as separate words
- An ampersand ("&") was considered as a word.
- Symbols (such as "%", "–", "_", "+") were counted as one word if they occurred between spaces.
- When the words in the logo were readable, they were counted.
- An alphanumeric sequence in the reference after the job title in the heading was counted as English if the job title was in English – for instance "Journey ambassador (Ref:ISTBH54)" – and as Turkish if the job title was Turkish.
- Dates with numbers for the day, month and year separated by points were counted as three words, for instance "21.11.2011" in Fig. 1.

2.2.2 Definition of "English" and other foreign languages

In order to determine whether a word was English or belonged to another foreign (non-Turkish) language, the following criteria were used:

- If a word was included in the latest version of an English dictionary, for example the Macmillan English dictionary (2007) and was not adapted to Turkish spelling conventions, the word was regarded as English.
- If an English word was included in the Turkish dictionary Türk Dil Kurumu (2019) and labelled as English ("*İngilizce*"), the word was regarded as an English word, for example "center", "Fast Food", "logo", "market" and "test".
- If words were included in a foreign-language dictionary (for example, Accademia della Crusca (2015) for Italian, Larousse (2022) for French and the Real Academia Española (2022) for Spanish) and were not adapted to Turkish spelling conventions, the words were regarded as foreign language words, for instance "casino" (Italian), "Chef de Partie" (French), "Técnicas Reunidas" (Spanish).
- If a word of foreign origin was included in the Turkish dictionary Türk Dil Kurumu (2019), and labelled as belonging to a particular foreign language, it was regarded as a foreign language word, for example, *hamburger* (German, "*Almanca*"), *pizza* (Italian, "*İtalyanca*").
- If an English word was included in Turkish spelling, the word was regarded as a Turkish word, for example "lider "[leader] and "ofis" [office] in "MS Ofis".
- Proper names were classified according to their language of origin. For example, English names of hotels such as "*Sheraton*" were regarded as English, while the hotel name "*Le Meridien*" was seen as consisting of French words.
- Software names of English origin (like "PPAP", "Solidworks", "Autodesk") were counted as English words. For example, the words "Microsoft Office" were both regarded as English words.
- Toponyms were counted as Turkish when the place to which they refer is in Turkey and follows Turkish spelling. Otherwise, a toponym was classified according to the language/country to which the toponym pertained. For example, *St. Regis* was counted as English, since it is a place name in Montana (USA) and, in turn, used as a name for a hotel chain.
- Compound nouns consisting of an English and a Turkish part were regarded as hybrids, for example "AKINSOFT", "Hotels'tir" and "NehirCell". Such compound nouns were labelled and counted as hybrid, so not as English nor as Turkish.
- URLs were regarded as hybrids. The majority were a combination of English and Turkish, such as "www.gulaylar.com" ("www" and "com" being English, and "gulaylar" being Turkish) and "facebook.com/çagdasholding". One URL ("www.rems.de") was a combination of German and English ("www" being English, and "REMS" and "de" being German).

- When a word was derived from a foreign language, but was adapted to Turkish spelling conventions, such as "lider" [leader] and "ofis" [office], the word was regarded as Turkish.

2.2.3 Sector of the organisation

The following sectors were distinguished, in accordance with the classification indicated on Kariyer.net: Danışmanlık (consultancy); Eğitim (education); Enerji (energy); Güvenlik (security); Perakende (retail); Bilişim (IT); Eğlence (entertainment); Kimya (chemicals); Reklam (advertising); Finans (finance); Maden (mining); Saglik (health care); Tekstil (textiles); Turizm (tourism); Gıda (food); Hızlı Tk. (fast moving consumer goods); Medya (media); Otomotiv (automotive); Sigortacılık (insurances); Telekom (telecommunications); Üretim (manufacturing); İnşaat (construction); Other; Unknown.

2.2.4 Criteria to determine the multinational nature of an organisation

An organisation was regarded as a multinational on the basis of the following criteria:

- The organisation indicated locations in Turkey as well as in other countries in the job advertisement or on the website of the organisation;
- A company was a subsidiary company of an organisation that had branches in Turkey and in other countries, according to the information in the job ad or on the organisation's website;
- The job ad indicated that the organisation operates internationally (that is, located outside Turkey).

When no sufficient information was given on any of the three points above, the organisation was classified as Turkish and therefore domestic or "national".

We made a distinction between "local" and "national" companies:

- We considered a company as "local" if the job ad or website of the company clearly specified that the company operated from just one location in Turkey;
- The scope of the company was classified as "national" if the job ad or the website of the company clearly specified that the company operated from more than one location in Turkey;
- The scope of the company was classified as "national" if the job ad or website of the company clearly specified that the company operated in Turkey.

When no sufficient information was given on any of the six points above, the scope of the organisation was classified as "unknown". The name of the organisation was missing in some advertisements. These cases were classified as "unknown" as well.

2.2.5 Statistical treatment

The Kolmogorov-Smirnov test showed that the data were not normally distributed, and, therefore, non-parametric statistical tests were conducted: the Mann-Whitney U test to determine statistically significant differences between two groups, and the Kruskal-Wallis test to determine statistically significant differences between more than two independent groups. Analyses were conducted at two levels: first for all 120 ads, and subsequently for ads containing at least one English word.

3. Results

3.1 Quantification of English, Turkish and other languages in the job ad corpus

The entire corpus consisted of 20,585 words, of which 2501 (12.15 %) were English words, 31 (0.15 %) were hybrids, 17,695 (85.96 %) were Turkish words, and 398 words (1.93 %) were in another language, mainly German. Per job ad, the mean number of words was 171.54 (min. 71, max. 372, SD = 62.62); the mean number of English words was 20.84 (min. 0, max. 345, SD = 59.03); the mean number of Turkish words was 147.46 (min. 2, max. 371, SD = 64.47); the mean number of hybrid Turkish-English words was 0.26 (min. 0, max. 5, SD = 0.95); and the mean number of words in other languages was 3.32 (min. 0, max. 214, SD = 23.85). The mean concentration of English in all 120 job ads was .09 (SD = .23) and in the 97 ads containing English it was .12 (SD = .25).

Of the 120 job advertisements, 22 (18.3 %) contained no English words, while 97 (80.8 %) contained one or more English words. None of the 120 job advertisements were completely in English. Five (4.2 %) advertisements were almost completely in English. Seventy-three advertisements (60.8 %) were partly in Turkish and partly in English. Eight ads (6.7 %) contained a mixture of Turkish, English and another language. Nine ads (7.5 %) combined Turkish, English and single hybrid English-Turkish words, and one ad in Turkish included a hybrid English-Turkish word (0.8 %). Two job ads (1.7 %) contained a mixture of Turkish, English, a foreign language (German, French) and single hybrid Turkish-English or German-English words. The remaining 22 advertisements (18.3 %) were fully in Turkish. See Table 1 for an overview.

Table 1: Frequency of English words used in 120 job ads from Kariyer.net with different language combinations.

Category	Total number of ads in this category	Number and % of total English words in the entire corpus
Almost completely English	5	1216 (48.62 %)
Partly English, partly Turkish	73	410 (16.39 %)
Turkish, English, another language	8	196 (7.84 %)
Turkish, English, hybrid English-Turkish	9	594 (23.75 %)
Turkish, hybrid English-Turkish	1	0 (0 %)
Turkish, English, hybrid English-Turkish, other language (German, French)	2	85 (3.40 %)
Completely Turkish	22	0 (0 %)
Total	**120 (100.0 %)**	**2.501 (100 %)**

In the 97 advertisements that contained one or more English words, the mean number of English words was 25.78 (min. 1, max. 345, *SD* = 64.73), while the mean total number of words in these 97 ads was 179.60 (min. 471 max. 372, *SD* = 65.29). The English used in the 97 job ads containing English ranged from a single word in a job title ("Steward"), headings of job ad elements ("Qualifications"), names of organisations ("Medicalpark"), names of software ("Microsoft Office"), phrases ("This is our point of view…"), completely English text under Turkish headings for job ad elements, to almost completely English text with only one Turkish word ("Başvur", meaning "apply") at the top of the job ad.

The ten most frequent English words in the 120 job ads are shown in Table 2. These words comprise common general vocabulary: a conjunction ("and"), definite and indefinite articles ("the", "a"), and prepositions ("to", "of", "in"). They also contain nouns that relate to the content of the vacancies: a proper noun for a company ("MS", as an abbreviation of "Microsoft") producing the software packages ("Office") applicants are expected to be able to use, and common nouns describing businesses offering the vacancies ("hotels") and what is relevant for the job offered ("experience").

Table 2: The ten most frequently used English words in 120 job ads from Kariyer.net.

	English word	Number of occurrences
1	and	101
2	the	71
3	to	56
4	of	53
5	in	44
6	MS	38
7	Office	36
8	a	33
9	hotel(s)	30
10	experience(s)	23

The English words and sentences used in the job ads sometimes deviated from the native norm in terms of spelling, grammar and vocabulary, for instance "Microsof [sic] offfice [sic]" and "We are looking for a 'junior' *but top talent* who wish [sic] to build his/her carrier [sic] to be a data scientist/analyst at [sic] finance", suggesting that the text was written by a non-native speaker of English.

3.2 The relationship between the use of English and the sector of the organisation offering the vacancy

For 116 of the 120 job advertisements, the organisations that offered the vacancies were found to be distributed across 19 sectors. For four ads, it was not possible to determine the sector to which the organisation belonged. A Kruskal-Wallis test (H (18, n = 116) = 48.99, $p < .001$) showed that there were significant differences in the concentration of English in these 116 ads depending on the sector of the organisation. Follow-up analyses (post-hoc pairwise comparisons with a Bonferroni correction) revealed that advertisements for jobs in the Tourism sector had a higher concentration of English (*Mean Rank* = 95.93) than ads in the Retail sector (*Mean Rank* = 30.19; p = .001), in the Manufacturing sector (*Mean Rank* = 43.17; p = .001), and the Healthcare sector (*Mean Rank* = 47.07; p = .016).

A Kruskal-Wallis test for the 97 ads containing one or more English words also revealed a significant difference in the mean concentration of English among the sectors (H(17, n = 97) = 37.43, p = .003). Follow-up post-hoc pairwise comparisons with a Bonferroni correction) revealed that advertisements for jobs in the Tourism sector had a higher concentration of English (*Mean Rank* = 74.73) than ads in the Manufacturing sector (*Mean Rank* = 31.36; p = .004).

Table 3 shows the number and percentage of job advertisements per sector, with the mean concentration and standard deviation of English per advertisement.

Table 3: Concentration of English per sector (a higher score in concentration of English indicates relatively more English words per job ad). The sectors are ordered according to the number of job ads per sector (high to low). 120 are all the ads in the corpus and 97 are the ads containing at least one English word.

Sector	**Number of advertisements 120 / 97**	**Percentage of total number of advertisements 120 / 97**	**Concentration English *M* (*SD*) in all 120 ads**	**Concentration English *M* (*SD*) in 97 ads with English**
Manufacturing	18 / 14	15.0 % / 14.4 %	.02 (.04)	.03 (.04)
Tourism	15 / 15	12.5 % / 15.5 %	.33 (.37)	.33 (.37)
Healthcare	14 / 11	11.7 % / 11.3 %	.01 (.01)	.02 (.01)
Construction	12 / 9	10.0 % / 9.3 %	.02 (.02)	.02 (.01)
Retail	8 / 4	6.7 % / 4,1 %	.01 (01.)	.02 (.01)
Finance	8 / 8	6.7 % / 8.2 %	.01 (.01)	.14 (.34)
Other	7 / 6	5.8.% / 6,2 %	.06 (.05)	.07 (.05)
Textiles	5 / 3	4.2 % / 3.1 %	.01 (.01)	.02 (.01)
IT	5 / 5	4.2 % / 5,2 %	.23 (.42)	.23 (.42)
Food	5 / 4	4.2 % / 4.1 %	.02 (.02)	.03 (.16)
Indeterminable	4 / 2	3.4 % / 2.1 %	.23 (.45)	.46 (.63)
Advertising	4 / 4	3.3 % / 4.1 %	.03 (.02)	.03 (.02)
Consultancy	3 / 2	2.5 % / 2.1	.01 (.01)	.02 (0.1)
Telecommunications	3 / 3	2.5 % / 3.1	.14 (.17)	.14 (.17)
Education	2 / 2	1.7 % / 2.1	.01 (.00)	.01 (.00)
Energy	2 / 2	1.7 % / 2.1 %	.49 (.68)	.49 (.68)
Security	2 / 0	1.7 % / 0.0 %	.00 (.00)	.00
Automotive	1 / 1	0.8 % / 1 %	.03	.03
Media	1 / 1	0.8 % / 1 %	.04	.04
FMCG	1 / 1	0.8 % / 1 %	.03	.03
Total	**120 / 97**	**100.0 %**		

3.3 The relationship between the use of English and the multinational nature of the organisation with the job advertisement

Of the 120 job advertisements, 107 job ads indicated the scope of the organisation; 44 (41.1 %) were from local organisations, 38 (35.5 %) from national organisations, and 25 (23.4 %) from multinational organisations. The mean concentration of English was .04 (SD = .15) in job ads by local organisations, .02 (SD = .02) in ads by national organisations, and .26 (SD = .35) in ads by multinational organisations. A Kruskal-Wallis test (H (2, n = 107) = 19.99, $p < .001$) showed that there were significant differences in the concentration of English according to the nature of the organisations. Post-hoc pairwise tests with Bonferroni corrections showed that ads by multinational organisations had a higher concentration of English words (Mean Rank = 77.70) than ads by local (Mean Rank = 43.84) ($p < .001$) and national organisations (Mean Rank = 50.17) (p =.002); between local and national organisations no differences were found (p = 1.0).

Of the 97 advertisements containing English, 88 indicated the scope of the organisation; 34 (38.6 %) were from local organisations, 31 (35.2 %) from national organisations and 23 (26.1 %) from multinational organisations. The mean concentration of English was .06 (SD = .17) in job ads by local organisations, .03 (SD = .02) in ads by national organisations, and .28 (SD = .36) in ads by multinational organisations. A Kruskal-Wallis test (H (2, n = 88) = 20.21, $p < .001$) showed that there were significant differences in the concentration of English according to the nature of the organisations. Post-hoc pairwise tests with Bonferroni corrections showed that ads by multinational organisations had a higher concentration of English words (*Mean Rank* = 64.89) than ads by local (*Mean Rank* = 35.44) ($p < .001$) and national organisations (*Mean Rank* = 39.31) (p =.001); between local and national organisations no differences were found (p = 1.0).

4. Conclusion and discussion

The purpose of this study was to quantify the use of English in Turkish job advertisements and to test the importance of two factors that could possibly determine the extent to which English was used. The results indicated that English was used in around 80 % of the 120 job ads on the Turkish job site Kariyer.net on one day in 2014 and that the factors studied (sector and multinational nature of the organisation) were indeed relevant to the use of English in Turkish job advertisements.

There were no completely English job advertisements in the current Turkish corpus. This contrasts with earlier findings in three Western European countries, where such fully English ads did occur, although they were a minority, ranging from 2.4 % and 4 % in the Netherlands (Korzilius et al., 2006; van Meurs et al., 2006, respectively), 8.11 % in Belgium (Zenner et al., 2013) to 11.1 % in Spain (van Hooft, 2015). However, it should be noted that 4.2 % of the Turkish job ads were almost completely in English, which is a percentage similar to the low end of the spectrum for all-English job ads in the Netherlands. Around 80 % of job ads in the present Turkish corpus contained one or more English words. This was higher than in paper job ads in the Netherlands (39 %; Korzilius et al., 2006), but similar to the percentages found in online job ads in the Netherlands (88.5 %; van Meurs et al., 2006) and Spain (87.5 %; van Hooft, 2015). The extensive use of English word in job ads in Turkey fits in with the increase in the spread, influence, and presence of English in Turkish from 1950 to the present, which can be explained by the modernization, westernization, and growing relevance of international communication in Turkish society (Arik 2020; Dogancay-Aktuna, 1998; Doğançay-Aktuna and Zeynep Kızıltepe, 2005).

Although the number of job ads with English was high, the concentration of English used was low. The mean concentration of English in all 120 job ads was .09 (*SD* = .23) and in the 97 ads containing one or more English words it was .12 (*SD* = .25). Earlier studies did not calculate the concentration of English, but Korzilius et al. (2006) reported that the mean percentage of the number of English words out of the total number of words in their corpus of 119 not completely English advertisements published in the Dutch national newspaper *de Volkskrant* was 0.71 %. It can, therefore, be concluded that a relatively large number of ads use English, but the proportion of English used is small, which has also been remarked about product ads in countries where English is not the first language (Hornikx and van Meurs, 2020: 108).

The presence of English words in the whole corpus of 20,000 words was 12 %. This is a considerably lower presence of English words than the 39.8 % found in the Spanish corpus of Monster.es (van Hooft, 2015). For the other countries that have been studied (Belgium and the Netherlands), no such data are available. It should be noted that the Spanish corpus was collected from a different job site and three years earlier than the current Turkish corpus. In order to have a solid basis for comparing findings across countries and languages, future research should extract data from similar job sites in the same period of time.

The present study provided evidence for the sector of the organisation being a factor determining the extent to which English is used. Advertisements for jobs in the Tourism sector had a higher concentration of English than ads in the

Manufacturing sector. This confirms earlier findings that the extent to which English is used differs among sectors in Belgium, the Netherlands (Zenner et al., 2013; van Meurs et al., 2006) and Spain (van Hooft, 2015), although the specific sectors that differ in the extent to which English is used were not the same in the various corpora.

The results of the current study show that the multinational nature of the organisation with the vacancy is a factor determining the use of English in job ads. Job ads by multinational organisations contained more English than job ads by local and national Turkish organisations. This result is in line with the findings by Korzilius et al. (2006), van Meurs et al. (2006) and van Hooft (2015) that English was used more extensively in job advertisements from multinationals than from domestic organisations. The cross-national similarity in this respect can be taken to indicate that an organisation's multinational nature is a robust factor that determines the presence of English in job ads across countries and languages. This use of English may be explained by multinationals' wish to create consistency in the terms and formulations in their advertising in different countries, as is suggested by Alm (2003: 150) and Gerritsen et al. (2000: 20), for product ads, and by Larson (1990: 268) for job ads. Another possible explanation relates to the fact that a number of the job ads from multinational organisations were almost completely in English and indicated that the applicants should have a high competence in English ("good command of English"; "strong proficiency in spoken and written English"). This suggests that the use of English in these cases is aimed at candidates who read English, perhaps including native speakers of English, or serves as a signal that the candidate should be proficient in English. These functions of the use of English have been mentioned for fully English jobs by job ad designers (van Meurs et al., 2015b: 93–95). Further research could explore whether potential applicants perceive completely or almost completely English job ads as signalling that they should be competent in English.

In addition to the two factors that the current study has investigated, there are other factors that could influence the use of English, such as the educational level of the job (cf. van Meurs et al., 2006 and van Hooft, 2015) and the type of job (cf. Zenner et al., 2013). The extent to which English is used may also be different in different parts of the job ad, such as job title or headline (cf. Korzilius et al., 2006; van Meurs et al., 2006; van Hooft, 2015). These factors were not taken into account for the Turkish job ads studied here, but their impact should be investigated in future research.

The current study is the first to list the most frequent English words found in job advertisements in a given corpus. The ten most frequent English words included common English function words as well as content words that could be related to the genre of job ads. The function words were the conjunction "and", the definite article "the", the indefinite article "a", and the prepositions "to", "of", and "in". The content words described the software packages ("Office") applicants are expected to be able to use, the company that produces them ("MS"), the businesses offering the vacancies ("hotels") and a job requirement ("experience"). In order to generalise these findings, future studies should compare the most frequent English words in job ads in different countries.

It should be noted that the definition of English in the current study, although similar to that used in van Hooft (2015), was not identical to the definitions used in Korzilius et al. (2006) and van Meurs et al. (2006), which, in turn, were different from the definition in Zenner et al. (2013). This makes it difficult to fully compare the results. It would be desirable if future studies reached consensus on the definition of English words. The question of how to define and determine if a word is an English word has also been raised in relation to the use of English in product ads, since different definitions lead to different results in terms of the number of English words that are identified (Hornikx & van Meurs, 2020: 106–107; Roberts et al., 2023: 3–5).

This study has attempted to shed more light on the use of English in job ads in Turkey by quantifying the presence of English and examining two factors on which it may depend. Future research should also consider what impact English in job ads has on relevant target groups, such as potential applicants. Thus far, such research only appears to have been conducted in the Netherlands (e.g. van Meurs et al., 2015a). The experiments could test the effects of the use of English versus Turkish on comprehension and evaluation of the ad, the organisation and the job offered. It is generally argued that one possible motivation for the use of borrowings is "social prestige" (Weinrich. 1968: 60). In line with this, Rodríguez González (1996: 114) remarks, "In our times English is the "lingua franca" *par excellence* and that confers a prestige and a positive connotation to its borrowings [...]". This prestige-enhancing function of English has also been commented on specifically in relation to English in job ads (see van Meurs, 2010: 68–70). One of the questions the experiments can answer is whether the use of English words instead of native-language equivalents in a job ad indeed makes the job that is advertised more prestigious in the eyes of possible applicants.

References

Accademia della Crusca (2015): "Tommaseo Online". http://www.tommaseobellini.it/#/items (accessed 20 January 2022).

Alm, Cecila O. (2003): "English in the Ecuadorian commercial context". *World Englishes,* 22 (2): 143–158.

Arik, Beril T. (2020): "English in Turkey". *World Englishes,* 39 (3): 514–527.

Cheshire, Jenny & Lise-Marie Moser (1994): "English as a cultural symbol: The case of advertisements in French-speaking Switzerland". *Journal of Multilingual & Multicultural Development,* 15 (6): 451–469.

Doğançay-Aktuna, Seran (1998): "The spread of English in Turkey and its current sociolinguistic profile". *Journal of Multilingual and Multicultural Development,* 19 (1): 24–39.

Doğançay-Aktuna, Seran & Zeynep Kızıltepe (2005): "English in Turkey". *World Englishes,* 24 (2): 253–265.

Genç, Ayten (2012): "Foreign language demand of the Turkish business world". *Hacettepe University Journal of Education,* 42 (1): 175–185.

Gerritsen, Marinel, Hubert Korzilius, Frank van Meurs, & Inge Gijsbers (2000): "English in Dutch commercials, not understood and not appreciated". *Journal of Advertising Research,* 40 (3): 17–31.

Gerritsen, Marinel, Catherine Nickerson Andreu van Hooft, Frank van Meurs, Ulrike Nederstigt, Marianne Starren, & Rogier Crijns (2007): "English in product advertisements in Belgium, France, Germany, the Netherlands and Spain". *World Englishes,* 26 (3): 291–315.

Görlach, Manfred (ed.) (2002): *An annotated bibliography of European Anglicisms.* Oxford: Oxford University Press.

Griffin, Jeff (1997): "Global English invades Poland. An analysis of the use of English in Polish magazine advertisements". *English Today,* 13 (2): 34–41.

Hornikx, Jos & Frank van Meurs (2020): *Foreign languages in advertising: Linguistic and marketing perspectives.* Cham: Palgrave MacMillan.

Kachru, Braj B. (1986): *The alchemy of English: The spread, functions, and models of non-native Englishes.* Urbana / Chicago: University of Illinois Press.

Korzilius, Hubert, Frank van Meurs, & José Hermans (2006): "The use of English in job advertisements in a Dutch national newspaper: On what factors does it depend?" In Rogier Crijns & Christian Burgers (eds.), *Werbestrategien in Theorie und Praxis. Sprachliche Aspekte von deutschen und niederländischen Unternehmensdarstellungen und Werbekampagnen* (pp. 129–145). Tostedt: Attikon Verlag.

Krippendorff, Klaus (2004): *Content analysis: An introduction to its methodology.* Thousand Oaks: Sage.

Larousse (2022): Dictionnaire de Français. https://www.larousse.fr/dictionnaires/francais-monolingue (accessed 19 January 2022).

Larson, Ben E. (1990): "Present-day influence of English on Swedish as found in Swedish job advertisements". *World Englishes,* 9 (3): 367–369.

Macmillan English dictionary (2007): Oxford: Macmillan.

Merriam-Webster Online Dictionary (2021): "word". https://www.merriam-webster.com/dictionary/word (accessed 1 June 2021)

Piller, Ingrid (2003): "Advertising as a site of language contact". *Annual Review of Applied Linguistics,* 23: 170–183.

Pulcini, Virginia, Cristiano Furiassi, & Félix Rodríguez González (2012): *The lexical influence of English on European languages.* Amsterdam: Benjamins.

Roberts, Gillian, Eline Zenner, & Laura Rosseel (2023): "Exploring English in TV product advertising for Dutch-speaking children". *World Englishes,* 42 (4): 661–678.

Rodríguez González, Félix (1996): "Functions of anglicisms in contemporary Spanish". *Cahiers de Lexicologie,* 68 (1): 107–128.

Real Academia Española (2022): *Diccionario de la lengua española*, 23.ª ed., [online version 23.5]. https://dle.rae.es (accessed 19 January 2022).

Türk Dil Kurumu (2019): Sözlükleri [Online Turkish Dictionary]. https://sozluk.gov.tr/ (accessed 18 January 2022).

van Hooft, Andreu (2015): "La presencia del inglés en la red de Internet en lengua española: Las ofertas de empleo en www.monster.es". *Revista Signos,* 48 (88): 250–269.

van Meurs, Frank (2010): *English in job advertisements in the Netherlands: Reasons, use and effects.* Utrecht: LOT.

van Meurs, Frank, Hubert Korzilius, & Liset Bergevoet (2015a): "English words and phrases in Dutch job advertisements: Do they function as peripheral persuasion cues?". *Dutch Journal of Applied Linguistics,* 4 (1): 21–38.

van Meurs, Frank, Hubert Korzilius, & Adriënne den Hollander (2006): "The use of English in job advertisements on the Dutch job site Monsterboard.nl and factors on which it depends". *ESP Across Cultures,* 3: 103–123.

van Meurs, Frank, Brigitte Planken, Hubert Korzilius, & Marinel Gerritsen (2015b): "Reasons for using English or the local language in the genre of job advertisements: Insights from interviews with Dutch job ad designers". *IEEE Transactions on Professional Communication,* 58 (1): 86–105.

Weinreich, Uriel (1968): *Languages in contact: Findings and problems.* The Hague: Mouton Publishers.

Zenner, Eline, Dirk Speelman, & Dirk Geeraerts (2013): "Macro and micro perspectives on the distribution of English in Dutch. A quantitative usage-based analysis of job ads". *Linguistics,* 51 (5): 1019–1064.

Biographical Note of Félix Rodríguez

Born in Frómista (Palencia, Spain, 1949), Félix Rodríguez González earned a degree in English Philology from the University of Valladolid in 1973, received a Ph.D. in Romance Linguistics from the University of Alberta (Canada) in 1980, and was awarded another, in English Linguistics, from the University of Salamanca in 1981.

He has had an extended career in the teaching profession. He taught Spanish at the University of Alberta (1977–1980) and moved on to become an English Linguistics instructor at the University of Valladolid (1974–1976) and, finally, at the University of Alicante (from 1983 until his retirement in 2022) of which he is now an Emeritus Professor.

Rodríguez' research has focused on the areas of Lexicology, Lexicography and Sociolinguistics of both Spanish and English. He has been either an author or editor of more than a hundred publications, among which are foremost his papers on acronyms, mostly derived from *Estudio lingüístico de las siglas en español actual* (Ph.D., 1980), Spanish youth slang (*El lenguaje de los jóvenes,* 2002), political language (*Prensa y lenguaje politico*, 1991), anglicisms (*Nuevo diccionario de anglicismos*, with Antonio Lillo, 1997; *Gran diccionario de anglicismos*, 2017; *Diccionario de anglicismos del deporte,* with Jesús Castañón, 2021), and dictionaries of slang (*soldiers'*, 2005, *gay-lebian*, 2008, *sex and erotism,* 2011, *drugs*, 2014), lexical hispanicisms (*Spanish Loanwords in the English Language* – awarded the 1996 National Prize for English Linguistics).
His contributions on Anglicisms are also represented in *A Dictionary of European Anglicisms* (2001) and *English in Europe* (2002), edited by Manfred Görlach for Oxford University Press, and (with Cristiano Furiassi and Virgini Pulcini) in *The Anglicization of European Lexis* (John Benjamins, 2012). Professor Rodríguez is currently preparing an *Encyclopedia of Anglicism* in several volumes for Peter Lang, the first two *Estudios del anglicismo en español contemporáneo: Una visión panorámica* and *Estudios sobre el anglicismos en español actual*: *Perspectivas lingüísticas* were published in 2022 and 2023, and the third "Reacciones ante el anglicismo en los medios de comunicación españoles", in collaboration with Jesús Castañón Rodríguez, will be published in 2024.

Professor Rodríguez González' interest in Anglicisms in Spanish and other languages was sparked at the University of Valladolid following the 1971 *Los anglicismos en el ámbito periodístico*, published by Pedro Jesús Marcos Pérez, one of his English language instructors. On pursuing graduate work at the University of Alberta, Rodríguez González studied under James Algeo, under whose supervision he wrote his dissertation, along with other professors of the stature of Gary Prideaux and Bernard L. Rochet, who contributed in orienting his interest to sociolinguistics and languages in contact. An additional research period in Salamanca was capped with another of his areas of interest, acronyms in Spanish, under the guidance of Antonio Llorente Maldonado, a well-known dialectologist.

For several years Rodríguez González has been an active supporter of the *Global Anglicism Database* (GLAD) project, of which he is a founding member, and whose objective is the compilation and study of Anglicisms in the main languages of Europe. In March 2016, he organized the second GLAD meeting at the University of Alicante, with attendees from representatives of many European languages and also from researchers working in unjustly neglected languages in the West, such as Chinese and Arabic.

A one-year research stint in Madrid, in 1981, drew Rodríguez González closer to Manuel Seco, the eminent Spanish lexicographer, who offered him guidance and support for his lexicographical projects in Spanish. As well, the request for collaboration by Manfred Görlach, professor of English Linguistics at the University of Köln, for his celebrated trilogy on Anglicisms in European languages, the forerunner of GLAD, was another great boost for his lexicographic studies, in this case those of English, particularly regarding language contrast and language contact.

As a professor at the University of Alicante, Rodríguez has advised on projects by both national and foreign researchers ranging from undergraduates to full-time scholars, and, in reaching out to a broader public, he has participated in various radio and television programs on youth slang and Anglicisms. At this university, where he taught for the last forty years, he created the research group "Lexicología y Lexicografía" (LyL) which included active members like Antonio Lillo Buades, José A. Sánchez Farjardo and Jesús Castañón Rodríguez, who collaborated in some of his works.

© Pepe Manchón

www.ingramcontent.com/pod-product-compliance
Ingram Content Group UK Ltd.
Pitfield, Milton Keynes, MK11 3LW, UK
UKHW021830100926
8556IPUK00004B/262

9 783631 915240